Lecture Notes in Computer Science 16912

The series Lecture Notes in Computer Science (LNCS), including its subseries Lecture Notes in Artificial Intelligence (LNAI) and Lecture Notes in Bioinformatics (LNBI), has established itself as a medium for the publication of new developments in computer science and information technology research, teaching, and education.

LNCS enjoys close cooperation with the computer science R & D community, the series counts many renowned academics among its volume editors and paper authors, and collaborates with prestigious societies. Its mission is to serve this international community by providing an invaluable service, mainly focused on the publication of conference and workshop proceedings and postproceedings. LNCS commenced publication in 1973.

Shengnan Han · Hongxiu Li · Samuli Pekkola
Editors

Work, Life, and Society in a Sustainable, Intelligent Future

25th IFIP WG 6.11 Conference
on e-Business, e-Services and e-Society, I3E 2026
Tampere, Finland, September 15–17, 2026, Proceedings

Springer

Editors
Shengnan Han
Stockholm University
Stockholm, Sweden

Hongxiu Li
Tampere University
Tampere, Finland

Samuli Pekkola
University of Jyväskylä
Jyväskylä, Finland

ISSN 0302-9743 ISSN 1611-3349 (electronic)
Lecture Notes in Computer Science
ISBN 978-3-032-38013-5 ISBN 978-3-032-38014-2 (eBook)
https://doi.org/10.1007/978-3-032-38014-2

This Springer imprint is published by the registered company Springer Nature Switzerland AG
The registered company address is: Gewerbestrasse 11, 6330 Cham, Switzerland

Preface

The papers in this volume constitute the proceedings of the 25th IFIP Conference on e-Business, e-Services, and e-Society (I3E 2026), convened under the theme "Work, Life, and Society in a Sustainable, Intelligent Future."

For a quarter-century, I3E has offered a meeting point where scholars, practitioners, and decision-makers examine how digital technologies are reshaping the conditions of economic, social, and civic life. As the flagship gathering of IFIP Working Group 6.11, the conference has built a lasting reputation for high-quality research and for convening varied disciplines and communities to advance scholarship across e-business, e-services, and e-society. With artificial intelligence now diffusing through everyday work and public life, and with sustainability pressing on every sector, the conference's guiding question—how intelligent services can strengthen rather than erode the way we work and live together—is especially timely.

For this edition (LNCS volume 16912), authors were asked to engage with the tensions and possibilities of a world that is at once more connected and more automated. Accepted studies reach across the future of work, digital platforms and service economies, AI-supported decision-making, public-sector and e-government services, and the ethical and ecological stakes of digital transformation. Together they illustrate how technology, society, and economy are being remade in concert.

Every manuscript was assessed through a double-blind peer review process, with three expert evaluations per manuscript. Sixty-four papers were submitted, and a Program Committee of 51 members and 16 reviewers contributed to the review work. Ultimately, 32 contributions were accepted for the proceedings, corresponding to a 50% acceptance rate. These papers combine conceptual, empirical, and methodological contributions and are organized into six thematic strands:

- **AI, Work, and Organizational Transformation** (8 papers)—AI-driven value and capabilities, human–AI collaboration, and the dynamics of digital service development.
- **Human–AI Interaction, Agents, and Companions** (4 papers)—experience, emotion, and satisfaction in interactions with conversational agents, companions, and avatars.
- **Immersive Technologies and the Metaverse** (4 papers)—XR, VR, and metaverse environments, and their cultural, value-creation, and ethical dimensions.
- **Data-Driven Services for Sustainability and Well-Being** (5 papers)—data features and persuasive design shaping sustainable behavior, health, and education
- **Responsible AI: Trust, Governance, and Accountable Use** (7 papers)—explainability, trust, governance, safety, and the trustworthy and rigorous use of AI.
- **Digital Government, Public Services, and Inclusion** (4 papers)—public-sector digitalization, e-government readiness, and the digital divide.

Beyond the scientific papers, I3E 2026 welcomed two keynote speakers: Virpi Tuunainen, from Aalto University, Finland, whose research centers on the platform economy and AI-based services, and Rainer Alt, from Leipzig University, Germany, whose work spans interorganizational networking, digital platforms and markets, and the convergence of technologies such as distributed ledger technologies and AI.

The conference was hosted by Tampere University, Finland, under the Unit of Information and Knowledge Management within the Faculty of Management and Business. Formed in 2019 from the merger of the University of Tampere and Tampere University of Technology and joined with Tampere University of Applied Sciences in the wider Tampere Universities community, the institution ranks among Finland's largest hubs for research and higher education, with a distinctive multidisciplinary reach across technology, society, and health.

Our thanks go first to the authors, reviewers, and Program Committee members, whose careful work and shared commitment to rigorous scholarship underpin the quality of this program. We are equally grateful to the local organizing team and to the institutional partners who made I3E 2026 possible. It is our hope that these proceedings will enrich the continuing conversation—and the exchange of ideas across disciplines and borders—on Work, Life, and Society in a Sustainable, Intelligent Future.

July 2026

Shengnan Han
Hongxiu Li
Samuli Pekkola

Organization

General Chair

Hongxiu Li	Tampere University, Finland

Conference Co-chairs

Matti Mäntymäki	University of Turku, Finland
Ilias Pappas	Norwegian University of Science and Technology, Norway

Program Committee Chairs

Shengnan Han	Stockholm University, Sweden
Samuli Pekkola	University of Jyväskylä, Finland

Program Committee

Samaneh Bagheri	Open University of the Netherlands, Netherlands
Edward Bernroider	WU Wien, Austria
Giuseppe Bisicchia	University of Pisa, Italy
Alessandro Bocci	University of Pisa, Italy
Stefano Bromuri	Open University of the Netherlands, Netherlands
Matteo Busi	University of Venice "Ca' Foscari", Italy
Roberto Casadei	University of Bologna, Italy
Antreas Dionysiou	Frederick University, Cyprus
Sunet Eybers	University of South Africa, South Africa
Thomas Fotiadis	University of Cyprus, Cyprus
Rouxan Fouche	University of Pretoria, South Africa
Shang Gao	Örebro University, Sweden
Frank Grave	Open University of the Netherlands, Netherlands
Carlos Guerrero	University of the Balearic Islands, Spain
Karan Gupta	T-Mobile, USA
Marié Hattingh	University of Pretoria, South Africa
Remko Helms	Open University of the Netherlands, Netherlands

Ronald van den Heuvel	Open University of the Netherlands, Netherlands
Antonio Ielo	University of Calabria, Italy
Christian Janiesch	TU Dortmund, Germany
Gustav Juell-Skielse	University of Borås, Sweden
Arpan Kar	Indian Institute of Technology Delhi, India
Georgia Kapitsaki	University of Cyprus, Cyprus
Laleh Kasraian	De Montfort University, UK
Karlheinz Kautz	Royal Melbourne Institute of Technology University, Australia
Ioannis Kiouvrekis	University of Thessaly, Greece
John Krogstie	Norwegian University of Science and Technology, Norway
Chrisostomi Maria Kyrillou	University of Nicosia, Cyprus
Isaac Lera	University of the Balearic Islands, Spain
Chenglong Li	Central China Normal University, China
Prashanth Madhala	Tampere University, Finland
Christos Markides	Frederick University, Cyprus
Jacopo Massa	University of Pisa, Italy
Riccardo Massidda	University of Pisa, Italy
Machdel Matthee	University of Pretoria, South Africa
Mohammad Merhi	Indiana University South Bend, USA
Christos Mettouris	University of Cyprus, Cyprus
Wynand Nel	University of Pretoria, South Africa
Alain El Osta	Université La Sagesse, Lebanon
Theodore Panagiotakopoulos	Hellenic Open University, Greece
Savvas Papagiannidis	Newcastle University, UK
Savvas Pericleous	Frederick University, Cyprus
Gehan Wishwajith Premathilake	Tampere University, Finland
Savvas Savvides	University of Cyprus & Fortanix, Cyprus
Laura Semini	University of Pisa, Italy
Jacopo Soldani	University of Pisa, Italy
AnnaMaria Souri	University of Nicosia, Cyprus
Paraskevi Tsoutsa	University of Thessaly, Greece
Evangelia Vanezi	University of Cyprus, Cyprus
Alexandros Yeratziotis	University of Cyprus, Cyprus
Hans-Dieter Zimmermann	OST Eastern Switzerland University, Switzerland

Additional Reviewers

Nasreen Azad
Maneesha Dias
Jenny Elo
Shan Feng
Mostafa Goudarzi
Rong Huang
Nard Janssens
Yong Liu
Ting Long
Stevens Phaphadi Mamorobela
Matti Minkkinen
Givemore Muchenje
Hanlie Smuts
Matti Vaarma
Jie Yang
Heng Zhang

Sponsors

City of Tampere

Finnish Foundation for Economic Education

The Finnish Work Environment Fund

Contents

AI, Work, and Organizational Transformation

The Role of DevOps and Decision Making in Advancing Software Delivery Capabilities

Nasreen Azad(✉), Jussi Kasurinen, and Sami Hyrynsalmi

Lappeenranta-Lahti University of Technology LUT, Lappeenranta, Finland
{nasren.azad,jussi.kasurinen,sami.hyrynsalmi}@lut.fi

Abstract. Digital transformation is a strategic priority for organizations, yet integrating DevOps with decision-making poses challenges. While much research focuses on the technical aspects of DevOps, less is known about how organizational factors influence successful transformation. This study investigates the relationship between DevOps practices, decision-making, and software delivery capabilities through semi-structured interviews with 17 industry practitioners. Using the Gioia methodology for analysis, the findings indicate that successful digital transformation relies on a collaborative culture, experimentation, digital awareness, and decentralized decision-making. DevOps practices like automation and continuous delivery improve software quality and organizational responsiveness. This study enhances the understanding of how culture, decision-making, and delivery capabilities shape transformation outcomes, offering valuable insights for organizations aiming for effective DevOps-driven digital transformation.

Keywords: DevOps · DevOps practice · Digital transformation · Digital innovation · Qualitative research

1 Introduction

Although DevOps is widely adopted for enhancing software delivery and digital transformation, organizations face significant challenges in implementation [4,6,8]. Many invest in automation tools and CI/CD pipelines but struggle to achieve consistent business value, as success also depends on factors like organizational culture, collaboration, leadership, and decision-making, leading to variable outcomes across organizations [1,5,15,26,33,35]. Existing studies have primarily examined DevOps from technical, process, or automation perspectives [4,6,8,26,33], while comparatively less attention has been paid to understanding how practitioners perceive the organizational and decision-making factors that influence successful digital transformation. Although previous research acknowledges the importance of culture, collaboration, and digital transformation, there remains limited empirical evidence explaining how these factors interact during

Published by Springer Nature Switzerland AG 2027
S. Han et al. (Eds.): I3E 2026, LNCS 16912, pp. 3–14, 2027.
https://doi.org/10.1007/978-3-032-38014-2_1

DevOps transformation and what outcomes practitioners associate with different transformation practices [5,15,30,35,41]. There is a need for qualitative studies that capture practitioners' experiences to better understand the organizational mechanisms that enable successful digital transformation in DevOps environments [11,31].

This research is motivated by the need to bridge the gap between the technical understanding of DevOps and the organizational realities faced by practitioners during digital transformation. Understanding these factors is important not only for advancing information systems research but also for providing practical guidance to organizations seeking to improve collaboration, decision-making, and transformation outcomes [5,15,30,41].

To address this gap, this study investigates the factors that influence digital transformation in organizations adopting DevOps practices and explores how practitioners perceive the outcomes of different transformation and decision-making approaches. We conducted semi-structured interviews with 17 industry professionals and analyzed the data using the Gioia methodology, which enables the development of theory grounded in practitioners' experiences [2,23]. By identifying the organizational and decision-making factors associated with successful DevOps transformation, this study contributes empirical evidence to the growing body of research on DevOps and digital transformation while offering practical insights for organizations undergoing digital change [4,5,8,11,31].

The study addresses the following research questions:

RQ1: What factors influence digital transformation in organizations adopting DevOps practices, particularly in relation to decision-making processes?
RQ2: What results do practitioners see from different DevOps transformation practices and decision-making methods?

The paper is organized as follows: Sect. 2 discusses the background, including digital transformation and its impact on DevOps and software development. Section 3 outlines the research methods, while Sect. 4 presents the results. Section 5 addresses future work implications, and the conclusion summarizes the research outcomes.

2 Background

2.1 Emergence of Digital Transformation

Digital transformation is about using new technologies to improve productivity, create value, and enhance well-being in society. Many governments, global groups, and industry coalitions are taking steps to shape their long-term plans for advancing digital change in the public sector [15,16,20,27]. Many people expect strong annual growth and rapid adoption, but several challenges are making widespread use difficult. These barriers include organizational structures or cultures that are either misaligned or overly varied, insufficient digital transformation strategies, and a lack of clear understanding regarding the process

[22]. Moreover, some individuals perceive disruptive technologies as threats to established businesses, leading to what is known as the innovator's dilemma. Additional external hurdles include a failure to recognize how digital transformation can positively impact society as a whole, a deficit of skilled and qualified personnel, inadequate infrastructure, insufficient regulation and consumer protection, and limited access to financing, particularly for small and medium-sized enterprises [16,20,31,43].

2.2 Decision-Making in DevOps Practices

Decision-making is essential in software development, influencing areas from requirements gathering to deployment. With the rise of DevOps in digital transformation, decision-making has shifted from a hierarchical structure to a collaborative and evidence-driven approach, enabling teams to respond swiftly to evolving business needs [11,13,15,29]. This collaboration involves input from various stakeholders, including developers, operations engineers, and business leaders, which is crucial for balancing technical and business considerations.

Data plays a critical role in supporting decision-making within DevOps, utilizing metrics such as deployment frequency and lead time to evaluate performance and drive enhancements. Research shows that organizations leveraging performance metrics achieve superior software delivery outcomes [11,31]. Continuous monitoring also helps identify bottlenecks and inform decisions across the development lifecycle. Collaboration enhances decision-making by breaking down silos between development, operations, and security teams. This shared ownership fosters better communication and faster, more informed decisions [28,31]. Careful selection of technologies and automation strategies is vital, as poor choices can impede the success of DevOps initiatives. Research highlights the significant impact of both architectural decisions and tool selection on achieving successful DevOps implementation and digital transformation [7,13,15].

2.3 DevOps and Digitalization Impact on Software Development

Digital transformation has significantly influenced entrepreneurship and business dynamics, particularly in technology-driven sectors. Companies operate in two modes: a standard mode, which focuses on maintaining traditional operations, and a disruptive mode, aimed at innovating and capturing new markets and technologies. Modern software technology is both a driver and indicator of this disruption. To remain competitive, industry leaders continually develop and deploy new technologies that meet evolving customer needs [15,17,20,31].

DevOps is a software development methodology that promotes collaboration between development and operations teams to ensure effective software performance in real-world environments. By involving database, system, and network administrators alongside programmers and QA teams, organizations enhance operational efficiency and minimize risks [6–10]. The shift toward digital transformation encourages innovation and entrepreneurship, compelling firms to adapt their strategies to leverage emerging opportunities.

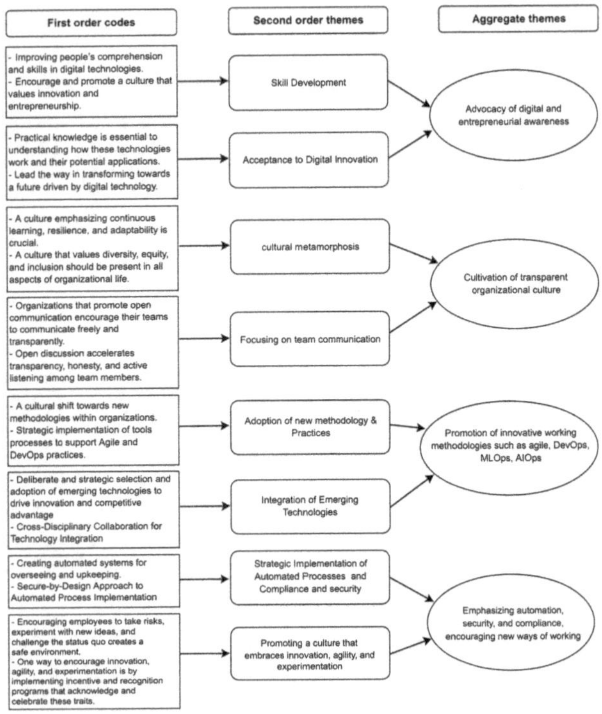

Fig. 1. Data analysis results

3 Research Method

3.1 Data Collection

In 2024, we conducted semi-structured interviews with 17 experienced professionals from Finland, Norway, and Sweden, focusing on digital transformation and DevOps practices [38]. Each interview lasted 45 min, was recorded with consent, and resulted in about 350 pages of transcripts. Participants were selected through purposive sampling to ensure they had relevant experience related to the research topic. A total of 17 semi-structured interviews were conducted. By the fifteenth interview, data saturation was nearly reached. We recruited 2 additional participants and concluded the process as no new themes or meaningful insights were emerging [32,36]. Table 1 summarizes each participant's country of origin, years of experience, and current role.

3.2 Data Analysis

We are using qualitative methods for our data analysis process. Three researchers have completed the coding and theme generation process. We have used the Gioia method for code generation, as proposed by Gioia et al. [23]. We use the open coding process suggested by Strauss and Cobin in the beginning of the process [40] to identify similar and dissimilar codes from different data segments in the interview transcripts. We have made constant comparisons to develop better codes based on the analysis. Table 2 presents the example coding process based on 17 interview segments.

We identified 16 first-order codes reflecting practitioners' views on digital transformation in DevOps. These codes, supported by participants' interviews, formed the basis of our analysis. We grouped related codes into higher-order themes that represented broader practices and phases of digital transformation. Using the constant comparison approach, we refined codes and themes for consistency. The data structure in Fig. 1 was developed with the Gioia methodology to illustrate the relationships between first-order concepts, second-order themes, and aggregate themes [23].

Table 1. Professional's country of origin, year of experience, and role in the company

Participants	Country of origin	Year of experience	Role in the company
P1	Finland	7	DevOps Operations
P2	Sweden	5	Tech Lead
P3	Sweden	3	Developer
P4	Norway	8	Developer
P5	Sweden	6	CTO
P6	Sweden	9	Lead Architect
P7	Finland	5	CEO
P8	Sweden	8	Developer
P9	Finland	9	Team Lead
P10	Norway	4	DevOps Engineer
P11	Finland	5	DevOps professional
P12	Finland	7	Tech Lead
P13	Norway	10	DevOps Engineer
P14	Finland	6	Team Lead
P15	Sweden	9	CEO
P16	Sweden	3	CTO
P17	Finland	8	Tech Lead

4 Findings and Results

4.1 Advocacy of Digital and Entrepreneurial Awareness

Participants highlighted that successful digital transformation begins with developing employees' digital skills, not just introducing new technologies. They emphasized the importance of digital and entrepreneurial awareness in helping employees adapt to change and drive innovation. Organizations that invest in training and continuous learning create an environment where employees can better adopt new technologies and meet evolving business needs. Thus, digital transformation is a human-centered process that requires ongoing capability development [16,20,30,37,41]. This finding addresses RQ1 by highlighting digital awareness as a key factor in DevOps digital transformation. While previous studies emphasize digital skills, our findings indicate that practitioners consider digital awareness crucial for organizational readiness and informed decision-making during the transformation process.

A professional stated that,

> *"Our organization was already taking steps towards digital transformation by implementing tech changes, allowing changes, and creating an innovative culture-P6 (Lead Architect)."*

4.2 Cultivation of a Transparent Organizational Culture and Decision Making

Participants identified organizational culture as a key factor in successful DevOps transformation. They emphasized the importance of transparency, communication, collaboration, and shared responsibility for enabling timely and informed decision-making. Transparent communication facilitates coordination among development, operations, and business teams, allowing for rapid responses to changing requirements, fostering an environment of experimentation, continuous learning, and innovation. [15,18,20,21,28,37,41]. This finding supports RQ1, showing that organizational culture impacts digital transformation by enhancing collaboration and decentralized decision-making. While prior studies highlight culture's role in DevOps, our research provides evidence that practitioners link transparency to quicker decision-making, better responsiveness, and increased agility during digital transformation. A professional stated that,

> *"cultural transformation is essential in organizations where teams were traditionally separate. It is crucial to emphasize communication, daily stand-up meetings, and getting people in sync to create a good working culture-P10 (DevOps Engineer)."*

4.3 Automation, Security, and Compliance, Encouraging New Ways of Working

Participants viewed automation as more than a means of accelerating software delivery. They described automation as an important mechanism for improving security, maintaining compliance, reducing manual effort, and supporting informed operational decision-making. Integrating security throughout the software development lifecycle enables organizations to identify vulnerabilities earlier, respond to incidents more effectively, and maintain continuous compliance

Table 2. Example coding derived from interview data

List of Codes	Description of Codes	Illustrated Examples
Digital Awareness Initiatives	Organizational efforts such as training, workshops, and knowledge-sharing programs aimed at improving digital literacy and entrepreneurial thinking among employees.	"Our organization introduced internal training sessions and innovation workshops to help employees understand digital tools and explore new ideas- P3."
Entrepreneurial Mindset Development	Encouraging employees to think creatively, take initiative, and identify new business or technological opportunities.	"Employees are encouraged to propose new solutions and experiment with ideas that can improve products or services- P7."
Transparent Communication Culture	Promoting open communication, knowledge sharing, and collaboration across teams to support alignment and trust.	"Daily stand-ups and open discussions help teams stay aligned and reduce misunderstandings-P15."
Collaborative Decision-Making	Involving cross-functional teams in decision-making processes to ensure diverse perspectives and better outcomes.	"Decisions about deployments and priorities are made collectively with input from development, operations, and business teams-P12."
Data-Driven Decision Making	Using data, metrics, and monitoring tools to guide strategic and operational decisions in software delivery and DevOps processes.	"We rely on system metrics and performance data to decide when to release updates or scale services-P1."
Automation of Processes	Implementation of automated tools and pipelines to reduce manual work, improve efficiency, and ensure consistency in development and deployment.	"CI/CD pipelines automate testing and deployment, reducing human error and speeding up delivery -P9."
Security and Compliance Integration	Embedding security practices and regulatory compliance into DevOps processes (DevSecOps) to ensure safe and reliable systems.	"Security checks are integrated early in the pipeline to detect vulnerabilities before production-P4."
Ethical Data Practices	Ensuring responsible data collection, storage, and usage aligned with privacy regulations and organizational values.	"The company defines clear policies on how user data is collected and used during development processes-P2."
Experimental and Learning Mindset	Encouraging experimentation, continuous learning, and acceptance of failure as part of innovation.	"Teams are allowed to test new tools and approaches without fear of failure, as long as they learn from it-P4."
Continuous Monitoring and Feedback	Use of monitoring tools and feedback loops to continuously improve system performance and development processes.	"Real-time monitoring helps identify issues quickly and improve system reliability-P8."
Leadership-Driven Transformation	The role of leadership in promoting cultural change, innovation, and adoption of new technologies and practices.	"Leadership actively supports transformation by investing in tools and encouraging cultural change-P11."

with organizational and regulatory requirements. Participants also emphasized that access to reliable operational data supports better decision making by enabling teams to monitor system performance and quickly address emerging issues [3,20,21,25,28][?].This finding contributes primarily to RQ2 by showing that practitioners associate automation not only with faster software delivery but also with improved software quality, security, compliance, and operational responsiveness.

"The role of automation in DevOps, particularly in streamlining processes, can reduce manual work and ensure efficient deployments-P12 (Tech Lead)."

To maintain privacy and security it should be aligned with the company's values, culture, and security checks.

A professional quoted that:

"For ethical considerations, a company should take into account where, and how to collect, store, and analyze data in our DevOps operations as that is an essential part for decision making process-P16(CTO)".

4.4 Promotion of Innovative Working Methodologies Such as Agile, DevOps, MLOps, AIOps

Participants described Agile, DevOps, MLOps, and AIOps as complementary approaches that collectively strengthen digital transformation rather than isolated methodologies adopted independently. Agile practices improve adaptability and customer responsiveness, while DevOps enhances collaboration and continuous software delivery. Emerging approaches such as MLOps and AIOps further enable organizations to automate operational processes, leverage data more effectively, and support proactive decision-making. Participants explained that adopting these methodologies allows organizations to continuously experiment with new technologies while improving software quality and operational efficiency [1,17,20,21,24,28,34,39]. This finding highlights that modern software engineering methodologies enhance digital transformation through improved collaboration, flexibility, and decision-making.

As a professional stated that,

" Adopting new technologies is good for any team to explore different ways of working. In our company, we try to adopt different tools like MLOPs based on the requirements of our project- P5 (CTO)."

5 Discussion

Digital transformation through DevOps involves adopting new technologies, improving operational efficiency, empowering teams, and changing the organizational culture. This approach results in benefits like increased speed, quality, and overall business performance [15,16,20,37].In regard to RQ1 (factors influencing digital transformation in DevOps), key enablers include teamwork for better communication, automation, and continuous testing for enhanced system reliability. Cultural elements such as ongoing learning, team empowerment, and decentralized decision-making are crucial, along with leadership, security, and compliance.

For RQ2 (outcomes of DevOps transformation and decision-making), benefits include faster software delivery, improved system reliability, and enhanced cost efficiency. Empowering teams drives productivity and innovation through iterative development. Effective decision-making in DevOps positively impacts software quality and organizational performance.

Theoretical Implications. This study extends the existing DevOps and digital transformation literature by demonstrating that successful digital transformation should be understood as a socio-technical process rather than a purely technical implementation of automation and continuous delivery practices. While previous studies have predominantly emphasized the technical dimensions of DevOps, such as CI/CD, automation, and deployment performance [4,6,8], our findings suggest that organizational culture, decentralized decision-making, collaboration, leadership, and continuous learning collectively shape transformation outcomes. Recent studies have acknowledged the importance of organizational capabilities in DevOps adoption [5,11,31]; however, this study further demonstrates that decision-making acts as a connecting mechanism through which technical practices translate into organizational transformation outcomes. By integrating software delivery capabilities with organizational and managerial perspectives, this study advances the theoretical understanding of DevOps by providing an empirical framework that links technical practices, organizational capabilities, and decision-making within the broader context of digital transformation [11,15,31].

Practical Implications. The findings offer practical recommendations for organizations adopting DevOps. First, view DevOps as an organizational transformation, aligning technology with culture and business goals for sustainable change [4,5,11]. Empower cross-functional teams to enhance responsiveness and innovation [29,31]. Second, invest in automation and continuous testing to improve software quality and deployment reliability, incorporating feedback mechanisms for quick adaptation to customer needs [4,11,21]. Finally, create a collaborative culture that promotes knowledge sharing and transparency among development, operations, security, and business teams. This enhances communication and trust, supporting continuous improvement throughout the software development lifecycle [5,15,31].

6 Future Directions

Our findings show that successful digital transformation in DevOps involves more than just technical practices like automation. Key elements include organizational culture, decentralized decision-making, collaboration, leadership, and continuous learning. Future research should examine how these factors develop and influence DevOps maturity and outcomes across different contexts [9,11,12]. Additionally, exploring the role of emerging technologies such as Artificial Intelligence (AI) and AIOps in improving decision-making during transformations is important. This study did not specifically assess how AI analytics and intelligent automation impact software delivery and operational efficiency [19,42,44].The importance of collaboration, continuous learning, and digital awareness should drive future research on developing digital competencies and leadership capabilities to support DevOps adoption, especially in regulated sectors like healthcare, finance, and manufacturing, which face unique compliance challenges [14,42].

7 Conclusion

This paper explores how DevOps practices facilitate digital transformation by emphasizing organizational values, collaborative culture, and software delivery. Based on interviews with 17 DevOps practitioners, it identifies crucial factors for success, such as digital awareness, transparency, continuous learning, and a focus on automation and security. The findings indicate that successful DevOps transformation depends on technical practices as well as organizational culture, leadership, and decentralized decision-making. This research provides insights for scholars and organizations looking to improve their digital transformation and software delivery.

Acknowledgement. The authors used ChatGPT and Gremmarly for language refinement grammar checks. All content was reviewed and validated by the authors.

References

1. Abrahamsson, P., Salo, O., Ronkainen, J., Warsta, J.: Agile software development methods: review and analysis. arXiv:1709.08439 arXiv preprint (2017)
2. Adeoye-Olatunde, O.A., Olenik, N.L.: Research and scholarly methods: semi-structured interviews. J. Am. College Clinic. Pharmacy **4**(10), 1358–1367 (2021)
3. Al-Nakeeb, A., et al.: Digital transformation and disruptive technologies: effect of cloud computing and devops on managing projects. In: Technology Innovation for Business Intelligence and Analytics (TIBIA) Techniques and Practices for Business Intelligence Innovation, pp. 39–62. Springer 2024
4. Almeida, F., Simões, J., Lopes, S.: Exploring the benefits of combining devops and agile. Fut. Internet **14**(2), 63 (2022)
5. Amaro, R.M.D., Pereira, R., da Silva, M.M.: Capabilities and practices in devops: a multivocal literature review. IEEE Trans. Softw. Eng. (2022)
6. Azad, N.: Understanding devops critical success factors and organizational practices. In: 2022 IEEE/ACM International Workshop on Software-Intensive Business (IWSiB), pp. 83–90. IEEE (2022)
7. Azad, N., Hyrynsalmi, S.: What are critical success factors of devops projects? a systematic literature review. In: Wang, X., Martini, A., Nguyen-Duc, A., Stray, V., (eds.), Software Business, volume 434 of Lecture Notes in Business Information Processing, Cham. Springer (2021)

8. Azad, N., Hyrynsalmi, S.: Devops challenges in organizations: through professional lens. In: Software Business: 13th International Conference, ICSOB 2022, Bolzano, Italy, 8–11 November 2022, Proceedings, pp. 260–277. Springer 2022
9. Azad, N., Hyrynsalmi, S.: Devops critical succes factors—a systematic literature review. Inf. Softw. Technol. 107150 (2023)
10. Azad, N., Hyrynsalmi, S.: Devops critical succes factors—a systematic literature review. Inf. Softw. Technol., 107150 (2023)
11. Azad, N., Hyrynsalmi, S.: Navigating challenges and pitfalls in devops-driven digital transformation. In: Conference on e-Business, e-Services and e-Society, pp. 115–128. Springer (2024)
12. Babar, Z.: A study of business process automation with devops: a data-driven approach to agile technical support. Am. J. Adv. Technol. Eng. Sol. **4**(04), 01–32 (2024)
13. Bass, L., Weber, I., Zhu, L.: DevOps: a Software Architect's Perspective. Addison-Wesley Professional (2015)
14. Betz, C., Olagunju, A.O., Paulson, P.: The impacts of digital transformation, agile, and devops on future it curricula. In: Proceedings of the 17th Annual Conference on Information Technology Education, pp. 106–106 (2016)
15. Bosch, J.: Towards a digital business operating system. In: 2019 13th International Conference on Research Challenges in Information Science (RCIS), pp. 1–9. IEEE (2019)
16. Bosch, J., Olsson, H.H.: Digital for real: a multicase study on the digital transformation of companies in the embedded systems domain. J. Softw. Evol. Process **33**(5), e2333 (2021)
17. Bosch-Sijtsema, P., Bosch, J.: User involvement throughout the innovation process in high-tech industries. J. Prod. Innov. Manag. **32**(5), 793–807 (2015)
18. Dekker, S., Edmondson, A.: Psychological safety. In: Restorative Just Culture in Practice, pp. 187–196. Productivity Press (2022)
19. Dos Santos, F.N., Sobreira, H., Campos, D., Morais, R., Paulo Moreira, A., Contente, O.: Towards a reliable robot for steep slope vineyards monitoring. J. Intell. Robot. Syst. **83**(3), 429–444 (2016)
20. Ebert, C., Duarte, C.H.C.: Digital transformation. IEEE Softw. **35**(4), 16–21 (2018)
21. Forsgren, N., Humble, J., Kim, G.: Accelerate: The Science of Lean Software and DevOps. IT Revolution Press (2018)
22. Gable, G.G.: Integrating case study and survey research methods: an example in information systems. Eur. J. Inf. Syst. **3**(2), 112–126 (1994)
23. Gioia, D.A., Corley, K.G., Hamilton, A.L.: Seeking qualitative rigor in inductive research: Notes on the Gioia methodology. Organ. Res. Methods **16**(1), 15–31 (2013)
24. Humble, J., Farley, D.: Continuous delivery: reliable software releases through build, test, and deployment automation. Pearson Education (2010)
25. Hüttermann, M.: DevOps for Developers. Apress (2012)
26. Jabbari, R., bin Ali, N., Petersen, K., Tanveer, B.: What is devops? a systematic mapping study on definitions and practices. In: Proceedings of the Scientific Workshop Proceedings of XP2016, pp. 1–11 (2016)
27. Kettunen, V., Kasurinen, J., Taipale, O., Smolander, K.: A study on agility and testing processes in software organizations. In: Proceedings of the 19th International Symposium on Software Testing and Analysis, pp. 231–240 (2010)

28. Kim, G., Humble, J., Debois, P., Willis, J.: The DevOps Handbook: How to Create World-Class Agility, Reliability, and Security in Technology Organizations. IT Revolution Press (2016)
29. Kim, G., Humble, J., Debois, P., Willis, J., Forsgren, N.: The DevOps Handbook: How to Create World-class Agility, Reliability, & Security in Technology Organizations. IT Revolution (2021)
30. Laato, S., Mäntymäki, M., Birkstedt, T., Islam, A.N., Hyrynsalmi, S.: Digital transformation of software development: implications for the future of work. In: Responsible AI and Analytics for an Ethical and Inclusive Digitized Society: 20th IFIP WG 6.11 Conference on e-Business, e-Services and e-Society, I3E 2021, Galway, Ireland, 1–3 September 2021, Proceedings 20, pp. 609–621. Springer (2021)
31. Leso, B.H., Cortimiglia, M.N., Ghezzi, A.: The contribution of organizational culture, structure, and leadership factors in the digital transformation of SMEs: a mixed-methods approach. Cogn. Technol. Work **25**(1), 151–179 (2023)
32. Mwita, K.: Factors influencing data saturation in qualitative studies. SSRN 4889752 (2022)
33. Riungu-Kalliosaari, L., Mäkinen, S., Lwakatare, L.E., Tiihonen, J., Männistö, T.: Devops adoption benefits and challenges in practice: a case study. In: International Conference on Product-Focused Software Process Improvement, pp. 590–597. Springer (2016)
34. Saar, S.: The role of devops in digital transformation: accelerating change. Int. J. Artif. Intell. Mach. Learn. **4**(2) (2017)
35. Sarah, A., Fakieh, B.: How devops practices support digital transformation. Int. J. **9**(3) (2020)
36. Saunders, B., et al.: Saturation in qualitative research: exploring its conceptualization and operationalization. Quality & Quantity **52**(4), 1893–1907 (2018)
37. Schwertner, K.: Digital transformation of business. Trakia J. Sci. **15**(1), 388–393 (2017)
38. Seaman, C.B.: Qualitative methods in empirical studies of software engineering. IEEE Trans. Softw. Eng. **25**(4), 557–572 (1999)
39. Shah, W., Abbas, A.: Dataops meets devops: AI-driven approaches for modernizing cloud enterprise architectures (2021)
40. Strauss, A., Corbin, J.: Basics of qualitative research techniques (1998)
41. Stryabkova, E.A., Lyshchikova, J.V., Chistnikova, I.V., Glotova, A.S., Kochergin, M.A.: Instruments to choose priorities of the spatial development of the region in the context of smart specialization. Amazonia Investiga **8**(24), 91–101 (2019)
42. Thomas, G.: AI and devops driven cloud enterprise networks for digital banking healthcare and government platforms. Int. J. Multidis. Res. Sci. Eng. Technol. Manag. **1**(01), 33–41 (2025)
43. Vial, G.: Understanding digital transformation: a review and a research agenda. Manag. Digital Transf., 13–66 (2021)
44. Zhou, J., Chen, F.: Human and Machine Learning. Springer (2018)

Technostress Responses in AI–Augmented Work: Emotional Exhaustion, Performance, and AI–Related Impostorism

Marieke Fiala(✉) and Christian Maier

University of Bamberg, Bamberg, Germany
marieke.fiala@uni-bamberg.de

Abstract. AI-augmented work creates a distinctive IS context in which the same work setting can support higher performance while increasing emotional exhaustion. We examine techno-eustress and techno-distress as distinct technostress responses and conceptualize AI-related impostorism through a competence-legitimacy lens. Using structural equation modeling and survey data from 207 employees who regularly use AI for professional work, we find a dual-response pattern: techno-eustress is associated with lower emotional exhaustion and higher performance, whereas techno-distress is associated with higher emotional exhaustion and lower performance. AI-related impostorism is positively associated with emotional exhaustion and selectively strengthens the techno-eustress–performance relationship, rather than broadly amplifying technostress relationships.

Keywords: Artificial Intelligence · Technostress · Impostor Phenomenon

1 Introduction

AI-augmented work creates a distinctive IS context in which the same work setting can support performance while increasing emotional exhaustion. The theoretical challenge is that AI can be experienced as both helpful and burdensome, and that AI-supported accomplishments may make employees less certain whether they reflect their own competence and contribution. This ambivalence stems from AI's capacity to replace or augment work tasks while remaining adaptive and opaque [1, 2]. IS research therefore needs an account of technostress responses in AI-augmented work that can explain performance and emotional exhaustion without treating them as contradictory outcomes.

Technostress, referring to stress arising from the use of information systems [3], offers a useful foundation for this ambivalence. Recent research on technostress shows that technology-related conditions should be understood through employee interpretations and daily variation, rather than treated as uniformly harmful [4, 5]. This view is useful for AI-augmented work because it distinguishes negative and positive responses to technology use. However, this account remains underspecified when technology use also affects how employees attribute AI-supported accomplishments.

Published by Springer Nature Switzerland AG 2027
S. Han et al. (Eds.): I3E 2026, LNCS 16912, pp. 15–26, 2027.
https://doi.org/10.1007/978-3-032-38014-2_2

In AI-augmented work, opacity and altered responsibilities may reshape how employees understand their work roles and evaluate their own competence and contribution [1, 2, 6]. Employees may have difficulty attributing AI-supported accomplishments to their own ability, the AI system, or both. We focus on AI-related impostorism, defined as persistent self-doubt and concern about being exposed as less competent when using AI tools, especially when AI-supported accomplishments raise questions about employees' own competence and contribution. This makes competence and legitimacy central to the construct. Although the broader impostor phenomenon is well established [7], its relevance for AI-augmented work is theoretical rather than only topical. It provides a competence-legitimacy lens for examining what technostress responses alone do not capture, namely whether AI-supported accomplishments are experienced as legitimate evidence of one's own competence and contribution.

We thus distinguish techno-eustress and techno-distress as positive and negative technostress responses and examine their relationships with emotional exhaustion and performance. We use a competence-legitimacy lens to conceptualize a role for AI-related impostorism in these relationships. This leads to our research question:

How do techno-eustress and techno-distress relate to emotional exhaustion and performance in AI-augmented work, and where does AI-related impostorism moderate these relationships?

We argue that techno-eustress and techno-distress relate differently to emotional exhaustion and performance in AI-augmented work, and that AI-related impostorism has a selective moderating role. Using structural equation modeling and survey data from 207 AI-using professionals, we examine the proposed relationships empirically.

2 Theoretical Background and Hypotheses Development

2.1 Techno-eustress and Techno-distress

Techno-eustress describes a positive technostress response in which employees experience technology use as motivating and beneficial. It encompasses mastery, autonomy, relatedness, and enrichment and is linked to favorable work states, including higher performance and lower strain [4, 8–10]. Techno-eustress captures how employees interpret AI use as enabling work execution, but it may still require effort and does not guarantee stable gains over time [2, 10, 11].

Techno-distress captures the draining counterpart, a negative technostress response. It arises when employees experience technology use as obstructive, burdensome, or difficult to cope with, and is reflected in overload, invasion, complexity, insecurity, and uncertainty. Prior research links techno-distress to lower job satisfaction, reduced performance, and burnout, with effects that may accumulate over time [3, 5, 11, 12].

Both constructs refer to responses to technology use rather than to objective AI demands. Their dimensions form the conceptual basis for modeling techno-eustress and techno-distress as reflective higher-order constructs. Distinguishing them matters because the same AI use context can be interpreted as enabling, obstructing, or both, preventing a simple beneficial versus harmful view of AI-augmented work.

2.2 The Influence of Techno-eustress and -distress on Emotional Exhaustion and Performance

Techno-eustress and techno-distress should relate differently to emotional exhaustion because they shape how employees experience AI use. In AI-augmented work, emotional exhaustion is the strain outcome examined in this study and reflects emotional overextension [13, 14]. As AI can reshape task and decision-making responsibilities [1, 6], it may absorb attention, coping resources, and emotional energy. Because techno-eustress reflects a positive technostress response [8, 9], it should be less likely to erode emotional resources. Techno-distress, by contrast, reflects a negative technostress response [8], and should therefore be associated with higher emotional exhaustion.

H1a: Higher techno-eustress is associated with lower emotional exhaustion.
H1b: Higher techno-distress is associated with higher emotional exhaustion.

Performance is represented through the first-order dimensions task performance and innovative performance, reflecting how technology helps employees complete tasks more effectively [15]. Because AI can reshape work processes, performance gains depend on how employees divide work with AI and use it [15, 16]. As techno-eustress is linked to favorable work outcomes [9, 10], employees who experience techno-eustress should be more likely to translate AI support into higher performance. By contrast, techno-distress can impair performance [15]. When AI use is experienced as obstructive or difficult to cope with, employees may have fewer resources available for effective work execution and may report lower performance.

H2a: Higher techno-eustress is associated with higher performance.
H2b: Higher techno-distress is associated with lower performance.

2.3 AI-Related Impostorism and Its Influence on Technostress

AI-related impostorism matters in AI-augmented work because AI-supported accomplishments may partly depend on system contributions, making competence attribution less clear. Prior research suggests that AI can reshape work roles and responsibilities, thereby affecting how employees understand their own contribution [1, 6]. This may link AI-augmented work to the impostor phenomenon, a persistent feeling of being a fraud despite objective success [7]. We use "impostor phenomenon" for the broader literature and "AI-related impostorism" for the AI-specific construct examined.

Building on this logic, AI-related impostorism captures a domain-specific self-evaluative tendency to doubt whether AI-supported accomplishments reflect one's own competence and contribution. We conceptualize it through a competence-legitimacy lens derived from this attributional context. By reshaping professional role identity [6] and work-related self-understanding [1], AI use may lead to uncertainty about whether AI-supported accomplishments reflect employees' own competence. Impostor phenomenon research shows that employees may explain success through factors other than their competence [7] and may minimize their responsibility for performance [17]. Together, these arguments make competence and legitimacy central.

We thus model AI-related impostorism as a moderator of selected technostress relationships, which specifies when it should matter for technostress responses. AI-related impostorism may also relate directly to emotional exhaustion and performance.

Prior work links the impostor phenomenon to emotional exhaustion, self-doubt, fear of exposure, and effortful overcompensation [7, 18]. For emotional exhaustion, AI-related impostorism should be associated with a self-evaluative burden around AI-supported accomplishments. Employees who question whether AI-supported accomplishments reflect their competence may spend emotional energy monitoring attribution. For performance, the expected association is narrower and less direct. Employees with stronger AI-related impostorism may invest additional effort to make AI-supported accomplishments defensible, which may be reflected in performance.

H3a: Employees with stronger AI-related impostorism report higher emotional exhaustion.
H3b: Employees with stronger AI-related impostorism report higher performance.

AI-related impostorism should matter most where technostress responses intersect with the interpretation of AI-supported accomplishments and may moderate how techno-eustress and techno-distress relate to emotional exhaustion and performance, consistent with person-level contingencies in technostress research [19]. For emotional exhaustion, AI-related impostorism may weaken the protective association of techno-eustress and should be especially consequential under techno-distress, as self-monitoring may limit recovery under techno-eustress [18], while concerns should intensify emotional exhaustion under techno-distress [3]. Under techno-eustress, employees high in AI-related impostorism may still monitor competence attribution; under techno-distress, these concerns add to an already burdensome experience.

H4a: AI-related impostorism moderates the relationship between techno-eustress and emotional exhaustion such that the negative association of techno-eustress with emotional exhaustion is attenuated at higher levels of AI-related impostorism.
H4b: AI-related impostorism moderates the relationship between techno-distress and emotional exhaustion such that the positive association of techno-distress with emotional exhaustion is amplified at higher levels of AI-related impostorism.

For performance, AI-related impostorism should matter most under techno-eustress, where higher performance may motivate employees concerned about anticipated exposure to make their contribution visible and defensible through additional effort [7, 18]. The expectation for techno-distress is more limited. Techno-distress should constrain performance, but AI-related impostorism may reduce the strength of this negative association if exposure concerns trigger additional effort to avoid appearing incompetent.

H4c: AI-related impostorism moderates the relationship between techno-eustress and performance such that the positive association of techno-eustress with performance is amplified at higher levels of AI-related impostorism.
H4d: AI-related impostorism moderates the relationship between techno-distress and performance such that the negative association of techno-distress with performance is attenuated at higher levels of AI-related impostorism.

3 Method

Sample and Data Collection. Data was collected through a cross-sectional single-source online survey targeting employees who use AI for professional work at least twice a week. Participation was voluntary and anonymous. Participants were recruited via Prolific. The final sample comprised 207 respondents from the United States and the United Kingdom. The sample was 58.5% male and 41.5% female, with a mean age of 39.36 years (SD = 11.06; range 20–78). 45.4% were IT professionals. Most used AI multiple times per day (58.5%), followed by two to four times per week (23.2%) and about once per day (18.4%). The sample represents recurring professional AI users rather than employees more broadly.

Measures. All constructs were operationalized using established scales. Differences in response scales reflect the original validated instruments and were retained to preserve their measurement logic. The study employed five multi-item reflective constructs. The full model comprised 61 items across all constructs. All measures were contextually adapted to AI-augmented work while preserving their original structure. The measurement model should therefore be read as an adaptation of established instruments to AI-augmented work.

Techno-eustress. Techno-eustress was measured as a reflective higher-order construct comprising four first-order dimensions, namely mastery, autonomy, relatedness, and enrichment, adapted from Tarafdar et al.'s [9] validated scale. All 16 items were measured on a five-point Likert scale ranging from 1 = strongly disagree to 5 = strongly agree. Adaptations were largely achieved by replacing "The IT applications and devices…" in the introductory sentence with "The AI I use for work challenges me in a positive way and motivates me to...". Three technology-explicit items were additionally adapted, for example "Prioritise my work (e.g., with the help of to-do list generation)".

Techno-distress. Techno-distress was operationalized as a reflective higher-order construct with five first-order dimensions, namely overload, boundary invasion, complexity, insecurity, and uncertainty, based on Ragu-Nathan et al.'s [3] technostress creators scale. Three items with outer loadings below .70 were removed after measurement model evaluation. They came from three different subdimensions, which reduced the risk that one facet was severely weakened. The final scale comprised 20 items, e.g. "I am forced to change my work habits to adapt to AI," and was measured on a five-point Likert scale ranging from 1 = strongly disagree to 5 = strongly agree.

Emotional Exhaustion. Emotional exhaustion was operationalized as a single first-order reflective construct based on Maier et al.'s [20] strain subscale. One item was removed because of a low outer loading. The final scale comprised 11 items measured on a seven-point Likert scale ranging from 1 = totally disagree to 7 = totally agree. Adaptations replaced the original reference to Facebook with AI, e.g., "I feel burned out from using AI." The measure therefore captures emotional exhaustion in the context of AI use at work rather than a broader burnout diagnosis.

Performance. Performance was measured as a reflective higher-order construct comprising two first-order dimensions, namely task performance and innovative performance, and was adapted from Tarafdar et al.'s [15] end-user performance scale. The scale comprised seven items measured on a five-point Likert scale ranging from 1 = strongly disagree to 5 = strongly agree. The adjustments replaced the generic reference to technology with explicit reference to AI, for example "AI helps me to accomplish more work than would otherwise be possible."

AI-related impostorism. AI-related impostorism was assessed using an adaptation of the Leary Impostorism Scale (LIS) [17] to the AI-augmented work setting by adding the situational frame "Using AI", e.g. "Using AI, I tend to feel like a phony." All seven items were measured on a five-point scale ranging from 1 = not at all characteristic of me to 5 = extremely characteristic of me. The scale should be interpreted as an adaptation of an established scale rather than as a fully independent development effort.

Analytical Approach. The analysis estimates associations in a structural model combining reflective higher-order constructs and latent interactions. Given the cross-sectional single-source survey design, the analysis assesses theorized relationships among latent constructs rather than identifying causal effects. PLS-SEM was selected because the model includes reflective higher-order constructs and interaction terms, requiring an approach that can estimate latent variable scores for moderation analysis without imposing distributional assumptions [21–23]. We applied a manual two-stage approach [23, 24]. In Stage 1, techno-eustress, techno-distress, and performance scores were estimated via the repeated indicators approach in Mode A, consistent with reflective specifications [21, 23]. In Stage 2, these scores were mean-centered and used to compute the interaction terms Techno-eustress × AI-related impostorism and Techno-distress × AI-related impostorism [25]. The structural estimates are interpreted as associations among latent constructs and conditional associations for the interaction terms.

4 Results

The results show three main patterns, namely that (a) techno-eustress and techno-distress have opposite associations with emotional exhaustion and performance, (b) AI-related impostorism is associated with emotional exhaustion, but not directly with performance, and (c) AI-related impostorism has a selective moderating role.

Measurement Model Assessment. Following established PLS-SEM guidelines, we examined internal consistency reliability, convergent validity, and discriminant validity [21, 22, 26, 27]. Internal consistency reliability was assessed using composite reliability, ρC. Convergent validity was assessed using outer loadings and average variance extracted; all retained items loaded above .70 on their respective constructs, with loadings ranging from .731 to .949, except for the items removed during measurement model evaluation. All AVE values were above .50 and composite reliability values exceeded .70, ranging from .881 to .972 [26] (Appendix, Table 1). Discriminant validity was assessed using the heterotrait-monotrait ratio of correlations, HTMT [22]. All HTMT values were below the conservative .85 threshold [27, 28], with the highest value observed for techno-eustress and performance (.755, 95% CI [.657, .846]); no confidence interval included 1.

Common Method Bias. We used both procedural and statistical precautions [CMB; 29]. Procedurally, respondents were assured of anonymity [29]. VIF values in the inner model were inspected as an indicator of pathological collinearity. All inner model VIF values ranged between 1.09 and 1.50, well below the threshold of 3.3 [30]. This result reduces concerns about the adverse influence of CMB on the results.

Structural Model Evaluation. Statistical inference was based on a bias-corrected bootstrap procedure with 5,000 resamples, seed = 42, two-tailed tests, and $\alpha = .05$ [22, 26]. Hypothesis support was determined primarily by 95% bootstrap confidence intervals. The model explained 47.4% of the variance in emotional exhaustion and 63.2% in performance (Fig. 1). The SRMR obtained via cSEM was .091.

Hypotheses Testing. Techno-eustress was associated with lower emotional exhaustion ($\beta = -.155, p = .008$, 95% CI [−.271, −.043]; supporting H1a), whereas techno-distress was associated with higher emotional exhaustion ($\beta = +.473, p < .001$, 95% CI [+.318, +.635]; supporting H1b). Techno-eustress was associated with higher performance ($\beta = +.594, p < .001$, 95% CI [+.512, +.683]; supporting H2a), whereas techno-distress was associated with lower performance ($\beta = -.208, p < .001$, 95% CI [−.334, −.091]; supporting H2b).

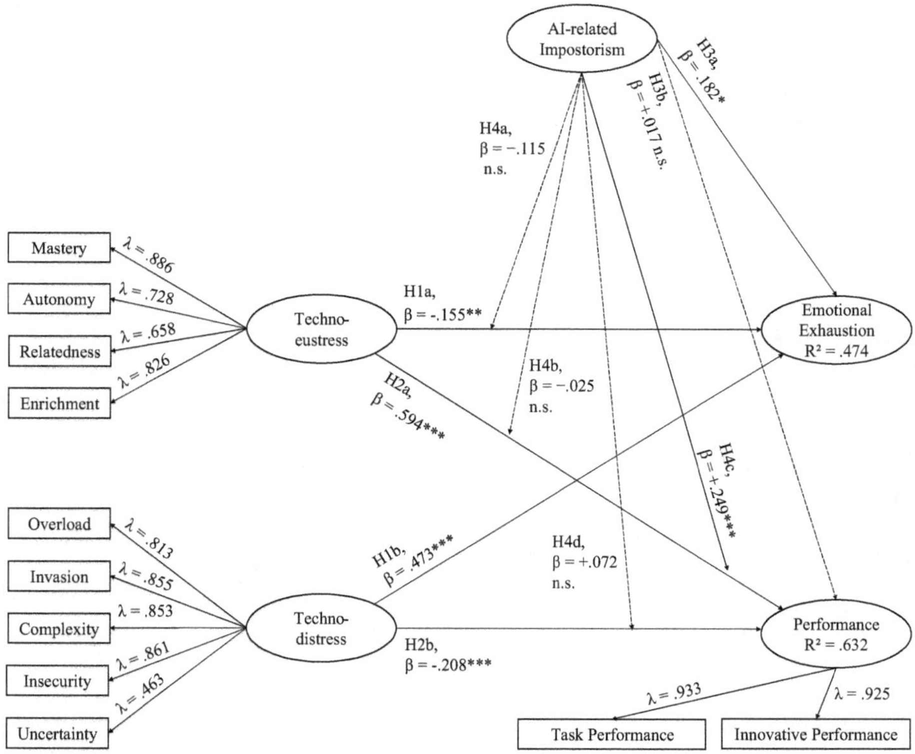

Fig 1. PLS-SEM Structural Model. *Note. Standardized path coefficients are shown. Dashed lines indicate non-significant paths. *p < .05; **p < .01; ***p < .001.*

AI-related impostorism was positively associated with emotional exhaustion ($\beta = +.182, p = .022$, 95% CI [+.028, +.321]; supporting H3a) but was not significantly related to performance ($\beta = +.017, p = .761$, 95% CI [−.095, +.137]; not supporting H3b). AI-related impostorism strengthened the positive relationship between techno-eustress and performance ($\beta = +.249, p < .001$, 95% CI [+.134, +.350]; supporting H4c).

Simple slope analyses (Fig. 2) showed that this relationship became stronger as AI-related impostorism increased, with $\beta = .346$ at low levels, $\beta = .594$ at mean levels, and $\beta = .843$ at high levels. The remaining interaction effects on emotional exhaustion and performance were not significant (H4a, H4b, H4d).

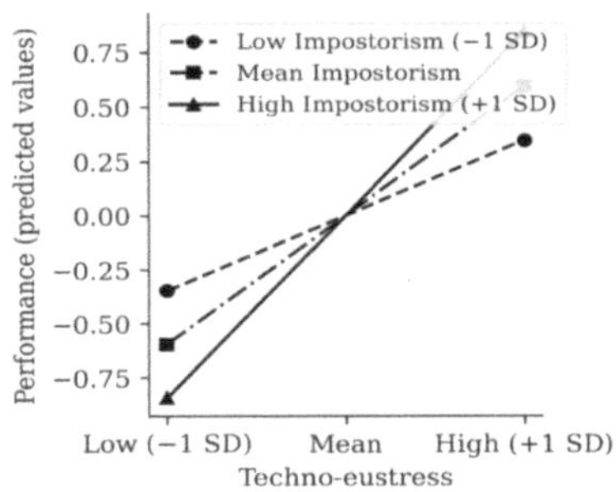

Fig 2. Simple Slope Analysis for the Interaction Effect of Techno-eustress and Impostorism on Performance (H4c). *Note. Slopes represent the effect of techno-eustress on performance at three levels of AI-related impostorism.* $\beta = .346$ *(low,* -1 *SD), .594 (mean), and .843 (high,* $+1$ *SD).*

5 Discussion

Theoretical Implications. For technostress research, the results specify how AI-augmented work can involve favorable and unfavorable technostress responses without treating emotional exhaustion and performance as interchangeable. Prior research has already moved beyond a purely negative view of technology-related experiences [4, 5, 8, 9]. Techno-eustress and techno-distress constitute distinct technostress responses with opposite relationships to emotional exhaustion and performance.

AI-related impostorism extends technostress accounts of AI-augmented work through a competence-legitimacy lens. Technostress research explains whether technology use is experienced as enabling or draining, but not whether AI-supported accomplishments are interpreted as legitimate evidence of one's own competence and contribution. Prior work suggests that AI can reshape work roles, make employees' contributions harder to evaluate, and challenge perceived competence [1, 2, 6]. The results position AI-related impostorism as a selective person-level contingency in technostress research [19], as it moderated the relationship between techno-eustress and performance. This suggests that AI-related impostorism is most relevant when enabling AI use makes AI-supported accomplishments attributionally meaningful.

AI-related impostorism was associated with emotional exhaustion, but it did not significantly condition the relationships between techno-eustress or techno-distress and emotional exhaustion. This suggests that AI-related impostorism may be emotionally relevant as a self-evaluative concern, while not necessarily altering how technostress responses relate to emotional exhaustion. Similarly, the non-significant techno-distress–performance interaction suggests that AI-related impostorism does not generally offset the performance constraints associated with techno-distress. Its moderating role appears more specific to situations in which AI use is experienced as enabling and is associated with higher performance.

Conceptually, AI-related impostorism concerns the legitimacy of one's competence when AI contributes to accomplishments. This supports the competence-legitimacy lens, which is particularly relevant in AI-augmented work, where opacity and task changes may challenge employees' understanding of their role and contribution [1, 2].

Practical Implications. Organizations should not treat high performance as evidence that employees are doing well in AI-augmented work. Because performance and emotional exhaustion are separate outcomes that can coexist [1, 12, 18], managers should monitor both outcomes and AI-related impostorism jointly. Practical responses should not stop at AI availability or technical training. Organizations should clarify work roles, contribution expectations, and attribution of AI-supported accomplishments, and provide task-relevant support [2, 16]. This is especially relevant under enabling AI use, where AI-related impostorism selectively strengthened the techno-eustress–performance relationship. Support should therefore distinguish technical proficiency from competence and contribution concerns linked to AI-related impostorism.

6 Limitations and Future Research

First, the cross-sectional design does not permit causal inference or establish temporal ordering, while technostress responses can vary over time [4, 11]. The findings should be interpreted as associations among latent constructs. Second, the study does not directly measure AI-related demands, task types, or forms of AI use, limiting inference to response-level mechanisms. Future research should measure AI-related demands and distinguish those demands from employees' technostress responses to AI use. It should also examine whether the relationships studied here differ across AI-supported tasks and work contexts. Third, all focal constructs were collected through self-reports in a single-source survey, which constrains interpretation of performance and leaves common method influences possible. Thus, the performance findings should not be interpreted as objective performance effects. Fourth, AI-related impostorism was modeled as a relatively stable domain-specific tendency, leaving its situational variability and distinction from related constructs open. Future research could examine episodic forms of AI-related impostorism. Finally, compensatory effort remains a plausible but untested mechanism in the performance-related arguments involving AI-related impostorism. Future research should measure compensatory effort directly and consider alternative explanations before treating it as an explanation for AI-related impostorism's direct or moderating links with performance.

7 Conclusion

This study clarifies that technostress research for AI-augmented work needs to account for both technostress response valence and competence attribution around AI-supported accomplishments. Techno-eustress and techno-distress related differently to emotional exhaustion and performance. AI-related impostorism was associated with emotional exhaustion and selectively moderated the techno-eustress–performance relationship. The results specify why AI-augmented work requires attention to both how employees experience AI use and how they interpret their own contribution to AI-supported accomplishments.

Appendix

Table 1. Subdimensional Correlations: Descriptive Statistics, AVE, and CR

		Construct	M	SD	AVE	CR	1	2	3	4	5	6	7	8	9	10	11	12	13
Techno-eustress	1	Mastery	4.15	0.63	0.663	0.887	**0.814**												
	2	Autonomy	3.60	0.88	0.720	0.911	0.500	**0.849**											
	3	Relatedness	2.89	1.13	0.829	0.951	0.428	0.589	**0.910**										
	4	Enrichment	4.00	0.70	0.700	0.903	0.620	0.427	0.395	**0.837**									
Techno-distress	5	Overload	2.23	0.92	0.696	0.919	-0.098	-0.031	0.110	-0.140	**0.834**								
	6	Invasion	1.70	0.76	0.684	0.896	-0.211	-0.038	0.116	-0.252	0.651	**0.827**							
	7	Complexity	1.89	0.77	0.690	0.899	-0.341	-0.158	-0.037	-0.315	0.541	0.625	**0.831**						
	8	Insecurity	2.03	0.86	0.649	0.881	-0.283	-0.149	0.038	-0.235	0.548	0.637	0.667	**0.806**					
	9	Uncertainty	2.83	1.10	0.827	0.935	0.078	0.162	0.323	0.063	0.469	0.335	0.287	0.348	**0.909**				
Exhaustion	10	Exhaustion	2.30	1.29	0.717	0.965	-0.375	-0.173	-0.049	-0.262	0.523	0.456	0.496	0.543	0.133	**0.847**			
Perfor-mance	11	Task Performance	4.15	0.61	0.707	0.906	0.668	0.294	0.270	0.556	-0.134	-0.235	-0.411	-0.324	0.028	-0.364	**0.841**		
	12	Innovative Performance	3.98	0.75	0.863	0.950	0.605	0.377	0.321	0.486	-0.074	-0.172	-0.370	-0.267	0.060	-0.376	0.726	**0.929**	
AI-related Impostor-ism	13	AI-related Impostorism	1.87	1.04	0.833	0.972	-0.174	-0.179	-0.115	-0.166	0.376	0.442	0.455	0.510	0.042	0.476	-0.205	-0.242	**0.913**

Note. Bold diagonal values represent the square root of AVE (√AVE). M = mean; SD = standard deviation; AVE = average variance extracted; CR = composite reliability (ρC). N = 207.

References

1. Selenko, E., Bankins, S., Shoss, M., Warburton, J., Restubog, S.L.D.: Artificial intelligence and the future of work: a functional-identity perspective. Curr. Dir. Psychol. Sci. **31**, 272–279 (2022). https://doi.org/10.1177/09637214221091823
2. Monod, E., Mayer, A.-S., Straub, D., Joyce, E., Qi, J.: From worker empowerment to managerial control: The devolution of AI tools' intended positive implementation to their negative consequences. Inf. Organ. **34**, 100498 (2024). https://doi.org/10.1016/j.infoandorg.2023.100498
3. Ragu-Nathan, T.S., Tarafdar, M., Ragu-Nathan, B.S., Tu, Q.: The Consequences of technostress for end users in organizations: conceptual development and empirical validation. Inf. Syst. Res. **19**, 417–433 (2008). https://doi.org/10.1287/isre.1070.0165
4. Benlian, A.: A Daily field investigation of technology-driven spillovers from work to home. MIS Q. **44**, 1259–1300 (2020). https://doi.org/10.25300/MISQ/2020/14911
5. Califf, C.B., Sarker, S., Sarker, S.: The Bright and dark sides of technostress: a mixed-methods study involving healthcare IT. MIS Q. **44**, 809–856 (2020). https://doi.org/10.25300/MISQ/2020/14818
6. Strich, F., Mayer, A.-S., Fiedler, M.: What Do I Do in a world of artificial intelligence? investigating the impact of substitutive decision-making AI systems on employees' professional role identity. J. Assoc. Inf. Syst. **22**, 304–324 (2021). https://doi.org/10.17705/1jais.00663

7. Clance, P.R., Imes, S.A.: The imposter phenomenon in high achieving women: dynamics and therapeutic intervention. Psychother. Theory Res. Pract. **15**, 241–247 (1978). https://doi.org/10.1037/h0086006
8. Tarafdar, M., Cooper, C.L., Stich, J.: The technostress trifecta - techno eustress, techno distress and design: Theoretical directions and an agenda for research. Inf. Syst. J. **29**, 6–42 (2019). https://doi.org/10.1111/isj.12169
9. Tarafdar, M., Stich, J., Maier, C., Laumer, S.: Techno-eustress creators: conceptualization and empirical validation. Inf. Syst. J. **34**, 2097–2131 (2024). https://doi.org/10.1111/isj.12515
10. Maier, C., Laumer, S., Tarafdar, M., Mattke, J., Reis, L., Weitzel, T.: Challenge and hindrance IS use stressors and appraisals: explaining contrarian associations in post-acceptance IS use behavior. J. Assoc. Inf. Syst. **22**, 1590–1624 (2021). https://doi.org/10.17705/1jais.00709
11. Salo, M., Pirkkalainen, H., Chua, C.E.H., Koskelainen, T.: Formation and mitigation of technostress in the personal use of IT. MIS Q. **46**, 1073–1108 (2022). https://doi.org/10.25300/MISQ/2022/14950
12. Pflügner, K., Maier, C., Thatcher, J.B., Mattke, J., Weitzel, T.: Deconstructing technostress: a configurational approach to explaining job burnout and job performance. MIS Q. **48**, 679–698 (2024). https://doi.org/10.25300/MISQ/2023/16978
13. Wright, T.A., Cropanzano, R.: Emotional exhaustion as a predictor of job performance and voluntary turnover. J. Appl. Psychol. **83**, 486–493 (1998). https://doi.org/10.1037/0021-9010.83.3.486
14. Xu, G., Xue, M., Zhao, J.: The Association between artificial intelligence awareness and employee depression: The mediating role of emotional exhaustion and the moderating role of perceived organizational support. Int. J. Environ. Res. Public Health. **20**, 5147 (2023). https://doi.org/10.3390/ijerph20065147
15. Tarafdar, M., Tu, Q., Ragu-Nathan, T.S.: Impact of technostress on end-user satisfaction and performance. J. Manag. Inf. Syst. **27**, 303–334 (2010). https://doi.org/10.2753/MIS0742-1222270311
16. Fügener, A., Grahl, J., Gupta, A., Ketter, W.: Cognitive challenges in human–artificial intelligence collaboration: investigating the path toward productive delegation. Inf. Syst. Res. **33**, 678–696 (2022). https://doi.org/10.1287/isre.2021.1079
17. Leary, M.R., Patton, K.M., Orlando, A.E., Wagoner Funk, W.: The Impostor phenomenon: self-perceptions, reflected appraisals, and interpersonal strategies. J. Pers. **68**, 725–756 (2000). https://doi.org/10.1111/1467-6494.00114
18. Whitman, M.V., Shanine, K.K.: Revisiting the impostor phenomenon: how individuals cope with feelings of being in over their heads. In: Perrewé, P.L., Halbesleben, J.R.B., Rosen, C.C. (eds.) Research in Occupational Stress and Well-being, pp. 177–212. Emerald Group Publishing Limited (2012). https://doi.org/10.1108/S1479-3555(2012)0000010009
19. Srivastava, S.C., Chandra, S., Shirish, A.: Technostress creators and job outcomes: theorising the moderating influence of personality traits. Inf. Syst. J. **25**, 355–401 (2015). https://doi.org/10.1111/isj.12067
20. Maier, C., Laumer, S., Eckhardt, A., Weitzel, T.: When social networking turns to social overload: explaining the stress, emotional exhaustion, and quitting behavior from social network sites' users. In: ECIS 2012 Proceedings (European Conference on Information Systems), pp. 1–12 (2012)
21. Henseler, J., Ringle, C.M., Sinkovics, R.R.: The use of partial least squares path modeling in international marketing. In: Sinkovics, R.R., Ghauri, P.N. (eds.) Advances in International Marketing, pp. 277–319. Emerald Group Publishing Limited (2009). https://doi.org/10.1108/S1474-7979(2009)0000020014
22. Sabol, M., Hair, J., Cepeda, G., Roldán, J.L., Chong, A.Y.L.: PLS-SEM in information systems: seizing the opportunity and marching ahead full speed to adopt methodological updates.

Ind. Manage. Data Syst. **123**, 2997–3017 (2023). https://doi.org/10.1108/IMDS-07-2023-0429
23. Sarstedt, M., Hair, J.F., Cheah, J.-H., Becker, J.-M., Ringle, C.M.: How to specify, estimate, and validate higher-order constructs in PLS-SEM. Australas. Mark. J. **27**, 197–211 (2019). https://doi.org/10.1016/j.ausmj.2019.05.003
24. Ringle, C.M., Sarstedt, M., Straub, D.W.: Editor's comments. a critical look at the use of PLS-SEM in MIS quarterly. MIS Q. **36**, iii–xvi (2012). https://doi.org/10.2307/41410402
25. Henseler, J., Fassott, G.: Testing moderating effects in PLS path models: an illustration of available procedures. In: Esposito Vinzi, V., Chin, W.W., Henseler, J., Wang, H. (eds.) Handbook of Partial Least Squares, pp. 713–735. Springer, Berlin Heidelberg, Berlin, Heidelberg (2010). https://doi.org/10.1007/978-3-540-32827-8_31
26. Hair, J.F., Ringle, C.M., Sarstedt, M.: PLS-SEM: Indeed a silver bullet. J. Mark. Theory Pract. **19**, 139–152 (2011). https://doi.org/10.2753/MTP1069-6679190202
27. Henseler, J., Hubona, G., Ray, P.A.: Using PLS path modeling in new technology research: updated guidelines. Ind. Manag. Data Syst. **116**, 2–20 (2016). https://doi.org/10.1108/IMDS-09-2015-0382
28. Henseler, J., Ringle, C.M., Sarstedt, M.: A new criterion for assessing discriminant validity in variance-based structural equation modeling. J. Acad. Mark. Sci. **43**, 115–135 (2015). https://doi.org/10.1007/s11747-014-0403-8
29. Podsakoff, P.M., MacKenzie, S.B., Lee, J.-Y., Podsakoff, N.P.: Common method biases in behavioral research: a critical review of the literature and recommended remedies. J. Appl. Psychol. **88**, 879–903 (2003). https://doi.org/10.1037/0021-9010.88.5.879
30. Kock, N.: Common method bias in PLS-SEM: a full collinearity assessment approach. Int. J. e-Collab. **11**, 1–10 (2015). https://doi.org/10.4018/ijec.2015100101

Using Generative AI in Knowledge Acquisition Within South African Insurance SMEs

Stevens Phaphadi Mamorobela(✉)

Department of Information Systems, College of Science Engineering and Technology, School of Computing, University of South Africa, Johannesburg, South Africa
mamorsp@unisa.ac.za

Abstract. The evolution of Generative Artificial Intelligence (GenAI) presents revolutionary learning and innovation opportunities in risk assessment, claims underwriting, and fraud management within the insurance industry. However, it is becoming increasingly difficult for SMEs to identify and extract valuable external knowledge signals from GenAI content to effectively support organisational learning and innovation. This study examines how GenAI contributes to enhancing Knowledge Acquisition in SMEs within the South African insurance industry. Drawing on absorptive capacity theory, this study adopts a qualitative approach and analyses data from 13 semi-structured interviews conducted with SME owners to gain a deeper understanding of the intricacies involved in integrating GenAI into Knowledge Acquisition processes. The thematical analysis was employed to identify common themes in the data, providing insights into the effective integration of GenAI with Knowledge Acquisition practices in SMEs within the South African insurance industry. The findings reveal that GenAI can enhance Knowledge Acquisition through three mechanisms. First, reasoning, which involves leveraging the high-order cognitive capabilities of GenAI to interpret and make sense of complex insurance terminologies. Second, experimentation, which requires SMEs to test GenAI outputs for accuracy and validity before adoption. Third, social learning, where GenAI outputs are used in conjunction with human expertise within collaborative environments to improve the quality of knowledge generated. This study provides valuable insights that can inform future research and development efforts aimed at understanding the evolving role of GenAI and its integration into Knowledge Management practices.

Keywords: Generative AI · Knowledge Acquisition · SME · Insurance

1 Introduction

Artificial intelligence (AI) has emerged as one of the most transformative forces in today's economy, fundamentally reshaping how organisations operate and compete. Although AI is not a new concept, its origins can be traced back to the 1940s, when early researchers sought to simulate the functioning of the human brain using simple input–output models to explore the computational capabilities of neurons [1]. From

Published by Springer Nature Switzerland AG 2027
S. Han et al. (Eds.): I3E 2026, LNCS 16912, pp. 27–37, 2027.
https://doi.org/10.1007/978-3-032-38014-2_3

these modest beginnings, AI has advanced significantly, leading to the development of technologies such as machine learning, deep learning, Human-centered AI, and GenAI [2–4]. These tools have gained widespread adoption across various industries due to their ability to rapidly process and analyse vast volumes of data.

In the insurance industry, GenAI is increasingly adopted for its potential to support intelligent underwriting, streamline claims management, and enhance insurance product analysis [5]. Its adoption is primarily driven by its unique advantages over other conventional technologies, particularly in areas such as risk management, customer needs analysis, insurance product consultation, personalised insurance product recommendations, automated underwriting, and customer communication [6]. The data relating to customers, claims, policies and regulations constitute critical sources of knowledge that must be systematically absorbed to support informed decision making [7]. Historically, absorptive capacity within insurance organisations has been slow and largely manual, with information dispersed across physical records, fragmented systems, and the personal experiences of employees [8]. This fragmentation often leads to the loss of valuable insights and reduces the efficiency of decision-making processes. As a result, insurance industries are increasingly expected to digitise processes to enhance absorptive capacity. Through digitisation, insurance organisations can better safeguard their knowledge assets, ensure continuity, and enhance their ability to make informed and strategic decisions.

GenAI now enables insurance small and medium-sized enterprises (SMEs) to process large volumes of information in seconds, identifying patterns and risks that would otherwise take human analysts days, if not weeks, to identify [7]. This advancement presents both significant opportunities and notable challenges for the insurance sector, as GenAI is disrupting traditional practices, transforming operational processes, and fostering innovation in ways that redefine how insurance SMEs create value. GenAI holds considerable potential for enhancing how SMEs acquire and use knowledge. However, despite growing scholarly and industrial interest, there remains a limited body of research that provides clear, practical guidance on how GenAI can be effectively integrated into Knowledge Acquisition processes. Much of the existing literature focuses on the broader impact of GenAI [2, 9, 10], with less attention given to actionable frameworks or strategies for its implementation within organisational Knowledge Acquisition practices.

Prior research has consistently highlighted the urgent need for SME-specific operational guidelines to support the responsible adoption and use of GenAI [11–15]. More specifically, empirical evidence on the use of GenAI to support Knowledge Acquisition in the SME context remains limited. SMEs in the South Africa's insurance industry face significant uncertainty regarding how to define appropriate GenAI use cases, assess associated risks, ensure regulatory compliance, safeguard data, and establish minimal yet effective socio-technical controls [8].

This lack of guidance increases the risk of mis-investment, compliance failures, and uneven performance outcomes, while also slowing the diffusion of productivity gains that GenAI could otherwise deliver in SMEs. The lack of contextual understanding limits the development of practical and responsible guidelines for use of GenAI tailored for SMEs in the South African insurance industry. Against this backdrop, the central question guiding this study is: *How is generative AI utilised to enhance Knowledge Acquisition in SMEs within the South Africa's insurance industry?*

Building on previous studies, this study contextualises how GenAI is utilised to enhance Knowledge Acquisition in SMEs within the South Africa's insurance industry. The structure of this study follows the introduction, problem identification and research question and objective in Sect. 1, Sect. 2 reviews theoretical foundations, Sect. 3 presents the methodology, Sect. 4 offers results and discussions, and conclusion, implications and recommendations for future research in Sect. 5.

2 Theoretical Foundations

The Absorptive Capacity theory was adopted as the theoretical foundation underpinning this study. Absorptive Capacity, as defined by [16], refers to an organisation's collective ability to acquire, assimilate, transform, and exploit knowledge in ways that fosters innovation. In essence, an organisation's innovative capability is strongly influenced by how effective it can identify, access, and utilise knowledge from external sources. Prior related knowledge, ranging from basic skills and shared language to an awareness of scientific and technological advancements, enhances an organisation's capacity to recognise the value of new knowledge, internalise it, and leverage it for competitive advantage [17]. This capability is particularly critical for SMEs in South Africa's insurance industry, where persistent economic inequalities intensify the need to develop absorptive capacity through alternative and adaptive approaches. The ability to make informed, data-driven decisions is therefore essential, as it directly influences not only the financial performance of insurance SMEs but also the trust and confidence of their customers.

In the SME context, Absorptive Capacity plays a critical role as a mediator between open innovation and performance outcomes [18]. A critical determinant of this capability is Knowledge Acquisition, which shapes how individuals and organisations evaluate, interpret, and apply new information. This capability also includes awareness of more advanced scientific and technological developments that enable organisations to recognise the value of new knowledge, integrate it more effectively, and leverage it to support innovation and competitive advantage. [19] also discovered that Absorptive Capacity enhances the relationship between Knowledge Acquisition and digital innovation in Software SMEs.

SMEs in the insurance industry often invest substantially in acquiring external knowledge and embedding it within their organisational structures [20]. They are increasingly becoming more equipped with advanced digital tools such as GenAI to understand, interpret, and integrate knowledge [21]. By leveraging insights derived from GenAI outputs, insurance SMEs are better positioned to recognise the value of new knowledge, assimilate it effectively, and translate it into viable commercial opportunities.

However, current research has often explored the role of GenAI in SME innovation and performance [5, 6, 11, 13, 22], leaving specific role of GenAI on Knowledge Acquisition in these aspects largely underexplored. For example, [6] discussed the relative advantage the GenAI brings to SME performance but did not explore the specific pathways through which external knowledge impacts actual SME performance. Furthermore, [22] discussed the impact of GenAI on enterprise innovation performance from the knowledge management perspective but raises concerns about organizational deficiencies in Absorptive Capacity that precipitates through ineffective human-AI collaboration, weak cross-boundary diffusion capabilities of AI-generated innovations, and imbalanced human-AI knowledge co-creation patterns. This gap in the literature necessitates a more granular investigation of how GenAI can be leveraged to enhance Knowledge Acquisition in SMEs, from the lenses of Absorptive Capacity.

3 Methodology

A qualitative approach was applied, using semi-structured interviews of purposively selected managers and executives in the insurance SMEs. To inform the sampling process, the corporate websites of potential SMEs were reviewed to gain insight into their background, size (number of permanent employees), location, annual turnover, and business profiles. Participants were selected based on specific criteria, focusing on founders, owners, directors, or managers with at least one year of experience in their roles and an established customer base. This ensured that respondents possessed sufficient organisational knowledge and experience to meaningfully contribute to the study. Table 1 tabulates the results of the recruitment process.

Table 1. Participant recruitment process

Recruitment process items	No.
Insurance SMEs shortlisted to participate in the study	21
SME participants who acknowledged the invitation to participate in the interview meetings	18
SME participants who honoured the invitation, signed the consent form and attended the interviews	13

An interview guide was developed, comprising semi-structured questions aligned with the absorptive capacity theory. This instrument was designed to explore the perceptions of respondents regarding the adoption of GenAI and its role in enhancing Knowledge Acquisition within their organisational processes. Each interview was scheduled to last between 45 and 60 minutes and was audio-recorded with participants' consent. The recordings were subsequently transcribed and analysed using a thematic analysis approach, following the methodological guidance outlined by [23]. Thematical analysis is a flexible method of qualitative data analysis that involves organising data into codes, themes, relationships, patterns, explanations, and interpretations to derive meaning. The process followed a systematic sequence of steps, including text familiarisation, coding, revision, theme creation and final revision of the identified themes, as illustrated in Fig. 1.

The first step involved text familiarisation in which the researcher listened to each of the 13 audio-recorded interviews multiple times to ensure clarity and accuracy. The recordings were then transcribed verbatim and imported into Atlas.ti version 25 software for subsequent analysis.

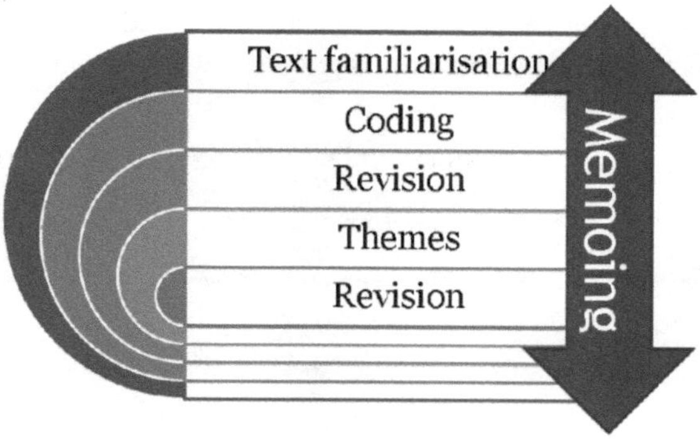

Fig 1. Thematical analysis process adapted from [23]

The second step entailed coding, which involved the development of a coding schema within Atlas.ti to extract text segments from each transcript that were relevant to addressing the research question. A theory-driven approach to code development was adopted [24, 25], whereby codes were developed "a priori" and used to guide the analysis. The central research question: *How is generative AI utilised to enhance Knowledge Acquisition in SMEs within the South African insurance industry?* informed the process. Key dimensions of Knowledge Acquisition, namely reasoning, social learning, and experimenting were identified as central ideas for guiding the analysis. Relevant text segments were systematically assigned to codes aligned with these dimensions, and a codebook was developed to document the codes and corresponding data text extracts.

In the third step, the codebook was reviewed and refined to ensure that all codes were relevant to the research question and that no significant text segments were omitted. Codes representing similar concepts were grouped into broader themes using the "code groups" function on Atlas.ti. Themes are parent codes used to organise related codes and subcodes. These themes were labelled as "GenAI-enabled Knowledge Acquisition:reasoning", "GenAI-enabled Knowledge Acquisition:experimenting", and "GenAI-enabled Knowledge Acquisition:social learning". The process of theme development was rigorous, ensuring that each theme captured distinct aspects of the data without conceptual overlap. Where necessary, codes were merged or removed to maintain analytical clarity and relevance to the research question.

Finally, the identified themes were further synthesised using the "smart groups" function on Atlas.ti to develop an overarching theme named "GenAI-enabled Knowledge Acquisition". This higher-order theme directly addresses the central research question by providing an integrated understanding of how GenAI can enhance Knowledge Acquisition in SMEs within the South African insurance industry.

4 Results and Discussions

The results are presented and discussed in accordance with the themes identified as most relevant to addressing the study's research question. A "network diagrams" function in Atlas.ti was utilised to visualise and consolidate the analytical findings, offering a clearer representation of how the codes and themes interrelate to address the research question. Figure 2 illustrates the thematic network diagram developed in this study.

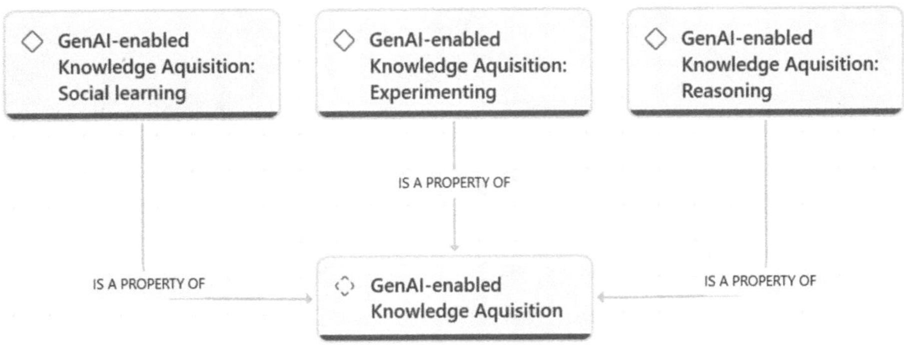

Fig 2. Generative AI enabled Knowledge Acquisition in SMEs

GenAI-enabled Knowledge Acquisition emerged as the central theme of the study, derived from the research question aimed at understanding how insurance SMEs utilise GenAI to identify and acquire new industry-related knowledge. The findings indicate that SMEs leverage GenAI for Knowledge Acquisition through three primary approaches: reasoning, experimentation, and social learning.

With respect to reasoning, the findings revealed that GenAI can support Knowledge Acquisition by applying conceptual and logical problem-solving capabilities to interpret complex insurance terminologies. In the context of large language models (LLMs), reasoning refers to the ability of the model to perform high-order cognitive processing, including decomposing problems, following logical steps, and making informed inferences, rather than merely reproducing learned text patterns [26, 27]. This suggests that GenAI does not simply replicate existing information but engages in a more structured, step-by-step analytical process, resembling human reasoning in problem solving contexts. These insights were further supported by the perspectives shared by the research participants as stated below:

> "*When I want to understand a new regulation or market shift, I can type a question and get a structured overview in seconds. It doesn't mean I stop verifying, but it gives me direction. It's like having a research assistant who never gets tired.*" [participant1]

> "*Insurance can get very jargon-heavy. Sometimes I'll paste a paragraph into GenAI and ask it to explain it like I'm talking to a client who's never heard of insurance before. It makes things less intimidating for the team too.*" [participant 4]

These sentiments indicate that SMEs in the insurance industry use GenAI as a sense-making tool to rapidly generate structured overviews of industry trends, thereby reducing the time required to review multiple source documents. The results further indicate that GenAI functions as a complementary layer that enhances situational awareness, broadens contextual understanding, and accelerates preliminary research processes, while final decisions continue to rely on human expertise. However, these observations also imply that GenAI does not truly perform genuine cognitive reasoning but simply simulates reasoning processes. Supporting this perspective, [28], in a study examining the challenges for generative AI in legal reasoning, argues that such systems lack the capacity to perform justifiable discretionary reasoning and instead operates within constrained parameters, responding to narrowly defined tasks rather than demonstrating genuine reasoning capabilities. Similarly, [29] reinforces this perspective by highlighting that LLMs often fail to exhibit consistent and reliable reasoning in complex scenarios. Collectively, these findings suggest that, due to their strong dependence on input data, the apparent reasoning capabilities of GenAI systems can vary significantly with even minor changes in input. This variability raises important concerns regarding inconsistencies and potential errors, particularly in complex decision-making contexts.

In terms of experimenting with newly acquired knowledge, existing literature suggests that GenAI can be used for experimentation through iteratively testing, validation, and refinement of its outputs within controlled environments [30]. Experimentation in the context of LLMs can be defined as the structured use of model in controlled settings to examine user interactions, perceptions, and outcomes, while systematically capturing conversations and participant feedback [31]. The findings of this study revealed that insurance SMEs primarily use GenAI to identify knowledge gaps between local practices and global industry trends. In doing so, SMEs compare GenAI insights with existing human expertise to enhance understanding and support collaborative knowledge development. The research participants explained their approach to experimenting with GenAI as follows:

> "*One example was when we were exploring wellness-linked insurance ideas. GenAI gave us international examples, and then we adapted those ideas to suit our local clients and regulatory environment. It wasn't copy and paste, more like inspiration that we reshaped*" [participant 8]

> "*One example was when we were reviewing coverage limits for commercial properties. GenAI gave us general market benchmarks, and then we compared that with our own historical claims data. The final adjustments came from blending both sources*" [participant 11]

These sentiments reflect informal experimentation with GenAI within everyday professional practices of insurance SMEs in South Africa. Participants indicated that they continuously test GenAI outputs across a range of insurance related tasks, including terminology translation, regulatory scanning, niche risk research, and market trend analysis, to evaluate where GenAI adds value. The results further indicate that, through repeated use, SMEs observe outcomes such as improved speed of comprehension, broader exposure to industry related knowledge, and reduced information overload. To support this, [32] adds that GenAI has the ability to navigate organisational complexity and capture fragmented knowledge that would otherwise remain inaccessible. Similarly, [33] highlights that organisations continuously engage in structural experimentations to explore how AI can support knowledge creation and decision making processes. Collectively, the findings suggest that the use of GenAI in organisations remain largely experimental, characterised by iterative testing, human in the loop, and continuous refinement of knowledge practices. While this process does not constitute formal scientific experimentation, it represents a practical, iterative trial and error process in which GenAI is applied within controlled work scenarios.

The third approach to Knowledge Acquisition identified in this study is social learning. According to [34], social learning can be described as a collaborative process of knowledge construction that emerges within learning communities, grounded in the principles of social constructivism and characterised by shared agency between humans and GenAI. This conceptualisation suggests that knowledge is co-created through dynamic interactions between human actors and GenAI systems within a collective learning environment. In this study, research participants explained how they use GenAI in a collaborative manner to support Knowledge Acquisition, as illustrated in the excerpts below:

> "*Yes, actually. We're more open about sharing information now. My staff will post short AI summaries in our WhatsApp group or bring them up during meetings. It's informal, but it keeps everyone updated.*" [participant 5]

> "*I'd say it's helped me see the bigger picture a bit quicker. Before, I'd jump between different websites or newsletters trying to understand what competitors were doing or what new products were coming up. Now I can ask one question and at least get a general overview*" [participant 13]

These sentiments suggest that GenAI is perceived as a supportive tool for information sharing and for generating rapid overviews of relevant knowledge in insurance SMEs. Participants further indicated that their organisations have become more open to knowledge sharing practices and the use of GenAI as a tool for Knowledge Acquisition. Although its application remains largely informal, participants acknowledged that GenAI enables them to stay informed by providing a broader perspective on industry trends and insights into the practices of other organisations. In a study of Human-centered Artificial Intelligence (HCAI) [3] advocates for human control over AI systems to ensure that human values are maintained when AI is used as a collaborative partner. Similarly, [35] laments that GenAI should adjust its responses based on real-time observations to maintain relevance as a cognitive collaborative partner in social learning environments. Collectively, these findings suggest that GenAI does not replace the expertise of humans and broader knowledge embedded within professional communities but aligns with social constructivist principles as a collaborative partner.

5 Conclusions and Recommendations

This paper explored the transformative role of GenAI on Knowledge Acquisition in SMEs within the South African insurance industry. Through a qualitative approach of 13 interviews with SME executives, the study demonstrated that GenAI could serve as a collaborative partner for Knowledge Acquisition through reasoning, experimentation, and social learning.

Whilst GenAI demonstrates capabilities that resemble reasoning, it was discovered that these systems do not possess true reasoning abilities but instead simulate reasoning through probabilistic pattern recognition, often leading to inconsistencies and errors in complex decision-making contexts. The research findings also revealed that approach of experimenting with GenAI in insurance SMEs reflects real-world experimentation focusing on understanding the capabilities and limitations of GenAI in supporting insurance related knowledge workflows. Moreover, the findings further indicated that GenAI aligns closely with social constructivist principles, enabling collaborative and interactive Knowledge Acquisition processes of insurance SMEs.

Although this study was limited to a qualitative approach, which may have excluded valuable insights that could have been obtained through quantitative and experimental research, it nevertheless makes meaningful contributions to both theory and practice. From a theoretical perspective, the study advances the understanding of the relationship between Knowledge Acquisition and GenAI by examining these constructs through the lens of Absorptive Capacity Theory. From a practical perspective, the findings provide SME owners and managers with key considerations for leveraging the potential of GenAI to enhance social learning, experimentation, and reasoning capabilities within knowledge acquisition activities. These insights may support SMEs in strengthening their knowledge management practices and improving their capacity for innovation.

It is recommended that future studies examine the impact of GenAI more broadly across additional Knowledge Management dimensions, as well as in relation to the goals and principles of industry 5.0. Furthermore, there is a need for further investigations into the development of policy frameworks and practical guidelines to support the ethical and responsible integration of GenAI in SME context.

Acknowledgments. This study received ethical clearance from the University of South Africa, College of Science, Engineering and Technology's Ethics Review Committee with a reference (ref.no.2024/CSET/SOC/6172).

Disclosure of Interests The author declares the use of AI in the paper titled "Exploring the role of Generative AI in Knowledge Acquisition within South African Insurance SMEs" to improve the English language. In addition, a professional language editing service, was used to further enhance the clarity and quality of the English language in the manuscript.

References

1. Daly, M.C.: The AI Moment? possibilities, productivity, and policy. FRBSF Econ. Lett. **2026**(06), 1–8 (2026)

2. Banh, L., Strobel, G.: Generative artificial intelligence. Electron. Mark. **33**(1), 63 (2023). https://doi.org/10.1007/s12525-023-00680-1
3. Schmager, S., Pappas, I.O., Vassilakopoulou, P.: Understanding human-centred AI: a review of its defining elements and a research agenda. Behav. Inf. Technol. **44**(15), 3771–3810 (2025). https://doi.org/10.1080/0144929X.2024.2448719
4. Taherdoost, H., Madanchian, M.: Artificial intelligence and knowledge management: impacts, benefits, and implementation. Computers. **12**, 72 (2023). https://doi.org/10.3390/computers12040072
5. Marano, P., Li, S.: Governing algorithmic insurance: reconciling the EU AI act with insurance-specific regulation. Connect. Insur. Law J. **32**(1), 62–114 (2026)
6. Zaijuan, X., Ramayah, T., Yubo, S.: Determinants of generative artificial intelligence adoption in insurance companies. Int. J. Bus. Soc. **26**(1), 272–291 (2025). https://doi.org/10.33736/ijbs.9562.2025
7. Jaiswal, R.: Impact of AI in the general insurance underwriting factors. Cent. Eur. Manag. J. **31**(2), 697–705 (2023). https://doi.org/10.57030/23364890.cemj.31.2.72
8. Jones, K.I., Sah, S.: The Implementation of machine learning in The insurance industry with big data analytics. Int. J. Data Informatics Intell. Comput. **2**(2), 21–38 (2023). https://doi.org/10.59461/ijdiic.v2i2.47
9. Behrend, T.S., Landers, R.N.: Participant interactions with artificial intelligence: using large language models to generate research materials for surveys and experiments. J. Bus. Psychol. **40**(6), 1275–1297 (2025). https://doi.org/10.1007/s10869-025-10035-6
10. Hou, I., et al.: All roads lead to ChatGPT': how generative AI is eroding social interactions and student learning communities. In: Annual Conference on Innovation and Technology in Computer Science Education, ITiCSE, pp. 79–85. Association for Computing Machinery (2025). https://doi.org/10.1145/3724363.3729024
11. Sánchez, E., Calderón, R., Herrera, F.: Artificial intelligence adoption in SMEs: survey based on TOE–DOI framework, primary methodology and challenges. Appl. Sci. **15**, 6465 (2025). https://doi.org/10.3390/app15126465
12. Le Dinh, T., Vu, M.C., Tran, G.T.C.: Artificial intelligence in SMEs: enhancing business functions through technologies and applications. Information. **16**, 415 (2025). https://doi.org/10.3390/info16050415
13. Rasdi, R.M., Baki, N.U.: Navigating the AI landscape in SMEs: overcoming internal challenges and external obstacles for effective integration. PLoS One. **20**, e0323249 (2025). https://doi.org/10.1371/journal.pone.0323249
14. Taeihagh, A.: Governance of generative AI. Policy Soc. **44**, 1–22 (2025). https://doi.org/10.1093/polsoc/puaf001
15. Schwaeke, J., Peters, A., Kanbach, D.K., Kraus, S., Jones, P.: The new normal: The status quo of AI adoption in SMEs. J. Small Bus. Manag. **63**(3), 1297–1331 (2025). https://doi.org/10.1080/00472778.2024.2379999
16. Zahra, S.A., George, G.: Absorptive capacity: a review, reconceptualization, and extension. Acad. Manag. Rev. **27**(2), 185–203 (2002)
17. Manesh, F.M.: Knowledge management in the fourth industrial revolution: mapping the literature and scoping future avenues. IEEE Trans. Eng. Manag. **68**(1), 289–300 (2021). https://doi.org/10.1109/tem.2019.2963489
18. Mubarak, M.F., Evans, R., Shabbir, M., Ghobakhloo, M., Petraite, M., Jucevicius, G.: Driving new product development performance: the mediating role of absorptive capacity in open innovation for SMEs. J. Manuf. Technol. Manag. **37**(3), 641–656 (2026)
19. Sherani, J., Zhang, M.U., Shehzad, S.A., Cao, Z.: Unlocking digital innovation: a moderated-mediation approach exploring the knowledge creation processes, IT-enabled capabilities and absorptive capacity in software SMEs. Bus. Process Manag. J. **31**(1), 170–201 (2025)

20. Carayannis, E.G., Dumitrescu, R., Falkowski, T., Zota, N.R.: Empowering SMEs 'harnessing the potential of gen AI for resilience and competitiveness. IEEE Trans. Eng. Manag. **71**, 14754–14774 (2024). https://doi.org/10.1109/TEM.2024.3456820
21. Mamorobela, S.P.: Evaluating the facilitating conditions towards the integration of GenAI in knowledge sharing for SMEs. In: 2025 IST-Africa Conference (IST-Africa), p. 2025 (2025) Online. Available: www.IST-Africa.org/Conference2025
22. Zhang, Q., Zuo, J., Yang, S.: Research on the impact of generative artificial intelligence (GenAI) on enterprise innovation performance: a knowledge management perspective. J. Knowl. Manag. **29**(7), 2238–2257 (2025)
23. Archer, E., van Vuuren, H.H.J., Van der Walt, H.D.: Introduction to Atlas. ti: Basic Operations, Tips and Tricks of Coding. Research Rescue (2017)
24. Fife, S.T., Gossner, J.D.: Deductive qualitative analysis: evaluating, expanding, and refining theory. Int. J. Qual. Methods. **23**, 1–12 (2024). https://doi.org/10.1177/16094069241244856
25. Bihu, R.: Qualitative Data Analysis: Novelty in Deductive and Inductive Coding (2024). https://doi.org/10.31124/advance.24143088.v2
26. Uçar, S.Ş., Lopez-Gazpio, I., Lopez-Gazpio, J.: Evaluating and challenging the reasoning capabilities of generative artificial intelligence for technology-assisted chemistry education. Educ. Inf. Technol. **30**(8), 11463–11482 (2025). https://doi.org/10.1007/s10639-024-13295-6
27. Wang, L., Shen, Y.: Evaluating causal reasoning capabilities of large language models: a systematic analysis across three scenarios. Electron. **13**(23), 4584 (2024). https://doi.org/10.3390/electronics13234584
28. Linna, E., Linna, T.: Judicial Requirements for Generative AI in Legal Reasoning, pp. 1–20 (2025) Online. Available: http://arxiv.org/abs/2508.18880
29. Mirzadeh, I., Alizadeh, K., Shahrokhi, H., Tuzel, O., Bengio, S., Farajtabar, M.: Gsm-symbolic: understanding the limitations of mathematical reasoning in large language models. In: 13th Int. Conf. Learn. Represent. ICLR, vol. 2025, pp. 18734–18756 (2025)
30. Lawsen, A.: Comment on The illusion of thinking: understanding the strengths and limitations of reasoning models via the lens of problem complexity, pp. 1–39 (2025) Online. Available: http://arxiv.org/abs/2506.09250
31. Laban, G., Laban, T., Gunes, H.: LEXI: Large language models experimentation interface. In: HAI 2024 - Proceedings of the 12th International Conference on Human-Agent Interaction, pp. 250–259. Association for Computing Machinery (2024). https://doi.org/10.1145/3687272.3688296
32. Zuin, G., Mastelini, S., Loures, T., Veloso, A.: Leveraging large language models for tacit knowledge discovery in organizational contexts. In: 2025 International Joint Conference on Neural Networks (IJCNN) (2025). https://doi.org/10.1109/IJCNN64981.2025.11227259
33. Grange, C., Demazure, T., Ringeval, M., Bourdeau, S., Martineau, C.: The Human-GenAI value loop in human-centered innovation: beyond the magical narrative. Inf. Syst. J. **36**(1), 29–51 (2026). https://doi.org/10.1111/isj.12602
34. Juan, Y.-C., Lee, Y.-H., Wu, J.-Y.: Generative artificial intelligence augments social interactivity and learning outcomes: advancing the framework of a scaffolded human–GenAI shared agency. Comput. Educ. **247**, 105564 (2026). https://doi.org/10.1016/j.compedu.2026.105564
35. Silva, R.R., Silva, H.D., Soares, A.L.: Generative AI as a catalyst for collaborative knowledge management: impacts across individual, intra, and inter-organizational levels. In: Working Conference on Virtual Enterprises, pp. 85–101. Springer (2025)

Human or AI Collaborator? An Experimental Comparison of Human and Machine Translators

Nora Nahr[1](✉) and Konstantin Hopf[2]

[1] University of Passau, Passau, Germany
nora.nahr@uni-passau.de
[2] Chemnitz University of Technology, Chemnitz, Germany
konstantin.hopf@wiwi.tu-chemnitz.de

Abstract. Artificial intelligence (AI) is beginning to take on increasingly knowledge-intensive and creative tasks and, thus, will automate entire functional roles in organizations. We currently lack evaluations of AI technology at the level of functional roles to better assess the implications of the proliferation of artificial agents on the work processes and collaboration modes of humans and AI. We propose an evaluation approach for AI tools for knowledge-intense tasks based on role theory, using established human-perceived quality metrics drawn from MT evaluation literature. We apply this approach to the evaluation of natural language translation services—a mature AI application which solves knowledge-intensity and partly creativity tasks—in direct comparison with human translators. Our lab experiment included 75 participants that rated 225 translations. Participants rated the performance of AI tools for translation tasks better than that of human translators, which suggests that current AI technology may outperform humans in selected but knowledge-intense tasks. This finding underscores the need for role-level evaluation frameworks for AI. Participants also showed a notable ability to identify translation sources, suggesting an intuitive human capacity to detect AI outcome. This study extends role theory to AI actors and proposes a role-theoretic evaluation methodology for AI in knowledge-intense work, informing task allocation in hybrid teams.

Keywords: Artificial Intelligence · Machine Translation · Human-Perceived Quality Evaluation · Role Theory · Experiment

1 Motivation

The current performance of artificial intelligence (AI) applications leads to the automation of knowledge-intense and creative tasks [1] and transforms our work environments [2]. Even complete functional roles like that of programmers [3], chip designers [4], and natural language translators [5] are performed by intelligent machines today. The performance of current AI systems led to fears of large-scale job losses due to AI [6, 7]. A dreaded "robo-apocalypse" [8, 9] have been a topic of discourse in research for several years. Up to now, however, there is little empirical evidence on situations in which entire functional roles in organizations are taken over by AI.

Published by Springer Nature Switzerland AG 2027
S. Han et al. (Eds.): I3E 2026, LNCS 16912, pp. 38–50, 2027.
https://doi.org/10.1007/978-3-032-38014-2_4

Research on the collaboration of humans with AI systems to date mainly focuses on a task level [10]. Hence, the evaluation of AI systems is based on rather technical metrics or user perceptions associated with the tasks. Recently, the focus shifted to the level of functional roles that AI systems can take [11]. While research on roles dates back to seminal works in the 1930s [12, 13], it has only begun to spark a new stream of empirical studies that explore how humans and AI can fulfil complete role functions [14] and work together as "co-workers" to accomplish knowledge work [15]. Gaining an understanding of AI's performance and human perceptions in situations where AI fulfils functional roles is crucial to develop human-centered AI applications, counteract a possible robo-apocalypse and develop differentiated skill sets especially in hybrid teams constellations performing knowledge-intense work [16].

The competences of intelligent machines to fulfil functional roles need adequate assessment. That is, checking the quality and performance of a person or system that perform a particular role with suitable metrics to ensure that the resulting outcomes are valid and beneficial [17]. The validation of AI systems takes place during development and is primarily based on technical metrics (e.g., predictive quality, speed). These are suitable for assessing the performance of intelligent systems for routine or highly structured tasks. Such metrics are, however, largely inappropriate for assessing the quality of knowledge-intensive tasks or those with a high degree of creativity and complexity. If AI systems are assumed to be able to successfully perform complex and knowledge-intense tasks in the future, it is necessary to expand the existing spectrum of performance evaluation metrics to include non-technical metrics that incorporate human-perceived quality as well. These non-technical metrics may vary depending on the task nature and the role assigned to the system, as well as the human expectations of the outcome. Currently, many studies do not consider a comparison of AI capabilities with those of human beings thus double standards are applied when AI systems are judged based on different metrics than humans. The extent to which humans are still able to distinguish results produced by AI from those of a human is unexplored so far.

Our study focuses on the *evaluation of natural language translations from a role perspective, that is, we use human-perceived metrics and assess the ability of current AI technologies focusing on the role of translators*. We conducted a laboratory experiment with the goal of empirically investigating MT systems' capabilities to compete with and assist humans in their knowledge work environments. In our experiment, 75 individuals performed 225 ratings of translations in three different application domains.

2 Related Work and Theoretical Background

The field of MT research has made strong technical advancements [18, 19] but also commercial translation services with offerings for corporate and private customers, e.g., Google Translator, Microsoft Translator, DeepL, and diverse generative AI tools. Such services are able to produce natural-sounding and authentic translations from different sources like simple text input and websites. Yet, the task of natural language translation requires a high degree of knowledge. Translators need a deep understanding of language context (e.g., for translating idioms), semantics, and (sometimes complex) sentence structures to produce correct and authentic results. Regardless of the large number of language families, translations are expected to sound natural and understandable to users with different backgrounds and expertise levels [20]. Translating technical terms or cultural references might be challenging for human experts and MT systems due to the difficulty of encoding knowledge about intercultural differences and the often sentence-by-sentence nature of translation processing [21]. In the following, we briefly describe diverse forms of MT systems and how they are evaluated in the literature.

2.1 Machine Translation: Approaches and Assessment

MT refers to the use of software "*to translate text from one natural (human) language to another.*" ([22], p. 159) and is a subfield of AI research and practice. Research distinguishes between rule-based, corpus-based, and neural-based methods to solve MT tasks [23]. Rule-based MT systems rely on hand-crafted rules, similar to early approaches of rule-based AI [24]. The rule bases are static and cannot adjust for language changes over time. Moreover, it is time consuming to create the rule bases with human experts. Systems can come as direct—involving a literal translation— and indirect —incorporating semantic and morphological information to contextualize words and perform the translation—[22]. Corpus-based MT allows to automatically extract translation rules from bilingual corpora. Statistical approaches determine the most likely translation y for a given text x (e.g., sentence) from a corpus using statistical models [25]. Neural-based MT [26, 27] use deep neural networks to learn associations between texts in the source and target language. Transformers brought significant performance increases in recent years, although this approach is computationally expensive ([21], pp. 33–35). Studies examining this category of MT systems found them to being able to handle sentence structure more correctly while requiring less domain knowledge [26].

MT quality evaluation can be performed, on the one hand, with the aid of technical metrics, which are considered as validation metrics [17]. These can be computed automatically (automated assessment metrics), and they are widely used in MT literature. On the other hand, human-perceived metrics can be employed, which count as evaluation metrics and are less frequently used due to their complexity [28]. Technical (validation) metrics focus on the overall quality of translations [29–31] or on the human-associated effort to proofread MT-based results [32, 33]. They typically help to measure how close a translation of an MT system is compared to one or several reference translations. The congruence of both texts is expressed in a numeric metric [28], most frequently the bilingual evaluation understudy (BLEU) score [34]. The metric quantifies the closeness of an MT translation to a reference translation in a range between 0 and 1. Quality evaluation metrics, which are collected with human-perceived scales (e.g., Likert), include the following ones: Whereas *accuracy* focuses on the source text and measures the extent to which the translation reproduces the information in the source text [35], *fluency* of a text, i.e., the well-formedness of the grammar of a translation in the target language indicates how precise rules and norms of the language are preserved during performing the translation [36]. *Comprehensibility* refers to the degree to which the (source or target) text can be easily understood by its audience [37], whereas *acceptability* measures the degree of a persons' satisfaction with the source or target text and how capable it is in fulfilling own needs and expectations [28]. By providing the user with the original source text and the target text(s), different versions of translations can also be ranked and prioritized. Finally, behavior-centered measures can be employed which can be subdivided into objective metrics (e.g., dwelling time on a page or website when performing the quality assessment for a translation) or subjective metrics (e.g., collecting the users' personal opinions towards the assessed target text).

2.2 Role Theory

To explore the actual quality of human and machine translators in comparison, we use role theory as it describes how humans fulfil roles and how other involved actors rate their competence in fulfilling their role. Role theory [38, 39] helps to understand how actors in the society perform certain roles (e.g., lecturer, physician, translator). Each role comes with a set of rights, responsibilities, expectations, norms, and behaviors [39, 40]. The fulfilment of roles has been studied from the internal actor perspective, e.g., the role behavior, the self-identity, and role breath self-efficacy [14] associated with the fulfilment of a certain role. Research also studied actors and their role behavior, expectations, and congruence from an external perspective [39, 41]. Role perceptions summarize that each actor behaves and accomplishes the respective duties and tasks according to own beliefs and ideals regarding this role. The degree of competence that an actor possesses (and which is perceived by other individuals) determines the status and level of power that others attributed to them [42]. In this respect, social norms and role expectations (i.e., external perspective) of other individuals in the actors' social environment can influence and shape a role image and lead to its acceptance or rejection.

Research has used role perspectives in a variety of phenomena e.g., to study the effect of role conflicts on the behavior of online communities [43] or investigate how the use of information technology may change role identity [44]. These studies share the characteristic that only humans perform certain roles. With current AI technology, however, novel actors emerge that imitate human behavior and competencies. Thus, humans start to delegate more and more decisions and actions to AI actors (e.g., [45–47]) and boundaries between human and AI actors are blurring. This puts contemporary assumptions of role theory into question, and studies begin to investigate the changes of AI systems on the role behavior of humans [14].

We operationalize role competence through output quality ratings, acknowledging that full role assumption encompasses additional dimensions such as professional judgment and accountability that are beyond the scope of this study. Considering our empirical context of natural language translation and the current progress in the AI field, we postulate the following hypothesis:

H1: The human-perceived quality of today's MT systems to fulfil the role of a natural language translator are at least equivalent to those of human translators.

To examine whether role competence perceptions depend on the assumed translation origin, we distinguish two competing hypotheses:

H2a: Individuals judge the results of current MT systems equal or better than that of a human translator when the origin of the translation is unknown, and participants assume a machine origin.

H2b: Individuals judge the results of current MT systems equal or better than that of a human translator, when the origin of the translation is unknown, and participants assume a human origin.

Beyond quality ratings, role theory implies that perceived competence depends on identifiability of the actor. We therefore propose:

H3: Individuals are unable to distinguish the translation of an actual MT system from that of a (professional) human translator.

3 Research Approach

We carried out a laboratory experiment to determine the perceived quality of DeepL and Google Translator, as representative MT systems, considering a human translation of a professional expert as a natural benchmark as we illustrate in Fig. 1.

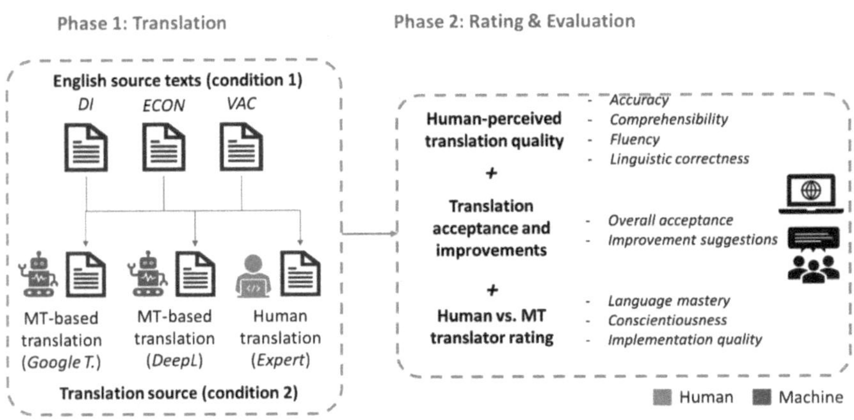

Fig. 1. Research approach

Our experiment has a 3 x 3 full factorial design, where the first factor consists of three translations of a source text, generated either by a human translator or by one of two MT systems. The second factor consists of three application domains from which we selected the source text. Participants evaluated three translations (i.e., translation as a within-subject condition) from one randomly assigned source text (i.e., source text as between-subject condition) each, according to a variety of items. Due to the participants' linguistic background (all were native German speakers), we used the language pair German/English, where English source texts were translated into German. For implementing the experiment, we obtained prior ethical approval from the *German Association for Experimental Economic Research.*

Condition 1- Translation Source (Two MT Systems and One Human Translation): We selected DeepL and Google Translator as two prominent MT systems [29, 31, 48], which both apply neural networks to fulfil translation tasks. We asked a state-certified and English native human translator to translate the original texts without any tool support and with the objective to stay close to the original text.

Condition 2- Source Text: We searched for publicly available English text corpora covering texts from different general domains. The texts had to be neither too complex nor too difficult to understand across disciplines (e.g., by using limited technical terms). The following three English texts from *OPUS* (https://opus.nlpl.eu/) [49] were selected and slightly shortened: DI: *Digital Infrastructure* (Domain: Transport and digital infrastructure) with 88 words, ECON: *Financial and Economic Crisis* (Domain: Financial news) with 90 words, and VAC: *Vaccine* (Domain: General healthcare) with 92 words. We translated the texts into German with two translations generated automatically with the MT systems and one manually by the human translator.

Based on MT evaluation literature and our theoretical lenses, we collected several variables. For example, we asked the participants to rate the original source text and measured the human-perceived translation quality using the metrics of 1) accuracy, 2) fluency 3) comprehensibility and 4) linguistic correctness of a translation. Content validity of these items is ensured by grounding them in established MT evaluation literature [28]. Furthermore, we asked items drawn from role theory and technology use literature. Free-text fields allowed us to gather qualitative ratings about the translation or improvement suggestions. To confirm our sampling approach, we queried the language skills of the participants in the beginning of the survey and collected demographic information and performance-based metrics where we tracked the intermediate reading and processing time per text and the total time per session and participant. These items served as control variables. We conducted a controlled laboratory experiment at one of our home institutions, in four individual sessions (30 min each). Each participant conducted the experiment on a randomly assigned desktop computer specially prepared for the experimental environment. We conducted the experiment in a LimeSurvey instance. Each participant received a randomly assigned source text (DI, ECON, VAC) and then three corresponding translation versions followed by rating questions. We rely on a sample of students (all native German speakers) who were enrolled in various degree programs of different faculties Altogether, 77 out of 100 students attended the experimental sessions, of which two participations were considered as invalid due to technical problems.

4 Key Findings

We evaluate our data with a multiple linear regression using ordinary least squares (OLS) estimation. Our analysis treats every translation rating of each participant as one observation i. Thus, the 75 participants with three stimuli each lead us to 225 observations in the following analyses. To mitigate the problem of heteroscedasticity, we use robust standard errors [50]. Analysis and tests were conducted using GNU R.

4.1 Overall Translation Quality (Test of H1)

We encode the translation source as a dummy-variable $s_D = 1$ for the case that the translation was created with DeepL and with $s_G = 1$ for the case of Google. Consequently, the human translation is represented when both dummy variables are zero. We use several control variables (CV_n) to vary the robustness of our findings. To test the first hypothesis, we focus on the human-perceived quality of the translated text as dependent variable y_i and use the following regression equation:

$$y_i = \beta_0 + \beta_1 * s_{Di} + \beta_2 * s_{Gi} + \beta_n * CV_{ni} + \epsilon_i \quad (1)$$

We found that the translation quality rating correlates with the order in which the translation is presented (Pearson's product moment correlation $r(223) = .18$, $p = .006$). This can be explained with memorization effects of the text content. Thus, we included the order in which the translation was displayed in the experiment as control variable in all analyses. We see a robust effect of the translation source, which means that participants perceived the quality of the translation from DeepL higher than the human translation ($p < .01$). The translation from Google similarly tends to be rated better than the human translation, yet, at lower statistical significance levels ($p < .05$) and not when we control for the reading time per word. The effect size of the translation source is $\eta^2 = 0.05$, which refers to a small effect [51]. Consequently, we find **support for hypothesis H1** that the translations of MT systems are considered qualitatively at least equivalent to those of human translators.

4.2 Human Quality vs. Machine Translation Quality (Test of H2a and H2b)

Using the model specification (1) with perceived software quality and human translator rating as dependent variable y_i, we obtain regression results. We see that the actual translation source has a significant impact on the perceived ratings in both cases, when participants assume a machine has made the translation and assuming a human has made the translation. This effect is significant (DeepL with $p < .01$) but with a small effect size of $\eta^2 = 0.02$, [51]. **In response to H2a and H2b**, we conclude that results of current MT systems are judged equal (Google Translate) or better (DeepL) by individuals when the origin of the translation is unknown and a machine (a) or human (b) origin is assumed.

4.3 Translation Ranking and Source Assignment (Test of H3)

To test H3, we asked the participants to state the source of each presented translation. In 105 (46.7%) of the cases, the assignment of the translator was correct. This lies clearly above a coincidence distribution, and we can confirm the result with $\chi^2(4)=31.188$, $p < .001$, Cramer's $V = 0.263$. Dividing the translation sources into human and machine only, the human translation was correctly identified in 43/75 (57.3%) cases and the machine translation in 117/150 (78.0%) cases. Thus, we **reject H3**.

We analyzed qualitative data, which we collected in free text fields. Participants were asked if they would use the translations in the presented form, or with corrections. 187 comments were submitted on the translations. Participants (P) criticized human translation as too close to the original. For instance, they repeatedly commented across all three domains that the human translation "*reads more like a word-to-word translation*" (ECON; P63), and that they "*would avoid using particular words of the translations*" (ECON; P68). Participants also reported that although the translation is basically "*correct*" (VAC; P16), the sentences were nested, less fluent, even annoying: "*had some very long sentence structures*" (DI; P46), "sounds artificial" (ECON; P64) or "awkward"

(VAC; P4). Some reported that in everyday life, they "*tend to not talk so pompous*" (DI; P18). For the MT translations, participants pointed to inconsistent translation of technical terms and comma misplacement. DeepL was criticized for not translating original English words like "*management*" or for inconsistently translating words like "*great depression*" (financial and economic crisis topic), "*services of general interest*" (digital infrastructure topic) or "*immunized*" (vaccine topic). Even if DeepL sometimes delivered somewhat odd translations, participants commented that these were "*basically well done*" (DI; P33) with "few improvements required" (VAC; P4). Google's translations were repeatedly criticized for the translation of the word "*governance*" (ECON; P24) or the term "*community immunity*" (VAC; P31).

5 Discussion and Summary

Our study investigates the role performance of current MT systems—a form of AI with a high technical stage and commercial use that can carry out knowledge-intensive and creative activities—in a blind-tasting-like experiment. As expected, current MT systems can produce creative and helpful output that humans rated to be better than that of a human translator using several quality criteria.

5.1 Theoretical Contribution

Expansion of Role Theory to Include AI Technologies: Regarding AI's role, research to date has mainly focused on human interaction with AI systems at the task level but has neglected situations where complete functional roles are taken over by AI. This will change in the future as new knowledge work forms emerge, no longer limited to routine tasks, but increasingly extending into the creative, knowledge-intensive domain. Our experiment has shown that people judge AI as competent as humans. They even considered DeepL more competent than the human translator across all texts. The translations of MT tools appeared to be a bit more colloquial and not as literal as the human one, which demonstrates a type of AI creativity. The MT system produced more intuitive, uncomplicated sentences, whereas human translation performed better with technical terminology. Future research needs to identify strengths and weaknesses of humans and AI, in different applications and traditional and new role models should undergo thorough examination or be redefined if necessary. Furthermore, the organizational embedding of AI in the translator's role requires closer examination. In addition to generating translations, factors such as the AI's professional judgment capability, ethically responsible application, the possibility for real-time interaction with users during translating, and context-specific customization of AI use needs more investigation.

New Procedures for the Evaluation of AI Role Performance: Research on the collaboration between humans and AI has focused primarily on task level [10]. Therefore, the evaluation of AI systems is usually based more on technical metrics or on user perception in connection with the tasks. MT systems, as well, are primarily validated using technical metrics or evaluated using task-related user evaluations. We argue that the evaluation of AI must also be performed from a functional role perspective to capture the impact of these systems on workplace.

Implications for the Current Debate on AI Use: One study contribution is that humans rated the translation of MT systems better than that of humans, without knowing their origin. The positive effect is that commercial MT systems are already performing well today. However, people could be fooled consequently into thinking that the result of an automatic translation is human. From an ethical perspective, this must be considered when designing information systems (e.g., by indicating text sources). A second finding is that individuals were quite capable of recognizing which translation came from a human or a machine in a direct comparison. This is a good indicator of the human ability to intuitively judge the text's origin. Participants gave the human translator more credit for translating technical terms and for translating correctly in context. The MT system translated more fluently and freely, which explains why these translations scored so well in the perceived ratings. Humans can benefit from the machine creativity—even if this only consists of the ability in recognizing and combining insights from discovered pattern [52]—and use the results as inspiration source to produce new ideas while considering ethical and legal concerns. Finally, applying role theory to the evaluation of AI applications is a valuable contribution to identifying requirements for AI systems and areas for future development. MT systems, for example, learn patterns and word contexts from the data (i.e., they learn word correlations), but they cannot map semantics or decide whether a translation in the training data may have been incorrect. To completely fill functional roles, AI must have mechanisms for identifying incorrect information and knowledge gaps (e.g., biased training data).

5.2 Practical Contribution

Study participants mentioned several linguistic weaknesses, such as incorrect comma placement or adequate translation of abbreviations. Such findings can be used to improve MT systems and technologies in general. Since the output of AI can hardly be distinguished from human text, the robustness and correctness of the output is crucial and should be validated more strongly, possibly also formally. Regarding the education of humans, the ability to evaluate a concrete AI output in terms of quality and truth requires a certain amount of prior education and technology awareness. Therefore, AI technology should already be addressed more strongly in school education and children should be given appropriate media competence. A helpful approach is also to label outputs of AI systems as such [53] if they have not undergone human review. This is important in that technical terms are often not translated correctly, or statements are translated too freely.

5.3 Limitations and Future Work

As our study opens a novel field of research, it comes with avenues for future research: *First*, we focused on an experiment with student participants. Future work should examine different groups of people with different language or education levels and should use the results of MT systems in real work environment. *Second*, the quality of the human reference translation should be controlled (e.g., using reference translations from multiple translators), which was not feasible due to the time it took each participant to read the original text and translations. *Third*, we presented participants with a static text rather than the dynamic features that translation tools already offer (e.g., suggestions for alternatives or for improvement when writing in a foreign language). Fourth, statistical analysis could be extended by using mixed effects models and further controls. *Fifth*, our study focused on the perceived quality of MT results compared to a human translation, without covering interactive correction features where participants could make their own improvements to the translations.

6 Annex - Original Source Texts

DI: Digital Infrastructure (Domain: Transport and Digital Infrastructure): Digital infrastructure is currently one of the most widely debated topics in public. Digital networks also provide innovative and smart solutions for services of general interest. The management of public and private passenger transport, for instance, is becoming more and more digital, so that congestion on motorways or long waiting times at stations can be reduced. Information and communications networks are key for the progress and development of a digital Germany be it in the field of business, mobility, health care, safety and security, education or energy supply.

ECON: Financial and Economic Crisis (Domain: Financial News): One Hundred Years of Ineptitude. – The global financial and economic crisis that began in 2008 was the greatest economic stress-test since the Great Depression, and the greatest challenge to social and political systems since World War II. It not only put financial markets and currencies at risk, it also exposed serious regulatory and governance shortcomings that have yet to be fully addressed. In fact, the 2008 crisis will most likely be remembered as a watershed moment, but not because it led to reforms that strengthened economic resilience and removed vulnerabilities.

VAC: Vaccine (Domain: General Healthcare): How do vaccines work? - This 'community immunity' can only work if enough people are vaccinated. Immunity through vaccination protects not only the immunised individual but also protects unvaccinated people in the community, such as infants who are too young to be vaccinated. Later, if the person comes into contact with the actual infectious virus or bacterium, their immune system will 'remember' it. Vaccines contain a greatly weakened or an inactivated (killed) form of a virus or bacterium that usually causes a disease, or a small part of the virus or bacterium.

References

1. Chen, J., Tajdini, S.: A moderated model of artificial intelligence adoption in firms and its effects on their performance. Inf. Technol. Manag. **26**, 407–419 (2024). https://doi.org/10.1007/s10799-024-00422-5
2. Ha, H.: When AI Meets AI: Analyzing AI Bills Using AI. AI Soc (2025)
3. Hassani, H., Silva, E.S.: The role of ChatGPT in data science: how AI-assisted conversational interfaces are revolutionizing the field. Big Data Cogn. Comput. **7**, 1–16 (2023). https://doi.org/10.3390/bdcc7020062

4. Zhang, Z., Yoo, Y., Lyytinen, K., Lindberg, A.: The unknowability of autonomous tools and the liminal experience of their use. Inf. Syst. Res. **32**, 1192–1213 (2021). https://doi.org/10.1287/isre.2021.1022
5. Jiao W, Wang W, Huang J, et al (2023) Is ChatGPT a Good Translator? Yes with GPT-4 as the Engine
6. Frey, C.B., Osborne, M.A.: The future of employment: how susceptible are jobs to computerisation? Technol Forecast Soc. Change. **114**, 254–280 (2017)
7. Spencer, D.A.: AI, automation and the lightening of work. AI Soc. **40**, 1237–1247 (2025)
8. Willcocks, L.: Robo-apocalypse cancelled? Reframing the automation and future of work debate. J. Inf. Technol. **35**, 286–302 (2020). https://doi.org/10.1177/0268396220925830
9. Willcocks, L.: Robo-apocalypse? Response and outlook on the post-COVID-19 future of work. J. Inf. Technol. **36**, 188–194 (2021). https://doi.org/10.1177/0268396220978660
10. Abedin, B., Meske, C., Junglas, I., et al.: Designing and managing human-AI interactions. Inf. Syst. Front. **24**, 691–697 (2022). https://doi.org/10.1007/s10796-022-10313-1
11. Blaurock, M., Caic, M., Okan, M., Henkel, A.P.: Robotic role theory: an integrative review of human–robot service interaction to advance role theory in the age of social robots. J. Serv. Manag. **33**, 27–49 (2022). https://doi.org/10.1108/JOSM-09-2021-0345
12. Linton, R.: The Study of Man: an Introduction. D. Appleton-Century (1936)
13. Mead, G.H.: Mind, Self and Society from the Standpoint of a Social Behaviorist. The University of Chicago Press, Chicago and London (1934)
14. Tang, P.M., Koopman, J., McLean, S.T., et al.: When conscientious employees meet intelligent machines: an integrative approach insipred by complementarity theory and role theory. Acad. Manag. J. **65**, 1019–1054 (2022). https://doi.org/10.5465/amj.2020.1516
15. Tarafdar, M., Page, X., Marabelli, M.: Algorithms as co-workers: human algorithm role interactions in algorithmic work. Inf. Syst. J. **33**, 232–267 (2023). https://doi.org/10.1111/isj.12389
16. Hopf, K., Nahr, N., Staake, T., Lehner, F.: The group mind of hybrid teams with humans and intelligent agents in knowledge-intense work. J. Inf. Technol. **40**, 9–34 (2025). https://doi.org/10.1177/02683962241296883
17. O'Keefe, R.M., O'Leary, D.E.: Expert system verification and validation: a survey and tutorial. Artif. Intell. Rev. **7**, 3–42 (1993). https://doi.org/10.1007/BF00849196
18. Lopez, A.: Statistical machine translation. ACM Comput. Surv. **8**, 8–49 (2008). https://doi.org/10.1145/1380584.1380586
19. Vaswani, A., Shazeer, N., Parmar, N., et al.: Attention is all you need. In: Guyon, I., Luxberg, U.V., Bengio, S., et al. (eds.) Advances in Neural Information Processing Systems, pp. 5998–6008. Curran Associates, Inc. (2017)
20. Chen, M.: Trust, understanding, and machine translation: the task of translation and the responsibility of the translator. AI Soc. **39**, 2307–2319 (2024)
21. Klimova, B., Pikhart, M., Benites, A.D., et al.: Neural machine translation in foreign language teaching and learning: a systematic review. Educ. Inf. Technol. **28**, 663–682 (2023). https://doi.org/10.1007/s10639-022-11194-2
22. Okpor, M.D.: Machine translation approaches: issues and challenges. Int. J. Comput. Sci. Issues. **11**, 159–165 (2014)
23. Xia, Y.: Research on statistical machine translation model based on deep neural network. Computing. **102**, 643–661 (2020). https://doi.org/10.1007/s00607-019-00752-1
24. Haenlein, M., Kaplan, A.: A brief history of artificial intelligence: on the past, present, and future of artificial intelligence. Calif. Manag. Rev. **61**, 5–14 (2019). https://doi.org/10.1177/0008125619864925
25. Poibeau, T.: Machine Translation. The MIT Press (2017)

26. Bentivogli, L., Bisazza, A., Cettolo, M., Federico, M.: Neural versus phrase-based MT quality: an in-depth analysis on english–German and english–French. Comput. Speech Lang. **49**, 52–70 (2018)
27. Luong, M., Manning, C.: Stanford neural machine translation systems for spoken language domain. In: Proceedings of the 12th International Workshop on Spoken Language Translation, pp. 76–79. Da Nang, Vietnam (2015)
28. Castilho, S., Doherty, S., Gaspari, F., Moorkens, J.: Approaches to human and machine translation quality assessment. In: Moorkens, J., Castilho, S., Gaspari, F., Doherty, S. (eds.) Translation Quality Assessment - from Principles to Practice, pp. 9–38. Springer International Publishing, Cham (2018)
29. Popovic, M., Avramidis, E., Burchardt, A., et al.: Learning from human judgments of machine translation output. In: Proceedings of the MT Summit XIV, pp. 1–8 (2013)
30. Li, Y., Thomas, M.A., Liu, D.: From semantics to pragmatics: where IS can lead in natural language processing (NLP) research. Eur. J. Inf. Syst. **30**, 569–590 (2020)
31. Farreús, M., Costa-jussà, M.R., Morse, M.P.: Study and correlation analysis of linguistic, perceptual, and automatic machine translation evaluations. J. Am. Soc. Inf. Sci. Technol. **63**, 174–184 (2012). https://doi.org/10.1002/asi.21674
32. Bentivogli, L., Bisazza, A., Cettolo, M., Federico, M.: Neural versus phrase-based machine translation quality: a case study. In: Proceedings of the Conference on Empirical Methods in Natural Language Processing, pp. 1–11 (2016)
33. Koponen, M., Salmi, L., Nikulin, M.: A product and process analysis of post-editor corrections on neural, statistical and rule-based machine translation output. Mach. Transl. **33**, 61–90 (2019). https://doi.org/10.1007/s10590-019-09228-7
34. Papineni, K., Roukos, S., Ward, T., Zhu, W.: BLEU: a method for automatic evaluation of machine translation. In: Proceedings of the 40th Annual Meeting of the Association for Computational Linguistics, pp. 311–318 (2002)
35. Fiederer, R., O'Brien, S.: Quality and machine translation: a realistic objective. J Spec Transl. **11**, 52–74 (2009)
36. Mitchell, L., Roturier, J., O'Brien, S.: Community-based post editing of machine-translated content: monolingual vs. bilingual. In: Proceedings of the European Association for Machine Translation, pp. 35–43 (2013)
37. Roturier, J., Bensadoun, A.: Evaluation of MT systems to translate user generated content. In: Proceedings of the 13th Machine Translation Summit, pp. 244–251 (2011)
38. Gross, N., McEachern, A.W., Mason, W.S.: Role conflict and its resolution. In: Biddle, B.J., Thomas, E.J. (eds.) Role Theory: Concepts and Research, pp. 287–296. Wiley, New York (1996)
39. Biddle, B.J.: Recent developments in role theory. Annu. Rev. Sociol. **12**, 67–92 (1986). https://doi.org/10.1146/annurev.so.12.080186.000435
40. Bates, F.L., Harvey, C.C.: The Structure of Social Systems. John Wiley & Sons Inc (1975)
41. Chiu, D.K., Cheung, S., Till, S., et al.: Workflow view driven cross-organizational interoperability in a web service environment. Inf. Technol. Manag. **5**, 221–250 (2004). https://doi.org/10.1023/B:ITEM.0000031580.57966.d4
42. Fiske, S.T., Cuddy, A.J., Glick, P., Xu, J.: A model of (often mixed) stereotype content: competence and warmth respectively follow from perceived status and competition. J. Pers. Soc. Psychol. **82**, 878–902 (2002). https://doi.org/10.1037/0022-3514.82.6.878
43. Nguyen, M., Septianto, F., Das, G., Malik, A.: Bridging role conflict and active lurking: the role of transformational leadership in B2B online communities. J. Knowl. Manag. **29**, 814–836 (2025)
44. Hassandoust, F., Techatassanasoontorn, A.A., Tan, F.B.: Importance of IT and role identities in information systems infusion. Inf. Syst. Front. **26**, 333–367 (2023). https://doi.org/10.1007/s10796-023-10378-6

45. Baird, A., Maruping, L.: The next generation of research on IS use: a theoretical framework of delegation to and from agentic IS artifacts. MIS Quartely. **45**, 315–341 (2021)
46. Jakesch, M., Bhat, A., Buschek, D., et al.: Co-writing with opinionated language models affects users' views. In: CHI '23: Proceedings of the 2023 CHI Conference on Human Factors in Computing Systems, pp. 1–15 (2023)
47. Wirtz, J., Patterson, P.G., Kunz, W.H., et al.: Brave new world: service robots in the frontline. J. Serv. Manag. **29**, 907–931 (2018). https://doi.org/10.1108/JOSM-04-2018-0119
48. Reber, U.: Overcoming language barriers: assessing the potential of machine translation and topic modeling for the comparative analysis of multilingual text corpora. Commun. Methods Meas. **13**, 102–125 (2019). https://doi.org/10.1080/19312458.2018.1555798
49. Tiedemann, J.: Parallel data, tools and interfaces in OPUS. In: Proceedings of the 8th International Conference on Language Resources and Evaluation (LREC 2012), pp. 2214–2218 (2012)
50. Zeileis, A.: Econometric computing with HC and HAC covariance matrix estimators. J. Stat. Softw. **11**, 1–17 (2004). https://doi.org/10.18637/jss.v011.i10
51. Field, A.: Discovering Statistics Using IBM SPSS Statistics, 4th edn. SAGE Publications, London (2013)
52. Kirkpatrick, K.: Can AI demonstrate creativity? Commun. ACM. **66**, 21–23 (2023). https://doi.org/10.1145/3575665
53. Dwivedi, Y.K., Kshetri, N., Hughes, L., et al.: "So what if ChatGPT wrote it?" multidisciplinary perspectives on opportunities, challenges and implications of generative conversational AI for research, practice and policy. Int. J. Inf. Manag. **71**, 102642 (2023). https://doi.org/10.1016/j.ijinfomgt.2023.102642

From System to Teammate: Human-Centered AI in the Industrial Internet of Things

Maximilian Nebel(✉)

TU Dortmund University, Dortmund, Germany
maximilian.nebel@tu-dortmund.de

Abstract. Human-centered AI (HCAI) aims to augment human expertise in decision-making rather than replace it, this is particularly relevant in complex IIoT environments. While AI technologies increasingly support operational decisions, their integration raises questions regarding technological suitability, human-AI interaction, and organizational governance. We synthesize and conceptualize existing research on HCAI in industrial decision-making through a systematic literature review. Identified publications are analyzed using a concept matrix informed by task-technology fit, social presence theory, and principal-agent theory. This perspective allows us to examine how the literature conceptualizes AI systems as moving from purely technical systems toward collaborative teammates in decision-making and identifies socio-technical conditions that shape this transition. We contribute to a conceptualization of HCAI in IIoT and highlight directions for future research on designing and governing such systems.

Keywords: Human-Centered AI · IIoT · Decision-Making · Human-AI Teaming

1 Introduction

Industrial environments are increasingly characterized by data-driven decisions enabled by the Industrial Internet of Things (IIoT). Sensors continuously generate operational data that support human decision-making in areas such as anomaly detection and predictive maintenance [1]. At the same time, Industry 5.0 emphasizes the importance of the reintroduction of human expertise into highly automated industry, highlighting the importance of human judgment and collaboration with AI [2].

AI is expected to enhance industrial decision-making by identifying patterns in complex data and providing recommendations to experts [3]. Yet, its increasing capabilities raise questions about the role of human decision-makers [4]. Human-centered AI (HCAI) addresses this issue by emphasizing AI systems that support rather than replace human judgment while preserving oversight and control [5, 6]. Accordingly, integrating HCAI into industrial decision-making raises technological, interactional, and organizational questions concerning transparency, collaboration, and governance [3, 4, 7, 8].

Information systems (IS) research examines various aspects of human-AI collaboration and HCAI design. Prior studies discuss technological capabilities of AI systems,

Published by Springer Nature Switzerland AG 2027
S. Han et al. (Eds.): I3E 2026, LNCS 16912, pp. 51–62, 2027.
https://doi.org/10.1007/978-3-032-38014-2_5

mechanisms of human-AI interaction, and organizational considerations deploying AI-supported decisions. However, the discussions are often distributed across different research streams, this makes it difficult to obtain a comprehensive understanding of HCAI's conceptualization and discussion in industrial decision-making.

To consolidate these distributed discussions, we conduct a systematic literature review and analyze the identified papers using a concept matrix informed by task-technology fit (TTF), social presence theory (SPT), and principal-agent theory (PAT). These lenses capture technological, interactional, and organizational perspectives on HCAI in decision-making. We address the following research questions (RQ):

RQ1: *How is HCAI conceptualized in IIoT decision-making?*
RQ2: *What socio-technical conditions shape the integration of HCAI into industrial decision environments?*

We contribute to IS research by synthesizing and conceptualizing the emerging field of HCAI in industrial decision-making, applying TTF, SPT, and PAT as a socio-technical lens that integrates technological, interactional, and organizational perspectives, and identifying key challenges and research themes in the design, interaction, and governance of HCAI systems.

2 Background

2.1 Conceptual Background

Decision Support in the IIoT. Decision support systems (DSS) support human decision-makers when situations cannot be fully formalized [9]. In the IIoT monitoring systems detect anomalies while human experts assess severity and determine appropriate responses [1]. Decisions are made under time pressure and are limited by human cognition [1, 7]. DSS structure decision-relevant information to support human judgment. Early work already cautioned that IS may degrade decisions when they increase information or interaction without improving task relevance [10]. This tension is visible in AI-supported decisions. HCAI promotes interactive decision support, yet excessive interaction may overload experts or distract from tasks [4, 11]. Conversely, highly automated systems can lead to automation bias, where users over-rely on algorithmic recommendations [4]. Designing AI-enabled decision support therefore requires balancing human involvement and algorithmic assistance.

Human-Centered AI. The concept of HCAI provides a design perspective for AI-enabled DSS that emphasizes strengthening human autonomy rather than replacing them [5, 6]. HCAI systems are socio-technical systems designed to augment human capabilities in goal-directed activities and support judgment while preserving human oversight [4–6]. Rather than opposing automation, HCAI reframes the role of humans in socio-technical systems. As automated systems assume operational tasks, humans operate at higher levels of abstraction, such as supervising processes and making strategic decisions [2]. This shift increases both responsibility and risk, as decisions often have far-reaching consequences and require substantial judgment [1, 7, 11]. Consequently,

HCAI aims to support human decision-makers in cognitively demanding tasks while preserving agency and decision authority [7, 12]. Approaches in this field include adapting information presentation to individual users or monitoring workload to provide support when cognitive demands increase [4, 12, 13].

2.2 Theoretical Background

To structure the analysis of HCAI systems, we employ three theoretical lenses. They capture key socio-technical dimensions of deploying HCAI in organizations.

Task-Technology Fit. TTF describes the degree to which technology's capabilities align with the requirements of the task it supports [14]. IS enhance performance when their functionalities match task demands and user needs, whereas misalignment can reduce effectiveness or adoption [14]. Introducing HCAI into IIoT decision-making changes how information is presented and how experts interact with decision support systems. Features such as conversational explanations or proactive recommendations may improve transparency [3, 4], but they can also introduce additional interaction steps. If poorly integrated into workflows, such mechanisms may interrupt decision processes or increase cognitive load in already complex environments [10].

The success of HCAI therefore depends on whether AI capabilities align with the characteristics of industrial decision tasks. The TTF lens helps identify conditions under which HCAI effectively supports decision-makers and where potential misfits arise.

Social Presence Theory. SPT explains how interaction with technology varies depending on the perception of another social entity being present [15]. Systems communicating human-like, for example through natural language, can create the impression of interacting with a social counterpart rather than a technical tool [16]. Perceived social presence, shaped by social cues and interactivity, influences how users interpret system behavior and rely on outputs [16]. For HCAI, this perspective is relevant because HCAI is designed to collaborate with human decision-makers. Through social cues, AI may be perceived less as a tool and more as an interaction partner. Consequently, the system's representation shapes users' expectations regarding its competence and role in the decision process [6, 16].

Principal-Agent Theory. PAT examines relationships where a principal delegates tasks to an agent who performs them on the principal's behalf [17]. Such relationships are characterized by information asymmetry and potentially diverging interests. Because principals cannot observe intentions of agents, governance mechanisms such as monitoring or reporting are introduced to reduce uncertainty. In IS research, AI systems are discussed as agents supporting human users. HCAI systems are therefore not only technical tools but participants in decision processes [4, 6]. Their representation influences how users interpret system behavior and attribute intentions to the AI [16, 18]. At the same time, HCAI systems are deployed and governed by organizations that pursue hidden objectives. Because these systems often rely on interaction data and operational decisions for improvement [3, 19], employees may perceive that their expertise contributes to training the system while they have limited visibility into how their data are used [8,

20]. This situation creates potential information asymmetries and concerns about organizational intentions. PAT therefore helps explain how perceived misalignment between organizational objectives and employee interests influences trust in the organization and acceptance of HCAI systems in IIoT decision-making.

3 Methodology

3.1 Systematic Literature Search

We conducted a systematic literature review following vom Brocke et al. [21]. The search was performed in March 2026 using the string *("human-centered AI" OR "AI assistant") AND ("industry 4.0" OR "industry 5.0" OR IIoT OR "industrial internet of things") AND ("decision making" OR "decision support")*, capturing HCAI, industrial contexts, and decision-making tasks. We searched IS-relevant databases (ACM, AISel, Scopus, IEEE Xplore, ScienceDirect, SpringerLink) without year restrictions and included only English journal articles and conference papers. The search returned 793 publications; after duplicate removal, 762 records remained and were screened by title (135), abstract (31), and full text, resulting in 13 publications. We included studies on HCAI in industrial contexts that addressed AI-supported organizational decision-making and human-AI interaction, and excluded papers limited to automation, algorithm development, model performance, non-industrial domains, or non-AI technologies.

3.2 Concept Matrix

Following the literature search, we analyzed the publications based on Webster and Watson's approach [22]. Rather than deriving concepts inductively, we structured the concept matrix deductively using the three theoretical lenses introduced in Sect. 2 to capture technological suitability, human-AI interaction, and organizational implications of HCAI. We operationalized these perspectives by reviewing the constructs proposed by the three theories and selecting those most relevant to the design and organizational integration of HCAI. To avoid an overly fine-grained coding scheme, we focused on constructs that could capture recurring themes across studies, as statements in the literature often relate to multiple concepts and require interpretive judgment. The resulting concept matrix is shown in Table 1.

From TTF, we included *task characteristics*, *technology characteristics*, and *fit* to capture IIoT decision tasks, AI capabilities and limitations, and their alignment in DSS. From SPT, we included *perceived social presence*, *social cues*, and *interactivity* to capture how HCAI systems are represented in interaction and how human-AI communication is structured. From PAT, we included *responsibility*, *information asymmetry*, *alignment of interests*, and *trust* to capture employee-organization relationships in HCAI deployment, including accountability, organizational intentions, and the use of employee data.

The concepts served as coding categories for the analysis (see Table 1). During coding, we identified passages addressing related problems, requirements, solutions, and design considerations. Following Gioia et al. [23], relevant excerpts were treated as first-order themes and provided in full in a digital appendix [24]. We then grouped similar themes into second-order themes and synthesized them into three aggregate dimensions characterizing current research on HCAI in IIoT decision-making contexts.

Table 1. Concept matrix showing problems (P), and solutions (S) in the reviewed literature.

References	Task-Technology Fit			Social Presence Theory			Principal-Agent Theory			
	Task characteristics	Technology characteristics	Fit	Perceived presence	Social cues	Interactivity	Responsibility	Information asymmetry	Alignment of Interest	Trust
[3]		P	S			P			P	S
[4]	P	P	S		S	S	S		P	P
[7]	S	P	S	S	S	S	P	P	P	S
[8]	P	S	S	P	S	P	S	S	P	P
[11]	P	S	P			P	P		S	S
[12]	P	P	P			P	P	P	S	P
[18]	P	P	P						P	
[19]	P				P	P				
[20]	P	P	P	S			P	S		
[25]	P		P							
[26]		P					P		S	P
[27]	P	P							P	P
[28]						P			P	P
Count(P + S)	**10**	**10**	**9**	**3**	**4**	**8**	**7**	**4**	**10**	**9**
Count(S)	**1**	**2**	**4**	**2**	**3**	**2**	**2**	**2**	**3**	**3**

4 Results

4.1 Overview of the Concept Matrix

For each concept, the matrix indicates whether a study discusses the concept as a problem (P) or proposes a solution (S). Overall, the literature more frequently identifies challenges related to HCAI than it proposes solutions. Across the three lenses, concepts related to TTF appear most often. Many publications discuss how HCAI technologies must align with the characteristics of decision tasks and how technological capabilities and task requirements influence the suitability of HCAI systems. Concepts derived from PAT are also addressed regularly. In particular, *alignment of interests* and *trust* appear frequently in the reviewed studies. These discussions often relate to concerns about how organizations use employee data and to uncertainties regarding the implications of HCAI adoption for employees' roles and job security. *Responsibility* is discussed in relation to accountability when AI systems influence or partially take over aspects of human decision-making. In contrast, SPT appears less frequent. While *interactivity* between humans and AI systems is discussed in several studies, the other constructs receive comparatively little attention.

4.2 Thematic Analysis and Aggregate Dimensions

While the concept matrix shows how frequently the concepts appear in the reviewed studies, it does not capture how these issues are discussed. We therefore conducted a thematic analysis of the coded passages [23]. Excerpts were condensed into first-order themes representing recurring problems (see Fig. 1 and our digital appendix [24]). Based on similarities among these themes, we developed second-order themes capturing broader patterns across the studies. These were finally synthesized into three aggregate dimensions representing overarching perspectives on HCAI in decision-making.

Human-Centered AI is not a Silverbullet. Across the publications it is consistently emphasized that HCAI does not automatically improve decision-making environments. Instead, the effectiveness of HCAI systems depends on several conditions related to *human factors*, *transparency and explainability*, and *technical capabilities*.

The first theme concerns *human factors*. Many studies highlight that HCAI systems must be designed in a way that supports human decision-makers rather than increasing their workload. Highly automated environments can lead to high cognitive load if human limitations are not considered [19, 25]. Consequently, HCAI systems should not create additional burdens for employees as they must retain autonomy to intervene in safety-critical situations [4, 7, 11]. A second recurring theme concerns *transparency and explainability*. Decision-makers need to understand how outputs are generated to rely on them [4, 20, 27]. Many powerful AI approaches function as black boxes, which restricts interpretability and makes it difficult for users to assess the reliability of outputs [12, 20, 26, 27]. These challenges are further amplified by biases or hallucinations, highlighting the need for explanations to critically assess outputs [3, 7, 8, 18, 20, 26]. The third theme relates to the technical capabilities of HCAI. Studies emphasize that AI faces limitations regarding context understanding, reasoning, and adaptability to dynamic environments [4, 11]. In addition, integration of HCAI into existing industrial infrastructures can be technically complex and requires continuous updates of models, knowledge bases, and data sources [4, 8, 11]. These constraints highlight that HCAI systems can only support tasks for which appropriate data and knowledge are available.

Taken together, these themes illustrate why the literature repeatedly emphasizes that HCAI should not be treated as a universal solution. Instead, effective decision support depends on how well AI systems account for human factors, provide transparent outputs, and address the technical constraints of industrial environments.

Human-Centered AI as a Teammate. Beyond technological capabilities, HCAI is framed in terms of interaction and collaboration with human users. Rather than acting solely as decision support tools, HCAI systems are described as participants in decision processes. We observed three recurring themes capturing how this shift is addressed in the literature: *interaction design*, *personalization*, and *human-AI collaboration*.

The first theme concerns *interaction design*. Several studies emphasize that HCAI systems must communicate with users in ways that is intuitive and appropriate to the operational context. Explanations and recommendations therefore need to be carefully designed in terms of format and timing to ensure effective communication [7]. Interaction should rely on natural and accessible communication channels, such as commonly used devices, while also considering environmental constraints and unavailable interfaces [8, 11, 19]. Importantly, the design of interaction and communication influences how users perceive the HCAI system and may shape expectations about its capabilities and role in the decision process [16].

A second theme relates to *personalization*. Several studies highlight that HCAI systems should adapt their behavior and interaction style to individual users. Customization through machine learning can allow systems to adjust explanations, interfaces, and interaction patterns to user preferences or cognitive load [12, 19, 20]. In addition, communicating the system's learning status or progress can help users understand how the HCAI evolves over time and support more effective interaction [7].

The third theme concerns *human-AI collaboration*. Here, HCAI systems are conceptualized as collaborative partners that participate in decision processes rather than merely providing analytical outputs. Interaction should enable bidirectional communication, allowing users to provide feedback, influence system behavior, and negotiate decisions with the AI [4, 7, 8].

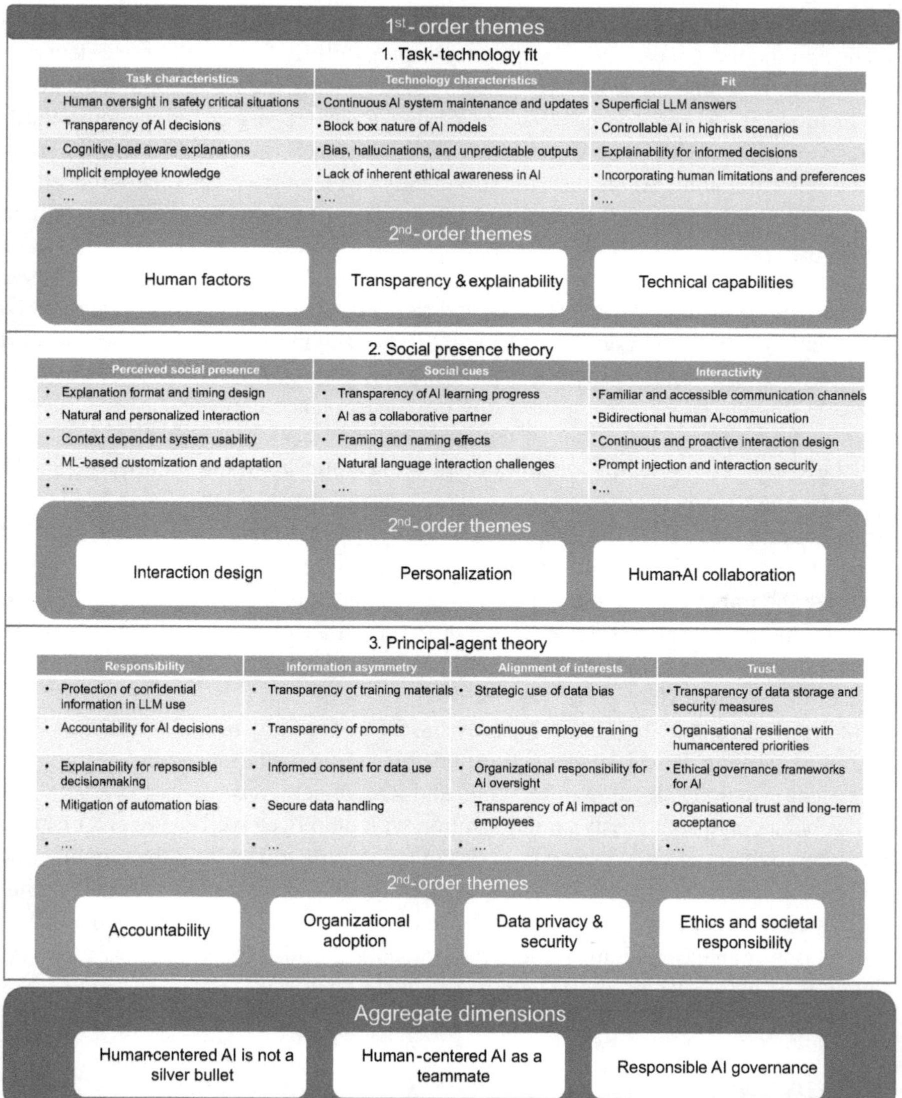

Fig. 1. First-order themes, second-order themes, and aggregate dimensions (see also [24]).

Responsible AI Governance. The literature further highlights that the deployment of HCAI raises important questions regarding the relationship between organizations and employees. Beyond technical design and interaction, organizations must establish governance structures that define responsibilities, regulate the use of employee data, and ensure that AI systems are deployed in ways that are perceived as legitimate and trustworthy by the workforce. Four recurring themes capture these governance considerations: *accountability*, *organizational adoption*, *data privacy and security*, and *ethics and societal responsibility*.

The first theme concerns *accountability*. Responsibilities for AI-supported decisions must be clearly defined, particularly when HCAI systems influence high-stakes decisions or produce incorrect outputs [4, 12, 26]. In such cases, organizations must clarify how responsibility is shared between human decision-makers and HCAI systems. Transparency and explainable AI are therefore frequently discussed as mechanisms that enable employees to understand AI outputs and justify their decisions within organizational contexts [4, 7].

A second theme relates to *organizational adoption*. The introduction of HCAI systems changes established work practices and requires organizations to actively involve affected employees in the adoption process. Studies highlight the importance of training, knowledge sharing, and mechanisms that allow employees to provide feedback or correct AI outputs [7, 8, 28]. At the same time, acceptance depends strongly on how employees perceive the intentions of the organization when deploying HCAI systems, particularly regarding potential changes to decision authority or job security [3, 8, 12].

A third theme concerns *data privacy and security*. Because HCAI systems rely on operational and interaction data generated by employees, organizations must establish transparent rules for how such data are collected, stored, and used. Several studies emphasize the importance of clear policies, secure data handling, and user control over personal data to prevent misuse or unintended surveillance [4, 11, 12, 20, 26]. In this context, concerns about data protection are closely tied to employees' trust in how the organization governs AI systems.

Finally, the literature highlights broader *ethical and societal responsibilities* of organizations deploying HCAI systems. Responsible implementation requires alignment with ethical principles, legal requirements, and human-centered values [3, 4, 28]. This includes balancing productivity and innovation with employee well-being and ensuring that the deployment of HCAI systems does not undermine trust within the organization.

Together, these themes illustrate that governing HCAI is not only a technical challenge but also a relational one. Successful implementation therefore depends on how organizations manage responsibilities, data practices, and transparency in ways that maintain trust between employees and the organization.

5 Discussion

The literature on HCAI in industrial decision-making increasingly moves beyond viewing AI merely as a technical system and instead frames it as a participant in decision-making. HCAI is conceptualized as a teammate collaborating with human experts.

Our findings indicate that this transition from system to teammate does not occur automatically. The literature highlights three conditions that shape whether HCAI systems can meaningfully participate in decision processes: alignment with human decision tasks, interaction mechanisms that enable effective human-AI collaboration, and organizational governance structures that ensure responsible deployment and maintain trust between employees and the organization. This transition can be compared to the integration of human team members in organizations. Just as employees must possess relevant capabilities, collaborate with colleagues, and operate within organizational structures, HCAI systems must support decision tasks, enable collaboration with users, and be embedded in governance structures that maintain trust.

Taken together, this reflects a socio-technical shift in the role of AI in industrial decision environments. HCAI systems become collaborative teammates not merely through technological capability but through the alignment of task suitability, human-AI interaction, and responsible organizational governance.

5.1 Implications for Theory and Practice

Our findings contribute to several streams of IS research. From a TTF perspective, the literature shows that HCAI does not automatically improve decision support through increasing technological sophistication. Instead, the effectiveness of HCAI depends on its alignment with decision tasks and the limitations of human decision-makers. This reinforces the view that HCAI systems are not universal solutions but technologies whose value emerges through their fit with specific work practices.

Insights from SPT highlight the importance of interaction design in shaping how users perceive HCAI systems. The way HCAI systems communicate, explain decisions, and present themselves influences whether users perceive them as tools or collaborative partners. Interaction design therefore acts as an important lever through which developers can shape the capabilities and intentions users attribute to the system [6, 16].

Our results also extend principal-agent perspectives on HCAI-supported work environments. The deployment of HCAI systems introduces governance challenges related to responsibility, data use, and organizational intentions. Employees often lack visibility into how interaction data are used or how HCAI may influence future work practices. Consequently, trust in HCAI-supported decision processes often reflect trust in the organization deploying the technology rather than trust in the technology itself.

Across the reviewed literature, technological and organizational aspects receive more attention than interaction. While human-AI collaboration is frequently acknowledged, the design of interaction mechanisms remains comparatively underexplored.

These findings also provide implications for organizations implementing HCAI in industrial environments. Organizations should evaluate how HCAI capabilities align with employees' decision tasks rather than treating AI as a universal solution. Interaction design should be considered a central design challenge, as explanation formats and communication mechanisms influence how employees collaborate with HCAI systems.

Finally, organizations must establish governance structures that ensure responsible deployment. Transparent data practices, clear responsibilities, and employee involvement in adoption processes are essential for maintaining trust between employees and organizations, particularly when concerns about data use or changes to job roles arise.

5.2 Limitations and Future Research

Our study has limitations. First, the analysis is based on the currently available publications addressing HCAI in industrial decision environments. As it is an emerging research field future developments are changing fast which highlights the need to further observe developments. Future studies could also extend the analysis to related domains. Second, our study relies on qualitative interpretation of the literature.

Future research could complement these findings with empirical studies examining how employees interact with HCAI systems in real industrial settings and whether users accept the technology. Future design science research could also investigate how organizations can design HCAI systems that function as teammates, particularly how task characteristics, interaction design, and organizational governance jointly shape human-AI collaboration in practice.

6 Conclusion

We examined how HCAI is conceptualized in IIoT decision-making and what sociotechnical conditions shape its integration into industrial decision environments. HCAI is increasingly framed not as a mere automation tool, but as a collaborative participant that augments human judgment while preserving oversight and accountability.

This role is conditional on understandable and contestable recommendations that align with industrial decision contexts. We identify task fit, interaction quality, and organizational governance as the key conditions shaping integration. HCAI must therefore fit workflows, enable collaboration through explanations and feedback, and be governed transparently regarding accountability, data use, and decision authority. Overall, we contribute to IS research by showing that HCAI's value emerges from the interplay of technical fit, collaborative interaction, and organizational trust.

Acknowledgments. This research and development project is funded by the German Federal Ministry of Research, Technology and Space (BMFTR) within the "Zukunft der Wertschöpfung – Forschung zu Produktion, Dienstleistung und Arbeit" (Funding No. 02K23A070/02K23A071) and managed by Projektträger Karlsruhe (PTKA). The authors are responsible for the contents of this publication.

Disclosure of Interests The authors have no competing interests to declare that are relevant to the content of this article.

References

1. Stahmann, P., Rodda, A., Nebel, M., van der Staay, A., Janiesch, C., Teuteberg, F.: Advanced analytics in real-time operational dashboards in smart manufacturing: effects on users' cognitive load and task load. J. Decis. Syst. **34**, 2593245 (2025). https://doi.org/10.1080/12460125.2025.2593245
2. Richardson, C.M.: Human-centric automation to intelligent information integration: a mixed-methods framework for industry 5.0 manufacturing. J. Ind. Inf. Integr. **51**, 101094 (2026). https://doi.org/10.1016/j.jii.2026.101094

3. Rožanec, J.M., et al.: Human-centric artificial intelligence architecture for industry 5.0 applications. Int. J. Prod. Res. **61**, 6847–6872 (2023). https://doi.org/10.1080/00207543.2022.2138611
4. Yan, J., et al.: Human-centric artificial intelligence towards industry 5.0: retrospect and prospect. J. Ind. Inf. Integr. **47**, 100903 (2025). https://doi.org/10.1016/j.jii.2025.100903
5. Shneiderman, B.: Human-Centered AI. Oxford University Press, Oxford (2022)
6. Nebel, M., Speckmann, P., Ciftci, S.A., Janiesch, C.: Standing on the shoulders of paperclips: a taxonomy of human-centered AI systems. In: ECIS 2026 Proceedings (2026)
7. Tsiakas, K., Murray-Rust, D.: Using human-in-the-loop and explainable AI to envisage new future work practices. In: Makedon, F. (ed.) Proceedings of the 15th International Conference on PErvasive Technologies Related to Assistive Environments, pp. 588–594. ACM, New York, NY, USA (2022). https://doi.org/10.1145/3529190.3534779
8. Kernan Freire, S., He, T., Wang, C., Niforatos, E., Bozzon, A.: Factory operators' perspectives on cognitive assistants for knowledge sharing: challenges, risks, and impact on work. Behav. Inform. Technol. **45**, 2248–2275 (2025). https://doi.org/10.1080/0144929X.2025.2574373
9. Gorry, G.A., Scott Morton, M.S.: A framework for information systems. Sloan Manag. Rev. **13**, 56–79 (1971)
10. Ackoff, R.L.: Management misinformation systems. Manag. Sci. **14**, B-147–B-156 (1967). https://doi.org/10.1287/mnsc.14.4.B147
11. Kernan Freire, S., Foosherian, M., Wang, C., Niforatos, E.: Harnessing large language models for cognitive assistants in factories. In: Lee, M., Munteanu, C., Porcheron, M., Trippas, J., Völkel, S.T. (eds.) Proceedings of the 5th International Conference on Conversational User Interfaces, pp. 1–6. ACM, New York, NY, USA (2023). https://doi.org/10.1145/3571884.3604313
12. Misra, S., Barik, K., Kvalvik, P.: A comprehensive review of human-centric AI, regulatory frameworks, and their role in shaping industry 5.0. Procedia Comput. Sci. **259**, 1672–1681 (2025). https://doi.org/10.1016/j.procs.2025.04.122
13. Demircan, F., Nebel, M., Janiesch, C.: Design principles for ethical automated mental workload monitoring in the industrial internet of things. In: vom Brocke, J., Chandra Kruse, L., Hevner, A., Rosemann, M., Chiarini Tremblay, M., Winter, R. (eds.) Design for Better Futures: Beyond the Science of the Artificial. Completed Research. DESRIST 2026 Lecture Notes in Computer Science, vol. 16606, pp. 59–76. Springer Nature, Switzerland, Cham (2026). https://doi.org/10.1007/978-3-032-28313-9_4
14. Goodhue, D.L., Thompson, R.L.: Task-technology fit and individual performance. MIS Q. **19**, 213–236 (1995). https://doi.org/10.2307/249689
15. Short, J., Williams, E., Christie, B.: The Social Psychology of Telecommunications. Wiley, New York (1976)
16. Logg, J.M., Minson, J.A., Moore, D.A.: Algorithm appreciation: People prefer algorithmic to human judgment. Organ. Behav. Hum. Decis. Process. **151**, 90–103 (2019). https://doi.org/10.1016/j.obhdp.2018.12.005
17. Eisenhardt, K.M.: Agency theory: an assessment and review. Acad. Manag. Rev. **14**, 57 (1989). https://doi.org/10.2307/258191
18. Toscani, G.: Future proofing expertise: AI as a power-up, not a takeover. Futures. **175**, 103728 (2026). https://doi.org/10.1016/j.futures.2025.103728
19. Hamdani, R., Chihi, I.: Integrating adaptive human computer interaction in fault detection and diagnosis systems: a human-centric approach for industry 5.0. In: Barolli, L. (ed.) Advanced Information Networking and Applications Lecture Notes on Data Engineering and Communications Technologies, vol. 245, pp. 444–457. Springer Nature, Switzerland, Cham (2025). https://doi.org/10.1007/978-3-031-87763-6_39

20. Usmani, U.A., Happonen, A., Watada, J.: Human-centered artificial intelligence: designing for user empowerment and ethical considerations. In: 2023 5th International Congress on Human-Computer Interaction, Optimization and Robotic Applications (HORA), pp. 1–7. IEEE (2023). https://doi.org/10.1109/HORA58378.2023.10156761
21. vom Brocke, J., Simons, A., Riemer, K., Niehaves, B., Plattfaut, R., Cleven, A.: Standing on the shoulders of giants: challenges and recommendations of literature search in information systems research. CAIS. **37**, 205–224 (2015). https://doi.org/10.17705/1CAIS.03709
22. Webster, J., Watson, R.T.: Analyzing the past to prepare for the future: writing a literature review. MIS Q. **26**, 13–23 (2002)
23. Gioia, D.A., Corley, K.G., Hamilton, A.L.: Seeking qualitative rigor in inductive research: notes on the Gioia methodology. Organ. Res. Methods. **16**, 15–31 (2013). https://doi.org/10.1177/1094428112452151
24. Nebel, M.: Appendix: From System to Teammate: Human-Centered AI in the Industrial Internet of Things (2026). https://doi.org/10.23728/b2share.dvcrq-zrt62
25. Waschull, S., Emmanouilidis, C.: Development and application of a human-centric co-creation design method for AI-enabled systems in manufacturing. In: IFAC-PapersOnLine, vol. 55, pp. 516–521 (2022). https://doi.org/10.1016/j.ifacol.2022.04.246
26. Besinger, P., Vejnoska, D., Ansari, F.: Responsible AI (RAI) in manufacturing: a qualitative framework. Procedia Comput. Sci. **232**, 813–822 (2024). https://doi.org/10.1016/j.procs.2024.01.081
27. Brückner, A., Hein, P., Hein-Pensel, F., Mayan, J., Wölke, M.: Human-centered HCI practices leading the path to industry 5.0: a systematic literature review. In: Stephanidis, C., Antona, M., Ntoa, S., Salvendy, G. (eds.) HCI International 2023 Posters. Communications in Computer and Information Science, vol. 1832, pp. 3–15. Springer Nature, Switzerland, Cham (2023). https://doi.org/10.1007/978-3-031-35989-7_1
28. Mihoubi, S., Benazzouz, T.: Assessing human-centricity in manufacturing supply chains: a framework for industry 5.0 transition. In: Benazzouz, T., Dahbi, S., Benmoussa, R. (eds.) Digital Transformation in Industrial and Logistics Systems Lecture Notes in Networks and Systems, vol. 1840, pp. 3–16. Springer Nature, Switzerland, Cham (2026). https://doi.org/10.1007/978-3-032-18548-8_1

Organizational Climate for Service Robot Integration

Dhyana Paramita[1(✉)], Amy Van Looy[1], and Peter Vlerick[2]

[1] Faculty of Economics and Business Administration, Ghent University, Ghent, Belgium
{dhyana.paramita,Amy.VanLooy}@UGent.be
[2] Faculty of Psychology and Educational Sciences, Ghent University, Ghent, Belgium
peter.vlerick@UGent.be

Abstract. The use of robots in service industries has sparked interest and attention among academia and industry. As its implementation often entails challenges for adaptation, the realization of the anticipated benefits of service robots (SRs) might be hindered. Based on organizational climate (OC) literature, well-managed OC for SR integration fosters integration within the organization and the realization of its benefits. However, empirical evidence on the effect of service-robot-oriented OC on organizational and employees' performance in service organizations remains limited. To fill the void, this study aims to assess the relationship of service-robot-oriented OC prevalent in service organizations on both organizational (i.e., processes, customers) and employees' performance (i.e., need satisfaction, work engagement). A cross-sectional survey is conducted with international data collection. Data analysis using PLS-SEM shows that internal process performance (IPP) statistically mediates the relationship between OC and customer performance (CP). Furthermore, employees' need satisfaction (NS) statistically mediates OC and employees' work engagement (WE). Theoretically, this study contributes by extending the mechanisms underlying the association between OC and organizational and employees' performance. In practice, study results suggest that shaping a proper service-robot-oriented climate is of strategic importance for service organizations' performance.

Keywords: organizational climate · service robots · employee engagement · self-determination theory · organizational performance

1 Introduction

The integration of service robots (SRs) in service industries offers advantages in organizational performance, particularly in service enhancements and financial performance [1]. However, their effect on employees has elicited mixed reactions. While some studies highlight employees' perceptions of SR benefits as task supports [2, 3], others highlight risks to SRs, including operational risks (e.g., malfunctions) [4, 5] and social aspects (e.g., social isolation) [6].

Published by Springer Nature Switzerland AG 2027
S. Han et al. (Eds.): I3E 2026, LNCS 16912, pp. 63–74, 2027.
https://doi.org/10.1007/978-3-032-38014-2_6

The integration of SRs shifts service dynamics in organizations, triggering uncertainty that affects both customer and employee experiences. Organizational climate (OC) plays an important role in addressing such unfamiliarity. The existing literature suggests that OC is shaped by employees' social-cognitive interpretations of the consequential social context in the workplace [7]. It shows that OC influences employees' inferences about organizational expectations and adapts their responses accordingly [8], including organizational performance (e.g., service performance) and employees' performance (e.g., employee engagement) (e.g., [8, 9]). Existing studies have demonstrated that OC influences both employees' performance and, subsequently, customer performance. Particularly, a service climate fosters employees' service orientation (e.g., work effort), which in turn enhances employee service quality (e.g., [10, 11]). This explains how employees' engagement can contribute to organizational performance (e.g., customer satisfaction).

While prior findings have indicated the effect of OC on organizational and employees' performance, these findings have not been extended to service-robot-oriented OC, where service encounters involve SRs. Since, to date, limited studies have examined service-robot-oriented OC or its effects on employee and organizational performance, it remains unclear how this specific OC influences performance outcomes. Consequently, the mechanisms or pathways connecting service-robot-oriented OC to these outcomes have not been investigated. Regarding employees' performance, self-determination theory (SDT) posits that employees in a supportive work environment are likely to be more motivated and subsequently more energized in their work [12]. Regarding organizational performance, performance literature posits that process performance (e.g., efficiency, productivity), driven by supportive organizational practices, will lead to improved customer performance [13]. Altogether, we propose that service-robot-oriented OC shapes employees' perceptions of the organizational performance and the extent of their engagement in their work.

To address this gap, this study empirically investigates the role of OC for enhancing employees' performance and organizational performance. In line with performance research, this study assesses the relationship between OC and customer performance (CP) that is mediated by internal process performance (IPP) (e.g., efficiency, quality). To assess employees' performance, this study uses SDT to examine the relationship between OC and employees' work engagement (WE) via need satisfaction (NS). Overall, this study examines the dual influence of OC on customers' and employees' outcomes. Accordingly, the research questions are:

- **RQ1.** To what extent does employees' need satisfaction (NS) mediate the relationship between organizational climate (OC) and their work engagement (WE) in the workplace?
- **RQ2.** To what extent does internal process performance (IPP) mediate the relationship between OC and customer performance (CP)?

To investigate these RQs, we provide international survey data to simulate the relationships among constructs. Theoretically, this study intends to advance the SR literature by examining the dual effects of service-robot-oriented OC on employee and customer performance in service organizations. We will therefore build and test a framework for explanation and prediction. The intended framework elucidates the mechanisms through which OC might shape employee and customer performance. In practice, the findings offer guidance for managers in fostering a work climate focused on well-managed SR integration, thereby enhancing both employees' engagement and organizational performance.

2 Theoretical Background

2.1 Organizational Climate

Organizational climate (OC) is defined as employees' shared perceptions of workplace policies, practices, and procedures, as well as the behaviors they observe as expected, supported, and rewarded within an organization ([14], p. 316). OC is characterized by organizational attributes, such as systems, structure, and managerial behaviors that shape employees' psychological states, behaviors, and perceptions of their work environment [7]. While OC was originally generic, studies have expanded and adapted its conceptualization and measurement into more context-specific forms of climate, aimed at measuring particular outcomes, such as safety climate and service climate [15].

For instance, service climate in IT has been measured by indicators such as service leadership, client communication, service vision, and service evaluation [9]. Safety climate has been measured by management values, communication, training, safety standard systems, and physical work environment [16, 17]. Meanwhile, robot integration in service settings has been perceived as a risk by service employees due to its safety and privacy risks [18], technical risks [19], and psychosocial risks [6]. Specific climates, particularly related to safety in services, can be measured by leadership, communication, commitment, resources, and risk awareness [20, 21]. Based on this perspective, it is reasonable to expect that leadership, communication, commitment, resources, and risk awareness are relevant to measure OC in an organization using SRs.

2.2 Organizational Performance

The literature on business process performance [22–24] has demonstrated that customer and financial performance typically form organizational performance, while internal business processes and organizational learning capacity are the typical drivers.

Customer performance (CP) remains an important antecedent of the ultimate firm goals [13]. CP is frequently measured by generic customer measures, such as customer satisfaction and company image [13, 23]. Measuring customer satisfaction is common in service settings, particularly to assess their experience in restaurants, hotels, and tourism [25]. Furthermore, customer satisfaction can be measured in the context where SRs are involved in service settings, particularly regarding customer interactions with service robots [26]. In prior studies, customer satisfaction has been mainly attributed to the SR characteristics (e.g., [26]). However, limited evidence exists on the effect of internal process performance (IPP) on customer satisfaction.

Additionally, internal business processes aim to identify critical activities in which organizations must excel to satisfy shareholder and customer expectations, such as service excellence (e.g., cycle time, cost), and productivity (e.g., efficiency) [23]. Meanwhile, service processes can be measured in terms of reliability (e.g., on-time service delivery), quality (e.g., fulfill customer needs), and flexibility (e.g., reduced waiting time) [27]. Accordingly, internal process performance (IPP) can be measured by time-related performance, cost per business process, internal quality, and flexibility [28]. As internal processes are essential in service delivery, it is plausible that OC, focused on the effective use of SRs, can improve IPP within service organizations.

2.3 Self-determination Theory (SDT) and Work Engagement (WE)

As a foundational theory for human motivation, self-determination theory (SDT) has been applied in a wide range of domains, including research on work organization [29]. Particularly, employees are more self-determined when their psychological basic needs for autonomy, competence, and relatedness are fulfilled [12]. Needs of autonomy reflect the freedom of choice of one's action. Competence needs refer to the feeling of being highly capable of performing tasks. Relatedness refers to the feeling of belongingness in one's social work environment. When these needs satisfaction (NS) are fulfilled, individuals become increasingly motivated (i.e., autonomous motivation) to perform tasks due to the enjoyment they experience [12]. With autonomous motivation, employees become more energized in their work activities. Therefore, the fulfillment of these psychological needs is typically associated with employee engagement [29].

Next, work engagement is defined as "*a positive, fulfilling, work-related state of mind that is characterized by vigor, dedication, and absorption*" ([30], p. 74). Overall, employees with high WE experience high levels of energy and involvement, and they feel happily engrossed in their work [30]. Employees' WE can be fostered through organizational attributes, such as work motivation, human resource management practices, and transformational leadership [31]. Furthermore, studies in service industries have shown that a work environment characterized by a supportive climate enhances employees' engagement at work [32, 33]. However, the mechanisms that activate WE remain unclear. Interestingly, SDT has not been extensively used in SR research focusing on employee well-being. This study thus uses SDT to examine the role of NS as the enabler of the relationship between OC and WE.

3 Hypotheses Development

This section develops hypotheses based on the theoretical foundations in OC, organizational performance, and SDT. Accordingly, the research model is shown in Fig. 1.

First, organizational performance encompasses organizational learning, process, and customer perspectives [13]. The learning perspectives refer to organizational procedures (i.e., leadership, training) that drive organizational capacity to improve and create value [13]. Accordingly, service-robot-oriented OC can be conceptually positioned as a component of learning perspectives, which drive process innovation of the organization [34]. As the learning perspectives focus on firms' capabilities to improve internal business processes [23], it is plausible to expect an important role for service-robot-oriented OC in optimizing service processes using service robots. Furthermore, internal business processes focus on critical customer outcomes [23], such as service productivity (e.g.,

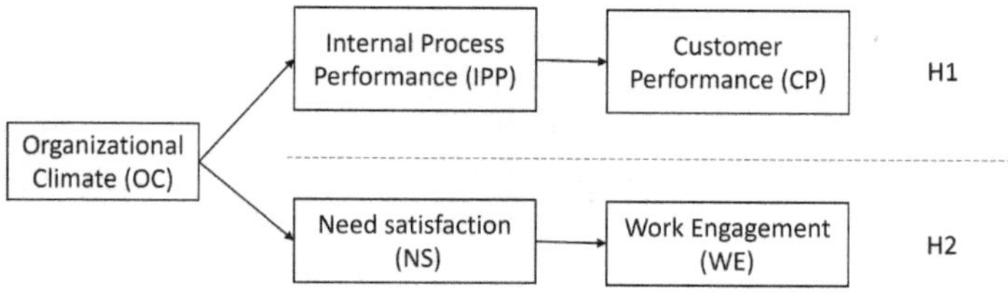

Fig. 1. Proposed research model

efficiency) and service quality [22, 24]. This, in turn, determines how customers experience service delivery, as typically measured by customer satisfaction [13]. Overall, we propose that process performance, driven by service-robot-oriented OC, would influence how customers experience robot-oriented service. Thus, we propose the first hypothesis as follows:

- **H1**. Internal process performance (IPP) mediates the positive relationship between organizational climate (OC) and customer performance (CP)

Next, SDT suggests that fostering a work climate in which employees feel supported will lead to greater employee satisfaction and increased engagement in their work [29]. Drawn from the business process literature, organizational learning originates from three primary sources: people, information systems, and organizational procedures (i.e., culture, leadership, alignment, and teamwork) [13, 22]. Particularly, employee metrics are measured within the learning perspective to assess employee-related outcomes, such as employee satisfaction and engagement [23]. These outcomes can be achieved by fostering an OC that is characterized by organizational procedures supporting the use of information technology (i.e., service robots) for employees' benefits. Supportive organizational procedures will allow employees to experience meaningful work, safety, and availability, motivating them to be physically, cognitively, and emotionally invested in their work [31]. Moreover, studies have shown that employees with autonomous motivation are more engaged in their work [29]. To that end, we assume that a work environment characterized by support for employee needs (i.e., empowerment, competence, relatedness) will foster higher levels of work engagement. Overall, we propose that employees' need satisfaction (NS), driven by service-robot-oriented OC, will be related to employee work engagement (WE).

- **H2**. Need satisfaction (NS) mediates the positive relationship between organizational climate (OC) and work engagement (WE)

4 Research Approach

We conducted a large-scale cross-sectional survey with international data, collected from third-party survey platforms (i.e., Prolific, Amazon Mechanical Turk, CloudResearch Connect). Prior to the main survey, the screening was carefully conducted to ensure that participants were working in service industries and had prior experience with physical SRs in the workplace. Of the 526 eligible participants invited to the main survey, 436 responded. With the exclusion of responses due to failed attention checks, incompleteness, or non-SR experiences, a total of 261 responses were considered valid for final analysis. Participation was voluntary, and the data were kept confidential. An information letter was provided to inform the description of the study and the rights regarding privacy and personal data. Informed consent was obtained from all subjects involved in the study. Participants varied in terms of region (Western Europe, 46%; North America, 53%; Asia, 1%), service sectors (healthcare, 48%; tourism and hospitality, 25%; retail, 11%; and others, 15%), and years of work experience (more than 5 years, 49%; 2–5 years, 31%; 1–2 years, 12%; less than 1 year, 8%)

Our online self-reported survey measured service-robot-oriented OC, drawing on organizational climate literature (e.g., [20]) and adapted to the context of SR integration. The adaptation process was conducted based on scale development guidelines (e.g., [35]), comprising a literature review and expert panel validation that resulted in 25 items across five dimensions namely leadership (e.g., "In my company, my direct daily leader actively promotes the use of service robots"); communication (e.g., "In my company, there has been transparent communication about the reasons for the use of service robots"); commitment (e.g., "In my company, top managers recognize the importance of the use of service robots"); resources (e.g., "In my company, adequate training has been provided to staff on how to use service robots"); and risk awareness (e.g., "In my company, employees are aware that service robots may have safety risks for humans"). These five dimensions captured key organizational attributes relevant to service robot integration, as aligned with prior service robot research (e.g., [36]).

Next, IPP was measured by four items adapted from [28] (e.g., "The use of service robots in our organization has made the service delivery more time efficient") while CP was assessed using five items built upon [26] (e.g., "The service provided with the support of service robots has met customer expectations"). NS was assessed using nine items across three dimensions (i.e., autonomy, competence, relatedness), as modified from [37] (e.g., "I feel capable of performing successfully when using service robots at my work"). WE was measured using nine items adapted from [38] (e.g., "I feel energized while working with service robots"). All items were measured on a five-point Likert scale (1 = strongly disagree, 5 = strongly agree).

The data were analyzed using Partial Least Squares, Structural Equation Modelling (PLS-SEM) with the SmartPLS 4 tool [39]. The data analysis included an assessment of both the measurement and structural models. The measurement instrument comprised lower-order constructs (LOCs) and higher-order constructs (HOCs). According to [40], the assessment of reflective LOCs involved the following metrics: (1) internal consistency reliability (Cronbach's alpha >0.70), (2) convergent validity, measured by average variance extraction (AVE > 0.50), and (3) discriminant validity, measured by Heterotrait-Monotrait (HTMT <0.85). The assessment of HOC in this study consisted of formative HOC (i.e., OC) and reflective HOC (i.e., NS). For formative HOC, the assessment involved a collinearity assessment using the variance inflation factor (VIF < 3). Furthermore, the outer weights of the constructs had to be statistically significant to be retained. When the outer weights were not significant, the constructs could be retained if the outer loadings were significant. For reflective HOC, the assessment followed the same criteria as the reflective LOCs, outlined in the previous paragraph.

Finally, the structural model was assessed as follows. First, the path coefficients and their significance measured the direct effects between constructs. The result captured specific indirect effects between constructs to assess the mediation relationship. Second, the R^2 was measured to assess the explanatory power of the model. Third, the f^2 was calculated to assess the effect size of the exogenous to endogenous constructs. Finally, the Q^2 was evaluated to assess the predictive capability of the model. For these metrics, we followed the thresholds described by [40]. The R^2 thresholds indicate weak (0.25), moderate (0.50), and substantial (0.75) explanatory power. For f^2, threshold ranges from 0.02 (small), 0.15 (medium), and 0.35 (large). The Q^2 values need to be larger than zero to exhibit predictive relevance for the given endogenous constructs.

5 Results

Based on full collinearity test [41], the VIF for all latent variables was below 3.3, suggesting that the common method bias was not a serious concern for this study. Next, the assessment first focused on the reflective LOCs (Table 1). The LOCs for the OC scale retained 23 items across five constructs, with all assessment criteria meeting the required thresholds (Cronbach's $\alpha > 0.70$, AVE > 0.50, HTMT <0.85). Similarly, the LOCs for the NS constructs retained all nine items across three constructs. This indicated that all constructs for OC and NS were reliable, valid, and empirically distinct.

Table 1. Assessment of the measurement scale (LOCs)

Constructs	Cronbach's α	AVE
OC (leadership; communication; commitment; resources; risk awareness)	0.705–0.842	0.531–0.618
NS (autonomy; competence; relatedness)	0.804–0.864	0.718–0.786
WE	0.951	0.72
IPP	0.862	0.644
CP	0.928	0.776

Next, Table 2 gives an overview of the HOC assessment. The assessment of formative HOC for OC showed no collinearity issues, with all VIF scores below three. All constructs showed significant outer weights, except for 'communication' and 'commitment'. These constructs were nevertheless retained because they showed significant outer loadings, demonstrating their absolute importance to the HOC. The assessment of reflective HOC for NS met the acceptable criteria, as the Cronbach's alpha and AVE were above the recommended thresholds (0.70 and 0.508, respectively).

Lastly, Table 3 provides an overview of the structural model assessment. Based on path analysis, all direct paths were significant and positively associated. The specific indirect effect of OC-IPP-CP was statistically significant ($\beta = 0.206$, $t = 4.041$, $p < 0.001$), suggesting partial mediation (H1 supported). The specific indirect effect between OC-NS-WE was statistically significant ($\beta = 0.287$, t-values = 5.666, $p < 0.001$), suggesting partial mediation (H2 supported). This was further supported by moderate explanatory power (R^2) (IPP, 0.430; CP, 0.516; NS, 0.46; WE, 0.466) and sufficient effect size ($f^2 > 0.10$). The Q^2 values were above zero (IPP, 0.409; CP, 0.435; NS, 0.434; WE, 0.352), suggesting the predictive relevance of the endogenous constructs.

Table 2. Assessment of the measurement scale (HOCs)

Lower-order construct (LOCs)	Outer weights	Outer loadings	VIF
Formative HOCs			
OC (Leadership)	0.325*	0.842**	2.124
OC (Communication)	0.186	0.81**	2.136
OC (Commitment)	0.173	0.827**	2.368
OC (Resources)	0.326*	0.868**	2.278
OC (Risk awareness)	0.207*	0.724**	1.650
	Cronbach's alpha	AVE	
Reflective HOCs			
NS	0.808	0.723	–

Notes: *$p < 0.01$, **$p < 0.001$

Table 3. Structural model and mediation analysis

Path	OC➔IPP	IPP➔CP	OC➔NS	NS➔WE	OC➔CP	OC➔WE
Coefficient	0.656	0.314	0.678	0.423	0.472	0.321
t-values	16.115	4.441	18.952	6	8.579	4.64
p-values	0	0	0	0	0	0
f^2	0.754	0.116	0.852	0.181	0.262	0.104

6 Discussion

Our study has shown that employees' perceptions of the service-robot-oriented OC are associated with customer performance and employee work engagement. Accordingly, this study has offered several theoretical contributions. First, regarding OC, our survey has extended the OC literature by investigating the potential dual effect of service-robot-oriented OC on customer and employees' performance. Moreover, this study is one of the first to apply OC to the specific context of service robot use in service organizations, in line with service encounters and workplaces that are becoming increasingly technologically oriented. This study extends prior research (e.g., [10]) by providing preliminary evidence, based on employees' perceptions, i.e., of the role of internal process performance in the association between service-robot-oriented OC and customer performance.

In terms of employees' performance, our findings extend existing studies (e.g., [11]) by showcasing that proper service-robot-oriented OC is associated with service employees' engagement through the fulfillment of their psychological basic needs. Regarding SRs, this study has advanced the SR literature by positioning OC as the primary antecedent of employees' performance and offering a deeper theoretical explanation. While existing SR studies typically examine organizational factors (e.g., leadership, organizational support) as moderators to alleviate perceived SR threats (e.g., [42]), this study has explored how such mechanisms can be explained through SDT.

Next, this study offers practical contributions from two perspectives. First, our study advises managers to consider the role of OC in shaping employees' interpretations of organizational performance. It is essential for managers to establish an OC that clearly articulates the expectations on service robot integration at work and how service robots contribute to improving work processes. We recommend that managers actively involve employees in service robot implementations through training sessions, knowledge sharing, and feedback mechanisms to help them better understand how service robots can optimize service encounters and improve the customer experience.

Furthermore, it is essential for managers to foster a specific climate by ensuring that employees feel empowered, competent, and included when working alongside SRs. This means that an autonomy-supportive climate can empower employees by involving them in decision-making related to SR integration. A competence-supportive climate can be fostered by providing adequate training and infrastructure that support employees' competences regarding the use of SRs. Finally, a relatedness-supportive climate can be reflected in strong support from both supervisors and colleagues, which can be reinforced through open communication and feedback practices. Addressing employees' psychological needs at work would help them be more engaged.

Nonetheless, we acknowledge some study limitations that can be addressed in future research. First, our survey has measured organizational performance through employees' perspectives, reflecting subjective perceptions. Future research could investigate actual service experiences to assess customer performance, as well as objective process performance metrics to assess internal process performance. Second, this study has not included control variables to account for potential boundary conditions. Future studies could include these variables to strengthen the findings. Third, future studies can benefit from longitudinal studies to strengthen claims about causal relationships among variables. Additionally, future studies can benefit from comparing different robot types or service contexts. Finally, while this scale has been developed for SR integration, it captures the core OC dimensions that may be applicable to other forms of technology adoption.

7 Conclusion

This study has aimed to assess the dual effect of service-robot-oriented OC on employee and organizational performance. Empirical data have shown that a proper service-robot-oriented OC seems associated with improved customer performance through internal business processes. Additionally, our data suggest that a proper service-robot-oriented OC is associated with employees' engagement through their psychological basic needs.

As a result, this study extends existing literature by exploring the mechanisms through which OC might influence both organizational and employees' performance in service organizations. This insight offers practitioners useful advice on the importance of establishing proper service-robot-oriented OC in service organizations.

Acknowledgments. This research is funded by a research grant number: BOF/24J/2023/023.

References

1. Belanche, D., Casaló, L.V., Flavián, C.: Frontline robots in tourism and hospitality: service enhancement or cost reduction? Electron. Mark. **31**, 477–492 (2021). https://doi.org/10.1007/s12525-020-00432-5
2. Melkas, H., Hennala, L., Pekkarinen, S., Kyrki, V.: Impacts of robot implementation on care personnel and clients in elderly-care institutions. Int. J. Med. Inform. **134**, 104041 (2020). https://doi.org/10.1016/j.ijmedinf.2019.104041
3. Mejia, C., Crandell, H.A., Broker, E., Shoss, M.: Working with service robots in the dining room: employees' perspectives and realities. J. Hosp. Tour. Technol. **15**, 878–896 (2024). https://doi.org/10.1108/JHTT-12-2023-0420
4. Ivkov, M., Blešić, I., Dudić, B., Pajtinková Bartáková, G., Dudić, Z.: Are future professionals willing to implement service robots? attitudes of hospitality and tourism students towards service robotization. Electronics (Basel). **9**, 1442 (2020). https://doi.org/10.3390/electronics9091442
5. El-Gazar, H.E., Abdelhafez, S., Ali, A.M., Shawer, M., Alharbi, T.A.F., Zoromba, M.A.: Are nurses and patients willing to work with service robots in healthcare? a mixed-methods study. BMC Nurs. **23**, 718 (2024). https://doi.org/10.1186/s12912-024-02336-7
6. Paluch, S., Tuzovic, S., Holz, H.F., Kies, A., Jörling, M.: "My colleague is a robot"–exploring frontline employees' willingness to work with collaborative service robots. J. Serv. Manag. **33**, 363–388 (2022). https://doi.org/10.1108/JOSM-11-2020-0406
7. Beus, J.M., Smith, J.H., Taylor, E.C.: Integrating organizational climate theory: a domain-independent explanation for climate formation and function. J. Appl. Psychol. **108**, 2018–2039 (2023). https://doi.org/10.1037/apl0001117
8. Schneider, B., White, S.S., Paul, M.C.: Linking service climate and customer perceptions of service quality: tests of a causal model. J. Appl. Psychol. **83**, 150–163 (1998). https://doi.org/10.1037/0021-9010.83.2.150
9. Jia, R., Reich, B.H.: IT service climate, antecedents and IT service quality outcomes: some initial evidence. J. Strateg. Inf. Syst. **22**, 51–69 (2013). https://doi.org/10.1016/j.jsis.2012.10.001
10. Schneider, B., Yost, A.B., Kropp, A., Kind, C., Lam, H.: Workforce engagement: what it is, what drives it, and why it matters for organizational performance. J. Organ. Behav. **39**, 462–480 (2018). https://doi.org/10.1002/job.2244
11. Hee Yoon, M., Beatty, S.E., Suh, J.: The effect of work climate on critical employee and customer outcomes. Int. J. Serv. Ind. Manag. **12**, 500–521 (2001). https://doi.org/10.1108/EUM0000000006095
12. Ryan, R.M., Deci, E.L.: Self-determination theory and the facilitation of intrinsic motivation, social development, and well-being. Am. Psychol. **55**, 68–78 (2000). https://doi.org/10.1037/0003-066X.55.1.68
13. Kaplan, R.S.: Conceptual foundations of the balanced scorecard. In: Handbook of Management Accounting Research. Elsevier (2009)

14. Schneider, B., Ehrhart, M.G., Macey, W.H.: Organizational climate and culture: history, current status, integration, and change. Annu. Rev. Organ. Psych. Organ. Behav. **13**(1), 309–335 (2025). https://doi.org/10.1146/annurev-orgpsych-020924-070545
15. Schneider, B., Ehrhart, M.G., Macey, W.H.: Organizational Climate and Culture. Annu. Rev. Psychol. **64**, 361–388 (2013). https://doi.org/10.1146/annurev-psych-113011-143809
16. Cheyne, A., Cox, S., Oliver, A., Tomás, J.M.: Modelling safety climate in the prediction of levels of safety activity. Work Stress. **12**, 255–271 (1998). https://doi.org/10.1080/02678379808256865
17. Neal, A., Griffin, M.A., Hart, P.M.: The impact of organizational climate on safety climate and individual behavior. Saf. Sci. **34**, 99–109 (2000). https://doi.org/10.1016/S0925-7535(00)00008-4
18. Vishwanath, A., Singh, A., Chua, Y.H.V., Dauwels, J., Magnenat-Thalmann, N.: Humanoid co-workers: how is it like to work with a robot? In: 2019 28th IEEE International Conference on Robot and Human Interactive Communication (RO-MAN), pp. 1–6. IEEE (2019)
19. Ali, F., Dogan, S., Chen, X., Cobanoglu, C., Limayem, M.: Friend or a foe: understanding generation Z employees' intentions to work with service robots in the hotel industry. Int. J. Hum. Comput. Interact. **39**, 111–122 (2023). https://doi.org/10.1080/10447318.2022.2041880
20. De Boeck, E., Jacxsens, L., Bollaerts, M., Vlerick, P.: Food safety climate in food processing organizations: development and validation of a self-assessment tool. Trends Food Sci. Technol. **46**, 242–251 (2015). https://doi.org/10.1016/j.tifs.2015.09.006
21. Davis, A.L. et al.: Moving FOCUS–the fire service organizational culture of safety survey–from research to practice. J. Saf. Res. **74**, 233–247 (2020). https://doi.org/10.1016/j.jsr.2020.06.011
22. Massingham, R., Massingham, P.R., Dumay, J.: Improving integrated reporting. J. Intellect. Cap. **20**, 60–82 (2019). https://doi.org/10.1108/JIC-06-2018-0095
23. Norton, D.P., Kaplan, R.S.: Balanced scorecard. In: The Palgrave Encyclopedia of Strategic Management, pp. 80–84. Palgrave Macmillan UK, London (2018)
24. Van Looy, A., Shafagatova, A.: Business process performance measurement: a structured literature review of indicators, measures and metrics. Springerplus. **5**, 1797 (2016). https://doi.org/10.1186/s40064-016-3498-1
25. Pizam, A., Shapoval, V., Ellis, T.: Customer satisfaction and its measurement in hospitality enterprises: a revisit and update. Int. J. Contemp. Hosp. Manag. **28**, 2–35 (2016). https://doi.org/10.1108/IJCHM-04-2015-0167
26. Seo, S.: When female (male) robot is talking to me: effect of service robots' gender and anthropomorphism on customer satisfaction. Int. J. Hosp. Manag. **102**, 103166 (2022). https://doi.org/10.1016/j.ijhm.2022.103166
27. Wouters, J.P.M.: Customer service strategy options: a multiple case study in a B2B setting. Ind. Mark. Manag. **33**, 583–592 (2004). https://doi.org/10.1016/j.indmarman.2003.12.003
28. Van Looy, A., Trkman, P., Clarysse, E.: A configuration taxonomy of business process orientation. Bus. Inf. Syst. Eng. **64**, 133–147 (2022). https://doi.org/10.1007/s12599-021-00700-4
29. Deci, E.L., Olafsen, A.H., Ryan, R.M.: Self-determination theory in work organizations: the state of a science. Annu. Rev. Organ. Psych. Organ. Behav. **4**, 19–43 (2017). https://doi.org/10.1146/annurev-orgpsych-032516-113108
30. Schaufeli, W.B., Salanova, M., González-romá, V., Bakker, A.B.: The measurement of engagement and burnout: a two sample confirmatory factor analytic approach. J. Happiness Stud. **3**, 71–92 (2002). https://doi.org/10.1023/A:1015630930326
31. Barrick, M.R., Thurgood, G.R., Smith, T.A., Courtright, S.H.: Collective organizational engagement: linking motivational antecedents, strategic implementation, and firm performance. Acad. Manag. J. **58**, 111–135 (2015). https://doi.org/10.5465/amj.2013.0227

32. Ancarani, A., Mauro, C., Di Giammanco, M.D.: Linking organizational climate to work engagement: a study in the healthcare sector. Int. J. Public Adm. **42**, 547–557 (2019). https://doi.org/10.1080/01900692.2018.1491595
33. Menguc, B., Auh, S., Yeniaras, V., Katsikeas, C.S.: The role of climate: implications for service employee engagement and customer service performance. J. Acad. Mark. Sci. **45**, 428–451 (2017). https://doi.org/10.1007/s11747-017-0526-9
34. Andersson, M., Moen, O., Brett, P.O.: The organizational climate for psychological safety: associations with SMEs' innovation capabilities and innovation performance. J. Eng. Technol. Manag. **55**, 101554 (2020). https://doi.org/10.1016/j.jengtecman.2020.101554
35. Van Looy, A.: Capabilities for managing business processes: a measurement instrument. Bus. Process. Manag. J. **26**, 287–311 (2019). https://doi.org/10.1108/BPMJ-06-2018-0157
36. Xu, S., Stienmetz, J., Ashton, M.: How will service robots redefine leadership in hotel management? a Delphi approach. Int. J. Contemp. Hosp. Manag. **32**, 2217–2237 (2020). https://doi.org/10.1108/IJCHM-05-2019-0505
37. Longo, Y., Gunz, A., Curtis, G.J., Farsides, T.: Measuring need satisfaction and frustration in educational and work contexts: the need satisfaction and frustration scale (NSFS). J. Happiness Stud. **17**, 295–317 (2016). https://doi.org/10.1007/s10902-014-9595-3
38. Schaufeli, W.B., Bakker, A.B., Salanova, M.: Utrecht Work Engagement Scale-9, (2011)
39. Ringle, C.M., Wende, S., Becker, J.M.: SmartPLS. **4** (2024)
40. Hair, J.F., Hult, G.T.M., Ringle, C.M., Sarstedt, M.: A Primer on Partial Least Squares Structural Equation Modeling (PLS-SEM). Sage, Thousand Oaks (2017)
41. Kock, N.: Common method bias in PLS-SEM. Int. J. e-Collab. **11**, 1–10 (2015). https://doi.org/10.4018/ijec.2015100101
42. Shum, C., Min, H. (Kelly), Sun, J., Yu, H. (Chandler), He, Z.: Kicking the robots: the roles of transformational leadership and fear on service robot risk awareness and robot abuse relationship. J. Hosp. Tour. Technol. 15, 934–946 (2024). https://doi.org/10.1108/JHTT-12-2023-0414

Tensions in Joint Projects: Examining an Innovative Digital Service Development

Markus Takamaa(✉) and Samuli Pekkola

University of Jyväskylä, Jyväskylä 40014, Finland
{Markus.k.t.takamaa,Samuli.j.pekkola}@jyu.fi

Abstract. When new innovative information systems are developed, unexpected tensions may rise between the project participants. This, in turn, may have an impact on the project outcome. To understand why and how these tensions surge, we conducted a qualitative case study with semi-structured interviews to understand what kind of tensions emerge on a development project where a service, that no stakeholder has earlier experiences, is developed to support the university students' mental wellbeing. Our findings suggest that various tensions rise between the project participants, each influencing the dynamics and relationship between the project participants. We address that these tensions need to be addressed to ensure the success of the project outcome.

Keywords: Tensions · ICT development · Digital social innovation · Psychological services · Paradox studies

1 Introduction

In information systems (IS) literature, information technologies (IT) have been seen as enablers for a variety of innovations, such as supporting new operations, reducing costs, and improving efficiency [16]. Digital social innovation thus represents an emerging focus point in IS research [2], where IS enabled innovations can be studied in their infancy. Digital social innovations are newly introduced digital technologies and solutions, which allows organizations to address larger societal challenges [2]. For example, these include innovations for mental health. Previous studies have shown that online wellbeing systems are often more effective in treating mental health issues than, for example, traditional face-to-face alternatives [3, 8, 20]. Thus, online mental health services show a promise in breaking the limitations of traditional face-to-face mental wellbeing intervention services, such as accessibility and concerns about privacy [3].

Developing such services is, however, challenging if the parties have no experience or even idea about those services and what they would look like. Different and unexpected conflicts and tensions may arise when stakeholders do not know what the others are talking about, what they want and expect, or what one can deliver. These conflicts may influence the tasks or the relationships between team members [4, 13]. While moderate levels of conflict can foster innovation within teams, having too much

S. Han et al. (Eds.): I3E 2026, LNCS 16912, pp. 75–86, 2027.
https://doi.org/10.1007/978-3-032-38014-2_7

conflict hinders innovation and makes collaboration very difficult, as the rising tensions limit the capacity for team members to perceive, process and evaluate information [4]. General awareness, and addressing these tensions, are consequently crucial in fostering innovative solutions to emerge. Unfortunately, IS literature has studied such situations sporadically. Especially studies have yet to address these in the context of digital social innovations, where their barriers of process are yet to fully be identified [19].

We seek to shed light on this unexplored area by answering the following research question: *When developing innovative digital services, what kinds of tensions emerge?*

We examine how tensions emerged during an innovative social IT service development. We especially focus on examining the first system version created in a brand-new context – a university-wide system to support the students' mental wellbeing – that started development internally back in 2012–2013. This means there were no prior examples of similar services which could have been used as a reference or an example. Such setting resulted in a need to explore unknown issues and discuss unfamiliar topics. An emergence of various tensions was therefore likely.

2 Literature Review

Digital social innovation allows organizations to address societal challenges with digital technologies. These digital processes, products, and services are used to create social and economic value [2], for example, in terms of better healthcare or education, or gender equality [1, 2, 19]. Digital social innovation thus provide means to solve socially pressing problems through the use of collaborative innovation [1]. Developing these innovations, however, creates new unexplored issues, which may, in turn, raise tensions within the development project.

These tensions have been studied from the perspective of paradoxes. Tensions emerge as contradictions in organizational environments. The viewpoint has motivated management researchers to study contradictions rising from organizational change [23, 27]. Within the IS field, paradoxes and contradictions have been used to describe challenging situations, such as examining tensions rising from either IS-related change or from IS development [27].

Paradox studies have explored how organizations manage competing demands simultaneously. The viewpoint suggests that the organizations' long-term sustainability requires continuous efforts to balance with multiple differing demands. For example, plurality may foster competing goals, as stakeholders seeks alternative ways for an organisation's success. Varying demands can also emerge from organizing activities as they may create competing designs and processes to reach the same outcome [23]. Handling such paradoxical tensions is crucial in providing a basis for successful teamwork.

IS development projects may also face various issues: technical complexities, uncertain or changing requirements, and socio-cognitive challenges. Socio-cognitive issues include differentiating conceptions of reality by the stakeholders, thus creating conflicts in the conceptions of IS projects [14]. Handling these processes involve navigating numerous, often contradicting values. This, in turn, may lead to interpersonal tensions and conflicts, as choices may benefit some stakeholders more than the others [6]. Technical issues, on the other hand, may relate to technical complexities, untried technologies, and system extendibility. Therefore, the problems associated with IS development are related to both technical and social systems within projects [28]. Addressing both dimensions is needed for the successful project outcomes, as unresolved tensions, for example, may steer towards failure [6].

Sociocognitive issues may sometimes be due to varying organisational frames. The project members use frames to assign make sense organisational tasks and the environment, and to create meaning for it. These frames also affect technologies, where they act as a basis for assumptions, expectation and knowledge for organisational technologies. These technological frames may cause varying interpretations by different groups, which in turn may cause difficulties and conflicts when developing new technologies if unaligned [17]. Therefore, addressing these differences and being aware of unaligned frames may provide solutions to these issues.

3 Research Methods

Based on previous research, managing tensions is crucial for organizing complex teams. However, little attention is paid to how these tensions manifest in IT projects where new, unexplored solutions are created. Our study explores this gap by using a qualitative case study approach [7]. The qualitative case study approach provides profound and comprehensive information and rich on a phenomenon, making it suitable in many IS studies [12, 26].

We study an innovative development project at a university. The project focused on creating a new online wellbeing service to improve the students' psychological wellbeing. During its initial developmental phases in the 2010s, the service was first of its kind in terms of target group, volume of potential users, context, and importantly, topic. The developers had to explore uncharted territory to create a unique service. As no example of similar service existed, the developer team had to scout its way by trial and error. We hypothesize that in this kind of novel situation, various tensions emerge. Consequently, we consider this service development to be ideal for our research goals.

The studied service was designed to provide tools for students to tackle various mental health issues, such as depression, anxiety, stress, and learning problems, and to improve their psychological resilience. Various tools mostly consist of self-guided exercises, implemented as a dedicated web service. The service also provides peer-support services for students in need of additional support to tackle their issues. In other words, the service aimed to provide cost-effective access for students and help them to manage mental issues affecting their studies.

To explore the tensions within the development team, we conducted a set of semi-structured interviews with the project team members. In these interviews, we aimed to create an overall understanding of the service development, the interviewees' approaches and understanding of the project, and how they collaborated in creating the service. By focusing on these points, we were able to discover emerging tensions. After identifying and interviewing the key stakeholders, we employed snowball sampling [18] to identify subsequent interviewees, i.e. those were recommended by the preceding informants.

The interviews were conducted during the fall of 2025. The interviewees had various roles within the creation of the wellbeing system, ranging from product owner and content creators to IT manager and software developers. They worked or had worked at the University and had a background either in psychology or in IT service development. We contacted all individuals (15) we knew being involved in the service development. Overall, we interviewed 11 people, as listed in Table 1.

Table 1. Interviewees with their major tasks in the project. Non-IT personnel had a background in the psychology field.

Name	Their main tasks
Professor K.	Managing the research team responsible for the development. The idea initiator.
Product owner J.	Managing & organizing the overall development project, handling user data & feedback, operating as the super user of the digital service.
IT manager I.	Responsible for managing IT development crew. They initially worked on the project as a software developer.
IT developer H.	Updating features after the initial launch until the first major update.
IT developer G.	Implementing the visual layout during the second major update.
IT developer F.	Working on software code during the second major update.
IT architect E.	Working as an IT system architect during the initial version and the first major update.
IT visual artist D.	Creating the visual layout design for the second major update. Worked as an outsourced independent contractor.
Content creator C.	Recent update of the service content and creating promotional material.
Content creator B.	Update of the service content during the second major update, working as a mental peer-coach for the service.
Content creator A.	Update of the service content during the second major update, working as a mental peer-coach for the service.

The interviews were done either face-to-face or online, based on the interviewees' preference. Overall, these interviews lasted an average of 66,5 min, ranging from 48 min to 93 min. The interviews were recorded with the interviewees' consent. The recordings were later transcribed using an AI tool. The transcriptions were manually checked to guarantee consistency with the recorded discussions. After the interviews, the data was supplemented by follow-up emails and documents. These included, for example, UI sketches, previous text-based conversations, and presentation slides.

The data analysis followed the interpretative data analysis [26]. First, the first author reviewed the transcripts to identify situations, persons or issues, which the interviews described as causing tensions. Then, indirect mentions of tensions were studied. We used words like "conflict", "difficult" and "challenging", as indicators of potential tensions. These insights were constantly discussed among the authors to guarantee the consistency of the analysis. Later, those discoveries that did not meet the subsequent definition of tensions were excluded.

For example, when professor K. stated: "I ended up in a conflict with [another] professor." This was coded as a potential instance of tension. When IT architect E. stated: "At beginning, there was some friction about the idea that the service had to be done with our content management system…", the quote was also coded as potential tension.

In this analysis of discovered tensions, the widely used Smith and Lewis (2011) framework was used as a research lens, as it provides in-depth understanding about emerging tensions. The framework divides tensions into four categories: learning, organizing, performing, and belonging, thus providing a comprehensive lens to understand different forms of tensions. First, learning tensions rise from efforts to renew, innovate and change. This gives tensions between building upon and destroying the past to create the desired future. Organizing tensions surface from competing designs and processes for achieving the desired outcome. Examples include tensions between collaboration and competition, as well as between routine and change. On the other hand, performing paradoxes rise from competing strategies and goals. These stem from the plurality of stakeholders, as they may have conflicting demands and priorities. Finally, belonging tensions are formed through identity. As individuals and groups seek both homogeneity and distinction, tensions may emerge due to these contradicting forces [23].

4 Findings

The development of the psychological wellbeing service begun in the early 2010s. Until today, the service is in its third generation, going through two major upgrades. They have transformed the service into more user-friendly and visually appealing versions.

The tensions varied depending on the people's roles and responsibilities. Figure 1 illustrates the tensions in the project. Overall, we discovered 10 issues causing tensions. These included one learning tension, two organizing tensions, five performing tensions, one belonging tension, and one tension not fitting into any category. Most tensions focus on the senior members of the development team. The tensions will be discussed next in the order of the different groups and their relationships.

4.1 Tensions for a Change

At the beginning of the development project, the service encountered strong opposition for its creation. Already before the actual development began, a fellow professor to Professor K expressed their strong disapproval. In these discussions, for example, the professor in question deemed the system unfit with the regulatory rules regarding psychological wellbeing services. This caused insecurities of whether the project can proceed at all, and whether and in which form the project can advance to development.

These learning tensions were carefully assessed by Professor K., responsible for the psychological research team. The situation was assessed and it was decided that the project could go ahead. To boost the start of the technical development, the team used their professorial authority (status) and ignored all resistance. In doing so, they proceeded with the development and accepted the presence of the tensions without diminishing them. The service's first proof-of-concept version concretized the initial

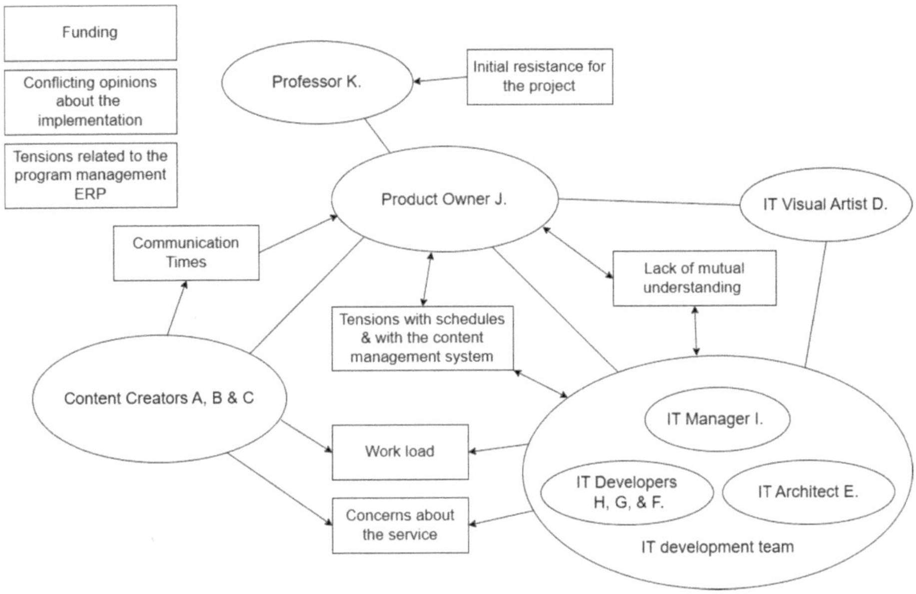

Fig. 1. Discovered tensions. The circles present the project personnel involved, while the squares present various tensions. The lines present direct work relationships between the team members, while the arrows indicate the direction of tensions.

ideas and gradually started to reduce disapproval and resistance. After a few years, the resistance was gone, and no further protests were expressed.

4.2 Tensions Between the Product Owner and the IT Development Team

The findings show that the most prominent tensions emerged between the product owner and IT development team. For example, tensions emerged when the product owner asked for major tasks to be done within a schedule that was not suiting for the development team. The product owner initially expected a major visual upgrade to be done in two weeks and had reserved this time for the development team to complete the task. The development team, however, deemed these deadlines unrealistic, citing the workload required to produce the service. We categorized these as performing tensions, as these were caused by conflicting scheduling demands by the personnel involved.

Similarly, organizing tensions emerged during the service's initial creation, due to conflicting designs for the service implementation. In these, the product owner expressed interest in deploying a particular content management system with the help of students. The IT development team, however, deemed the system unsuitable due to information security concerns. The team preferred to use a familiar content management system – familiar for them.

Both previously mentioned tensions were solved by the product owner adhering to the needs of the IT development team; the deadlines were extended, and the development team's preferences were acknowledged. Although such tensions and coping mechanisms are well known in the project management literature, the issues emerged due to the product owner's and the IT development team's mutual lack of understanding of the other party, their ideas, work, and constraints.

IT architect E observed that communication between the development team and the product owner also worked like a broken phone. For example, after the initial service version was completed, the IT development team was unaware of the amount of manual labor required to maintain the service. In the initial version, the product owner administrated the system and entered all users manually and copied all the necessary files to each users' individual folder. After a couple of years, the IT development team was shocked by surprise as they were completely unaware of the need. As the product owner did not know that the task could be automated, s/he did not ask for it. This notion led to the first major system update.

The IT development team members and the product owner stated that at the initial development phases, there was a lack of common understanding and an absence of common language between the parties. This lack of understanding was expressed by IT developer H who felt the planning meetings were left open-ended and very generic. The IT developers felt they needed additional talks with their fellow developers to understand what needed to be done on a functional level. They felt that this was sometimes a guess. This caused tensions among the project participants, which do not fit neatly into any Smith & Lewis category. IT developer H. articulated:

"*I can argue that more than once I made a change and tried to get it approved. I'm pretty sure the others didn't understand what I meant. So I just published something. And then, maybe someday, it will become clear whether it was what was wanted. At least I never felt like I could say with certainty: "Hey! I was asked to do this, and I solved it this way. I'm pretty sure I did it right and as it was wanted." There was never such feeling in that project.*"

The lack of understanding was seen being caused by people's diverse backgrounds. IT developer H claimed the others to be people from outside the IT field with no previous experiences on IT development projects. Although the product owner softened his/her argument and said that this might be also due to themselves being more technically oriented, and therefore s/he may lack the knowledge needed to understand the project's vision–guided by the methods of psychological therapy.

4.3 Tensions Between Content Creators and the Product Owner

The content creators expressed tensions towards the product owner, particularly concerning his/her communication. Oftentimes, the content creators receive work related messages after normal working hours, such as late evenings or during weekends. This made them feel that these messages interfered with their time off from work. For example, Content creator C felt that this reduced the predictability of their work, although s/he expressed that these tasks were not required to be completed immediately. S/he expressed that this was about preliminary information for the forthcoming tasks. Content creator B also expressed his/her frustration. S/he felt this made him/her feel disoriented due to numerous changes to schedules and objectives. Handling these changes requires a lot of flexibility with their personal schedules and tasks. These tensions fit neatly into belonging tensions, as these rise between individual's and project's needs.

On the other hand, Content creators A and B expressed positive attitude towards this kind of communication: It made it easy to know about the forthcoming work tasks. They also understood that communication times were the results of the product owner's long workdays with his/her other tasks, and that work tasks concerning the project needed to proceed accordingly. Such communication made knowledge sharing easy as the threshold to communicate was low. Product owner replied to their questions quickly if they needed his/her support with some tasks. However, at times they felt this type of communication made them work at late hours. Content creator B partly objected and said that most tasks were not urgent, and their free time should be sanctified.

4.4 General Tensions

Most common tensions, not directed toward any particular person, focused on the lack of resources. For example, most interviewees expressed a lack of work time capacity as they also had other tasks and projects. Content creator B said this made him/her feel disorientated when developing the service. IT developer H felt that other IT development team members overworked. S/he felt that their team cannot put their focus on the project as they were leaping back and forth with various project demands. These tensions fit neatly into performing tensions, as these stem from the demands of stakeholders of other tasks and projects outside the examined one in our study.

Also, the lack of funding was mentioned. Particularly the project owner emphasized that due to limited funding, some features are not yet implemented. S/he said that they have many features they would like to add, but it is not yet possible. Some updates, for example, have been on the list for years. We categorized this as performing tensions, as they were based on conflicting priorities for the University's funding. On the other hand, IT developer G expressed that it is sometimes challenging to decide how to implement ideas, as others may have conflicting opinions. S/he said that it is impossible to satisfy everyone on the project. We categorized them as organization tensions, based on these competing implementation designs.

Some tensions emerged after the implementation of a program management ERP at the IT unit. IT developer G. said that although the ERP provides a good tool for managing their time and tasks, the process is cumbersome to the product owner and stakeholders. As the program management process is laborious and time-consuming, many IT developers (also outside our project) do not attend the prioritization meetings, despite praising the process for bringing structure to their work. This absence resulted in their projects not being prioritized – for example the wellbeing project. These created further performing tensions for the project, as conflicting stakeholders' needs influenced the project's schedule.

Despite the ultimate acceptance of the service, some interviewees still expressed their concerns. IT developer H worried about information security, focusing on providing examples of how this could be improved. Content creator B, on the other hand, showed concerns about the effectiveness of the service. They felt that the service was used to replace personal face-to-face therapy sessions. This made them concerned of the students, who lack sufficient functional or initiative capacity to use online services. Therefore, they felt that the University should also provide additional face-to-face therapy in support of the service to better cater to these people in question. As these tensions rise from conflicting demands for service implementation, we categorized these concerns as performing tensions.

5 Discussion

In this paper, we studied tensions influencing the development of innovative information systems. We show most tensions focus on sociocognitive elements of the development organizations rather than the solution itself or its technical details. These insights show more focus is needed on sociocognitive elements to guarantee a successful outcomes from IS development projects [21]. These may include, for example, focusing on stakeholder commitment to the project's means and ends [9].

In our project, most tensions emerged among project members, as well as with the stakeholders. These make performing tensions the most common category. We hypothesize this is due to various conflicting technological frames [17]. As the frames affect interpretations of technologies, they in turn create different priorities with project members and stakeholders. These, in turn, raise additional tensions in development projects, as priorities cause unsatisfied needs in decision making.

Concerning project personnel, we discovered that tensions are likely to emerge between the product owner ("customer") and the IT development team. These were mostly focused on communication issues, and conflicting expectations and visions in the project planning. This reflects the communication effects on the development process alongside technological frames [10, 17]. We hypothesize that these communication issues are caused by the lack of understanding and vision of the goal, of what kind of solution should be developed. As no party had previous experiences in developing an online psychological service, none had a clear vision of what the innovative solution should be. Cultural differences between the fields of psychology and IT may also be a contributing factor. Therefore, analyzing the influence of cultural differences on the communication barriers may be one way to mitigate these issues at innovative development [5, 10].

Conflicts and tensions in innovative development projects are also connected to power dynamics. As our findings show, most tensions were directed towards managerial personnel.. This was, for example, the case concerning content creators and the project owner, or from a different point of view, between the product owner (customer) and the IT developers. It seems that power over personnel causes tensions due to its restrictive nature over employees' daily schedules. Therefore, emerging tensions and conflicts may help team members to express these hidden issues in projects. Power tensions may, therefore, play also a role in future role in conflict management [11].

Other tensions also focused on the IS project management and the resistance towards the service. Project and program management issues cause tensions when the "customer" does not understand the constraints and content of the IT team: constant balancing between individual projects and their needs. Also, innovative projects themselves may face resistance. In our case, this may be due to the personnel's normative beliefs of how psychological services should be offered and implemented, or to the perceived loss of power by the psychologist. Therefore, managers focusing on innovative IS development should focus on improving perceived value of change as well as promote the necessity for the change to managing these issues [15].

6 Summary and Conclusions

We have studied tensions in an innovative IS development project. Our findings highlight various tensions and why they arise. We show that tensions are likely due to inappropriate communication, lack of resources, and other working related aspects. Addressing these will be therefore important for sustaining reasonable level of tensions and providing successful project outcomes.

Managing tensions in innovative social projects require compromises or adhering to the needs of others. This implies that accepting and understanding other's viewpoints are crucial in reducing tensions. However, this might be very difficult due to the lack of shared vision and common language, and different technological frames. As our case illustrates, many tensions were the result of the absence of earlier experiences: no one knew what they, or the others want, and how that unknown can be implemented.

This paper contributes by increasing our understanding of tensions in IS projects. The tensions originate from people, not even touching the technologies or project deliverables. These bring insights into digital social innovation research, showing potential issues stem from social aspects of projects. Our insights can be used also by project managers to anticipate potential project issues, while developing innovative solutions. They can apply this knowledge by putting special emphasis on managing social-issue-related tensions, such as stakeholder commitment and the creation of common understanding.

Our study also provides a basis for future studies. These include understanding legitimization practices [25], i.e. how new innovative services are legitimized, how common understanding is established [22], or how the new service is used as a boundary object [24]. More research is also needed to shed light on best practices in developing digital social innovation. Future studies could also explore further the effects of technological frames [17] on emerging tensions.

Our study has some limitations. As it is a single case study in a democratic, western country where a certain type of service was implemented, different tensions may emerge in other contexts, such as business and environmental innovations.

References

1. Bonina, C., et al.: Social, commercial, or both? an exploratory study of the identity orientation of digital social innovations. Inf. Syst. J. **31**(5), 695–716 (2021). https://doi.org/10.1111/isj.12290
2. Buck, C., et al.: Doing good by going digital: a taxonomy of digital social innovation in the context of incumbents. J. Strateg. Inf. Syst. **32**(4), 101806 (2023). https://doi.org/10.1016/j.jsis.2023.101806
3. Cha, B.S., et al.: Peer perspectives on challenges encountered during a multi-site digital mental health intervention project. Admin. Pol. Ment. Health. **52**(4), 603–618 (2025). https://doi.org/10.1007/s10488-025-01441-2
4. De Dreu, C.K.W.: When too little or too much hurts: evidence for a curvilinear relationship between task conflict and innovation in teams. J. Manag. **32**(1), 83–107 (2006). https://doi.org/10.1177/0149206305277795
5. Dingley, S., et al.: Tribes of users and systems developers. Australas. J. Inf. Syst. **7**, 2 (2000)

6. Durani, K., et al.: Navigating value conflicts: how developers at varied levels of moral development approach decision-making in information systems development. JAIS. **26**(5), 1294–1336 (2025). https://doi.org/10.17705/1jais.00949
7. Feldman, G., et al.: Technological, organisational, and environmental drivers for enterprise systems upgrade. IMDS. **116**(8), 1636–1655 (2016)
8. Ferrari, M., et al.: Digital interventions for psychological well-being in university students: systematic review and meta-analysis. J. Med. Internet Res. **24**(9), e39686 (2022). https://doi.org/10.2196/39686
9. Gilchrist, A., et al.: The process of social alignment and misalignment within a complex IT project. Int. J. Proj. Manag. **36**(6), 845–860 (2018). https://doi.org/10.1016/j.ijproman.2018.04.004
10. Gunatilake, H., et al.: The impact of human aspects on the interactions between software developers and end-users in software engineering: a systematic literature review. Inf. Softw. Technol. **173**, 107489 (2024)
11. Hekkala, R., et al.: Power and conflict in inter-organisational information systems development. Inf. Syst. J. **32**(2), 440–468 (2022). https://doi.org/10.1111/isj.12335
12. Iyamu, T.: Collecting qualitative data for information systems studies: the reality in practice. Educ. Inf. Technol. **23**(5), 2249–2264 (2018). https://doi.org/10.1007/s10639-018-9718-2
13. Jehn, K.A., et al.: The effects of conflict types, dimensions, and emergent states on group outcomes. Group Decis. Negot. **17**(6), 465–495 (2008). https://doi.org/10.1007/s10726-008-9107-0
14. Jenkin, T.A., et al.: Mutual understanding in information systems development: changes within and across projects. MIS Q. **43**(2), 649–671 (2019)
15. Kim, H.-W.: Kankanhalli: investigating user resistance to information systems implementation: a status quo bias perspective. MIS Q. **33**(3), 567 (2009)
16. Neirotti, P., Pesce, D.: ICT-based innovation and its competitive outcome: the role of information intensity. EJIM. **22**(2), 383–404 (2019)
17. Orlikowski, W.J., Gash, D.C.: Technological frames: making sense of information technology in organizations. ACM Trans. Inf. Syst. **12**(2), 174–207 (1994). https://doi.org/10.1145/196734.196745
18. Parker, C., et al.: Snowball sampling. In: SAGE Research Methods Foundations. SAGE Publications Ltd, 1 Oliver's Yard, 55 City Road, London EC1Y 1SP United Kingdom (2020)
19. Qureshi, I., et al.: Digital social innovation: an overview and research framework. Inf. Syst. J. **31**(5), 647–671 (2021). https://doi.org/10.1111/isj.12362
20. Räsänen, P., et al.: An online guided ACT intervention for enhancing the psychological well-being of university students: a randomized controlled clinical trial. Behav. Res. Ther. **78**, 30–42 (2016). https://doi.org/10.1016/j.brat.2016.01.001
21. Sawyer, S.: Effects of intra-group conflict on packaged software development team performance. Inf. Syst. J. **11**(2), 155–178 (2001)
22. Seidel, S., et al.: Sensemaking and sustainable practicing: functional affordances of information systems in green transformations1. MIS Q. **37**(4), 1275–1300 (2013). https://doi.org/10.25300/MISQ/2013/37.4.13
23. Smith, W.K., Lewis, M.W.: Toward a theory of paradox: a dynamic equilibrium model of organizing. Acad. Manag. Rev. **36**(2), 381–403 (2011). https://doi.org/10.5465/AMR.2011.59330958
24. Star, S.L., Griesemer, J.R.: Institutional ecology, "translations" and boundary objects: amateurs and professionals in Berkeley's museum of vertebrate zoology, 1907-39. Soc. Stud. Sci. **19**(3), 387–420 (1989)
25. Suchman, M.: Managing legitimacy: strategic and institutional approaches. Acad. Manag. Rev. **20**, 3 (1995)

26. Walsham, G.: Doing interpretive research. Eur. J. Inf. Syst. **15**(3), 320–330 (2006). https://doi.org/10.1057/palgrave.ejis.3000589
27. Ylinen, M.: Digital Transformation in a Finnish Municipality: Tensions as Drivers of Continuous Change (2021)
28. Yu, C.-P., Lin, W.-Y.: Risks associated with the development process of in-house information system projects. IJISPM. **10**(2), 66–78 (2022)

Translating Strategic AI Use into Business Value in Organizations: A Qualitative Study

Jie Yang(✉) and Marko Seppänen

Unit of Information and Knowledge Management, Faculty of Management and Business, Tampere University, Tampere 33721, Finland
{jie.yang,marko.seppanen}@tuni.fi

Abstract. Artificial intelligence (AI) is increasingly regarded as a transformative technology with the potential to unlock significant business value for organizations. However, many organizations are struggling to generate real business value from AI adoption. This study therefore investigates how organizations translate AI's potential into meaningful business value from a strategic use perspective. We conducted a qualitative study based on 11 interviews from European companies engaged in AI initiatives. We find that AI initiation should be problem-driven rather than technology-driven, and organizations can develop AI-enabled exploitative and exploratory capabilities to gain business value. We propose a conceptual framework to structure how organizations initiate, apply, and scale AI for business value realization. This study contributes to our understanding of the mechanisms of AI value translation and offers practical guidance for organizations seeking to produce meaningful business value from AI use.

Keywords: Artificial Intelligence · Business Value · Dynamic Capabilities

1 Introduction

Artificial intelligence (AI) is increasingly being integrated into organizational strategy, enabling firms to automate processes, enhance decision-making and innovate business models [1, 2]. Despite significant investments in AI initiatives, many firms struggle to translate the potential of AI into tangible business value, raising important questions about how business value can be realized through AI use.

Prior studies have examined AI adoption and its organizational implications from multiple perspectives. Some studies drawing on the technology-organization-environment (TOE) framework have identified key factors influencing AI adoption in organizations [3, 4]. Some studies have explored the impact of AI on business value [5, 6], mainly focusing on value in terms of efficiency improvements, innovation outcomes, or financial performance. Research on AI-enabled capabilities has emphasized the roles of exploitative and exploratory capabilities in shaping organizational outcomes [7].

While prior research provides valuable insights into AI's effect on business outcomes, many of the existing quantitative studies adopt a variance-based approach, focusing on

S. Han et al. (Eds.): I3E 2026, LNCS 16912, pp. 87–104, 2027.
https://doi.org/10.1007/978-3-032-38014-2_8

whether and to what extent AI influences business outcomes, which may not explain how AI generates organizational outcomes. Although existing qualitative studies have explored AI adoption in organizations, there remains a limited understanding of how firms translate AI's potential into business value in practice from a strategic use perspective. Strategic use of AI, which highlights the alignment between AI initiatives and business priorities, is critical for realizing business value [8]. This issue is particularly important given that AI technologies are still evolving rapidly and are implemented in dynamic and uncertain organizational contexts, where process-oriented and qualitative insights are valuable.

This study is, therefore, aiming to reveal how strategic use of AI is translated into business value in organizations. Specifically, this study seeks to address the following research question: How do firms strategically use AI to realize business value? To answer this research question, this study adopts a qualitative approach to examine how firms translate the strategic use of AI into business value. We conducted 11 interviews with managers and executives from multiple organizations in Europe. By investigating the processes through which AI initiatives are developed, implemented, and aligned with organizational objectives, this study advances research on AI use in organizations. It shifts attention from the antecedents and outcomes of AI use to the mechanisms through which AI generates business value. This study delivers practical insights for organizations seeking to produce meaningful business value from AI use.

2 Literature Review

2.1 AI Use in Organizations

AI refers to systems that mimic human cognitive functions such as learning, reasoning, and problem-solving, enabling them to perceive their environment, process information, and take actions or make decisions to achieve specific objectives [9]. Scholars and practitioners have recognized AI's potential to transform how organizations operate and compete [10, 11]. As a result, a growing body of literature has examined organizational AI adoption and AI-related initiatives as part of broader digital transformation efforts.

Prior studies on AI adoption focus on the factors that drive or hinder AI adoption in organizations. From a technology-centric perspective, prior research emphasizes that technology readiness can shape organizational decisions regarding AI adoption [12]. An organization-centric perspective shifts the focus to internal factors, such as organizational resources [13], capabilities [14], and culture [15]. This perspective often draws on resource-based view (RBV) or dynamic capabilities theory (DCT) to explain how organizational attributes influence AI adoption in organizations [14, 16]. Evidence suggests that digital and innovation capabilities of firms can drive AI adoption in organizations [14]. From an environmental perspective, external pressures play an important role in influencing organizational AI adoption. For example, institutional pressures, including coercive, mimetic, and normative forces, were found to increase managers' willingness to adopt AI [17]. A human-centric perspective highlights the role of individuals in AI adoption, such as employee skills [13], employee motivation and leadership support

[18]. Some studies adopt the TOE framework, which integrates technological, organizational, and environmental factors to provide a holistic understanding of AI adoption in organizations [3].

While prior research has examined the drivers and barriers of organizational AI adoption from different perspectives, these studies treat AI adoption primarily as an outcome rather than exploring how AI is leveraged strategically in organizations. In practice, however, the debate over whether to adopt AI has shifted. The main challenge is no longer AI adoption itself but the strategic integration of AI into core business processes to achieve measurable business outcomes.

From a strategic management perspective, technologies alone do not create business value. It emphasizes the need to embed technology such as AI into organizational processes, routines, and decision-making that generates real value [19]. Strategic use of AI refers to the intentional alignment of AI with business strategies to create business value [8, 20]. However, there remains limited understanding of how AI is strategically used in organizational practices and how strategic AI use translates into meaningful business outcomes. Addressing this gap is essential because it helps explain why organizations with similar AI resources may achieve different outcomes in practice from a strategic use perspective.

2.2 AI Capabilities

The literature on AI capabilities in organizations describes them not only as a technological asset, but as a firm's ability to select, orchestrate, and leverage AI-specific resources to achieve strategic goals [21]. Prior scholars employ the RBV theory to conceptualize AI capability, viewing it as a bundle of complementary resources, including AI-related tangible, human, and intangible resources, that are difficult for competitors to imitate [21]. Organizations do not gain competitive advantages from AI technology alone, as software and data are often tradable; rather, the advantage stems from how these resources are integrated [22]. DCT therefore has been used to understand AI capabilities and explain how organizations use AI to sense market opportunities, seize them through business model innovation, and reconfigure internal resources [23]. Some studies adopt a socio-technical system or contingency theory, highlighting that AI capabilities operate through the interaction of technology, organizational processes, and social factors, and that environmental conditions moderate their impact on performance [6].

Prior studies have categorized the components of an organization's AI capabilities from different perspectives. According to RBV, AI capability can be viewed as a bundle of organizational resources [21]. From an organizational learning perspective, AI capabilities can be categorized into exploitative and exploratory capabilities [7]. AI capabilities can be classified into process automation, cognitive insights, and cognitive engagement from a task-oriented perspective [24] and into algorithm development capability, data pipeline capability, and AI democratization capability from a co-evolutionary perspective [25].

Prior research on AI capabilities offers a valuable theoretical lens for understanding how AI resources and competencies are structured within organizations. These studies indicate that AI capabilities are shaped by resources, organizational routines, business tasks, functional roles, co-evolutionary processes, and environmental contingencies, and should not be treated as static technical attributes. Thus, it is necessary to explore how AI technologies are strategically used to enhance organizational practices and generate business value from an AI-enabled capabilities perspective.

2.3 Business Value of AI

Business value has been widely studied in the information systems literature. In the context of information technology (IT), business value is defined as the organizational performance impacts of IT by improving organizational processes as well as overall organizational performance, including both efficiency- and competitiveness-related benefits [26]. Following the IT business value perspective, the business value of AI refers to the organizational benefits generated through the use of AI technologies.

Prior research has explored the business value brought by AI in organizational contexts. Studies show that AI contributes to operational improvements by enhancing process optimization [27] and operational efficiency [5]. Research also highlights the strategic and innovation value of AI. For instance, empirical evidence from natural disaster shocks suggests that AI can improve firm resilience [28]. AI can improve rational decision-making in B2B marketing by integrating AI into the organizational knowledge creation process [29]. Strong AI capabilities of firms can increase organizational creativity [21], improve open innovation practices [6], and enable business model innovation (BMI) [25]. Empirical studies also demonstrate positive associations between AI and firm performance outcomes. For instance, prior research indicates that AI use can boost financial performance [30], enhance firms' profitability [31], and improve the environmental sustainability performance of organizations [32].

In summary, prior empirical studies provide evidence on the effect of AI on business value. However, this stream of research focuses on establishing the associations between AI and business outcomes, leading to an insufficient understanding of the process through which AI is translated into business value in organizations. Moreover, despite the perceived value of AI, many firms still struggle to realize the business value of AI in practice. The gap between potential and realized business value underscores the need for qualitative research to uncover the mechanisms through which AI can be strategically used to generate business value in organizations.

3 Methodology

3.1 Data Collection

In this study, we conducted semi-structured interviews between March and April 2026 via online Microsoft Teams. Semi-structured interviews, a common type of interview process, allow flexibility in adapting the sequence and wording of interview questions to the flow of conversation. This form of interview encourages participants to share detailed narratives and allows researchers to examine complex organizational phenomena from different perspectives.

Before the formal data collection, we conducted three informal exploratory interviews with industry practitioners, each lasting approximately one hour, to gain initial insights into organizational AI use. These informal discussions helped refine the interview questions for the formal data collection. The informal interviews were not recorded and were not included in the final analysis, but they helped enhance the researchers' contextual understanding of AI adoption practices and inform the design of the formal interviews.

For the formal data collection, we employed purposive sampling to recruit participants with experience in strategic AI use. Specifically, we selected participants whose work responsibilities are closely associated with AI strategy, implementation, and operations, so that the interviews could provide rich insights into how AI initiatives are enacted, how AI-related capabilities are developed, and how business value is realized in organizations. Participants were recruited through professional networks and LinkedIn.

Before the interviews, we explained the research goals to the participants and asked them to provide their written consent via email. At the start of each interview, we reconfirmed their willingness to participate in the study and obtained verbal consent. We then asked questions about the interviewees' background and role in their organizations, the context and motivations of introducing AI in their home organizations, the current practices in using AI, and observed outcomes and impacts of AI initiatives. After each interview, we reviewed the interview data to assess whether the emerging evidence adequately covered the research themes of interest. Additional interviews were conducted when further evidence was needed to enrich and clarify the emerging themes.

In total, we conducted 11 online interviews with senior managers and specialists engaged in AI from European companies. Each interview lasted approximately 30–60 min, and all sessions were recorded and transcribed to ensure accuracy and reliability of the data. The participants are from different areas across various industries, such as information technology, consultancy, banking, and industrial equipment, allowing us to gather diverse perspectives that reflect both strategic and operational insights of AI use in various organizations. Table 1 shows the interviewee information.

Table 1. Interviewee information.

#	Role	Responsibilities	Industry	No. of employees	Duration
1	Product owner	Data & analytics	Industrial equipment	>10,000	56 min
2	Business leader	AI business design	Digital & Technology consulting	1000–5000	59 min
3	CEO	Strategic consulting	Construction consulting	2–10	60 min
4	Head of AI	AI & Engineering design	Information technology	50–200	33 min
5	DevOps leader	Data & AI strategy	Technology consulting	>10,000	58 min

(*continued*)

Table 1. *(continued)*

#	Role	Responsibilities	Industry	No. of employees	Duration
6	CTO	AI vision & Enterprise access management	Computer systems design	10–50	43 min
7	Product manager	Enterprise AI governance & Implementation	Software development	1000–5000	53 min
8	Senior data scientist	AI & Data science	Banking	> 10,000	50 min
9	Consulting manager	Data & AI strategy	Business consulting	> 10,000	60 min
10	Vice president	AI strategy & Transformation	Cybersecurity	500–1000	32 min
11	CCO	AI & Business transformation	Digital & Strategy consulting	2–10	57 min

Notes: CEO, Chief executive officer; CTO, Chief technology officer; CCO, Chief commercial officer.

3.2 Data Analysis

Our analysis followed an abductive logic, iterating between existing theoretical concepts and empirical observations. While initial sensitizing concepts were derived from the literature, including strategic use of AI, AI-enabled capabilities, business-AI alignment and business outcomes, the interview data revealed a processual pattern that reshaped our analytical structure.

We adopted template analysis following King's (2004) [33] approach. Template analysis is a flexible analysis method, allowing researchers to begin with an initial coding template while remaining open to modifying the structure as new themes emerge from the data [34]. Based on insights from prior literature and aligned with the purpose of this study, we developed an initial template including the four types of strategic use of AI (decision support, new products and services offering, customer and employee engagement, and automation) [8], the two types of AI-enabled capabilities (AI-enabled exploitative and exploratory capabilities) [7], and potential business outcomes (e.g., business model innovation, BMI) brought by AI [25]. The first author then read the interview transcripts repeatedly and coded the data by organizing participants' accounts into preliminary themes. The initial template was continuously refined as new themes emerged from the data, and earlier coded transcripts were revisited to ensure consistency throughout the analysis. The revised coding structure and thematic interpretations were then reviewed by the co-author. Differences in interpretation were discussed until agreement was reached on the final hierarchical structure of themes, which captures how

AI is strategically used in practice and how it translates into business value in organizations. During this process, we observed that interviewees' accounts reflected a process from strategic considerations to capability development and then to meaningful business outcomes. This emergent pattern informed the structure of our findings.

The final coding template (see Fig. 1) consists of four main themes that capture the key aspects of strategic AI use in organizations, including AI initiation, AI-enabled capabilities, AI scaling, and feedback loops. For example, interview data were coded under the subtheme "strategic mindset" within the main theme "AI scaling" when interviewees emphasized the need to rethink their business logic.

We followed Lincoln and Guba (1985)'s [35] trustworthiness criteria for evaluating the rigor of this study, including credibility, transferability, dependability and confirmability. Credibility was enhanced through iterative engagement with the recorded interviews and their transcripts, continuous refinement of the coding template, and informal discussions with industry practitioners before the formal interviews to gain familiarity with organizational AI practices. This process ensured that the findings and interpretations reflect participants' accounts. Transferability was addressed by presenting findings from different perspectives and organizational contexts. Therefore, readers can assess the transferability of this study's findings to other similar contexts based on the contextual information provided. Dependability was ensured through an iterative coding process based on template analysis, where codes and themes were developed and refined iteratively. Confirmability was supported by providing direct participant quotes to illustrate the findings and interpretations.

1. ***AI initiation***
1.1. Motivations of AI adoption
1.1.1. Internal, goal-oriented adoption
1.1.2. External, pressure-oriented adoption
1.2. Drivers of AI implementation
1.2.1. Top-down managerial push
1.2.2. Bottom-up initiative
1.3. AI initiation strategies
1.3.1. Problem framing
1.3.2. Planning-first approach
1.3.3. Doing-first approach
1.4. Perceptions of AI's potential
1.4.1. High expectations of AI
1.4.2. Perceived irrelevance of AI
2. ***AI-enabled capabilities***
2.1. AI-enabled exploitative capabilities
2.1.1. Automation
2.1.2. Streamlined workflows
2.1.3. Accelerated decision-making
2.1.4. Faster task execution
2.2. AI-enabled exploratory capabilities
2.2.1. Business model innovation
2.2.2. Prototype generation
2.2.3. Insights generation
2.2.4. New product/services offering
2.3. Organizational ambidexterity
3. ***AI scaling***
3.1. Strategic mindset
3.2. Leadership
3.3. Supportive organizational culture
3.3.1. Openness to change
3.3.2. Encourage experimentation and learning
3.3.3. Trust in new technologies
3.3.4. Startup spirit
3.4. Business-AI alignment
3.4.1. Shared vision
3.4.2. AI governance
3.4.2.1. Internal established routines
3.4.2.2. External policy regulations
3.4.3. Measurement of AI's business value
3.4.3.1. Cost-saving
3.4.3.2. Time-saving
3.4.3.3. Reduced workforce requirements
3.4.3.4. Customer retention
3.4.3.5. Revenue growth
3.5. Data foundation
3.5.1. Data quality
3.5.2. Data availability
3.5.3. Data accessibility
3.5.4. Data governance
3.6. Building partnership
4. ***Feedback loops***
4.1. Continuous learning from AI use
4.2. Rapid experimentation and iteration

Fig. 1. The final coding template.

4 Findings

This section presents the findings from the interviews on how organizations translate the strategic use of AI into business value. The interviewees' responses reveal a process through which organizations gradually make sense of AI, experiment with its use, and attempt to scale it to amplify AI's impact on business value.

Across the interviews, AI transformation in organizations was widely perceived as being in an early stage. Some of the interviewees noted that the value of AI is still unclear for organizations (Interviewees 1, 2, 9). At the same time, all the interviewees perceived that adopting AI is essential for organizations; otherwise, the organizations risk falling behind in the long run. As a result, organizations are learning how to understand business problems, rethink business processes, and make sense of data in ways that make AI useful, rather than simply implementing AI tools.

The findings are organized into three parts to reflect the process of translating the strategic use of AI into business value in organizations. We first describe how organizations initiate AI by forming their motivations, key drivers, initial strategies, and expectations for AI use. We then examine how organizations build AI-enabled capabilities in their contexts. Finally, we analyze how organizations attempt to scale AI to generate organizational business value, identifying the main challenges they face at this stage.

4.1 Initiation: Starting AI in Organizations

Organizations approach AI differently at the initiation stage, shaped by motivations, key drivers, initial strategies, and expectations.

Motivations. Organizations adopt AI for two main reasons. From an internal, goal-oriented perspective, organizations aim to use AI to achieve specific objectives, such as increasing productivity, generating revenue or reducing costs (Interviewee 1, 5, 6, 8). Interviewee 1 stated that their main target is to grow revenue, which is a key factor driving interest in AI. Interviewee 5 explained that their organization aims to derive greater value from the same amount of investment through AI adoption. Interviewee 6 described that adopting new AI technologies can speed up their own development, leading to a significant leap in productivity.

From an external, pressure-oriented perspective, organizations adopt AI in response to industry trends and competitive pressures. As interviewee 3 put it, "*I think that it's more like when everybody's using AI, maybe we should also see what it's all about*" (N3). Interviewee 7 described a market push for AI adoption. "*There is a market push that if you are a company that does not have AI in your branding or something, then you are seen as being behind... The investors also push for that...*" (N7). Interviewee 6 also stated, "*because our competitors will use it anyway. So, in order to keep up with the competition, we are forced to use these [AI] tools and we somehow try to use them more cleverly than the others*" (N6).

Drivers. Strategic AI use requires a clear internal owner to drive AI initiatives. Interviewee 11 discussed that, in one of their use cases, the CEO acted as the owner of the AI initiative. However, interviewee 11 further noted that this role does not have to be filled by a C-level person. In most cases, the ownership is held by other senior leaders or managers who understand the organizational context, have a holistic view of the process, and are willing to champion innovative approaches.

Initiation Strategies. Interviewees consistently emphasized that AI initiation should begin from defined problems rather than from AI technology itself. As one interviewee explained, "*AI is not the solution tier, but the problem tier. I said that AI is a technology. Before it reaches the solution, it needs to find a problem to solve...*" (N7).

Following a problem-driven perspective, organizations differ in how business problems are clarified and how AI initiatives are launched. Interviewees indicated two ways to initiate AI in organizations: the ideal way it should begin (planning-first approach) and the way it often unfolds in practice (doing-first approach).

In a planning-first approach, problems should be carefully defined in advance and in line with their business strategy. Organizations should form a solid understanding of processes, people, workflows and AI capabilities before launching AI initiatives (Interviewees 9 and 10). Interviewee 10 recalled their experiences during the first month of an AI initiative, "*What I did in the first month was a quite broad maturity assessment. Where do we stand as a company? How do our data assets, processes, people, talent, and tech stack look, and how good are our foundations for moving forward? As the pace of AI development is so fast at the moment, we wanted to focus in the beginning on having solid foundations. This means the data platform, unified data access, having AI gateways in place, having a knowledge repository in place, and these kinds of things that enable us to take in all the new things that are coming in a fast and robust way*" (N10). Interviewee 9 emphasized the importance of having clear objectives from the outset and systematically tracking value through all stages of the AI journey, from ideation to implementation and to scaling.

In a doing-first approach, problems are gradually identified through hands-on experimentation with AI tools. Understanding of the problems and potential solutions emerges through practice and feedback. As interviewee 2 reflected, "*my perfect world answer would be to start by making sure that people understand what they can do with AI, what kind of technology it is, what it is capable of doing, what it is good at, and what it is not good at. But in reality, where it usually starts is that there are individuals who are curious and not afraid of new technologies. They just take the tools and start testing them, and then they learn what they can do, what is easy, what is difficult*" (N2).

Expectation Management. Interviewees noted that there is significant AI hype, highlighting the importance of expectation management (Interviewees 1, 2, 3, 5). "*In some organizations, top management doesn't understand the technology and where it is at, and because they listen to all the hype around AI, they have too high expectations. They think they can replace people with AI without understanding what it actually means*" (N3). This perspective highlights the need for managers to understand AI in their business context, including its potential and limitations, and to focus on practical steps. At the same time, interviewee 10 described that managers in some more traditional industries may underestimate AI's relevance to their business. "*...in more traditional industries, they are somehow living in the mindset that AI does not touch their business at all, which is a mistake*" (N10). These accounts suggest that, in managing expectations, managers need not only to address AI hype and avoid overestimating its immediate impact, but also to be aware of how AI may affect their own business rather than overlooking its relevance.

In summary, interviewees agreed that AI initiation is problem-driven, and it is rarely a one-time decision; organizations need to refine their strategies through iterative practices as they progress. As interviewees stated, "*...people too often think just about the end result. But before we get there, there will be many iterative set points*" (N1). "*...because many of these things [related to AI] are still being mapped out. So, it's not like everything has been decided and already in some places*" (N8).

4.2 Application: AI-Enabled Capabilities

Following initiation, organizations begin to develop AI-enabled capabilities that support their operational and strategic goals. We categorized interviewees' responses into two types of capabilities: AI-enabled exploitative capabilities, which focus on improving existing processes and efficiency, and AI-enabled exploratory capabilities, which focus on generating new insights, opportunities, or innovative solutions. We also discussed their relationship from the perspective of organizational ambidexterity.

AI-Enabled Exploitative Capabilities. Interviewees reported several AI applications in the business environment across industries. For instance, interviewee 5 expressed that in healthcare, doctors and nurses spent a lot of time on documentation. AI was then used to automate note-taking during patient consultations, to summarize texts in structured formats, and to process healthcare records. Interviewee 2 also mentioned that AI has been used to improve their daily work efficiency, "*we can actually transcribe everything and then analyze and summarize that [using embedded AI tools]*" (N2). Interviewee 7 mentioned that AI can assist with payment automation in finance. Interviewee 3 expressed that in physical construction, most use cases of AI are related to document analysis and on-site safety analysis. "*Traditionally, bidding documents are really extensive, often hundreds of pages of legal and technical text, and LLMs [Large language models] provide a good basis for analyzing those documents and supporting the bidding process*" (N3). Interviewee 6 described an AI solution based on optical character recognition (OCR) and camera systems installed at port terminals. The system automatically reads container IDs, license plates, and hazard labels as containers are unloaded from vessels, while cameras capture images at the same time. Each image is linked to a unique container ID, creating a visual record of the container's condition on arrival and departure. This enables terminal operators to quickly retrieve evidence in case of damage claims, clarify responsibility, and improve operational transparency and efficiency.

AI-Enabled Exploratory Capabilities. This type of capability focuses on using AI to generate new insights and explore possibilities that were not visible before. Interviewee 1 described that AI enables predictive capabilities in maintenance activities that allow organizations to anticipate potential issues and plan resources. Interviewee 1 further mentioned that "*AI can also be used to create and test use case scenarios*" (N1). This may open possibilities for those who currently do not see clear AI-related use cases. Interviewee 2 highlighted the role of AI in creating prototypes, which helps possibilities exploration and insights generation. "*...with the recent AI tools, we can quite quickly, and* *without having specific coding skills, create prototypes that can be used as hypotheses for testing. This way, we can get insights faster about what the end result could look like or be like*" (N2). Interviewee 3 described how AI may transform construction management in the long term, "*In the long run, I think AI can help with the management of the construction project. Nowadays, construction management is very much based on oral communication. Everybody messages through WhatsApp on construction projects. AI could help automate part of that management. If we have a system that understands the schedule, understands the current situational awareness of the site, knows where everybody is, and what is supposed to happen next, then it can instruct everyone on site what to do next. It could kind of become a co-manager in a way*" (N3). Interviewee 6 described a use case where the company developed a new AI solution for their customers. The product solution is an AI-enabled visual tracking system for trailer terminals that detects where trailers are actually parked and supports the correct loading sequence onto vessels. "*...this new AI solution that I described, we developed it completely using the new AI tools, large language models, coding assistance, not even looking into the code too often. So, it has given enormous flexibility, speed of development, and also customer satisfaction because of that*" (N6).

Organizational Ambidexterity. The existence of both AI-enabled exploitative and exploratory capabilities observed in the interviews reflects organizational ambidexterity. In practice, most organizations right now focus on exploitative use of AI. As interviewee 2 observed, "*I would say mostly it's [AI] seen as a tool for operational efficiency, at least that's the narrative at the moment that I recognize*" (N2). However, interviewee 3 emphasized the importance of building exploration capabilities enabled by AI. "*...you also have to experiment to get to know the technology. But if you're just exploiting it, I think that you run out of value in the long run*" (N3). Interviewee 7 perceived exploitative and exploratory capabilities as complementary, "*I see it as complementary...AI is the same thing. At the moment, we need people to use it for internal productivity. Once they start using it, they will start to see, 'Wait a minute, if I can use it that way, my client can get this, that, and the other'. Then we can implement it for the client. This is a natural progress. You use the technology, understand what it can do, and then create solutions out of it*" (N7).

4.3 Scaling: Generating Organizational Business Value with AI

AI value scaling can be viewed as a change management process. As interviewee 11 stated, "*It is still a change management process in general, where we talk about people, their jobs, the tasks they operate daily, and their lives. So, I would say, a very important thing to consider when starting to operate with AI is the change management and human aspect*" (N11). To better understand how organizations scale AI value, we further conceptualize this change management process into four interrelated dimensions: strategic mindset, business-AI alignment, data foundation, and partnership.

Strategic Mindset. To realize broader business value of AI, interviewees consistently pointed to a necessary strategic shift (Interviewees 1, 2, 3, 4, 7, 8, 9, 10, 11). As interviewee 3 explained, "*I think that is a strategic shift...I don't think any technology per se* *can be strategic unless you have the idea of how you can basically rethink your business and the way you work. If you just keep doing things the way you do, just adding some automation here and there, it doesn't radically improve anything*" (N3).

To enable this strategic shift, interviewee 2 suggested that strong leadership is essential. "*Leadership needs to understand what we are aiming to achieve. What will our organization look like in three, five, or ten years, or what do we want it to look like, so that we actually gain value from AI. This also means understanding how the business environment, customer expectations, and competitors are changing, and what our position is in that ecosystem*" (N2). Interviewee 8 highlighted that the top management team should understand technologies such as AI and be aware of its potential and limitations. Interviewee 5 emphasized the importance of a supportive organizational culture, and interviewee 11 highlighted the need for a positive mindset toward AI, where employees are willing to trust AI tools and explore new ways of working.

Business-AI Alignment. Successful value scaling depends on alignment between AI initiatives and organizational goals. Interviewee 2 explained that while AI can improve individual efficiency, a lack of coordination may create confusion at the organizational level. To address this, it is essential to build a shared vision of the future business environment and then define the organization's desired position in this vision. Interviewee 8 described that at the highest level, their company has set a vision to become an AI-first bank by 2030. Interviewee 11 also pointed out that organizations initiating AI pilots have realized the need to be more consistent in the way they utilize AI to scale its value. AI use should be connected to the bigger picture rather than solving isolated problems somewhere in the organization.

To achieve business-AI alignment, interviewees highlighted the role of AI governance in organizations (Interviewee 2, 5, 6, 7, 8, 10). Interviewee 2 explained that, "*For example, if everyone creates their own assistant to do almost the same thing, a lot of similar tools are created, which leads to unnecessary energy use, IT costs, and maintenance effort without real added value. It can also happen that someone creates something to speed up one part of the process, but this then blocks the next part of the process because the whole workflow has not been considered. These kinds of situations are why AI governance is important*" (N2). Interviewee 10 shared that alignment is maintained through established routines, "*So now that we are rolling out the [AI] strategy, we have weekly touch points on how things are progressing, with all the major stakeholders involved in what's happening on the operational level*" (N10). From the regulation side, interviewee 8 described that in highly regulated domains such as banking, AI governance is critical, as risk and compliance considerations take priority over all else, which can influence technological choices and the deployment of AI initiatives.

Value measurement is essential for organizations to confirm whether business-AI alignment leads to real impact. Interviewees were in consensus that top-level metrics for measuring AI's business value remain unchanged (Interviewees 3, 5, 6, 7, 10, 11). Organizations continue to use traditional metrics such as time saved, headcount, cost reduction, revenue, and customer retention. At the operational level, interviewee 5 and 10 expressed that there are defined AI-specific Key Performance Indicators (KPIs) in their organizations; however, some of those indicators still need to be improved. But interviewee 5 also emphasized that, "*On a high level, we still rely on the same old metrics*" (N5). Overall, as interviewee 11 described, "*The metrics [of AI value] are not that different from the existing ones. You might set up some additional KPIs to understand the effect, but overall, the metrics are very much the same as the ones you would normally use in business*" (N11).

Data Foundation. Interviewee 10 described a data-related challenge when implementing AI. "*We also struggled quite a bit in the beginning when we had a poor data foundation. It was very hard to attach a KPI to something we did, and that's why we needed to take the data foundation as the starting point of our focus... You need to have the data in place and the KPIs defined to be able to do this kind of AB testing setup to understand whether it actually moved anything*" (N10). Interviewee 2 highlighted that organizations should identify what kind of data in their specific contexts is critical and ensure that the data is available, representative, and usable for AI implementation. Interviewee 3 stated that there is a large volume of data and information floating around in the construction processes. The priority is to understand what the data is and how it creates value through workflows, not only in one project but across the entire project portfolio. Interviewee 4 suggested that one challenge in AI development is not the availability of data in general, but the limited access to high-quality, domain-specific datasets. One possible approach is the use of synthetic or simulated data generated through virtual environments. This shifts the emphasis from data collection to data generation for model training.

Partnership. Partnership is a critical enabler for scaling AI value. Interviewee 6 emphasized that, as a small software company, partnership helps them overcome two major bottlenecks in scaling AI value, namely hardware infrastructure expansion and cross-border solution delivery. The company leveraged partners to handle the scaling of hardware components, allowing them to focus on core AI solution design. At the same time, through their partner's local networks, the company was able to deliver integrated AI solutions to client sites across countries or regions. Therefore, in this case, partnership is essential for scaling both technical capabilities and geographic reach. "*We are a software company, but we need the hardware to enable the full functionality...in that case, the hardware component is not as scalable as software is. And for that, we need some kind of assistance from our partners...but in our case, the scalability also requires smooth delivery of the hardware and installation of the hardware and super the maintenance as well. So that partners bear a critical role here. Also, scalability globally*" (N6). Interviewee 4 emphasized that scaling AI value at an industrial level relies on collaboration. By coming together to define use cases and reflect on the fundamental changes AI could bring, organizations are more likely to achieve successful AI adoption outcomes.

To provide an overview of the main findings, we present a conceptual framework (see Fig. 2) to explain how strategic use of AI is translated into business value in organizations. The process of strategic AI use unfolds through three interrelated stages: initiation, application and scaling. Transitions between stages are driven by learning in the early phase and diffusion in the later phase. Notably, the process is non-linear, as cross-stage feedback loops among stages enable iterative refinement of AI practices in response to changing conditions.

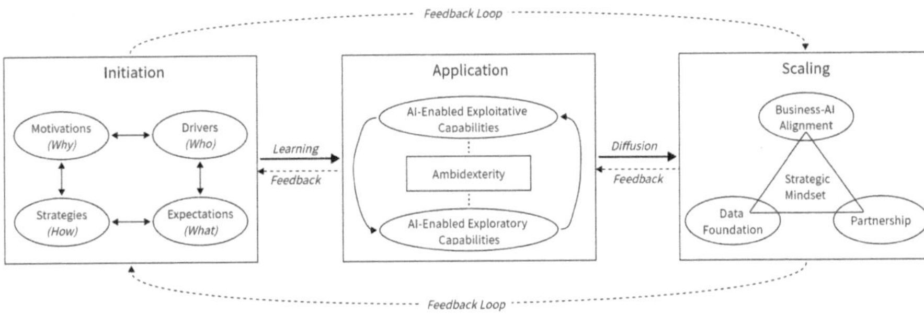

Fig. 2. A conceptual framework of translating strategic AI use into business value.

5 Discussion

AI has the potential to contribute to meaningful business outcomes for organizations. However, this study shows that many firms are struggling to generate business value from AI adoption. While prior studies have demonstrated the positive impacts of AI on organizational performance outcomes [5, 28, 30], this study provides insights into how business value is realized through the strategic use of AI.

This study suggests that business value is not produced in a straightforward way. Based on the analysis of interview data, this study identifies three stages for AI value creation: initiation, application, and scaling. First, AI initiation is problem-driven and iterative in organizations, regardless of whether the motivation is internal value-seeking or external pressure. Second, AI application in most organizations currently emphasizes efficiency-focused exploitation, but exploration for new opportunities is growing. AI implementation is a continuous learning process, not a one-time event. It takes time to see the big impact of AI transformation in organizations. Third, AI scaling is not mere technical scale-up but a structural upgrade from cognition to operation. It demands leaders' mindset shift to understand their business environment and rethink workflows. From there, organizations need to build a shared vision, assess their current position, and then formulate aligned business and AI strategies. AI governance should be in place to ensure ongoing alignment. A high-quality data foundation enables initiation, applications, and scaling. A strong partnership helps organizations overcome internal constraints and scale AI value.

The interviewees' answers also reflect that the AI journey as a learning process does not occur in a linear way, which is in line with prior research [25]. Instead, each stage evolves through iterative experimentation, adjustments, and reflections on what works in practice. Transitions from AI initiation to AI application are enabled by learning processes, while transitions from AI application to AI scaling are enabled through diffusion of validated practices across the organization. Cross-stage feedback loops connect the three stages and enable continuous adaptation across the process.

Unexpectedly, when asked about industry differences in AI use, most interviewees did not emphasize strong industry-specific distinctions. Instead, interviewees mentioned that AI applications are often driven by similar functional needs across industries, leading to improvements in operational efficiency and process quality regardless of the industry context (Interviewees 2 and 11). This also indicates that more innovative uses of AI in organizations may emerge in the future, especially as organizations develop a deeper understanding of industry-specific contexts and shift toward innovation-oriented use of AI. At the same time, differences in how AI is perceived across industries still emerged in the interview. Interviewee 10 noted that the media industry tends to be more forward-looking and open to AI adoption, whereas more traditional sectors such as manufacturing are often perceived as less prepared to implement AI or as viewing AI as less relevant to their core business activities. In addition to industry differences, interviewees also pointed to organizational size as an important factor shaping strategic AI use. Interviewee 7 explained that small firms tend to be more agile in AI adoption, supporting faster experimentation and innovation but facing challenges in scaling AI solutions; in contrast, large enterprises have stronger capabilities in scaling AI solutions but lower agility, which may slow down their pace of innovation. This reflects a trade-off between agility and scalability in organizational AI implementation.

6 Conclusion

6.1 Implications for Research and Practice

From a theoretical perspective, this study contributes to the literature by offering a nuanced understanding of how strategic AI use in organizations translates into meaningful business value. First, this study contributes a conceptual framework for AI value creation in organizations, including three dynamic phases: Initiation, application, and scaling. Second, this study highlights a problem-driven perspective on AI initiatives, in contrast to a technology-push perspective. Third, this study contributes to the organizational learning literature by demonstrating how organizations use AI strategically to generate business value through AI-enabled exploitative and exploratory capabilities. This study integrates exploitation and exploration into the AI application phase. This moves beyond the view that AI serves either efficiency or innovation, showing that the two capabilities coexist and complement each other. Finally, this study adopts a dynamic perspective on scaling AI value by proposing four interacting layers. Strategic mindset enables alignment between business and AI strategies; business-AI alignment specifies data requirements and serves as a bridge between strategic mindset and execution; data foundation constrains or enables both; and partnership leverages external resources and capabilities, enabling AI value to scale across organizational boundaries.

From a practical perspective, our findings highlight the importance of strategic thinking in turning AI use into meaningful business value. Successful AI implementation does not depend on being the first to adopt AI. Leaders need to recognize that the core of strategic AI use lies in human-centered thinking rather than in the technology itself. In the face of AI hype, organizations need to focus on concrete business requirements to ensure that AI initiatives deliver meaningful value. Managers should develop a deep understanding of their business environment, rethink workflows, and identify relevant business problems. Building an innovative culture can encourage employees to embrace and creatively use AI in their daily work. For organizations concerned about risk and who do not want to disrupt their existing business models, one suggestion can be to adopt a dual-track approach. One track applies AI to existing processes for efficiency gains, while the other runs separate exploratory experiments (e.g., an AI lab or AI innovation unit). Our findings also reveal that the AI journey is a learning process. Organizations benefit from using AI to enhance both exploitative and exploratory capabilities. Managers should ensure that fundamental elements, such as high-quality data, technical infrastructure, and employee training, are in place to support both exploitative and exploratory AI initiatives. Alignment between business and AI strategy is essential. Managers should establish feedback loops to ensure continuous learning and ongoing improvement. Organizations should strengthen AI governance, not only as an end in itself for compliance, but as a means to support value creation from AI initiatives. Organizations should develop collaborations with external partners to compensate for internal data and capability gaps, building a scalable AI value ecosystem.

6.2 Limitations and Future Research

This study has several limitations. First, this study is based on interviews with 11 European companies of varying sizes and industries, nine of them serving global customers. Despite this diversity, generalizability may be limited. Future research could extend to companies from other countries and explore how AI use and value generation vary across national, industrial, and organizational contexts. Second, this study analyzes organizational AI use from an organizational learning capability perspective and views AI-enabled exploitative and exploratory capabilities as key mechanisms for business value generation. Future research could adopt complementary perspectives such as socio-technical systems theory or value co-creation theory. Finally, this study is cross-sectional; given the rapid evolution of AI technologies, the mechanism of value creation may also change over time. Future research could adopt longitudinal studies to reveal how AI-enabled capabilities and organizational practices evolve and their influence on business value realization.

Acknowledgments. We acknowledge the financial support of the Finnish Ministry of Education and Culture through the Intelligent Work Machines Doctoral Education Pilot Program (IWM VN/3137/2024-OKM-4).

References

1. Bahoo, S., Cucculelli, M., Qamar, D.: Artificial intelligence and corporate innovation: a review and research agenda. Technol. Forecast. Soc. Chang. **188**, 122264 (2023)
2. Loureiro, S.M.C., Guerreiro, J., Tussyadiah, I.: Artificial intelligence in business: state of the art and future research agenda. J. Bus. Res. **129**, 911–926 (2021)
3. Hughes, L., Davies, F., Li, K., Gunaratnege, S.M., Malik, T., Dwivedi, Y.K.: Beyond the hype: organisational adoption of generative AI through the lens of the TOE framework–a mixed methods perspective. Int. J. Inf. Manag. **86**, 102982 (2026)
4. Kinkel, S., Baumgartner, M., Cherubini, E.: Prerequisites for the adoption of AI technologies in manufacturing–evidence from a worldwide sample of manufacturing companies. Technovation. **110**, 102375 (2022)

5. Yao, N.C., Bai, J., Yu, Z., Guo, Q.: Does AI orientation facilitate operational efficiency? A contingent strategic orientation perspective. J. Bus. Res. **186**, 114994 (2025)
6. Sahoo, S., Kumar, S., Donthu, N., Singh, A.K.: Artificial intelligence capabilities, open innovation, and business performance–empirical insights from multinational B2B companies. Ind. Mark. Manag. **117**, 28–41 (2024)
7. Ritala, P., Aaltonen, P., Ruokonen, M., Nemeh, A.: Developing industrial AI capabilities: an organisational learning perspective. Technovation. **138**, 103120 (2024)
8. Borges, A.F., Laurindo, F.J., Spínola, M.M., Gonçalves, R.F., Mattos, C.A.: The strategic use of artificial intelligence in the digital era: systematic literature review and future research directions. Int. J. Inf. Manag. **57**, 102225 (2021)
9. Chakravorti, B., Bhalla, A., Chaturvedi, R.S.: Which countries are leading the data economy. Harv. Bus. Rev. **1**(1), 2–8 (2019)
10. Grewal, D., Satornino, C.B., Davenport, T., Guha, A.: How generative AI is shaping the future of marketing. J. Acad. Mark. Sci. **53**(3), 702–722 (2025)
11. Krakowski, S., Luger, J., Raisch, S.: Artificial intelligence and the changing sources of competitive advantage. Strateg. Manag. J. **44**(6), 1425–1452 (2023)
12. Uren, V., Edwards, J.S.: Technology readiness and the organizational journey towards AI adoption: an empirical study. Int. J. Inf. Manag. **68**, 102588 (2023)
13. Abadie, A., Roux, M., Chowdhury, S., Dey, P.: Interlinking organisational resources, AI adoption and omnichannel integration quality in Ghana's healthcare supply chain. J. Bus. Res. **162**, 113866 (2023)
14. Arroyabe, M.F., Arranz, C.F., De Arroyabe, I.F., de Arroyabe, J.C.F.: Analyzing AI adoption in European SMEs: a study of digital capabilities, innovation, and external environment. Technol. Soc. **79**, 102733 (2024)
15. Fountain, T., McCarthy, B., Saleh, T.: Building the AI-powered organization technology isn't the biggest challenge, culture is. Havard Bus. Rev. **97**(4), 62 (2019)
16. Madan, R., Ashok, M.: AI adoption and diffusion in public administration: a systematic literature review and future research agenda. Gov. Inf. Q. **40**(1), 101774 (2023)
17. Rodriguez Müller, A.P., Tangi, L., Lerusse, A.: Understanding the adoption of artificial intelligence in local government decision-making: the influence of institutional pressures and managerial perceptions. Public Adm. 1–17 (2025). https://doi.org/10.1111/padm.70033
18. Tursunbayeva, A., Gal, H.C.B.: Adoption of artificial intelligence: a TOP framework-based checklist for digital leaders. Bus. Horiz. **67**(4), 357–368 (2024)
19. Kelley, D.J., Rice, M.P.: Advantage beyond founding: the strategic use of technologies. J. Bus. Ventur. **17**(1), 41–57 (2002)
20. Hjaltalin, I.T., Sigurdarson, H.T.: The strategic use of AI in the public sector: a public values analysis of national AI strategies. Gov. Inf. Q. **41**(1), 101914 (2024)
21. Mikalef, P., Gupta, M.: Artificial intelligence capability: conceptualization, measurement calibration, and empirical study on its impact on organizational creativity and firm performance. Inf. Manag. **58**(3), 103434 (2021)
22. Teece, D.J.: Explicating dynamic capabilities: the nature and microfoundations of (sustainable) enterprise performance. Strateg. Manag. J. **28**(13), 1319–1350 (2007)
23. Abou-Foul, M., Ruiz-Alba, J.L., López-Tenorio, P.J.: The impact of artificial intelligence capabilities on servitization: the moderating role of absorptive capacity-a dynamic capabilities perspective. J. Bus. Res. **157**, 113609 (2023)
24. Ayala, N.F., da Silva, J.R., Tinoco, M.A.C., Saccani, N., Frank, A.G.: Artificial intelligence capabilities in digital servitization: identifying digital opportunities for different service types. Int. J. Prod. Econ. **284**, 109604 (2025)
25. Sjödin, D., Parida, V., Palmié, M., Wincent, J.: How AI capabilities enable business model innovation: scaling AI through co-evolutionary processes and feedback loops. J. Bus. Res. **134**, 574–587 (2021)

26. Melville, N., Kraemer, K., Gurbaxani, V.: Information technology and organizational performance: an integrative model of IT business value. MIS Q. **28**(2), 283–322 (2004)
27. Nayak, M., Dhanarajan, G., Dineshkumar, R., Sen, R.: Artificial intelligence driven process optimization for cleaner production of biomass with co-valorization of wastewater and flue gas in an algal biorefinery. J. Clean. Prod. **201**, 1092–1100 (2018)
28. Han, M., Shen, H., Wu, J., Zhang, X.: Artificial intelligence and firm resilience: empirical evidence from natural disaster shocks. Inf. Syst. Res. **36**(4), 2116–2133 (2025)
29. Bag, S., Gupta, S., Kumar, A., Sivarajah, U.: An integrated artificial intelligence framework for knowledge creation and B2B marketing rational decision making for improving firm performance. Ind. Mark. Manag. **92**, 178–189 (2021)
30. Gyau, E.B., Appiah, M., Gyamfi, B.A., Achie, T., Naeem, M.A.: Transforming banking: examining the role of AI technology innovation in boosting banks financial performance. Int. Rev. Financ. Anal. **96**, 103700 (2024)
31. Alnofeli, K.K., Akter, S., Yanamandram, V., Hani, U.: AI-powered CRM capability model: advancing marketing ambidexterity, profitability and competitive performance. Int. J. Inf. Manag. **86**, 102981 (2026)
32. Kumar, S., Kumar, V., Chaudhuri, R., Chatterjee, S., Vrontis, D.: AI capability and environmental sustainability performance: moderating role of green knowledge management. Technol. Soc. **81**, 102870 (2025)
33. King, N.: Using templates in the thematic analysis of texts. In: Symon, G., Cassell, C. (eds.) Qualitative Methods and Analysis in Organizational Research, pp. 256–270. Sage, London (2004)
34. Nielsen, K., Agate, C., Yarker, J., Lewis, R.: It's business: a qualitative study of moral injury in business settings; experiences, outcomes and protecting and exacerbating factors. J. Bus. Ethics. **194**(2), 233–249 (2024)
35. Lincoln, Y., Guba, E.G.: Naturalistic Inquiry. Sage, Newbury Park, CA (1985)

Human–AI Interaction, Agents, and Companions

Human-AI Interactions in Digital Customer Service: Exploring the Role of Interaction Modality

Khadija Ahmed, Yuanyuan Lai(✉), Alexander Reppel, Krisanee Meechao, and Mark Lycett

Royal Holloway, University of London, Egham TW20 0EX, UK
Yuanyuan.lai@rhul.ac.uk

Abstract. Organisations are rapidly adopting AI-enabled customer-service interfaces such as text-based chatbots and, increasingly, embodied digital human replicas that mimic real humans in appearance and behaviour. However, a knowledge gap persists around modality-scenario fit, that is, where chatbots are preferred over digital humans, and vice versa. Given that a poor match can be detrimental to the user experience, we explore how modality shapes user perceptions under realistic customer service contexts. While our exploratory qualitative interviews with 20 participants indicated that users preferred text-based chatbots for both information-seeking and emotion management scenarios, digital humans have potential in high-arousal encounters, which we discuss in an outlook for future digital human research and application.

Keywords: AI-enabled Customer Services · Digital Humans · Text-based Chatbots · Modalities

1 Introduction

Artificial intelligence (AI)-enabled applications are reshaping customer interaction and business process optimisation. A particularly promising area is what Gartner (2023) refers to as digital customer service, with AI offering the potential to create intuitive and empathetic interactions between human customers and digital service representatives. Against this backdrop, companies are experimenting with AI-powered interfaces for customer service roles that take multiple forms, such as the text-based chatbots now widely used and, more recently, embodied conversational agents and digital humans such as WHO's Florence and Qatar Airways' Sama.

Offering potential to transform human-machine interactions (Mills and Liu, 2020), conversational agents benefit from recent advances in Generative AI. Though various experiments have tested the general viability of more advanced AI-enabled virtual service agents like digital humans, further investigations around their effectiveness and boundary conditions are needed. To leverage the full potential of AI for businesses, organisations

Published by Springer Nature Switzerland AG 2027
S. Han et al. (Eds.): I3E 2026, LNCS 16912, pp. 107–113, 2027.
https://doi.org/10.1007/978-3-032-38014-2_9

must think about how they can align the unique technical affordances of virtual service agents with customers' preferences and needs when fulfilling tasks (Jobanputra, 2024; Rashid and Kausik, 2024). For instance, while text-based chatbots can deliver speed and efficiency, they are often associated with a lack of social presence (Rosengren et al., 2024), as text-based interactions limit the use of non-verbal social cues. Digital humans, in contrast, can combine verbal (e.g., voice, tone, and accent) and non-verbal cues (e.g., facial expressions, eye gazes, body movements). However, a trade-off exists where digital humans are (potentially) better at showing empathy and/or engagement towards the customer (Ischen et al., 2022) but may also result in a sensation of eeriness. So, while digital humans have the potential to add a "human touch" (Seymour et al., 2023) to automated customer interactions, their use may result in a feeling of discomfort if not done right.

Although there are studies discussing the impact of communication modalities on human-AI interactions, most are focused on comparing voice-only with text-only chatbot interfaces in a single-task scenario (e.g., Przegalinska et al., (2025); Rzepka (2022)). To the best of our knowledge, only one paper investigated the differences between text-based chatbots and digital human interaction – albeit for a single task scenario (Rosengren et al., 2024). However, as the technology-task fit (TTF) theory indicates, technology can only achieve the highest utilisation when the task matches the technology (Goodhue and Ronald, 1995). Addressing this paucity, our research question here is whether there is a complementary effect between interaction modalities (chatbot vs. digital human) and customer service task types (information provision vs. emotion management). In response, we conducted an exploratory qualitative study with 20 participants to examine how different interface modalities affect their use experience across two different service contexts. We aim to contribute to designing engaging interactions between (human) customers and (artificial) service representatives.

We begin by outlining the current literature on modalities and task-modality fit (Sect. 2), followed by an overview of our methodology (Sect. 3) and preliminary results (Sect. 4). We conclude with an outlook on the next steps for our study (Sect. 5).

2 Literature Background

2.1 Modalities of Human-AI Interactions

In human-AI interaction, modality refers to the way in which human users and AI systems exchange information (e.g., via a mode or channel). Put differently, it describes how users express intentions (input) and how the AI system presents responses (output). A common distinction is made between voice-based agents, text-based agents, and multimodal interfaces like virtual avatars and digital humans (Terblanche et al., 2023). Considering the promise of the latter two and their increasingly widespread use in digital customer services, we focus on those as the context of our work.

Text-Based Chatbots. Chatbots are conversational agents that use Natural Language Processing (NLP) to interpret user input and converse via text in a human-like manner (Rosengren et al., 2024). Key drivers are their potential to provide cost-efficient yet personalised responses and efficiency around information-seeking needs. However, while chatbots excel in certain task-oriented, direct customer service queries, their performance often degrades when faced with complex or ambiguous issues (Zhang et al., 2024). One of the reasons for this is that text-based chatbots can be perceived as less empathetic and friendly, leading to reduced trust, satisfaction, and perceived (overall) usefulness (Rosengren et al., 2024). These limits have thus motivated the deployment of embodied options that are commonly referred to as digital humans, virtual humans, and virtual avatars (Loveys et al., 2022).

Digital Humans. Digital humans (DH), also known as virtual humans and virtual avatars, are embodied conversational agents that are presented with a human-like face, voice, and body (Rosengren et al., 2024). DHs can be thought of as chatbots augmented with emotional and cognitive intelligence (Rosengren et al., 2024; Whittaker et al., 2025; Seymour et al., 2023). Their potential is in combining cognitive capabilities with emotional intelligence – this is largely associated with the ability to convey verbal and non-verbal cues, leading to suggestions that they are superior in socio-emotional contexts (e.g., Ischen et al., 2022). However, increased human-likeness in artificial agents introduces risks, such as the feeling of eeriness and inauthenticity.

2.2 From Task-Technology Fit to Task-Modality Fit

While the potential of both chatbots and digital humans is now well established, comparative studies have reported both benefits and risks associated with both modalities. For example, when used for collecting customer reviews, Rosengren et al., (2024) showed that a digital human increased perceived humanness, positive emotion, satisfaction, effectiveness and efficiency, with stronger reuse intentions than a text chatbot. On the flip side, studies also reveal the negative effects of increased embodiment. Ciechanowski et al., (2019), for example, reported that avatar cues heightened discomfort, while the text bot was judged more competent. Found that a text-only LLM agent was perceived as more competent, useful, and trustworthy than an embodied counterpart with identical capabilities, with excessive agreement from the avatar reducing perceived authenticity. Other work shows that as avatars approach realism, eeriness increases rather than decreases (e.g., Thaler et al., 2020), and salient physical features can overpower perceived intellect, simultaneously increasing humanness and unease (Stein et al., 2020).

To explain the inconsistencies in the effect of virtual embodiment on user interaction outcomes, we referred to the task-technology fit theory (TTF). This theory proposes that technology leads to performance improvements only when a technology's capabilities fit the demands of the task (Goodhue and Ronald, 1995). Researchers have started extending TTF into AI-augmented work frameworks. For example, Przegalinska et al., (2025) integrated TTF and the Resource-Based View to examine how AI, human capabilities, and task types influence organisational outcomes. Drawing on TTF, Rzepka (2022) conducted a laboratory experiment with 116 participants who had to complete an information search task with a voice-based agent or a chatbot and found that speech exhibits higher perceived efficiency, lower cognitive effort, higher enjoyment, and higher service satisfaction than text-based interaction. However, among the customer service-related studies, most of them still focus on varying modalities (voice vs. text) for chatbots. In addition, most studies, including the one with digital humans (Rosengren et al., 2024), compared the modality effect with a single task. None of these studies has considered matching the interaction modality with different types of task scenarios to identify when each modality is preferable. To fill in this gap, we draw from social support theory that separates two fundamental forms of support in customer service settings (Wang et al., 2021): informational support (to reduce uncertainty, incl. advice, recommendations, and product knowledge) and emotional support (incl. expressions of care and empathy). Recent HCI research on chatbots and online communities shows that both forms of support are conceptually distinct yet complementary and jointly shape user experience and knowledge (Lin et al., 2024). To extend this line of research, this study aims to explore the complementary effect of the two interaction modalities (chatbot vs. digital human) when solving different customer service tasks (information provision vs. emotion management).

Fig. 1. Two modalities: Text-based chatbot (left) and digital human (right).

3 Methodology

To achieve the above research goal, we conducted scenario-based, semi-structured interviews with 20 participants recruited via a convenience sample consisting of 14 females and 6 males. Their age ranged from 19 to 34. All of the interviews were conducted via MS Teams by the first author. Two identical WordPress website prototypes were developed for a fictitious telecom company, SkyNet Telecom, differing only in the interaction format of the customer service agent (Fig. 1).

The study instructions for participants: "Your SIM-card contract with another carrier is about to expire, and you are considering switching to SkyNet Telecom. You plan to contact Skynet's customer service agent on their website to learn about current plans and promotions and request personalised recommendations that will help you decide whether to switch or not". To enhance behavioural realism, the digital human was designed to display facial animations, gaze, and gestures (e.g., listening pose, waving hands). Both agents were called 'Dan'. To ensure both agents responded consistently, an identical knowledge base and OpenAI's API configurations were used, built around detailed scenario scripts and contextual responses for the fictitious mobile phone service provider.

After filling out the questionnaire for collecting demographics, each participant interacted with the two agents using two different approaches. In scenario 1 (S1: information seeking), the participant was told to only ask for plan details and personalised guidance to decide; the agent was designed to attend to requirements and propose tailored bundles to persuade a switch to SkyNet. In scenario 2 (S2: emotion management), the participant was told to express frustration, be emotionally charged and seek both resolution and reassurance. Both agents were prompted to empathise, acknowledge the issue, and commit to a resolution. In this way, each participant would go through four different conditions. To mitigate the carryover and order effects of the within-subject design, the order of modalities varied for participants. After each interaction, participants were invited to share their perceptions and use experiences with the researcher.

Thematic analysis was selected to analyse the interview data because it provides a flexible yet rigorous approach for examining qualitative data and generating themes that capture shared meanings across participants while remaining grounded in their accounts. Following the six-phase framework proposed by Braun and Clarke (2006), the analysis involved iterative familiarisation with the transcripts, systematic coding, theme development, theme refinement, and interpretation.

4 Preliminary Results

Four recurring themes were observed through the thematic analysis. The first one was **speed and efficiency**. All of the participants favoured the chatbot for quick responses and efficiency in information-seeking scenarios, while the digital human often took longer to process the answer, as relaying information verbally slowed resolution.

Clarity and information retention were commonly raised by the participants in the information-seeking scenario, where verbal delivery from the digital human felt overwhelming. Besides, participants struggled to concentrate and retain the details needed to decide. Text-based interactions let them skim, re-read, and extract specifics. However, one participant expressed a different viewpoint: *"For me, receiving information verbally was so much easier to retain than reading through a bunch of paragraphs which the user might not even read through out, it was a lot"* (P 3).

The **trade-off between empathy/social presence and authenticity** was another recurring theme. On the positive side, it was acknowledged by participants that the digital human did a good job at mirroring their emotions, showed empathy, and helped ease their frustration in S2. Some participants also appreciated the opportunity to speak verbally to an agent, stating it was a more natural way of interacting, especially during S2, where they felt it was easier to verbally display anger rather than type. Particularly, several participants also highlighted that, while the words used by both agents were the same, they felt the verbal medium of communication had a stronger impact than reading those words alone. On the negative side, participants also suggested that, in some cases, the chatbot expressed more empathy. Participants partly attributed this to the hyper-realistic and, in their perception, exaggerated expressions and gestures that made the conversation seem genuine. This was particularly true for S2, where this heightened their sense of frustration. For example, a participant described: *"At one point it wasn't even looking at me and looking side to side, which pissed me off more. It was okay when I was calm and seeking information; I let that slide, but it was still very annoying"* (P 20).

Turn-taking and flexibility were also mentioned by participants. They disliked being interrupted by the digital human and valued time to compose thoughts in text. Several noted that the digital human didn't let them finish or ask follow-up questions, breaking their train of thought.

Overall, qualitative feedback showed a strong preference for the chatbot in information-seeking scenarios where speed, efficiency, and visual aids were key, and empathy was only an added advantage. Emotionally charged scenarios, in contrast, revealed mixed feedback. While some participants felt that additional human-like traits, such as a face and voice, can help pacify anger, others felt that these cues were unnecessary and even uncanny, and that speed remains key for any service scenario. However, different views also emerged, such as: *"When I was frustrated, and I wanted to take my anger out, it was easier for me to vocalise and take my frustration out because I thought someone was listening. In the chatbot, I would write one message after another to take my frustration out, but it would give big paragraphs, which made me even angrier. Digital human would listen and wait for me to stop talking, so I preferred that even though the resolution was the same"* (P 19).

5 Discussion and Future Plans

Although the qualitative results did not answer our research question directly, they implied the importance of the service agent's clarity, pace, and visual additions to user-perceived ease of use and usefulness of the interaction. Another key insight arising from the qualitative data was the potential of digital human technology for "high arousal" service scenarios if technological challenges could be overcome (e.g., low latency and visual aids for information retrieval). These findings will help us design follow-up factorial experiments to test the interaction effect between task types and interaction modalities.

Practical implications of these findings recommend moving away from the 'one-size-fits-all' approach in designing digital customer service agents and focusing efforts on matching the agents' affordances with users' different communication demands. For high-volume, low-affect queries where speed and clarity matter most, chatbots could be a better choice, whereas digital humans can excel selectively in high-involvement, emotion-management scenarios after tightening delivery (lip-sync, prosody, context-sensitive expressions, strict turn-taking).

References

Braun, V., Clarke, V.: Using thematic analysis in psychology. Qual. Res. Psychol. **3**(2), 77–101 (2006)

Ciechanowski, L., et al.: In the shades of the Uncanny valley: an experimental study of human–chatbot interaction. Futur. Gener. Comput. Syst. **92**, 539–548 (2019)

Gartner: Gartner Reveals Three Technologies That Will Transform Customer Service and Support By 2028. Gartner (2023)

Goodhue, D.L., Ronald, L.T.: Task-technology fit and individual performance. MIS Q. **19**(2), 213 (1995)

Ischen, C., et al.: Is voice really persuasive? The influence of modality in virtual assistant interactions and two alternative explanations. Internet Res. **32**(7), 402–425 (2022)

Jobanputra, K.: Customer Service: How AI Is Transforming Interactions. Forbes. https://www.forbes.com/councils/forbesbusinesscouncil/2024/08/22/customer-service-how-ai-is-transforming-interactions/ (2024). Accessed 28 Oct 2025

Lin, X., et al.: How chatbots augment human intelligence in customer services: a mixed-methods study. J. Manag. Inf. Syst. **41**(4), 1016–1041 (2024)

Loveys, K., et al.: Exploring empathy with digital humans. In: 2022 IEEE Conference on Virtual Reality and 3D User Interfaces Abstracts and Workshops (VRW), pp. 233–237, Christchurch, New Zealand (2022)

Mills, A., Liu, L.: Trust in digital humans. In: ACIS 2020 Proceedings (2020)

Przegalinska, A., et al.: Collaborative AI in the workplace: enhancing organizational performance through resource-based and task-technology fit perspectives. Int. J. Inf. Manag. **81**, 102853 (2025)

Rashid, A.B., Kausik, A.K.: AI revolutionizing industries worldwide: a comprehensive overview of its diverse applications. Hybrid Adv. **7**, 100277 (2024)

Rosengren, W., et al.: Using chatbots and digital humans to collect online reviews. In: Hawaii International Conference on System Sciences (HICSS) (2024)

Seymour, M., Lovallo, D., Riemer, K., Dennis, A.R., Yuan, L.: AI with a Human Face: The case for and against digital employees. Harv. Bus. Rev. **101**(3–4), 49–54 (2023)

Rzepka, C., et al.: Voice assistant vs. Chatbot – examining the fit between conversational agents' interaction modalities and information search tasks. Inf. Syst. Front. **24**(3), 839–856 (2022)

Stein, J.-P., et al.: Matter over mind? How the acceptance of digital entities depends on their appearance, mental prowess, and the interaction between both. Int. J. Hum.-Comput. Stud. **142**, 102463 (2020)

Terblanche, N.H.D., et al.: Talk or text? The role of communication modalities in the adoption of a non-directive, goal-attainment coaching chatbot. Interact. Comput. **35**(4), 511–518 (2023)

Thaler, M., et al.: Agent vs. Avatar: comparing embodied conversational agents concerning characteristics of the Uncanny valley. In: IEEE International Conference on Human-Machine Systems (ICHMS), pp. 1–6, Rome, Italy (2020)

Whittaker, L., et al.: Avatars, assemble! Digital human avatars for public figure engagement and marketing. Bus. Horiz. **69**, 449–461 (2025)

Wang, X., et al.: Understanding the emotional and informational influence on customer knowledge contribution through quantitative content analysis. Inf. Manage. **58**(2), 103426 (2021)

Zhang, R.W., et al.: When chatbots fail: exploring user coping following a chatbots-induced service failure. Inf. Technol. People. **37**(8), 175–195 (2024)

Emotional Design of AI Avatar and AI-Enabled Knowledge Service Assistant Use Experience

Yang Bai[1(✉)], Xiaoqi Qin[1], Yuhan Li[1], and Rong Huang[2]

[1] School of Information Management, Central China Normal University, Hubei, Wuhan, China
yang.bai@ccnu.edu.cn

[2] International Business School, South China Normal University, Foshan, China

Abstract. This study explores the impact of the emotional design of AI avatar's facial expression and voice on user experience in the context of knowledge services. A couple of experiments were conducted to examine the effects of different emotion intensity combinations (calm/warm avatars × calm/warm voices) in AI avatar's facial expression and voice design. The findings indicate that the warmth design in AI avatar's facial expression and voice design can trigger user perceptions of the warmth of AI avatar following the Warmth Primacy Theory. Under the condition of neutral avatar expressions, a warm voice significantly enhances user satisfaction and continuance intention. In contrast, under the warm avatar expressions, variations in voice emotion did not lead to significant differences in user experience. The findings indicate that warm visual emotion could play a dominant role in user experience in AIGC use when integrated with warm voice in emotional AI avatar design. The study enriches the literature on emotional design AI avatar by combining of facial expression and voice design and provides practical insights for the emotional design of AI avatar in AIGC-based knowledge services.

Keywords: Knowledge Services · AI Avatar · AIGC · Emotional Design

1 Introduction

The mechanisms shaping the effectiveness of knowledge services and strategies for improving such effectiveness have long been central issues in knowledge management. These mechanisms, however, may vary considerably across informational and technological contexts. Against the backdrop of rapidly expanding knowledge, the evaluation of knowledge service quality has gradually moved beyond an earlier emphasis on the amount of knowledge acquired and users' ability to access knowledge, shifting toward a more comprehensive assessment of service outcomes. In this process, increasing attention has been paid to users' cognitive and affective experiences during knowledge service interactions. In recent years, the rapid advances in artificial intelligence have given rise to artificial intelligence (AI)-generated content (AIGC), which has emerged as a new mode of content production following professionally generated content (PGC) and user-generated content (UGC) and has been widely applied in various knowledge service contexts. AIGC can provide users with intelligent, convenient, and personalized knowledge services.

S. Han et al. (Eds.): I3E 2026, LNCS 16912, pp. 114–125, 2027.
https://doi.org/10.1007/978-3-032-38014-2_10

The literature has investigated individuals' AIGC use experience in knowledge service contexts from outcome perspective. Such as, AI's strong capacity for content integration and generation (e.g., AIGC) can relieve users from the workload in information retrieval and filtering, thereby substantially improving the efficiency of accessing and absorbing such knowledge [1]. Some scholars argued that individuals' interaction with anthropomorphic AI leads to users' certain degree of emotional support and companionship in their use of AIGC [2]. As AIGC has become an important source for knowledge acquisition, it is meaningful to examine how the anthropomorphic design of AI avatar influences individuals' AIGC use experience.

Anthropomorphic design of AI has mainly focused on the anthropomorphism of appearance of AI avatars in AIGC context; recently "emotional anthropomorphism" has garnered increasing attention from researchers. Emotional anthropomorphism can be viewed as extending visual anthropomorphism [3]. However, how emotional design of AI avatar influences user perception and experience across different application contexts remains unclear. There is a lack of knowledge about how different anthropomorphic designs, such as emotional audio and visual design of AI avatar, shape user experience in AIGC use.

Although abundant existing works have explored emotional AI agents, digital humans, virtual assistants and chatbot personalities, most multi-modal emotional design studies isolate visual facial cues and vocal warmth as separate single variables and rarely discuss their joint matching effects in professional knowledge service scenarios, leaving the interactive influence of cross-modal emotional signals underexplored.

Therefore, this paper aims to explore the effect of combined emotional design of the facial expression and voice of AI avatar on user perception of AI as well as their satisfaction and continuance intention to use AIGC in the context of AI-enabled knowledge services.

2 Literature Review

The user experience of knowledge services has evolved alongside technological progress. Originally, knowledge resources were largely concentrated in institutions like libraries, where accessibility constituted the core demand. Consequently, experience optimization focused on resource allocation structures and service models, such as tailoring library collections based on reader needs [4]. As the scale of available knowledge increased, users shifted their goals from mere information retrieval to solving practical problems through high-quality knowledge services. Related studies have explored achieving precise service delivery by identifying and addressing personalized needs [5]. Open and interconnected knowledge environments have developed with social media development, and convenience of access to knowledge has driven user expectations beyond information quality toward emotional experience. Such experience is closely related to their continuance intention to use different knowledge service technologies or systems [6].

The emergence of AI has introduced new means of knowledge service, which also affects user experience. Regarding content quality, AI-generated information may vary in quality, which can affect user experience and even lead to adverse outcomes [7]. For instance, some studies indicate that AIGC may be apparently correct but meaningless content to individual users [8], and low-quality information may weaken user trust and undermine users' overall experience [9].

From an interaction perspective, AI can enhance users' emotional engagement through multi-channel interfaces such as visual and auditory systems [10]. Studies have suggested that AI assistants with more human-like appearances are likely to elicit trust [11], while other studies show significant interaction effects between voice types and user gender on emotional preferences [12]. Additionally, conversational strategies, personality traits, and other design features are closely associated with user preferences and experience in using AIGC [13].

Building on the discussion of the effects of multichannel interaction on emotional engagement, the influence of these emotional design elements on users' trust in AI or perceived support can be further explained from the perspective of social cognition. The warmth primacy theory argues that individuals tend to rely first on warmth-related affective perceptions when making judgments and decisions, rather than following a purely rational decision-making pattern [14]. This perspective has demonstrated the positive role of warmth in research on product design and service experience. For example, individuals tend to favor advisors who convey greater warmth or positivity, even when they are less competence-oriented, rather than relying solely on advisors with higher competence but lower warmth, suggesting the primacy of warmth in interpersonal relationship formation [15]. Extending this principle to product design, appearance-related elements such as shape, color, and material can attract users' attention and trigger purchase impulses, while affective design can help strengthen the emotional connection between users and products through the integration and optimization of appearance-related elements [16]. Similarly, in human–computer interaction services, beyond functional usability, perceived service warmth also contributes significantly to users' system preferences [17].

In summary, existing studies indicate that knowledge service experience is shaped by multiple factors, including information quality and emotional support. With the advancement of artificial intelligence, emotional support in virtual interactions within AI-enabled knowledge services – often delivered through anthropomorphic design – may help enhance user satisfaction and trust. However, few studies examined how differences in the emotional intensity expressed by AIGC influence user experience. Therefore, this study uses avatar-voice combinations with different warmth levels and investigates how such design combinations shape user experience in AIGC-enabled knowledge service interactions from the perspective of perceived warmth.

3 Research Hypotheses

Warmth primacy theory [14] suggests that warmth judgments usually precede and significantly shape competence judgments when people evaluate a perceptual target. Trust in artificial intelligence also shares psychological mechanisms with interpersonal trust, in which perceived warmth helps establish and enhance user trust [18]. Grounded in warmth primacy theory, this study treats the warmth level of AI avatar's affect emotional design as the independent variable and manipulates it through different emotional levels of avatar facial expression and voice.

Based on the warmth primacy theory, when interacting with an anthropomorphic AI service assistant with human-like social attributes, users may evaluate it along the two dimensions of warmth and competence of such AI assistant. Warmth is usually evaluated first and may further affect competence judgments [19]. In addition, emotional states conveyed by avatars and voices, such as smiling or serious expressions, can be transmitted to users. In virtual service settings, such emotional transmission may further shape the service experience [12]. For example, warm virtual robots have been found to elicit more positive user evaluations [20]. Accordingly, the following hypotheses are proposed:

H1: In the neutral-avatar condition, the warm voice of AI knowledge service assistant will elicit higher perceived warmth, satisfaction, and continuance intention regarding the AI knowledge service assistant than neutral voice.
H2: In the warm-avatar condition, the warm voice of AI knowledge service assistant will elicit higher perceived warmth, satisfaction, and continuance intention regarding the AI knowledge service assistant than neutral voice.

4 Research Methodology

4.1 Experiment Design

The experimental stimuli consisted of avatar and voice materials with different emotional designs. Two emotional design conditions were used: neutral and warm, corresponding to lower and higher levels of warmth, respectively. Accordingly, a 2 × 2 factorial design was adopted, resulting in four experimental conditions: neutral avatar with neutral voice, neutral avatar with warm voice, warm avatar with neutral voice, and warm avatar with warm voice (NA × NV / NA × WV / WA × NV / WA × WV). By using avatar and voice stimuli with different emotional designs, this study examines their effects on users' cognition, satisfaction, and continuance intention to use such AI knowledge service assistant.

Voice Materials. The intelligent speech generation platform "Moyin Workshop" [21] was applied in this study to generate the voice materials. The software can control the emotional style of voice by selecting different emotion labels under a character with a specific vocal timbre. In this way, a set of voice recordings with the same timbre but different emotional expressions were obtained and used as experimental voice stimuli. In this study, two voice materials with neutral and warm emotions were developed.

Avatar Materials. The avatar stimuli were generated using OpenAI's DALL-E3 [22] with specified prompts. The prompts constrained the avatars' hairstyle, facial expression, clothing, and other appearance-related features while varying the smile expression on the face. In this way, avatar materials with the same appearance-related features but different emotional expressions (neutral and warm) were obtained.

Knowledge Service Task Materials. To control for the potential influence of knowledge service task on the interaction, all participants were invited to interact on the same three topics in the experiment. Three topics with a degree of novelty were selected: "Digital Publishing and Print Publishing", "Low-Altitude Economy", and "Flow Experience". For each topic, three sub-questions were derived and designed to guide users in deeper interaction and allow them to experience the AI-enabled knowledge-service process.

4.2 Construct Measures and Questionnaire

Three constructs were included in the experiment, including perceived warmth, satisfaction, and continuance intention. This study adapted established measurement scales for the three constructs from prior studies. Table 1 reports the construct measurement sources and the measurement items. Based on these scales, the survey questionnaire was developed. A seven-point Likert scale was applied in this study. Some questions regarding users' demographic background were also included in the survey questionnaire.

Table 1. Scale Sources and Original English Wording of Measurement Items

Variable	Measurement Items		Source
Perceived Warmth	The AI assistant is very rigid (reverse)		[23, 24]
	The AI assistant is very cold (reverse)		
	The AI assistant is very nice		
	The AI assistant is very likable		
Continuance intention	I intend to continue using the AI assistant in my job.		[25]
	I intend to continue using the AI assistant for processing more applications		
	I intend to continue using the AI assistant for more of my job responsibilities.		
Satisfaction	How do you feel about your overall experience of using the AI assistant		[26]
	very dissatisfied	very satisfied	
	very displeased	very pleased	
	very frustrated	very contented	
	absolutely terrible	absolutely delight	

4.3 Data Collection

This study used Doubao as the experiment platform. The platform allows users to create AI agents and configure their avatars and voices according to needs. Based on the avatar-voice combinations with different warmth levels, four AIGC knowledge service assistants were created and labeled N1, N2, N3, and N4. Through prompt constraints, the four agents were kept consistent in terms of role setting, response structure, and linguistic style.

Participants were recruited through a combination of online and offline channels using convenience sampling, with the sample mainly drawn from student populations. To ensure consistency in the experimental environment, all participants completed the experiment in a designated quiet and low-stress setting. They were required to install the Doubao application on their smartphones and use earphones throughout the experiment. Participants were randomly assigned to one of four groups, each corresponding to one AI knowledge service assistant (N1, N2, N3, and N4). Each participant voluntarily wore earphones, interacted with the knowledge service assistant by entering three knowledge topics and corresponding sub-questions, and completed a measurement questionnaire after they have interacted with the AI assistant for 10 min.

To examine whether the voice and avatar stimuli showed sufficient differentiation in warmth level, the neutral and warm avatar and voice stimuli were randomly presented to 60 participants for evaluation. Participants rated the stimuli using a seven-point Likert scale. The results of the nonparametric tests showed that all p-values were below 0.05, indicating significant differences in perceived warmth between the neutral and warm voice stimuli and between the neutral and warm avatar stimuli. These results indicated that the stimuli were suitable for constructing the multimodal emotional design conditions for AI assistant and used in the main experiment.

*Four experiments were implemented, and a total of 298 responses were collected. After excluding 13 invalid responses based on the attention-check item and short completion-time screening, 285 valid responses remained and 72(N1), 74(N2), 70(N3), and 69(N4) participants for each experiment, yielding a valid response rate of 95.6%. The sample sizes across the four groups were generally balanced.

5 Results

Among the valid participants, the gender distribution was relatively balanced. In terms of educational background, undergraduate and master students accounted for most of the sample (96.14%). The sample profile is presented in Table 2.

Table 2. Demographic Characteristics of the Sample

Demographics	Category	Frequency	Percentage
Gender	Female	154	54.04%
	Male	123	43.16%
	Prefer not to say	8	2.8%
Educational Background	High school or below	3	1.05%
	Junior college student	6	2.11%
	Undergraduate student	216	75.79%
	Master's student	58	20.35%
	Doctoral student	2	0.70%

To ensure that participants could understand the AI-based knowledge-service experimental environment, the study investigated participants' use of AI tools and found that 91.58% of the participants frequently used AI tools, while no participant had never used such tools. In addition, 77.89% had previously used Doubao, the platform used in this study. These results suggest that Doubao is a relatively appropriate platform for the experimental interaction in this study.

To examine the effects of the four different AI avatar designs on each latent construct, descriptive statistics were conducted separately for the data of each group, as shown in Table 3. The results show that the variables in the four experimental groups generally met the normality criteria, with absolute skewness values below 3 and absolute kurtosis values below 10, indicating that the questionnaire samples were representative of the corresponding population.

Table 3. Descriptive Statistics of Latent Variables by Experimental Group

Experiment	Latent Variable	N	Mean	SD	Median	Skewness	Kurtosis
N1	Perceived Warmth	72	5.01	0.79	5.00	−0.46	0.12
	Continuance Intention		4.76	1.23	5.00	−1.08	1.12
	User Satisfaction		4.99	0.83	5.00	−0.91	1.39
N2	Perceived Warmth	74	4.93	0.98	4.75	0.01	−0.36
	Continuance Intention		4.67	1.33	5.00	−0.53	−0.17
	User Satisfaction		4.85	1.12	4.75	−0.72	0.43
N3	Perceived Warmth	70	5.08	0.95	5.25	−0.37	−0.32
	Continuance Intention		5.25	1.07	5.33	−0.73	0.05
	User Satisfaction		5.34	0.82	5.5	−0.07	−0.89
N4	Perceived Warmth	69	4.98	1.13	5.25	−1.09	1.88
	Continuance Intention		4.92	1.44	5.33	−0.70	−0.27
	User Satisfaction		5.07	1.08	5.25	−1.17	2.50

Reliability and validity analyses were conducted to assess the quality of the questionnaire measurements. As shown in Table 4, the values for Cronbach's alpha, composite reliability (CR), and AVE exceeded the recommended thresholds of 0.7, 0.7, and 0.5 respectively, indicating good convergent validity of the measurement model. In addition, the factor loadings for all measurement items exceeded the threshold of 0.70, indicating reliability of the measurement model. In addition, all variables met the discriminant validity requirement of the Fornell-Larcker criterion, as shown in Table 5, indicating good discriminant validity among the variables.

Table 4. Reliability and Validity Test

Variable	Item	Factor Loading	α	CR	AVE
Perceived Warmth	WAR1	0.827	0.794	0.869	0.624
	WAR2	0.753			
	WAR3	0.716			
	WAR4	0.855			
Continuance Intention	SAT1	0.870	0.882	0.92	0.742
	SAT2	0.849			
	SAT3	0.875			
	SAT4	0.850			
User Satisfaction	CON1	0.944	0.929	0.955	0.875
	CON2	0.937			
	CON3	0.926			

Table 5. Discriminant Validity Based on the Fornell-Larcker Criterion

	Perceived Warmth	Continuance Intention	User Satisfaction
Perceived Warmth	0.790		
Continuance Intention	0.610	0.936	
User Satisfaction	0.814	0.710	0.861

We conducted t-tests to compare the mean differences of the three latent constructs across the 4 experimental groups (See Tables 6 and 7). We first compared the two groups that shared the same neutral-avatar face expression design but with neutral and warm voice design. The results showed that the difference in perceived warmth was not statistically significant (See Table 6). Specifically, under the neutral-avatar condition, user perceived warmth score in the warm-voice condition was 5.08, which was higher than that in the neutral-voice condition. User satisfaction and continuance intention to use AI knowledge service assistant are higher in the warm voice design than in the neutral voice design and their difference is statistically significant (See Table 6). The findings partly support H1.

Table 6. t-Test Results: Neutral Avatar with Different Voice Types

	Experimental Group (Mean ± SD)		t	p
	NA × NV (n = 72)	NA × WV (n = 70)		
Perceived Warmth	5.01 ± 0.79	5.08 ± 0.95	−0.489	0.626
User Satisfaction	4.99 ± 0.83	5.34 ± 0.82	−2.560	0.012*
Continuance Intention	4.76 ± 1.23	5.25 ± 1.07	−2.522	0.013*

$p < 0.05, p < 0.01$

As shown in Table 7, we also conducted the t-test to compare the two groups that shared the same warm-avatar facial expression design but differed in voice emotional design. The results showed that the difference in perceived warmth was not statistically significant. However, the comparison of means and standard deviations still indicated a small descriptive difference. Specifically, under the warm-avatar condition, users in the warm-voice condition perceived slightly higher warmth toward the AI knowledge-service assistant than those in the neutral-voice condition. However, user satisfaction and continuance intention to use AI knowledge service assistant are higher in the warm voice design than in the neutral voice design but their difference is not statistically significant (See Table 7). The findings partly support H2.

Table 7. t-Test Results: Warm Avatar with Different Voice Types

	Experimental Group (Mean ± SD)		t	p
	WA × NV(n = 74)	WA × WV (n = 69)		
Perceived Warmth	4.93 ± 0.98	4.98 ± 1.12	−0.3	0.765
User Satisfaction	4.85 ± 1.12	5.07 ± 1.08	−1.197	0.233
Continuance Intention	4.67 ± 1.33	4.92 ± 1.44	−1.108	0.27

$p < 0.05, p < 0.01$

6 Discussion

When the avatar facial expression is designed neutral and paired with voice of different warmth levels, it did not lead to statistically significant differences in users' perceived warmth toward the AI assistant. One possible explanation is that, although the pretest showed significant differences in respondents' perceived warmth toward the voice and avatar materials when they were compared separately, users in the experiments allocated more cognitive resources to processing the knowledge task itself and less to distinguishing the external design differences among the AIGC assistants, ultimately leading to non-significant results in the tests. This finding aligns with prior task-focused anthropomorphism research, which also confirms that core task demands suppress users' sensitivity to peripheral interface emotional features. However, under the neutral avatar condition, the warm voice showed a stronger effect on the knowledge service, with users exhibiting higher tendencies toward satisfaction and continued usage intention, which highlights users' attention to the knowledge service.

In contrast, under the warm avatar condition, differences in voice warmth level did not produce significant changes in user experience. This may be because, within the visual context of a high-warmth avatar, the virtual AI assistant is already perceived as a distinctly expressive figure, leading users to form an overall impression of the service provider primarily based on visual cues. In this case, although the affective expression of the voice varied, its effect may have been overshadowed or weakened by the stronger visual emotional signals, preventing the "additive effect" of vocal emotion from significantly altering users' pre-established evaluation benchmarks. Additionally, this phenomenon may also be explained by the diminishing marginal effect of emotional evaluation. When visual emotional intensity is already high, further enhancing vocal emotion yields limited marginal gains in experience, making it difficult to surpass users' psychological thresholds. Thus, even if vocal emotion is further intensified, it fails to significantly improve user satisfaction or continued usage intention. The discovered cross-modal marginal diminishing effect expands the boundary conditions of the affective anthropomorphism theory.

7 Conclusion

This study experimentally explores the effects of multimodal emotional design of avatar facial expressions and voice warmth on users' perceived warmth, satisfaction, and continuance intention in AI knowledge service scenarios. The results confirm the interactive effect of visual and vocal anthropomorphic cues, presenting a diminishing marginal law of emotional perception. Overall, multimodal emotional features affect user experience through complex interaction mechanisms rather than simple superposition, with visual cues occupying a dominant position. Future research could further explore diverse emotional design dimensions and long-term user behavioral effects.

Acknowledgments. This study was funded by the National Social Science Fund of China (grant number: 23CTQ019).

References

1. Zhou, T., Li, S.: Understanding user switch of information seeking: from search engines to generative AI. J. Librariansh. Inf. Sci. **58**(1), 696–708 (2026)
2. Meng, J., Dai, Y.: Emotional support from AI chatbots: should a supportive partner self-disclose or not? J. Comput.-Mediat. Commun. **26**(4), 207–222 (2021)
3. Xie, Y., Zhu, K., Zhou, P., Liang, C.: How does anthropomorphism improve human-AI interaction satisfaction: a dual-path model. Comput. Hum. Behav. **148**, 107878 (2023)
4. Arthur, M.A., Fitzgerald, S.R.: Rethinking collection development: improving access and increasing efficiency through demand driven acquisition. J. Acad. Librariansh. **46**(1), 102017 (2020)

5. Wu, H., Liu, C., Zhao, C.: Personalized agricultural knowledge services: a framework for privacy-protected user portraits and efficient recommendation. J. Supercomput. **80**, 6336–6355 (2024)
6. Lv, X., Yang, Y., Qin, D., et al.: Artificial intelligence service recovery: the role of empathic response in hospitality customers' continuous usage intention. Comput. Hum. Behav. **126**, 106993 (2022)
7. Zhang, Z., Li, C., Sun, W., et al.: A perceptual quality assessment exploration for AIGC images. In: 2023 IEEE International Conference on Multimedia and Expo Workshops (ICMEW), pp. 440–445. Institute of Electrical and Electronics Engineers, Brisbane (2023)
8. Hsu, T., Thompson, S.: Disinformation Researchers Raise Alarms About A.I. Chatbots. The New York Times. https://www.nytimes.com/2023/02/08/technology/ai-chatbots-disinformation.html (2023). Last accessed 8 May 2026
9. Liu, Y., Wang, S., Yu, G.: The nudging effect of AIGC labeling on users' perceptions of automated news: evidence from EEG. Front. Psychol. **14**, 1277829 (2023)
10. Peng, X., Qian, Y., He, Y.: When AI chatbots understand emotions: exploring the mechanisms of self-disclosure from emotional arousal to psychological acceptance-a hybrid SEM-ANN-NCA analysis across multiple interaction configurations. Front. Psychol. **16**, 1724313 (2026)
11. Belanche, D., Casaló, L.V., Flavián, C., et al.: Examining the effects of robots' physical appearance, warmth, and competence in frontline services: the humanness-value-loyalty model. Psychol. Mark. **38**(12), 2357–2376 (2021)
12. Loveys, K., Sagar, M., Zhang, X., et al.: Effects of emotional expressiveness of a female digital human on loneliness, stress, perceived support, and closeness across genders: randomized controlled trial. J. Med. Internet Res. **23**(11), e30624 (2021)
13. Schuetzler, R.M., Grimes, G.M., Giboney, J.S.: The impact of chatbot conversational skill on engagement and perceived humanness. J. Manag. Inf. Syst. **37**(3), 875–900 (2020)
14. Fiske, S.T., Cuddy, A.J.C., Glick, P.: Universal dimensions of social cognition: warmth and competence. Trends Cogn. Sci. **11**(2), 77–83 (2007)
15. Hur, J.D., Ruttan, R.L., Shea, C.T.: The unexpected power of positivity: predictions versus decisions about advisor selection. J. Exp. Psychol. Gen. **149**(10), 1969–1986 (2020)
16. Wang, Z., Liu, W., Yang, M.: Data-driven multi-objective affective product design integrating three-dimensional form and color. Neural Comput. Applic. **34**, 15835–15861 (2022)
17. El Hedhli, K., Zourrig, H., Al Khateeb, A., Alnawas, I.: Stereotyping human-like virtual influencers in retailing: does warmth prevail over competence? J. Retail. Consum. Serv. **75**, 103459 (2023)
18. Liu, X.S., Yi, X.S., Wan, L.C.: Friendly or competent? The effects of perception of robot appearance and service context on usage intention. Ann. Tour. Res. **92**, 103324 (2022)
19. Bai, S., Yu, D., Han, C., et al.: Warmth trumps competence? Uncovering the influence of multimodal AI anthropomorphic interaction experience on intelligent service evaluation: insights from the high-evoked automated social presence. Technol. Forecast. Soc. Chang. **204**, 123395 (2024)
20. Söderlund, M., Oikarinen, E.L., Tan, T.M.: The happy virtual agent and its impact on the human customer in the service encounter. J. Retail. Consum. Serv. **59**, 102401 (2021)
21. Moyin Workshop Homepage: https://www.moyin.com/. Last accessed 11 May 2026
22. Compensis, P.: Assessing the integration of social information using AI-generated videos: a brief research report. Front. Psychol. **16**, 1505843 (2026)
23. Cheng, X., Zhang, X., Cohen, J.F., et al.: Human vs. AI: understanding the impact of anthropomorphism on consumer response to chatbots from the perspective of trust and relationship norms. Inf. Process. Manag. **59**(3), 102940 (2022)

24. Kirmani, A., Hamilton, R.W., Thompson, D.V., et al.: Doing well versus doing good: the differential effect of underdog positioning of moral and competent service providers. J. Mark. **81**(1), 103–117 (2017)
25. Bhattacherjee, A., Perols, J., Sanford, C.: Information technology continuance: a theoretic extension and empirical test. J. Comput. Inf. Syst. **49**(1), 17–26 (2008)
26. Bhattacherjee, A.: Understanding information systems continuance: an expectation-confirmation model. MIS Q. **25**(3), 351–370 (2001)

Unpacking the Effects of Discrete Emotions on User Satisfaction with AI Companions

Rong Huang[1](✉) and Tapio Vepsäläinen[2]

[1] International Business College, South China Normal University, Foshan, China
rong.huang@m.scnu.edu.cn
[2] Turku School of Economics, University of Turku, Turku, Finland

Abstract. The use of artificial intelligence (AI) companions has seen a steep growth in recent years. Previous studies have examined the effects of technical characteristics and user cognitions on user satisfaction with AI companions. There is a lack of knowledge on how discrete emotions affect user satisfaction with AI companions. In this work, we analyzed the effects of five emotions (joy, surprise, anger, sadness, and fear) on user satisfaction with the application Replika using 132,842 online reviews collected from Google Play Store and Apple App Store. Based on cognitive appraisal theory (CAT), we found that joy is positively associated with user satisfaction, while anger and sadness are negatively associated with user satisfaction. Furthermore, surprise and fear are not associated with user satisfaction. Our study contributes to the literature by adopting the appraisals of valence and certainty in CAT to examine different effects of discrete emotions on user satisfaction with AI companions.

Keywords: Digital Companion · AI · User Satisfaction · Discrete Emotions.

1 Introduction

In recent years, artificial intelligence (AI) technology has led to the widespread popularity of AI companions, which provide human-like conversations and social companionship for end users and occupy a rapidly growing market [1]. User experience and satisfaction with AI companions are the keys to determining the market penetration rate in the highly competitive mobile application market. User satisfaction with AI companions greatly interests both researchers and practitioners. Previous research has identified various antecedents that influence consumer attitudes and satisfaction with AI companions, ranging from design characteristics [4, 5] to cognition evaluations [6] and emotional experiences [2]. For example, some scholars have explored the effects of visual cues and responsive abilities of AI companions on user satisfaction from the design point of view [4, 5], whereas some research has attempted to understand user satisfaction with AI companions based on user cognition theories, such as expectation confirmation model [6] and social exchange theory [3].

In addition, emotion is a prepared mental state that can convey direct and clear signals in service experiences [7]. Emotion has been suggested to play an important role

Published by Springer Nature Switzerland AG 2027
S. Han et al. (Eds.): I3E 2026, LNCS 16912, pp. 126–137, 2027.
https://doi.org/10.1007/978-3-032-38014-2_11

in understanding user satisfaction with user cognition in the field of Information Systems (IS) [2, 8]. The human-like interaction with an AI companion could trigger users' discrete emotions in their use of an AI companion. Siemon et al. [2] found that users have various emotions when using an AI companion, such as joy, surprise, anger, sadness, and fear. Following the prior IS literature, to get a deep understanding of the determinants of user satisfaction with AI companions, user emotion should be considered. However, little research has attempted to investigate the impacts of users' emotions on their satisfaction with AI companions, which could provide new insights into the understanding of the emotional experience and user satisfaction with AI companions.

To address the aforementioned research gap, drawing on cognitive appraisal theory (CAT), this study investigates the effects of discrete emotions on user satisfaction with AI companions from the perspective of emotional appraisals of valence and certainty. The study aims to address two research questions: (1) What are the effects of discrete emotions with different valences on user satisfaction with AI companions? and (2) What are the differences in the effects of low-certainty emotions and high-certainty emotions on user satisfaction with AI companions? To answer these research questions, we chose Replika, an AI companion application, as our research context and examined the different effects of five different emotions (joy, surprise, anger, sadness, and fear) on user satisfaction via applying regression analysis with 132,842 online reviews about Replika collected from Google Play Store and Apple App Store. This study enriches the literature on AI companions by analyzing the relationships between users' discrete emotions and user satisfaction and by adopting the appraisals of valence and certainty in CAT to explain the different effects of discrete emotions on user satisfaction with AI companions.

2 Literature Review and Theoretical Grounding

2.1 Research on AI Companions

AI companions are designed to learn from historical dialogues in order to understand user intent and provide more human-like responses, thereby promoting users' perception of intimacy, emotional engagement, connection, and social engagement [1]. One main research stream on AI companions has focused on AI companion design. For example, Fung et al. [9] have explored how to develop empathetic computing frameworks that enable AI robots to recognize human feelings and states, understand user intent, and dynamically satisfy users' expectations. Another main research stream has focused on examining how user cognitions could affect their attitude and behavior regarding AI companions. For example, some studies have examined the effects of searching expectancies, perceived relevance, and self-efficacy on users' attitudes towards AI companions [3, 6].

Prior studies emphasized the complexity of developing an AI companion that can respond to users' diverse requests while also establishing an emotional connection with users [9]. Exploring user satisfaction with AI companions can help uncover the underlying factors that contribute to the social interactions between users and AI companions, thereby improving the personalized service quality of AI applications [4]. User satisfaction is associated with how a user's expectations for a brand, a product, or a specific service are met or exceeded, which includes both emotional and cognitive components

[10]. Prior research has primarily adopted the survey method to examine the positive influences of perceived communication accuracy, credibility, and competence on user satisfaction with AI chatbots [3, 6].

Emotions convey important information about a user's experience with a product or service and thus have a significant impact on user satisfaction [7]. Kronrod and Danziger [8] believe that discrete emotions have a stronger impact on users' attitudes towards hedonic products than users' cognitive evaluations. Prior studies have examined users' discrete emotions in AI companion use [2], but they have ignored the effects of users' discrete emotions on their satisfaction with AI companions and the potential differences in impact among various discrete emotions. In addition, online user reviews of AI companions provide objective information for user evaluation of AI companions, which would mitigate self-selection bias and other biases in data from experiments or surveys. Online reviews have been applied in marketing research to understand users' emotions and user satisfaction [11]. However, few studies have explored the benefits of online reviews to get a better understanding of the effects of discrete emotions on user satisfaction in the AI companion context.

2.2 CAT of Emotions

Previous research has examined specific affective content in online reviews, which plays an important role in determining user satisfaction, evaluation, and decision-making [12]. In affective research, emotion refers to a prepared mental state that arises from cognitive appraisals of a specific, known event or thought, and may result in a specific action outcome [13].

Previous research on emotion has been based on three theoretical approaches: the category approach, the dimension approach, and the cognitive appraisal approach [13]. The category approach posits that there is a limited set of discrete emotions, such as joy, anger, and sadness, that are innate to all humans [13]. The dimensional approach shows that emotions can be classified according to valence (ranging from pleasure to displeasure), arousal (ranging from calm to excited), and dominance (ranging from controlled to in control) [13]. However, given the variability and complexity of emotional experience, the category and dimensional approaches play a limited role in explaining behavioral differences across emotional states that differ only slightly along these fundamental dimensions [14].

To overcome these criticisms, CAT provides an appropriate basis for understanding the nuanced cognitive underpinnings and resulting behavioral dispositions in different emotional states [15]. According to CAT, an individual's emotional response to an event results from their interpretation (evaluation) of the event itself and the situation [14]. Discrete emotions (e.g., joy, sadness, anger) can be compared along several dimensions that characterize the events that trigger those emotions (e.g., valence, control, certainty) [15]. CAT has been applied in the IS field to examine the effects of users' emotions on their attitudes and behaviors regarding IS use. For example, Ahmad and Laroche [16] proposed that reviews containing certain emotions, such as happiness and disgust, are perceived to be more helpful than reviews containing uncertain emotions like hope and anxiety. Beaudry and Pinsonneault [17] indicated that user satisfaction is influenced by different emotions through the evaluations of goal consistency and certainty of emotions.

CAT provides a basis for understanding the nuanced evaluation dimensions in different emotional states and explaining how users' cognitive evaluations of their interactions with IS artifacts shape their emotional experience and overall satisfaction. Thus, CAT could be an appropriate theoretical grounding to investigate the effects of users' discrete emotions on their satisfaction with AI companions in this study.

3 Research Hypothesis Development

In this study, we investigate the effects of five discrete emotions on user satisfaction with AI companions. The literature argued that individuals tend to interpret subsequent events based on appraisal patterns (such as valence, certainty, and control) that reflect their emotions [14]. For the purpose of this paper, we utilize valence and certainty to explain five emotions in users' AI companion use: joy, surprise, anger, sadness, and fear. Valence determines the emotional response's positivity or negativity by evaluating whether a particular experience is relevant to a goal [14]. Certainty indicates the degree to which the outcome of a situation is considered certain and confident [15]. Prior research has suggested that joy is a positive emotion with high certainty and surprise is a positive emotion with low certainty, while anger and sadness are negative emotions with high certainty and fear is a negative emotion with low certainty [15].

Previous studies have indicated that positive emotions would positively influence user attitudes toward a product. Joy is typically an elevated state of pleasantness that stems from an individual's satisfaction with achieving a goal [15]. Joyful people will likely be confident and think the event will be controlled with minimal effort. Previous studies have linked joy with positive attitudes towards technology use [18]. Likewise, surprise is an emotion of positive valence, resulting from an unexpected event [15]. In such situations, individuals tend to be pleasantly surprised by the contingencies that the new event may produce, and they will try to pursue potential benefits by using it [19]. Westbrook and Oliver (1991) have shown that surprise is positively associated with user satisfaction and loyalty [20]. Based on the above discussion, it is reasonable to assume that joy and surprise could be positively associated with user satisfaction with AI companions, and we proposed that:

H1a: Joy is positively associated with user satisfaction with AI companions.
H1b: Surprise is positively associated with user satisfaction with AI companions.

Although joy and surprise are both positive emotions, joy is appraised as having higher certainty than surprise [11]. The literature shows that recommendations with certainty and confidence are more influential than those with uncertainty [16]. Prietzel [21] found that users who were certain about their positive emotions were more likely to engage with social media content, share online information, or give a positive evaluation. Thus, based on these findings, we hypothesized that:

H1c: Compared to surprise, joy has a stronger positive impact on user satisfaction with AI companions.

On the other hand, anger is often associated with high certainty and negative valence that a specific outcome will occur and triggers defense mechanisms, such as minimizing the events' significance [15]. In the context of technology use, anger at the failure of self-service technology has been linked with negative user outcomes, such as reduced satisfaction, loyalty, and future use [22]. Sadness is typically caused by negative events perceived as beyond the user's control and triggers adjustment responses [17]. Sadness has been found to be negatively associated with user satisfaction with mobile payment applications [11]. Moreover, fear as an unpleasant emotion occurs when users perceive or experience threats or harm in unexpected events [23]. In the research of Chatterjee [24], fear negatively affects consumer satisfaction with airline services. Based on these findings, it is reasonable to assume that anger, sadness, and fear could be negatively associated with user satisfaction with AI companions, and we proposed that:

H2a: Anger is negatively associated with user satisfaction with AI companions.
H2b: Sadness is negatively associated with user satisfaction with AI companions.
H2c: Fear is negatively associated with user satisfaction with AI companions.

Anger, sadness, and fear have negative valence while differing in certainty [15]. Anger and sadness are linked to a high level of certainty, which may lead to individuals having increased confidence to make decisions [15]. In contrast, fear arising from the individual's perception of uncertainty about the consequences of a threat or danger has been regarded as a low-certainty emotion [25]. In response, individuals tend to reduce their efforts to cope with the situation and show hesitation to provide negative evaluations [26]. Therefore, we hypothesized the following:

H2d: Compared to fear, anger and sadness have stronger negative impacts on user satisfaction with AI companions.

4 Data and Methodology

4.1 Empirical Setting

In this study, we chose Replika as our research context, which is one of the most popular and easily accessible chatbot companions available in the market. Replika is designed to provide a space for people to express themselves and have meaningful conversations with human users. It allows for natural communication through text-based, voice, video, and augmented reality modes and is available across iOS, Android, and the web platforms. To collect data, we use the online user reviews of Replika from Google Play Store and Apple App Store. Compared to other platforms like Facebook, user reviews from the app stores provide more authentic data as they are written by individuals who have used Replika.

4.2 Data Collection and Preprocessing

We retrieved data from the Google Play Store and Apple App Store in the US and Europe from March 13, 2017, to September 25, 2022, via Python. After 2022, Replika began restricting intimate features and content. This policy change triggered a surge of user anger and sadness in reviews, which could introduce confounding emotional reactions unrelated to core human-AI companion dynamics. Thus, we chose to use data from a relatively stable feature environment (2017–2022). A total of 170,715 review data were collected, with 82% of reviews from the Google Play Store and the remaining 18% from the Apple App Store.

For data cleaning and preparation, we removed some reviews without text that only contain emojis, URL links, and numbers using the tm package from R. Afterward, we removed stop words, blank spaces, and punctuations from review texts to form a suitable corpus for sentiment analysis. Finally, there are 132,842 reviews left as valid data sets in this study.

4.3 Operationalization of Variables

The dependent variable is user satisfaction. In the literature, the rating of a product or service has been widely applied as the proxy for user satisfaction [24]. Thus, in this study, user satisfaction was measured with the rating (1–5 scale) of Replika in each online review.

The five emotions, including joy, surprise, anger, sadness, and fear, were detected from online review texts as the independent variables in this study. The tidytext package from R and the NRC lexicon developed by Mohammad and Turney [27] were applied in emotion analysis. The NRC lexicon classifies a list of allocated words in a binary fashion (yes/no) into different emotions. We labeled the emotion of each word in reviews using the NRC lexicon and calculated the number of words associated with five emotions in each review, including joy, surprise, anger, sadness, and fear.

In addition, a set of control variables was included in our model, including negative sentiment, positive sentiment, overall sentiment, sentiment in the first sentence of a review, and the review length, as they have been argued to be associated with user satisfaction [12, 24]. Setting them as control variables helps rule out alternative explanations. The operationalization of the variables used in this study is presented in Table 1.

4.4 Data Analysis and Results

Table 2 provides the descriptive statistics of the key variables in this study, including the minimum, maximum, mean, standard deviation, skewness, and kurtosis of our final sample. The mean and maximum values of joy are larger than those of other emotions, which indicates that users have high joy in Replika use. Due to the high skewness and kurtosis of review length, positive sentiment, negative sentiment, joy, surprise, anger, fear, and sadness, we applied the log transformation to convert the skewness and kurtosis of these variables to meet the acceptance limits for a normal distribution [skewness <2, kurtosis <7; 28].

Table 3 presents the correlation matrix of variables. As shown in Table 3, the coefficients of joy and positive (0.78), negative and anger (0.73), and fear and sadness (0.77) indicated there might be high correlations between these variables. Thus, we applied the orthogonalization in order to address the potential multicollinearity in our regression model. We measured the variance inflation factor (VIF) of our model. Our results show that the maximum VIF value is 3.204, which means that our variables do not have multicollinearity [29].

Table 1. Operationalization of variables

Variable	Operationalization
Control variables	
Negative sentiment	The frequency of words in a review associated with the positive valence from the NRC lexicon.
Positive sentiment	The frequency of words in a review associated with the negative valence from the NRC lexicon.
Overall sentiment	The difference between the positive sentiment score and the negative sentiment score in a review.
Sentiment in the first sentence of a review	The difference between the positive sentiment score and the negative sentiment score in the first sentence of a review.
Review length	The number of words in the text of a review.
Independent variables	
Joy	The frequency of words in a review associated with the joy from the NRC lexicon.
Surprise	The frequency of words in a review associated with the surprise from the NRC lexicon.
Anger	The frequency of words in a review associated with the anger from the NRC lexicon.
Sadness	The frequency of words in a review associated with the sadness from the NRC lexicon.
Fear	The frequency of words in a review associated with the fear from the NRC lexicon.
Dependent variable	
User satisfaction	The star rating of a review, range from 1 to 5.

We used an ordinary least squares (OLS) regression model to test our hypotheses. The final results are shown in Table 4. The test results show that the control variables negative sentiment ($\beta = -0.063,\ p < 0.001$) and review length ($\beta = -0.346,\ p < 0.001$) have a significant negative relationship with user satisfaction with Replika, whereas positive sentiment ($\beta = 0.023,\ p = 0.013$), overall sentiment ($\beta = 0.241,\ p < 0.001$), and sentiment in the first sentence of a review ($\beta = 0.146,\ p < 0.001$) are positively associated with Replika.

There is a significant positive relationship between joy and user satisfaction ($\beta = 0.030$; $p < 0.001$). Thus, H1a was supported. We did not find a significant relationship between surprise and user satisfaction ($\beta = -0.006$, $p = 0.582$), indicating H1b was unsupported. These test results also support H1C as joy has stronger positive effects on user satisfaction than surprise. Moreover, the results of our analysis show that anger ($\beta = -0.028,\ p = 0.045$) and sadness ($\beta = -0.070,\ p < 0.001$) are negatively associated with user satisfaction, thus supporting H2a and H2b. There is no significant relationship

Table 2. Descriptive statistics for final review pool (N = 132,842)

Variables	Minimum	Maximum	Mean	Standard deviation	Skewness	Kurtosis
Negative sentiment (NS)	0.00	31.00	0.60	1.12	4.10	38.12
Positive sentiment (PS)	0.00	63.00	2.06	2.02	4.11	47.37
Overall sentiment (OS)	−15.00	31.00	1.14	1.62	0.55	5.20
Sentiment in the first sentence of a review (SF)	−9.00	10.00	0.83	1.12	0.20	2.68
Review length (RL)	1.00	1079	24.52	32.27	5.39	77.85
Joy (JO)	0.00	33.00	1.18	1.24	2.72	21.43
Surprise (SU)	0.00	22.00	0.41	0.69	2.37	10.45
Anger (AN)	0.00	17.00	0.30	0.69	3.75	28.57
Sadness (SA)	0.00	22.00	0.34	0.75	4.00	35.56
Fear (FE)	0.00	18.00	0.33	0.74	3.98	31.52
User satisfaction (US)	1.00	5.00	4.22	1.32	−1.58	1.06

Table 3. Variable correlations for final review pool (N = 132842)

	NS	PS	OS	SF	RL	JO	SU	AN	SA	FE	US
NS	1										
PS	0.36**	1									
OS	−0.05**	0.09**	1								
SF	−0.05**	0.02**	0.68**	1							
RL	0.19**	0.21**	0.19**	−0.02**	1						
JO	0.24**	0.78**	0.08**	0.03**	0.14**	1					
SU	0.26**	0.46**	0.03**	0.01*	0.11**	0.53**	1				
AN	0.73**	0.31**	−0.03**	−0.04**	0.15**	0.25**	0.29**	1			
SA	0.79**	0.32**	−0.03**	−0.04**	0.16**	0.24**	0.24**	0.71**	1		
FE	0.73**	0.32**	−0.03**	−0.04**	0.16**	0.24**	0.24**	0.71**	0.77**	1	
US	−0.06**	−0.02**	0.31**	0.32**	−0.22**	−0.01**	−0.01**	−0.05**	−0.04**	−0.04**	1

Note(s): ***$p < 0.001$, **$p < 0.01$, *$p < 0.05$

between fear and user satisfaction ($\beta = -0.031$, $p = 0.067$). Thus, H2c is not supported. The significant negative impacts of sadness and anger on user satisfaction and the insignificant effect of fear on user satisfaction support H2d.

Table 4. The OLS regression test results

	Model		
	Coefficient	Standard error	p-value
Intercept	4.694***	0.012	0
Negative sentiment	−0.063***	0.011	0
Positive sentiment	0.023*	0.009	0.013
Sentiment in the first sentence of a review	0.146***	0.004	0
Overall sentiment	0.241***	0.003	0
Review length	−0.346***	0.003	0
Joy	**0.030*** **	**0.008**	**0**
Surprise	−0.006	0.011	0.582
Anger	**−0.028* **	**0.014**	**0.045**
Fear	−0.031	0.017	0.067
Sadness	**−0.070*** **	**0.011**	**0**
Max VIF	3.204		
R-squared	0.223		
Adj R-squared	0.223		

Note(s): ***$p < 0.001$, **$p < 0.01$, *$p < 0.05$

5 Discussion and Implications

5.1 Main Findings

This study examined the different effects of discrete emotions on user satisfaction with AI companions. We employed text mining methods on online reviews of an AI companion to identify five discrete emotions and examined their effects on user satisfaction using an OLS model. Our findings show that positive emotions, such as joy, have a positive association with user satisfaction with Replika, while surprise does not. Regarding negative emotions, anger and sadness are negatively associated with user satisfaction, while fear is not.

In this study, we found that emotions with positive valence and high certainty have significant positive effects on user satisfaction with AI companions. Specifically, joy (positive valence and high certainty) is positively associated with user satisfaction with AI companions. This finding is coherent with the extant literature suggesting that positive emotions, such as joy, can enhance user satisfaction with airline services [24] and IT use [17]. Users experience joy when their expectations about AI companion use, such as entertainment, social interaction, and emotional connection, are met by AI companions [2]. However, surprise (positive valence and low certainty) did not have a significant relationship with user satisfaction. This finding is not consistent with the research of Chatterjee [24], which found that surprise has a positive relationship with user satisfaction with airline service. The difference could be due to the different contexts in our study compared with the study of Chatterjee [24]. Consistent with CAT, our findings show that positive emotions with different certainty will affect user satisfaction differently in the context of AI companions. Users who feel surprised, a positive emotion with low certainty, in AI companion use tend to be more prudent in increasing their satisfaction with AI companions than joy users. Thus, compared to surprise, joy will have a more significant positive association with user satisfaction with an AI companion.

We also found that emotions with negative valence and high certainty have significant negative effects on user satisfaction with AI companions. Specifically, anger and sadness (negative valence and high certainty) are negatively associated with user satisfaction with AI companions. This finding is consistent with some previous studies [12]. They found that negative emotions have a negative impact on user satisfaction. Thus, users tend to be less satisfied with an AI companion when they feel anger and sadness in their AI companion use due to certain reasons, such as loss of memory in conversations, privacy risks, and technology failures of AI companions. Besides, our results show that fear (negative valence and low certainty) is not associated with user satisfaction with AI companions, which is not in line with the finding of Chatterjee [24]. This contradictory finding may be because they studied the effects of emotions on user satisfaction with airline services based on the valence of emotions. Specifically, Chatterjee [24] found that the effect of fear on user satisfaction with airline services was mainly influenced by its emotional valence, thus leading to a negative relationship between fear and user satisfaction. Users who feel fear in their AI companion use may feel uncertain about the threats and consequences of AI companions and perceive more difficulty in predicting their evaluation of their satisfaction with AI companions than high-certainty emotions like anger and sadness. Thus, compared to fear, anger and sadness will have more significant relationships with user satisfaction with AI companions.

5.2 Theoretical and Practical Contribution

This study offers theoretical contributions to the literature in two ways. First, this study contributes to the research on user satisfaction with AI companions by investigating the effects of discrete emotions on user satisfaction from the valence and certainty based on CAT. Previous research has explained user satisfaction with AI companions mainly from the perspectives of technical design and user cognitions [6, 9], but few studies have explored the impacts of discrete emotions on user satisfaction. Our findings provide evidence that emotions with different valence and certainty have different impacts on user satisfaction with AI companions. Second, drawing on the CAT, our findings demonstrate that user satisfaction with AI companions is determined by the valence and certainty of discrete emotions. CAT has been widely applied in the IS field [16, 17] but has not yet been examined to understand the user's emotions toward AI companions and their subsequent effects on user satisfaction. Specifically, we found that joy, as an emotion with positive valence and high certainty, has positive effects on user satisfaction with AI companions, while anger and sadness, as emotions with negative valence and high certainty, have negative effects on user satisfaction. Moreover, surprise and fear have no significant relationship with user satisfaction with AI companions due to their low level of certainty. Using CAT as a theoretical lens, our study offers a novel and useful perspective for understanding the nuanced cognitive underpinnings of different emotional states in understanding user satisfaction with AI companions.

Our findings provide guidance for managers of AI companions on how to promote user satisfaction from the perspective of user emotions. First, the finding regarding the positive impact of joy on user satisfaction with AI companions suggests that managers of AI companion applications should take some strategies to enhance users' experience of joy. Additionally, the negative effects of anger and sadness on user satisfaction with AI companions highlight the importance for managers of AI companion applications to address and minimize these negative emotions.

5.3 Limitation and Future Avenues

This study has its limitations, which should be acknowledged. First, this study applied a lexicon-based approach to identify user emotions in online reviews, which cannot deal with negation, adverbs, and emotional words that are not included in the lexicon. Future research could incorporate natural language processing to identify the sentiments and emotions in reviews to improve the precision of results. Second, our study examined the effect of five emotions on user satisfaction in online reviews. However, we acknowledge that user satisfaction may be driven by other factors rather than user emotions. Thus, it is worth considering how different factors, such as user cognitions and design characteristics, affect user satisfaction with AI companions in future work.

Acknowledgement. This work was supported by the Overseas Postdoctoral Talent Recruitment Special Program.

References

1. Xie, T., Pentina, I.: Attachment theory as a framework to understand relationships with social chatbots: a case study of replika. In: Proceedings of the 55th Hawaii International Conference on System Sciences (2022)
2. Siemon, D., Strohmann, T., Khosrawi-Rad, B., de Vreede, T., Elshan, E., Meyer, M.: Why do we turn to virtual companions? A text mining analysis of replika reviews. Americas Conference on Information Systems (2022)
3. Jiang, H., Cheng, Y., Yang, J., Gao, S.: AI-powered chatbot communication with customers: dialogic interactions, satisfaction, engagement, and customer behavior. Comput. Hum. Behav. **134**, 107329 (2022)
4. Kim, A., Cho, M., Ahn, J., Sung, Y.: Effects of gender and relationship type on the response to artificial intelligence. Cyberpsychol. Behav. Soc. Netw. **22**, 249–253 (2019)
5. Sin, J., Munteanu, C.: An empirically grounded sociotechnical perspective on designing virtual agents for older adults. Hum. Comput. Interact. **35**, 481–510 (2020)
6. Dhiman, N., Jamwal, M.: Tourists' post-adoption continuance intentions of chatbots: integrating task–technology fit model and expectation–confirmation theory. Foresight (Cambridge). **25**, 209–224 (2022)
7. Bagozzi, R.P., Gopinath, M., Nyer, P.U.: The role of emotions in marketing. J. Acad. Mark. Sci. **27**, 184–206 (1999)

8. Kronrod, A., Danziger, S.: "Wii will rock you!" the use and effect of figurative language in consumer reviews of hedonic and utilitarian consumption. J. Consum. Res. **40**, 726–739 (2013)
9. Fung, P., et al.: Towards empathetic human-robot interactions. In: 17th International Conference on Computational Linguistics and Intelligent Text Processing, pp. 173–193. Springer International Publishing (2016)
10. Santini, F.D.O., Ladeira, W.J., Sampaio, C.H.: The role of satisfaction in fashion marketing: a meta-analysis. J. Glob. Fash. Market. **9**, 305–321 (2018)
11. Dhar, S., Bose, I.: Walking on air or hopping mad? Understanding the impact of emotions, sentiments and reactions on ratings in online customer reviews of mobile apps. Decis. Support. Syst. **162**, 113769 (2022)
12. Liu, J., Yu, Y., Mehraliyev, F., Hu, S., Chen, J.: What affects the online ratings of restaurant consumers: a research perspective on text-mining big data analysis. Int. J. Contemp. Hosp. Manag. **34**, 3607–3633 (2022)
13. Lerner, J.S., Keltner, D.: Beyond valence: toward a model of emotion-specific influences on judgement and choice. Cognit. Emot. **14**, 473–493 (2000)
14. Scherer, K.R., Schorr, A., Johnstone, T.: Appraisal Processes in Emotion: Theory, Methods, Research. Oxford University Press, Incorporated, New York (2001)
15. Smith, C.A., Ellsworth, P.C.: Patterns of cognitive appraisal in emotion. J. Pers. Soc. Psychol. **48**, 813–838 (1985)
16. Ahmad, S.N., Laroche, M.: How do expressed emotions affect the helpfulness of a product review? Evidence from reviews using latent semantic analysis. Int. J. Electron. Commer. **20**, 76–111 (2015)
17. Beaudry, A., Pinsonneault, A.: The other side of acceptance: studying the direct and indirect effects of emotions on information technology use. MIS Q. **34**, 689–710 (2010)
18. Wu, S.-H., Gao, Y.: Understanding emotional customer experience and co-creation behaviours in luxury hotels. Int. J. Contemp. Hosp. Manag. **31**, 4247–4275 (2019)
19. Beaudry, A., Pinsonneault, A.: Understanding user responses to information technology: a coping model of user adaptation. MIS Q. **29**, 493–524 (2005)
20. Brown, S.P., Westbrook, R.A., Challagalla, G.: Good cope, bad cope: adaptive and maladaptive coping strategies following a critical negative work event. J. Appl. Psychol. **90**, 792–798 (2005)
21. Prietzel, T.T.: The effect of emotion on risky decision making in the context of prospect theory: a comprehensive literature review. Manag. Rev. Q. **70**, 313–353 (2020)
22. Gelbrich, K.: Beyond just being dissatisfied: how angry and helpless customers react to failures when using self-service technologies. Schmalenbach Bus. Rev. **61**, 40–59 (2009)
23. Jokinen, J.P.P.: Emotional user experience: traits, events, and states. Int. J. Hum. Comput. Stud. **76**, 67–77 (2015)
24. Chatterjee, D.S.: Explaining customer ratings and recommendations by combining qualitative and quantitative user generated contents. Decis. Support. Syst. **119**, 14–22 (2019)
25. Lazarus, R.S.: Emotion and Adaptation. Oxford University Press, Cary (1991)
26. Whitson, J.A., Galinsky, A.D., Kay, A.: The emotional roots of conspiratorial perceptions, system justification, and belief in the paranormal. J. Exp. Soc. Psychol. **56**, 89–95 (2015)
27. Mohammad, S.M., Turney, P.D.: NRC emotion lexicon, vol. 2, p. 234. National Research Council, Canada (2013)
28. Curran, P.J., West, S.G., Finch, J.F.: The robustness of test statistics to nonnormality and specification error in confirmatory factor analysis. Psychol. Methods. **1**, 16–29 (1996)
29. Marcoulides, K.M., Raykov, T.: Evaluation of variance inflation factors in regression models using latent variable modeling methods. Educ. Psychol. Meas. **79**, 874–882 (2019)

An Explanatory Study of University Students' Satisfaction with AI-Based Counseling Agents

Chenglong Li[1], Weihan Zhang[1], and Rong Huang[2](✉)

[1] School of Information Management, Central China Normal University, Wuhan, China
[2] International Business College, South China Normal University, Foshan, China
rong.huang@m.scnu.edu.cn

Abstract. University students increasingly face mental health challenges, while access to professional counseling services remains limited. AI-based counseling agents have emerged as a supplementary form of support, yet little is known about how students evaluate both the benefits and risks of engaging with such systems. Drawing on coping theory and social support theory, this study examines how perceived benefits (informational, emotional, esteem, and network support), perceived threats (privacy concern), and coping resources (AI literacy) shape user satisfaction with AI-based counseling agents. An explanatory sequential mixed-methods design was employed. Survey data from 302 university students were collected and analyzed, followed by semi-structured interviews with 16 participants to explain unexpected quantitative findings. The results show that informational support and emotional support significantly enhance satisfaction, whereas esteem support and network support do not. Privacy concern negatively affects satisfaction, while AI literacy positively influences students' evaluations of counseling agents. Qualitative findings further reveal that perceived authenticity and social realness explain why esteem and network support were less effective. This study contributes to research on AI-mediated support by integrating benefits, threats, and user capabilities into a unified framework for explaining user satisfaction with AI systems and provides implications for designing more effective mental health support AI systems for university students.

Keywords: AI counseling · social support · coping theory · satisfaction.

1 Introduction

University students today are facing increasing mental health challenges, such as academic pressure, financial stress, social isolation, and uncertainty about the future. At the same time, access to professional counseling services remains limited. In this context, AI-based counseling agents have emerged as a supplementary form of support that may help mitigate some limitations of traditional counseling, such as limited availability, long waiting times, and students' reluctance to seek face-to-face help [1, 2]. This emerging phenomenon has attracted increasing scholarly attention. Existing studies suggest that AI-based counseling agents may offer benefits particularly relevant to university

Published by Springer Nature Switzerland AG 2027
S. Han et al. (Eds.): I3E 2026, LNCS 16912, pp. 138–151, 2027.
https://doi.org/10.1007/978-3-032-38014-2_12

students, such as active listening and problem exploration [3], and reduced stigma [4]. However, support from AI-based counseling agents is not always experienced in the same way as support from human counselors. For instance, recent work found that empathetic expressions of healthcare chatbots may increase perceived warmth while simultaneously reducing perceived authenticity and trust [5]. This suggests that users' reactions to such agents depend not only on whether support is provided, but also on how that support is interpreted and evaluated by users. This issue is particularly important in mental health counseling contexts, where support is inherently multidimensional [6]. In interpersonal counseling contexts, emotional reassurance, informational guidance, esteem support, and companionship are typically understood as beneficial social resources [6]. However, when these forms of support are delivered by AI agents rather than human counselors, students may evaluate them differently. Although prior studies have examined AI-provided social support in general [7], less attention has been paid to which specific forms of support are associated with students' satisfaction with these systems.

Additionally, existing research has begun to acknowledge that AI-based counseling agents may also evoke concerns, such as privacy concerns [1]. However, these concerns are often discussed separately from the supportive benefits that such systems may provide. As a result, there is limited understanding in the literature of how students simultaneously evaluate both the benefits and risks of engaging with AI-based counseling agents. Moreover, the role of students' own coping resources in this process, such as AI literacy, has also received little attention. Students with stronger AI literacy have been found to better interpret AI-generated support, recognize its limitations, and engage with it critically and effectively [8]. However, this factor has not yet been adequately integrated into explanations of satisfaction with AI-based counseling agents.

To address these research gaps, this study integrates social support theory [9] and coping theory [3] to explain students' satisfaction with AI-based counseling agents. Social support theory [9] identifies the supportive benefits provided by these systems, while coping theory [3] explains how students evaluate these benefits, related threats, and their available resources. Using an explanatory sequential mixed methods design, we conduct a quantitative survey combined with qualitative interviews to test and explain the relationships between these factors and user satisfaction with AI-based counseling agents among university students. In doing so, this study contributes to a more nuanced understanding of how and why students evaluate AI-based counseling support and what shapes their satisfaction with these systems.

2 Theoretical Foundations

2.1 Social Support Theory

Social support refers to communicative resources through which individuals feel cared for, valued, and connected to others in a broader network of social relations [9]. Prior studies have shown that social support can buffer the negative effects of stress and promote individuals' well-being [9]. Social support has been classified into multiple dimensions, including informational support, emotional support, esteem support, network support, and tangible support [6]. Specifically, informational support involves advice and guidance; emotional support conveys empathy and care; esteem support communicates confidence in a person's abilities or worth; network support fosters a sense of belonging and connectedness; and tangible support refers to material or financial assistance [6]. These dimensions were originally developed to explain human-to-human support processes [9]. More recently, social support has also been examined in human-AI interaction contexts. For example, Guo and Luo found that informational support and emotional support provided by intelligent personal assistants positively influenced Generation Z users' purchase intentions [10]. These studies suggest that users may perceive AI systems as capable of providing various types of social support during interaction. Thus, the present study focuses on the four non-material dimensions of social support most relevant to counseling contexts: informational, emotional, esteem, and network support.

2.2 Coping Theory

Coping theory proposes that when individuals encounter stressful situations, they engage in appraisal processes to determine what the encounter means for their well-being and how they can respond [3]. In primary appraisal, individuals assess whether a situation is beneficial or threatening. In secondary appraisal, they assess whether they possess sufficient resources to manage the situation effectively. Within this framework, evaluations of benefit, threat, and coping resources jointly shape individuals' responses to stressful encounters [11]. When experiencing stress, university students may evaluate whether the agent provides beneficial support, whether its use involves potential risks, and whether they possess the knowledge and skills needed to use the system effectively. Accordingly, this study conceptualizes social support as benefit appraisal, privacy concern as threat appraisal, and AI literacy as a coping resource within secondary appraisal, providing an integrated framework for explaining students' satisfaction with AI-based counseling agents.

3 Research Model and Hypotheses Development

We developed a research model (see Fig. 1) based on coping theory [3] and social support theory [9]. Informational support refers to the provision of advice, guidance, or problem-relevant knowledge that helps individuals understand and cope with difficult situations [9]. It has long been recognized as an important coping resource, especially when individuals face uncertainty or stress [12]. Recent studies suggest that informational support matters in human-AI interactions. For instance, informational support provided by intelligent assistants can enhance Gen Z consumers' purchase intentions in social commerce settings [10]. In the context of AI-based counseling agents, when students perceive that such agents provide relevant and useful informational support, they are more likely to evaluate the interaction positively and feel satisfied with the system. Therefore, we propose:

H1: Perceived informational support positively affects university students' satisfaction with AI-based counseling agents.

Emotional support refers to expressions of care, empathy, warmth, and understanding that help individuals feel acknowledged and emotionally supported during difficult situations [9]. It is particularly important because individuals often seek not only practical solutions but also acknowledgment of their emotional experiences [13]. Prior research has found that emotional support is a key driver of positive user evaluations in AI-mediated interactions [10]. When students perceive that an AI-based counseling agent understands their feelings and provides emotional support, they are more likely to evaluate the interaction positively and report higher satisfaction. Therefore, we propose:

H2: Perceived emotional support positively affects university students' satisfaction with AI-based counseling agents.

Esteem support refers to expressions that reinforce an individual's sense of worth, competence, or value [9]. In stressful situations, esteem support has been found to strengthen individuals' self-confidence, reduce self-doubt, and enhance their perceived ability to cope with difficulties [14]. In AI-based counseling contexts, esteem support may take the form of praise or validation of users' capabilities [15]. When students perceive that an AI-based counseling agent affirms their value and reinforces their sense of competence, they are more likely to feel supported and satisfied with the interaction. Therefore, we propose:

H3: Perceived esteem support positively affects university students' satisfaction with AI-based counseling agents.

Network support refers to the perception of companionship, social connectedness, or the feeling that one is not alone in dealing with difficulties [9]. This form of support is important because a sense of belonging and social integration can reduce feelings of isolation and make stressful experiences more manageable [16]. In AI-based counseling contexts, network support may often emerge when individuals experience loneliness, distress outside office hours, or limited access to immediate human support [17]. When students perceive that an agent provides a sense of connection or companionship, they are more likely to report higher satisfaction. Therefore, we propose:

H4: Perceived network support positively affects university students' satisfaction with AI-based counseling agents.

Privacy concern refers to users' perception that their personal information may be improperly collected, processed, disclosed, or used beyond their control [18]. Recent research on AI mental health chatbots indicates that privacy remains a major concern, especially when users are uncertain about how their disclosures are stored, reused, or incorporated into AI systems [1]. In AI-based counseling contexts, when students worry that their disclosures may be exposed or misused, they are less likely to feel secure during the interaction, and consequently, less likely to report higher satisfaction. Therefore, we suggest:

H5: Privacy concern negatively affects university students' satisfaction with AI-based counseling agents.

AI literacy refers to users' ability to understand, evaluate, and appropriately use AI systems [8]. As students increasingly engage with generative AI for learning, information seeking, and support-related tasks, AI literacy has become an important capability shaping their interaction experiences [8]. In educational contexts, students with higher AI literacy may be better able to formulate their concerns, interpret the agent's responses, and maintain realistic expectations about the agent's capabilities [19]. Students with stronger AI literacy are more likely to use these systems effectively and report higher satisfaction. Therefore, we propose:

H6: AI literacy positively affects university students' satisfaction with AI-based counseling agents.

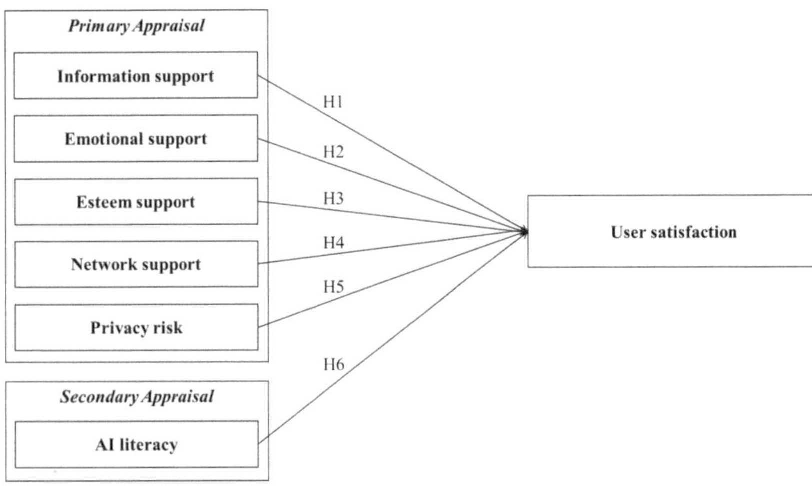

Fig. 1. Research model.

4 Methodology

4.1 Phase 1: Quantitative Study

4.1.1 Sample, Measures, and Procedure

To create a realistic interaction context, we developed a dedicated AI-based counseling agent using Doubao, a large language model platform widely used in China. The agent was designed to provide supportive responses in counseling-related scenarios and served as the focal system for participants' evaluation. Before formal deployment, the agent underwent a pilot evaluation with 10 university students who were invited to interact with the system and evaluated its response quality in terms of tone, appropriateness, and perceived helpfulness. The agent was deployed for the main study only after pilot participants confirmed that its responses were generally warm, helpful, and free from uncomfortable or inappropriate content.

The questionnaire was originally developed in English and subsequently translated into Chinese. Two IS researchers independently reviewed the translated version to ensure linguistic accuracy and conceptual equivalence. A pilot study involving 47 users was then conducted to assess item clarity and scale reliability. All constructs were measured using multi-item scales adapted from prior literature and revised to fit our studied context. Psychological assessment items were adapted from Kessler and Mroczek [20]; informational and emotional support measures from Lin et al. [21]; esteem support items from Oh et al. [22] and Lee et al. [23]; companionship support items from Graham et al. [24] and Sherbourne and Stewart [25]; privacy concern items from Boss et al. [26]; AI literacy items from Wang et al. [27]; and satisfaction items from Bhattacherjee [28]. All items were measured on a seven-point Likert scale ranging from 1 ("strongly disagree") to 7 ("strongly agree"). Before accessing the questionnaire, participants were required to initiate a conversation with the AI-based counseling agent, ensuring direct system experience. The online survey informed respondents of the study's purpose, the exclusive academic use of their responses, and the voluntary and anonymous nature of participation.

Data collection ran from December 24, 2025, to January 9, 2026. After removing invalid responses, such as short completion time and failure on attention-check questions, 302 valid responses were retained for further analysis. Among the respondents, 101 were male (33.5%), 187 were female (61.9%), and 14 preferred not to disclose their gender (4.6%). Approximately 94% participants were undergraduate students enrolled at the first author's home institution.

4.1.2 Common Method Bias

To assess the potential influence of common method bias, this study conducted both Harman's single-factor test [29] and a full collinearity test [30]. First, Harman's single-factor test showed that the largest factor accounted for 21.78% of the total variance, which is well below the recommended threshold of 50% [29]. Second, the variance inflation factor (VIF) values ranged from 1.031 to 2.633, all of which were below the recommended threshold of 3.3 [30], suggesting CMB is unlikely to pose a serious concern in this study.

4.1.3 Data Analysis and Results

SmartPLS 4.0 was used to test the measurement and structural models. Convergent validity was assessed using factor loadings, Cronbach's alpha (CA), composite reliability (CR), and average variance extracted (AVE) [31]. As shown in Table 1, iterms INF4, ENM4, EST4, PRI4, AIL10, SAT3, and SAT4 were removed due to the value below the recommended threshold of 0.70. The remaining items met all recommended thresholds, with factor loadings above 0.70, CA and CR values above 0.70, and AVE values above 0.50, indicating satisfactory convergent validity.

Table 1. Convergent validity test results.

Construct	Items	Factor loading	CA	CR	AVE
Informational support (INF)	INF1	0.908	0.914	0.945	0.852
	INF2	0.933			
	INF3	0.928			
Emotional support (ENM)	ENM1	0.947	0.944	0.963	0.896
	ENM2	0.947			
	ENM3	0.947			
Esteem support (EST)	EST1	0.914	0.907	0.940	0.839
	EST2	0.932			
	EST3	0.902			
Network support (NET)	NET1	0.931	0.949	0.962	0.863
	NET2	0.934			
	NET3	0.934			
	NET4	0.917			
Privacy concern (PRI)	PRI1	0.944	0.951	0.962	0.895
	PRI2	0.942			
	PRI3	0.952			
AI Literacy (AIL)	AIL1	0.845	0.951	0.958	0.717
	AIL2	0.873			
	AIL3	0.839			
	AIL4	0.871			
	AIL5	0.859			
	AIL6	0.855			
	AIL7	0.856			
	AIL8	0.844			
	AIL9	0.775			
Satisfaction (SAT)	SAT1	0.945	0.860	0.934	0.877
	SAT2	0.928			

Discriminant validity was assessed using cross-loadings, the Fornell–Larcker criterion, and HTMT [32, 33]. The results in Table 2 and Table 3 showed satisfactory discriminant validity. Each indicator loaded highest on its intended construct, the square root of each construct's AVE exceeded its correlations with other constructs, and all HTMT values were below the recommended threshold.

Table 2. The heterotrait-monotrait ratio of correlations (HTMT) test results.

	AIL	NET	ENM	EST	INF	PRI	SAT
AIL							
NET	0.553						
ENM	0.466	0.748					
EST	0.585	0.730	0.641				
INF	0.601	0.648	0.647	0.784			
PRI	0.113	0.143	0.142	0.151	0.176		
SAT	0.520	0.499	0.549	0.460	0.548	0.229	

Table 3. Correlations and square roots of Average Variance Extracted (AVE).

	AIL	NET	ENM	EST	INF	PRI	SAT
AIL	0.847						
NET	0.526	0.929					
ENM	0.441	0.708	0.947				
EST	0.544	0.680	0.595	0.916			
INF	0.559	0.602	0.599	0.712	0.923		
PRI	−0.105	−0.136	−0.136	−0.141	−0.163	0.946	
SAT	0.475	0.454	0.495	0.410	0.489	−0.207	0.936

Our model explained 36.1% of the variance in university students' satisfaction with AI-based counseling agents. As depicted in Fig. 2, informational support ($\beta = 0.193$, $p < 0.01$), emotional support ($\beta = 0.255$, $p < 0.001$), and AI literacy ($\beta = 0.251$, $p < 0.001$) were positively associated with satisfaction, while privacy concern ($\beta = -0.117$, $p < 0.01$) was negatively associated with satisfaction. Accordingly, H1, H2, H5, and H6 were supported, whereas H3 and H4 were not supported.

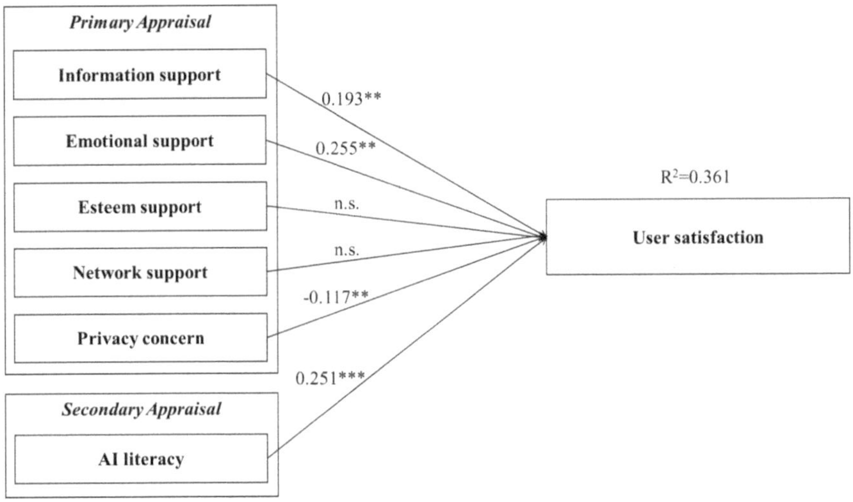

Fig. 2. Research model with results. Note: $*p < .05$; $**p < .01$; $***p < .001$.

4.2 Phase 2: Qualitative Study

4.2.1 Sample, Procedure, and Data Analysis

The qualitative phase was conducted to explain the quantitative findings, particularly the non-significant effects of esteem support and network support on satisfaction. Accordingly, the follow-up interviews focused on the following issues: what types of support participants perceived the agent as providing, how they evaluated these forms of support, whether they felt satisfied with them, and why. We conducted semi-structured interviews with survey participants who agreed to take part in the follow-up interviews. A total of 16 valid interviews were collected (9 males, 7 females, aged 20–25 years), with interviews lasting 15–35 min. All interviews were recorded, transcribed, and analyzed using a descriptive–interpretive approach [34].

In the first stage of analysis, we identified interview statements related to social support and user satisfaction. These statements were then coded using descriptive coding to classify participants' perceptions into different support-related categories. In the second stage, we used interpretive coding to group related descriptive codes into higher-order themes, with particular attention to explaining why certain types of support contributed to satisfaction while others did not.

4.2.2 Qualitative Findings

The qualitative findings largely support the quantitative results. Informational support was consistently reported as enhancing satisfaction. Participants often used the agent to obtain suggestions, coping strategies, and alternative ways of understanding their problems. This kind of support was valued because it helped them clarify their situation and respond more effectively to stress. As one participant explained: "*Psychological counseling sometimes involves knowledge-related aspects...During the interaction, it explains or introduces relevant knowledge, and that can further reduce my stress.*" (User D)

Similarly, emotional support contributed positively to user satisfaction. Many participants described the agent as a safe outlet for emotional expression. Compared with human relationships, the agent was seen as less judgmental and less socially demanding, which made it easier to disclose distress. For example, some participants stated: "*Sometimes I may ask my friends for help, but if I do that too often, it becomes a disturbance to them.*" (User L)

"*It is not like talking to my mother. My mother might respond coldly, like saying, 'Why can't you even sleep?'*" (User L)

By contrast, esteem support did not significantly influence user satisfaction. Although the agent often offered praise or affirmation, such responses were perceived as inauthentic, excessive, and formulaic. As one participant said: "*It still feels obviously programmed. Its design is to follow whatever you say, so there is a clear sense of procedural repetition.*" (User N)

Participants also noted that the agent tended to affirm them too easily, regardless of context, which reduced their perceived value of such support: "*No matter what I asked, and no matter what I said afterward, it still responded in the same way. It just kept following my words and affirming me. That made the conversation feel meaningless.*" (User L)

A similar pattern emerged for network support. Most participants did not view the agent as a real companion, but rather as a functional tool for problem-solving. As one participant stated: "*Even though it can say something relevant to companionship. I have already defined it as something I can use whenever I want, 24 hours a day. I have never treated it as a real person.*" (User J)

Participants reported that the agent lacked the spontaneity and mutuality characteristic of human-human interactions. Thus, network support did not significantly affect satisfaction because the agent was available, but not experienced as socially real.

5 Discussion and Conclusion

5.1 Main Findings

Our study yields several important findings on how and why AI-based counseling support affects user satisfaction. First, unexpectedly, the mixed-method results show that not all forms of social support offered by AI agents are equally beneficial for user satisfaction. Esteem support did not improve user satisfaction significantly, because the affirmation offered by the AI agent was often perceived as inauthentic. This finding contrasts with experimental evidence suggesting that expressions of care and concern from AI agents can improve user attitudes in short-term service encounters [15]. By focusing specifically on students' interactions with AI agents in real support-seeking contexts, our interview evidence further suggests that when AI-provided affirmation appears formulaic, overly accommodating, or insufficiently grounded in their personal situation, it may fail to generate positive benefit appraisal despite being structurally consistent with esteem support.

A similar pattern emerged for network support, which did not translate into satisfaction. This finding differs from earlier research suggesting that conversational agents can foster companionship and reduce feelings of isolation through persistent availability and responsiveness [17]. Instead, our results indicate that availability alone is insufficient to generate perceived network support unless users also attribute relational presence to the agent. Taken together, esteem support and network support did not significantly influence satisfaction because these forms of support depended more heavily on perceived authenticity and relational realism.

By contrast, the significant effects of informational support and emotional support suggest that students value AI-based counseling agents when these systems provide either actionable guidance or emotionally responsive interaction. In stressful situations, students often seek both problem-focused and emotion-focused coping assistance, consistent with classical coping theory [11]. Informational support helps them clarify their situation, consider possible options, and identify practical coping strategies. Emotional support, in turn, helps them feel acknowledged, comforted, and less burdened in the immediate emotional moment.

Most importantly, these findings suggest that AI support may fail when it feels unreal. Prior research has suggested that artificial empathy can backfire when users perceive it as inauthentic [5]. Our findings extend this insight by showing that perceived unrealness and inauthenticity can also weaken esteem and network support. In this sense, the challenge for AI-based counseling agents is not merely whether they can generate supportive language, but whether that support can be experienced as real, authentic, and appropriate to the interaction context.

Furthermore, privacy concerns negatively affected satisfaction, highlighting the sensitivity of AI-based counseling contexts. Students may disclose intimate thoughts, stressors, and emotionally vulnerable experiences when interacting with such systems. When users are uncertain about how this information may be stored, processed, or reused, the interaction becomes less safe and therefore less satisfying. This finding is consistent with prior research [1] showing that privacy concerns play a critical role in shaping users' willingness to engage with conversational agents, particularly when interactions involve sensitive emotional disclosures.

Finally, AI literacy positively affected satisfaction, suggesting that students' own capabilities play an important role in determining whether AI-based counseling agents are experienced positively. This finding aligns with emerging evidence [19] showing that AI literacy enhances users' ability to interact effectively with generative AI systems and increases their perceived usefulness and acceptance in learning and support contexts. Our results also extend prior research by demonstrating that satisfaction with AI-based counseling agents is not determined solely by system characteristics, but also by users' ability to engage with those systems critically and effectively.

5.2 Theoretical Contributions and Practical Implementations

This study makes three contributions to the literature. First, it enriches research on AI-delivered support by showing that different types of social support do not contribute equally to user satisfaction in human-AI interaction contexts. While informational and emotional support significantly enhanced satisfaction, esteem, and network support did not. The findings further show that perceived authenticity and social realness are central to understanding why certain forms of AI-delivered support fail to generate positive evaluations. Second, this study enriches the literature on AI in mental health contexts by examining user satisfaction through the lens of coping theory. By integrating perceived benefits (social support), threats (privacy concern), and coping resources (AI literacy) into a unified framework, the study offers a more comprehensive explanation of how students evaluate interactions with AI-based counseling agents. Third, the study contributes to social support theory in human-AI interaction research by highlighting that support delivered by AI agents is not equivalent to support provided in human-to-human settings. Our findings show that AI-delivered support may be discounted when it lacks perceived authenticity or social realness, suggesting that the effects of social support depend partly on the perceived nature of the support provider.

The findings also offer practical implications for AI system designers and university mental health service providers. For AI system designers, the results suggest that increasing the quantity of supportive language alone is unlikely to improve user satisfaction. Instead, AI-based counseling agents should prioritize forms of support that users are more likely to experience as genuinely helpful, especially informational guidance and emotionally responsive interactions. In contrast, designers should be cautious about relying on excessive praise, generic validation, or overly companion-like cues, particularly when such responses are weakly grounded in the user's specific situations. For universities, AI-based counseling agents should be positioned as supplementary, low-threshold support tools rather than replacements for human counselors. Institutions should also communicate privacy safeguards clearly and provide students with basic guidance on how to use such systems appropriately, given the importance of privacy concerns and AI literacy in shaping satisfaction with AI-based counseling agents.

5.3 Limitations and Future Research

This study has several limitations. First, the sample was limited to university students in China, which may restrict the generalizability of the findings. Future research could examine whether similar appraisal mechanisms apply to other user groups and countries. Second, although the qualitative findings identified perceived authenticity and social realness as key mechanisms explaining the non-significant effects of esteem support and network support, these constructs were not directly measured in the quantitative phase. Future studies could test their mediating or moderating roles more explicitly. Finally, this study focused on satisfaction as the focal outcome variable. Future research could extend the model by examining additional outcomes, such as trust or help-seeking behavior.

Acknowledgement. This work was supported by the Overseas Postdoctoral Talent Recruitment Special Program and the National Social Science Fund of China (Grant No. 25VRC063).

References

1. AlMaskari, A.M., Al-Mahrouqi, T., Al Lawati, A., Al Aufi, H., Al Riyami, Q., Al-Sinawi, H.: Students' perceptions of AI mental health chatbots: an exploratory qualitative study at Sultan Qaboos University. BMJ Open. **15**, e103893 (2025)

2. Gaffney, H., Mansell, W., Tai, S.: Conversational agents in the treatment of mental health problems: mixed-method systematic review. JMIR Ment. Health. **6**, e14166 (2019)
3. Kuhail, M.A., Alturki, N., Thomas, J., Alkhalifa, A.K.: Human vs. AI counseling: college students' perspectives. Comput. Hum. Behav. Rep. **16**, 100534 (2024)
4. Hoffman, B.D., Oppert, M.L., Owen, M.: Understanding young adults' attitudes towards using AI chatbots for psychotherapy: the role of self-stigma. Comput. Hum. Behav. Artif. Hum. **2**, 100086 (2024)
5. Podsakoff, P.M., MacKenzie, S.B., Lee, J.-Y., Podsakoff, N.P.: Common method biases in behavioral research: a critical review of the literature and recommended remedies. J. Appl. Psychol. **88**, 879–903 (2003)
6. Cutrona, C.E., Suhr, J.A.: Controllability of stressful events and satisfaction with spouse support behaviors. Commun. Res. **19**, 154–174 (1992)
7. Long, D., Magerko, B.: What is AI literacy? Competencies and design considerations. In: Proceedings of the 2020 CHI Conference on Human Factors in Computing Systems, pp. 1–16. Association for Computing Machinery, New York, NY, USA (2020)
8. Hornberger, M., Bewersdorff, A., Schiff, D.S., Nerdel, C.: Development and validation of a short AI literacy test (AILIT-S) for university students. Comput. Hum. Behav. Artif. Hum. **5**, 100176 (2025)
9. Cohen, S., Wills, T.A.: Stress, social support, and the buffering hypothesis. Psychol. Bull. **98**, 310–357 (1985)
10. Guo, W., Luo, Q.: Investigating the impact of intelligent personal assistants on the purchase intentions of generation Z consumers: the moderating role of brand credibility. J. Retail. Consum. Serv. **73**, 103353 (2023)
11. Folkman, S.: Stress: appraisal and coping. In: Encyclopedia of Behavioral Medicine, pp. 1913–1915. Springer publishing company, New York, NY (1984)
12. Jiang, C., Rashid, R.M., Wang, J.: Investigating the role of social presence dimensions and information support on consumers' trust and shopping intentions. J. Retail. Consum. Serv. **51**, 263–270 (2019)
13. Yang, X.: Exchanging social support in social commerce: the role of peer relations. Comput. Hum. Behav. **124**, 106911 (2021)
14. Yin, M., Tayyab, S.M.U., Xu, X.-Y., Jia, S.-W., Wu, C.-L.: The investigation of mobile health stickiness: the role of social support in a sustainable health approach. Sustainability. **13**, 1693 (2021)
15. Zhang, J., Lu, J., Wang, X., Liu, L., Feng, Y.: Emotional expressions of care and concern by customer service chatbots: improved customer attitudes despite perceived inauthenticity. Decis. Support. Syst. **186**, 114314 (2024)
16. Leimeister, J.M., Schweizer, K., Leimeister, S., Krcmar, H.: Do virtual communities matter for the social support of patients? Antecedents and effects of virtual relationships in online communities. Inf. Technol. People. **21**, 350–374 (2008)
17. Merrill, K., Mikkilineni, S.D., Dehnert, M.: Artificial intelligence chatbots as a source of virtual social support: implications for loneliness and anxiety management. Ann. N. Y. Acad. Sci. **1549**, 148–159 (2025)
18. Bansal, G., Zahedi, F.".M."., Gefen, D.: The impact of personal dispositions on information sensitivity, privacy concern and trust in disclosing health information online. Decis. Support. Syst. **49**, 138–150 (2010)
19. Wang, C., Wang, H., Li, Y., Dai, J., Gu, X., Yu, T.: Factors influencing university students' behavioral intention to use generative artificial intelligence: integrating the theory of planned behavior and AI literacy. Int. J. Hum. Comput. Interact. **41**, 6649–6671 (2025)
20. Kessler R.C., Mroczek D.K.: Final versions of our non-specific psychological distress scale (1994)

21. Lin, T.C., Hsu, S.C., et al.: Exploring the relationship between receiving and offering online social support: a dual social support model. Inf. Manag. **52**(3), 371–383 (2015)
22. Oh, H.J., Lauckner, C., Boehmer, J., et al.: Facebooking for health: an examination into the solicitation and effects of health-related social support on social networking sites. Comput. Hum. Behav. **29**(5), 2072–2080 (2013)
23. Lee, C.T., Pan, L.Y., Hsieh, S.H.: Artificial intelligent chatbots as brand promoters: a two-stage structural equation modeling-artificial neural network approach. Internet Res. **32**(4), 1329–1356 (2022)
24. Graham, A.L., Papandonatos, G.D., Kang, H., Moreno, J.L., Abrams, D.B.: Development and validation of the online social support for smokers scale. J. Med. Internet Res. **13**(3), e69 (2011)
25. Stewart, S.A.L.: The MOS social support survey. Soc. Sci. Med. **32**(6), 705–714 (1991)
26. Boss, S.R., Galletta, D.F., Lowry, P.B., Moody, G.D., Polak, P.: What do systems users have to fear? Using fear appeals to engender threats and fear that motivate protective behaviors in users. MIS Q. **39**(4), 837–864 (2015)
27. Wang, B., Rau, P.L.P., Yuan, T.: Measuring user competence in using artificial intelligence: validity and reliability of artificial intelligence literacy scale. Behav. Inform. Technol. **42**(9), 1324–1337 (2023)
28. Bhattacherjee, A.: Understanding information systems continuance: an expectation-confirmation model. MIS Q. **25**(3), 351–370 (2001)
29. Myers, M.D., Newman, M.: The qualitative interview in IS research: examining the craft. Inf. Organ. **17**, 2–26 (2007)
30. Kock, N.: Common method bias in PLS-SEM: a full collinearity assessment approach. Int. J. e-Collab. **11**, 1–10 (2015)
31. Fornell, C., Larcker, D.F.: Structural equation models with unobservable variables and measurement error: algebra and statistics. J. Mark. Res. **18**, 382 (1981)
32. Chin, W.W.: The partial least squares approach for structural equation modeling. In: Modern Methods for Business Research, pp. 295–336. Lawrence Erlbaum Associates Publishers, Mahwah, NJ, US (1998)
33. Henseler, J.: PLS-MGA: a non-parametric approach to partial least squares-based multi-group analysis. In: Gaul, W.A., Geyer-Schulz, A., Schmidt-Thieme, L., Kunze, J. (eds.) Challenges at the Interface of Data Analysis, Computer Science, and Optimization, pp. 495–501. Springer, Berlin, Heidelberg (2012)
34. Myers, M.D.: Qualitative Research in Business & Management. Sage Publications Ltd, Thousand Oaks, CA (2009)

Immersive Technologies and the Metaverse

When Immersion Obscures Ethics: An Empirical Study of End User Perceptions of Data Practices in Metaverse Marketing

Muhammad Irfan Khalid[1,2(✉)]

[1] Department of Information Systems, University of Agder, 4630 Kristiansand, Norway
muhammad.i.khalid@uia.no, mikhalid@singularlogic.eu

[2] Department of Research and Development and Innovation, Singular Logic, 15561 Athens, Greece

Abstract. This study explores how end users perceive ethical issues in metaverse marketing, an area that existing information systems (IS) theories have not sufficiently addressed. We conducted semi-structured interviews with 16 metaverse users from Decentraland, Roblox and Meta Horizon. Using the Gioia methodology, our thematic analysis identified four key dimensions shaping user experience: gaps in privacy awareness and lack of control, problems with consent including dysfunction and fatigue, imbalances of trust and power, and concerns about transparency and fairness. Based on these findings, we make three theoretical contributions grounded in IS research. First, we introduce the concept of immersive blindness, describing how users ability to evaluate privacy trade-offs is significantly constrained in highly immersive environments. Second, we propose spatial capitalism, a conceptually distinct extension of surveillance capitalism that addresses embodied, presence-triggered data extraction in three dimensional (3D) environments; a form of data collection that is qualitatively different from two dimensional (2D) behavioral tracking and requires new theoretical tools. Third, we argue that the sociotechnical design of metaverse platforms disrupts contextual integrity in ways that existing general data protection regulation (GDPR) consent mechanisms do not fully address at the level of user experience, perceived legitimacy, or ethical adequacy even where formal legal compliance is maintained. These contributions have important implications for future IS research on privacy, platform governance and the design of ethical information systems particularly those used for marketing in the metaverse.

Keywords: Metaverse Marketing · Privacy Calculus · Immersive Blindness · User Perceptions · Platform Governance · Sociotechnical Systems.

1 Introduction

The metaverse is reshaping how brands engage consumers. Platforms such as Decentraland, Roblox and Meta Horizon now host virtual stores, sponsored events and immersive branded experiences through which major companies such as Nike, Gucci, Coca-Cola

Published by Springer Nature Switzerland AG 2027
S. Han et al. (Eds.): I3E 2026, LNCS 16912, pp. 155–170, 2027.
https://doi.org/10.1007/978-3-032-38014-2_13

have established permanent commercial presences [1]. The market for virtual goods alone is projected to reach USD 56 billion by 2030 [2]. The nature of data which is generated due to these marketing campaigns makes this commercially significant development also theoretically urgent. Unlike traditional digital marketing, metaverse marketing operates through 3D embodied environments where users produce spatial, behavioral and biometric data simply by being present, not through discrete disclosure acts [3]. These novel marketing practices raise ethical concerns that go beyond conventional digital marketing and require examination from an IS perspective. The design properties of the information technology (IT) artifact not merely platform intentions or user choices determine what data is collected, what users can know about that collection and what risks they face [4]. Yet IS scholarship has produced relatively little empirical work on how ordinary users actually perceive and navigate this immersive and embodied landscape.

That gap carries specific theoretical consequences. For example, the privacy calculus which is one of the most cited frameworks in IS privacy research [5, 28] assumes that users engage in deliberate cost-benefit reasoning before disclosing personal information. That assumption is significantly challenged when a user is cognitively absorbed in a branded virtual experience with no discrete moment at which to weigh costs against benefits. While IS research has examined privacy, consent and fairness in digital contexts [6], the immersive and embodied nature of metaverse environments introduces complications that existing frameworks are not designed to address. The problem is further shaped by platform architecture such that blockchain based environments like Decentraland, corporate walled gardens like Meta Horizon and user-generated content ecosystems like Roblox each instantiate distinct governance philosophies that determine what data is collected, by whom and under what accountability conditions [7]. Prior research has focused primarily on technical architectures and theoretical frameworks [8, 9], thereby leaving the user perspective empirically unexamined. This omission is significant, as user trust fundamentally shapes the commercial viability of these platforms [3] and understanding user perceptions is essential for the development of ethical design principles and effective governance.

This study addresses that gap by examining how end users perceive and experience ethical issues in metaverse marketing across three architecturally distinct platforms. For the purposes of this study, end users are defined broadly as individuals who interact with metaverse platforms in any capacity that involves direct exposure to marketing practices. This includes general users, platform developers participating as users, professionals and governance participants, all of whom encounter and must navigate marketing related data collection in their platform use. This broad definition is consistent with IS research traditions that treat the user perspective as the primary analytical lens regardless of role [26], and is justified by this study's focus on perceived ethical experiences across the full range of platform engagement rather than a narrower consumption only perspective. This study is situated in the European Union (EU) where GDPR grants users formal rights to consent, erasure and data minimization that should in principle constrain the practices described above. Our study is guided by the question: **how do end users in GDPR-regulated contexts perceive and experience ethical issues related to marketing practices across diverse metaverse platform architectures?** We address this question through interviews with 16 metaverse end users and contribute to IS scholarship in three ways: by identifying conditions under which the privacy calculus model is significantly challenged in immersive contexts, by introducing new theoretical constructs grounded in the affordances of immersive IT artifacts, and by offering practical implications for platform designers, marketers and regulators. The rest of the paper is organized as: Sect. 2 develops the theoretical background; Sect. 3 describes the methodology; Sect. 4 presents findings; Sect. 5 discusses implications and limitations while Sect. 6 concludes.

2 Theoretical Background

Understanding why metaverse marketing is an IS problem requires beginning with the IT artifact. Orlikowski and Iacono (2001) [4] argued that IS research must engage with the material properties of technology rather than treating it as a black box. The ethical problems recognized in this study are produced by specific artifact properties such as the spatial continuity of virtual environments, embodied avatar mediated interaction and the capacity to generate behavioral, spatial and biometric data continuously as a function of presence rather than discrete user action. When a user walks through a branded virtual store, the movement trajectories, product gaze duration and social proximity data generated are actually the artifacts of design. The ethical consequences are therefore IS problems in the precise sense which Orlikowski and Iacono intended [4]. The dominant IS privacy lens is the privacy calculus model, formalized for e-commerce contexts by Dinev and Hart (2006) [28].

A related and influential construct, internet users information privacy concerns (IUIPC) was developed by Malhotra et al. (2004) [10] to measure the antecedent privacy concerns that feed into this calculus and was later integrated into the broader APCO framework *(Antecedents → Privacy Concerns → Outcomes)* formalized by Smith et al. (2011) [11]. Bélanger and Crossler (2011) identify this stream as the central contribution of IS privacy research [5]. The privacy calculus model assumes that users can identify disclosure moments and engage in deliberate cost-benefit reasoning. Both conditions are undermined in immersive environments since sensory immersion, social presence and narrative engagement consume the cognitive resources required for privacy reasoning, while data is generated passively and continuously rather than through discrete disclosure acts. Acquisti et al. (2015) [6] and Kokolakis (2017) [12] further note that the privacy calculus struggles when deliberation is compromised. The metaverse represents a particularly severe case of this compromise. The artifact's design properties actively reduce users deliberative capacity, which the model assumes to be intact. We treat this as an empirically observed constraint on privacy reasoning, not as a categorical refutation of the model.

Sociotechnical systems theory (Bostrom and Heinen, 1977) [13] explains why this failure is systemic: consent fails not because users are irrational or platforms simply exploitative but because the sociotechnical configuration of immersive platforms produces failure simultaneously across technical design, organizational interests, user cognition and regulatory frameworks.

Platform governance failures are best analyzed through Nissenbaum's (2010) [14] contextual integrity framework which is adopted in IS research for platform privacy analysis. The framework holds that privacy is respected when information flows match the norms of the context in which information was shared. Metaverse platforms architecturally collapse contextual distinctions such that a user attending a brand sponsored virtual concert concurrently inhabits entertainment, social and commercial context yet the platform provides no architectural signal indicating which informational norms govern each context. This collapse takes platform specific forms. For example, on Decentraland the public blockchain ledger exposes commercial transaction data in ways users associate with decentralization but do not anticipate as disclosure. On Meta Horizon, integration of VR behavioral data with Meta's advertising infrastructure produces cross platform flows grounded in a documented GDPR enforcement history. While on Roblox distributed content creation across operators, developers and brand sponsors produces accountability diffusion that makes identifying responsibility for specific data practices practically impossible.

It is important to distinguish here between four levels at which contextual integrity may break down: (a) formal legal compliance, where platforms satisfy the letter of GDPR through initial registration consent; (b) user understanding, where users are unaware of what data flows occur and why; (c) perceived legitimacy, where users who do understand the flows judge them as unfair or unexpected; and (d) ethical adequacy, where practices may technically comply with regulation but fail to meet the contextual norms users reasonably hold. The findings in this study speak primarily to levels (b), (c) and (d), and our theoretical claims should be interpreted accordingly. These are architecturally differentiated that fundamentally require platform-comparative analysis. The regulatory dimension further connects these IS theoretical concerns to the European context of this study. The EU GDPR requires end users consent to be freely given, specific, informed and unambiguous and grants users rights of access, rectification and erasure (Regulation EU 2016/679) [16]. Yet IS research has examined GDPR primarily in data management and compliance contexts [17] and has not theorized how its consent architecture performs when data collection is triggered by spatial presence rather than discrete user action. This misalignment is compounded by temporal consent decay. Users consented at registration under earlier policy versions even though platforms notify users of subsequent updates but those notifications are routinely clicked through without reading. Formal legal consent is preserved while substantive informed consent erodes over time. IS research on consent fatigue [11, 27] has not addressed this temporal dimension. Documenting its mechanisms and consequences in a metaverse marketing context is one of this study's contributions to IS privacy and regulatory research.

3 Research Methodology

3.1 Data Collection

This study adopts an interpretive qualitative research design treating metaverse users subjective perceptions and lived experiences as the primary unit of analysis. We conducted semi-structured interviews with 16 participants between September 2025 and March 2026. Participants recruited with the help of professional networks, industry collaborations and targeted LinkedIn outreach. Inclusion criteria required active use of at least one of the three focal platforms within the six months preceding interview. The sample was purposively constructed to represent a range of platform experience levels, primary use patterns and marketing exposure contexts. As noted in Sect. 1, end users are defined broadly in this study to include general platform users, developers who actively participate in platform experiences, professionals using Meta Horizon for workplace purposes and governance participants in Decentraland; all of whom are directly exposed to marketing related data collection in their platform activities.

This inclusive definition enables theoretical breadth across diverse exposure contexts, which is the objective of purposive sampling in interpretive IS research [26]. Interviews were conducted via Microsoft Teams platform and lasted between 45 and 60 min. The interview guide was developed through a comprehensive literature review [18] that entailed scenario based questioning protocol to ground discussions in specific platform experiences rather than abstract attitudes. Participants were asked to recount particular marketing encounters, describe their understanding of data collection practices during those encounters and reflect on their experience of consent and transparency mechanisms. Table 1 presents interview participant characteristics.

3.2 Data Analysis

The interview transcripts were analyzed using Gioia methodology [19] which is well suited to theory building from rich qualitative data in IS research contexts [20]. The analysis begin with open coding that stayed close to participants own language producing first order codes grounded in informant experience rather than determined categories. These codes were then systematically grouped into second order themes that reflect researcher level theoretical interpretation before being consolidated into aggregate dimensions that represent this study's core theoretical contributions. MAXQDA data analysis tool was used in order to manage and code all transcripts. All transcripts were coded by a single researcher, with the full code list reviewed against the dataset after the initial coding pass to ensure consistent application. The final data structure presented in Table 2 yielded 38 first order codes 14 second-order themes and 4 aggregate dimensions.

Table 1. Details of the interview participants along with their marketing exposures

ID	Platform	Experience	Primary activities	Marketing exposure	Profile
P1	Decentraland	14 months	Virtual events, NFT trading	Brand activations, virtual wearables	General user
P2	Decentraland	22 months	Land ownership, partnerships	Sponsored spaces, digital fashion	General user
P3	Decentraland	18 months	Gaming, social interaction	In-game advertising	General user
P4	Decentraland	20 months	Virtual shopping, exploration	Brand showrooms, virtual products	General user

(*continued*)

Table 1. (*continued*)

ID	Platform	Experience	Primary activities	Marketing exposure	Profile
P5	Roblox	36 months	Game creation, community	Branded games, sponsorships	Developer/user
P6	Roblox	28 months	Gaming, customization	Virtual items, influencer content	General user
P7	Roblox	42 months	Gaming, purchases	In-game ads, premium features	General user
P8	Meta Horizon	10 months	Social VR, meetups	Branded experiences, ads	General user
P9	Meta Horizon	12 months	Entertainment, events	Sponsored events, product placements	General user
P10	Meta Horizon	16 months	Gaming, social experiences	VR advertising, branded worlds	General user
P11	Decentraland	24 months	Art galleries, exhibitions	Brand art commissions, NFT partnerships	General user
P12	Decentraland	30 months	DAO governance, community	Branded governance proposals	Governance user
P13	Decentraland	16 months	Virtual real estate, leasing	Brand land leasing, sponsored districts	Developer/user
P14	Roblox	48 months	Game development, monetization	Branded game creation, dev partnerships	Developer/user
P15	Roblox	24 months	Competitive gaming, tournaments	Sponsored tournaments, branded prizes	General user
P16	Roblox	32 months	Social hangouts, avatar styling	Branded avatar items, influencer exp.	General user

4 Findings

4.1 Privacy Awareness Gaps and Control Deficits

Across all three platforms, participants knowledge of what data was being collected during branded interactions was significantly thinner than the actual scope of collection. Transactional data, account information and purchase history was generally recognized. Spatial behavioral data was not. When the extent of marketing-related monitoring was explained during the interviews, participants frequently expressed surprise and discomfort. As one participant put it, *"I know they track what I buy but I never thought about them tracking where my avatar goes in their virtual store or what products I look at. That seems invasive when you say it out loud"* [P6]. A Decentraland user was more direct: *"They are watching where I walk in their branded space? Who I hang out with at their virtual events? That is surveillance"* [P3]. These reactions are not simply expressions of discomfort but rather point to an information asymmetry between platforms and users that is structurally produced by the IT artifact's design. The metaverse collects data as a byproduct of presence rather than action which means users have no natural cue to trigger awareness of collection. The GDPR regulatory context created an interesting dynamic among several participants. Users familiar with their rights under the regulation expressed expectations of transparency and control that were not being met which produced a specific form of institutional distrust. *"Under GDPR I have the right to know what data is collected and why. But I have no idea what data Meta Horizon sends to its advertising partners when I visit a branded virtual space. That should not be legal"* [P10].

A qualitatively distinct concern emerged from participants who used platforms for governance or professional purposes. P12 who was a Decentraland governance participant identified a data collection mechanism that had not been anticipated in this study's protocol: *"I vote in DAO proposals and attend governance meetings that brands sponsor. My governance participation, which proposals I support, which I oppose, could be a marketing signal. But it is all on-chain, visible to anyone"* [P12]. This finding is significant because it suggests that in blockchain based platforms the boundary between civic participation and commercial profiling is architecturally absent rather than merely poorly enforced. In the same way another person using Meta Horizon for client meetings raised a related concern about professional data exposure: *"If Meta is using behavioral data from my professional VR meetings for advertising purposes, that is a different kind of violation than personal use. There is nothing in the terms that separates professional from personal data"* [P8]. The phenomenon we term *immersive blindness* emerged across all platforms though its character varied by platform architecture. Participants described a pattern in which cognitive absorption during branded virtual experiences reduced their awareness of data collection with privacy concern returning only after the experience ended: *"When I am in VR experiencing a branded environment, I am just in the moment. I forget about the tech side. But then later I think, 'Wait, what just happened? What did I share with that brand?"* [P8]. This comparative observation implies that immersive blindness is not simply a user characteristic but a platform specific effect produced by particular design affordances.

4.2 Consent Dysfunction and Fatigue

No participant reported reading platform terms of service before accepting them. The pattern was universal and largely unreflective: *"I just clicked 'I Agree.' Everyone does. What choice do you have?"* [P2]. Several participants expressed awareness of the contradiction between their stated privacy values and their actual consent behavior which maps onto what IS researchers have called the privacy paradox [12]. *"I worry about privacy but I also click 'Accept All Cookies' everywhere. I know it is contradictory. I have just given up"* [P7]. Under GDPR this kind of blanket acceptance is supposed to be legally insufficient for consent to be valid. In practice participants experienced no meaningful difference between the GDPR compliant consent prompts they encountered on European platforms and the click through culture that predates GDPR. Beyond initial terms participants frequently entered branded experiences with no additional consent moment. In Meta Horizon branded spaces and sponsored content simply appeared in the environment: *"One day there were just ads and branded spaces in Horizon. No one asked me. They were just there"* [P8]. In Roblox the embedding of branded content within user generated games made it structurally impossible to identify consent decision points: *"In Roblox branded games, there is never a consent moment because it is framed as part of the game not an ad"* [P16]. This observation reveals that consent dysfunction in metaverse marketing is not simply a user interface problem. It is a governance problem produced by the multi actor architecture of platforms that distribute content creation across operators, developers and brands. A temporal dimension of consent dysfunction emerged that was specific to long-term platform users. Several participants described a progressive normalization of consent over time in which the effort invested in reading consent materials at registration had decayed entirely by the time of interview. *"When I first started I would at least try to read what I was consenting to. Now I just click through automatically. The longer you use these platforms the less you care about what you agreed to"* [P12, P13]. This finding has a specific GDPR relevance. The same person also noted that Decentraland had substantially revised its terms of service twice since they registered and that each revision had been accompanied by a notification requiring re-acceptance. *"I got an email saying the terms had changed. I clicked accept on the new ones in about three seconds. I have no idea what changed"* [P12]. The temporal decay of consent is a distinct problem from initial consent dysfunction and one that GDPR's formal notification requirements have not resolved in practice.

4.3 Trust Asymmetries and Power Imbalances

Participants trust in the three platforms varied substantially shaped by reputational factors, architectural characteristics and personal experience with data protection failures. Meta Horizon occupied the lowest trust position across the sample. The explanation given was consistent: Meta's history of privacy scandals including the Cambridge Analytica [29] case had established a priority against which all subsequent platform behavior was interpreted. *"Facebook has had how many data breaches and scandals? Why would I trust them with VR data?"* [P8]. Several participants framed this explicitly in terms of GDPR enforcement. *"Meta has already been fined multiple times by European data protection authorities. Why would I trust that Horizon is any different?"* [P10]. This reputational distrust is significant from an IS perspective because it suggests that trust in a metaverse platform is not determined solely by the platform's own design or policies but by users broader assessments of the corporate entity that controls it. Decentraland generated a qualitatively different trust dynamic such that participants who had chosen it specifically for its decentralized architecture expressed qualified trust in the technical system while acknowledging practical vulnerabilities: *"If someone hacks my wallet and steals my non fungible tokens there is no customer service to call. That terrifies me"* [P4]. The absence of centralized accountability which decentralization theoretically offers as protection against corporate data exploitation, simultaneously removes the recourse mechanisms that users rely on when things go wrong. Several participants articulated this tension unprompted which suggest that it is a structurally salient feature of blockchain based platform governance rather than an incidental concern. Multi-platform participants developed comparative trust frameworks that were notably more sophisticated than those of single platform users. *"I trust Decentraland the most because the rules are in the code. I trust Roblox for basic child safety because they have regulatory exposure. I trust Meta the least because their business model depends on monetizing my attention. But none of them have my full trust. They just have different failure modes"* [P1, P5]. This relational approach to trust calibrated across platforms rather than assessed in isolation suggests that extensive metaverse experience produces a form of platform literacy that may function as a partial protective factor against the worst effects of privacy asymmetry. A participant who attended virtual concerts in Meta Horizon described a qualitatively different kind of distrust from those centered on behavioral or transactional data: *"At a virtual concert I was fully immersed feeling emotions responding physically. If Meta is capturing my biometric responses during that experience and feeding them to concert sponsors they are not just getting my behavior. They are getting my emotional state"* [P9]. This concern for affective data commodification extends the spatial capitalism construct beyond physical movement into the domain of emotional experience and raises questions about whether existing IS privacy frameworks have adequate conceptual tools to address this form of data collection.

4.4 Transparency Deficits and Fairness Concerns

The distinction between branded marketing content and organic user generated content was unclear to a majority of participants, particularly in Decentraland and Roblox. *"Is this someone's creative project or is it an ad? Half the time I cannot tell"* [P2]. In traditional media editorial and advertising content are formally separated which is a requirement that extends to digital advertising under EU regulations. In metaverse environments branded content is spatially integrated into the virtual landscape in ways that defeat those disclosure norms. A brand's virtual store may be architecturally impossible to differentiate from a users creative build. A sponsored game may carry no visible indication of its commercial origins. Participants consistently reported that this ambiguity was not accidental since platforms had commercial incentives to present branded content as organic and they had no technical requirement to do otherwise. The dominant assumption was that targeting was based on demographic information, age and location rather than behavioral inference. *"They probably show me brand ads based on my age and what I have bought before. Beyond that I do not know"* [P6]. When the actual scope of behavioral targeting in metaverse contexts was described to participants including spatial movement in branded areas, gaze duration on products and social proximity during sponsored events the reaction was consistently one of distress. *"Just tell me why you are showing me this ad. 'We are showing you this Nike ad because you visited their virtual store.' That would be honest"* [P7]. Several participants extended the transparency deficit beyond advertising into platform governance. One person identified a form of opacity that is specific to blockchain platforms: *"Decentraland brands sponsor governance proposals. If a brand is funding the infrastructure vote I am participating in and that participation is being used to build a marketing profile the governance process is corrupted. Nobody tells you that"* [P12].

5 Theoretical and Practical Implications

From a theoretical perspective, this study contributes to IS research in three ways. First, it extends the privacy calculus tradition by identifying an empirically observed boundary condition for the model. Specifically, in immersive branded experiences, the technological artifact may reduce users exposure to the privacy-relevant cues that are necessary for awareness and consequently for the formation of privacy concerns [10, 11]. The deliberative cost-benefit process that the privacy calculus assumes [28] is therefore constrained by the very design of the IT artifact which is a condition the model was not originally formulated to address. We term this as "*immersive blindness*", which is a consequence of artifact design rather than user motivation. Our findings suggest that immersive blindness is reinforced by a broader design logic that treats seamlessness, immersion and uninterrupted engagement as inherently desirable. Human computer interaction researchers increasingly argue that "frictionless" or ultra-seamless online experiences can undermine human agency by encouraging habitual action, poorly reflected decisions and forms of engagement that do not align with users values [23–25]. In metaverse marketing, this concern becomes especially important because users do not merely browse or click; they move, look, speak, interact and socialize within immersive commercial environments. The seamlessness of these environments can therefore obscure the moments at which users embodied behavior becomes datafied and commercially valuable. In metaverse marketing, friction may be ethically necessary because immersion reduces the users capacity to recognize and evaluate data extraction as it occurs. This implies that dual process extensions of the privacy calculus are needed for next-generation computing environments and carries regulatory consequences since GDPR's consent framework assumes the deliberative mode that immersive blindness structurally bypasses.

Second, we introduce "*spatial capitalism*" as an IS construct extending Zuboff's (2023) [21] surveillance capitalism into immersive 3D environments. We justify spatial capitalism as a conceptually distinct construct rather than treating the metaverse as a new context for surveillance capitalism, on three grounds. First, spatial capitalism extracts embodied data, including physical movement, gaze direction and physiological response whereas surveillance capitalism extracts behavioral data such as clicks, searches and purchase history. Second, spatial capitalism is triggered by a users presence in a virtual space, whereas surveillance capitalism is triggered by a discrete user action such as a click or a page visit. This removes the disclosure moment that surveillance capitalism's behavioral modification logic depends on. Third, in spatial capitalism the avatar is the users presence in the environment not a proxy for it, so there is no perceptual separation between the user and the data generating entity, unlike in 2D interfaces where a profile or account stands in for the user. Together, these three differences, embodied rather than behavioral data, presence-triggered rather than action-triggered collection and the absence of user-avatar separation produce an extraction logic that surveillance capitalism does not theorize and that requires a dedicated construct.

Third, we develop "*contextual integrity breakdown*" as an IS governance failure mode. As noted in Sect. 2, our claims about GDPR and contextual integrity concern primarily levels of user understanding, perceived legitimacy and ethical adequacy not formal legal compliance, which platforms may technically satisfy through registration consent. The governance problem we identify is that GDPR's action-triggered consent architecture does not address the continuous, presence-triggered collection that follows from initial consent. Technical compliance at registration does not govern the continuous data collection that follows during the user experience. Two further findings extend these contributions: the temporal decay of consent, whereby click-through normalization separates formal legal consent from actual platform practices; and the governance-commercial conflation (P12), wherein blockchain civic participation data becomes commercial marketing data with no transaction boundary marking the conversion.

From a practical point of view, there are several implications for the involved entities in this metaverse marketing ecosystem. For platform designers, users must be provided with contextual consent triggers at the point of entry into branded spaces rather than just at registration; this aligns consent with actual data collection, often referred to as dynamic consent. This points to the potential role of design frictions in ethical metaverse marketing. Design frictions intentionally insert moments of resistance into otherwise seamless flows, helping users slow down, reflect and make more deliberate choices [23]. Rather than viewing friction as a usability problem, our findings suggest that carefully designed friction may support user agency by making data practices visible when they become contextually relevant. Such frictions could include context-sensitive prompts when gaze, movement, proximity, voice, gestures, or interaction patterns are collected for marketing purposes. This is especially important in cognitively demanding environments where users may struggle to evaluate privacy trade-offs in real time. Similarly, real-time session-level privacy dashboards would tackle the awareness asymmetry which is detailed in Sect. 4.1. Blockchain platforms require architectural separation of governance participation data from commercial data streams.

For marketers, spatial behavioral data collected during branded experiences almost certainly constitutes personal data under GDPR and its collection without specific consent corresponds to unaddressed legal exposure. Users who feel surveilled in branded environments also develop negative brand associations, which is a commercial risk independent of regulatory penalty. For regulators, GDPR's consent architecture requires extension to presence-triggered data collection. The European Data Protection Board's shift toward opt-in requirements for web behavioral tracking [30] provides a partial model; following that equivalent guidance for spatial and biometric data in immersive environments is needed. By linking *immersive blindness* to design friction, we extend current discussions of metaverse governance. Existing consent mechanisms often assume that users can understand data practices through privacy notices, consent banners, or abstract disclosures. However, our findings show that in immersive environments, the problem is not only a lack of information, but also the weakening of users capacity to recognize when information matters. A capacity-by-design approach would therefore evaluate metaverse platforms not only by whether they provide transparency or obtain formal consent, but also by whether they preserve users ability to pause, understand

and act in accordance with their values. This suggests that ethical metaverse marketing requires governance mechanisms that are embedded in the interaction itself, rather than separated from the experience of immersion.

Table 2. Data structure using Gioia method showing the main findings

Representative First Order Codes	Second Order Themes	Aggregate Dimensions
1. Unaware of spatial/behavior tracking 2. Blockchain transparency paradox (*public ledger*) 3. Meta cross platform data integration fears 4. VR biometric and gaze data concerns 5. GDPR expectations unmet in immersive contexts 6. Immersive absorption hides privacy awareness 7. No meaningful control over marketing data 8. Governance participation as commercial signal 9. Professional context data exposed to advertising 10. Intergenerational awareness gap/parental concern	• Limited understanding of behavior tracking • Platform specific privacy concerns • Immersive blindness phenomenon • Perceived lack of data control • GDPR entitlement vs. platform reality gap • Governance surveillance conflation	Privacy Awareness Gaps and Control Deficits
11. Terms of service never read 12. Consent perceived as functionally unavoidable 13. Branded spaces entered without consent moment 14. Permission prompt exhaustion 15. Creator-side consent chain fragmentation 16. Temporal decay of initial consent 17. GDPR re-consent notifications clicked through 18. Parental proxy consent ineffective for minors	• Click-through consent culture • Invisible marketing agreements • Permission prompt fatigue • Fragmented multi-actor consent chains • Temporal consent decay in evolving platforms • Intergenerational consent deficits	Consent Dysfunction and Fatigue

(*continued*)

Table 2. (*continued*)

Representative First Order Codes	Second Order Themes	Aggregate Dimensions
19. Meta's regulatory and reputational history 20. Blockchain security vs. recourse absence 21. Cross platform data aggregation fears 22. Learned helplessness and resignation 23. GDPR enforcement failures referenced by users 24. Comparative / relational trust hierarchies 25. Emotional and biometric data distrust 26. Professional data asymmetry concern	• Platform credibility variations • Cross-platform data flow fears • Learned helplessness • Structural power concentration • Relational comparative trust • Emotional data commodification fears	Trust Asymmetries and Power Imbalances
27. Cannot distinguish ads from organic content 28. Algorithmic targeting criteria opaque 29. Demographic targeting assumed 30. Manipulative game design in financed experiences 31. Accountability diffused across platform actors 32. Governance integrated branded content opacity 33. Flow state targeting in competitive contexts 34. Cross platform inference without disclosure 35. Emotional state targeting in entertainment events 36. Predatory design targeting minors cognitive limits	• Content ambiguity and marketing disguise • Algorithmic opacity in ad delivery • Perceived manipulation • Accountability gaps • Governance commercial conflation • Flow state and emotional targeting • Cross platform inference opacity	Transparency Deficits and Fairness Concerns

5.1 Limitations and Future Research

With 16 participants, the sample falls within the 15 to 30 range typically associated with theoretical saturation in Gioia-based research, a judgment supported here by the absence of new first-order codes in the final four interviews and is comparable to published IS research using similar methods in related contexts [22]. The findings should be read as theoretical propositions grounded in a purposive sample rather than as claims about how common these phenomena are across the broader population of metaverse users. The constructs we introduce are theoretically transferable rather than statistically generalizable and validation through larger-scale survey or experimental designs with samples of 100 or more remains an important next step.

Restricting the sample to EU jurisdictions made the GDPR context analytically tractable, but it also means that findings cannot speak to users in other regulatory environments. China's Personal Information Protection Law, the US patchwork of state-level regulation and Brazil's general personal data protection law each create substantially different conditions for how users understand and experience data privacy and comparative research across these contexts would be a valuable extension of this work. The study is also bounded by timing: platform privacy policies changed before and during data collection and the gap between when participants first registered on their platform and when they were interviewed was not controlled. Longitudinal research tracking user perceptions across policy changes would help clarify how consent understanding evolves over time. Finally, this study relied on what participants reported without auditing what platforms actually collect. Combining user interviews with a technical review of real platform data practices would give a more accurate picture of the gap between platform behavior and user understanding.

6 Conclusion

This study examined how end users experience ethical issues in metaverse marketing through 16 interviews across Decentraland, Roblox and Meta Horizon. The findings reveal that existing IS privacy frameworks face significant structural challenges in immersive contexts. The metaverse artifact's design reduces users capacity for the deliberative reasoning that the privacy calculus assumes, platform architectures distribute consent responsibility across multiple actors in ways that erode meaningful consent and GDPR's action-triggered consent architecture does not address presence-triggered data collection. These are empirically grounded observations that point to the need for theoretical extension rather than definitive refutations of existing frameworks. To capture these dynamics, this study introduces *immersive blindness, spatial capitalism and contextual integrity breakdown* as theoretically grounded starting points for future IS research and regulatory development in immersive digital marketing environments.

Acknowledgement. This research was funded by the European Union's Horizon Europe research and innovation programme "Training Young Researchers on Shaping Metaverse for Business and Social Value (AGORA)" under the Marie Skłodowska-Curie grant agreement No 101119937.

References

1. Dwivedi, Y.K., et al.: Metaverse marketing: how the metaverse will shape the future of consumer research and practice. Psychol. Mark. **40**(4), 750–776 (2023)
2. Business Insider: Luxury NFTs could become a $56 billion market by 2030 (2022)

3. Hadi, R., Melumad, S., Park, E.S.: The metaverse: a new digital frontier for consumer behavior. J. Consum. Psychol. **34**(1), 142–166 (2024)
4. Orlikowski, W.J., Iacono, C.S.: Research commentary: desperately seeking the 'IT' in IT research. Inf. Syst. Res. **12**(2), 121–134 (2001)
5. Bélanger, F., Crossler, R.E.: Privacy in the digital age: a review of information privacy research in information systems1. MIS Q. **35**(4), 1017–A36 (2011)
6. Acquisti, A., Brandimarte, L., Loewenstein, G.: Privacy and human behavior in the age of information. Science. **347**(6221), 509–514 (2015)
7. Nambisan, S., Wright, M., Feldman, M.: The digital transformation of innovation and entrepreneurship. Res. Policy. **48**(8), 103773 (2019)
8. Di Pietro, R., Cresci, S.: Metaverse: security and privacy issues. In: 2021 Third IEEE International Conference on Trust, Privacy and Security in Intelligent Systems and Applications (TPS-ISA), pp. 281–288. IEEE (2021)
9. Wang, Y., Su, Z., Zhang, N., et al.: A survey on metaverse: fundamentals, security, and privacy. IEEE Commun. Surv. Tutor. **25**(1), 319–352 (2023)
10. Malhotra, N.K., Kim, S.S., Agarwal, J.: Internet users' information privacy concerns (IUIPC): the construct, the scale, and a causal model. Inf. Syst. Res. **15**(4), 336–355 (2004)
11. Smith, H.J., Dinev, T., Xu, H.: Information privacy research: an interdisciplinary review1. MIS Q. **35**(4), 989–A27 (2011)
12. Kokolakis, S.: Privacy attitudes and privacy behaviour: a review of current research on the privacy paradox phenomenon. Comput. Secur. **64**, 122–134 (2017)
13. Bostrom, R.P., Heinen, J.S.: MIS problems and failures: a socio-technical perspective. MIS Q. **1**(3), 17–32 (1977)
14. Nissenbaum, H.: Privacy in Context: Technology, Policy, and the Integrity of Social Life. Stanford University Press (2010)
15. Xu, H., Teo, H.H., Tan, B.C., Agarwal, R.: Research note: effects of individual self-protection, industry self-regulation, and government regulation on privacy concerns. Inf. Syst. Res. **23**(4), 1342–1363 (2012)
16. Regulation (EU) 2016/679 of the European Parliament and of the Council (General Data Protection Regulation). Official Journal of the European Union, L 119, 27 April 2016 (2016)
17. Politou, E., Alepis, E., Patsakis, C.: Forgetting personal data and revoking consent under the GDPR: challenges and proposed solutions. J. Cybersecur. **4**(1), tyy001 (2018)
18. Khalid, M.I., Pappas, I., Mahmoud, M., Rizou, S.: The convergence of digital marketing, ethics, and the metaverse: an integrative systematic literature review of reviews. AIS Trans. Hum. Comput. Interact. **18**(2), 269–318 (2026)
19. Gioia, D.A., Corley, K.G., Hamilton, A.L.: Seeking qualitative rigor in inductive research: notes on the Gioia methodology. Organ. Res. Methods. **16**(1), 15–31 (2013)
20. Langley, A., Abdallah, C.: Templates and turns in qualitative studies of strategy and management. Res. Methodol. Strateg. Manag. **6**, 201–235 (2011)
21. Zuboff, S.: The age of surveillance capitalism. In: Social Theory Re-Wired, pp. 203–213. Routledge (2023)
22. Roider, H., Widjaja, T.: Privacy concerns in the metaverse context: an examination of real and virtual identity (2025)
23. Bermúdez, J.P.: Autonomy by design: preserving human autonomy in AI decision-support. Philos. Technol. **38**, 97 (2025)
24. Ericson, J.: Reimagining the role of friction in experience design. J. User Exp. **17**(4), 131–139 (2022)
25. Mathiesen, H.: What's human agency, anyway? Overly seamless UX routinely erodes user agency. UX Collective (2025)
26. Walsham, G.: Interpretive case studies in IS research: nature and method. Eur. J. Inf. Syst. **4**(2), 74–81 (1995)

27. Obar, J.A., Oeldorf-Hirsch, A.: The biggest lie on the internet: ignoring the privacy policies and terms of service policies of social networking services. Inf. Commun. Soc. **23**(1), 128–147 (2020)
28. Dinev, T., Hart, P.: An extended privacy calculus model for e-commerce transactions. Inf. Syst. Res. **17**(1), 61–80 (2006)
29. Isaak, J., Hanna, M.J.: User data privacy: Facebook, Cambridge Analytica, and privacy protection. Computer. **51**(8), 56–59 (2018)
30. European Data Protection Board: Report of the work undertaken by the cookie banner taskforce. Adopted 17 January 2023 (2023). Available at: https://www.edpb.europa.eu

Making the Metaverse Viable: Vendor Framings and the Conditional Realisation of Sustainable Value

Iordanis Lainidis[1,2](✉)

[1] University of Agder, Kristiansand, Norway
iordanis.lainidis@uia.no
[2] Maggioli S.p.a., Rimini, Italy

Abstract. Extended reality (XR) and digital twin (DT) solutions are increasingly presented as technologies that can create organisational value and support sustainability. Yet these claims are often made in emerging and uncertain markets, where clients may not immediately understand what the technologies are for, how they may generate value, or under what conditions that value becomes relevant for sustainability. Vendors are therefore important because they translate XR/DT possibilities into client-facing value propositions. However, less is known about how vendors present these technologies as valuable for clients and connect such value claims to sustainability. This qualitative exploratory study draws on semi-structured interviews with 16 domain experts involved in the development, provision, implementation, or organisational use of Metaverse-related solutions. The data were analysed using reflexive thematic analysis. The findings identify a vendor-side conditional value pathway in which vendors first made XR/DT commercially recognisable and justifiable and then emphasised technological possibilities. Whether these possibilities became practically valuable depended on organisational, technical, material, and ecosystem conditions. Sustainability implications were associated with substitution, reconfigured participation, and context-dependent trade-offs. The study therefore interprets XR/DT as conditional sustainability mediators. Particular uses can connect technological possibilities to sustainability implications, but these implications are neither inherent nor automatic. The study contributes an account of how vendors connect XR/DT value propositions to sustainability, while recognising that the findings reflect participants' accounts rather than independently verified client outcomes or sustainability impacts.

Keywords: Metaverse · Extended Reality · Digital Twin · Value Realisation · Sustainability · IT Business Value · Information Systems

1 Introduction

Digital technologies are increasingly discussed in information systems (IS) research as tools that can support sustainability. This discussion has contributed to the emergence of digital sustainability as a broader perspective for examining the environmental, social,

Published by Springer Nature Switzerland AG 2027
S. Han et al. (Eds.): I3E 2026, LNCS 16912, pp. 171–191, 2027.
https://doi.org/10.1007/978-3-032-38014-2_14

and economic implications of digital technologies [1]. At the same time, organisations face growing regulatory and societal pressure to improve their sustainability performance [2]. This makes it important to understand not only how digital technologies may support sustainability goals, but also how they generate value for the organisations that adopt them since their continued adoption and use are likely to depend on the organisational value they create. Information technology (IT) business value research is relevant here because it examines how the potential value of digital technologies is converted into realised organisational value through their implementation and use within organisations [3]. One emerging area in which IT business value and sustainability are increasingly examined is the Metaverse and its foundational technologies, such as extended reality (XR) and digital twins (DTs) [4].

The Metaverse has been described as an evolving concept that fuses physical reality with digital virtuality, while XR integrates the physical and digital to different degrees through virtual reality (VR), mixed reality, and augmented reality (AR) [5]. In industrial settings, the Industrial Metaverse has been described as an immersive and data-driven ecosystem built on technologies such as AR, VR, DTs, and artificial intelligence (AI) to connect physical and digital environments [6]. XR allows users to visualise and interact with virtual models, while DTs connect physical entities to their digital counterparts to simulate behaviour, monitor real-time operating conditions, and generate analytical insights [7]. These capabilities are therefore relevant to organisational activities such as training, monitoring, and remote assistance.

Existing research has begun to examine value creation among organisations within Metaverse ecosystems [8]. Research has also considered how value is realised in specific XR/DT applications. For example, an empirical study has examined how value is realised in shop-floor applications of DT-based AR [9]. However, less attention has been paid to how vendors present XR/DT value propositions to client organisations and to the conditions under which the proposed value becomes relevant for sustainability. This issue is important for emerging technologies because client organisations may be unfamiliar with what these technologies can offer [10]. They may lack the expertise required to identify appropriate organisational processes in which these technologies can be applied, and to connect the technologies' capabilities to their concrete organisational needs. Vendors therefore not only provide technical solutions but also seek to support the adoption of these complex technologies and the potential realisation of organisational value within client organisations. This vendor perspective is particularly relevant because digital technologies are increasingly developed and implemented through wider ecosystems involving technology providers, complementors, service firms, and users [11].

To address this gap, this study asks: How do vendor organisations present XR and DT solutions as sources of value for client organisations, and what conditions shape whether this value becomes relevant for sustainability?

The main research question is addressed through the following secondary research questions:

SRQ1: How do vendors make XR/DT solutions commercially recognisable and justifiable for client organisations?

SRQ2: Which technological possibilities do vendors emphasise when presenting the value of XR/DT solutions?
SRQ3: What conditions shape whether XR/DT value can be realised in practice?
SRQ4: What sustainability implications are associated with XR/DT solutions?

The study addresses these questions through semi-structured interviews with domain experts possessing substantial knowledge of the vendor side of the XR/DT solutions sector. The interview data were analysed using reflexive thematic analysis.

The study contributes to IS research by showing that XR/DT sustainability should not be treated as a direct or guaranteed technological outcome. Instead, XR/DT value becomes relevant to sustainability through a conditional value pathway involving commercial translation, technological possibilities, organisational, technical, material, and ecosystem conditions, and context-dependent sustainability implications. By unpacking this pathway, the study links IT business value research with digital sustainability and shows how vendors shape the connection between emerging technologies, potential organisational value, and sustainability.

2 Background

IT business value research examines how the application of information technology affects organisational performance [12]. A central argument in the literature is that IT does not create value on its own, but as part of a business value-creating process in which technological resources interact with organisational resources, business processes, and management practices [13]. Consequently, IT-based value may take time to emerge following adoption, learning, and organisational adjustment, while its effects can be difficult to isolate and attribute directly to the technology [14]. Value realisation is therefore shaped by factors such as IT use, organisational and process change, information sharing, organisational capabilities, and complementary resources [12, 13]. From this perspective, the capabilities associated with emerging technologies such as XR and DTs represent potential sources of organisational value.

Digital sustainability is defined as the development and deployment of digital resources and artefacts towards improving environmental, social, and economic welfare [15]. This perspective brings digitalisation and sustainability into the same analytical frame by directing attention to how digital resources are developed, deployed, governed, and used in relation to sustainability objectives [16]. The sustainability relevance of digital technologies is therefore not intrinsic to the technologies themselves, but depends on how they are configured and used within organisational and wider institutional contexts [16]. Accordingly, the sustainability implications of digital technologies may be desirable or undesirable, intended or unintended, and may involve tensions within and between sustainability objectives [1].

Together, IT business value and digital sustainability offer complementary perspectives for this study. Vendor value propositions describe the potential organisational value of XR/DT solutions: IT business value provides a basis for understanding how such value may be realised, while digital sustainability directs attention to its environmental, social, and economic implications. This combination enables the study to examine how vendors present XR/DT as sources of organisational value and how that value may become relevant to sustainability.

3 Research Method

3.1 Research Design

This study followed a qualitative exploratory interview strategy in multiple organisational contexts. It sought to understand how professionals involved in XR and DT solutions described how these technologies were applied in organisations, the value they associated with these solutions for client organisations, the challenges affecting their implementation, and their possible sustainability implications. Semi-structured interviews were appropriate because they enabled participants to explain, from their professional positions, these issues in detail [17].

The interview guide was initially developed around a broader exploratory interest in how metaverse-related technologies, specifically XR and DTs, enter organisations and how their use may affect organisational sustainability. Through iterative engagement with the interview material, the research question was subsequently refined to focus on how vendors present XR/DT solutions as sources of value and how that value becomes relevant to sustainability. This refined focus remained within the substantive areas addressed by the original interview guide. The resulting interview data were analysed using reflexive thematic analysis, following Braun and Clarke's approach [18] and informed by Byrne's worked example [19].

3.2 Sampling and Recruitment

Participants were selected through purposive sampling based on the relevance of their professional knowledge and experience and on their potential to provide rich information relevant to the research question [20]. Relevant experience included involvement in the development, provision, commercialisation, implementation, research, or organisational application of XR and DT solutions. Recruitment followed two pathways. First, potential interviewees were identified through LinkedIn using keywords such as "metaverse", "digital twin", "extended reality", "virtual reality", and "augmented reality". Public profiles were reviewed to assess relevance, and suitable participants were contacted through private messages and invited to participate. Second, potential participants were identified through colleagues and professional contacts associated with the author's industrial supervisor's company. These pathways led to the recruitment of 16 domain experts across industrial, cultural, and creative contexts, who took part in 15 initial interviews and one additional follow-up interview (P5). One initial interview involved two participants from the same organisation. Most participants worked directly for organisations that developed or provided XR/DT solutions, while two were not directly employed by vendors but had substantial experience of, or close engagement with, the vendor side of the sector. One represented an XR industry association and ecosystem intermediary, while the other had direct experience as a client and co-producer of XR solutions. Table 1 summarises their professional and organisational backgrounds. Organisational size was grouped as micro (<10 employees), small (10–49), medium (50–249), and large (250 or more).

Table 1. Overview of participants and their organisational contexts

ID	Position / Role	XR/DT Exper. (Years)	Organisational Size	Domain / Sector	Actor Type
P1	CTO	10	Medium	Industrial / enterprise	Vendor
P2	Head of Research	2	Medium	Industrial / enterprise	Vendor
P3	Project Manager	2	Medium	High-tech ICT / R&D firm	Vendor
P4	Innovation Officer	2.5	Medium	ICT / telecom / industrial IoT-OT solutions	Vendor
P5	COO	6.5	Medium	Location-based VR platform and content studio	Vendor
P6	(1) Head of Business Development, (2) CTO	10	Micro	Metaverse / immersive-tech studio	Vendor
P7	Founding partner	3	Micro	Art-tech / social-impact / climate-oriented creative organisation	Vendor
P8	Managing Director	9	Micro	XR industry association / ecosystem intermediary	European XR industry association
P9	Chief Innovation Officer	7	Large	Public-sector digital solutions and R&D	Vendor
P10	Researcher and Consultant	8	Large	Public-sector digital solutions and R&D	Vendor
P11	Owner	9	Micro	Cultural heritage / creative industries digital storytelling	Vendor
P12	CEO	6.5	Micro	Cultural heritage / museum XR design and technical art services	Vendor

(*continued*)

Table 1. *(continued)*

ID	Position / Role	XR/DT Exper. (Years)	Organisational Size	Domain / Sector	Actor Type
P13	CEO	6	Small	XR development/services	Vendor
P14	Technical Manager	16	Large	Consulting / digital transformation	Vendor
P15	Digital Technology and Development Lead	10	Micro	Cultural heritage / archives / library	Client/XR Co-producer

3.3 Data Collection

Interviews were conducted online and recorded via the Microsoft Teams application and lasted 44 min on average. Oral informed consent was obtained and recorded at the beginning of each interview. Participants were informed of their right to withdraw while their data remained identifiable. Names and other identifying information were removed from the transcripts, and the research data were stored and handled in accordance with the University of Agder's data-protection requirements. The interviews were open-ended and there were no "right" or "wrong" answers. The semi-structured interview guide provided an initial set of topics and questions, while the order, wording, and follow-up questions remained flexible and were adapted to the information provided by each participant. The main topics included participants' professional involvement with XR/DT technologies, the solutions and use cases provided by their organisations, organisational and client value, adoption and implementation challenges, effects on client organisations, and potential sustainability implications. Probing questions were used to obtain clarification or further detail when responses were unclear or analytically relevant. For example, when a participant discussed the increasing maturity of DT/XR through AI-enabled analytics, prediction, and asset failure forecasting, the interviewer followed up by asking how such solutions were positioned to clients. This prompted further discussion of cost reduction, remote inspection, safety, and sustainability.

4 Theoretical Assumptions of the Reflexive Thematic Analysis

When conducting thematic analysis, epistemological and analytical assumptions should be made explicit because they shape how the researcher understands and interprets the data [19]. The following paragraphs present the assumptions guiding this study in accordance with the "continua" outlined by Byrne [19].

This study adopted a constructionist epistemology. Participants' accounts were not treated as reports of fixed or objective meanings of XR/DT, but as situated professional interpretations shaped by their roles, backgrounds, organisational settings, and sector-specific understandings of the technologies. Meaning and meaningfulness were central to the coding process and development of the themes. Differences in language and framing were treated as analytically meaningful. Accordingly, theme development was guided not only by the recurrence of ideas, but also by their relevance to how XR/DT value and sustainability were understood across different contexts.

An experiential orientation was adopted because the study aimed to understand participants' experiences, professional judgements, and their interpretations of the value associated with XR/DT technologies. The analysis was predominantly inductive, as codes and candidate themes were developed through repeated engagement with the interview data. However, when clarification was needed, the environmental, social, and economic dimensions of the triple bottom line [21] were introduced to create a shared understanding of what sustainability entailed. The triple bottom line and its dimensions were not applied as deductive coding categories during the analysis.

Both semantic and latent coding were used to interpret the data. Semantic coding captured participants' claims regarding XR/DT applications, associated value, implementation challenges, and sustainability implications. Latent coding was used to interpret underlying assumptions, tensions, and relationships through which participants connected XR/DT value with sustainability.

5 Data Preparation and Analysis

Data preparation, coding and analysis followed the methodological guidance in [18], with Byrne's worked example providing additional procedural guidance [19]. Familiarisation involved listening to each interview before and during transcription. Automatically generated transcripts were checked against the recordings, corrected, and anonymised. Initial coding was conducted in Microsoft Word using comments to retain links between codes and transcript excerpts. Codes were then transferred to an Excel file containing the participant identifier, excerpt, assigned code, and analytical notes.

Coding was iterative. Codes were revised through repeated engagement with the data as their relevance to the research questions, relationships with other codes, and position within the developing thematic structure became clearer. For example, the initial code "XR promotes realistic and immersive viewing of 3D products limiting the need for physical prototyping" was revised to "XR product visualisation can reduce the need for physical prototypes before production".

To support theme development, codes were temporarily organised into broader groups such as "training", "decision making", and "safety". These provisional groups helped identify relationships between codes and supported the development of candidate themes and subthemes. The thematic structure was later reviewed to assess whether each theme and subtheme had a clear central organising concept. This process led to revisions of theme and subtheme names and the removal of three subthemes whose analytical points could be incorporated elsewhere. The final themes were defined and organised into a vendor-side value pathway presented in the following section.

Table 2 illustrates the analytical progression from selected transcript excerpts and codes to subthemes, final themes, and research questions. It is intended to demonstrate analytical traceability rather than provide an exhaustive codebook. Numerical frequency was not used to determine theme importance because themes were developed according to patterned meaning and analytical relevance to the research questions rather than prevalence alone.

6 Findings

The findings are organised into five themes that together form a vendor-side conditional value pathway, moving from commercial translation and technological possibilities to client-side and ecosystem conditions shaping value realisation, and finally to sustainability implications conditional on how the technologies are implemented and used.

Table 2. Illustrative analytical progression from participant excerpt to final theme structure

Participant Excerpt	Code	Subtheme	Theme - SRQ
P11: It can, in some cases, be subscription-based, while offering additional services to end users.	DT solutions can be offered through a subscription model	Making offerings commercially recognisable	Theme 1: Making XR/DT commercially viable - SRQ1
P4: The greatest value we have seen, and the reason companies prefer it as a solution, is the saving of time and cost, improved productivity, better quality control, and a major improvement in training.	Vendors target organisational processes where benefits are visible and easier to justify	Selective targeting due to uneven market maturity	
P3: The physical trial site has capacity for three teams over six months … with virtual trial sites, the limitation becomes what the server can support.	Virtual trial sites shift capacity constraints from physical access to server capacity	Viability depends on configuring the use environment	

(continued)

Table 2. (*continued*)

Participant Excerpt	Code	Subtheme	Theme - SRQ
P5: Users can customise a photorealistic 3D avatar… because LBVR is not easily shareable on social media, the giveaway provides shareable content from the experience.	LBVR visibility through well-known IP and personalised shareable content	Creating interest through experiential visibility	
P2: Instead of people standing in hazardous areas, you can have someone remotely controlling things, with AR and AI assistance.	XR enables remote operation in hazardous industrial environments	Making inaccessible, dangerous or hidden realities experientially available	Theme 2: Generated and Malleable Realities - SRQ2
P10: Transitioning from 2D CAD to 3D helps pinpoint faults, conflicts, and a lack of meeting specifications.	During design XR helps identify faults, conflicts, and unmet specifications	Turning products, spaces, and procedures into testable simulations	
P4: It reduces a lot of back-and-forth, communications and misunderstandings, because we all see the same image at the same time	Shared visual information accelerates decisions and reduces errors	Creating a shared view for remote coordination	
P14: We have enough data … 3D models, CAD models … and analytical data. Everything needs to be integrated into a single platform.	DT use depends on integrating existing digital assets within a single platform	Integrating XR/DT into client technical systems	Theme 3: XR/DT use requires organisational and technical reworking - SRQ3

(*continued*)

Table 2. (*continued*)

Participant Excerpt	Code	Subtheme	Theme - SRQ
P8: It still represents, for a lot of companies, a fundamental change initiative to how they do training, whether they do it in-house, who runs it, and who manages the equipment for it	VR training adoption requires organisational changes to training, responsibility, and equipment management	Reworking organisational processes and roles around XR/DT use	
P15: Even having ten headsets is difficult … would I bring them here for a twenty-minute experience?	Limited headset availability constrains the scaling of group VR experiences	The material reality of XR/DT: hardware and infrastructure as barriers to use	
P6: What data can you take with you from one application to another? … This does not happen automatically with the current technology.	Limited cross-platform data and asset portability creates interoperability barriers	Interoperability shapes XR/DT cross-system viability	Theme 4: Ecosystem interdependence shapes XR/DT viability - SRQ3
P12: Museums are still a little bit dependent on other experts like externals to manage the headsets and to provide updates to applications.	Dependence on external experts for headset management and software updates	External support sustains XR/DT viability	
P1: You spare physical prototypes … you already see them realistically and immersively in 3D without producing them.	XR product visualisation can reduce the need for physical prototypes	Sustainability through substitution	Theme 5: Sustainability as conditional, indirect and context-dependent - SRQ4
P13: They look down and see the height … and are then asked to do hazard identification … or for fire protocol.	XR simulation training prepares workers for safety scenarios	Reconfiguring participation through training, learning, accessibility, and inclusion	

(*continued*)

Table 2. (*continued*)

Participant Excerpt	Code	Subtheme	Theme - SRQ
P9: Environmental sustainability is a matter of the context in which the solution is used and what we want to do with it.	DT environmental value depends on context-specific use	Ambiguity, trade-offs, and context-dependence	

6.1 Making XR/DT Commercially Viable

Commercial viability was an initial condition in the vendor-side value pathway, meaning that before presenting XR/DT as producing organisational benefits, vendors had to make these technologies understandable, purchasable, and justifiable to clients.

The first form, "Making offerings commercially recognisable", involved translating unfamiliar technologies into familiar commercial and organisational forms. For example, one participant described XR streaming as a move away from early AR/VR projects and proofs of concept towards a more productised model, sold through "a sort of either licensed or seat-based model" and described as "an established model, a seat-based subscription" (P1). Similar translations appeared in service-based framings, where XR/DT was presented as "AR remote support as a service", "VR training modules" and hybrid IoT-Metaverse packages for monitoring or inspection (P4). In these accounts, XR/DT became commercially legible by being connected both to familiar revenue models and to established organisational functions such as support, training, monitoring, inspection, and problem resolution.

The second form, "Selective targeting due to uneven market maturity", shows that vendors targeted specific use cases and markets where value was easier to demonstrate. Training was one of the clearest examples. One participant explained that VR works best for "process-based things" where users need "muscle memory to a sequence" such as health and safety training or preparing an operating room. Because these procedures are relatively standardised, the participant described health and safety training as "the easiest area for VR to sell" (P8). This suggests that vendors responded to uneven market maturity by concentrating on use cases that were comparatively established and easier to sell, rather than presenting XR/DT as equally viable across all applications.

The third form, "Viability depends on configuring the use environment", shows that XR/DT offerings became commercially viable only when the environment of use could be configured to support practical deployment. In the case of virtual trial sites, one participant explained that a physical trial site could host only "up to three teams for a period of six months". By creating a virtual trial site, the constraint changed so that "the problem is then limited only to what your server can handle" rather than how many physical cars were available for testing (P3). This shows that viability could improve when the use environment shifted from a "limited in capacity" setting to a more scalable digital one, although the capacity limitation was relocated rather than eliminated.

The fourth form, "Creating interest through experiential visibility", shows how vendors presented XR as a way of attracting attention and renewing interest in cultural offerings. One participant described digital experiences as bringing people into physical institutions, functioning as "its own revenue stream" but also as "a hook to attract people" (P7). Another participant explained that museums with static offerings face "a big gap" between visits because returning visitors may find "nothing new to see" (P12). In this context, XR made cultural offerings experientially visible in new ways and renewed what visitors could experience without requiring substantial changes to the physical site itself. A similar mechanism appeared in product sales, where XR allowed potential customers to "experience your product" and "visualize the outcome or even simulate an experience with the outcome", particularly when the product was expensive, customised, or not readily available in physical form (P10). In both settings, experiential visibility made offerings more tangible and engaging, thereby creating or renewing interest that could support visits, purchasing decisions, and revenue opportunities.

Together, Theme 1 answers SRQ1 by showing that vendors made XR/DT commercially viable through four forms of commercial translation. They translated offerings into recognisable and justifiable forms, targeted comparatively mature use cases, configured the environment of use, and created interest through experiential visibility.

6.2 Generated and Malleable Realities

After showing how vendors made XR/DT commercially understandable, the next theme looks at the technological possibilities that vendors used to explain why these technologies could be valuable for clients. Across the interviews, vendors framed XR/DT as technologies that could change how clients access, test, and coordinate around digital representations of real or possible situations.

The first capability was "Making inaccessible, dangerous, or hidden realities experientially available". Vendors described XR/DT as ways of giving clients access to places, situations, or processes that would otherwise be difficult, not safe, or impossible to encounter directly. In cultural settings, one participant explained that the value of such experiences lay in giving audiences "something they will never experience in their life", such as "getting into a painting" or entering "the artist mind" (P5). In industrial settings, another participant described XR as enabling workers to operate remotely around hazardous production tasks without standing inside the danger zone, explaining that "one person instead of 100 people" could work in "hazardous areas" and "dangerous environments" through remote control, AR assistance, and AI assistance (P2). Other participants extended this mechanism to visibility and preparation. VR could show "something that is difficult to show in the physical environment", such as complex construction methods (P12), while workers could "walk around" an "entire production process" virtually before entering the actual workplace (P14). Digital twins and VR were also presented as enabling remote training, allowing personnel to "learn our equipment" and understand "our way of working" (P3), while "there is no need for everyone to go to training rooms" because training could take place through a "VR simulator" (P4). Across these accounts, vendors located potential value in making otherwise unreachable, hazardous, hidden, or unfamiliar realities experientially available without requiring direct physical presence.

The second capability was "Turning products, spaces, and procedures into testable simulations". Vendors framed XR/DT as valuable because they allowed clients to evaluate designs, layouts, and operational procedures before committing to physical production, construction, or implementation. One participant described this as a move away from "a 2D screen-based work environment" towards an "immersive scene or scenario" where product planning, facility planning, or training could be experienced at "one to one scale" (P1). This allowed clients to assess whether a product's "surface" and "texture" felt right, whether workers could "reach certain" parts, whether they would "collide with something", and whether the action was "ergonomically healthy" (P1). Other participants extended this mechanism to design revision and procedural rehearsal. One participant explained that "we design it and we check the architecture in VR because this thing will be built physically" (P5), while XR was presented as helping identify "faults", "conflicts", and unmet specifications during design (P10). Virtual scenarios were also presented as allowing personnel to rehearse procedures, undertake assessment, and practice "real-time crisis management" in a virtual environment "as if it were reality" (P11). Across these accounts, vendors presented the potential value as lying in making products, spaces, and procedures testable while they remained open to modification and before resources were committed to implementation.

The third capability was "Creating a shared view for remote coordination". Vendors framed XR/DT as ways of allowing multiple actors to see, discuss, and act around the same digital object or situation. In industrial remote support settings, one participant described a technician wearing smart glasses while an expert in a control centre could see "exactly what the technician sees in the field" and provide AR annotations, such as "arrows" or "circles" directly on the machine (P4). The proposed value was that expert guidance no longer depended only on verbal explanation. The same mechanism supported collaborative review, allowing distributed experts to look at "the same car at the same time" (P3) and enabling products to be shown directly to stakeholders rather than explained through lengthy presentations (P15). Across these accounts, vendors located potential value in giving distributed actors a shared visual reference for guidance, discussion, and decision-making.

Together, Theme 2 answers SRQ2 by showing that vendors presented XR/DT as technologies able to reconfigure how organisational actors engaged with real or possible situations by making them experientially accessible, open to testing before implementation, and available as shared reference points for remote coordination.

6.3 XR/DT Use Requires Organisational and Technical Reworking

Theme 3 shifts from value proposition to value realisation. It shows that XR/DT value depended on whether client organisations could make these technologies work within their existing technical systems and organisational arrangements, and with hardware and infrastructure that supported practical use.

The first condition was "Integrating XR/DT into client technical systems". Participants presented XR/DT value as limited when solutions remained standalone applications rather than becoming embedded in the technical systems and connected to the data used by client organisations. One participant explained that XR became valuable when it was integrated into the product pipeline "starting from the design" and treated as "a necessarily required part of the pipeline" rather than as "an ornamental tool" (P2). The participant contrasted this with earlier projects in which XR remained "an independent application" before users returned to "traditional ways of manufacturing or designing". Similarly, another participant argued that XR/DT should not be treated in isolation, as "its real strength is shown when connected with IoT, real data, and everyday business operations" (P4). Technical integration therefore shaped whether XR/DT moved beyond isolated applications and became part of routine organisational activity.

The second condition was "Reworking organisational processes and roles around XR/DT use". Even VR training, which was described as a relatively mature use case, required organisational change. One participant explained that VR was still not "the most common form" of training because, for many companies, it represented "a fundamental change initiative" concerning "how they do training", whether training is done in-house, "who runs it", and "who manages equipment" (P8). Similar issues appeared in service and inspection contexts, where the proposed benefits of remote expert guidance depended on technician adoption and on making the new practice "part of the process" (P4). Sustained use also depended on internal ownership, since projects with no "clear champion from the company" would "almost always" sit "on the shelf" (P13).

The third condition was "The material reality of XR/DT: Hardware and infrastructure as barriers to use". Hardware and infrastructure shaped whether the proposed value could be realised in practice. Participants noted that newer devices with "very high resolution" displays and "stable tracking" made experiences more natural and realistic (P1). However, others stressed that devices could still be "expensive" and "not reliable", which meant that users did not always "trust and adopt it" (P2). Smooth use could also require "expensive instruments", including headsets, special computers, or "a very fast internet line" (P7). Hardware therefore created trade-offs between accessibility and usability, as cheaper headsets made XR more affordable but offered fewer functions than more expensive devices and made interaction harder for first-time users (P6). Practical use was also constrained by headset fit and availability, including cases where only "70%" of users had a "good experience" (P10) or where even providing "10 headsets" was considered difficult to justify for a 20-min experience (P15).

Together, Theme 3 answers SRQ3 by showing that, in participants' accounts, XR/DT value depended on integration into technical systems, organisational routines and responsibilities, and hardware and infrastructure that worked well in practice.

6.4 Ecosystem Interdependence Shapes XR/DT Viability

Theme 4 moves beyond the client organisation by showing that value realisation also depended on wider ecosystem conditions. XR/DT viability was shaped by whether the wider ecosystem could support the transfer, reuse, maintenance, and continued development of XR/DT solutions over time.

The first condition, "Interoperability shapes XR/DT cross-system viability", concerned interoperability across platforms and device ecosystems. Viability was restricted when assets, experiences, or data could not be transferred or reused across contexts. This was visible in both device platforms and digital assets. One participant explained that "you have the Meta glasses, you have the Snap glasses", but these brands are "not interoperable", meaning that an experience developed for Meta could not be transferred to Snap (P7). Another participant raised the same issue for digital assets by asking "what data can you take with you?" when moving between Metaverses, noting that the transfer of skins or clothing "does not happen automatically with the current technology" (P6). Together, these examples show that confining XR/DT experiences and assets to specific platforms made their value dependent on remaining in those ecosystems.

Interoperability problems were also presented as affecting the long-term viability of XR technology. One participant argued that many XR functions remained "not yet covered by the standardization approach" and were organised around a "fragmented provider-based, SDK-based approach", which they considered detrimental to "the economic sustainability of XR technology" (P10). They therefore emphasised the need for interoperability frameworks and protocols, while stressing that this was "not just a technical discussion" because their design also depended on use cases, organisational needs, and decisions about which data should be shared and in what format. Their image of separate Metaverses needing "gates" or "contact points" illustrates how XR/DT viability depends on creating connections across otherwise fragmented systems.

The second condition was "External support sustains XR/DT viability". One participant described the XR ecosystem as "not fully mature yet" to be "truly accessible for a business" without external "know-how", "support", "a tool set", and "raw assets" to help clients get started (P10). This dependence continued after deployment. For example, museums often needed "external" experts to "manage the headsets" and "provide updates to applications", as XR experiences had a "maintenance tail" shaped by operating system updates and changes in output mechanisms (P12). If clients feared that they "may not get support for this", they might decide to "do something else" (P12).

Together, Theme 4 answers SRQ3 by showing that XR/DT value realisation depended on conditions beyond client organisations. Interoperability shaped whether systems, assets, and experiences could move across platforms, while external support shaped whether clients could access the expertise, tools, and maintenance needed to implement and keep XR/DT solutions usable over time.

6.5 Sustainability as Conditional, Indirect and Context-Dependent

Theme 5 examines how vendors associated XR/DT with sustainability through substitution, reconfigured participation, and context-dependent trade-offs, while presenting these implications as conditional rather than automatic.

The first subtheme, "Sustainability through substitution", shows how XR/DT could become relevant for sustainability when digital alternatives were presented as reducing the need for physical presence, travel, material production, or transport. In AR-enabled support, one participant described how a process that previously required "about two hours and the movement of two people" could now be completed in "about 30 minutes" with one technician in the field (P4). Similarly, by integrating IoT sensors with DT applications, workers were "not required to be there on the site" because factory or oil and gas equipment could be monitored remotely (P14). Substitution was also visible in product visualisation. One participant explained that XR could have both an "economic" and "ecologic" impact because organisations could "spare physical prototypes". Instead of building the prototype first, clients could view it "realistically" and "immersively" in 3D, potentially reducing both costs and the need to produce a physical prototype

(P1). Here, XR was presented as shifting part of the development process from physical prototyping to virtual iteration.

The second subtheme, “Reconfiguring participation through training, learning, accessibility, and inclusion”, shows how XR/DT could become relevant to sustainability by changing how people prepared for work and hazardous or emergency situations, how they learned and retained knowledge, and how they could access and participate in work and cultural activities. One participant described VR as a form of “safety kind of training” provided before employees entered hazardous areas in manufacturing and oil and gas environments (P14). Another participant explained that training simulations could use real data to help users “gain experience”, reduce training time, and “avoid mistakes”, with similar applications in assessment and real-time crisis management (P11). In another account, the daily use of AR recordings was associated with “better retention of technical knowledge” (P4). Other accounts associated simulated exposure with greater familiarity, confidence, and mental preparation. Training therefore reconfigured participation by allowing workers to rehearse tasks and situations and develop preparedness before entering real work environments.

In cultural settings, participation was reconfigured through learning, accessibility, and inclusion. One participant explained that cultural heritage reconstructions could have “social impact” because people could learn about the ancient world or experience a monument remotely “from home” (P11). Another described VR as giving archival material “another form”, making it more “tangible”, and helping to “democratise” access to it (P15). The same participant emphasised the importance of enabling someone who could not physically visit a cultural location to “see it and experience it” and reported that older visitors were “glad” to have participated and felt they had understood what a historical period was like (P15). In these accounts, XR/DT became relevant to sustainability by making cultural material more accessible, supporting learning, and broadening participation to include older visitors and people facing mobility or geographical barriers.

The third subtheme, “Ambiguity, trade-offs, and context-dependence”, shows that XR/DT sustainability was not always straightforward. Beyond cases where XR/DT replaced travel or physical materials, sustainability depended on the specific use context, operational purpose, and balance between benefits and costs. This was visible in relation to DTs, where one participant described environmental impacts as “more indirect” because they depended on “how the solution is being used” and on “what we want to do from this solution” (P9). DT environmental value therefore appeared when users applied the technology to problems such as reducing the “energy footprint in industry” or including “sustainability metrics” in decision-making (P9). In “energy intense cases”, optimisation services were applied on top of DTs to consider “not only performance but also environmental aspects like energy consumption”, although the participant stressed that the benefits “depend on where” the solution is implemented and were stronger in “very energy intense industries” than in industries that were “not so much energy aware” (P9). This suggests that DT sustainability was conditional on implementation context and energy intensity, rather than a general property of the technology. A related environmental trade-off appeared when AI was combined with AR, with another participant warning that its carbon footprint might be “not as good as we can believe” and describing the use of AI as "a choice", while acknowledging that the available evidence was "not very precise yet" (P7).

Together, Theme 5 answers SRQ4 by framing XR/DT sustainability as conditional, indirect, and context-dependent. Sustainability implications were associated with substitution, reconfigured participation through training, learning, accessibility, and inclusion, and trade-offs that varied across industrial and cultural settings.

7 Discussion

This study examined how vendors presented XR/DT solutions as sources of organisational value and how this value became relevant for sustainability. Synthesised as a conditional value pathway, the findings answer the main research question. Vendors first made XR/DT commercially recognisable and connected their technological possibilities to specific organisational purposes. Whether these possibilities became practically valuable then depended on complementary organisational, technical, material, and wider ecosystem conditions. Sustainability relevance emerged when XR/DT use substituted for physical presence or materials, or reconfigured possibilities for participation, while remaining subject to trade-offs. Therefore, sustainability was not an inherent outcome of XR/DT, but a conditional implication of how the solutions were positioned, implemented, supported, and used. Figure 1 synthesises this pathway.

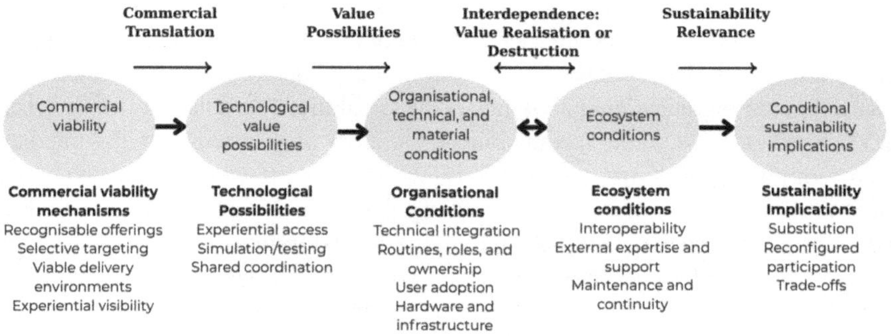

Fig. 1. Vendor-side conditional value pathway

The findings addressing SRQ1 and SRQ2 show that the pathway began before adoption through vendors' commercial translation of technological possibilities. Vendors translated unfamiliar technologies into recognisable offerings, prioritised comparatively established use cases and markets, configured viable delivery environments, and generated interest by making XR/DT experientially visible. Through these commercially framed offerings, they presented XR/DT as providing access to otherwise inaccessible situations, enabling testing before physical implementation, and creating shared reference points for coordination. This connects with IT business value research, which treats digital value as a process rather than as a direct effect of the technology itself [22]. The findings add that vendors shape which technological possibilities become available and credible for organisational evaluation. These possibilities represented potential value rather than organisational or sustainability outcomes.

The findings addressing SRQ3 show that value realisation and sustained use required organisational adaptation alongside technical and material conditions. XR/DT solutions had to be integrated with technical systems, embedded in routines, assigned responsibilities, and supported by hardware and infrastructure. Participants also emphasised user adoption, internal ownership, and organisational champions in moving solutions beyond pilots. Change management, understood as adapting routines, roles, capabilities, and user practices, therefore became a condition of sustained value realisation. This connects with IT business value research, which emphasises that value realisation depends on complementary organisational and technological conditions [12]. The findings specify this relationship for XR/DT by showing that organisational adaptation was inseparable from device functionality, connectivity, and infrastructure availability.

Theme 4 extends this argument beyond the client organisation. Value realisation also depended on interoperability, external expertise, support, and maintenance, indicating that XR/DT viability was distributed across interdependent actors. This aligns with research conceptualising Metaverse platforms as emergent platform ecosystems in which value depends on alignment among partners [23], while the interoperability constraints identified in the findings reflect an unresolved Metaverse challenge [24]. Given this interdependence, the Theory of Multi-Realization of IT Value (MUIT) may be relevant, as it explains value realisation in large-scale, co-developed digital platforms [25]. Whether XR/DT or Metaverse platforms meet MUIT's boundary conditions remains an open empirical question.

The findings addressing SRQ4, considered together with Themes 3 and 4, explain why the possibilities identified in Theme 2 did not translate automatically into sustainability implications. The conditions identified in these themes shaped whether XR/DT use reconfigured organisational activities in sustainability-relevant ways. In this sense, XR/DT acted as conditional sustainability mediators. An example of this mediation appeared in cultural settings, where XR/DT renewed what visitors could experience without requiring substantial physical reconfiguration of the site, potentially reducing some of the costs associated with changing physical exhibitions.

However, the findings did not establish net sustainability benefits. Participants noted that environmental value depended on use context and energy intensity, while economic value remained uncertain relative to hardware, infrastructure, implementation, and maintenance costs. More broadly, digital use may also supplement rather than replace corresponding physical activities, while hardware obsolescence may shift impacts towards equipment lifecycles and electronic waste [26]. The interaction between client-side and ecosystem conditions also suggested a point of vulnerability where value could be destroyed rather than merely remain unrealised. Where organisational adaptation depended on external actors, misalignment across these relationships could erode prior investments and reduce the value available to both clients and ecosystem actors. This is consistent with IT ecosystem research showing that value co-creation and value destruction can be intertwined rather than treated as separate outcomes [11].

Finally, this study contributes to IS research on digital sustainability by conceptualising a vendor-side value pathway through which XR/DT can act as conditional sustainability mediators rather than as "green" technologies by default. Although they can support sustainability, their sustainability relevance remains indirect and context-dependent. This interpretation is consistent with Green IS research, which argues that IS can support sustainability through new practices, monitoring, and decision-making [27, 28], and with work showing that sustainability benefits depend on how environmental strategies are translated into concrete Green IS initiatives [29]. The pathway shows how emerging technologies become commercially recognisable, practically realisable, and connected to specific sustainability implications.

8 Implications and Limitations

These findings have implications for both research and practice. For research, the study suggests that XR/DT sustainability should be studied as a conditional value pathway rather than as a direct technology outcome. This means examining how technological possibilities, organisational use, technical integration, ecosystem support, and a clear sustainability purpose come together in specific settings. For practice, the findings are most relevant to vendors, managers, and client organisations that evaluate or implement XR/DT solutions. They suggest that sustainability claims should be assessed against the specific value mechanism, implementation setting, ecosystem dependencies, and trade-offs involved. XR/DT may support sustainable value, but only when organisational use, technical integration, ecosystem support, and a clear sustainability purpose are aligned. Commercial justification may help the technology enter the organisation, but it does not by itself secure sustainable value.

Five limitations should also be acknowledged. First, consistent with reflexive thematic analysis, the themes reflect the researcher's interpretation of participants' accounts rather than objective categories. Second, the findings mainly reflect vendor framings of XR/DT value, not direct evidence of client outcomes or measured sustainability impacts. Future research should include additional client organisations and end users to examine whether this value pathway is experienced in practice. Third, the sample was concentrated in Europe, with two participants in India, limiting global generalisability. Fourth, because the study was exploratory and the research question was refined after data collection, sustainability measurement, long-term maintenance, and client-side value realisation were not examined as systematically as they would be in a study designed around these issues from the beginning. Fifth, LinkedIn-based purposive recruitment may have favoured highly visible XR/DT professionals, underrepresenting less visible organisations and stakeholders.

Acknowledgements. This research was funded by the European Union's Horizon Europe research and innovation programme under the Marie Skłodowska-Curie grant agreement No 101119937 and UKRI EPSRC Grant Ref: EP/Y032454/1.

ChatGPT, GPT-5.5 model, was used to improve language and support the clarification of methodological descriptions. All substantive methodological decisions, interpretations, and conclusions were made and reviewed by the author, who remains responsible for the final content.

Disclosure of Interests The author declares no competing interests.

References

1. Schoormann, T., Möller, F., Hoppe, C., Brocke, J.V.: Digital sustainability: understanding and managing tensions. Bus. Inf. Syst. Eng. **67**, 429–438 (2025). https://doi.org/10.1007/s12599-025-00937-3
2. Aragón-Correa, J.A., Marcus, A.A., Vogel, D.: The effects of mandatory and voluntary regulatory pressures on firms' environmental strategies: a review and recommendations for future research. Acad. Manag. Ann. **14**, 339–365 (2020). https://doi.org/10.5465/annals.2018.0014
3. Davern, M.J., Kauffman, R.J.: Discovering potential and realizing value from information technology investments. J. Manag. Inf. Syst. **16**, 121–143 (2000). https://doi.org/10.1080/07421222.2000.11518268
4. Brenk, K., Tomini, N., Kanbach, D.K., Stubner, S., Pinelli, M.: From virtual vision to business reality: embracing the metaverse revolution. Rev. Manag. Sci. **20**, 81–107 (2026). https://doi.org/10.1007/s11846-025-00878-x
5. Lee, L.H., et al.: All one needs to know about metaverse: a complete survey on technological singularity, virtual ecosystem, and research agenda (2021). http://arxiv.org/abs/2110.05352
6. Henkel, D.A., Ivens, B.S.: Conceptualizing the industrial Metaverse: from technological layers to business value. Ind. Mark. Manag. **131**, 58–72 (2025). https://doi.org/10.1016/j.indmarman.2025.10.003
7. Lowry, P.B., Boh, W.F., Petter, S., Leimeister, J.M.: Long live the Metaverse: identifying the potential for market disruption and future research. J. Manag. Inf. Syst. **42**, 3–38 (2025). https://doi.org/10.1080/07421222.2025.2455770
8. Tingelhoff, F., Schultheiss, R., Schöbel, S.M., Leimeister, J.M.: Qualitative insights into organizational value creation: decoding characteristics of Metaverse platforms. Inf. Syst. Front. **27**, 467–486 (2025). https://doi.org/10.1007/s10796-024-10494-x
9. Stacchio, L., Angeli, A., Marfia, G.: Empowering digital twins with extended reality collaborations. Virtual Real. Intell. Hardw. **4**, 487–505 (2022). https://doi.org/10.1016/j.vrih.2022.06.004
10. Hasani, T., Rezania, D., Mohammadi, M.: Towards a framework for successful metaverse adoption in small and medium-sized enterprises: an exploratory study. Int. J. Eng. Bus. Manag. **16**, 18479790241257118 (2024). https://doi.org/10.1177/18479790241257118
11. Sahaym, A., Vithayathil, J., Sarker, S., Sarker, S., Bjørn-Andersen, N.: Value destruction in information technology ecosystems: a mixed-method investigation with interpretive case study and analytical modeling. Inf. Syst. Res. **34**, 508–531 (2023). https://doi.org/10.1287/isre.2022.1119
12. Melville, N., Kraemer, K., Gurbaxani, V.: Review: information technology and organizational performance: an integrative model of IT business value. MIS Q. **28**, 283–322 (2004). https://doi.org/10.2307/25148636
13. Kohli, R., Grover, V.: Business value of IT: an essay on expanding research directions to keep up with the times. J. Assoc. Inf. Syst. **9**, 23–39 (2008). https://doi.org/10.17705/1jais.00147
14. Schryen, G.: Revisiting IS business value research: what we already know, what we still need to know, and how we can get there. Eur. J. Inf. Syst. **22**, 139–169 (2013). https://doi.org/10.1057/ejis.2012.45
15. Kotlarsky, J., Oshri, I., Sekulic, N.: Digital sustainability in information systems research: conceptual foundations and future directions. J. Assoc. Inf. Syst. **24**, 936–952 (2023). https://doi.org/10.17705/1jais.00825
16. Höllerer, M.A., et al.: "Digital sustainability": addressing managerial, organizational, and institutional challenges. Acad. Manag. Perspect. **40**, 241–251 (2026). https://doi.org/10.5465/amp.2025.0278

17. Myers, M.D., Newman, M.: The qualitative interview in IS research: examining the craft. Inf. Organ. **17**, 2–26 (2007). https://doi.org/10.1016/j.infoandorg.2006.11.001
18. Braun, V., Clarke, V.: Thematic analysis. In: Cooper, H., Camic, P.M., Long, D.L., Panter, A.T., Rindskopf, D., Sher, K.J. (eds.) APA Handbook of Research Methods in Psychology, pp. 57–71. American Psychological Association, Washington, DC (2012). https://doi.org/10.1037/13620-004
19. Byrne, D.: A worked example of Braun and Clarke's approach to reflexive thematic analysis. Qual. Quant. **56**, 1391–1412 (2022). https://doi.org/10.1007/s11135-021-01182-y
20. Kemper, E.A., Stringfield, S., Teddlie, C.: Mixed methods sampling strategies in social science research. In: Tashakkori, A., Teddlie, C. (eds.) Handbook of Mixed Methods in Social & Behavioral Research, pp. 273–296. SAGE, Thousand Oaks, CA (2003)
21. Elkington, J.: Partnerships from cannibals with forks: the triple bottom line of 21st-century business. Environ. Qual. Manag. **8**, 37–51 (1998). https://doi.org/10.1002/tqem.3310080106
22. Soh, C., Markus, M.L.: How IT creates business value: a process theory synthesis. In: ICIS 1995 Proceedings, pp. 29–41. ICIS, Amsterdam (1995)
23. Schöbel, S., Karatas, J., Tingelhoff, F., Leimeister, J.M.: Not everything is a Metaverse?! A practitioners perspective on characterizing metaverse platforms. In: Proceedings of the 56th Hawaii International Conference on System Sciences, pp. 544–553 (2023). https://doi.org/10.24251/HICSS.2023.070
24. Peukert, C., et al.: Metaverse: a real change or just another research area? Electron. Mark. **34**, 32 (2024). https://doi.org/10.1007/s12525-024-00711-5
25. Flak, L.S., Solli-Sæther, H., Straub, D.W.: A theory of multi-realization of IT value: toward construct clarity in the co-development of large platforms. MIS Q. **46**, 1739–1758 (2022). https://doi.org/10.25300/MISQ/2022/14492
26. Itten, R., et al.: Digital transformation—life cycle assessment of digital services, multifunctional devices and cloud computing. Int. J. Life Cycle Assess. **25**, 2093–2098 (2020). https://doi.org/10.1007/s11367-020-01801-0
27. Melville, N.P.: Information systems innovation for environmental sustainability. MIS Q. **34**, 1–21 (2010). https://doi.org/10.2307/20721412
28. Watson, R.T., Boudreau, M.C., Chen, A.J.: Information systems and environmentally sustainable development: energy informatics and new directions for the IS community. MIS Q. **34**, 23–38 (2010). https://doi.org/10.2307/20721413
29. Loeser, F., Recker, J., vom Brocke, J., Molla, A., Zarnekow, R.: How IT executives create organizational benefits by translating environmental strategies into green IS initiatives. Inf. Syst. J. **27**, 503–553 (2017). https://doi.org/10.1111/isj.12136

Location-Based Entertainment Research: A Review and Future Directions

Chenglong Li[1], Zeyu Wu[1], Ting Long[1], and Wen Yang[2(✉)]

[1] Central China Normal University, Wuhan 430079, China
[2] Hubei University of Education, Wuhan 430205, China
vaniayang7@163.com

Abstract. Location-Based Entertainment (LBE) has emerged as an increasingly important form of immersive digital experience in museums, heritage sites, and theme parks. Although LBE often draws on VR, AR, and XR technologies, it differs from general immersive technology applications in its reliance on site-specific environments, physical-digital integration, and embodied on-site participation. Despite its growing practical relevance, research on LBE remains fragmented. This study addresses this gap through a literature review. Following the PRISMA 2020 guidelines, the review selected 20 relevant publications, and examined their publication trends, methodologies, application contexts, and theoretical foundations. The review develops an analytical framework that organizes the literature around LBE features, user responses, and interaction outcomes. The findings show that current research focuses mainly on system design and immediate user experience, while broader organizational, societal, and critical issues remain underexplored. By synthesizing the current knowledge landscape and identifying key gaps, this review contributes to a clearer understanding of LBE as an emerging interdisciplinary field and outlines directions for future research.

Keywords: Location-Based Entertainment · Literature Review · Immersive Service · Virtual Reality

1 Introduction

Location-Based Entertainment (LBE) is rapidly emerging as a prominent form of immersive digital experience in cultural settings, such as museums, heritage sites, and theme parks, where digital content is no longer consumed only through personal screens but is staged within physical environments and experienced through embodied and on-site participation [1]. LBE generally refers to a form of entertainment experience that takes place in specific physical locations and is characterized by immersive, interactive, and on-site engagement [2]. Although LBE often draws on the technological foundations of virtual reality (VR), augmented reality (AR), or extended reality (XR), it should not be treated simply as an instance of VR/XR application. Rather, LBE is distinguished by its dependence on a particular site, the integration of digital content with physical infrastructures, and the orchestration of embodied, co-located, and often multisensory

Published by Springer Nature Switzerland AG 2027
S. Han et al. (Eds.): I3E 2026, LNCS 16912, pp. 192–203, 2027.
https://doi.org/10.1007/978-3-032-38014-2_15

participation [3]. In other words, while VR/XR emphasizes the immersive capability of the medium itself, LBE places greater emphasis on how immersion is produced through the alignment of space, movement, immersion, and narrative within a particular venue (see Fig. 1). The development of LBE is reflected in markets, and a recent report suggests that the global LBE market will continue expanding over the next decade, and may reach USD 88.27 billion by 2034 [4].

Despite this growing practical importance, academic research on LBE has not yet developed into a coherent body of knowledge. Reviews on VR/XR tend to synthesize research around technology adoption, imagination, immersion, or educational effects [5, 6]. However, these studies are not well suited to understanding LBE, where physical setting, spatial choreography, fixed equipment, and social co-presence become central to value creation.

Fig. 1. An example of LBE (source: https://www.jiemian.com/article/12143151.html)

Current work on LBE can be grouped into two research streams. The first stream examines LBE from the design side, such as immersion, presence, and site-specific experience design. For instance, Ford (2022) suggests that the value of LBE resides in site-specific experience design, where spatial staging, environmental cues, and multisensory staging collectively produce a situated immersive experience rather than relying solely on end-user devices [3]. The second stream investigates LBE from the user behavior side, focusing on how users perceive, interpret, and respond to these experiences. For instance, Kleftodimos et al. (2023) demonstrate that LBE experiences significantly enhance cultural understanding and learning motivation, particularly when narrative content is embedded directly into the physical heritage site [7]. Similarly, Guo et al. (2023) suggest that immersion, affective experience, and social presence significantly shape visitors' intentions to use LBE [8].

However, prior LBE studies have not yet produced a clear overview. Although they have advanced understanding of design features and user responses, it remains unclear how LBE scholarship is structured overall, which themes have received sustained attention, which methods and theoretical approaches dominate current research, and which important issues remain insufficiently examined. In particular, the literature still lacks a systematic review capable of consolidating the field's research status, and identifying the gaps that should inform future work [9]. Thus, to address the issue, this study aims to conduct a literature review to answer the following questions:

RQ1: What are the main research themes and topics in existing LBE literature?
RQ2: How has LBE research been conducted in terms of methods, theoretical foundations, and application contexts?
RQ3: What major gaps and future directions emerge from the current body of LBE research?

The rest of the paper is organized as follows. Section 2 describes the research methodology used for selecting and analyzing the literature. Section 3 presents the descriptive results, including publication trends, methods, contexts, and theories. Section 4 summarizes research theme distribution and identifies gaps in the current body of knowledge. Section 5 proposes a future research agenda. Finally, Sect. 6 summarizes the contributions and limitations of this study.

2 Methodology

The literature review followed the PRISMA 2020 (Preferred Reporting Items for Systematic Reviews and Meta-Analyses) guidelines [10] (see Fig. 2). First, a systematic search was conducted across three prominent academic databases, including Web of Science, Science Direct, and EBSCO. The search query was defined as:

TS = ("location-based entertainment" OR LBE OR "location-based VR" OR LBVR OR "immersive entertainment" OR "spatial entertainment" OR "location-based AR" OR "LBAR")

The search targeted peer-reviewed publications published between 2016 and 2026. This initial search yielded 1,925 records. After all records were exported to a reference management database and duplicates were removed, 1,657 studies remained for the subsequent screening stage. Second, a two-round evaluation process was conducted to exclude irrelevant literature. In the first round, titles and abstracts were reviewed against inclusion criteria, that is, studies had to be peer-reviewed articles, published in English, and directly related to LBE, digital immersive experiences, or VR/AR applications in physical contexts. Based on this screening, 1,451 records were excluded, leaving 206 studies for full-text review. In the second round, the full texts of these studies were examined in depth. Articles were excluded if they focused on peripheral areas rather than the core development, experiential features, or interactive design of LBE, as well as user experiences and reactions in-depth. For example, studies were excluded if they treated VR/AR solely as an online or home-based personal entertainment medium without site-specific interaction, or if they involved mixed digital-physical experiences but without VR/AR headsets, such as research on Pokémon GO. Following this process, 20 studies were selected for the final analysis. Third, in the data extraction and synthesis stage, a structured coding scheme was developed using Microsoft Excel to categorize each article based on seven dimensions, including research questions, theoretical foundations, methodologies, data sources, applied technologies, research contexts, and primary findings. To further analyze the studies, thematic focus was classified into three types, including LBE Side, User Side, and Outcomes.

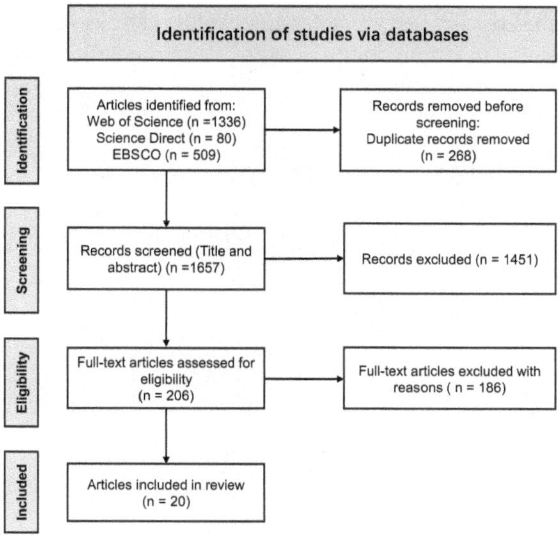

Fig. 2. PRISMA 2020 flowchart for systematic reviews

3 Descriptive Results

3.1 Publication Trends and Venues

The distribution of the 20 selected publications suggests that LBE remains an emerging but increasingly visible area of research (see Table 1). Although publications appeared as early as 2017, approximately 70% of the research was published between 2023 and 2025, suggesting that LBE has become a more visible research topic in recent years. Regarding publication venues, the distribution of publications across journals and conference proceedings in a range of fields, such as computer science, human–computer interaction, tourism, hospitality, and education, suggests that the topic has not yet consolidated around a single disciplinary core. Rather, LBE research is developing through multiple disciplinary lenses, with different fields approaching the topic from technological, experiential, cultural, and service-related perspectives. Overall, this distribution indicates that interest in LBE is increasing, but the field has not yet developed into a stable and unified academic domain.

3.2 Research Methodologies

Among the included studies, questionnaire-based quantitative research was the most prevalent approach, employed in nine studies [8, 11–18]. These studies predominantly relied on large-scale survey data, with structural equation modeling serving as the core analytical technique to examine hypothesized theoretical models and path relationships among variables [8, 11–15, 19]. In addition, one study employed a scenario-based within-subjects experimental design, manipulating variables such as spatial context, content dimensionality, and dynamism to compare users' perceptual differences toward various LBE content presentation formats [17].

Table 1. Publication count by year and venue

Venue	2017	2018	2019	2020	2021	2022	2023	2024	2025	2026	Total
Current Issues in Tourism		1									1
Telematics and Informatics					1						1
Computers							1		1		2
Applied Sciences								1	1		2
Design Journal			1								1
Media Practice and Education								1			1
International Journal of Distributed Systems and Technologies				1							1
Information Resources Management Journal										1	1
ISPRS Archives									1		1
Multimedia Tools and Applications	1										1
Virtual Reality							1		2		3
Frontiers in Virtual Reality									1		1
Human–Computer Studies	1										1
The XXXIII ISPIM Innovation Conference "Innovating in a Digital World"						1					1
2017 IEEE 3rd VR Workshop on Sonic Interactions for Virtual Environments (SIVE)	1										1
Sustainability							1				1
Total	3	1	1	1	1	1	3	2	6	1	20

Qualitative research methods were adopted in seven studies. These encompassed semi-structured interviews [20–22], focus groups [19], case studies [23–25], and typological analysis based on observations and secondary data [3].

Four studies adopted a mixed-methods approach, integrating the collection and analysis of both quantitative and qualitative data. The specific combinations included surveys combined with gameplay performance log data analysis [15], surveys combined with post-hoc explanatory interviews [11], the System Usability Scale and Game Experience

Questionnaire combined with user feedback [26], and usability testing combined with a laboratory experience questionnaire evaluation [27].

3.3 Research Contexts

In the selected studies, cultural heritage sites and museums appear most frequently, accounting for over half of the reviewed literature. In these contexts, LBE technology is primarily utilized to reconstruct inaccessible, damaged, or no-longer-existing historical spaces, such as the Peking Man site at Zhoukoudian [20], the Longmen Grottoes in Luoyang [14], and the Nanjing Qinhuai River Scenic Belt [13], allowing visitors to move through and engage with digitally mediated historical narratives. Additionally, several studies adopted entire urban districts or public spaces as venues for situated learning and experience, for instance, the urban pathways designed for sustainability education in Aveiro, Portugal [15], and the local knowledge inheritance project conducted at the Hitachi City Museum in Japan [28]. Beyond heritage settings, the reviewed studies also include dedicated entertainment environments, such as commercial location-based VR gaming spaces [23], theme parks, such as Lotte World Adventure in Seoul, Korea [24], and the "Star Wars: Galactic Starcruiser" immersive hotel by Disney [25], as well as university laboratories used for technological development and testing [22, 26].

3.4 Theoretical Foundations

The reviewed LBE studies draw on a range of theories. From the user experience and psychological perspective, Immersion Theory, particularly Brown and Cairns' three-level model (Engagement-Engrossment-Total Immersion) and its derivative ARI questionnaire, serves as a core measurement framework across multiple studies [8, 18, 19]. Flow Theory [8, 19] and Presence Theory [8, 21, 22] are also employed to explain users' deep engagement and spatial perception. Technology Acceptance Model (TAM) [13], Elaboration Likelihood Model (ELM) [13], Media Richness Theory [13], and Intrinsic and Extrinsic Motivation Theory [12] are utilized to explain the formation of user attitudes and adoption behaviors toward LBE. Social Presence Theory and Social Touch Theory [22] are applied to analyze social mechanisms in multi-user shared AR environments. Service-Dominant Logic of Value Co-Creation Theory [11] and the Experience Economy framework [3] are employed to examine the production and consumption of LBE experiences. Narrative Theory [28], the Hero's Journey framework [25], and Narrative Transportation Theory [20] are adapted to examine the design of heritage education and entertainment experiences. Additionally, the GreenComp competence framework for sustainability education [15], along with concepts such as Digital Twin and Photogrammetry [18, 22], provide further theoretical grounding for the technological implementation and educational application of LBE.

4 The Framework for the Interaction Between LBE and Users

4.1 Analytical Framework

This study developed a three-part analytical framework consisting of LBE Side, User Side, and Interaction Outcomes. This framework was designed to capture the main concerns of the existing literature and to provide a clearer basis for identifying the research focus and underexplored areas in current LBE research. Specifically, LBE Side, includes studies that focus on the characteristics of LBE, such as system architecture, spatial design, interaction design, tracking technologies, multisensory elements, and the integration of digital content with physical settings. User Side, includes studies that examine how users perceive and respond to LBE experiences. This category is mainly concerned with users' subjective experiences during their interaction with LBE, such as perceived presence, enjoyment, and other immediate psychological or experiential responses. Interaction Outcomes, refers to studies that investigate the consequences or value generated through the interaction between LBE and users, such as learning, satisfaction, cultural understanding, visit intention, and other forms of experiential or behavioral outcomes. Compared with the second category, which focuses on immediate user reactions, this category is more concerned with broader effects and post-experience outcomes. Each of the 20 selected studies was classified according to the category that best reflected its primary analytical focus. To improve the reliability of the classification process, the authors reviewed the studies independently and discussed any inconsistencies when they arose.

4.2 LBE Side

In the LBE side dimension, studies focus on physical and technical configurations, which can be grouped into three categories. First, IS features, addresses system architecture and multisensory aspects, with literature highlighting field of view (FoV) [16], real-time tracking technologies [11], integrated audio-visual modalities [20], the pacing of slow progression [21], immersive audio design [23], and aesthetic auditory design [23]. Second, content features center on narrative design, such as storytelling [11, 20], and contextualized character and venue elements [20]. Third, space features, concerns physical configurations and user interaction within the environment and other users, such as entrance design [24], expansive spatial design [20], and free-roaming interaction [20], collision safety and spatial awareness [22], tangible interaction [22], haptic engagement and presence [22], social meeting [21], multi-user collaboration [20], social gesture and social touch [22].

4.3 User Side

Research on the User Side focuses on users' features and psychological and experiential responses. First, some studies examine user perceptions prior to the interaction with LBE, such as intrinsic and extrinsic motivation [12], awareness and knowledge [11], social relevance [11], and AR psychological engagement [11]. Additionally, some studies focus on perceptions during the interaction, such as immersion [23, 27], presence [18,

19], flow [18, 19], focus of attention [18, 19], usability [18, 19], and social interaction, expression, and interpersonal distance [22]. Other research highlights emotional perspectives during interaction, such as emotional attachment [18, 19], empathy [26], and the ability to generate memories of positive verse negative states [11]. Moreover, some studies examine perception in the post-interaction stage, such as competence, sensory, tension, tiredness, and the transitional state of returning to reality [26].

4.4 Outcomes

Regarding outcome, the research explores the consequences of LBE through four dimensions. First, the cognitive dimension, studies examine meaningfulness of the virtual content [21], effectiveness of using museum materials [28], understanding of local knowledge [28], and quality of experience [16]. Second, the emotional dimension, such as emotional resonance [11]. Third, attitude dimension, such as attitude toward sponsors [11], and different types of user satisfaction, for instance, overall satisfaction, tourist satisfaction, personalized satisfaction, immersion satisfaction, and satisfaction with technical experience [14]. Finally, in the behavior dimension, studies examine intention to use LBE [12], intention to visit [12, 27], intention to recommend [27], intention to consume [17], content sharing [17], intention to visit sponsor [11], education of sustainability [15], overall co-creation of value experience [11], behavioral involvement [26], and engagement with the history and culture [20]. Figure 3 illustrates our research framework and findings.

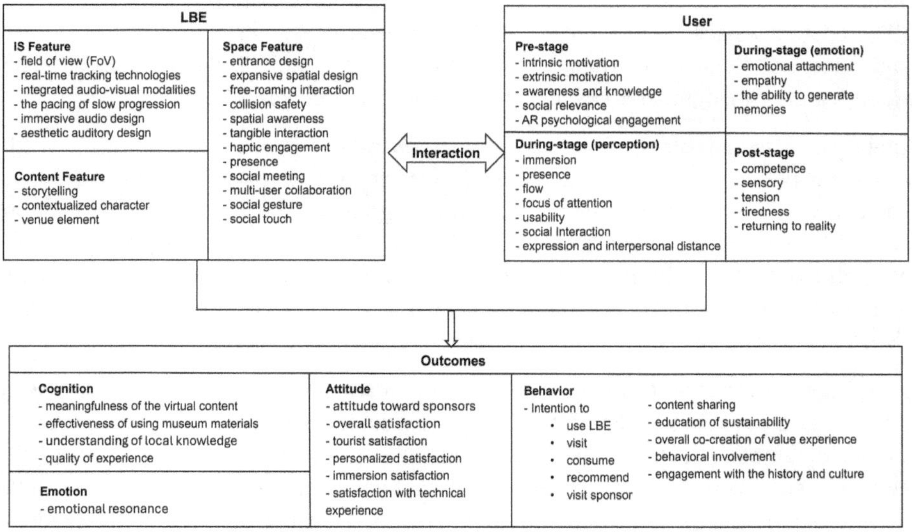

Fig. 3. Research framework and findings

5 Discussion

5.1 Future Agenda

Methodological Agenda. The reviewed literature is dominated by empirical evaluation, with experiments and surveys occupying an important place. While these methods have provided valuable insights into user behaviors, future research could benefit from a broader range of methods. There is room for more longitudinal studies that examine how LBE experiences influence users and institutions over time, rather than focusing mainly on one-time encounters. There is also scope for more mixed-methods designs that combine standardized scales with observational, interview-based, or behavioral data to capture both measurable responses and richer experiential processes. Additionally, the integration of design science research could offer a more rigorous framework for the iterative development of LBE, allowing researchers to evaluate not just the final user outcome, but the specific affordances of the tracking systems (e.g., SLAM, OptiTrack) and rendering engines (e.g., Unity and Unreal) throughout the creation process. By adopting these multi-dimensional and longitudinal methodologies, scholars can get a deeper understanding of the long-term impact and operational resilience of LBE installations.

Agenda on LBE Features. Given the strong concentration of studies on LBE characteristics, future research on LBE Features could move beyond describing technical components and focus more explicitly on how different design elements work together. Existing studies often examine spatial features, IS features, and content features as separate features. Future work could pay greater attention to the relationships among these elements and explore how they jointly shape the quality, coherence, and reliability of LBE experiences across different contexts. Comparative studies across museums, heritage sites, and themed entertainment venues may be especially helpful for clarifying which features are context-specific and which are more generalizable.

Agenda on User Features. Prior studies focus on immediate reactions during or shortly after the experience. Future research could examine user responses in a more differentiated way by considering variations across user groups, prior experience, motivation, cultural background, and social settings. There is also room to investigate how users interpret LBE differently in heritage, tourism, and commercial entertainment contexts. Such work would deepen understanding of not only whether users respond positively to LBE, but also how and why these responses vary across settings and populations.

Agenda on Interaction Outcomes. Studies on interaction outcomes remain relatively limited and are concentrated mainly at the individual level. Existing work has primarily examined outcomes such as satisfaction and intention. By contrast, organizational-level outcomes, such as service quality and operational value, have received much less attention. Research on societal-level outcomes is even more limited, and few studies address issues such as cultural participation, public value, and social inclusion. Future research should therefore adopt a more multi-level perspective on outcomes, moving beyond individual users to examine how LBE creates value, or generates consequences, for organizations and society more broadly.

Critical Agenda on Challenges and Practical Constraints. Current LBE research pays limited attention to practical challenges and constraints involved in the development, deployment, and long-term operation of LBE. This suggests a tendency to emphasize technological innovation and positive user experience while giving less attention to the conditions that shape whether LBE can be implemented sustainably in real-world venues. Future research should therefore examine barriers that may affect adoption, operation, and maintenance, such as hardware costs, equipment durability, technical instability under high-frequency public use, staff training, user throughput, and the physical safety and physiological comfort of users moving within hybrid physical–virtual environments. Also, privacy and ethical issues should also be considered, although their significance is likely to vary across LBE settings. In many LBE experiences, data collection may be limited, temporary, and primarily operational. However, where systems involve persistent user profiles, full-body tracking, gaze tracking, video monitoring, biometric recognition, or third-party analytics, questions of informed consent, data minimization, transparency, and responsible data use become more important. Rather than treating LBE as inherently risky, future studies should identify the specific technical and organizational conditions under which privacy, safety, and ethical concerns become salient. Addressing these practical and responsible-use issues would support a more balanced understanding of LBE and contribute to its sustainable development.

6 Conclusions

This review makes three main contributions. First, it synthesizes the existing literature and provides an overview of the main themes, methods, contexts, and theoretical foundations of LBE research. Second, it develops an analytical framework that organizes prior studies around the LBE side, the user side, and interaction outcomes. This framework clarifies the current structure of LBE research and highlights several imbalances in the field. Existing studies have focused mainly on LBE features and users' immediate experiential responses, while giving less attention to how different design elements work together, how user responses vary across contexts and populations, and how LBE generates broader organizational or societal outcomes. Third, building on this synthesis and framework, the review proposes a future research agenda that identifies conceptual, methodological, outcome-related, and practical gaps for further investigation.

This study has several limitations. The review is based on a relatively small sample of 20 publications. Although these studies were selected for their strong relevance to site-dependent immersive LBE, they may not capture the full breadth of a rapidly evolving field. Some adjacent work on mobile AR, mixed reality, or industry-led LBE development may not be fully represented in the academic literature reviewed here. In addition, because LBE is developing quickly in commercial practice, especially in museums and themed entertainment contexts, there may be a gap between current industry developments and what is currently documented in peer-reviewed publications. Further reviews will therefore be needed to track new developments in LBE and their implementation in practice.

Acknowledgement. This work was supported by the Overseas Postdoctoral Talent Recruitment Special Program and National Social Science Fund of China (Grant No. 25VRC063).

References

1. Mendoza-Ramírez, C.E., Tudon-Martinez, J.C., Félix-Herrán, L.C., Lozoya-Santos, J.D.J., Vargas-Martínez, A.: Augmented reality: survey. Appl. Sci. **13**(18), 10491 (2023)
2. Kim, Y.-J., Lu, J., Höllerer, T.: Dynamic theater: location-based immersive dance theater, investigating user guidance and experience. In: Proceedings of the 29th ACM Symposium on Virtual Reality Software and Technology, pp. 1–11. Association for Computing Machinery, New York, NY, USA (2023)
3. Ford, S.: Experience design and the characteristics of location-based entertainment. In: Innovating in a Digital World: Proceedings of the XXXIII ISPIM Innovation Conference, pp. 1–16. ISPIM, Copenhagen (2022)
4. Location based entertainment market size, share, trends [2034], https://www.fortunebusinessinsights.com/location-based-entertainment-market-110163 (2026). Last accessed 07 May 2026
5. Angra, S., Jangra, S., Gulzar, Y., Sharma, B., Singh, G., Onn, C.W.: Twenty-two years of advancements in augmented and virtual reality: a bibliometric and systematic review. Front. Comput. Sci. **7**, 1470038 (2025)
6. Huang, T.-C., Tseng, H.-P.: Extended reality in applied sciences education: a systematic review. Appl. Sci. **15**(7), 4038 (2025)
7. Kleftodimos, A., Evagelou, A., Triantafyllidou, A., Grigoriou, M., Lappas, G.: Location-based augmented reality for cultural heritage communication and education: the doltso district application. Sensors. **23**(10), 4963 (2023)
8. Guo, J., Pan, Y.: What factors impact visitors' intentions to use location-based AR games? An empirical study from Chinese cultural heritage sites. Sustainability. **15**(19), 14328 (2023)
9. Pratisto, E.H., Thompson, N., Potdar, V.: Immersive technologies for tourism: a systematic review. Inf. Technol. Tour. **24**, 181–219 (2022)
10. Page, M.J., et al.: The PRISMA 2020 statement: an updated guideline for reporting systematic reviews. BMJ. **372**, n71 (2021)
11. Guo, J., Xu, J., Pan, Y.: How do location-based AR games enhance value co-creation experiences at cultural heritage sites? a process perspective analysis. Appl. Sci. **14**(15), 6812 (2024)
12. Lacka, E.: Assessing the impact of full-fledged location-based augmented reality games on tourism destination visits. Curr. Issues Tour. **23**, 345–357 (2018)
13. Yan, Y., Du, Q.: From digital imagination to real-world exploration: a study on the influence factors of VR-based reconstruction of historical districts on tourists' travel intention in the field. Virtual Real. **29**, 85 (2025)
14. Lan, F., Liu, J., Sun, Z.: Data-driven information resource optimization for cultural tourism. Inf. Resour. Manag. J. **39**, 1–25 (2026)
15. Marques, M.M., Ferreira-Santos, J., Rodrigues, R., Pombo, L.: Mobile augmented reality games towards smart learning City environments: learning about sustainability. Computers. **14**(7), 267 (2025)
16. Kasapakis, V., Gavalas, D.: Occlusion handling in outdoors augmented reality games. Multimed. Tools Appl. **76**, 9829–9854 (2017)
17. Hirsch, L., Mueller, F., Kruse, M., Butz, A., Welsch, R.: Social MediARverse: investigating users' social media content sharing and consuming intentions with location-based AR. Virtual Real. **29**(2), 110 (2025)
18. Duric, I., Medic, S., Ecet, D., Grgic, S., Jelicic, J.A.: Enhancing public space experiences: evaluating perception of digital and digitized sculptures in augmented reality. Appl. Sci. **15**(2), 743 (2025)

19. Georgiou, Y., Kyza, E.A.: The development and validation of the ARI questionnaire: an instrument for measuring immersion in location-based augmented reality settings. Int. J. Hum.-Comput. Stud. **98**, 24–37 (2017)
20. Wei, J., et al.: Innovative digital technology in education about paleolithic sites: a case study of the peking man site at Zhoukoudian. In: The International Archives of the Photogrammetry, Remote Sensing and Spatial Information Sciences (ISPRS Archives), pp. 1599–1606 (2025)
21. Laato, S., Inaba, N., Hamari, J.: Convergence between the real and the augmented: experiences and perceptions in location-based games. Telemat. Inform. **65**, 101716 (2021)
22. Zhang, J., Ma, F., Pi, Y., Du, H., Pan, X.: Digital twin embodied interactions design: synchronized and aligned physical sensation in location-based social VR. Front. Virtual Real. **6**, 1502311 (2025)
23. Summers, C., Jesse, M.: Creating immersive and aesthetic auditory spaces in virtual reality. In: 2017 IEEE 3rd VR Workshop on Sonic Interactions for Virtual Environments (SIVE), pp. 1–6 (2017)
24. Yoon, S.: Entrance as a non-peripheral space in a theme park design-focusing on Lotte world adventure in Seoul, Korea. Des. J. **22**, 371–382 (2019)
25. Gröppel-Wegener, A.: Immersive protagonists – exploring the notion of the "hero" in theme parks. Media Pract. Educ. **25**, 137–148 (2024)
26. Oriti, D., Manuri, F., Pace, F.D., Sanna, A.: Harmonize: a shared environment for extended immersive entertainment. Virtual Real. **27**, 3259–3272 (2023)
27. Kleftodimos, A., et al.: Creating location-based augmented reality games and immersive experiences for touristic destination marketing and education. Computers. **12**(11), 227 (2023)
28. Ishida, T., Ito, H.: Implementation and evaluation of local knowledge inheritance system. Int. J. Distrib. Syst. Technol. **11**, 1–22 (2020)

Beyond Immersion: How Location-Based Virtual Reality Affordances Enable User Engagement with Jingchu Culture

Ting Long, Yihong Zhan, and Chenglong Li(✉)

Central China Normal University, Wuhan 430079, China
chenglong.li@ccnu.edu.cn

Abstract. Location-based virtual reality (LBVR) is increasingly used in museums and cultural settings, yet limited research explains how LBVR shapes users' cultural experience. This study examines Jingchu culture-related LBVR from an affordance perspective. Drawing on a qualitative multiple-case study of three location-based LBVR projects in Hubei, China, and 11 semi-structured interviews, it analyzes how participants perceived and actualized the possibilities enabled by LBVR. The findings show that immersive cultural experience is shaped through an unfolding process of affordance enactment. The findings identify a three-stage process of affordance enactment. First, immersive, sensory, and exploratory affordances helped participants enter, perceive, and explore virtual cultural worlds. Second, embodied and interactive affordances enabled participants to act within these worlds. Third, narrative, interpretive, affective, and learning affordances supported participants in making sense of cultural content, developing emotional resonance, and deepening cultural understanding. These findings show that LBVR shapes cultural experience through a progressive process of entering, acting within, and interpreting and internalizing cultural experiences. The study contributes to IS research by offering a more process-sensitive account of immersive technologies and their role in shaping users' cultural experience.

Keywords: Virtual Reality · Affordance · Immersive Experience · Jingchu Culture

1 Research Background

Virtual reality (VR) is increasingly used in tourism, museums, and heritage attractions to create immersive cultural experiences. By enabling users to enter computer-generated environments, VR can enhance presence, interactivity, narrative engagement, and learning [1, 2]. Prior research has shown that VR can create new possibilities for cultural communication and experience design by transforming cultural content into vivid, participatory, and emotionally engaging encounters [3–5]. Recently, location-based virtual reality (LBVR) has become visible in cultural and commercial venues. Unlike home-based or mobile VR, LBVR is deployed in dedicated physical venues where users wear

Published by Springer Nature Switzerland AG 2027
S. Han et al. (Eds.): I3E 2026, LNCS 16912, pp. 204–215, 2027.
https://doi.org/10.1007/978-3-032-38014-2_16

head-mounted displays, move through designed spaces, and engage with curated virtual worlds. Although LBVR often draws on the technological foundations of VR, it is distinguished by the integration of digital content, physical space, bodily movement, social co-presence, and often multisensory stimulation. In cultural settings, LBVR is used not only for entertainment but also for reconstructing historical scenes, dramatizing cultural narratives, and transforming heritage resources into embodied and interactive experiences [3, 4, 6]. Therefore, LBVR should not be understood merely as another application of VR technology. Rather, it represents a distinctive form of cultural experience in which technology, space, user, and cultural content are jointly orchestrated.

Existing research on VR has generated valuable insights into immersive cultural experiences. One research stream examined experiential qualities from the design angle, such as immersion, presence, embodiment, and interactivity [5–7]. Another focused on user side, such as user satisfaction and behavioral intention [3, 5, 8], as well as broader outcomes beyond information systems use, such as learning and understanding of cultural content [4, 8]. However, while these studies offer useful insights, they remain limited in explaining how LBVR works as a culturally situated process. In the LBVR contexts, the central question is not simply whether VR features increase satisfaction or behaviors, but how users actualize the possibilities offered by LBVR and how this actualization leads to meaningful cultural consequences.

To address this gap, the present study adopts the affordance theory, which shifts analytical attention from technological features to the action possibilities that emerge through the relationship between users, technologies, and use contexts [9–11]. This perspective is well suited to LBVR because immersive cultural experiences are produced through the interaction of users, devices, physical settings, and cultural narratives. It enables us to explain how LBVR affordances are perceived and actualized, and how this process leads to cultural outcomes. Empirically, this study examines Jingchu culture-themed LBVR as the research context. Rooted in the ancient state of Chu, Jingchu culture constitutes an important part of Chinese culture and offers rich historical, symbolic, and narrative resources for immersive interpretation. The current development of Jingchu-themed LBVR projects therefore provides a meaningful context for our study. In so doing, this study contributes to VR tourism and heritage research by shifting attention from isolated experiential outcomes to the process through which immersive cultural experiences are enacted. It also contributes to information systems research by extending the affordance theory to LBVR as an emerging form of culturally situated digital experience.

2 Literature Review

2.1 Immersive VR Experiences in Tourism and Cultural Settings

Research on immersive VR experiences can be broadly classified into two streams. The first stream focuses on a design-side perspective, focusing on experiential qualities such as immersion, presence, embodiment, interactivity, and realism, and examines how these qualities shape users' responses to virtual environments [5–7]. In tourism and cultural contexts, this stream shows that immersive VR can support more direct, vivid, and involving forms of cultural communication by enhancing users' sense of being present, engaged, and connected with cultural content [3, 4, 8].

The second stream takes a user-side perspective, focusing on why users engage with immersive VR and what outcomes they derive from the experience. Prior research suggests that users may enter immersive VR with multiple motives, such as novelty, enjoyment, learning, and cultural interest [12, 13]. Prior studies also examine the outcomes, such as satisfaction, loyalty, behavioral intention, and revisit intention [5, 6, 8]. However, existing research has not sufficiently connected the design side and the user side. Limited attention has been paid to how users perceive and actualize the possibilities embedded in immersive VR design, and how this process connects their initial motivations with culturally meaningful outcomes. Thus, a further investigation is needed.

2.2 An Affordance Perspective on Immersive VR Cultural Experiences

In IS filed, affordance theory explains how technologies matter by focusing on the action possibilities they make available to users in specific contexts [11, 14]. Affordances are generally understood as relational rather than inherent properties, emerging through the interaction among users, technologies, and situated goals [11, 14]. Prior research suggests that affordances must be actualized through use and can be understood as part of a broader process of perception and enactment [10, 11]. This perspective is particularly useful for studying LBVR experiences. Existing constructs such as immersion, presence, embodiment, authenticity, and behavioral intention capture important aspects of VR experience [5, 6], but they do not fully explain what LBVR enables users to do, feel, and understand in culturally themed settings. An affordance lens helps clarify how users engage with the possibilities offered by LBVR and how such engagement may generate culturally meaningful outcomes.

In the specific context of immersive VR cultural experiences, prior studies have proposed several affordance dimensions that help explain how users engage with virtual cultural environments. For instance, studies on digital heritage and VR museums identify interactive affordance and sensory affordance, suggesting that immersive VR influences user engagement by enabling direct interaction and vivid multisensory experience [15]. Recent research also highlights interactivity and embodiment as core affordances of VR [7]. Some studies suggest narrative affordance and interpretive affordance, showing that immersive scenes, role-based progression, and reconstructed historical environments can help users understand cultural stories, historical contexts, and symbolic meanings [4, 5, 8]. We summarize these affordance dimensions in Table 1. To sum up, these dimensions of affordance provide a useful conceptual basis for examining LBVR cultural experiences. Specifically, these affordance dimensions help identify what LBVR enables users to do, perceive, feel, understand, and explore in culturally themed settings. In this study, these affordance dimensions are treated as sensitizing concepts for examining how LBVR shapes users' cultural experience in Jingchu-related settings.

3 Research Methodology

3.1 Research Design

This study adopts a qualitative multiple-case design to examine how LBVR affordances shape users' cultural experience in context. Specifically, the study examines how users engage with Jingchu culture-related LBVR experiences and how the possibilities enabled by LBVR contribute to connecting their initial motivations with subsequent cultural outcomes. The case study approach is selected for the following reasons. First, LBVR is still emerging and can be viewed as a contemporary phenomenon embedded in real-world cultural and commercial settings. Case study research is appropriate when the phenomenon under investigation cannot be separated from its context [16]. Second, LBVR cultural experiences involve the interaction of technology, physical space, bodily movement, cultural content, and user interpretation. A case study approach is therefore suitable for capturing this contextual complexity [16]. Semi-structured interviews were used as the primary data collection method because they are well suited to capturing how users describe what LBVR enabled them to do, feel, and understand during the experience, as well as how they reflected on the experience afterward [16].

Table 1. Summary of prior studies on different dimensions of affordance

Affordance	Affordance concept	Sources
Immersive affordance	The possibility for users to feel experientially inside a mediated cultural world rather than observing it from the outside.	[5, 7]
Sensory affordance	The possibility for users to experience vivid multisensory stimulation, especially through visual and auditory cues.	[3, 17]
Navigational affordance	The possibility for users to move through and orient themselves within virtual cultural space.	[7]
Embodied affordance	The possibility for users to engage through bodily movement and sensorimotor involvement.	[6, 18]
Interactive affordance	The possibility for users to manipulate or respond to virtual cultural elements instead of passively receiving content.	[5, 7]
Participatory affordance	The possibility for users to become active participants in the cultural or historical scene.	[3]
Narrative affordance	The possibility for users to encounter cultural content through unfolding stories, roles, and scene progression.	[4, 8]
Interpretive affordance	The possibility for users to understand and contextualize cultural or historical meaning through the experience.	[4, 5]
Affective affordance	The possibility for users to experience emotional resonance, attachment, or felt closeness through VR.	[4, 5]
Exploratory affordance	The possibility for users to discover cultural details and pursue curiosity through movement and observation.	[3, 5]
Learning affordance	The possibility for users to acquire knowledge and deepen cultural understanding through immersion and interaction.	[3, 8]

3.2 Case Context

This study examines three Jingchu culture-related LBVRs in Hubei, including Crossing the Bronze Age, Crossing Hanyang Arsenal, and Xiaoyao Wudang. All three cases are location-based, delivered through head-mounted immersive VR, and embedded in highly visible public venues in Hubei, China.

Specifically, Crossing the Bronze Age, hosted by the Hubei Provincial Museum, reconstructs bronze-age scenes associated with major relics such as the Sword of Goujian and Marquis Yi's chime bells. Crossing Hanyang Arsenal, located in the Xinhai Revolution Museum, immerses users in a wartime industrial setting linked to the relocation of Hanyang Arsenal during the Battle of Wuhan. Xiaoyao Wudang, deployed in Wuhan MixC, draws on the cultural imagery of the Wudang Mountains and presents a stylized immersive experience shaped by Daoist and martial traditions.

3.3 Data Collection and Analytical Approach

Data were collected through 11 semi-structured interviews conducted between December 31, 2025 and January 22, 2026. Participants were recruited primarily through Chinese social media platforms, including Xiaohongshu and Douban, where the researcher posted recruitment messages inviting users who had experienced Jingchu culture-related LBVR projects. Before each interview, the researcher informed participants of the study aim, explained the confidentiality of the research, and obtained their consent. The researcher then confirmed the relevance of each participant's experience and collected basic background information. All interviews were conducted online via Tencent Meeting and typically lasted 29–45 min. To protect participants' privacy, only audio was recorded, and no video was used. Participants were asked how they entered the LBVR experience, how they engaged with the possibilities offered by the technology, and how they reflected on the experience afterward. Attention was paid to descriptions of what LBVR enabled participants to do, feel, and understand during the experience (Table 2).

Table 2. Profile of Interview Participants

Participant	Gender	Age	Experienced Immersive VR	Interview Time
1	Male	27	*Crossing the Bronze Age*	33 min
2	Female	26	*Crossing the Bronze Age*	29 min
3	Female	21	*Crossing Hanyang Arsenal*	40 min
4	Male	23	*Crossing the Bronze Age*	44 min
5	Female	30	*Crossing the Bronze Age*	45 min
6	Male	21	*Crossing the Bronze Age*	34 min
7	Female	24	*Crossing the Bronze Age*	36 min
8	Female	24	*Crossing the Bronze Age*	42 min
9	Male	28	*Crossing Hanyang Arsenal*	29 min
10	Male	26	*Xiaoyao Wudang*	34 min
11	Female	26	*Xiaoyao Wudang*	40 min

The data were analyzed using an abductive thematic approach [19, 20]. The interview recordings were transcribed into text and then deleted to protect participants' privacy.

The transcripts were read repeatedly, and passages related to participants' experience processes were coded iteratively. The analysis focused on descriptions of the possibilities enabled by LBVR and how these were connected to participants' experiences. The affordance dimensions identified in the literature review were used as sensitizing concepts rather than predefined findings. This allowed the analysis to move between empirical evidence and theoretical interpretation, generating richer and more explanatory insights across the three cases.

4 Research Findings and Discussion

The findings show that LBVR affordances shaped participants' cultural experiences in three ways. First, affordances for entering and perceiving cultural worlds, enabled participants to enter and perceive the virtual cultural world. Second, affordances for acting within cultural worlds, enabled bodily engagement and interaction with the virtual cultural world. Third, affordances for interpreting and internalizing cultural experience, supported interpretation and internalization through narrative understanding, emotional response, and learning. These affordances functioned as an interconnected process rather than as isolated components (see Fig. 1).

4.1 Affordances for Entering and Perceiving Cultural Worlds

The findings suggest that participants' initial entry into immersive cultural experiences was shaped by the combined enactment of immersive, sensory, and exploratory affordances. Across the three cases, these affordances enabled participants to experience LBVR as a virtual world that could be entered, vividly perceived, and spatially explored. Specifically, immersive affordance refers to the possibility for users to feel present inside a culturally themed virtual world. This affordance was evident when participants described the experience as a form of "entering" or "being placed within" a historical or cultural scene. For instance, in Crossing the Bronze Age, one participant said that "*it felt as if I had really stepped into that era*" (P2). Similar descriptions appeared in Crossing Hanyang Arsenal, where participants described "*being placed inside a wartime industrial setting*" (P3). In Xiaoyao Wudang, participants described "*moving through temples, mountains, and stylized Daoist landscapes as if they were physically present*" (P10). These descriptions show that immersive affordance made cultural scenes feel experientially accessible.

Sensory affordance refers to the possibility for users to experience cultural scenes through vivid visual, auditory, and atmospheric stimulation. This affordance was reflected in participants' descriptions of how sensory cues intensified the perceived reality of cultural content. Participants repeatedly emphasized that sound, visual scale, lighting, and environmental effects made the experience feel immediate and striking. One participant in Crossing the Bronze Age described floating bronze artifacts as so visually powerful, saying that "*it felt as if the bronze objects were about to fall on me*" (P7), indicating that the integration of visual scale, motion, and proximity made the relics feel physically present. Another participant stated that "*the combination of music and scene transitions made the final sequence especially impactful*" (P1). These descriptions indicate that sensory affordance strengthened vividness and realism of cultural content.

Exploratory affordance refers to the possibility for users to encounter cultural content through movement, spatial orientation, and curiosity-driven discovery. This affordance was particularly visible in Xiaoyao Wudang. One participant noted that "*the designated route and spatial position shaped our experience, which depended on spatial navigation rather than passive viewing*" (P11). Another described such experience as "*almost like actually touring and exploring Wudang Mountain temples*" (P10). The cultural content was encountered through movement across different sites. These statements suggest that exploratory affordance enabled participants to approach culture as something to be encountered through spatial movement, orientation, and discovery.

Overall, immersive, sensory, and exploratory affordances shaped the opening stage of the immersive cultural experience. They helped transform cultural content into a world that participants could enter, perceive, and explore.

4.2 Affordances for Acting Within Cultural Worlds

The findings indicate that participants' transition from spectatorship to active involvement was primarily by embodied affordance and interactive affordance. These affordances allowed participants to act within the virtual cultural world as situated actors. Embodied affordance refers to the possibility of engaging with virtual cultural content through bodily movement and bodily feedback. This affordance was especially visible in Crossing the Bronze Age, where participants described swinging hammers, touching objects, and striking ritual instruments. One participant recalled that "*when I swung the hammer, there was vibration feedback; and when striking the instrument, there was the original sound*" (P6). Participant's bodily action was connected with tactile and auditory feedback, making the cultural activity physically experienceable. Another emphasized that being able to "*reach out and touch those instruments*", made the experience "*feel more real*" (P2). In Xiaoyao Wudang, a participant described "*following gestures, pressing handprints, and practicing Tai Chi movements*" (P10). Bodily movement was a central way through which participants became involved in the cultural scene.

Interactive affordance refers to the possibility of manipulating, responding to, or directly engaging with virtual elements in ways that influence the unfolding experience. This affordance was reflected in actions that required participants to complete tasks, respond to prompts, or cooperate with the virtual scenario. For instance, in Crossing the Bronze Age, one participant described that they should "*personally hand over the Sword of Goujian*" and that this was "*not simply something to watch from the outside*" (P1). Participants were required to perform a culturally meaningful action within the scene. In Crossing Hanyang Arsenal, interaction was more closely tied to scenario-based tasks. A participant described "*moving with teammates, following commands, passing ammunition, and taking part in evacuation and defense tasks*" within the wartime setting (P3). These accounts support interactive affordance because they show that users responded to virtual objects, characters, and tasks in ways that made their responses matter within the cultural-historical scene.

Overall, the two affordances emphasize different aspects of action. Embodied affordance concerns how users engage through bodily movement and sensorimotor feedback, while interactive affordance concerns how users respond to virtual objects, characters, and tasks in ways that shape the experience. Through these affordances, cultural content became something participants could enact through bodily and situated involvement.

4.3 Affordances for Interpreting and Internalizing Cultural Experience

The findings indicate that participants' movement from immersion and participation to cultural understanding was shaped primarily by narrative affordance, interpretive affordance, affective affordance, and learning affordance. These affordances helped participants organize what they encountered into meaningful cultural experiences. In the studied cases, narrative and interpretive affordances mainly structured and clarified cultural content, affective and learning affordances strengthened participants' emotional and cognitive connection to that content.

Narrative affordance refers to the possibility of encountering cultural content through stories, roles, and scene progression. This was especially visible in Crossing Hanyang Arsenal, where a participant emphasized that the "*experience unfolded through the perspective of ordinary workers, making the historical event easier to follow and personally relevant*" (P9). In Crossing the Bronze Age, a participant also mentioned "*forging sequences, ritual scenes, and the story of Goujian as helping them grasp the cultural logic behind the artifacts*" (P5). These accounts suggest that narrative affordance turned cultural content from isolated information into a structured experiential sequence.

Interpretive affordance refers to the possibility of understanding and contextualizing cultural meaning through the immersive experience. In Crossing the Bronze Age, one participant stated that previously they had understood Jingchu culture "*only at a surface level, knowing what it was, but not why it was so*" (P5). Another explained that "*the experience moved me beyond the textual Jingchu culture and enabled deeper understanding*" (P7). LBVR helped participants connect cultural symbols with their historical and cultural significance. Interpretive affordance therefore supported meaning-making beyond simple exposure to cultural content.

Affective affordance refers to the possibility of developing emotional resonance and felt closeness through the experience. In Crossing Hanyang Arsenal, one participant described the bonfire scene in direct emotional terms, stating that "*the moment of declaring our resolve around the bonfire moved me even more... it gave me a strong sense of devotion to family and nation*" (P3). In Crossing the Bronze Age, another participant explained the emotional effect of the experience by saying that "*the feeling it created was greater reverence, and also a greater sense of closeness*" (P2). These responses indicate that LBVR supported cultural experiences not only cognitively, but also emotionally.

Learning affordance refers to the possibility of acquiring knowledge and deepening cultural understanding through immersion and interaction. In Crossing the Bronze Age, one participant stated that the experience made him feel "*the important place of bronze artifacts in history*" and see them as "*an important symbol of Chinese civilization*" (P4). Another participant described this shift more broadly by noting that the experience enabled her to move beyond "*Jingchu culture at the level of text*" and instead "*understand it more deeply*" (P7). These accounts suggest that learning in immersive VR was embedded in the process of narrative understanding, interpretation, and emotional engagement rather than occurring separately from them.

Overall, these four affordances therefore shaped the interpretive stage of the immersive cultural experience. Narrative affordance organized cultural content into stories and roles, interpretive affordance clarified cultural meaning, affective affordance created emotional resonance, and learning affordance deepened cultural understanding. Through these affordances, participants interpreted and internalized cultural content during the LBVR experience.

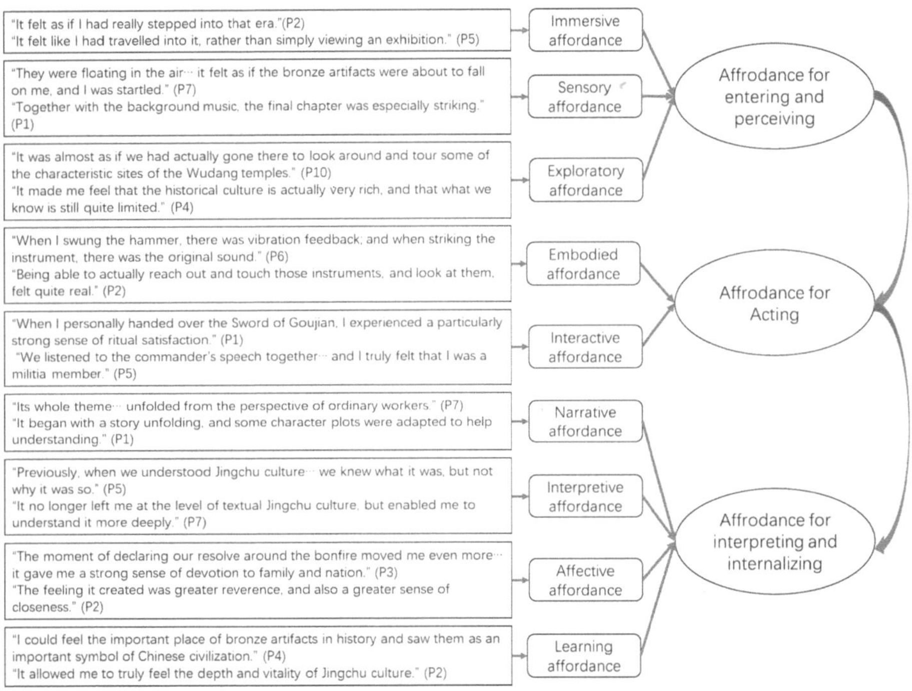

Fig. 1. LBVR Affordances Across the Immersive Experience Process

4.4 Affordance Enactment Across the Experience Process

The results suggest that the identified affordances were enacted as a connected process. Participants' immersive cultural experiences unfolded through three stages. First, immersive affordance, sensory affordance, and exploratory affordance shaped how participants entered and perceived culturally themed virtual worlds. At this stage, cultural content and elements became something participants could enter, sense, and explore via LBVR. Second, embodied affordance and interactive affordance shaped how participants acted within LBVR. Bodily movement, tactile feedback, gesture, task completion, and direct responses made cultural content actionable and participatory. Third, narrative affordance, interpretive affordance, affective affordance, and learning affordance shaped how participants interpreted and internalized what they encountered. At this stage, stories, roles, historical contexts, emotional scenes, and knowledge cues within LBVR helped participants develop cultural understanding, emotional resonance, and learning.

To sum up, the findings suggest that LBVR shaped cultural experience through an unfolding affordance process. Its cultural significance lies in its capacity to guide users through a process of entering, acting within, and making sense of cultural virtual worlds.

5 Conclusion

5.1 Theoretical Contribution

This study makes two main theoretical contributions. First, it explains how LBVR affordances shape cultural experience through an unfolding process. The findings show that users' experience developed through three connected stages: entering and perceiving virtual cultural worlds, acting within them, and interpreting and internalizing what they encountered. This extends prior research by showing that LBVR in cultural settings is shaped by a connected process of affordance enactment. Second, the study reframes the role of LBVR in culturally themed settings. Prior research has often emphasized experience enhancement through constructs such as immersion, presence, authenticity, and enjoyment. The present findings suggest that LBVR should also be understood as a medium that structures cultural engagement by enabling users to enter, participate in, and interpret cultural content in meaningful ways. This provides a more process-sensitive account of immersive VR in IS research on technology-enabled experience.

5.2 Practical Implications

The findings suggest that Jingchu culture-related LBVR should be designed and managed as a process of cultural engagement, not as a collection of impressive technical effects. The practical value of LBVR lies in how it structures users' involvement from entering a virtual cultural world, participating in it, and then interpreting its cultural meaning. For museums, cultural institutions, and immersive content developers, effective LBVR design should therefore support the whole experience process instead of relying mainly on immersion or visual spectacle.

More specifically, different affordances become important at different stages of the experience. Immersive, sensory, and exploratory affordances help users enter and perceive cultural virtual worlds. Embodied and interactive affordances help transform users from viewers into participants. Narrative, interpretive, affective, and learning affordances help users understand, emotionally connect with, and internalize cultural content. Therefore, LBVR design should integrate strong virtual environmental design, meaningful bodily interaction, and clear narrative and interpretive support. For instance, cultural interpretation could be embedded throughout the experience. Key cultural meanings can be explained through voice-over, character dialogue, scene transitions, object labels, or even interactive actions.

5.3 Limitations and Future Research

This study has several limitations. First, it is based on a qualitative multiple-case design with 11 interviews from three Jingchu culture-related LBVR projects in China. Because the three cases are situated in a specific cultural and regional context, the findings may need further examination in other cultural settings. Future studies could examine a broader range of LBVR, compare different cultural themes, venue types, and audience groups. Second, the study relies on retrospective interviews. Although this method is useful for capturing participants' interpretations, they are less able to trace affordance enactment in real time. Future studies could combine interviews with observation, behavioral tracking, and post-experience survey data to provide a more comprehensive account of users' experience processes. Third, although this study identifies an unfolding process of affordance enactment, further research is needed to examine whether this process appears in other immersive cultural experiences. Future studies could also investigate how different stages of affordance enactment relate to cultural engagement outcomes, such as cultural learning, cultural affinity, revisit intention, and long-term cultural participation.

Acknowledgement. This work was supported by the Overseas Postdoctoral Talent Recruitment Special Program and the Fundamental Research Funds for the Central Universities at Central China Normal University (Grant No. CCNU26XJ046).

References

1. Slater, M.: Immersion and the illusion of presence in virtual reality. Br. J. Psychol. **109**(3), 431–433 (2018)
2. Slater, M., Sanchez-Vives, M.V.: Enhancing our lives with immersive virtual reality. Front. Rob. AI. **3**, 74 (2016)
3. Jangra, S., Singh, G., Mantri, A., et al.: Exploring the impact of virtual reality on museum experiences: visitor immersion and experience consequences. Virtual Reality. **29**(2), 84 (2025)
4. Jiang, L., Chen, Y., Sun, Y.: Influences of VR technology on the effect of museum narrative based on embodied cognitive theory: a case study of the opium war museum. J. Hosp. Tour. Technol. **16**(2), 269–285 (2025)
5. Li, M., Sun, X., Zhu, Y., et al.: Real in virtual: the influence mechanism of virtual reality on tourists' perceptions of presence and authenticity in museum tourism. Int. J. Contemp. Hosp. Manag. **36**(11), 3651–3673 (2024)
6. Lin, Y.Q., Suh, A., Wagner, C.: Increasing immersive virtual reality platform loyalty: the role of embodiment. Inf. Manag. **63**(1), 104255 (2026)
7. Dincelli, E., Yayla, A.: Immersive virtual reality in the age of the metaverse: a hybrid-narrative review based on the technology affordance perspective. J. Strateg. Inf. Syst. **31**(2), 101717 (2022)
8. Chang, S., Suh, J.: The impact of digital storytelling on presence, immersion, enjoyment, and continued usage intention in VR-based museum exhibitions. Sensors. **25**(9), 2914 (2025)
9. Lichti, C., Tumasjan, A.: "My precious!": a values-affordances perspective on the adoption of bitcoin. J. Assoc. Inf. Syst. **24**(3), 629–663 (2023)
10. Strauss, L.M., Klein, A.Z., Scornavacca, E.: Adopting emerging information technology: a new affordances process framework. Int. J. Inf. Manag. **76**, 102772 (2024)

11. Strong, D.M., Volkoff, O., Johnson, S.A., et al.: A theory of organization-EHR affordance actualization. J. Assoc. Inf. Syst. **15**(2), 53–85 (2014)
12. Kim, M.J., Hall, C.M.: A hedonic motivation model in virtual reality tourism: comparing visitors and non-visitors. Int. J. Inf. Manag. **46**, 236–249 (2019)
13. Lee, S.A., Lee, M., Jeong, M.: The role of virtual reality on information sharing and seeking behaviors. J. Hosp. Tour. Manag. **46**, 215–223 (2021)
14. Leonardi, P.M.: When flexible routines meet flexible technologies: affordance, constraint, and the imbrication of human and material agencies 1. MIS Q. **35**(1), 147–167 (2011)
15. Jia, W., Li, H., Jiang, M., et al.: Melting the psychological boundary: how interactive and sensory affordance influence users' adoption of digital heritage service. Sustainability. **15**(5), 4117 (2023)
16. Yin, R.K.: Case Study Research: Design and Methods. Sage (2009)
17. Flavián, C., Ibáñez-Sánchez, S., Orús, C.: The impact of virtual, augmented and mixed reality technologies on the customer experience. J. Bus. Res. **100**, 547–560 (2019)
18. Tussyadiah, I.P., Wang, D., Jung, T.H., et al.: Virtual reality, presence, and attitude change: empirical evidence from tourism. Tour. Manag. **66**, 140–154 (2018)
19. Braun, V., Clarke, V.: Using thematic analysis in psychology. Qual. Res. Psychol. **3**(2), 77–101 (2006)
20. Thompson, J.: A guide to abductive thematic analysis. Qual. Rep. **27**(5), 1410–1421 (2022)

Data-Driven Services for Sustainability and Well-Being

From Data to Decision: How Data Features of Digital Product Passport Influence Consumers' Intention to Use Digital Product Passport for Circular Consumption

Maneesha Dias(✉) and Gehan Wishwajith Premathilake

Unit of Information and Knowledge Management, Faculty of Management and Business, Tampere University, Tampere, Finland
{maneesha.dias,gehan.ethugalapathiranage}@tuni.fi

Abstract. This study examines how data features of Digital Product Passport (DPP) influence consumers' intention to use DPP for circular consumption. Drawing on the norm activation model and signaling theory, this study investigates how data features of DPP, including data completeness, accuracy, reliability, and relevance, shape consumers' awareness of consequences of circular economy and ascription of responsibility for circular economy, which in turn affect personal pro-environmental norm regarding sustainability and influence consumers' intention to use DPP for circular consumption. Using a scenario-based survey with 281 valid responses, it reveals that data relevance significantly enhances both awareness of consequences of circular economy and ascription of responsibility for circular economy, while data accuracy positively affects only ascription of responsibility for circular economy. In contrast, data completeness and reliability show no significant effects. Furthermore, awareness of consequences of circular economy and ascription of responsibility for circular economy positively influence personal pro-environmental norm, which subsequently drives consumers' intention to use DPP for circular consumption. This study enriches the literature by examining the role of data in DPP in shaping consumers' intention to use DPP for circular consumption at the individual level from norm activation perspective.

Keywords: Circular consumption · Data features · Digital product Passport · Norm Activation Model · Signaling theory

1 Introduction

Data can be used to support data-driven decision making across different levels of stakeholders, including individuals, organizations, and societies. However, data-driven decision making is closely related to data features, data quality, data analytics capability and effective interaction between human cognition and decision support systems [1].

Circular economy practices encourage the extension of the life of materials and continuous use of a product via strategies such as reduce, reuse and recycle [2]. Circular

Published by Springer Nature Switzerland AG 2027
S. Han et al. (Eds.): I3E 2026, LNCS 16912, pp. 219–239, 2027.
https://doi.org/10.1007/978-3-032-38014-2_17

consumption, which stems from circular economy, extends these principles from organizational and societal level to the individual consumer level, encouraging consumers to engage in product choices that minimize environmental impact, retain material value, and prolong product lifecycles [3]. However, the adoption of circular consumption practices can be hindered by fragmented, inconsistent, and inaccessible data and information about product life cycles and environmental impacts at the individual consumer level.

Digital product passport (DPP) has emerged as a digital solution that addresses data-related challenges by providing a digital identity for products and offering standardized lifecycle-wide information accessible to consumers [4]. By providing product data related to its material composition and circular performance, DPP aims to support data-driven decision making for both organizations and end consumers. While prior research on DPP has extensively investigated how DPP enables data-enabled circular economy practices and circular decision making at the organizational level, these studies overlook the role of DPP in supporting consumers' circular consumption. The effectiveness of DPP in promoting circular consumption depends not only on the availability of product data but also on the features of data communicated to consumers. It is meaningful to examine the role of data features of DPP in shaping individuals' intention to use DPP for circular consumption.

This study addresses the above research gap by examining how four data features of DPP (data completeness, data accuracy, data reliability and data relevance) affect consumers' intention to use DPP for circular consumption based on the Norm Activation Model (NAM) and signaling theory. According to signaling theory, data features can serve as informational signals that reduce information asymmetry and shape consumers' perceptions of product sustainability, while NAM explains how these perceptions activate consumers' awareness of environmental consequences and personal responsibility, ultimately influencing their circular consumption.

2 Theoretical Background

2.1 Data in Data-Driven Decision Making for Circular Consumption

Data plays a central role in data-driven decision and acts as the foundation for generating insights. Availability of data alone is not sufficient for successful data-driven decision making. It requires enhanced data quality and data analytics capabilities to generate meaningful insights and improve decision quality [6]. Data quality can be conceptualized based on data features, such as data completeness, data accuracy, data relevance and data reliability [7–10]. These data features can affect consumers' perception of data quality. Data completeness reflects whether sufficient information is available, data accuracy reflects whether information correctly represents reality, data reliability reflects whether information can be trusted consistently, and data relevance reflects whether information is applicable to the consumers' decision context. Together, these dimensions capture fundamental data attributes [7]. In addition, data analytics capability enables transforming raw data into actionable insights and making better insights and more informed decisions, leading to substantial value creation [11]. Beyond these technical dimensions, research has also uncovered that organizational and behavioral factors, such as data-driven culture and human cognitive skills affect how data is utilized and interpreted [1, 5].

Circular economy is a sustainable development strategy that promotes products and materials use in continuous circulation along its value chain via strategies such as reuse, remanufacturing, refurbishment and recycling [2]. Data sharing and data analytics can enable circular economic performance monitoring and linking circular practices to firm performance [12]. Empirical evidence also shows that data enables decision support and trust building among individuals in circular economic practice. Data supports consumer evaluation on the quality of reused goods and environmental impact of the product in their circular consumption decisions [13] [14].

Meanwhile, the use of data in circular economy is not without its share of challenges. Data is often fragmented, inconsistent and inaccessible across the value chain of a product throughout its life cycle. Furthermore, the lack of standardization of data and unreliability of provided data makes consumers not trust the data and use their intuition for circular decision making. DPP has emerged as an ideal solution that overcomes these data related challenges and provides consumers with standardized, trustworthy data across the value chain throughout the product life cycle for data-driven circular decision making.

2.2 DPP for Data-Driven Decision Making for Circular Consumption

DPP has been introduced by the European Union as a digital identification solution under the Ecodesign for Sustainable Products Regulation of the European Union [4]. DPP assigns digital identity to products, enabling the sharing of relevant product information throughout their lifecycle. Consumers can access DPP by scanning a QR code or tapping NFC tag available on products or by visiting the online platform for DPP of products.

Empirical studies have highlighted the contribution of DPP towards data-driven decision making. Much attention has been given to organizational level studies that focus on data integration in DPP and product lifecycle decision making. They have found that data in DPP enables material traceability and supports data sharing among actors towards improving lifecycle visibility of the product [15]. Lifecycle data embedded in DPP supports recycling and remanufacturing decisions for organizations [16]. Further, DPP acts as a shared data platform through which product data are collected by stakeholders along the value chain of a product and distributed across value chain partners and are accessible to end consumers as well. Prior studies extensively examine DPP enabled decision-making at the organizational level. For instance, existing research has examined the role of DPP on enhancing organizational traceability and transparency for decision making and improving circularity through product life cycle from data perspective [17]. DPP could also facilitate individuals' circular decision making when product circularity related data is available in DPP. However, there is a lack of knowledge on how end consumers engage with data in DPP to support their circular consumption. It is unclear how the data features of DPP shape consumers' perceptions and support their circular consumption decision making.

2.3 Norm Activation Model

NAM posits that personal norm influence altruistic behavior [18]. According to the theory, personal norm, which is an internalized standard of behavior, is a determinant of the pro-social behavioral intention. Awareness of consequences and ascription of responsibility shape personal norm. Awareness of consequences refers to the human awareness that actions have consequences and ascription of responsibility means that individuals must feel personally responsible for the outcome. NAM suggests that individuals engage in pro-social behaviors when they become aware of the consequences of their actions for others and accept personal responsibility for addressing those consequences, thereby activating their personal norms [18].

This perspective has been applied across various contexts, including charitable giving and volunteering demonstrating that moral norms are strong predictors of behaviors intended to benefit society [45] [46]. has investigated consumers' energy-saving intentions during vehicle usage. Their findings confirmed the application of NAM in explaining pro-environmental intentions in the transportation context.

Prior research has defined pro-environmental behavior as a pro-social behavior [19] and applied NAM in research in the sustainability context to understand individuals' sustainable behavior. Thus, NAM is an appropriate theory to understand consumers' intention to use DPP for circular consumption.

2.4 Signaling Theory

Signaling theory [20] explains how signals effectively reduce uncertainty and facilitate efficient matching between market participants. The signaling theory consists of signaler, signal and receiver. Signaler is defined as an insider who obtains information that is not available to an outsider. Receiver is regarded as an outsider who does not have the necessary information but would like to obtain the information. The signal represents positive and negative information that the signaler is aware of and decides whether to communicate to the receiver or not [21].

Signaling theory has been applied as a theoretical foundation in information systems (IS) field to explain how digital cues acting as credible signals reduce perceived uncertainty and guide user decisions [22]. The research [47] has applied signaling theory to explain how digital technologies, such as blockchain, communicate credible information about product attributes and sustainability performance, thereby reducing consumers' uncertainty and fostering trust.

This study applies signaling theory to understand the data provided through the DPP as signals communicated by product manufacturing stakeholders to end consumers. It further examines how these signals shape consumers' perceptions and their intention to use DPP for circular consumption.

3 Research Model and Hypotheses

Based on the theories of NAM and signaling theory, we investigate the effect of data features in DPP on consumers' intention to use DPP for circular consumption. The integration of signaling theory and NAM can explain how data features in DPP act as signals that active consumers' personal pro-environmental norm regarding sustainability and support their pro-environmental decision-making. Following NAM, we assume that data features in DPP can shape consumers' awareness of consequences of circular economy and ascription of responsibility for circular economy, which further influence their personal pro-environmental norm regarding sustainability. Personal pro-environmental norm will lead to their intention to use DPP for circular consumption. Specifically, four distinct data features of data in DPP were selected in this study, including data completeness, data accuracy, data reliability and data relevance. The conceptual model is depicted in Fig. 1.

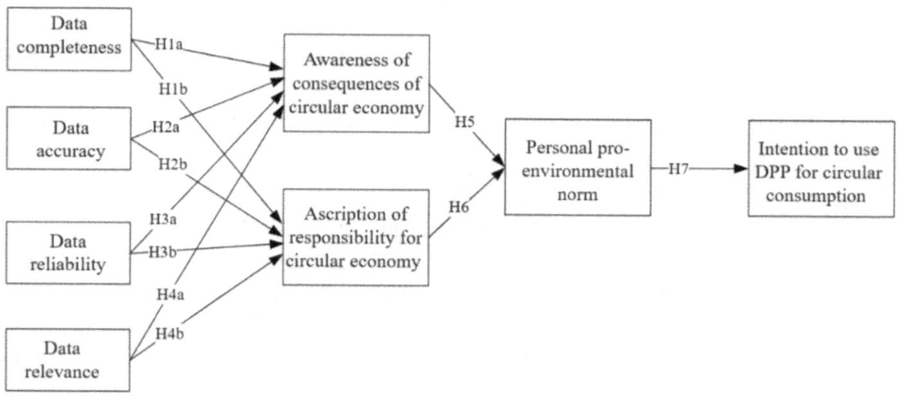

Fig. 1. Research model

Data completeness refers to the extent to which all the required information are present in a digital solution without omission of necessary information, thereby providing complete data for a task or a decision [9, 10]. DPP consists of data related to product information, product life cycle information from origin to end of life, circular options possible for the product, sustainability performance of the product etc. [16]. In DPP, the availability of complete data improves consumers' interpretation of the product and its circular performance [23]. Consequently, the completeness of DPP data enhances consumers' ability to assess the environmental consequences of circular consumption decisions. Further, by making consequences of circular consumption visible, data completeness showcase the moral responsibility initiated by the consumer for the circular consumption practices that benefit the environment. It enhances the link between consumption decisions and their environmental impact, which in turn increases consumers' perceived responsibility for the positive environmental consequences [19]. Better data completeness supports stronger ascription of responsibility for circular economy. Therefore, we hypothesize:

H1a: *Data completeness of DPP is positively associated with consumers' awareness of consequences of circular economy.*
H1b: *Data completeness of DPP is positively associated with consumers' ascription of responsibility for circular economy.*

Data accuracy is interpreted as a data attribute that reflects how the data represent the real situation correctly and is free from errors [7]. Accurate data in DPP reduces ambiguity and ensures consumers of the real consequences of circular consumption decisions. Thereby, consumers can more effectively anticipate positive outcomes of their circular behavior, leading to better awareness of environmental consequences [24]. Accurate data in DPP can also support consumers to understand the positive environmental responsibility initiated by consumers when deciding to make circular consumption with the support of DPP. By providing precise information about the environmental impact associated with products, DPP allows consumers to understand the positive outcomes of responsible consumption, reinforcing ascription of responsibility for circular economy. Therefore, we hypothesize:

H2a: *Data accuracy of DPP is positively associated with consumers' awareness of consequences of circular economy.*
H2b: *Data accuracy of DPP is positively associated with consumers' ascription of responsibility for circular economy.*

Data reliability refers to the credibility and trustworthiness of information presented in DPP [7]. Data reliability can help consumer build confidence in their circular consumption. For instance, consumers can effectively assess the positive environmental consequences of their circular consumption, leading to better awareness of its consequences related to sustainability. Further, by providing reliable information about the environmental impact associated with products, DPP allows consumers to understand the positive outcomes of responsible consumption, reinforcing ascription of responsibility for circular economy [25]. It allows consumers to link their circular consumption to broader environmental effects, fostering a sense of responsibility. Therefore, we hypothesize:

H3a: *Data reliability of DPP is positively associated with consumers' awareness of consequences of circular economy.*
H3b: *Data reliability of DPP is positively associated with consumers' ascription of responsibility for circular economy.*

Data relevance is defined as the extent to which the data is pertinent for a consumer's intended analysis or decision [8]. Relevance of data is an important consideration for DPP since DPP aims to provide all the relevant data related to product specifications, product composition, product circularity and product life cycle, which can enable consumers to make informed circular consumption [16]. When DPP provides data relevant to circular consumption of a product, consumers can better understand the environmental consequences of their purchase decision, thereby increasing their awareness of its consequences related to sustainability. Furthermore, when DPP provides data relevant to circular consumption of a product, consumers can recognize the responsibility rendered towards the environment in ensuring circular consumption, thus enhancing their ascription of responsibility for circular economy. Therefore, we hypothesize:

H4a: *Data relevance of DPP is positively associated with consumers' awareness of consequences of circular economy.*

H4b: *Data relevance of DPP is positively associated with consumers' ascription of responsibility for circular economy.*

According to prior literature, when individuals recognize that their behavior can contribute to positive environmental benefits, it directly impacts the moral obligation to act, considering the positive outcomes that may occur by their pro-environmental choice [26]. When consumers consider the positive environmental outcome of circular consumption, it strengthens their personal pro-environmental norm [27] and reinforces a commitment to use DPP in ways that support environmental sustainability. Therefore, we argue that awareness of positive environmental consequences caused by conducting circular consumptions from DPP benefits an individual's development of personal pro-environmental norm. We posit the subsequent hypothesis:

H5: *Awareness of consequences of circular economy is positively associated with personal pro-environmental norm.*

When individuals understand the beneficial impact of engaging in pro-environmental behavior, individuals perceive such actions as meaningful and rewarding [24]. This increased awareness makes individuals feel responsible for the positive environmental outcomes caused by their decisions, thereby fostering the internalization of personal pro-environmental norms and encouraging individuals to act in accordance with pro-environmental behavior [18]. Therefore, when DPP users are personally feeling the responsibility of their circular consumption, they will be more likely to initiate an internalized pro-environmental norm. Thus, we posit the following hypothesis:

H6: *Ascription of responsibility for circular economy is positively associated with personal pro-environmental norm.*

When individuals have internalized personal pro-environmental norm, they experience a moral obligation to engage in behaviors that benefit the environment [19] [38]. When the consumers using the DPP feel the urge to conduct circular consumption as a personal pro-environmental norm, this internalized sense of duty converts into behavioral intention towards circular consumption using the DPP. Therefore, it is assumed that personal pro-environmental norm can shape consumers' intention to use DPP to support their circular consumption, and it is proposed that:

H7: *Personal pro-environmental norm is positively associated with consumers' intention to use DPP for circular consumption.*

4 Research Methodology

4.1 Research Design

This study employs a scenario-based survey design to investigate how data features in DPP influence consumers' intention to use DPP for circular consumption. Since DPP is a digital solution at the initial stage and research participants might have no DPP use experience, the scenario-based survey method is a suitable approach to study consumers' use of DPP for circular consumption. The scenario-based survey design includes a vignette that provides research participants a context of DPP use, which ensures uniformity of the details available for research participants and help them get understanding of DPP use [28, 29].

To operationalize the scenario, we developed six graphical user interface (GUI) artifacts corresponding to the interfaces that a consumer may interact with when using DPP. The GUIs represent product information, material composition, circular consumption options of the product and product lifecycle information of a product. Then a scenario was developed by combining the GUIs to mimic the way a user may interact with the six GUIs of DPP (see Appendix B).

The questionnaire consists of a consent form, reading material on DPP, questions to filter respondents interested in DPP and circular practices, demographic information related questions, and consumer perceptions about using DPP for circular consumption. The scenario was presented to respondents prior to the questionnaire. Prior to data collection, the questionnaire was pre-tested through a pilot study to understand the clarity of the questionnaire. The survey instrument was modified to improve its readability and overall quality based on the feedback gathered from the pilot study.

4.2 Operationalization of Constructs

The research model includes eight constructs: data completeness, data accuracy, data reliability, data relevance, awareness of consequences of circular economy, ascription of responsibility for circular economy, personal pro-environmental norm and consumers' intention to use DPP for circular consumption. To ensure content validity, these constructs were measured by adopting the measurement items from literature and slightly adjusting them to match the study context of DPP. The items for measuring data completeness were adopted from [10]. Data accuracy and data reliability were measured with items taken from [7], and data relevance was measured with items from [8]. The measurement items of awareness of consequences of circular economy, ascription of responsibility for circular economy and personal pro-environmental norm were adopted from [26] and consumers' intention to use DPP for circular consumption was adopted from [44] (see Appendix A). Construct items were measured using a seven-point Likert scale ranging from 1 (strongly disagree) to 7 (strongly agree).

4.3 Data Collection

A scenario-based online survey was conducted to collect empirical data through the online research platform Prolific, which is considered a reliable and a valid platform for collecting empirical data [30]. An introduction to the concept DPP was provided before starting the questionnaire to establish familiarity with the topic among research participants. To ensure relevance of responses, eligibility was further assessed through screening questions that evaluated respondents' understanding of the provided DPP description as well as their prior involvement in circular economy practices. Only respondents meeting these criteria were allowed to continue the survey. Three attention-check questions were embedded at different points in the survey, and any participant failing these checks was removed from the final dataset.

A total of 292 responses were collected, and 11 responses were identified as extreme outliers in terms of survey completion time and therefore excluded. Consequently, we obtained 281 valid responses for analysis. The final dataset consisted of 148 male respondents (52.7%), 131 female respondents (46.6%), and 2 participants (0.7%) who did not disclose gender. The sample covered a broad age distribution from 18 to 60 years and above, with a dominant share (80.1%) in the 18–39 age group. Regarding prior engagement in circular economy activities, 54.8% of respondents reported participating more than five times in such practices over the past five years. Demographic analysis of the dataset is available in Table 1.

Table 1. Demographic information of the respondents

Measurement	Item	Count	Percentage (%)
Gender	Male	148	52.7
	Female	131	46.6
	Prefer not to say	2	0.7
Age	18–29	130	46.3
	30–39	95	33.8
	40–49	26	9.3
	50–59	17	6
	60 or more	13	4.6
Education	Upper secondary school or vocational school	7	2.5
	Bachelor's degree	186	66.2
	Master's degree	72	25.6
	Doctorate	16	5.7
Income	Less than $20,000	90	32
	$20,000–$39,999	91	32.4
	$40,000–$59,999	41	14.6
	$60,000–$79,999	24	8.5
	$80,000–$99,999	20	7.1
	$100,000 or more	15	5.4
Circular economic practices during last 5 years	Once	10	3.6
	2–3 times	70	24.9
	4–5 times	47	16.7
	More than 5 times	154	54.8

4.4 Validity and Reliability

Following the guidelines of [31], common method bias (CMB) was examined considering the self-reported nature of data. First, Harman's single factor test revealed that the first factor accounted for 38.93% of the total variance, which is below the threshold of 50% [32]. Additionally, a marker variable was integrated to the endogenous constructs to assess CMB [33]. The model's significant path coefficients remained unchanged after controlling for the marker variable. Further, the R^2 value of ascription of responsibility for circular economy remained unchanged and R^2 values of consumers' intention to use DPP for circular consumption ($\Delta R^2 = +0.001$), awareness of consequences of circular economy ($\Delta R^2 = +0.004$), and personal pro-environmental norm ($\Delta R^2 = +0.002$) were slightly changed. The test results indicate that model's constructs were not substantially affected by CMB. In addition, the inner variance inflation factor (VIF) values for all constructs were between 1.000 to 2.336, below the recommended threshold of 3.3, indicating no significant concerns related to multicollinearity [34].

Convergent validity tests were conducted to verify whether construct items accurately represent the theoretical stance of the study following reliability and validity guidelines [35]. Two construct measurement items were removed as their factor loading values are lower than 0.7. Other factor loading values exceeded the threshold of 0.7 as suggested by [35]. The Cronbach alpha values and composite reliability (CR) values of all constructs exceeded 0.7 respectively, indicating satisfactory internal consistency reliability. Furthermore, average variance extracted (AVE) values of all constructs exceed the threshold of 0.5, confirming convergent validity of the research instrument [37] (see Table 2).

Table 2. Confirmatory factor analysis

Construct	Item	Factor loading	Cronbach's alpha	CR	AVE
Data completeness (DCOM)	DCOM1	0.894	0.866	0.872	0.788
	DCOM2	0.892			
	DCOM3	0.877			
Data accuracy (DACC)	DACC1	0.916	0.87	0.882	0.793
	DACC2	0.885			
	DACC3	0.869			
Data reliability (DREL)	DREL1	0.896	0.879	0.929	0.802
	DREL2	0.927			
	DREL3	0.863			
Data relevance (DRLV)	DRLV1	0.919	0.942	0.945	0.852
	DRLV2	0.927			
	DRLV3	0.917			
	DRLV4	0.928			
Awareness of consequences of circular economy (PBAV)	PBAV1	0.868	0.801	0.857	0.629
	PBAV2	0.819			
	PBAV3	0.884			

(continued)

Table 2. (*continued*)

Construct	Item	Factor loading	Cronbach's alpha	CR	AVE
Ascription of responsibility for circular economy (ASRP)	ASRP1	0.954	0.935	0.938	0.885
	ASRP2	0.935			
	ASRP3	0.933			
Personal pro-environmental norm (PNOM)	PNOM1	0.852	0.919	0.919	0.757
	PNOM2	0.909			
	PNOM3	0.825			
	PNOM4	0.871			
	PNOM5	0.889			
Intention to use DPP for circular consumption (BHIN)	BHIN1	0.930	0.934	0.939	0.883
	BHIN2	0.937			
	BHIN3	0.952			

Following the guidelines of [35], the discriminant validity was evaluated using the Fornell–Larcker criterion and the Heterotrait-Monotrait ratio (HTMT). Each construct's square root of the AVE exceeds its correlations with other constructs, indicating adequate discriminant validity (see Table 3). Furthermore, all HTMT values were below the threshold of 0.90, confirming that the latent constructs are empirically distinct [37] (see Table 4).

Table 3. Discriminant validity-latent variable correlations and square roots of AVEs

	ASRP	BHIN	DACC	DCOM	DREL	DRLV	PBAV	PNOM
ASRP	0.941							
BHIN	0.444	0.940						
DACC	0.254	0.421	0.890					
DCOM	0.125	0.369	0.446	0.888				
DREL	0.172	0.443	0.710	0.513	0.896			
DRLV	0.395	0.687	0.478	0.446	0.514	0.923		
PBAV	0.484	0.547	0.258	0.273	0.313	0.387	0.793	
PNOM	0.653	0.470	0.260	0.192	0.230	0.401	0.542	0.87

Table 4. Discriminant validity-Heterotrait-Monotrait ratio (HTMT)

	ASRP	BHIN	DACC	DCOM	DREL	DRLV	PBAV
BHIN	0.473						
DACC	0.275	0.470					
DCOM	0.138	0.409	0.511				
DREL	0.178	0.476	0.807	0.581			
DRLV	0.418	0.732	0.527	0.490	0.556		
PBAV	0.540	0.607	0.281	0.301	0.337	0.418	
PNOM	0.702	0.505	0.287	0.214	0.249	0.429	0.610

5 Research Results and Discussion

The proposed relationships were tested through bootstrapping in PLS-SEM algorithm and with 5000 subsamples [36]. Data relevance has a significant positive impact on both consumers' awareness of consequences of circular economy ($\beta = 0.288$, $p < 0.01$) and consumers' ascription of responsibility for circular economy ($\beta = 0.406$, $p = 0.000$). Data accuracy has a positive impact on consumers' ascription of responsibility for circular economy ($\beta = 0.184$, $p < 0.05$) but not on consumers' awareness of consequences of circular economy ($\beta = -0.006$). In addition, both awareness of consequences ($\beta = 0.295$, $p = 0.000$) and ascription of responsibility for circular economy ($\beta = 0.510$, $p = 0.000$) positively affect personal pro-environmental norm while personal pro-environmental norm positively affects consumers' intention to use DPP for circular consumption ($\beta = 0.470$, $p = 0.000$). Therefore, hypotheses H2b, H4a, H4b, H5, H6 and H7 were supported while H1a, H1b, H2a, H3a and H3b were not supported (see Fig. 2). The model explains 17.2% of the variance in consumers' awareness of consequences of circular economy, 17.6% of the variance in consumers' ascription of responsibility for circular economy, 49.2% of the variance in personal pro-environmental norm, and 22.1% of the variance in consumers' intention to use DPP for circular consumption.

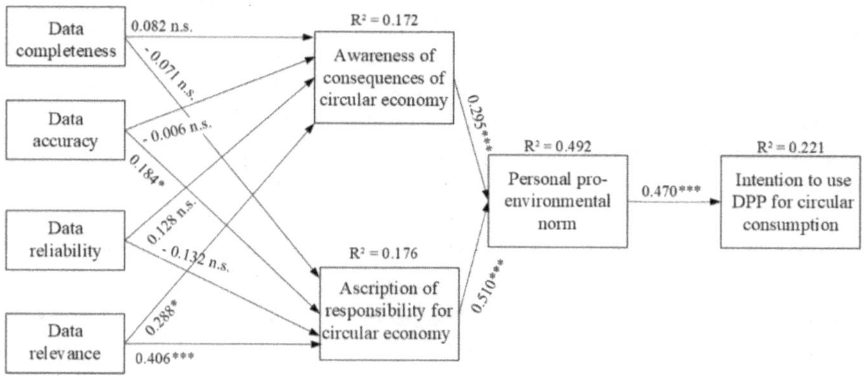

Fig. 2. Hypothesis test results (Note: n.s.: not significant, * p <0.05, *** p <0.001)

Data completeness was found to have no significant effect on consumers' awareness of consequences of circular economy and consumers' ascription of responsibility for circular economy. This could be because data completeness mainly captures whether the DPP provides a complete, comprehensive, or full set of sustainability and circularity information about a product. However, providing only the complete information may not be sufficiently enough for consumers to understand the environmental consequences of their consumer decision or foster a sense of responsibility for their pro-environmental behavior. Awareness of consequences of circular economy and ascription of responsibility for circular economy require consumers to understand the environmental meaning and personal relevance of the information, not only its completeness. Additionally, consumers may not have capacity to process the complete information and connect it with their social responsibility and environmental consequences.

Data accuracy has no significant effect on awareness of consequences of circular economy. This suggests that accurate DPP information may not be sufficient to increase consumers' general awareness of the environmental consequences. In addition, consumers may perceive information based on the way information is framed and communicated [40], neglecting their accuracy. When data is presented accurately in an informative way without emphasizing and framing relevant environmental outcome, consumers may not understand the connection between accurate data and awareness of consequences of circular economy. However, data accuracy has a positive and significant effect on ascription of responsibility for circular economy, indicating that when sustainability and circularity information in DPP is perceived as correct, accurate, and credible, consumers are more likely to attribute responsibility to themselves for their consumption decisions. Accuracy of data in DPP can reduce information asymmetry and reduce any uncertainty regarding pro-environmental consumption. When consumers get clear about the impact of products on environment, they can feel they are responsible for environment sustainability [21, 40].

Data relevance was found to affect consumers' awareness of consequences of circular economy and their ascription of responsibility for circular economy positively. This could be because data relevance captures whether DPP provides applicable, related, or pertinent sustainability and circularity information about the product. Prior research states that information that is tailored and relevant to the users' information need can be effective in improving user understanding and user judgement [41, 42]. Relevant information will be cognitively processed by consumers and lead to their increased awareness of positive outcomes of pro-environmental consumption. Further, when consumers perceive the information as directly relevant for circular consumption, they are more likely to internalize the implications of their actions and feel personally accountable for the environmental impact of their circular consumption. It aligns with prior research of [43] which states that individuals are more likely to ascribe responsibility when information connects directly to their personal values and actions. It further complies with the signaling theory by reducing information asymmetry [21, 39], in making relevant circular data available in DPP for consumers to make them feel responsible for, and bring awareness to the consequences of their circular behavior.

Contrary to expectations, data reliability has no significant effect on consumers' awareness of consequences of circular economy and consumers' ascription of responsibility for circular economy. This could be because data reliability captures whether data in DPP provides believable, trustworthy or credible sustainability and circularity information about the product. It may suggest that even though data reliability is perceived as a feature of credible information it may not necessarily lead to consumers' cognitive and moral engagement towards circular consumption consequences and responsibility of circular consumption. It could be due to the following reasons. First, data reliability may be considered as a qualifying factor for the information available on DPP rather than considering it as an important data feature that will lead to consumers' active increase of awareness of consequences of circular economy or ascription of responsibility for circular economy. Second, considering DPP as an authorized digital solution, its data should be reliable. Consumers might need to have highly relevant data to encourage their awareness of consequences of circular economy and consumers' ascription of responsibility for circular economy towards circular consumption.

Awareness of consequences of circular economy was found to positively and significantly affect personal pro-environmental norm. This finding suggests that consumers' awareness of the environmental consequences of their consumption choices motivate them in a moral sense to act in an environmentally responsible manner and strengthens their personal pro-environmental norms for circular consumption. This finding is consistent with prior research finding that awareness of consequences of circular economy leads to personal pro-environmental norm in acting environmentally friendly manner [26]. Therefore, when consumers become aware of these consequences, they are more likely to feel personally obliged to reduce unsustainable consumption and use DPP for sustainable and circular product choices.

The results indicate that ascription of responsibility for circular economy has a positive and significant effect on personal pro-environmental norm. This suggests that when consumers feel personally responsible for the environmental consequences, they are more likely to develop a moral obligation to support sustainable and circular consumption practices. Ascription of responsibility for circular economy captures consumers' feelings of guilt when they do not make sustainable and circular consumption choices. These feelings appear to strengthen their personal pro-environmental norms, reflected in their perceived obligation to support sustainable and circularity initiatives and use DPP for sustainable and circular product decisions.

Personal pro-environmental norms exert positive effect on intention to use DPP for circular consumption. When consumers have stronger personal pro-environmental norm towards pro-environmental consumption, they will have stronger intention to perform sustainable consumption, such as circular consumption. Consumers' internal sense of responsibility toward the environment strengthens their willingness to use DPP as a tool for making sustainable and circular consumption.

The findings in this study indicate that data relevance can serve as signal to activate both awareness of consequences of circular economy and ascription of responsibility for circular economy, but data accuracy as a signal can only activate ascription of responsibility for circular economy when data in DPP is applied as signal to activate consumers' personal pro-environmental norm and their intention to use DPP for circular consumption.

6 Conclusion

This study investigates the role of data features in influencing awareness of consequences of circular economy, ascription of responsibility for circular economy, and personal pro-environmental norm, which further affect consumers' intention to use DPP for circular consumption. Theoretically, the findings contribute to a more comprehensive understanding of how data influence circular consumption decisions in the DPP context at the individual consumer level. Specifically, the findings demonstrate how data features of DPP can influence individual decision-making in the circular economy context by explaining how data can activate consumers' awareness of consequences of circular economy and ascription of responsibility for circular economy which further trigger personal pro-environmental norm and their intended use of DPP for circular consumption. In addition, the current study provides a deeper understanding of how data trigger consumers' norms related to the circular economy and their circular consumption decision by integrating signaling theory and NAM.

The study has practical implications. The finding on the role of data accuracy and data relevance in activating consumers' pro-environmental norm and promoting consumers' intention to use DPP for circular consumption indicates that stakeholders should provide accurate and relevant information about product circularity in DPP to activate consumers' personal pro-environmental norm and support consumers' circular consumption decisions in CE practice.

The study has certain limitations which should be acknowledged. First, this study examined only four data features in activating personal pro-environmental norm and understanding consumers' intention to use DPP for circular consumption. Future scholars could consider including other data features and IS artifact in the DPP context. Second, the scenario used in this study were based on fabricated DPP GUIs, since DPP are not yet commercially available. Future research could utilize real-world DPP to explore consumers' use of DPP in circular economy practices. Lastly, the research sample includes only respondents who have prior experience with circular economy practices, which could limit the generalizability of the findings to the broader population of consumers with lower awareness of circular economy.

Appendix A

Construct	Measurement items	Reference
Data completeness	The DPP provides me with complete set of sustainability and circularity information of the product.	[10]
	The DPP provides me comprehensive sustainability and circularity information of the product.	
	The DPP provides me with all the sustainability and circularity information of the product.	
Data accuracy	The sustainability and circularity information provided in the DPP for the product is correct	[7]
	The sustainability and circularity information provided in the DPP for the product is accurate.	
	The sustainability and circularity information provided in the DPP for the product is credible.	
Data reliability	The sustainability and circularity information provided in the DPP for the product is believable.	[7]
	The sustainability and circularity information provided in the DPP for the product is trustworthy.	
	The sustainability and circularity information provided in the DPP for the product is credible.	
Data relevance	The sustainability and circularity information provided in the DPP for the product is applicable to my purchase decision.	[8]
	The sustainability and circularity information provided in the DPP for the product is related to my purchase decision.	
	The sustainability and circularity information provided in the DPP for the product is pertinent to my purchase decision.	

(*continued*)

(*continued*)

Construct	Measurement items	Reference
Awareness of consequences of circular economy	The sustainability and circularity information provided in the DPP for the product is relevant to my purchase decision.	[26]
	I am aware that my unsustainable and linear consumption habits influence the depletion and scarcity of limited resources.	
	My circular consumption can be a contribution to the protection of the environment.	
	When I do not make circular consumption, I contribute to the pollution of the environment.	
	I think that my circular consumption contributes to the protection of the environment.	
Ascription of responsibility for circular economy	I have a bad conscience when I think of the pollution to the environment I might cause if I do not make circular consumption.	[26]
	I have a bad conscience toward the environment if I do not make circular consumption frequently.	
	When I do not make circular consumption, I feel guilty in view of the environment.	
Personal pro-environmental norm	I have an obligation to reduce unsustainable consumption.	[26]
	I have an obligation to support sustainable consumption and circularity initiatives.	
	I have an obligation to use DPP for my sustainable consumption and circulating products.	
	I have a responsibility for quality of environment of others.	
	I have a responsibility for sustainability of the environment.	

(*continued*)

(*continued*)

Construct	Measurement items	Reference
Intention to use DPP for circular consumption	I intend to use DPP to support my circular consumption decisions in the future.	[44]
	I will always try to use DPP to support my circular consumption decisions in my daily life.	
	I plan to use DPP to support circular consumption decisions.	

Appendix B

Imagine you are planning to buy a new laptop and need detailed product information to guide your purchase decision. Below is an example of a DPP interface and information for the laptop that you can obtain by scanning the QR code. Please review the details carefully and share your opinions on the role of the DPP in supporting your purchase decision.

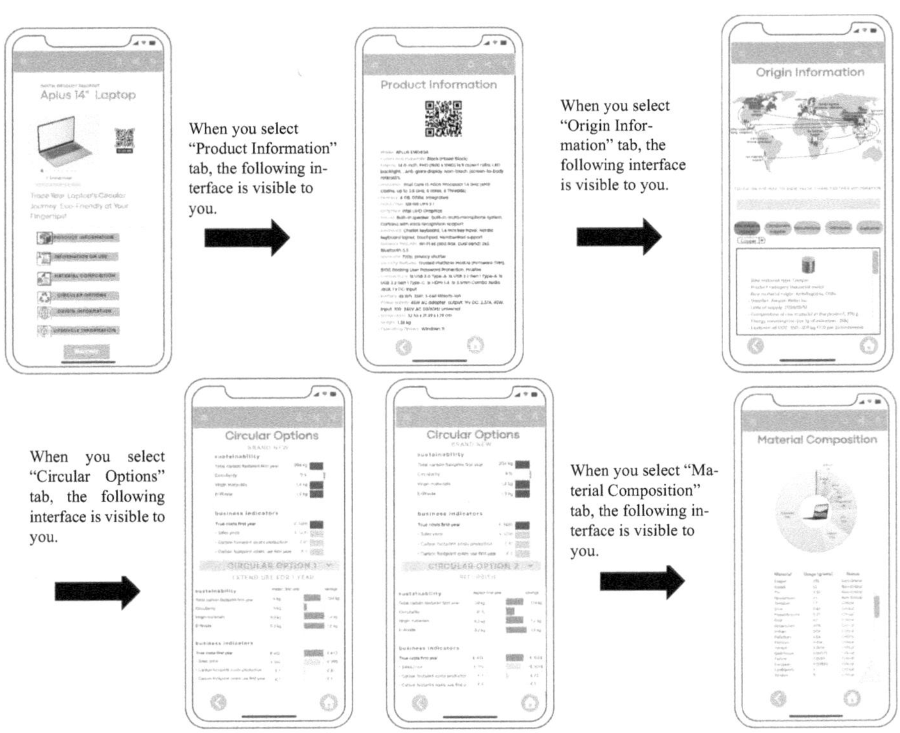

References

1. Chatterjee, S., Chaudhuri, R., Vrontis, D.: Does data-driven culture impact innovation and performance of a firm? An empirical examination. Ann. Oper. Res. [New York]. **333**(2–3), 601–626 (2024). https://doi.org/10.1007/s10479-020-03887-z
2. The Ellen MacArthur Foundation.: The circular economy glossary, Circular economy introduction. [Online]. Available: https://www.ellenmacarthurfoundation.org/topics/circular-economy-introduction/glossary. Accessed: 13 Mar 2025
3. Camacho-Otero, J., Boks, C., Pettersen, I.N.: Consumption in the circular economy: a literature review. Sustainability. **10**(8), 2758 (2018). https://doi.org/10.3390/su10082758
4. European Union: EU's Digital Product Passport: Advancing transparency and sustainability. [Online]. Available: https://data.europa.eu/en/news-events/news/eus-digital-product-passport-advancing-transparency-and-sustainability. Accessed: 5 Feb 2025
5. Zaitsava, M., Marku, E., Di Guardo, M.C.: Is data-driven decision-making driven only by data? When cognition meets data. Eur. Manag. J. **40**(5), 656–670 (2022). https://doi.org/10.1016/j.emj.2022.01.003
6. Li, L., Lin, J., Ouyang, Y., Robert Luo, X.: Evaluating the impact of big data analytics usage on the decision-making quality of organizations. Technol. Forecast. Soc. Chang. **175**, 121355 (2022). https://doi.org/10.1016/j.techfore.2021.121355
7. Lee, Y.W., Strong, D.M., Kahn, B.K., Wang, R.Y.: AIMQ: a methodology for information quality assessment. Inf. Manag. **40**(2), 133–146 (2002). https://doi.org/10.1016/S0378-7206(02)00043-5
8. McKinney, V., Yoon, K., Zahedi, F.".M.".: The measurement of web-customer satisfaction: an expectation and disconfirmation approach. Inf. Syst. Res. **13**(3), 296–315 (2002). https://doi.org/10.1287/isre.13.3.296.76
9. Nelson, R.R., Todd, P.A., Wixom, B.H.: Antecedents of information and system quality: an empirical examination within the context of data warehousing. J. Manag. Inf. Syst. **21**(4), 199–235 (2005). https://doi.org/10.1080/07421222.2005.11045823
10. Wixom, B.H., Todd, P.A.: A theoretical integration of user satisfaction and technology acceptance. Inf. Syst. Res. **16**(1), 85–102 (2005). https://doi.org/10.1287/isre.1050.0042
11. Sharma, R., Mithas, S., Kankanhalli, A.: Transforming decision-making processes: a research agenda for understanding the impact of business a. Eur. J. Inf. Syst. **23**(4), 433–441 (2017). https://doi.org /10.1057/ejis.2014.17
12. Ganzi, A., Sarkis, J., Molinaro, M., Woschank, M.: Linking circular economy practices to circular economy outcomes: empirical evidence from the manufacturing sector. Prod. Manuf. Res. **14**(1), 2618343 (2026). https://doi.org/10.1080/21693277.2026.2618343
13. Jäger-Roschko, M., Petersen, M.: Advancing the circular economy through information sharing: a systematic literature review. J. Clean. Prod. **369**, 133210 (2022). https://doi.org/10.1016/j.jclepro.2022.133210
14. Ta, A.H., Aarikka-Stenroos, L., Litovuo, L.: Customer experience in circular economy: experiential dimensions among consumers of reused and recycled clothes. Sustainability. **14**(1), 509 (2022). https://doi.org/10.3390/su14010509
15. Petrik, D., Strobel, G., Schoormann, T., Möller, F., Hoppe-Ludwig, C., Springer, V.: Digital product passports. Electron. Mark. **36**(1), 25 (2026). https://doi.org/10.1007/s12525-026-00877-0
16. Jensen, S.F., Kristensen, J.H., Adamsen, S., Christensen, A., Waehrens, B.V.: Digital product passports for a circular economy: data needs for product life cycle decision-making. Sustainable Prod. Consumption. **37**, 242–255 (2023). https://doi.org/10.1016/j.spc.2023.02.021

17. Berger, K., Schöggl, J.-P., Baumgartner, R.J.: Digital battery passports to enable circular and sustainable value chains: conceptualization and use cases. J. Clean. Prod. **353**, 131492 (2022). https://doi.org/10.1016/j.jclepro.2022.131492
18. Schwartz, S.H.: Normative influences on altruism. In: Advances in Experimental Social Psychology, vol. 10, pp. 221–279. Elsevier (1977). https://doi.org/10.1016/S0065-2601(08)60358-5
19. Gärling, T., Fujii, S., Gärling, A., Jakobsson, C.: Moderating effects of social value orientation on determinants of proenvironmental behavior intention. J. Environ. Psychol. **23**(1), 1–9 (2003). https://doi.org/10.1016/S0272-4944(02)00081-6
20. Spence, M.: Job market signaling. Q. J. Econ. **87**(3), 355 (1973). https://doi.org/10.2307/1882010
21. Spence, M.: Signaling in retrospect and the informational structure of markets. Am. Econ. Rev. **92**(3), 434–459 (2002). https://doi.org/10.1257/00028280260136200
22. Mavlanova, T., Benbunan-Fich, R., Koufaris, M.: Signaling theory and information asymmetry in online commerce. Inf. Manag. **49**(5), 240–247 (2012). https://doi.org/10.1016/j.im.2012.05.004
23. Duong, C.D.: Balancing awareness and responsibility: cognitive mechanisms shaping electric vehicle purchase intentions. Transp. Res. Interdiscip. Perspect. **31**, 101440 (2025). https://doi.org/10.1016/j.trip.2025.101440
24. Fang, W.-T., Chiang, Y.-T., Ng, E., Lo, J.-C.: Using the norm activation model to predict the pro-environmental behaviors of public servants at the central and local governments in Taiwan. Sustainability. **11**(13), 3712 (2019). https://doi.org/10.3390/su11133712
25. Bamberg, S., Schmidt, P.: Incentives, morality, or habit? Predicting students' car use for university routes with the models of Ajzen, Schwartz, and Triandis. Environ. Behav. **35**(2), 264–285 (2003). https://doi.org/10.1177/0013916502250134
26. Hunecke, M., Blöbaum, A., Matthies, E., Höger, R.: Responsibility and environment: ecological norm orientation and external factors in the domain of travel mode choice behavior. Environ. Behav. **33**(6), 830–852 (2001). https://doi.org/10.1177/00139160121973269
27. Onwezen, M.C., Antonides, G., Bartels, J.: The norm activation model: an exploration of the functions of anticipated pride and guilt in pro-environmental behaviour. J. Econ. Psychol. **39**, 141–153 (2013). https://doi.org/10.1016/j.joep.2013.07.005
28. Trevino, L.K.: Experimental approaches to studying ethical-unethical behavior in organizations. Bus. Ethics Q. **2**(2), 121–136 (1992). https://doi.org/10.2307/3857567
29. Alexander, C.S., Becker, H.J.: The use of vignettes in survey research. Public Opin. Q. **42**(1), 93 (1978). https://doi.org/10.1086/268432
30. Palan, S., Schitter, C.: Prolific.Ac—a subject pool for online experiments. J. Behav. Exp. Financ. **17**, 22–27 (2018). https://doi.org/10.1016/j.jbef.2017.12.004
31. Podsakoff, P.M., Organ, D.W.: Self-reports in organizational research: problems and prospects. J. Manag. **12**(4), 531–544 (1986). https://doi.org/10.1177/014920638601200408
32. Harman, H.H., Jones, W.H.: Factor analysis by minimizing residuals (Minres). Psychometrika. **31**(3), 351–368 (1966). https://doi.org/10.1007/BF02289468
33. Lindell, M.K., Whitney, D.J.: Accounting for common method variance in cross-sectional research designs. J. Appl. Psychol. **86**(1), 114–121 (2001). https://doi.org/10.1037/0021-9010.86.1.114
34. Kock, N.: Common method bias in PLS-SEM: a full collinearity assessment approach. Int. J. e-Collab. **11**(4), 1–10 (2015). https://doi.org/10.4018/ijec.2015100101
35. Fornell, C., Larcker, D.F.: Evaluating structural equation models with unobservable variables and measurement error. J. Mark. Res. **18**(1), 39–50 (1981). https://doi.org/10.1177/002224378101800104

36. Hair, J.F., Sarstedt, M., Ringle, C.M., Mena, J.A.: An assessment of the use of partial least squares structural equation modeling in marketing research. J. Acad. Mark. Sci. **40**(3), 414–433 (2012). https://doi.org/10.1007/s11747-011-0261-6
37. Henseler, J., Ringle, C.M., Sarstedt, M.: A new criterion for assessing discriminant validity in variance-based structural equation modeling. J. Acad. Mark. Sci. **43**(1), 115–135 (2015). https://doi.org/10.1007/s11747-014-0403-8
38. Pavlou, P.A., Fygenson, M.: Understanding and predicting electronic commerce adoption: an extension of the theory of planned behavior 1. MIS Q. **30**(1), 115–143 (2006). https://doi.org/10.2307/25148720
39. Connelly, B.L., Certo, S.T., Ireland, R.D., Reutzel, C.R.: Signaling theory: a review and assessment. J. Manag. **37**(1), 39–67 (2011). https://doi.org/10.1177/0149206310388419
40. Levin, I.P., Schneider, S.L., Gaeth, G.J.: All frames are not created equal: a typology and critical analysis of framing effects. Organ. Behav. Hum. Decis. Process. **76**(2), 149–188 (1998). https://doi.org/10.1006/obhd.1998.2804
41. Haugtvedt, C.P., Petty, R.E., Cacioppo, J.T.: Need for cognition and advertising: understanding the role of personality variables in consumer behavior. J. Consum. Psychol. **1**(3), 239–260 (1992). https://doi.org/10.1016/S1057-7408(08)80038-1
42. Morris, J.D., Woo, C., Singh, A.J.: Elaboration likelihood model: a missing intrinsic emotional implication. J. Target. Meas. Anal. Mark. **14**(1), 79–98 (2005). https://doi.org/10.1057/palgrave.jt.5740171
43. Stern, P.C.: New environmental theories: toward a coherent theory of environmentally significant behavior. J. Soc. Issues. **56**(3), 407–424 (2000). https://doi.org/10.1111/0022-4537.00175
44. Venkatesh, V., Thong, J.Y.L., Xu, X.: Consumer acceptance and use of information technology: extending the unified theory of acceptance and use of technology 1. MIS Q. **36**(1), 157–178 (2012). https://doi.org/10.2307/41410412
45. Steg, L., De Groot, J.: Explaining prosocial intentions: testing causal relationships in the norm activation model. Br. J. Soc. Psychol. **49**(4), 725–743 (2010). https://doi.org/10.1348/014466609X477745
46. Liu, S., Gong, H., Zheng, C.: Are you an energy saver? Investigating consumers' energy saving intention during vehicle usage by extending the norm activation model. Transport. Res. F: Traffic Psychol. Behav. **115**, 103335 (2025). https://doi.org/10.1016/j.trf.2025.103335
47. Hina, M., Islam, N., Luo, X.R.: Towards sustainable consumption decision-making: Examining the interplay of blockchain transparency and information-seeking in reducing product uncertainty. Decis. Support Syst. **189**, 114370 (2025). https://doi.org/10.1348/014466609X477745

Understanding the Persuasive System Design Model Features: The Case of Duolingo

Courtney Hart, Marie Hattingh(✉), and Danie Smit

Department of Informatics, University of Pretoria, Pretoria, Hatfield 0002, South Africa
marie.hattingh@up.ac.za

Abstract. Persuasive technologies are a tool that can assist people in achieving their future goals or targets. A persuasive technology uses a system to persuade a person to alter their behaviors, actions, or thoughts to reach a desired result. The persuasive systems design model is a theoretical framework that guides system engineers and developers to develop a persuasive technology by providing a set and clear persuasive principles that should be developed within a persuasive system. This research study aims to analyze the degree of influence persuasive design features have on a system user. 25 respondents participated in this research study to identify the degree of persuasion and reasoning for each design feature using the Duolingo application. The results indicated that encouragement, subconscious features, and visibility were the most persuasive. The most influential features were those directly related to the user's main goal, although goal achievement itself was not the dominant theme in how features should be developed for full persuasive impact. This suggests an additional layer in the PSD Model: the development themes of persuasive design features.

Keywords: persuasive system design features · persuasion · impact of persuasive features · influence of persuasive features · persuasive system design model · PSD Model · persuasive technology · persuasive systems

1 Introduction

Goal setting is a conscious decision and a means to welcome change [1], but reaching goals and sticking to new habits is not simple [41]. To reach a goal, individuals must change thoughts, behaviors, and actions and maintain focus [42]. Behavior modification has long been studied [3], with theories and models exploring motivation and traits for change [11, 42], yet modifying behavior is not easy or immediate [33].

New technologies and web applications to assist users in achieving personal goals are increasing [26]. Examples include smart watches, water tracker apps, and online shopping recommendations, with advancements leading to persuasive technology [28].

Persuasive technologies modify a person's attitude, behavior, or thoughts [30] and can support goal achievement by creating focus and constant reminders. For example, Quit Tracker highlights progress, benefits, and savings for users quitting smoking (Ortis

Published by Springer Nature Switzerland AG 2027
S. Han et al. (Eds.): I3E 2026, LNCS 16912, pp. 240–253, 2027.
https://doi.org/10.1007/978-3-032-38014-2_18

et al., 2020). Studying persuasive technology is increasingly important as applications grow [26]. While they can support positive change, they can also contribute to harmful or addictive behaviors if misused [5], making it essential to understand their effects [28].

The Persuasive Systems Design (PSD) Model explains system features that influence behavior and how developers can implement them to persuade users to achieve goals [30]. Understanding these features can help design systems that positively influence users. This study aims to answer: *"What key design features influence the effectiveness of persuasive technology in changing user behavior?"*

The study is limited to users who speak English and German to ensure clear communication and analysis during interviews.

The rest of the paper is structured as follows: Sect. 2 provides a short literature review on the concept of persuasion and persuasive technologies and the PSD model. Section 3 details the study design, case application description and the data collection process. Sections 4 and 5 presents and discuss data analysis and future research. Section 6 concludes the study.

2 Literature Background

The literature review covers the following important concepts: the concept of persuasion and persuasive technology, the persuasive systems design model and the design of persuasive features. Each of these aspects will be briefly discussed below.

2.1 The Concept of Persuasion and Persuasive Technologies

Persuasion is the act of altering or modifying a person's thoughts, emotions, attitudes, or behaviors [12]. The Fogg Behavior Model (FBM) for Persuasive Design was developed to understand the factors required to successfully alter a person's behavior [11]. It is important as it is the basis for understanding how to alter a person's behavior and the considerations involved. FBM is comprised of three factors: motivation, ability, and trigger. All these factors must exist and act in unison for the persuasive act to be successful, and the stronger the three factors are individually, the higher the degree of persuasion [13].

A persuasive technology is the use of an interactive computer system to alter a person's thoughts, emotions, attitudes, or behaviors without coercion or deception [11, 13, 30]. Persuasive Technologies are all around us, such as disease management and early detection applications [31], monitoring your diet and promoting you to eat healthy [35], or health apps assisting with exercise routines or quitting smoking [26]. When discussing how to implement persuasive technology, we should consider persuasion and FBM to ensure the necessary factors are included. However, FBM alone is not enough, as it does not give guidance on how the factors should be implemented or how the system should look to keep a user's focus and attention [19].

2.2 Persuasive Systems Design (PSD) Model

The persuasive systems design (PSD) model was designed to enhance the understanding of how a persuasive system can be designed and engineered [29, 39]. The PSD Model is a conceptual and theory-based model developed from the by Oinas-Kukkonen and Harjumaa [30], and is an expansion of the FBM [12], describing the process and considerations developers must consider when implementing a persuasive system and how it can successfully persuade a user to achieve their desired goal [32, 38].

There are three phases within the PSD Model: understanding key issues; analyzing the context; and the design of system features [29]. Four categories and twenty-eight design features are defined: primary task; dialogue support; system credibility; and social support, each comprising seven design features to be considered when developing a persuasive system [29]. The more features a system can incorporate and successfully implement, the higher the chances of persuasion.

Due to space limitations, each of these categories is explained in Sect. 3.3.

3 Research Methodology

3.1 Research Design

The study adopted an interpretivist approach to collect both quantitative and qualitative data from the participants. Duolingo, see Sect. 3.2, was identified as the case application for this study. Participants were identified through purposive and snowball sampling [10, 44] by sending an advertisement on the Duolingo community group, of which the lead author is a member. Purposive sampling was required as the study requires users who are familiar with and use Duolingo on a regular basis as they would be able to reflect on and suggest which of the design principles they felt, influenced their Duolingo usage and if the specific feature motivated and persuaded them to reach their desired goal. To identify the initial sample users, an advertisement was sent out to a community group, where users were able to sign up to be sample users in the research study.

The lead author mapped the Duolingo system features to the design principles within the PSD Model, see Table 1 with an extract of the mapping for the Primary Tasks. This mapping was used during the interview process. Once the study participants were identified, they were invited for an online interview.

The interview consisted of two parts: Part one was concerned with identifying the Duolingo features the participant felt had an influence on their continued use of the application. Part two was concerned with ranking the identified features that had the most influence on their Duolingo usage.

Throughout the process the participants were asked to verbally explain their decisions, as per the Think-Aloud Protocol (TAPs) [7]. The data collected through the TAP; allowed the researchers to understand why these features are more influential and have a higher influence on the user. While the user was trying to complete the activity, they were encouraged to speak aloud and guide the interviewer through their thoughts while trying to separate and rank the features; it was important to navigate the user to describe what they were thinking, and not explain why they were thinking it [7].

3.2 Use Case-Duolingo

Duolingo is a language learning application with the mission to provide free language lessons globally [9]. Its main goal is to help users learn new languages and support

Table 1. Matching the PSD Model Feature to Duolingo Features

Primary Tasks	
Reduction	Learning is divided into simple, doable sections.
Tunneling	The daily quests.
Tailoring	Selecting the reason or personal motivation to learn a language.
Personalization	Choosing the language to learn. Choosing a daily goal of how many minutes to practice.
Self-Monitoring	The day streaks.
Simulation	Realizing personal development through visual completion of different levels to identify progress.
Rehearsal	The ability to practice targeted areas (speaking, reading, writing, listening, roleplay).
Dialogue Support	
Praise	Messages after completing a lesson and sound after getting a question correct.
Rewards	The rewards, Badges, XP a user receives after completing a lesson.
Reminders	Emails and notifications to start a lesson.
Suggestion	The Duolingo Widget and characterized Duolingo Owl in the screen icon.
Similarity	The user's personal avatar.
Liking	UX/UI of the Duolingo application.
Social Role	Learning content and Blog.
Credibility	
Trustworthiness	The degree to which the user trusts Duolingo.
Expertise	Duolingo website and blog where expertise and improvements are mentioned.
Surface Credibility	UX/UI of the Duolingo application.
Real-World Feel	Duolingo website and blog where the team is mentioned.
Authority	Duolingo is a top application for language learning.
Third-Party Endorsements	A display of the third parties that endorse or sponsor Duolingo.
Verifiability	As Duolingo follows the Language Certification System.
Social Support	
Social Learning	A user can view another user's profile to see their stats, streaks, total XP, and achievements.
Social Comparison	A user can compare their daily XP collection with other users.

(continued)

Table 1. *(continued)*

Primary Tasks	
Normative Influence	A user's fellow learners can 'Nudge' them or send me rewards to use.
Social Facilitation	Via the weekly league board, users move up or down in real time based on XP points obtained.
Cooperation	Friend quests.
Competition	The league boards.
Recognition	Users can share achievements (streak, badges, etc.) with fellow learners and friends and send and receive high fives from fellow learners.

millions of users worldwide. Duolingo offers over 40 languages and is available in more than 120 countries, with over 500 million users, 74 million monthly active users, and 21.4 million daily active users (Q3 2023) [34].

Duolingo combines gamification with micro-learning lessons to keep users engaged while learning reading, writing, listening, and speaking skills. It is free for users aged 4 and above, with optional subscriptions for additional features. The app also includes features such as daily streaks, encouraging consistent use through consecutive daily engagement.

3.3 Data Collection Process

A total of 25 Duolingo users were identified. According to Guest et al. [17], if participants have a standard set of questions and are homogenous, a minimum of 12 users is sufficient. An interview was scheduled with each sampling user, where they were introduced to the research study, informed of their rights of withdrawal, that no personal data would be collected, and that they would remain anonymous. Users were then asked questions to understand their usage and purpose of using Duolingo before being introduced to the interview activity.

The sampling user was asked to go through Duolingo features one-by-one and place each feature card into a green box (influence on usage) or red box (no influence). A Card Explanation to Visual Duolingo Feature matching was available to standardize understanding and ensure equal assessment.

In the second stage, users retrieved cards in the green box and ranked features from highest to lowest influence on their usage and motivation to reach their goal. A template designed in Figma guided the activity (refer to Fig. 1), ensuring a consistent process, reducing bias or external influence, and allowing the natural ranking process and opportunity for TAPs [7].

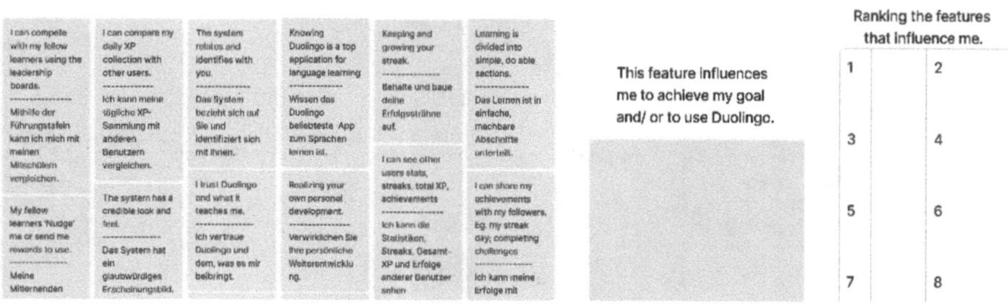

Fig. 1. Duolingo Feature Ranking Template

4 Data Analysis and Findings

A total of 25 users participated in the interview activity, and the users' daily usage streak ranged from the lowest daily usage streak of 25 days to the highest daily usage streak of 2912 days, with an average daily usage streak of 559 days. Sections 4.1 and 4.2 presents the data analysis of the ranking and TAP data, respectively.

4.1 PSD Model Principle and Duolingo Feature Ranking Analysis

After each interview, the ranking of the design features was added to an Excel spreadsheet template. The PSD Model principles were listed according to each Duolingo feature, and a point system was used based on the user's ranking. First place received 20 points, second place 19 points, continuing down to 20th place, while 20th and below received 1 point. Features with no impact received 0 points. Points were awarded for all sampling users' rankings. Once completed, the points were summed to generate a total score for each PSD Model design principle, and the average points per user were calculated for each principle (refer to Table 2).

Based on the point system, the PSD Model design principles with the highest persuasive influence have the highest total score and highest average points.

From the analysis, Tailoring, followed by Self-Monitoring and Simulation, are the top three design principles with the highest persuasive influence. In the top ten, six out of seven principles in the Primary Task category are listed, and the top five are all from the Primary Task Category. The lowest ranked design principles are Third-Party Endorsements, Real-World Feel, and Social Role. The bottom ten include principles from system credibility (three ranked 19, 27, 28), dialogue support (two ranked 25, 26), and social support (five ranked 20–24). Design principles rated as having no user influence were identified by users placing features in the red box. After analysis, the number of "no influence" responses were compared with total points per design principle. Some principles had fewer users reporting no influence but were ranked lower overall, while others had more "no influence" votes but higher rankings from users who did perceive influence. The two design principles 96% of users ranked as having no influence are Real-World Feel and Third-Party Endorsements, while Reduction and Tailoring were ranked by all users as having influence.

Table 2. PSD Model Principle Rating Overview

		Total Points	Average Points	No influence votes	Ranking Position
Primary Task	Rehearsal	273	10.92	4	5
	Simulation	389	15.56	1	3
	Reduction	367	14.68	0	4
	Self-Monitoring	418	16.72	2	2
	Personalization	167	6.68	12	13
	Tailoring	455	18.2	0	1
	Tunneling	241	9.64	7	7
Dialog Support	Social Role	40	1.6	19	26
	Liking	256	10.24	3	6
	Similarity	57	2.28	18	25
	Suggestion	119	4.76	14	17
	Reminders	215	8.6	11	10
	Rewards	240	9.6	5	8
	Praise	127	5.08	12	15
System Credibility	Authority	126	5.04	10	16
	Real World Feel	2	0.08	24	27 / 28
	Surface Credibility	197	7.88	4	11
	Expertise	128	5.12	14	14
	Trustworthiness	231	9.24	3	9
	Verifiability	109	4.36	14	19
	Third-Party Endorsements	2	0.08	24	27 / 28
Social Support	Recognition	88	3.52	12	23
	Competition	186	7.44	7	12
	Cooperation	115	4.6	14	18
	Normative Influence	94	3.76	16	21
	Social Facilitation	72	2.88	10	24
	Social Comparison	104	4.16	15	20
	Social Learning	93	3.72	14	22

4.2 Think-Aloud Protocol and Natural Ranking Analysis

To understand the ranking and effectiveness of the persuasive system design features, the comments made by sampling users during the think aloud method were analyzed to explain why users ranked features the way they did and to interpret the combined ranking results. During the interviews, think-aloud protocol comments were recorded, and themes for each persuasive system design feature were identified and discussed. The themes provide insight into why each feature was ranked in a particular position and why users felt it could or could not be persuasive. Identifying common themes can support future development of persuasive systems by ensuring features are designed effectively and to their full persuasive potential. The most common themes which were identified across the design features can be seen in Table 3.

Table 3. Common Themes Across Design Features

Theme	Design Features the Theme was Identified Within
Encouragement, subconscious	9
Visibility	6
Aversion, daily achievement and gratification, goal achievement, redundant	4
Skepticism	3
Complexity, variety	2
Competition, realization, personalization, simplicity, live interactions, reliance, loyalty, trigger, quick, choice of lesson quantity	1

5 Discussion

Previous studies have investigated how the PSD Model is integrated into system applications with specific goals, such as a health monitoring system [2]. Oyibo [32] identified the categorization of individualist and collectivist users, where individualists preferred self-monitoring design principles and collectivists preferred dialogue support design principles. While this provides insight into user group preferences, a gap remains in evaluating individual PSD Model features and how to enhance them to reach their full persuasive potential. This section addresses this gap by discussing the top themes identified for PSD Model features and how they should be considered in system development. The discussion focuses only on themes identified in four or more PSD Model features (see Table 3), although other themes should still be considered as they may also impact feature influence.

5.1 Encouragement

For users to achieve their goals, the persuasive system needs features that continuously encourage and support users. Encouragement can come in many forms, such as family or friends doing the same diet and motivating each other, or a partner taking on an extra chore to give additional time to focus on a goal.

In Duolingo and the PSD Model features, the encouragement theme took the form of earning rewards to keep users engaged in language classes and working with friends and peers to achieve goals through extra classes. Within this theme, four features are in the Dialogue Support category, four in the Social Support category, and one in the Primary Task category. Although the most influential features were within the Primary Task category, without encouragement and support, users may lack motivation, focus, and enjoyment to complete the required work and time needed to achieve their goals. This aligns with user engagement in digital games [37], where engagement refers to keeping users motivated and reducing early drop-out or low/non-usage [8].

5.2 Conscious vs. Subconscious Design Principles

The subconscious controls decision-making [20] and is responsible for 95% of brain activity [24]. Within the first phase of the PSD model, understanding key issues behind persuasive systems, Oinas-Kukkonen and Harjumaa [29] defined seven postulates of persuasive systems, including direct and indirect routes of persuasive strategies. This postulate states that persuasive systems should use both direct and indirect strategies to draw user attention, as direct features make users consciously aware of influence, while indirect features influence users subconsciously. User comments in this category indicated that if the feature did not exist, users would still not be using the application. An example of a subconscious feature is Liking, such as whether the user likes the look and feel of the application. Visual design influences perceptions of usability, credibility, and quality subconsciously [22], and can evoke emotional responses [40], affecting whether users continue using the application. By incorporating both subconscious and direct/indirect persuasive features, a system can better influence users and support them in sticking to their goals and continuously using the system.

5.3 Visibility of Design Features

A direct design feature cannot be influential to a user if the user does not know it exists in the first place. With system applications becoming more complex and incorporating more functionalities, some features can be lost, and the system may fail to represent them accurately and visibly [36]. The main reason the lowest ranked features were ranked lowest was because users did not know those features existed. If users did not see the feature or information within Duolingo, it could not influence them, as they were unaware of it. This aligns with findings by Sankar et al. [36], where system complexity can reduce feature visibility. To fully utilize PSD Model features, developers must ensure features are presented in a way that users can see, understand, and use them. One approach is a dynamic user interface, which adapts based on user interest and needs, ensuring relevant features and information are always visible [36].

5.4 Aversion

All PSD Model features are intended to have a positive persuasive effect on the system user. However, if a feature is perceived differently by the user, or is not relatable, wanted, or enjoyable, it may have the opposite effect and deter users from the application instead of persuading them. Frommel and Mandryk [14] found that engagement rewards in games can lead to frustration, annoyance, and disappointment when users cannot achieve them. A similar pattern is seen in Duolingo's weekly leadership board, where users who cannot spend as much time collecting enough XP, or access subscriptions may feel frustrated and deterred from using the app. In-app advertising is another feature shown to decrease user experience and deter users [16], despite generating income for developers [23], highlighting the need to balance revenue with user experience. A way to prevent negative effects and improve user control is to include enable/disable options for features. For example, Duolingo balances in-app advertising through a subscription model that removes ads, giving users control over whether they experience certain features.

5.5 Daily Achievement and Gratification

Milestone and step planning are important when a person is trying to reach a goal. If an application can create milestones and handle daily planning, it helps users visualize how they will achieve their overall target. This aligns with Goal-Setting Theory [42] where achieving a goal requires completing smaller tasks and setting attainable milestone goals that build toward the overall goal [41]. This also supports users who thrive on daily achievements and have an achiever strength, allowing them to feel good about small daily progress. The Gallup StrengthsFinder framework by Clifton [6] highlights individual strengths and how people should use them. In particular, the achiever's strength reflects a constant need for accomplishment and daily success. This theme also aligns with Usage and Gratification Theory, where users engage with media to fulfil needs and seek gratification [27].

5.6 Goal Achievement

The goal of a persuasive technology is to assist users in changing a personal behavior or attitude [29]. According to Fogg [11], the most crucial aspect of successfully altering behavior is having a clearly defined target or goal to guide behavior change. This aligns with Goal-Setting Theory [42], which states that a clear goal must be identified and supported by relevant actions or tasks needed to achieve it. An important mechanism in goal achievement is maintaining direct attention to the goal, ensuring it remains visible and in focus [18]. Therefore, a persuasive system must keep the overall goal at its core and make it visible to the user. The interesting finding within this theme is that features directly related to the overall goal ranked the highest, even though this theme appeared only four times across the twenty-eight PSD Model features. This shows it is crucial that the goal remains central and visible in a persuasive system. However, for successful persuasion, additional themes are also required to ensure users choose and continue using the system.

5.7 Redundancy in Persuasive Techniques

Video gaming is a daily activity for a large population and represents a global market of over 150 billion USD [25]. Games such as Super Mario, Crash Bandicoot, Grand Theft

Auto, Spyro, Call of Duty, and Final Fantasy all have an end once a user completes all levels or activities. After completion, users either replay the game or stop playing [15]. This relates to the concept of redundancy. Duolingo users aim to complete language levels, reach leaderboards, or maintain streaks, but users reported that once courses are finished or goals are achieved, features can feel predictable and repetitive, reducing motivation. This mirrors real-life behavior, where routines such as exercise become boring over time [4]. Fitness training advice often recommends diversifying or changing routines to maintain motivation and enjoyment [21]. By ensuring motivational features remain relevant, persuasive systems can maintain user engagement. One approach to avoiding redundancy is using AI for Procedural Content Generation (PCG) [43], allowing systems to continuously adapt and evolve content to sustain user interest.

5.8 Future Research

Within this research study, the focus was to understand the influence of design principles on system users in general, without differentiating between user characteristics such as background, culture, or nationality. Considering user traits could provide further understanding of which design principles have specific influence across different user groups.

During the interviews, a common comment from users with Duolingo Family Pro and children using the application was: *"I notice my child completes more lessons in one sitting than I do...they are not necessarily absorbing the lessons and language...so we wonder if the application is as effective for our children to learn a language, or if they just use the application for the game."* This suggests future research could examine the impact of Duolingo's design principles on adolescents compared to adults.

This study focused on one application. The sampled users were current Duolingo users, and the system meets their needs and expectations based on its design principles. However, to better understand persuasive system design influence more generally, another similar application such as Babbel should be examined to determine whether design principle influence is consistent across systems or specific to how an application implements them.

Additionally, expanding the sample to include users who previously used Duolingo but stopped would provide further insight into whether the themes that initially persuaded users also contributed to disengagement over time.

6 Conclusion

While it is important to understand which PSD Model features are most persuasive and influential, it is also necessary to understand how to effectively implement them. Without this, the features will not achieve their intended persuasive effect. By analyzing why certain features are more influential, common themes can be identified, which can guide system developers in implementing features more effectively.

The main themes identified in the most persuasive features were encouragement, subconscious features, and visibility of design features. The most influential features were those directly related to the user's main goal, although goal achievement itself was not the dominant theme in how features should be developed for full persuasive impact. This suggests an additional layer in the PSD Model: the development themes of persuasive design features.

This additional layer distinguishes between what users find influential (feature rankings) and how features should be developed to maximize persuasive impact (themes). Lower-ranked features or less frequent themes should not be considered less important, as all features support different user needs and preferences. By considering both design features and development themes, system developers can create more effective persuasive technologies that better support user goals.

References

1. Aarts, H.: Goal setting theory and the mystery of setting goals. Motiv. Sci. **5**, 106–107 (2019)
2. Hussian, A., Mateen, A., Amin, F., Abid, M.A., Ullah, S.: Health monitoring apps: an evaluation of the persuasive system design model for human wellbeing. Information. **14**(7), 412 (2023). https://doi.org/10.3390/info14070412
3. Bandura, A.: Self-efficacy: toward a unifying theory of behavioral change. Psychol. Rev. **84**, 191–215 (1977)
4. Barkley, J.E., Roemmich, J.N., Ryan, E.J., Bellar, D., Bliss, M.V., Rittenhouse, M.A.: The effect of increasing the variety of exercise equipment on the physical activity level of children. Med. Sci. Sports Exerc. **40**, 320 (2008)
5. Chen, X., Hedman, A., Distler, V., Koenig, V.: Do persuasive designs make smartphones more addictive? A mixed-methods study on Chinese university students. Comput. Hum. Behav. Rep. **10**, 100299 (2023). https://doi.org/10.1016/j.chbr.2023.100299
6. Clifton, D.R.: StrengthsFinder 2.0. https://www.gallup.com/cliftonstrengths/en/254033/strengthsfinder.aspx (2021). Last accessed 2 Jul 2026
7. Cowan, J.: The potential of cognitive think-aloud protocols for educational action-research. Act. Learn. High. Educ. **20**, 219–232 (2019)
8. Crutzen, R., Van't Riet, J., Short, C.E.: Enjoyment: a conceptual exploration and overview of experimental evidence in the context of games for health. Games Health J. **5**, 15–20 (2015)
9. Duolingo: Duolingo brand glossary. https://design.duolingo.com/writing/glossary#definitions (2024). Last accessed 2 Jul 2026
10. Emmel, N.: Sampling and Choosing Cases in Qualitative Research: A Realist Approach. SAGE Publications, London (2013)
11. Fogg, B.: A behavior model for persuasive design. In: Proceedings of the 4th International Conference on Persuasive Technology. Association for Computing Machinery, Claremont, CA, USA. New York (2009)
12. Fogg, B.J.: Persuasive Technology: Using Computers to Change What we Think and Do. Morgan Kaufmann, Amsterdam (2003)
13. Fogg, B.J., Euchner, J.: Designing for behavior change—new models and moral issues: an interview with B.J. Fogg. Res. Technol. Manag. **62**, 14–19 (2019)
14. Frommel, J., Mandryk, R.L.: Daily quests or daily pests? The benefits and pitfalls of engagement rewards in games. Proc. ACM. Hum. Comput. Interact. **6**, 1–23 (2022). https://doi.org/10.1145/3549489
15. Funk, J.B.: Video games. Adolesc. Med. Clin. **16**, 395–411 (2005)
16. Gao, C., Zeng, J., Lo, D., Xia, X., King, I., Lyu, M.R.: Understanding in-app advertising issues based on large-scale app review analysis. Inf. Softw. Technol. **142**, 106741 (2022)
17. Guest, G., Bunce, A., Johnson, L.: How many interviews are enough? An experiment with data saturation and variability. Field Methods. **18**, 59–82 (2006)

18. Gutt, D., von Rechenberg, T., Kundisch, D.: Goal achievement, subsequent user effort and the moderating role of goal difficulty. J. Bus. Res. **106**, 277–287 (2020)
19. Harjumaa, M., Oinas-Kukkonen, H.: An analysis of the persuasiveness of smoking cessation web sites. In: Proceedings of the Second International Symposium on Medical Information and Communication Technology, pp. 1–5. CWC, University of Oulu (2007)
20. Johann, G.: The subconscious mind—a marketing tool. Eur. J. Contemp. Econ. Manag. **1**(2), 113–128 (2014). https://doi.org/10.19044/elp.v1no2a9
21. J Juvancic-Heltzel, J.A., Glickman, E.L., Barkley, J.E.: The effect of variety on physical activity: a cross-sectional study. J. Strength Cond. Res. **27**(1), 244–251 (2013). https://doi.org/10.1519/JSC.0b013e3182518010
22. Lima, A.L.S., von Wangenheim, C.G.: Assessing the visual esthetics of user interfaces: a ten-year systematic mapping. Int. J. Hum.-Comput. Interact. **38**(2), 144–164 (2022). https://doi.org/10.1080/10447318.2021.1926118
23. Maddodi, C.B., Upadhyaya, P.: In-app advertising: a systematic literature review and implications for future research. Span. J. Mark.–ESIC. **28**, 334–355 (2024)
24. Marra, G.: 9 interesting facts about your subconscious mind. https://www.gailmarrahypnotherapy.com/9-interesting-facts-about-your-subconscious-mind/ (2021). Last accessed 2 Jul 2026
25. Martinez, L., Gimenes, M., Lambert, E.: Video games and board games: effects of playing practice on cognition. PLoS One. **18**, e0283654 (2023). https://doi.org/10.1371/journal.pone.0283654
26. Matthews, J., Win, K.T., Oinas-Kukkonen, H., Freeman, M.: Persuasive technology in mobile applications promoting physical activity: a systematic review. J. Med. Syst. **40**, 1–13 (2016)
27. Md Alamgir, H., Minho, K., Nusrat, J.: Can "liking" behavior lead to usage intention on Facebook? Uses and gratification theory perspective. Sustainability. **11** (2019). https://doi.org/10.3390/su11041166
28. Oinas-Kukkonen, H.: A foundation for the study of behavior change support systems. Pers. Ubiquit. Comput. **17**, 1223–1235 (2013)
29. Oinas-Kukkonen, H., Harjumaa, M.: Persuasive systems design: key issues, process model, and system features. Commun. Assoc. Inf. Syst. **24**, 485–500 (2009)
30. Giudici, M., Crovari, P., Garzotto, F.: Persuasive conversational agents for environmental sustainability: a survey. ACM Comput. Surv. **58**(6), 139–1–37 (2025). https://doi.org/10.1145/3774751
31. Orji, R., Moffatt, K.: Persuasive technology for health and wellness: state-of-the-art and emerging trends. Health Informatics J. **24**, 66–91 (2018)
32. Oyibo, K.: Investigating the key persuasive features for fitness app design and extending the persuasive system design model: a qualitative approach. Proc. Int. Symp. Hum. Factors Ergon. Health Care. **10**(1), 47–53 (2021). https://doi.org/10.1177/2327857921101022
33. Perloff, R.M.: The Dynamics of Persuasion: Communication and Attitudes in the 21st Century. Routledge, New York (2014)
34. Piedrahíta, P.: Essential Duolingo statistics for 2024: monthly users, revenue, and time spent. https://cooljugator.com/blog/duolingo-statistics/ (2023). Last accessed 2 Jul 2026
35. Pollak, J.P., Gay, G., Byrne, S., Wagner, E., Retelny, D., Humphreys, L.: It's time to eat! Using mobile games to promote healthy eating. IEEE Pervasive Comput. **9**, 21–27 (2010)
36. Sankar, S., Amudha, S., Madhavan, P., Lamba, D.K.: Personalized dynamic user interfaces. Mater. Sci. Eng. **1130**(1), 012070 (2021). https://doi.org/10.1088/1757-899X/1130/1/012070
37. Schwarz, A.F., Huertas-Delgado, F.J., Cardon, G., Desmet, A.: Design features associated with user engagement in digital games for healthy lifestyle promotion in youth: a systematic review of qualitative and quantitative studies. Games Health J. **9**, 150–163 (2020)
38. Shevchuk, N., Oinas-Kukkonen, H.: Aiding users in green IS adoption with persuasive systems design. Urban Sci. **4**, 52 (2020)

39. Sittig, S., McGowan, A., Iyengar, S.: Extensive review of persuasive system design categories and principles: behavioral obesity interventions. J. Med. Syst. **44**, 189 (2020). https://doi.org/10.1007/s10916-020-01656-9
40. Šola, H.M., Qureshi, F.H., Khawaja, S.: Eye-tracking analysis: college website visual impact on emotional responses reflected on subconscious preferences. Int. J. Adv. Comput. Sci. Appl. **14**(1), 813–821 (2023). https://doi.org/10.14569/IJACSA.2023.0140192
41. Swann, C., Rosenbaum, S., Lawrence, A., Vella, S.A., McEwan, D., Ekkekakis, P.: Updating goal-setting theory in physical activity promotion: a critical conceptual review. Health Psychol. Rev. **15**, 34–50 (2021)
42. Tosi, H.L., Locke, E.A., Latham, G.P.: A Theory of Goal Setting and Task Performance. Prentice Hall, Englewood Cliffs (1991)
43. Warpefelt, H., Salge, C., Eladhari, M.P., El-Nasr, M.S., Zhu, J.: Guest editorial: special issue on user experience of AI in games. IEEE Trans. Games. **14**, 539–542 (2022). https://doi.org/10.1109/TG.2022.3225731
44. Bekele, W., Ago, F.: Sample size for interview in qualitative research in social sciences: a guide to novice researchers. Res. Educ. Policy Manag. **4**(1), 42–50 (2022). https://doi.org/10.46303/repam.2022.3

User Perceptions of Behavior Change Support Systems for Physical Activity and Weight Management: A Scoping Review

Sharon Nabwire(✉), Renata Savian Colvero de Oliveira, and Harri Oinas-Kukkonen

Faculty of Information Technology and Electrical Engineering, University of Oulu, Oulu, Finland
{sharon.nabwire,renata.deoliveira,harri.oinas-kukkonen}@oulu.fi

Abstract. Behavior change support systems (BCSS) offer a scalable way to promote health behaviors, such as physical activity and other weight-management behaviors. Many of these systems are designed and evaluated using the Persuasive Systems Design (PSD) model, yet sustaining long-term user engagement remains difficult. Using the PRISMA-ScR guidelines and the Joanna Briggs Institute methodology, we searched four databases (PubMed, Scopus, Web of Science, and Elsevier) from 2015 to 2025. A total of 13 qualitative studies that met the inclusion criteria were reviewed to synthesize evidence on users' perceptions of implemented PSD features in physical activity and weight management BCSS, as well as the factors that influence engagement and continued use. Across the included studies, users most often reported that *Reminders*, *Self-monitoring*, *Goal-setting*, *Liking,* and *Personalization* supported behavior change. In contrast, some features were even perceived as discouraging or demotivating if poorly aligned with users' needs or contexts. Dialogue and social support features were commonly linked to engagement. Beyond software features, system characteristics of *Ease of use* and *Unobtrusiveness*, user context, and habit formation also influenced continued use. The findings highlight the importance of centering design processes on users' characteristics and experiences when developing health BCSS.

Keywords: Persuasive systems design · Weight management · Physical activity · User experience · Scoping review

1 Introduction

Well-being technologies have become a go-to solution for supporting health behavior changes, particularly in areas such as physical activity [1] and disease-related self-management, including weight management [2]. These systems, commonly referred to as "health behavior change support systems (HBCSS) [3]," offer scalable alternatives to traditional approaches by allowing users to continuously monitor their behavior, receive feedback, and establish new habits [4]. Such interventions have been described

S. Han et al. (Eds.): I3E 2026, LNCS 16912, pp. 254–272, 2027.
https://doi.org/10.1007/978-3-032-38014-2_19

as "social-technical" systems intended to influence not only users' behavior but also their attitudes while avoiding coercive or deceptive approaches [3]. Many of these interventions are based on design frameworks such as the Persuasive Systems Design (PSD) model for designing, developing, and assessing their effectiveness [5]. Within this model, engagement and behavior change can be facilitated through persuasive features such as *Self-monitoring* and *Reminders.*

A growing body of literature suggests that PSD plays an important role in the effectiveness of HBCSS. For instance, a study of randomized controlled trials in overweight and obesity management has shown that primary task support features, particularly *Self-monitoring*, are among the most frequently implemented strategies in successful long-term weight-loss interventions [6]. Similarly, a scoping review of PSD trends in coronary heart disease management found that primary task and dialogue support features were widely used across interventions, signifying their importance [7]. Moreover, emerging work has attempted to classify persuasive features by levels of scientific evidence, demonstrating that features such as *Self-monitoring, Personalization, Reminders,* and *Expertise* show strong empirical support in HBCSS [8].

Prior studies have also examined how specific persuasive design procedures influence a system's persuasiveness, effectiveness, and users' willingness to continue using it [9–13]. For example, a recent study found that integrating cognitive consistency principles into a weight-loss application through dialogue support features and *Self-monitoring* increased perceived persuasiveness and strengthened users' intention to continue using the system [11]. Also, when people believe a platform is credible, they are more likely to continue using it [13]. These findings highlight the potential of persuasive features to change behaviors and influence health outcomes [9].

Although persuasive features are widely implemented in HBCSS, user engagement remains a challenge, especially in the long term. Moreover, previous studies have mainly examined the effectiveness, characteristics, and prevalence of software features [2, 9, 14]. Less attention is paid to how users perceive the implemented persuasive features and how these perceptions may influence the use of these systems. Existing studies have often evaluated whether features such as *Reminders* enhance adherence and behavioral outcomes in the short and long term [15, 16]. Additionally, individual qualitative studies assess users' experiences with behavior change interventions [17, 18]; however, the synthesis of users' perceptions of design features remains limited. Consequently, evidence on users' experiences with persuasive features is still fragmented across individual studies.

As a result, this review aims to systematically explore and synthesize users' perceptions of PSD features and the factors influencing engagement and sustained use of HBCSS targeting physical activity and/or weight management. Specifically, the review examines (**RQ1**) how users perceive persuasive features as supportive or challenging, and (**RQ2**) which user-reported factors, including these perceptions, influence engagement with and continued use of the system. By integrating evidence from users' experiences, this review complements research on intervention effectiveness and offers implications for user-centered approaches that minimize unintended disengagement and increase the long-term effectiveness of HBCSS.

2 Related Work

Different frameworks guide the design and development of behavior change systems. For example, the Capability, Opportunity, and Motivation-Behavior (COM-B) model and the Behavior Change Wheel explain behavior change through the interaction of capability, opportunity, and motivation [19]. Behavior Change Taxonomies, like Behavior Change Techniques, present different categorizations of intervention components [20]. In persuasive technology, Fogg's model describes behavior change as centered on three interacting elements: user motivation, ability, and system triggers [21]. Building on these principles, the PSD model conceptualizes software design features and interaction elements that support behavior change [5]. Because the review focuses on users' perceptions of persuasive software features in digital health interventions, the PSD model offers an appropriate framework for organizing and interpreting the findings.

2.1 Persuasive Systems Design Model

The PSD model, introduced by Oinas-Kukkonen and Harjumaa [5], is an important design approach for creating and assessing systems that influence behaviors and attitudes, known as "*Behavior Change Support Systems*" (BCSS). The model outlines seven key principles related to system users (e.g., commitment and consistency), persuasion strategies (e.g., direct and indirect routes to persuasion), and system characteristics (e.g., *Unobtrusiveness* and *Ease of use*) to consider when creating or assessing systems. Secondly, the model emphasizes the need to consider the context in which persuasion occurs, including the system's intended function, the technologies employed, and the users involved, when selecting the system's persuasive elements. This requires an understanding of the users, the situations in which they interact with the system, and the most effective ways to engage them.

Finally, the model presents a collection of persuasive software features organized into four categories: Primary task support (PRIM), Computer-human dialogue (DIAL), System credibility support (CRED), and Social support (SOCI) [5]. PRIM features, such as *Self-monitoring* and *Personalization*, assist users in executing the system's main functions. DIAL components, such as *Reminders, Rewards*, or *Suggestions,* improve user interaction while CRED elements (for example, *Transparency* and *Trustworthiness*) enhance user trust in the system. SOCI features, including *Competition*, rely on principles of social influence to motivate and encourage behavior change [5]. These features have been widely applied in well-being interventions and have been associated with improved engagement, system compliance, and health outcomes [16, 22]. For example, research shows that utilizing these fundamental PSD software categories is important for system compliance [22]. In particular, dialogue-enhancing features have been shown to promote task completion or engagement with the system (e.g., self-weighing or reading content), which, in turn, may influence overall health outcomes [16].

3 Methods

In this study, we conducted a scoping review to synthesize the existing evidence on user-perceived persuasive system features in behavior change interventions for physical activity and weight management, and to identify gaps for future research and design practice. A scoping review explores the breadth and characteristics of research within a particular field. Unlike systematic reviews, which focus on specific questions and evaluate study quality, scoping reviews address broader topics and incorporate a range of study designs. Their goal is to offer an overview of existing evidence and highlight research gaps rather than assess effectiveness [23]. This review adhered to the Preferred Reporting Items for Systematic Reviews and Meta-Analyses for Scoping Review (PRISMA-ScR) guidelines [24] and the methodology of the Joanna Briggs Institute [25].

3.1 Research Questions

The research questions were formulated using the PCC (Population, Concept, Context) acronym, as advised by the Joanna Briggs Institute, to guide scoping reviews [24, 25], and establish a clear, focused review scope. In this study, the population comprises adult users of behavior change interventions aimed at physical activity and/or weight management. The concept involves user-perceived persuasive system design features based on the PSD model, and the context concerns BCSS delivered via mobile or web technologies. Guided by this model, the research questions for this review were:

RQ1: Which PSD features do users perceive as supportive or challenging in behavior change interventions targeting physical activity and/or weight management?
RQ2: What user-reported factors influence engagement and sustained use of behavior change interventions?

3.2 Search Strategy

This scoping review executed a systematic search across four electronic databases (PubMed, Scopus, Web of Science, and Elsevier) on November 27, 2025, to identify relevant studies published between 2015 to 2025. The search approach utilized controlled vocabulary from the Medical Subject Headings (MeSH) thesaurus (National Library of Medicine, 2025). Keywords and their synonyms were categorized into three conceptual groups: (1) behavior change interventions delivered through mobile and web applications, (2) weight management and physical activity, and (3) persuasive system design and behavior change interventions. Boolean operators (AND, OR) were used to combine these terms across PubMed (n = 62), Scopus (n = 201), Web of Science (n = 87), and Elsevier (n = 28), yielding a total of 378 references.

3.3 Inclusion and Exclusion Criteria

This review included peer-reviewed qualitative or mixed-methods studies published in English and available in full text that examined behavior change interventions targeting weight management, obesity, and/or physical activity. Only studies with a qualitative component were included to explore users' perceptions and experiences of persuasive features, rather than their effectiveness. This approach captures how users experience these features and the factors that influence continued use. This review focused on weight management and physical activity because they are established lifestyle behavior-change domains that share self-regulatory strategies and are closely linked in supporting weight-loss maintenance [26].

Studies were included if they reported user-perceived design elements or factors related to engagement, sustained use, or behavior change, thereby addressing at least one of the review's research questions. For mixed-methods studies, only the qualitative results were evaluated. Studies were excluded if they met any of the following criteria: 1) study type (purely quantitative, reviews, protocols, app development without evaluation, gray literature); 2) population (children or adolescents (under 18 years), athletes (i.e., runners), pregnant women, individuals with cognitive health conditions); 3) clinical conditions outside this review's scope (including Type 2 diabetes and prediabetes management, cardiovascular rehabilitation, cancer-related populations, musculoskeletal conditions); 4) interventions focusing exclusively on dietary behaviors, SMS-only interventions, or group-based interventions without a digital component.

3.4 Final Selection

The *Rayyan* platform was utilized to organize and review the files [27]. Figure 1 presents the PRISMA flow diagram outlining the literature review process [28]. The first author conducted the screening and selection of studies and resolved any doubts through discussion and agreement with the second author. Initially, duplicate records were removed. During the screening phase, titles, abstracts, and keywords were assessed against the inclusion and exclusion criteria, resulting in the exclusion of records that did not meet the criteria. In the full-text review phase, the remaining articles were meticulously evaluated, and only those that satisfied all inclusion criteria were included in the final analysis.

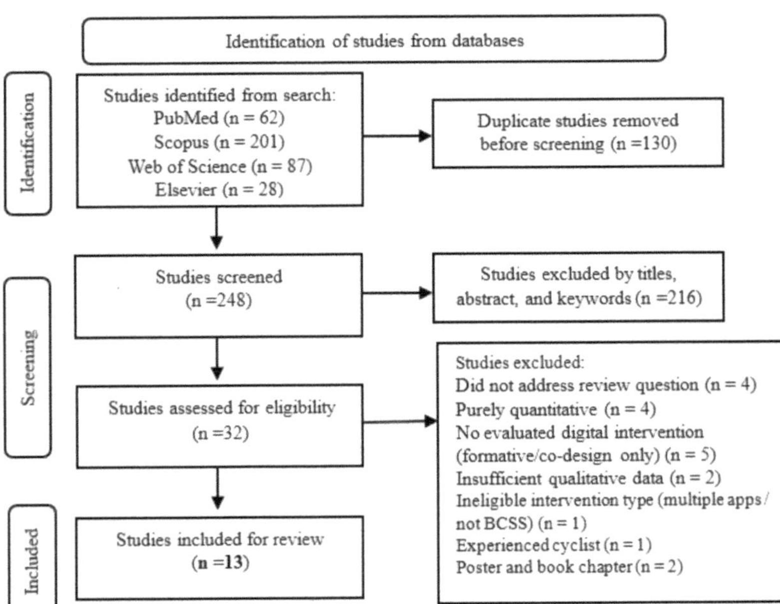

Fig. 1. PRISMA flow diagram of identified studies

3.5 Analysis

The analysis followed a qualitative scoping review approach to synthesize the findings [21]. Data extraction was performed systematically to capture and integrate information from the included studies (n = 13). The extracted study characteristics included author(s), year, study design, aims, sample characteristics (e.g., size and population), study duration, and type of behavior-change intervention. Each article included in the study was thoroughly read multiple times to extract qualitative findings related to (1) users' perceptions of the PSD features and (2) factors influencing engagement and continued use. These findings were then summarized and organized in Notion, a project management and note-taking platform, to facilitate detailed comparisons and discussions among the authors. The initial coding and grouping were performed by the first author and subsequently reviewed by the second author. Users' perceptions of persuasive features (RQ1) were categorized according to the PSD model [5] to ensure consistent classification and minimize potential bias. Any uncertainties in interpreting or assigning PSD features were discussed by the first and second authors; if no consensus was reached, the third author was included. This collaborative process was similarly applied to identify and refine factors related to engagement and continued use (RQ2).

4 Results

4.1 Characteristics of Included Studies

A total of 13 studies (see, Table 1) met the inclusion criteria and reported qualitative user perceptions of BCSS; these were included in the review. Most studies (9/13) focused on promoting physical activity through various intervention approaches, including mobile apps, augmented reality, and gamified systems. Four studies focused on weight management (i.e., weight loss maintenance) and metabolic syndrome. Sample sizes varied considerably between the two studies, ranging from four to 1383 participants. However, the qualitative samples in the remaining studies typically included 10–30 participants. Most studies employed a mixed-methods approach (9 articles), while the rest used purely qualitative methods, including interviews and focus groups. Two studies were 12-month long-term interventions, while two were short-term evaluations (30–45 min). The remaining study durations ranged from two weeks to three months. Overall, this corpus of included studies provides a solid foundation for synthesizing user experiences with persuasive design features that support or hinder engagement with physical activity and weight management HBCSS.

Table 1. Overview of Extracted Studies

Study	Sample Size (n)	Study Design & Duration
StepsBooster-S [29]	30	Mixed methods; 10 days
eCHANGE [30]	15	Mixed methods; 3 months
MoveDaily: Iterative Design Study [31]	26/4 (Phases 2 & 3)	Mixed methods; 10 weeks/ 45 min (Phases 2 & 3)

(continued)

Table 1. (*continued*)

Study	Sample Size (n)	Study Design & Duration
Personalized Coaching [32]	4	Interviews; 2 weeks
BCSS for metabolic syndrome prevention [18]	43	Interviews; 12–52 weeks
Habit formation BCSS [33]	43	Interviews: 12–52 weeks
Healthier Lifestyle App [34]	10	Focus groups
NoHoW Web-Based Toolkit [35]	1383	Mixed methods; 12 months
The Journey [36]	29 / 12	Mixed methods; 30 min
AR Dancee [37]	27	Mixed methods; 15 days
TreeCare [38]	23	Mixed method; 3 weeks
PetBuddy [39]	17	Mixed-methods, 10 days
Competition, Cooperation, or Both? [40]	15	Mixed methods; 2 weeks

4.2 User Perceptions of Persuasive System Features

System features perceived as supportive (i.e., valued by users) or challenging (i.e., experienced as difficult or undesirable) in HBCSS targeting physical activity and/or weight management were identified and categorized according to the PSD model. As shown in Table 2, the identified features were classified into four predefined PSD categories: PRIM, DIAL, SOCI, and CRED.

Across the studies, the PRIM features of *Self-monitoring*, *Personalization*, *Simulation*, and *Tunneling* were identified as supportive. *Self-monitoring*, or tracking, was frequently (7/13) highlighted as motivating and beneficial for increasing awareness of progress, self-reflection, and accountability, and for recognizing behavioral triggers [18, 30, 33–36, 39]. *Personalization* improved alignment with daily schedules and increased perceived control, largely through customizable reminders [29, 30, 34, 36]. Additionally, tailored feedback was found to reinforce behavior [30]. *Simulation* was considered motivating when user actions visibly influenced outcomes (e.g., a virtual tree) or when virtual tours/augmented reality interactions boosted motivation [36, 38]. Similarly, structured (*Tunneling*) content was perceived as supportive because it provided continuity and a stable rhythm [18, 33]. Users also described *Goal-setting* as useful and motivating, as it increased commitment and awareness and helped sustain user efforts [29, 30, 36, 38–40].

In various studies, users have also appreciated *Reminders, Suggestions, Rewards, Liking*, and *Social Role* within the DIAL category. *Reminders,* including prompts, were largely seen as beneficial for encouraging activity, aiding task completion, and maintaining routines [18, 29, 30, 33–36, 39]. When these reminders are personalized, they provide a sense of control and convenience. Likewise, *Rewards*, often presented as badges or gamified incentives, were effective at reinforcing goal achievement, particularly when paired with social *Competition* [29, 30, 39]. Users also reported enjoying the messages, finding them entertaining, and appreciated designs that were visually appealing and minimal (*Liking*) [32, 34, 35, 38, 39]. Finally, *Suggestions* were perceived as supportive and encouraged additional physical activity [29, 36], as well as *Social Role* (implemented through a virtual coach), which helped stay on track [30].

The credibility-related (CRED) features of *Trustworthiness* and *Expertise*, which pertain to trust in educational content, not only boosted engagement but also helped users understand their habits [18, 30, 36]. Additionally, the SOCI features of *Competition* and *Social Comparison*, and *Cooperation* were often perceived as motivating, increasing accountability, and effort [29, 36, 38–40].

In contrast, some persuasive features were perceived by users as challenging or undesirable. The most reported difficulties included the effort required for *Self-monitoring*, such as maintaining a food log; discouragement from setbacks in weight monitoring; and fear or anxiety related to monitoring in weight-management contexts [18, 33, 35]. Users also reported challenges with DIAL and SOCI features. Some found gamified *Rewards* less desirable, while *Praise* was sometimes seen as trivial [30, 33]. In the social support category, *Cooperation* was not universally positive; some users felt uncomfortable with team-based dynamics, and, in some cases, it demotivated them [29]. Moreover, low *Transparency* (CRED) was associated with reduced honesty in self-reporting [32].

Table 2. Supportive vs Challenging PSD Features

PSD Category	PSD Feature	Supportive perceptions (what users valued)	Challenging perceptions (what users struggled with)	Study
Primary Task Support (PRIM)	Goal-setting	Useful and motivating; increases commitment and awareness; goals can drive continued effort.	N/A	[29, 30, 36, 38–40]
	Self-monitoring	Beneficial and motivating; supports progress control, self-awareness, reflection, accountability, and habit change.	Can be too effortful (manual logging/food diaries); setbacks or weight-monitoring difficulties can discourage use; self-monitoring alone may not sustain engagement for everyone.	[18, 30, 33–36, 39]

(*continued*)

Table 2. (*continued*)

PSD Category	PSD Feature	Supportive perceptions (what users valued)	Challenging perceptions (what users struggled with)	Study
	Personalization	Enhances perceived control and helps the system fit users' routines.	N/A	[29, 30, 34, 36]
	Tunneling	Provides continuity and a stable rhythm; can feel supportive through structure, i.e., less effort	N/A	[18, 33]
	Simulation	Can motivate the user when user actions produce meaningful virtual outcomes.	N/A	[36, 38]
Dialogue Support (DIAL)	Reminders	Motivate activity and task completion; support adherence and routine maintenance; personalizable reminders increase convenience.	N/A	[18, 29, 30, 33–36, 39]
	Suggestions	Motivating and supportive when working toward goals.	N/A	[29, 36]
	Praise	N/A	Praise can be perceived as trivial.	[33]

(*continued*)

Table 2. (*continued*)

PSD Category	PSD Feature	Supportive perceptions (what users valued)	Challenging perceptions (what users struggled with)	Study
	Rewards	Can reinforce goal completion and increase engagement for some users.	Some users find gamified rewards undesirable.	[29, 30, 39]
	Liking	Application is visually appealing; messages are entertaining & enjoyable		[32, 34, 35, 38, 39]
	Social Role	Supports staying on track and motivation to maintain healthy habits (Virtual coach)	N/A	[30]
Social Support (SOCI)	Competition & Social Comparison	Motivates exercise and performance; can strengthen accountability and effort.	N/A	[29, 36, 38, 39]
	Cooperation	Encourages accountability and motivation.	Discouraged users are uncomfortable in group settings	[29, 38, 40]
System credibility support (CRED)	Trustworthiness & Expertise	Trust in content and expertise increases acceptance; trustworthy educational information supports understanding habits and motivation.	N/A	[18, 30, 36]
	Transparency	N/A	Low transparency can reduce honest self-reporting	[32]

(*continued*)

Table 2. (*continued*)

PSD Category	PSD Feature	Supportive perceptions (what users valued)	Challenging perceptions (what users struggled with)	Study

Note. N/A = Not applicable

4.3 Factors Influencing Engagement and Continued Use

In the studies reviewed, factors influencing engagement and continued use were categorized by **1**) system-related aspects and **2**) user context and behavioral factors (see Table 3). From a system design perspective, characteristics related to *Ease of use* (7/13 studies) and *Unobtrusiveness* (4/13 studies) influenced how individuals used the system. Perceived *Ease of use* and low effort facilitated continued interaction in several studies [29, 33, 34, 38], whereas usability issues and high effort requirements (e.g., content-heavy modules and manual logging) undermined engagement [31, 35, 36]. Regarding *Unobtrusiveness*, when a system fits smoothly into users' existing routines while minimizing disruptions to daily activities, it supports engagement [29–31, 37].

At the feature level, *Reminders* helped users adhere to personal goals and minimize forgetting [29, 30]. For instance, one study found that users reported insufficient notifications and feedback [30], whereas general motivational messages increased system interaction [32]. *Rewards* reinforced continued app use and adherence, although their removal reduced engagement for some users [29]. Under SOCI, competitive ranking (*Competition*) on leaderboards increased engagement [29], whereas its absence was associated with dropout [31]. Similarly, a lack of social support affected the use of some applications [18, 33, 35]. Insufficient or a lack of *Personalization/Tailoring* was also highlighted as a hindrance to engagement [35, 37].

Beyond system-related influences, contextual factors (such as life circumstances and emotional experiences) and habitual mechanisms also affected how people used systems. Personal life stressors, including demanding work and health-related issues, influenced system usage [18, 33, 35]. Emotional experiences related to commitment to using the system and improved mood were also linked to engagement [33, 37]. In some cases, system use evolved into a habit [33, 37, 38]. On the other hand, when the intervention reinforced established habits, successful users perceived less need for continued support, often leading to its discontinued use [18].

Table 3. Factors Influencing Engagement and Continued Use

Category	Sub-Category	Factor	Direction	Studies
Feature-related	DIAL	Reminders	Facilitated engagement	[29, 30]

(*continued*)

Table 3. (*continued*)

Category	Sub-Category	Factor	Direction	Studies
		Rewards (or Loss of)	Facilitated & reduced engagement	[29]
		Motivational messages	Increased engagement	[32]
	SOCI	Competitive ranking	Increased engagement	[29]
		Absence of competition	Linked to dropout	[31]
		Lack of social support	Reduced use	[18, 33, 35]
	PRIM	Lack of personalization/ Tailoring	Reduced engagement	[35, 37]
Postulate	Ease of use	Ease of use/ Reduced effort	Supported continued use	[29, 33, 34, 38]
		High effort, usability issues	Caused disengagement	[31, 35, 36]
	Unobtrusiveness	Fit with routine	Sustained engagement	[29–31, 37]
User Context	Life circumstances	Time constraints, Life Stressors, Low perceived value of content	Hindered use	[18, 33, 35]
	Emotional experiences	Positive mood; Commitment	Increased engagement	[33, 37]
Behavior maintenance	Habit formation	The system had become habitual	Sustained use	[33, 37, 38]
		Reduced perceived need	Discontinuation	[18]

5 Discussion

In this scoping review, we systematically synthesized qualitative evidence on users' perceptions of PSD features in behavior change interventions for physical activity and weight management, as well as factors influencing engagement and continued use. The findings revealed a set of features most frequently perceived as supportive of behavior change: *Reminders, Self-monitoring, Goal-setting, Personalization*, and *Liking*. Moreover, social support was highlighted as an effective means of altering behavior.

However, users encountered difficulties with certain features, including team-based elements (*Cooperation*) and *Rewards*, which some found discouraging and demotivating. Also, computer-human dialogue support (i.e., motivational messages, *Reminders,* and *Rewards*) and social support features appeared to facilitate user engagement. Beyond the PSD features, engagement was also influenced by system design characteristics of *Ease of use* and *Unobtrusiveness*, user context factors, and habit formation.

Overall, the findings suggest that DIAL and PRIM features were generally perceived positively, as they facilitated self-regulation and helped users achieve their goals. *Reminders*, *Self-monitoring*, and *Goal-setting* appeared to improve awareness, accountability, and motivation, thereby supporting task completion and continued engagement. *Goal-setting* was often implemented alongside *Self-monitoring*, enabling users to establish targets and track progress, reinforcing accountability and commitment to behavior change [39]. The findings are consistent with previous research showing that *Reminders* are among the most widely implemented DIAL features in behavior change interventions [6, 7], and that *Self-monitoring* is associated with improved weight-loss and maintenance outcomes [41]. Taken together, this evidence highlights the value of these persuasive features in helping users monitor their progress, establish goals, and maintain healthy routines. Recent evidence from weight-focused BCSS interventions further shows the contributions of *Goal-setting* and *Reminders* to adherence and behavior change outcomes [16, 42]. For example, *Goal-setting* accounted for 15.3% of the variance in body mass index reduction among participants living with obesity [42], further emphasizing its importance in HBCSS.

The findings also revealed mixed user perceptions of several persuasive features, including *Self-monitoring*, *Rewards,* and *Cooperation.* While these features were often viewed as supportive, some participants found them challenging, often triggering feelings of discouragement, guilt, or even unwanted pressure. These observations align with previous research highlighting the benefits of *Self-monitoring* in increasing behavioral awareness while acknowledging the potential downsides, including monotony, tediousness, and even risks of health disorders [43]. Similarly, social support and dialogue elements of *Cooperation* and gamified *Rewards* motivated some users and reinforced goal attainment, whereas others perceived them as less favorable. These results highlight the dual nature of these features, suggesting that their effect is neither inherently positive nor negative but may depend on individual preferences, user characteristics, and/or contextual factors.

Moreover, users perceived credibility-supporting features (in particular, *Trustworthiness* and *Expertise*) as especially helpful when reflected in the content's quality and reliability. Trust in the content increased system acceptance by boosting motivation and supporting a better understanding of users' habits. On the other hand, low *Transparency* was linked to reduced honesty in self-reporting, suggesting that users may provide inaccurate inputs when intervention goals are unclear [32]. Recent research on transparency in a weight-focused BCSS indicates that transparent and open systems (i.e., communicating system goals, explaining strategies used, and disclosing data use) can improve both persuasiveness and overall effectiveness [12]. Likewise, transparent content has been shown to strengthen user trust, increase engagement, and improve overall user experience [44]. This evidence suggests that credibility-supporting features influence not only system adoption but also the quality and continued use.

The findings indicated that engagement and sustained use were influenced by system design factors (including persuasive features and system characteristics), user context, and behavioral mechanisms. *Ease of use* and reduced effort consistently supported continued interaction, suggesting that persuasive features alone may not sustain engagement if the system is perceived as time-consuming or demanding. In line with the PSD model, systems should provide useful and convenient user experience [5]. Feedback features such as *Reminders* and *Rewards* may reinforce system interaction by helping users adhere to their goals, but their effectiveness appears to depend on being integrated into systems that require minimal effort and fit naturally into users' daily routines. Repeated interactions sometimes evolved into routines or habits, suggesting that persuasive systems can support habit formation when seamlessly incorporated into everyday life. Consistent with the PSD principle of *Unobtrusiveness*, persuasive strategies should be delivered at the right moment without disrupting the user's primary activities [5]. Furthermore, a system's unobtrusive nature was found to significantly influence users' perceptions of dialogue support messages [42].

At the same time, the user context played a key role in the continued use of HBCSS. Factors related to life circumstances, such as time constraints and work-related stress or illness, could limit engagement regardless of system design. Interestingly, once desired health behaviors and habits were established, some users perceived less need for the system and subsequently discontinued its use [18]. These findings suggest that disengagement may not always indicate intervention failure and may, in some cases, reflect successful behavior change.

5.1 Implications

This work advances understanding of Persuasive System Design and health behavior change support systems by showing that features across PSD categories (PRIM, DIAL, CRED, and SOCI) may contribute to sustained use and behavior change. The findings further suggest that the persuasive potential of these features depends on how well they align with users' characteristics, situational context, and everyday routines. Consequently, designers should consider persuasive features alongside system design postulates of *Ease of use* and *Unobtrusiveness,* as they appear to enable the effective delivery of strategies such as *Self-monitoring.* This may be achieved by minimizing user burden through simplified interactions and low-effort self-monitoring approaches such as automated tracking using wearable devices.

The findings also have some implications for how the success of HBCSS interventions is evaluated. Some users stopped using the system once their actions had become habitual or after they achieved their goals [18]. This indicates that a decrease in system usage might not always represent failure; instead, it could signify successful change or the adoption of the desired behaviors. Therefore, evaluations of HBCSS should extend beyond user perceptions to include factors like goal achievement, engagement indicators, and objective outcomes to accurately assess sustained behavior change.

Persuasive features such as *Cooperation* and *Rewards* should be implemented with flexibility. Given differences in user preferences (i.e., some found these features supportive, while others felt they reduced engagement), these features may be most effective when optional and adjustable. For example, users could choose whether to receive *Rewards* or adjust the intensity of *Cooperation* features. This would allow users to decide whether to participate in competitive or group-based elements. Designers should therefore provide opportunities to tailor persuasive features to individual needs, as the absence of *Personalization* was associated with reduced use [35, 37]. At the same time, insufficient opportunities for social support were reported as barriers [18, 35], suggesting that designers should balance customizable competitive elements with accessible forms of social support.

Designers should integrate complementary persuasive features rather than implementing them in isolation. For example, users valued the ability to set goals and track their progress [39], as well as receiving prompts to complete monitoring tasks and personalize these features to fit their needs [34]. Combining features such as *Goal-setting, Self-monitoring,* and personalized *Reminders* into a consistent intervention structure may therefore strengthen user commitment and long-term engagement.

5.2 Limitations and Future Work

We acknowledge some limitations of this study. The review included a wide range of intervention types, from early-stage prototypes to fully developed randomized controlled trials, with study durations ranging from 30 min to 12 months. Users generally use applications more during initial adoption and gradually reduce their usage over time [45]. As such, this may have influenced how users experienced and evaluated the systems, as short-term use may yield different perceptions than long-term engagement in full-fledged interventions. Consistent with the scoping review's purpose, we did not assess the effectiveness of the included studies [25]. Therefore, the results reflect perceived value and challenges rather than demonstrated behavioral outcomes. Conclusions cannot be drawn, as these persuasive features may not have been the most effective in promoting physical activity or supporting weight management. Even so, the review provides an overview of how users perceive software features and highlights both supportive and challenging aspects that may influence sustained use, offering valuable insights for designers and developers of these applications. Future studies can explore the relationship between users' perceptions and objective outcomes to better understand how perceptions explain sustained engagement and health behavior change. Given the mixed responses to several persuasive features, future research could examine how user characteristics and preferences influence these perceptions. In addition, future studies could also distinguish between negative attrition and intentional discontinuation after successful habit formation, as disengagement may not always reflect intervention failure.

6 Conclusion

This review compiled qualitative evidence on users' views of persuasive features in HBCSS for physical activity and weight management, as well as on factors affecting engagement and sustained use. *Reminders, Self-monitoring, Goal-setting, Liking* and

Personalization were most frequently perceived as supportive features. However, some features, including *Self-monitoring*, *Rewards*, and team *Cooperation*, were described as both supportive and challenging, indicating their dual nature. Features such as *Reminders, Rewards,* and *Competition*, along with system aspects like *Ease of use* and *Unobtrusiveness*, facilitated continued engagement. In contrast, limited social support and usability issues, particularly when interventions required high effort, negatively affected user experience. Aside from PSD features and design characteristics, user context and the ability to maintain new habits also played important roles in continued engagement. Overall, the findings emphasize the importance of a flexible, user-centered approach to persuasive features rather than universal design. These insights have practical implications for designers, practitioners, and health experts by supporting the need to place users' characteristics and experiences at the center of health behavior change interventions.

References

1. Lee, S.A., Park, J.H.: Systematic review and meta analysis of standalone digital behavior change interventions on physical activity. NPJ Digit. Med. **8**, 436 (2025). https://doi.org/10.1038/s41746-025-01827-4
2. Markkanen, J.O., et al.: Mobile health behaviour change support system as independent treatment tool for obesity: a randomized controlled trial. Int. J. Obes. (2023). https://doi.org/10.1038/s41366-023-01426-x
3. Oinas-Kukkonen, H.: A foundation for the study of behavior change support systems. Pers. Ubiquit. Comput. **17**, 1223–1235 (2013). https://doi.org/10.1007/s00779-012-0591-5
4. Turkkila, E., et al.: Five-year follow-up of a randomized weight loss trial on a digital health behaviour change support system. Int. J. Obes. **49**, 949–953 (2025). https://doi.org/10.1038/s41366-025-01742-4
5. Oinas-Kukkonen, H., Harjumaa, M.: Persuasive systems design: key issues, process model, and system features. Commun. Assoc. Inf. Syst. **24**, 485–500 (2009). https://doi.org/10.17705/1cais.02428
6. Sittig, S., McGowan, A., Iyengar, S.: Extensive review of persuasive system design categories and principles: behavioral obesity interventions. J. Med. Syst. (2020). https://doi.org/10.1007/s10916-020-01591-w
7. Agyei, E.E.Y.F., Ekpezu, A., Oinas-Kukkonen, H.: Persuasive systems design trends in coronary heart disease management: scoping review of randomized controlled trials. JMIR Cardio. **8** (2024). https://doi.org/10.2196/49515
8. de Oliveira, S.C.R., Oinas-Kukkonen, H.: Evidence levels for persuasive software features in digital health interventions: insights from a scoping review regarding T2DM. In: ICIS 2024 Proceedings (2024). https://aisel.aisnet.org/icis2024/ishealthcare/ishealthcare/15
9. Nabwire, S., Agyei, E., Merikallio, H., Savolainen, M.J., Hukkanen, J., Oinas-Kukkonen, H.: Evaluating the influence of persuasive systems design on continuance intention, perceived effectiveness, and weight loss. Digit. Health. **12** (2026). https://doi.org/10.1177/20552076261461365
10. Oduor, M., Oinas-Kukkonen, H.: Committing to change: a persuasive systems design analysis of user commitments for a behaviour change support system. Behav. Inform. Technol. **40**, 20–38 (2021). https://doi.org/10.1080/0144929X.2019.1598495

11. Nabwire, S., de Oliveira, S.R., Merikallio, H., Savolainen, M., Hukkanen, J., Oinas-Kukkonen, H.: Cognitive consistency as a facilitator of perceived persuasiveness and continuance intention in digital weight management. In: ICIS 2025 Proceedings. Association for Information Systems (2025). https://aisel.aisnet.org/icis2025/user_behav/user_behav/5
12. Nabwire, S., de Oliveira, R., Merikallio, H., Savolainen, M.J., Hukkanen, J., Oinas-Kukkonen, H.: Enhancing the perceived effectiveness of health behaviour change support systems through transparency in persuasive systems design. Behav. Inform. Technol. (2026). https://doi.org/10.1080/0144929X.2026.2638915
13. Wiafe, I., Koranteng, F.N., Kastriku, F.A., Gyamera, G.O.: Assessing the impact of persuasive features on user's intention to continuous use: the case of academic social networking sites. Behav. Inform. Technol. **41**, 712–730 (2020). https://doi.org/10.1080/0144929X.2020.1832146
14. Agyei, E., Miettunen, J., Oinas-Kukkonen, H.: Effective interventions and features for coronary heart disease: a meta-analysis. Behav. Inform. Technol. (2023). https://doi.org/10.1080/0144929X.2023.2213342
15. Foster, J.M., Reddel, H.K., Usherwood, T., Sawyer, S.M., Smith, L.: Patient-perceived acceptability and behaviour change benefits of inhaler reminders and adherence feedback: a qualitative study. Respir. Med. **129**, 39–45 (2017). https://doi.org/10.1016/j.rmed.2017.05.013
16. Nabwire, S., de Oliveira, R.S.C., Merikallio, H., Savolainen, M.J., Hukkanen, J., Oinas-Kukkonen, H.: Evaluating persuasive reminders and suggestions in a weight management mHealth intervention. In: 59th Hawaii International Conference on System Sciences, pp. 3777–3786 (2026). https://doi.org/10.24251/HICSS.2026.452
17. Asbjørnsen, R.A., et al.: Identifying persuasive design principles and behavior change techniques supporting end user values and needs in eHealth interventions for long-term weight loss maintenance: qualitative study. J. Med. Internet Res. **22**, e22598 (2020). https://doi.org/10.2196/22598
18. Karppinen, P., et al.: Persuasive user experiences of a health behavior change support system: a 12-month study for prevention of metabolic syndrome. Int. J. Med. Inform. **96**, 51–61 (2016). https://doi.org/10.1016/j.ijmedinf.2016.02.005
19. Michie, S., van Stralen, M.M., West, R.: The behaviour change wheel: a new method for characterising and designing behaviour change interventions. Implement. Sci. **6**, 42 (2011). https://doi.org/10.1186/1748-5908-6-42
20. Michie, S., et al.: The behavior change technique taxonomy (v1) of 93 hierarchically clustered techniques: building an international consensus for the reporting of behavior change interventions. Ann. Behav. Med. **46**, 81–95 (2013). https://doi.org/10.1007/s12160-013-9486-6
21. Fogg, B.J.: A behavior model for persuasive design. In: ACM International Conference Proceeding Series (2009). https://doi.org/10.1145/1541948.1541999
22. Ekpezu, A.O., Oinas-Kukkonen, H., Wiafe, I.: Investigating the determinants of compliance intention in behavior change support systems. In: AMCIS 2023 Proceedings. AIS Electronic Library (AISeL) (2023)
23. Arksey, H., O'Malley, L.: Scoping studies: towards a methodological framework. Int. J. Soc. Res. Methodol. **8**, 19–32 (2005). https://doi.org/10.1080/1364557032000119616
24. Tricco, A.C., et al.: PRISMA extension for scoping reviews (PRISMA-ScR): checklist and explanation. Ann. Intern. Med. **169**, 467–473 (2018). https://doi.org/10.7326/M18-0850
25. Aromataris, E., Lockwood, C., Porritt, K., Pilla, B., Jordan, Z.: JBI Manual for Evidence Synthesis. JBI (2024). https://doi.org/10.46658/JBIMES-24-01
26. Annesi, J.J.: Effects of increased physical activity/exercise on long-term losses in weight and waist circumference: serial mediation from changes in exercise-related to eating-related

self-regulation. Int. J. Behav. Med. **30**, 334–344 (2023). https://doi.org/10.1007/s12529-022-10106-5

27. Ouzzani, M., Hammady, H., Fedorowicz, Z., Elmagarmid, A.: Rayyan—a web and mobile app for systematic reviews. Syst. Rev. **5**, 210 (2016). https://doi.org/10.1186/s13643-016-0384-4
28. Page, M.J., et al.: The PRISMA 2020 statement: an updated guideline for reporting systematic reviews. BMJ, n71 (2021). https://doi.org/10.1136/bmj.n71
29. Almutari, N.S., Alqahtani, F., Orji, R., Chan, G.: StepsBooster-S: a culturally tailored step-based persuasive application for promoting physical activity. Int. J. Hum. Comput. Interact., 1–24 (2024). https://doi.org/10.1080/10447318.2024.2331874
30. Asbjørnsen, R.A., et al.: Digital behaviour change intervention for weight loss maintenance in adults with obesity: a feasibility pilot study of eCHANGE. Behav. Inform. Technol. **44**, 2577–2595 (2025). https://doi.org/10.1080/0144929X.2024.2399299
31. Hooglugt, F., Ludden, G.D.S.: A Mobile app adopting an identity focus to promote physical activity (MoveDaily): iterative design study. JMIR Mhealth Uhealth. **8**, e16720 (2020). https://doi.org/10.2196/16720
32. Janols, R., Guerrero, E., Lindgren, H.: A pilot study on personalised coaching to increase older adults' physical and social activities. In: De Paz, J.F., Julián, V., Villarrubia, G., Marreiros, G., Novais, P. (eds.) 8th International Symposium on Ambient Intelligence. Springer International Publishing, Cham (2017). https://doi.org/10.1007/978-3-319-61118-1
33. Karppinen, P., et al.: Opportunities and challenges of behavior change support systems for enhancing habit formation: a qualitative study. J. Biomed. Inform. **84**, 82–92 (2018). https://doi.org/10.1016/j.jbi.2018.06.012
34. Ladwa, S., Grønli, T.M., Ghinea, G.: Towards encouraging a healthier lifestyle and increased physical activity – an app incorporating persuasive design principles (2018). https://doi.org/10.1007/978-3-319-91244-8_13
35. Mattila, E., et al.: Users' experiences with the NoHoW web-based toolkit with weight and activity tracking in weight loss maintenance: long-term randomized controlled trial. J. Med. Internet Res. **24**, e29302 (2022). https://doi.org/10.2196/29302
36. Odenigbo, I.P., Reen, J.K., Eneze, C., Friday, A., Orji, R.: The journey: an AR gamified mobile application for promoting physical activity in young adults. In: Adjunct Proceedings of the 30th ACM Conference on User Modeling, Adaptation and Personalization, pp. 342–353. ACM, New York, NY, USA (2022). https://doi.org/10.1145/3511047.3537652
37. Odenigbo, I.P., Alslaity, A., Chan, G., Orji, R.: AR Dancee: an augmented reality-based mobile persuasive intervention for promoting physical activity through dancing. Int. J. Hum. Comput. Interact. **41**, 6765–6785 (2025). https://doi.org/10.1080/10447318.2024.2384136
38. Oyebode, O., Ganesh, A., Orji, R.: TreeCare: development and evaluation of a persuasive Mobile game for promoting physical activity. In: 2021 IEEE Conference on Games (CoG), pp. 1–8. IEEE (2021). https://doi.org/10.1109/CoG52621.2021.9619035
39. Srivastava, P., Chan, G., Oyebode, O., Orji, R.: PetBuddy: an examination of augmented reality mobile health game for promoting physical activity (2025). https://doi.org/10.1007/978-3-031-94959-3_19
40. Zhao, J., Yao, J., Guo, X., Xiao, T.: Competition, cooperation, or both? a field study on a persuasive smartwatch fitness application with intergroup competition for promoting physical activity (2025). https://doi.org/10.1007/978-3-031-93221-2_17
41. Hallock, R., Ufholz, K., Patel, N.: Self-monitoring of weight as a weight loss strategy: a systematic review. Curr. Cardiovasc. Risk Rep. **18**, 163–172 (2024). https://doi.org/10.1007/s12170-024-00746-5

42. de Oliveira, R.S.C., Nabwire, S., Merikallio, H., Savolainen, M., Hukkanen, J., Oinas-Kukkonen, H.: Behind the software: the impact of unobtrusiveness, goal setting and persuasive features on BMI. Int. J. Med. Inform. **196**, 105795 (2025). https://doi.org/10.1016/j.ijmedinf.2025.105795
43. Orji, R., Lomotey, R., Oyibo, K., Orji, F., Blustein, J., Shahid, S.: Tracking feels oppressive and 'punishy': exploring the costs and benefits of self-monitoring for health and wellness. Digit. Health. **4** (2018). https://doi.org/10.1177/2055207618797554
44. Almohanna, A.A.S., Meedya, S., Vlahu-Gjorgievska, E., Win, K.T.: Exploring user experiences with a persuasive mHealth app for breastfeeding: an empirical investigation. Int. J. Hum. Comput. Interact., 1–18 (2025). https://doi.org/10.1080/10447318.2024.2394726
45. Lee, K., et al.: Effect of self-monitoring on long-term patient engagement with mobile health applications. PLoS One. **13**, e0201166 (2018). https://doi.org/10.1371/journal.pone.0201166

Adopting Smart Grid Services Under Uncertainty: A Mixed-Method Study of Privacy Calculus in Household Decision-Making

Gauri Shankar(✉), Prabhat Kumar, and Najmul Islam

LUT University, Yliopistonkatu 34, 53850 Lappeenranta, Finland
gauri.shankar@lut.fi

Abstract. Smart Grid Technology (SGT) can support sustainable energy use by offering households personalized energy insights, consumption monitoring, and financial incentives. However, its adoption remains uncertain because SGT relies on detailed household energy data, raising privacy, security, and control concerns. Drawing on Privacy Calculus Theory (PCT), this study examines how household decision-makers evaluate SGT adoption under uncertainty. We used an exploratory sequential mixed-method design. Phase 1 involved five focus group interviews with 23 urban European household decision-makers to identify perceived benefits, risks, and assurance needs. Phase 2 used a privacy-assuring User Interface (UI) and a scenario-based pilot survey with 52 European respondents, along with PLS-SEM analysis. The findings show that households value personalized benefits and monetary rewards but remain concerned about profiling, cyber attacks, data misuse, and loss of control. Pilot results suggest that trust reduced privacy and control concerns, while transparency increased perceived personalized benefits. The study conceptualizes SGT adoption as an assurance-driven privacy calculus process and highlights the role of privacy-assuring interfaces in supporting sustainable smart energy adoption.

Keywords: Smart Grid Technology · Privacy Calculus Theory · User Assurance · Privacy and Security Concerns · Smart Energy Services

1 Introduction

As societies move toward more sustainable and consumer-oriented energy systems, governments and utility providers are increasingly adopting SGT [20]. SGT refers to the integration of data-intensive information systems and communication technologies with automated control mechanisms into electricity supply networks [25]. SGT balances supply and demand through continuous monitoring and real-time feedback, enabling personalized energy services that help households to optimize consumption and reduce energy costs while contributing to broader sustainability goals [25].

Published by Springer Nature Switzerland AG 2027
S. Han et al. (Eds.): I3E 2026, LNCS 16912, pp. 273–285, 2027.
https://doi.org/10.1007/978-3-032-38014-2_20

However, the benefits of SGT depend entirely on the collection and processing of detailed household energy data [25]. SGT operates through continuous data-collection flows among connected entities such as households, utility providers, service operators, and third-party actors [25]. These data contain very detailed energy usage information linked to a household's profile and can constitute sensitive personal information [11]. While this data is crucial for offering personalized energy insights and demand-response services, collecting and sharing it also poses significant privacy and security risks [22,25]. These risks are particularly significant because households often lack sufficient knowledge of SGT service providers' data management practices [9,27]. In such situations, information asymmetry may increase uncertainty and reduce users' confidence in SGT adoption [13]. It raises concerns about data misuse and its security and privacy [11]. Therefore, prior research has identified privacy and security concerns as major barriers to the adoption of smart energy services [22]. Additionally, these concerns are also influenced by perceived loss of control, lack of transparency, and unclear consent practices by the SGT service provider [25].

Households may recognize SGT-enabled personalized services and financial benefits from usage optimization, motivating them for adoption [25]. On the other hand, they may be concerned about privacy and security of collected data [22,25]. Such a situation develops a privacy dilemma for households [8]. Therefore, households must evaluate whether the expected benefits of SGT outweigh the perceived risks of data disclosure and digital monitoring [8]. This decision-making process is challenging because households differ in their technical knowledge, prior experience, and awareness of data protection issues [11]. Accordingly, users with prior experience of cyber incidents may evaluate SGT services more cautiously [6]. Similarly, users with greater privacy awareness may demand transparency in data practices before adopting smart energy services [1,27]. Consequently, the adoption of SGT also relies on households' assurance regarding SGT services [23,25].

Building on this reasoning, this study investigates how household decision-makers evaluate SGT adoption under privacy and security uncertainty [8]. Although prior studies have emphasized the technological usefulness and financial benefits of SGT services, less is known about how households evaluate these services under information asymmetry [25]. Therefore, this study examines how perceived benefits, perceived risks, and assurance mechanisms such as transparency and trust shape household evaluations [13,27]. In doing so, it conceptualizes SGT adoption as an assurance-driven privacy calculus process. Further, it identifies UI-based assurance features through which transparency and trust may reduce privacy and security uncertainty [2,8,25]. To address these gaps, this study investigates the following research questions:

RQ1. *How do household decision-makers evaluate the perceived benefits and perceived privacy risks associated with SGT service adoption?*

RQ1(a). *How do UI-based assurance mechanisms, transparency, and trust-building features shape households' evaluation of perceived benefits and perceived privacy risks in SGT service adoption?*

RQ1(b). *How do prior privacy experiences and awareness influence households' evaluations of perceived benefits and perceived privacy risks for SGT adoption under uncertainty?*

2 Background

SGT adoption faces significant challenges, including skepticism and disengagement due to privacy and security concerns as seen in the Netherlands [11,17,25]. Beyond these concerns, lower engagement, digital literacy gaps, and limited trust in service providers further increase uncertainty around adoption [18]. Failure to address these issues can undermine trust in digital energy services [11,25]. Evidence suggests that educating users about SGT and ensuring transparent communication by utilities about data management practices may reduce users' sensitivity to risk [1,25]. Moreover, strong data protection and governance frameworks can foster trust in SGT, as observed in Germany [17,18]. Factors such as informed consent and user control may enhance trust and reduce perceived risks associated with adoption [1,25]. However, the absence of these elements may hinder the early implementation of SGT [11,17]. Thus, utility providers and smart energy service operators should offer privacy assurances and transparent communication to reduce uncertainty in SGT adoption [1,6]. When users believe their data is protected, they may become more willing to consider the benefits of SGT services and adopt them [25].

Prior research on privacy concerns in smart energy systems, such as smart meters, has mainly used technology adoption models, Organismic Integration Theory, and Self-Determination Theory, focusing on constructs such as perceived usefulness to explain adoption [25]. However, these approaches often overlook consumer-level decision-making around privacy and security concerns. Factors such as privacy invasion experiences and control concerns remain underexplored [6]. To address this gap, this study applies Privacy Calculus Theory to examine how household decision-makers evaluate SGT services [14].

2.1 Theoretical Framework: Privacy Calculus Theory

To understand how households adopt SGT, it is essential to examine the socio-technical and privacy factors that influence user acceptance. SGT improves energy services for users and enables more efficient power grid management [25]. Thus, SGT supports personalized benefits and broader sustainability goals [20]. However, because SGT collects detailed data, its adoption also raises security and privacy concerns over energy-related and personal information [22]. Privacy Calculus Theory provides a framework for how households evaluate the tradeoff between perceived risks and perceived benefits. Specifically, PCT suggests that individuals make disclosure and technology adoption decisions by weighing perceived benefits against perceived privacy risks [9]. In the SGT context, *perceived benefits* include personalized energy recommendations, monetary rewards, and cost savings over energy consumption. Conversely, *perceived risks* involve personal information profiling, security breaches, unauthorized data access, and reduced control over household energy information. Thus, households are likely to assess whether the expected value of SGT services outweighs the perceived privacy and security costs [8,25].

However, many households may lack the technical knowledge needed to evaluate data management practices and assess benefit–risk trade-offs. This uncertainty can be reduced through *assurance mechanisms* that support informed decision-making. Thus, this study conceptualizes SGT adoption as an assurance-driven privacy calculus process. In this process, transparency and trust serve as key assurance mechanisms. Transparency helps households understand how utility and service providers manage data [1,27], while trust reflects confidence that these actors will handle energy data responsibly and for legitimate purposes [12,18]. Further, this assurance mechanism is visualized to the user as UI-based assurance features and treated as practical mechanisms through which transparency and trust can be communicated to households during SGT service evaluation. Together, they reduce information asymmetry and provide households with greater assurance when evaluating SGT services. Households' privacy calculus evaluations may also depend on contextual factors such as *prior privacy experiences* and *awareness*. Users who have experienced privacy violations may assess SGT services more cautiously. Similarly, users with greater awareness of data-intensive systems may pay closer attention to consent, transparency, control, and data protection before adoption [4,6,16]. These factors shape how households interpret SGT-related risks, benefits, and assurances without replacing the core benefit–risk logic of PCT. By focusing on this *assurance-driven privacy calculus*, the study explains why households may remain uncertain about SGT despite recognizing its benefits. SGT adoption depends not only on usefulness and cost savings but also on perceptions of transparency, trust, control, privacy, and security.

3 Methods

In this study, we adopted an exploratory sequential mixed-method design. Phase 1 used semi-structured focus group interviews (FGIs) [15] and an interactive feature-elicitation activity to identify household expectations for safer and more trustworthy SGT services. Building on Phase 1 insights, Phase 2 used a scenario-based pilot survey [26] to assess initial user perceptions of the privacy-assuring SGT interface and identify preliminary patterns for future larger-sample testing. The results from Phase 1, *Understanding Users' Perceptions of Benefits, Risks, and UI Elicitation*, informed the development of the UI-based scenario. The survey constructs were developed based on users' perceived benefits and risks and were aligned with Privacy Calculus Theory. Participants evaluated these scenario-based UI features using validated items adapted from prior research [26]. All items were measured on a 7-point Likert scale, ranging from 1 = "strongly disagree" to 7 = "strongly agree" [7]. The measurement constructs, item sources, and adaptations sources are presented in Table 1. The Appendix provides details of construct items, UI, and UI-based scenarios.

4 Phase 1: Understanding Users' Perceptions of Benefits, Risks, and UI Elicitation

4.1 Data Collection

Data were collected through five focus group interviews with 23 urban European household decision-makers, after which thematic saturation was reached. Participants were recruited through purposive screening to include households responsible for paying or closely monitoring electricity bills and those who had encountered SGT-related offerings, such as smart meters or utility demand-response programs, within the past 12 months. Each focus group included 4–5 participants and lasted approximately 60 min. The interview began with consent information and an introduction to smart-grid technology. The questions then addressed appliance-level monitoring, user control, data-sharing transparency, trust in utility providers, cybersecurity risks, and billing transparency. Sessions used semi-structured open-ended questions and ended with a Miro-based feature-elicitation task. On the Miro board, participants proposed UI features that would make them feel safer about adopting SGT services, particularly regarding transparency, privacy, and control.

4.2 Analysis and Results

The collected transcript data were analyzed using the Gioia methodology [10]. The analysis followed an iterative and abductive process, moving between the empirical data and the PCT lens. First, transcripts were manually screened to understand the data within the PCT framework. Open coding was then used to develop first-order concepts while preserving participants' original meanings where possible [21]. Next, an interactive, theory-informed coding strategy was applied to cluster related first-order concepts into second-order codes. Finally, aggregate themes were developed by merging second-order codes to connect the coding structure with the adopted theory. These themes include *Perceived Benefits*, *Perceived Risks*, *User Assurance*, and *Informed Engagement* for SGT adoption. The final data structure, shown in Fig. 1, visualizes these three analytical steps and clarifies how participants' perspectives link to the aggregate PCT dimensions.

Perceived Benefits: Many participants expressed positive views about the *benefits* of SGT services. We identified two key factors encouraging SGT adoption: personalized benefits and monetary rewards, where *personalized benefits* refer to smart grid systems' ability to provide tailored insights and usage feedback that help households manage their electricity consumption more effectively. As one participant from FGI 2 noted, *"With a smart grid, I get access to detailed reports*

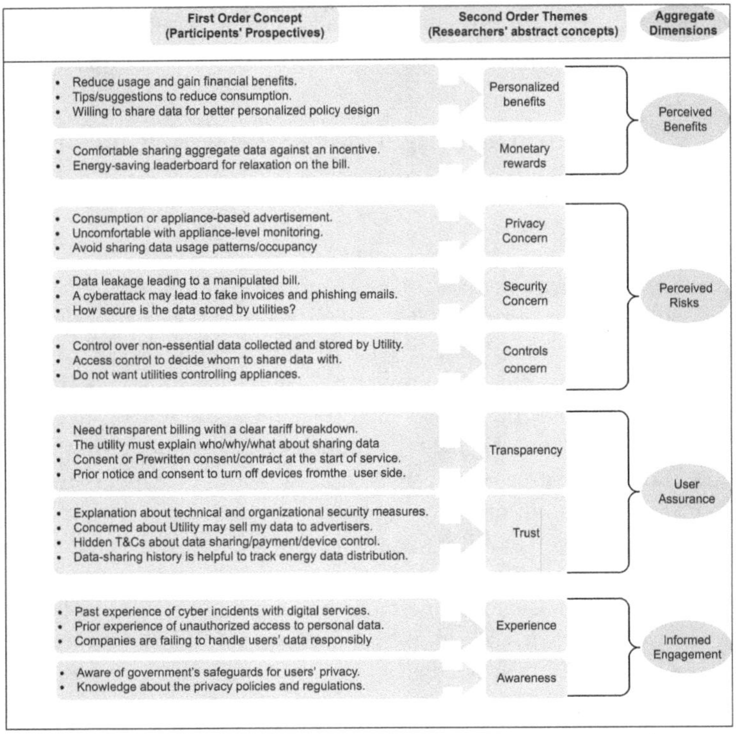

Fig. 1. Data structure of factors affecting SGT adoption.

about my energy use. We can spot when I'm using the most power and tweak my habits to save money." Second, *monetary rewards* emerged as another key factor influencing participants' willingness to share energy data. Many respondents indicated they would be comfortable sharing certain levels of consumption data if doing so led to financial benefits, such as discounts or rewards for energy-efficient behaviors. As one participant from FGI 2 highlighted *"In my case, I would be willing to share my data if I receive compensation. If my data is collected, there should be some form of incentive or payment."*

Perceived Risks: Although participants recognized the benefits of SGT, they also expressed concerns about privacy, security, and control. First, *privacy concerns* related to the collection and sharing of detailed energy consumption data. As one participant from FGI 5 noted, *"Smart grid service providers could easily profile me from my energy consumption data and infer my daily routines and habits."* and other participants shared similar sentiments. Second, *security risks* associated with cyber incidents and data breaches. As one participant from FGI 2 noted: *"If a cyberattack occurs and my energy data is compromised, it could be used to create fake invoices or other scams, which is a serious con-*

cern." Third, participants raised *Control Concern* regarding how utilities or SGT service providers store, share, and use household energy data.

User Assurance: Participants emphasized that *assurance mechanisms* are vital in reducing uncertainty around adopting SGT services. Further, *Transparency* is identified as crucial for building trust between consumers and utilities. While *trust* in utility providers emerged as a key factor in adoption, it was strengthened by responsible data governance and clear safeguards for personal information. As one participant from FGI 4 stated *"I think it is very important for consumer to be informed when and why our data is accessed by a third party. Having a clear data-sharing history would increase transparency and trust. It would also give me control to review and manage how my information is being used and which parties are using my information and for what purpose."*

Informed Engagement: Participants highlighted how their past experiences and awareness of privacy and security in digital services influenced their evaluation of the risks and benefits of adopting SGT services. Participants from FGI 1 and 2, supported by others in their groups, stated that."No matter what check boxes or consent options are there, in almost every case I still end up receiving marketing emails, which suggests that my data is being shared somewhere."

4.3 Proposed Solution from Participants' Perspective

Participants collaboratively described smart-grid application features that could mitigate their concerns and reduce uncertainty about SGT adoption. The resulting features are presented in Fig. 2, which links participants' concerns to proposed UI features and the aggregate PCT dimensions. These features provided the basis for the Phase 2 UI-based scenario and pilot survey by translating them into an SGT UI interface presented in the Appendix.

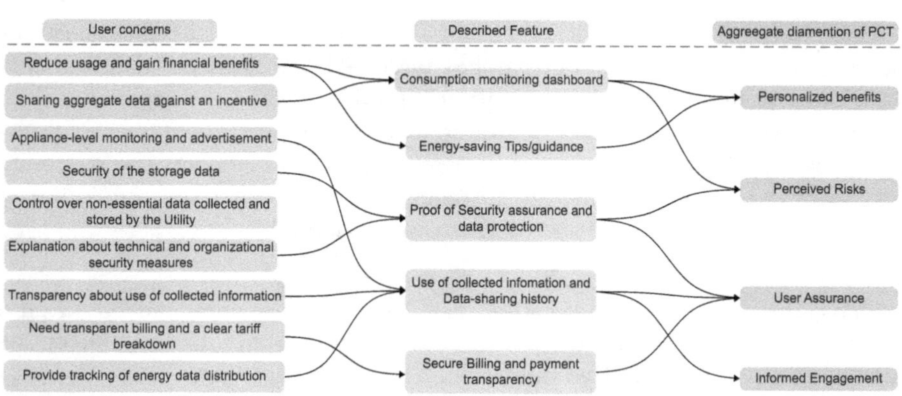

Fig. 2. Participant-derived system features linking user concerns, proposed UI features, and PCT aggregate dimensions.

5 Phase 2: Pilot Assessment of the Privacy-Assuring UI

5.1 Pilot Data Collection and Analysis

Phase 2 was designed as a pilot assessment of users' perceptions of the proposed privacy-assuring SGT interface, rather than as a full confirmatory validation of the structural model. Data were collected via Prolific, yielding 52 valid responses from European households. Respondents were demographically diverse in age, education, residence, and income, reflecting variation in technology-related knowledge, experience, and affordability (see the Appendix). Further, given the limited sample size, the quantitative analysis was used to examine measurement plausibility and preliminary patterns among the constructs. Accordingly, the PLS-SEM [5] results are interpreted cautiously and treated as exploratory evidence that complements the qualitative findings from Phase 1. The Phase 2 constructs presented in Table 1 operationalized the Phase 1 Gioia dimensions rather than introducing unrelated variables. Personalized Benefit and Monetary Reward captured perceived benefits; Privacy Concerns, Security Concerns, and Control Concern captured perceived risks; Transparency and Trust captured UI-based user assurance; Awareness and Privacy Experience captured informed engagement; and Adoption Intention captured willingness to adopt the proposed privacy-assuring SGT service.

5.2 Pilot Results

The Pilot Measurement Model showed acceptable reliability and convergent validity. Following PLS-SEM guidelines, Cronbach's alpha and composite reliability values above 0.70 indicate acceptable internal consistency, while AVE values above 0.50 indicate acceptable convergent validity [5]. In this study, Cronbach's alpha ranged from 0.795 to 0.963, composite reliability from 0.878 to 0.976, and AVE from 0.655 to 0.932. Given the limited sample size, these results are interpreted as preliminary rather than confirmatory. The item wording, loadings, means, standard deviations, and measurement-item sources are provided in the Appendix. Further, results suggested that trust reduced privacy and control concerns, while transparency increased perceived personalized benefit. However, direct effects on adoption intention were not significant. Thus, the pilot findings indicate that the interface may support adoption evaluation mainly by strengthening trust and transparency. Table 1 reports the reliability and convergent validity results; the "Measurement-item source" column indicates prior studies from which the survey items were adapted.

For the Pilot Structural Model, as Phase 2 was a pilot and based on a limited sample, the structural results are interpreted as preliminary perception patterns rather than definitive validation. The model showed explanatory power for Adoption Intention ($R^2 = 0.477$). The clearest patterns were observed for UI-based assurance mechanisms: Trust reduced Privacy Concerns ($\beta = -0.609$, $p < 0.001$) and Control Concern ($\beta = -0.502$, $p < 0.001$), while increasing

Table 1. Construct Reliability and Validity

Construct	Cronbach's α	Composite Reliability	AVE	Source
Adoption Intention	0.952	0.969	0.912	[23]
Awareness	0.800	0.878	0.706	[27]
Control Concern	0.941	0.962	0.893	[24]
Monetary Reward	0.830	0.883	0.655	[19]
Personalized Benefit	0.795	0.880	0.710	[9]
Privacy Concerns	0.940	0.957	0.847	[25]
Privacy Experience	0.898	0.936	0.830	[16]
Security Concerns	0.963	0.976	0.932	[4]
Transparency	0.901	0.936	0.830	[3]
Trust	0.934	0.950	0.791	[25]

Monetary Reward perception ($\beta = 0.515$, $p < 0.001$). Transparency increased Personalized Benefit ($\beta = 0.398$, $p = 0.005$). The model also explained variance in Control Concern ($R^2 = 0.181$), Monetary Reward ($R^2 = 0.340$), Personalized Benefit ($R^2 = 0.312$), and Privacy Concerns ($R^2 = 0.274$). Effect-size results showed that Trust had the strongest effects on Privacy Concerns ($f^2 = 0.365$), Monetary Reward ($f^2 = 0.287$), and Control Concern ($f^2 = 0.220$), while Transparency had a moderate effect on Personalized Benefit ($f^2 = 0.165$). However, the direct paths from Monetary Reward, Personalized Benefit, Privacy Concerns, and Security Concerns to Adoption Intention were not significant. Overall, the pilot findings suggest that the proposed UI may reduce uncertainty by strengthening trust, transparency, and perceived benefits, while the direct paths to Adoption Intention require larger-sample validation.

6 Discussion

This study emphasizes that household adoption of SGT is shaped by an assurance-driven privacy calculus, where perceived benefits, perceived risks, transparency, and trust jointly influence adoption evaluations [8,14]. In response to RQ1, the findings show that households evaluate SGT services through a benefit–risk trade-off. Households recognized the value of SGT, especially cost optimization through personalized energy insights and financial incentives, but these benefits were weakened by privacy and security concerns [14]. Participants were particularly concerned about privacy-related cyberattacks or data misuse, and loss of control over household energy data [25]. This tension reflects the core logic of Privacy Calculus Theory, where users evaluate whether expected benefits justify the risks of data disclosure [8].

Regarding RQ1(a), findings from Phase 1 showed that households expected clear explanations of data collection, access histories, consent options, and control over data sharing [12]. These expectations suggest that uncertainty arises mainly from information asymmetry between households and utility or service providers [13]. Accordingly, transparency and trust become essential mechanisms for reducing uncertainty and supporting informed decision-making [18,27]. Phase 2 complemented these insights through a pilot assessment of the proposed privacy-assuring UI. The pilot results suggest that trust reduced privacy and control concerns, while transparency increased perceived personalized benefit. Trust also strengthened perceptions of monetary reward. However, the direct paths from benefits and concerns to adoption intention require larger-sample validation; therefore, these findings are interpreted as preliminary perception patterns rather than definitive behavioral evidence. Regarding RQ1(b), prior privacy experiences and awareness shaped households' evaluations by making users more cautious about privacy risks and more attentive to consent, accountability, transparency, and control before accepting SGT-related benefits [6,16]. Overall, the pilot findings suggest that the proposed UI supports adoption evaluation by strengthening assurance-related perceptions, especially trust, transparency, and perceived benefits.

The study extends Privacy Calculus Theory by conceptualizing SGT adoption as an assurance-driven privacy calculus rather than a simple benefit–risk trade-off. The main contribution lies in identifying household privacy, security, and control concerns and translating them into a privacy-assuring SGT interface framework. In practice, SGT providers and policymakers should strengthen transparent data practices, verifiable privacy indicators, user-centric data governance, and accountability mechanisms to support sustainable, broader societal trust in SGT infrastructures.

7 Conclusion

This study highlights the adoption of SGT services under uncertainty. Households acknowledge the personalized and monetary benefits. However, these benefits are limited by privacy and security risks. Interpreted through PCT, the findings show that SGT adoption is not merely an evaluation of financial gain, but a decision-making process in which households weigh perceived benefits against privacy and security risks. Further, findings emphasize the role of assurance mechanisms in SGT adoption. Phase 1 showed that households seek transparency, data-access records, and verifiable privacy and security safeguards, while Phase 2 provided preliminary support that trust reduces privacy and control concerns and transparency strengthens perceived personalized benefits. Together, these findings support a user-informed privacy-assuring interface framework for SGT adoption under uncertainty.

However, the study is limited by its qualitative sample of 23 participants and pilot survey sample of 52 respondents. As Phase 2 was a pilot, the multi-country sample was used to capture initial patterns of perception rather than country-level or regulatory differences. Given the limited sample and ten-construct model, the non-significant paths may reflect limited statistical power or Type II error. Future studies should validate these relationships with larger, stratified European samples and examine how regulatory contexts, digital literacy, and prior privacy experiences shape privacy-calculus evaluations. Future studies should also test the proposed UI assurance features (available in Appendix), in real-world SGT settings to examine whether transparency dashboards, consent controls, and data-access histories can reduce uncertainty and support sustained adoption. Overall, this study underscores the role of assurance-oriented design in the adoption of trustworthy smart grids.

Acknowledgment. This work was supported by the Research Council of Finland with CHIST-ERA, grant agreement no–359790, Di4SPDS-Distributed Intelligence for Enhancing the Security and Privacy of Decentralized and Distributed Systems.

Use of AI. The authors used AI-integrated Grammarly tools only for grammatical editing and improving readability. The authors reviewed all content and take full responsibility for the manuscript.

Disclosure of Interests. The authors have no competing interests to declare that are relevant to the content of this article.

Appendix. can be found at https://doi.org/10.5281/zenodo.20719764

References

1. Awad, N.F., Krishnan, M.S.: The personalization privacy paradox: an empirical evaluation of information transparency and the willingness to be profiled online for personalization. MIS Q. **30**(1), 13–28 (2006)
2. Bui, N., Castellani, A.P., Casari, P., Zorzi, M.: The internet of energy: a web-enabled smart grid system. IEEE Network **26**(4), 39–45 (2012). https://doi.org/10.1109/MNET.2012.6246751
3. Chen, T., Chen, J.: Exploring college students' perceptions of privacy and security in online learning: a comprehensive questionnaire-based study. Int. J. Human-Comput. Interaction **41**(10), 6481–6494 (2025)
4. Chen, Y., Zahedi, F.M.: Individuals' internet security perceptions and behaviors: poly contextual contrasts between the united states and china. MIS Q. **40**(1), 205–222 (2016)
5. Chin, W.W.: The partial least squares approach to structural equation modeling. In: Modern Methods for Business Research, pp. 295–336. Psychology Press (1998)
6. Cichy, P., Salge, T.O., Kohli, R.: Privacy concerns and data sharing in the internet of things: mixed methods evidence from connected cars. MIS Q. **45**(4), 1863–1891 (2021)
7. Dawes, J.: Do data characteristics change according to the number of scale points used? an experiment using 5-point, 7-point and 10-point scales. Int. J. Mark. Res. **50**(1), 61–104 (2008)
8. Dinev, T., Hart, P.: An extended privacy calculus model for e-commerce transactions. Inf. Syst. Res. **17**(1), 61–80 (2006)
9. Dinev, T., Xu, H., Smith, J.H., Hart, P.: Information privacy and correlates: an empirical attempt to bridge and distinguish privacy-related concepts. Eur. J. Inf. Syst. **22**(3), 295–316 (2013)

10. Gioia, D.A., Corley, K.G., Hamilton, A.L.: Seeking qualitative rigor in inductive research: Notes on the GIOIA methodology. Organ. Res. Methods **16**(1), 15–31 (2013)
11. Hoenkamp, R., Huitema, G.B., de Moor-van Vugt, A.J.: The neglected consumer: The case of the smart meter rollout in the Netherlands. Renewable Energy Law Policy Rev. 269–282 (2011)
12. Kehr, F., Kowatsch, T., Wentzel, D., Fleisch, E.: Blissfully ignorant: the effects of general privacy concerns, general institutional trust, and affect in the privacy calculus. Inf. Syst. J. **25**(6), 607–635 (2015)
13. Kim, D.J., Ferrin, D.L., Rao, H.R.: A trust-based consumer decision-making model in electronic commerce: the role of trust, perceived risk, and their antecedents. Decis. Support Syst. **44**(2), 544–564 (2008)
14. Kim, D., Park, K., Park, Y., Ahn, J.H.: Willingness to provide personal information: perspective of privacy calculus in IoT services. Comput. Hum. Behav. **92**, 273–281 (2019)
15. Kvale, S., Brinkmann, S.: Interviews: learning the craft of qualitative research interviewing. Sage (2009)
16. Li, Y.: The impact of disposition to privacy, website reputation and website familiarity on information privacy concerns. Decis. Support Syst. **57**, 343–354 (2014)
17. von Loessl, V.: Smart meter-related data privacy concerns and dynamic electricity tariffs: evidence from a stated choice experiment. Energy Policy **180**, 113645 (2023)
18. Märtins, J., Kehl, R., Westmattelmann, D., Schewe, G.: A multi-dimensional theory of transparency, trust, and risk in technology adoption. In: Proceedings of the 43rd International Conference on Information Systems (ICIS 2022). Association for Information Systems, Copenhagen, Denmark (2022)
19. Shi, J., et al.: Factors influencing the sharing of personal health data based on the integrated theory of privacy calculus and theory of planned behaviors framework: results of a cross-sectional study of Chinese patients in the Yangtze river delta. JMIR **25**, e46562 (2023)
20. Sim, J., Lee, J., Cho, D.: On the effectiveness of smart metering technology adoption: evidence from the national rollout in the united kingdom. J. Assoc. Inf. Syst. **24**(2), 555–591 (2023)
21. Strauss, A.L., Corbin, J.M.: Basics of Qualitative Research: Techniques and Procedures for Developing Grounded Theory, 2nd edn. Sage Publications Inc, Thousand Oaks, CA (1998)
22. Strüker, J., Kerschbaum, F.: From a barrier to a bridge: Data-privacy in deregulated smart grids. In: Proceedings of the 33rd International Conference on Information Systems (ICIS 2012). Association for Information Systems, Orlando, Florida, USA (2012)
23. Venkatesh, V., Morris, M.G., Davis, G.B., Davis, F.D.: User acceptance of information technology: toward a unified view. MIS Q. **27**(3), 425–478 (2003)
24. Wang, T., Duong, T.D., Chen, C.C.: Intention to disclose personal information via mobile applications: a privacy calculus perspective. Int. J. Inf. Manage. **36**(4), 531–542 (2016)
25. Warkentin, M., Goel, S., Menard, P.: Shared benefits and information privacy: what determines smart meter technology adoption? J. Assoc. Inf. Syst. **18**(11), 3 (2017)

26. Weber, J.: Scenarios in business ethics research: review, critical assessment, and recommendations. Bus. Ethics Quarterly. 137–160 (1992)
27. Xu, H., Dinev, T., Smith, J., Hart, P.: Information privacy concerns: linking individual perceptions with institutional privacy assurances. J. Assoc. Inf. Syst. **12**(12), 1 (2011)

Predictive Dropout Research Through a Data-Based Value-Creation Taxonomy: Patterns and Blind Spots

Matti Vaarma(✉)

Tampere University, Tampere, Finland
matti.vaarma@tuni.fi

Abstract. Predictive dropout research uses data-based, individual-level predictions for the early identification of at-risk students with the general aim of improving student retention. Yet it lacks a systematic understanding of the specific types of value that its data-driven approaches are expected to create. This study addresses this gap by applying Baecker et al.'s data-based value-creation taxonomy to a purposive sample of 23 predictive dropout studies in higher education contexts. Using the taxonomy as an analytical lens, this study examines how existing research conceptualizes institution-level value-creation through its data foundations, proposed value-creation approaches, and proposed business value. The findings reveal strong convergence, characterized by recurring data foundations and a dominant focus on targeted interventions. In contrast, financial value and institution-level strategic value are rarely articulated. The study contributes a precise conceptual vocabulary for analyzing prediction-based value-creation and clarifies structural patterns and blind spots within predictive dropout research, thereby supporting future empirical work beyond predictive accuracy.

Keywords: data-based value-creation · dropout prediction · higher education

1 Introduction

Dropout research in higher education examines why students discontinue their studies and what kinds of measures could reduce attrition. One stream of this literature is predictive dropout research, which aims to increase student retention by producing data-driven, individual-level risk estimates that enable the early identification of at-risk students. Most studies in this stream concentrate on the performance metrics of machine-learning models, and the evidence consistently indicates that at-risk students can be identified with high accuracy (e.g., [1]). However, despite repeated calls for more empirical work (e.g., [2, 3]), this research stream is becoming notorious for its lack of evaluations examining how these data-driven insights can be transformed into tangible value and what such value entails. Thus, existing value-creation approaches and targets largely remain proposed rather than demonstrated and are often formulated in ways that lack conceptual precision.

Published by Springer Nature Switzerland AG 2027
S. Han et al. (Eds.): I3E 2026, LNCS 16912, pp. 286–298, 2027.
https://doi.org/10.1007/978-3-032-38014-2_21

Another research stream, data-based value-creation, focuses on how organizations transform data into value with operational, strategic, or economic benefits (e.g., [4]). Within this stream, Baecker et al [5] developed a comprehensive taxonomy that captures key data requirements, value-creation approaches, and resulting business value, offering a structured analytic lens for investigating organization-level value-generation mechanisms with conceptual clarity.

This study examines the stream of predictive dropout research through the lens of the value-creation taxonomy proposed by Baecker et al [5]. This structured analysis provides insights into the current state of the research stream and offers suggestions regarding which specific organization-or institution-level[1] value-creation characteristics could and should be explored in future empirical studies. Although some studies examine value-creation frameworks in learning analytics more broadly (e.g., [6, 7]), as far as can be ascertained, no research has applied such frameworks to predictive dropout research.

The applicability of a taxonomy developed in a business context to higher education can be justified as follows. Although higher education institutions are not primarily profit-maximizing, their funding is often strongly performance-based. For example, in the Finnish system, approximately 56% of the funding of universities of applied sciences and around 30% of university funding are allocated based on completed degrees. Consequently, phenomena such as student dropouts have direct financial implications, creating incentive structures that resemble those found in business contexts.

This study makes two key contributions. First, it provides the first application of a data-based value-creation taxonomy within predictive dropout research, thereby forming a conceptual bridge between the narrower stream and the broader data-driven value-creation literature. Second, by illustrating how prediction-based value-creation can be systematically characterized in terms of its data foundations, value-creation approaches, and resulting business value, the study offers predictive dropout researchers a structured vocabulary as an aid to guide future empirical work. Accordingly, the study addresses the **RQ**: What does applying Baecker et al.'s [5] taxonomy to the predictive dropout literature reveal about the current state of research—specifically, which value-creation aspects have been addressed and which remain underexplored?

2 Research Background

Predictive dropout research is characterized by data-driven, machine-learning based estimates of individual students' dropout risk and related phenomena. It can be further divided into course-level (e.g., [8]) and degree program-level dropout research, with a focus here on the latter. While the majority of the literature shows that early identification of at-risk students can be achieved with high reliability (e.g., [9]), complementary research themes have also emerged, such as the development of interpretable dashboards [10] and the application of explainable artificial intelligence (AI) techniques [11]. Despite technological maturity, the stream lacks empirical evaluations examining how predictive insights translate into measurable value. Indeed, empirical evidence on whether prediction-informed interventions reduce dropout rates remains sparse, with only a small

[1] Predictive performance and targeted interventions are conceptualized in this paper as mechanisms through which institutional value is realized, rather than as distinct types of value.

number of studies explicitly addressing this question, including [12]. Moreover, possibly due to the absence of an established framework for systematically structuring value-creation approaches—despite comparable frameworks in related fields such as learning analytics (e.g., [6, 7])—its value propositions remain conceptually underdeveloped beyond the general goal of "improved retention".

Data-based value-creation research investigates how organizations convert data resources into tangible value. It is usually applied in business settings such as optimizing processes [13] and creating new revenue models [14]. However, it also provides frameworks for analyzing the pathways and mechanisms of value-creation generally. For example, Baecker et al. [5] developed a taxonomy that synthesizes 78 empirical cases into a structured classification of data foundations, value-creation approaches, and resulting business value across 13 dimensions, and 44 characteristics. The taxonomy provides a conceptually clear and empirically grounded framework for analyzing how organizational data are transformed into meaningful organization-level value.

Taken together, predictive dropout research and data-based value-creation research address closely related but currently disconnected questions. The limited integration of these perspectives has resulted in predictive dropout research advancing value propositions without systematically characterizing the value-creation approaches or the concrete value outcomes through which such propositions are realized. This indicates a need for an analytical framework capable of structuring and clarifying value-creation within the stream in a more systematic and conceptually grounded manner.

3 Methods

This study analyzed 23 recent predictive dropout studies in higher education and examined how each study addressed the 44 characteristics of the data-based value-creation taxonomy of Baecker et al [5]. Based on the observed distribution of these characteristics, the current state of research on predictive dropout was assessed.

3.1 Sample Selection and Analysis

This study used *purposive sampling*—where sample items are selected based on their relevance to predefined criteria rather than through a comprehensive literature review [15]—to assemble a sample of 23 recent (published 2019 or later) predictive dropout studies. Purposive sampling is a well-established qualitative strategy that focuses on analytically relevant, information-rich cases [15], and it has been applied specifically to samples consisting of academic publications [16]. The criteria were: (1) the study incorporates an individual-level predictive dropout model; (2) dropout is defined at the degree program level (as opposed to course-level dropout); and (3) the institutional context is a higher education institution.

Relevant studies were identified through searches in Scopus and Web of Science using search strings combining the terms *dropout*, *predict**, and *higher education/university*. The searches were limited to English-language journal articles and conference papers published between 1 January 2019 and 13 February 2026. The Scopus search returned

926 papers, and the Web of Science search returned 776 papers. After removing duplicates, 1,115 records remained. These articles were screened by the author based on titles and abstracts against the predefined criteria to assess relevance and identify key trends in the field, and 478 papers were included. From the included records, studies were selected through purposive sampling for detailed analysis. The sample was further supplemented with relevant studies known to the author from prior engagement with the literature. This process resulted in a final sample of 23 studies, which was considered sufficient to capture key trends in predictive dropout research.

The characteristics of the taxonomy were coded as present if a study articulated a corresponding value-creation proposition, even when no empirical validation was provided. To ensure consistency, explicitness was required: only clearly stated value propositions or data-related claims were mapped to characteristics, whereas vague formulations—such as general references to "financial burden"—were excluded. Moreover, only propositions originating from the study itself, rather than from the literature it cited, were coded. While some inclusion decisions involved subjective judgment, the explicitness requirement made the classification unambiguous in most cases.

In the following, all 44 data-based value-creation characteristics across the 13 dimensions and 3 meta-dimensions (see Table 1) are defined based on Baecker et al [5], *using verbatim definitions or minor contextual adaptations* (e.g., replacing "firm" with "institution" and "customer" with "student"). For each characteristic, one illustrative example from the sample studies is provided; these examples serve to clarify coding decisions and are not reported as empirical findings.[2]

3.2 Data for Data-Based Value-Creation: Definitions

The first meta-dimension focuses on the data used by predictive models. It comprises 4 dimensions—data origin, data source, data format, and data generation—each consisting of several characteristics. *Only the data that were fed into the predictive models were included*, excluding, for instance, any follow-up survey data.

Data Origin. **Internal data** originates from institutional processes, systems, or actions stored in (self-)managed databases *(survey data was also classified as internal when institution-administered; e.g.,* [17]*).* Sosa-Alonso et al. [18] utilized academic performance data sourced from databases maintained by the participating universities. **External data** comes from sources outside the institution (partners, students, suppliers, free available, etc.). Mustofa et al. [9] incorporated macroeconomic indicators from a Portuguese database.

Data Source. **Operations and Transactions** create data based on internal processes or business transactions usually stored in internal systems. Cannistrà et al. [19] used static (e.g., gender) and dynamic (e.g., grades) institutional data collected regularly by the university. **Customers** (students) provide data *directly* by consuming institutional

[2] It is acknowledged that some characteristics (e.g., breakthrough or weapon-level strategic value) do not align well with the higher-education context. However, these characteristics were retained to preserve the structural integrity of the original taxonomy and to avoid unsystematic modification of an established framework.

products or services, e.g., via mobile devices *(institution-assigned data such as demographics or transcript data was not counted as customer-provided).* Vaarma and Li [20] used learning management system activity data (e.g., clickstream data). **Commercial Providers** are specialized in offering data (such as social media data, genomic data, etc.) as an asset. Matz et al. [1] used student engagement data collected via *READY Education* company's app. **Public and open data** includes all (external) data that an institution can freely access (e.g., weather, maps, or governmental data). Jiménez-Gutiérrez et al. [21] downloaded open census data from the National Institute of Statistics and Geography of Mexico.

Data Format. **Structured data** are usually managed in relational database management systems following a defined data model making it easier to input, query, store, and analyze. Kiss et al. [22] used tabulated data containing numerical and categorical features. **Unstructured data** does not follow a specified format, such as text messages or video data. **Semi-Structured data** does not follow a conventional database system, but, for instance, provides self-describing elements. None of the studies in the sample employed unstructured or semi-structured data.

Data Generation. **Collected data** comprises all passively recorded and stored data usually arising from institutional operations. Song et al. [23] used routinely collected Korean institutional data (e.g., military service status and absences). **Tracked data** requires additional up-font investments (and/or equipment) to generate data for a specific purpose. Wild and Heuling [24] combined survey data with administrative records. **Acquired data** is purchased with financial expenses from or traded with external providers. Matz et al. [1] acquired behavioral student data generated through an app provided by *READY Education.* **Aggregated data** can be actively sourced from external sources without (additional, data-related) costs. Buñay-Guisñan et al. [10] sourced inflation rate and GDP data from an open database.

3.3 Approaches for Data-Based Value-Creation: Definitions

The second meta-dimension examines the proposed value-creation approaches across 4 dimensions: development approach, development structure, value target, and partner structure, each comprising several characteristics.

Development Approach. **Inductive Orientation:** Higher education institutions examine (existing) data exploratively to identify unknown patterns or insights that serve innovation or a general business objective rather than solving a concrete task. None of the analyzed studies contained examples of this characteristic. **Deductive Orientation:** An institution primarily analyzes (and often generates) data to target a specific and pre-defined business case. Berka and Marek [25] explicitly frame their study around addressing student dropouts.

Development Structure. **Centralization:** The institution employs a central unit that houses the necessary capabilities and provides expertise as a service to the business units. **Managed Decentralization:** To promote close interaction and communication within (specified) business areas, the units manage their capabilities and projects while remaining centrally controlled. None of the studies in the sample mentioned characteristics related to characteristics of this dimension.

Value Target. **Business Processes Improvement:** The institution targets the improvement of its existing operational processes. Buñay-Guisñan et al. [10] proposed a visual dashboard with predictions to automate selected support processes. **Product/Service Improvement:** Data can create value by optimizing existing (incl. non-data) products or services (such as quality improvements). Villar and de Andrade [26] argue that predictive insights can support planning interventions. **Developing Information Goods:** In combination with new data-based value propositions (e.g., data-based services or insights), the institution has to develop corresponding processes of value-creation. Plak et al. [12] developed a dashboard visualizing individual dropout predictions. **Customization and Targeting:** Data can be used to adapt the way value is delivered to (and perceived by) customers, thereby increasing satisfaction and loyalty or even generating data-related lock-in effects. Nagy and Molontay [11] advocate targeting at-risk students with personalized interventions based on explainable individual predictions. **Organizational Transparency & Conformance:** An institution can create additional value through an improved understanding of internal actions (e.g., transparency gained from process mining). Matz et al. [1] highlight monitoring the perceived fairness of predictive models. **Strategic Decision Support:** In contrast to (repetitive) decisions inherent in standardized operational processes, an organization can leverage data to support managerial decision-making in complex (often one-time) situations with significant impact on organizational performance. Song et al. [23] suggest that tuition fee reductions may lower dropout rates. **Means of Reputation:** Besides targeting students, data-based value can emerge beyond the institution boundaries by a general increase in visibility and perception (e.g., leading to more qualified applicants or lasting partnerships). Maldonado et al. [27] propose that reducing dropout rates enhances external perceptions among prospective and current students. **Value Co-Creation:** By sharing data or capabilities with partners, an institution can specifically target the co-creation of value based on (company's) data. Jiménez-Gutiérrez et al. [21] highlight the potential for cross-sector use of predictive models.

Partner Structure. **Autonomous:** Value from data can be created independently, i.e. without the involvement of external expertise *(a relaxed explicitness criterion was applied here: references to institutional staff were considered sufficient for inclusion).* Plak et al. [12] advocate dashboards to support timely counsellor interventions. **Interdependent:** The institution can use valuable partnerships to (co-) create value. Sihare [28] suggests cross-institutional collaboration to improve resource allocation. **Orchestrating:** (Parts of) an institution's data-based value-creation can be outsourced (permanently) to third parties that provide the necessary know-how. None of the studies analyzed referred to this characteristic.

3.4 Data-Based Business Value: Definitions

The third meta-dimension examines the proposed business value-creation dimensions across 5 dimensions: strategic direction, value type, strategic value, innovativeness and financial benefit, each comprising several characteristics.

Strategic Direction. **Functional:** Value an institution realizes by performance improvements directly resulting from the involvement of dropout predictions to a corresponding part of an institution's value-creation. Park and Yoo [29] developed a model producing weekly at-risk student predictions in an online university. **Symbolic:** Value that occurs from the signalling effect, the perception of which depends on the recipient (such as students, competitors, partners, employees, or others). Maldonado et al. [27] suggest that low student attrition enhances the institution's status or ranking.

Value Type. **Efficiency Gain:** Value emerges through savings within (existing) processes to produce and deliver value to students more efficiently (e.g., by reducing times, failures and resources etc.). Plak et al. [12] explicitly state that predictive models make individualized student interventions possible, which is currently often infeasible as counsellors are responsible for hundreds of students. **Risk Mitigation:** Using data appropriately can support the institution in mitigating or avoiding various risks (e.g., fraud, security, operational, legal, preventing compliance or audit and accreditation issues). None of the analyzed papers mentioned this characteristic. **Increase in Market Share:** Value emerges through stable or new students in existing market segments or by entering new segments (e.g., with new data-based services). Yu et al. [30] clearly state that the common objective of data-driven support systems is the early identification of at-risk students to reduce dropout rates. **Increased Customer Loyalty:** Students are more strongly and positively connected with or even locked-in to an institution's offerings or status leading to higher retention *(in the sense of stronger student-institution connection, distinct from dropout-retention as an outcome variable).* Hoca and Dimililer [2] associate reduced dropout with improved academic environments and motivation. **Improved Perception:** In addition to students, value can emerge through accompanying effects (such as workforce satisfaction or more rewarding and trustful partnerships). Nagy and Molontay [11] and Buñay-Guisñan et al. [10] argue that explainable AI can make predictions more transparent, thereby increasing staff trust. **Leveraged Partner Capabilities:** Co-created through the effort and capabilities of partners using institution data, value occurs through innovations and new insights (while preventing organizational blindness). Von Hippel and Hofflinger [31] mention partnership with external vendors to generate risk scores.

Strategic Value. **Support:** By supporting single stages of the (co-)existing primary value-creation, the resulting value is important particularly within specific areas of the institution. *For this characteristic, the explicitness requirement was relaxed: studies that cited dropout reduction or similar outcomes as their value proposition were included, as these outcomes naturally align with a university's primary value-creation objective: education.* **Breakthrough:** In combination with predominant value-creation, the financial performance of an institution is highly dependent on the value created by data. **Weapon:** Value received from data-based value-creation forms the heart of the institutions' business model and turnover. None of the sample papers mentioned Breakthrough or Weapon characteristics.

Innovativeness. **Competitive Advantage:** Value that can hardly be replicated by competitors (due to highly specific data, partner structures, or institution characteristics). None of the studies in the sample exhibited this characteristic. **Industry Trends**: Specific pioneer value that can be created similarly by (leading) competitors. Olaya et al. [3] introduced an uplift model to target students most responsive to interventions. **Follow the Leader:** Value that is created in particular to defend a market position usually following the technological state of the art. Sihare [28] used standard, widely available machine-learning models—such as decision trees and support vector machines—as the basis for the predictive model.

Financial Benefit. **Revenue Gains**: An increase in earnings. Maldonado et al. [27] note that tuition fees are the main source of income for private institutions, which naturally increase with improved student retention; moreover, in many countries such as the Czech Republic, governmental financial support is tied to graduation numbers [25]. **Cost Reduction:** A reduction in institutional expenditure, for example, resulting from improved processes. Plak et al. [12] consider predictive models promising for lower-cost interventions compared to current practices.

4 Results and Discussion

Table 1 presents the observed frequencies of all 44 characteristics—together with the original taxonomy—in a heatmap-style format (hue range: 0 = white to 18 = green). The main trends and noteworthy findings are highlighted in the following.

Data for Data-Based Value-Creation. It is no surprise that nearly all studies feed their models with **internal**, **structured** and **collected** data generated through the regular **operations and transactions** of the higher education institution. Such data are often large—including datasets covering tens of thousands of students [30]—rich in multiple dimensions, and conveniently accessible through institutional databases [18]. More notably, only 5 studies used data directly generated by **customers**, despite evidence that such data (e.g., learning-management-system activity) can have strong predictive power [1, 20, 29]. None of the analyzed studies used **unstructured** or **semi-structured** data—such as written student messages—which is curious given its availability in higher-education. Moreover, semi-structured data have been shown to offer substantial predictive power in secondary-education dropout research [32].

Approaches for Data-Based Value-Creation. All studies employed a **deductive orientation**, which is unsurprising given that the stream has been active for nearly twenty years. None of the papers referenced **centralization** or **managed decentralization** within institutions. However, although *institutional level* structures were not discussed—such as faculties managing their own intervention workflows under central policies and shared infrastructure—analogous structures at *multi institutional* or *national levels* were mentioned. In Spain, a new Psycho-Pedagogical Office unifying all student support services has been established [17], and in the United States, a managed-decentralization-type model has been proposed in which clusters of universities jointly collect data and develop predictive models that individual institutions can adapt to their own resources and goals

[1]. The most common proposed value targets are **customization and targeting** as well as **product/service improvements**, which, again, are no surprise, as the predictive models can very precisely identify the at-risk students, and such information is most directly applicable to improving student-support services. While most studies emphasize customized interventions at either the individual level (e.g., [9, 11]) or group level (e.g., [2, 27]), it is important to note that predictive insights can also inform improvements to general support strategies aimed at all students—for instance, curriculum design [26]. By contrast, fewer studies emphasize institution-oriented value targets such as **business process improvement** or **strategic decision support**. This is somewhat surprising, given that some studies note that predictive model outputs have potential for supporting institutional resource allocation in student counselling [1, 12], teaching staff and lecture-room resources [25]. Only 3 studies mention **organizational transparency and conformance**, typically in relation to ethical considerations [1, 30] or model transparency [10]. Yet dashboards developed through **information goods** [10, 12] could be expanded to support process monitoring (e.g., who contacted which students, with what interventions, and with what outcomes), thereby enhancing institutional understanding of internal actions. Finally, only a few papers mention **interdependent** partnerships for **value co-creation**—either commercial [1, 31] or cross-institutional [21, 28]. Most studies implicitly assume an autonomous partner structure in which institutions generate predictions and take corresponding actions internally.

Table 1. Observed frequencies of the 44 characteristics of the taxonomy of Baecker et al. [5] in a sample of 23 predictive dropout studies.

	Dimension	Characteristics					
Data for Data-Based Value-Creation	Data Origin	Internal (22)	External (9)				
	Data Source	Operations and Transactions (22)	Customers (5)	Commercial Providers (1)	Public and Open Data (5)		
	Data Format	Structured (23)	Unstructured (0)	Semi-structured (0)			
	Data Generation	Collected (20)	Tracked (7)	Acquired (1)	Aggregated (6)		
Approaches for Data-Based Value-Creation	Development Approach	Inductive Orientation (0)	Deductive Orientation (23)				
	Development Structure	Centralization (0)	Managed Decentralization (0)				
	Value Target	Business Processes Improvement (13)	Product / Service Improvement (21)	Developing Information Goods (7)	Customization and Targeting (19)		
		Organizational Transparency and Conformance (3)	Strategic Decision Support (2)	Means of Reputation (1)	Value Co-Creation (4)		
	Partner Structure	Autonomous (20)	Interdependent (4)	Orchestrating (0)			
Data-Based Business Value	Strategic Direction	Functional (23)	Symbolic (4)				
	Value Type	Efficiency Gain (9)	Risk Mitigation (0)	Increase in Market Share (23)	Increased Customer Loyalty (4)	Improved Perception (3)	Leveraged Partner Capabilities (1)
	Strategic Value	Support (22)	Break Through (0)	Weapon (0)			
	Innovativeness	Competitive Advantage (0)	Industry Trends (9)	Follow the leader (21)			
	Financial Benefit	Revenue Gains (6)	Cost Reduction (5)				

Data-Based Business Value. All studies propose that predictive models generate **functional** and **support**ive business value aimed at an **increase in market share**—in this context, improving student retention. Omissions of these characteristics are likely unintentional and due to the explicitness of requirement. Only a few studies promote **symbolic** business value, which in this context is closely intertwined with **improved perception**. Nevertheless, Nagy and Molontay [11] offer an important insight: predictive models with explainable outputs can build trust among decision makers, a key precondition for adoption and collaboration. Possibly due to ethical considerations, relatively few studies explicitly mention **increased customer loyalty**—that is, positive student level effects beyond mere retention—such as enhancing students' awareness of their own performance and dropout risk [12]. None of the analyzed papers refer to **breakthrough** or **weapon**-level strategic value, which is understandable, as it would be unrealistic to claim that predictive models could ever "form the heart" of a university's business model or even that an institution's financial performance would become highly dependent on such models. An emerging **industry trend** is the use of explainable AI to complement numerical risk scores with explanations [10, 11, 18]. Additionally, two profit oriented models specifically designed for dropout prediction [3, 27] stand out from the more typical **follow the leader** use of standard machine learning models, which otherwise dominates the stream. One of the more surprising findings is that only 6 papers explicitly discuss financial benefits—whether through **revenue gains** or **cost reduction**. Despite ethical considerations, optimizing savings or revenue remains a central component of data-based value-creation [27]. Predictive models can provide a low-cost means of targeting students and improving resource allocation [1, 12]. For this reason, costs should be systematically assessed in predictive-dropout research [3].

To summarize, the findings reveal clear and recurring patterns in the current state of predictive dropout research. Across studies, recurring data foundations and value-creation approaches indicate strong convergence and a dominant focus on targeted interventions with comparatively limited attention given to institution-level strategic value, suggesting substantial potential for broader data-driven value transformation. Moreover, considerations related to financial benefit are addressed in only a small subset of studies, even though such aspects are central to understanding the full value-creation potential of predictive models in higher-education institutions, and crucial for assessing their scalability and long-term sustainability.

5 Conclusions and Limitations

This study examined the stream of predictive dropout research through the lens of Baecker et al.'s [5] data-based value-creation taxonomy to determine which aspects of institution-level value-creation have been addressed and which remain underexplored. The findings show that the stream displays strong convergence, with heavily recurring data and value-creation patterns and a consistent focus on targeted, individual-or group-level interventions. At the same time, the analysis highlights a relative scarcity of financial considerations and a lack of attention to strategic value within institutions, suggesting substantial opportunities to broaden the understanding of how predictive models can create value in higher-education settings.

The findings suggest an important implication: applying a value-creation taxonomy offers a precise conceptual vocabulary for describing value-creation approaches and targets in predictive dropout research. By using this vocabulary to systematically analyze the literature, the study makes visible both dominant patterns and underexplored areas of value-creation, thereby enabling future empirical work to more directly address the specific gaps identified.

This study has limitations. The analysis is based on a purposive sample of 23 studies, which may not fully capture the diversity of predictive dropout research. As a result, the observed prominence of some value creation patterns may be over- or underestimated. Furthermore, applying the taxonomy required contextual interpretation, and alternative classifications may be possible in some cases.

Future research should move beyond evaluations of model performance and examine how predictive insights are used to generate and measure value in practice. In particular, empirical studies addressing financial value are needed to assess the practical scalability and sustainability of predictive models in higher-education contexts. Furthermore, drawing on Table 1, future research could explore underexamined value-creation characteristics, such as the use of semi-structured data and value co-creation approaches.

Disclosure of Interests. No competing interests relevant to the content of this article are declared.

References

1. Matz, S.C., Bukow, C.S., Peters, H., Deacons, C., Dinu, A., Stachl, C.: Using machine learning to predict student retention from socio-demographic characteristics and app-based engagement metrics. Sci. Rep. **13**(1), 5705 (2023). https://doi.org/10.1038/s41598-023-32484-w
2. Hoca, S., Dimililer, N.: A machine learning framework for student retention policy development: a case study. Appl. Sci. **15**(6), 2989 (2025). https://doi.org/10.3390/app15062989
3. Olaya, D., Vásquez, J., Maldonado, S., Miranda, J., Verbeke, W.: Uplift modeling for preventing student dropout in higher education. Decis. Support. Syst. **134**, 113320 (2020). https://doi.org/10.1016/j.dss.2020.113320
4. Grover, V., Chiang, R.H., Liang, T.-P., Zhang, D.: Creating strategic business value from big data analytics: a research framework. J. Manag. Inf. Syst. **35**(2), 388–423 (2018)
5. Baecker, J., Böttcher, T.P., Weking, J.: How companies create value from data: a taxonomy on data, approaches, and resulting business value. In: ECIS 2021–29th European Conference on Information Systems (2021)
6. Sheikh, R.A., Bhatia, S., Metre, S.G., Faqihi, A.Y.A.: Strategic value realization framework from learning analytics: a practical approach. J. Appl. Res. High. Educ. **14**(2), 693–713 (2022). https://doi.org/10.1108/JARHE-10-2020-0379
7. West, D., Heath, D., Huijser, H.: Let's talk learning analytics: a framework for implementation in relation to student retention. Online Learn. J. **20**(2), 30–50 (2015). https://doi.org/10.24059/olj.v20i2.792
8. Basnet, R.B., Johnson, C., Doleck, T.: Dropout prediction in MOOCs using deep learning and machine learning. Educ. Inf. Technol. **27**(8), 11499–11513 (2022). https://doi.org/10.1007/s10639-022-11068-7

9. Mustofa, S., Emon, Y.R., Mamun, S.B., Akhy, S.A., Ahad, M.T.: A novel AI-driven model for student dropout risk analysis with explainable AI insights. Comput. Educ.: Artif. Intell. **8**, 100352 (2025). https://doi.org/10.1016/j.caeai.2024.100352
10. Buñay-Guisñan, P., Lara, J.A., Cano, A., Cerezo, R., Romero, C.: Towards accessible AI for addressing students' academic dropout: an auto machine learning and explainable artificial intelligence approach. Univ. Access Inf. Soc. **25**(1), 19 (2026). https://doi.org/10.1007/s10209-025-01278-4
11. Nagy, M., Molontay, R.: Interpretable dropout prediction: towards XAI-based personalized intervention. Int. J. Artif. Intell. Educ. **34**(2), 274–300 (2024). https://doi.org/10.1007/s40593-023-00331-8
12. Plak, S., Cornelisz, I., Meeter, M., Van Klaveren, C.: Early warning systems for more effective student counselling in higher education: evidence from a Dutch field experiment. High. Educ. Q. **76**(1), 131–152 (2020). https://doi.org/10.1111/hequ.12298
13. Popovič, A., Hackney, R., Tassabehji, R., Castelli, M.: The impact of big data analytics on firms' high value business performance. Inf. Syst. Front. **20**(2), 209–222 (2018). https://doi.org/10.1007/s10796-016-9720-4
14. Schüritz, R.M., Seebacher, S., Satzger, G., Schwarz, L.: Datatization as the next frontier of servitization: understanding the challenges for transforming organizations. In: International Conference on Information Systems (ICIS) (2017)
15. Patton, M.Q.: Qualitative Research & Evaluation Methods: Integrating Theory and Practice. Sage, Thousand Oaks (2014)
16. Suri, H.: Purposeful sampling in qualitative research synthesis. Qual. Res. J. **11**(2), 63–75 (2011). https://doi.org/10.3316/QRJ1102063
17. Lizarte Simón, E.J., Gijón Puerta, J.: Prediction of early dropout in higher education using the SCPQ. Cogent Psychol. **9**(1), 2123588 (2022). https://doi.org/10.1080/23311908.2022.2123588
18. Sosa-Alonso, J.J., López-Aguilar, D., Álvarez-Pérez, P.R., González-Morales, O.: Predicting university dropout: connecting big data and structural models. Stud. High. Educ. **51**(1), 210–227 (2026). https://doi.org/10.1080/03075079.2025.2462675
19. Cannistrà, M., Masci, C., Ieva, F., Agasisti, T., Paganoni, A.M.: Early-predicting dropout of university students: an application of innovative multilevel machine learning and statistical techniques. Stud. High. Educ. **47**(9), 1935–1956 (2022). https://doi.org/10.1080/03075079.2021.2018415
20. Vaarma, M., Li, H.: Predicting student dropouts with machine learning: an empirical study in Finnish higher education. Technol. Soc. **76**, 102474 (2024). https://doi.org/10.1016/j.techsoc.2024.102474
21. Jiménez-Gutiérrez, A.L., Mota-Hernández, C.I., Mezura-Montes, E., Alvarado-Corona, R.: Application of the performance of machine learning techniques as support in the prediction of school dropout. Sci. Rep. **14**(1), 3957 (2024). https://doi.org/10.1038/s41598-024-53576-1
22. Kiss, B., Nagy, M., Molontay, R., Csabay, B.: Predicting dropout using high school and first-semester academic achievement measures. In: 17th International Conference on Emerging eLearning Technologies and Applications (ICETA), pp. 383–389 (2019). https://doi.org/10.1109/ICETA48886.2019.9040158
23. Song, Z., Sung, S.-H., Park, D.-M., Park, B.-K.: All-year dropout prediction modeling and analysis for university students. Appl. Sci. **13**(2), 1143 (2023). https://doi.org/10.3390/app13021143
24. Wild, S., Heuling, L.S.: Student dropout and retention: an event history analysis among students in cooperative higher education. Int. J. Educ. Res. **104**, 101687 (2020). https://doi.org/10.1016/j.ijer.2020.101687
25. Berka, P., Marek, L.: Bachelor's degree student dropouts: who tend to stay and who tend to leave? Stud. Educ. Eval. **70**, 100999 (2021). https://doi.org/10.1016/j.stueduc.2021.100999

26. Villar, A., de Andrade, C.R.V.: Supervised machine learning algorithms for predicting student dropout and academic success: a comparative study. Discov. Artif. Intell. **4**(1), 2 (2024). https://doi.org/10.1007/s44163-023-00079-z
27. Maldonado, S., Miranda, J., Olaya, D., Vásquez, J., Verbeke, W.: Redefining profit metrics for boosting student retention in higher education. Decis. Support. Syst. **143**, 113493 (2021). https://doi.org/10.1016/j.dss.2021.113493
28. Sihare, S.R.: Student dropout analysis in higher education and retention by artificial intelligence and machine learning. SN Comput. Sci. **5**(2), 202 (2024). https://doi.org/10.1007/s42979-023-02458-w
29. Park, H.S., Yoo, S.J.: Early dropout prediction in online learning of university using machine learning. Int. J. Inf. Vis. **5**(4), 347–353 (2021). https://doi.org/10.30630/joiv.5.4.732
30. Yu, R., Lee, H., Kizilcec, R.F.: Should college dropout prediction models include protected attributes? In: Proceedings of the Eighth ACM Conference on Learning @ Scale, pp. 91–100 (2021). https://doi.org/10.1145/3430895.3460139
31. Von Hippel, P.T., Hofflinger, A.: The data revolution comes to higher education: identifying students at risk of dropout in Chile. J. High. Educ. Policy Manag. **43**(1), 2–23 (2021). https://doi.org/10.1080/1360080X.2020.1739800
32. Zerkouk, M., Mihoubi, M., Chikhaoui, B., Wang, S.: Predicting online education dropout: a new machine learning model based on sentiment analysis, socio-demographic, and behavioral data. Int. J. Artif. Intell. Educ. **35**(4), 2345–2371 (2025). https://doi.org/10.1007/s40593-025-00472-y

Responsible AI: Trust, Governance, and Accountable Use

Governance by Negotiation: How Organizations Translate AI Ethics into Practice

Teemu Birkstedt(✉), Matti Minkkinen, and Matti Mäntymäki

University of Turku, Turku School of Economics, Turku, Finland
{teemu.birkstedt,matti.minkkinen,matti.mantymaki}@utu.fi

Abstract. Governing artificial intelligence (AI) within organizations has become an imperative, driven by the rapid proliferation of AI systems and the emergence of binding regulation such as the EU AI Act. Despite the growing volume of normative AI ethics guidelines, there remains a gap in empirical understanding of how organizations translate these principles into operational governance practices. This research addresses that gap by applying Actor-Network Theory (ANT) to examine organizational AI governance as an emergent socio-technical phenomenon. Drawing on 27 semi-structured interviews conducted across two empirical studies (13 interviews in 2020 and 14 in 2022–2023) with experts from 23 Nordic organizations, we analyze AI governance as a network involving human actors (regulators, managers, developers) and non-human actors (AI systems, ethical guidelines, regulatory frameworks). Using ANT's translation process framework, we identify 'organizational practices' as the focal actor that mediates between external demands and internal AI operations through four key phases: problematization, interessement, enrollment, and mobilization. Our findings show that organizational AI governance appears to take shape through ongoing negotiations between diverse stakeholders, and that AI systems and technology themselves actively shape governance processes. This study contributes to AI governance theory by providing an ANT-based framework that explains differences in organizational approaches and highlights the active role of AI systems in shaping governance practices.

Keywords: Actor-Network Theory · AI Governance · EU AI Act · Organizational AI · Translation Process

1 Introduction

AI-based algorithmic systems have demonstrated high potential to provide advancements such as self-driving vehicles, intelligent assistants, and highly advanced robotics [1–3]. However, achieving these benefits while mitigating risks associated with safety, discrimination, and lack of transparency requires approaches and actions to govern AI systems and ensure alignment with human and societal values [4–8]. The swift progress in AI technologies has triggered concerns about broader implications of universally accessible AI, including issues like deepfakes and misinformation. These concerns, supported by documented incidents, have highlighted the importance of ethical considerations in AI development and deployment.

Published by Springer Nature Switzerland AG 2027
S. Han et al. (Eds.): I3E 2026, LNCS 16912, pp. 301–312, 2027.
https://doi.org/10.1007/978-3-032-38014-2_22

In response, multi-stakeholder groups, governmental and international entities, professional organizations, and numerous companies have issued sets of principles and guidelines for ethical AI use (see [5, 6, 9, 10]). The principle-based development of AI ethics and increasing recognition of potential risks have led to regulatory developments. The EU AI Act [11] entered into force on 1 August 2024 as the world's first comprehensive legal framework for AI, with its obligations phased in from 2025 through 2027 (prohibited practices first, then governance and general-purpose AI rules, and high-risk requirements originally set for 2026, since deferred to December 2027 under the 2026 Digital Omnibus proposal). With the emergence of this binding AI legislation, coupled with existing laws on non-discrimination and privacy, AI governance has become a priority for organizations to manage risks, ensure compliance, and uphold business ethics.

Substantial scholarly work has been devoted to bridging the gap between AI ethics principles and organizational practice. This includes mappings of ethics principles [6, 12], conceptual layered governance models [13, 14], defining frameworks for organizational AI governance [7, 15], taxonomies of governance practices [16], and translations of ethics into operational practice [17, 18]. What has been comparatively under-developed, however, is empirical evidence on how organizations actually enact these governance arrangements in practice, particularly under the conditions of binding regulation now imposed by the EU AI Act. There is a continuing need for empirical studies of AI governance within organizations, as they are the entities expected to oversee AI systems throughout their entire lifecycles, balancing ethical principles, regulations, and stakeholder expectations.

The central aim of this research is to understand organizations' different approaches to AI governance and how they translate ethical principles and regulations into strategic decisions and organizational actions. This research contains two rounds of empirical research: the first conducted in autumn 2020, capturing organizational AI governance practices during the period of normative ethics guidelines but prior to binding regulation; and the second conducted in 2022–2023, as organizations began preparing for the anticipated EU AI Act.

2 Theoretical Approach

2.1 AI Governance

AI governance has been defined as "a system of rules, practices, processes, and technological tools that are employed to ensure that an organization's use of AI technologies aligns with the organization's strategies, objectives, and values; fulfils legal requirements; and meets principles of ethical AI followed by the organization" [15]. This definition captures the multi-layered character of AI governance, which operates simultaneously at the level of individual AI systems, organizational strategy, and the broader regulatory and societal environment [13].

2.2 Actor-Network Theory

To explore the complex and dynamic nature of AI governance, this research adopts Actor-Network Theory (ANT) as its theoretical framework. ANT is a theoretical and methodological approach in which everything in the social and natural worlds exists in constantly shifting networks of relationships [19–21]. It posits that nothing exists outside these relationships. All factors involved in a social situation are on the same level, and thus there are no external social forces beyond what and how network participants interact at present [19, 22].

Key concepts deployed in this study are: *Actors*, human and non-human entities able to act and be acted upon (in our context, regulators, AI systems, ethical principles, organizations, and developers) [19]; *Translation*, the process by which actors' interests are aligned to form a stable network, unfolding through four moments: problematization, interessement, enrollment, and mobilization [22]; and *Obligatory Passage Point (OPP)*, a situation, formulation, or commitment through which all relevant actors must pass for the focal actor's problematization to hold, and through which their otherwise divergent interests are made compatible [22]. In our study, the OPP is the formulation that "organizations need a fit-for-purpose approach to *AI* governance", one that translates external regulatory and ethical demands into context-specific operational arrangements, not uniform organization-wide rules.

ANT is particularly relevant to this study for three reasons: (1) it avoids pre-defined hierarchies, enabling a nuanced understanding of how diverse elements interact and influence governance; (2) it highlights the process of 'translation,' aligning with the study's focus on how organizations operationalize ethical principles; and (3) it acknowledges the fluid, evolving nature of networks, mirroring the rapidly changing landscape of AI and its governance.

3 Research Approach

3.1 Methodology and Research Design

We adopt an interpretive, ANT-informed research approach [19, 23], appropriate for tracing the heterogeneous actors and translation processes through which AI governance is constituted in organizational settings. Two rounds of expert interviews were conducted between 2020 and 2023, forming a repeated cross-sectional, two-wave design that captures AI governance practices at two points during a period of significant regulatory development. Because the two rounds sample different organizations, comparisons across rounds speak to shifts in the governance field rather than to change within individual organizations.

3.2 Data Collection

The empirical material used in this study was collected from multiple sources. The primary source is two rounds of expert interviews (described below). To triangulate the interview findings, we obtained publicly available AI policy documents from the participating organizations. We additionally followed the development of the EU AI Act from its initial draft in 2021 onwards to situate our empirical observations within the evolving regulatory context.

The first round (October–November 2020) comprised 13 semi-structured interviews lasting 30–70 min with experts from 12 Finnish frontrunner organizations. The second round (August 2022–December 2023), drawn from a broader European study of retail banking and insurance, focused on the Nordic subset: 14 semi-structured interviews lasting 42–93 min with experts from 11 organizations headquartered in Finland, Norway, and Sweden. The total empirical material consists of 27 interviews across 23 Nordic organizations. The Round 1 sample comprised software services and AI platforms (3 organizations, including a maritime software provider; O1, O7, O10), IT consultancy (3), public sector (3), and one organization each in financial services, higher education, and retail; Round 2 comprised retail banking (6) and insurance (5) organizations across Finland, Norway, and Sweden. Participants were selected through purposive sampling [24], targeting individuals in strategic, managerial, or technical decision-making roles over AI systems — including CEOs and Chairpersons, Heads of AI and Data, Lead Data Scientists, and Analytics Directors, or with operational experience in implementing AI governance. Initial contacts were identified through professional networks and extended via snowball sampling. All interviews except one (26 of 27) were recorded with participant consent and transcribed; for the remaining interview, detailed contemporaneous notes were used. Table 1 provides an anonymized overview of all participating organizations, their sector, country, and informant roles.

Table 1. Sample organizations (anonymized).

ID	Round	Period	Sector	Country	Informant role(s)
O1	R1	2020	Software/AI platforms	FI	Chairperson; CEO
O2	R1	2020	IT consultancy	FI	Analytics Executive
O3	R1	2020	Public sector	FI	Analytics Lead
O4	R1	2020	IT consultancy	FI	CEO
O5	R1	2020	IT consultancy	FI	Lead Consultant
O6	R1	2020	Financial services	FI	Lead Data Scientist
O7	R1	2020	Maritime software	FI	CEO
O8	R1	2020	Public sector	FI	Chief Innovation Officer
O9	R1	2020	Higher education	FI	Chief Information Officer
O10	R1	2020	Software/AI platforms	FI	CEO
O11	R1	2020	Public sector	FI	Senior Specialist
O12	R1	2020	Retail	FI	Head of Analytics
O13	R2	2022–23	Banking	FI	Head of AI; Lead Data Scientist
O14	R2	2022–23	Insurance	NO	Head of Data and AI
O15	R2	2022–23	Insurance	NO/SE	Head of AI; Lead Data Scientist
O16	R2	2022–23	Banking	FI	Head of AI and Digital
O17	R2	2022–23	Banking	FI	Head of AI

(*continued*)

Table 1. (*continued*)

ID	Round	Period	Sector	Country	Informant role(s)
O18	R2	2022–23	Insurance	NO	Head of AI
O19	R2	2022–23	Insurance	FI	Director, Analytics
O20	R2	2022–23	Banking	FI	Head of Data and AI
O21	R2	2022–23	Banking	FI	Head of AI and Data
O22	R2	2022–23	Insurance	FI	Director, Analytics
O23	R2	2022–23	Banking	FI	Head of Data and AI

3.3 Interview Design

Both rounds of interviews followed semi-structured protocols designed to elicit accounts of how AI governance was understood, organized, and operationalized within the participating organizations. The protocols were structured around four thematic areas, derived from the study's ANT orientation: (1) actors and roles: who is involved in AI-related decisions in the organization, what is their role, and which external parties influence AI development or deployment; (2) translation of principles into practice: how ethical AI principles or regulatory expectations enter the organization, and how they are converted into concrete practices, processes, or controls; (3) tensions and negotiations where friction occurs between regulatory demands, business goals, technical realities, or organizational values, and how such tensions are resolved; and (4) AI systems as actors, how the characteristics of specific AI systems (e.g., opacity, autonomy, performance variability) shape the governance arrangements built around them. The 2022–2023 protocol additionally included questions on organizational preparation for the EU AI Act, reflecting the more concrete regulatory horizon at the time of the second study.

3.4 Data Analysis

Data analysis followed an ANT-informed interpretive approach. Interview transcripts were analyzed using a structured coding template applied by the author. Coding proceeded in two stages. First, an open coding pass identified the actors, relationships, and tensions present in each interview. Second, a focused coding pass mapped these elements onto Callon's [22] four moments of translation: problematization, interessement, enrollment, and mobilization, and identified candidate obligatory passage points (OPPs) emerging across the data. Coding followed a written template (codebook) and was carried out by a single researcher; inter-coder reliability was therefore not applicable, and analytical rigour was instead pursued through a documented audit trail and constant comparison across cases [23]. The mapping was abductive rather than confirmatory. For example, the statement that 'regulation is not something that makes compromises' was coded as regulation acting as a non-negotiable actor and mapped to interessement. Not every case fit cleanly, however, as several organizations never reached stable mobilization (see Sect. 4.4).

The two data sets were analyzed iteratively. The 2020 data provided a baseline picture of AI governance practices during a period of normative but non-binding AI ethics guidance, while the 2022–2023 data captured organizations' responses to an increasingly concrete regulatory horizon, including active preparation for the anticipated EU AI Act. The comparison across rounds was used to identify emerging patterns and shifts in governance network configurations rather than to make strict longitudinal claims, since the two samples involve different organizations and partially different sectoral focus.

4 Results

We apply Callon's [22] four-phase translation process (problematization, interessement, enrollment, and mobilization) as the analytical lens for our empirical findings. The selection of a focal actor and the definition of an OPP are the first analytical tasks; the subsequent phases trace how diverse actors are progressively aligned around that OPP. Law [20] notes that translation strategies are always local and contingent, which is reflected in the variation we observe across organizations.

4.1 Problematization

Identifying the relevant actors and selecting the focal actor for the research theme, understanding organizations' different approaches to AI governance, is itself an interpretive task. A first option would be to view organizations as primarily under external pressure from forces such as evolving ethical AI principles and forthcoming regulation, encouraging them toward a 'principles-to-practice' transformation. A second option would be that organizational practices themselves are at the core of the transformation, driving alignment dialogue with the external environment and AI systems. A third option would be to consider the AI system itself as the focal actor, being the place where AI governance actions hit the ground operationally. By analyzing the communication and power dynamics between actors against the main research question, we selected the second option: 'organizational practices' as the focal actor. Organizational practices is the actor that takes external demands as well as strategy- and value-based requirements for AI governance into account and drives the translation process toward systems and operations. Figure 1 depicts the resulting actor network, with organizational practices as the focal actor and the obligatory passage point through which the surrounding actors must pass for the network to stabilize.

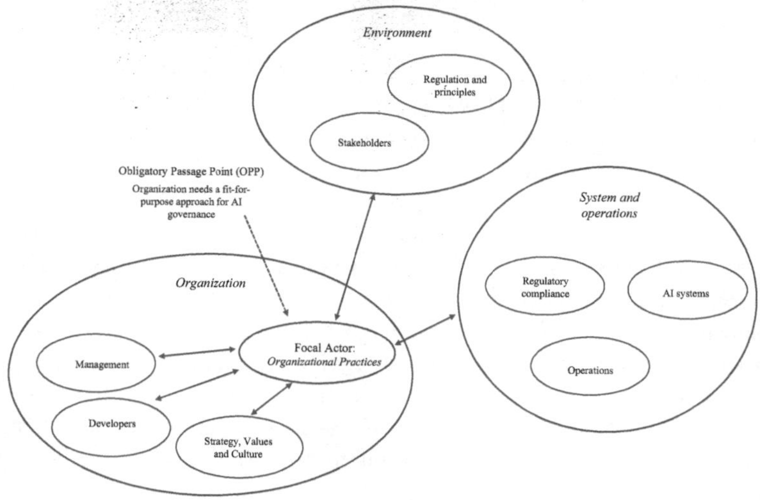

Fig. 1. Identified actor network with focal actor and obligatory passage point

Defining the OPP is the next key action in the problematization phase. The OPP should be defined in a way that supports the identified focal actor's dialogue with a multitude of actors and helps to avoid obstacles in discussions. In our case we defined the OPP as: 'organizations need a fit-for-purpose approach to AI governance.'

4.2 Interessement

Callon [22 , p. 208] described the second moment of translation as interessement: 'the group of actions by which an entity attempts to impose and stabilize the identity of the other actors it defines through its problematization'. This step involves convincing actors to agree on the interests defined for them by the focal actor.

The OPP 'organizations need a fit-for-purpose approach to AI governance (as one size does not fit)' was iteratively assessed against the positions of the surrounding actors. Regulation enters the network as a non-negotiable force ('regulation is not something that makes compromises'), to which the focal actor responds that while regulation is identical for all organizations, the operational approaches available are heterogeneous. Strategy, values, and culture conditionally accept the OPP insofar as governance remains aligned with the organization's identity, while AI systems and operations accept the framing on the condition that the organization invests in it.

"Regulatory or administrative pressure blocks quite clearly any black box AI and drives us more towards rule-based solutions." (Informant, banking sector)

"It's about... culture. It's about training. It's about constant focus on us being an ethical company." (Informant, senior leadership role)

4.3 Enrollment

The third moment of translation is enrollment, when actors are willing to anchor themselves to the network [22 , p. 211]. Successful interessement is followed by enrollment, which involves defining the roles of each actor in the transformed or newly created actor-network [22]. This further strengthens the OPP as actors accept the focal actor's definition.

A key conflict identified between the focal actor and other actors during alignment for the OPP concerned the relationship between regulation and organizational practices. Regulation, in its fundamental nature, should not be approached in a way that organizations make their own 'versions of regulation.' Through analysis and dialogue between actors, it was identified that regulatory compliance management at the level of individual AI systems or use cases is needed. This shifts the locus of compliance toward context-sensitive system-level governance, allowing the heterogeneous operational approaches anticipated in the interessement phase to materialize without compromising the uniformity of the underlying regulation.

4.4 Mobilization

Mobilization is the final phase of the translation process, in which the key actors ensure that supposed spokespersons for relevant collective entities adequately represent all members of the network that are acting as a single agent [25]. In our case, the role of 'organizational practices' as a focal actor and its impact on the creation of organizational AI governance capability was confirmed across the analyzed cases. Organizations that established stable spokespersons for the focal actor, typically an AI governance function or a multi-disciplinary AI governance committee with explicit decision rights were able to translate the OPP into durable governance arrangements that linked external regulatory expectations, internal strategy, and AI system-level controls. Conversely, organizations that lacked such institutionalized representation experienced repeated re-negotiation of the same governance issues, indicating that mobilization had not been achieved.

5 Discussion

Our application of Actor-Network Theory reveals AI governance as a processual accomplishment: rather than a top-down implementation of predefined principles, it emerges through negotiations between diverse actors (both human and non-human) each bringing their own interests and capabilities to the governance network.

With organizational practices as the focal actor, the translation process explains why AI governance cannot be a one-size-fits-all solution: each organization must navigate its own constellation of regulatory pressures, strategic priorities, technological capabilities, and cultural values, which accounts for the variation we observed even within similar regulatory environments. The OPP; 'organizations need a fit-for-purpose approach to AI governance', emerged not as a predetermined goal but through ongoing negotiations between competing interests and constraints.

Our analysis illustrates how AI systems themselves actively shape governance practices, challenging traditional conceptions of governance as a purely human-driven activity. The AI systems in our study were not passive objects to be governed but active participants in the network. For example, the opacity of certain banking-sector models forced organizations to develop rule-based fallback solutions and to redefine which decisions could be delegated at all (see Interessement, above), a case of the AI system materially shaping its own governance arrangement. Effective AI governance must therefore account for the agency of the technologies being governed.

The dynamic nature of the governance networks we observed also highlights a critical tension in current AI governance discourse. While regulatory frameworks tend toward standardization and predictability, the reality of organizational AI governance is characterized by continuous adaptation and renegotiation. The entry into force of the EU AI Act intensifies this dynamic. The Act's phased implementation through 2025–2027 (see Sect. 1) requires ongoing re-enrollment of actors as new obligations come into scope. Organizations that developed adaptive translation capabilities may be better positioned to respond, though confirming this requires follow-up research after binding enforcement progresses.

Our findings further suggest that organizational AI governance appears to take shape through what we term 'productive friction', the constructive tensions between different actors that force ongoing refinement and adaptation of governance practices. The Mobilization phase makes this visible: organizations that established designated AI governance functions or multi-disciplinary committees did not eliminate friction between regulation, strategy, AI systems, and operations, but kept it open and worked through it iteratively. Conversely, organizations that lacked such institutionalized representation experienced repeated re-negotiation of the same governance issues. Productive friction, in this sense, is a sign that organizations have achieved mobilization without collapsing the network into rigid procedures. In ANT terms, this reflects that translation is never final: productive friction is a generative variant of the residual instability ANT associates with incomplete translation.

5.1 Implications for Research and Practice

These findings have implications for both theory and practice. Theoretically, the study extends ANT's application to the governance of an emerging and now legally regulated technology. The four-moment translation lens proves productive for analyzing how heterogeneous actors: regulators, AI systems, organizational strategies, and operational routines, are progressively aligned, and it complements existing structural and procedural accounts of responsible AI governance [7, 15] by foregrounding the dynamics of alignment rather than the components of governance frameworks.

For practice, three implications follow. First, organizations should invest in translation capabilities, the ability to continuously negotiate and realign interests across the governance network, as opposed to treating AI governance as a one-off compliance project. Second, mobilization requires institutional anchoring: an AI governance function or a designated committee with explicit decision rights provides the stable spokesperson the network needs to convert principles and regulatory expectations into durable practice. Third, regulatory compliance is more effectively managed at the level of individual AI systems or use cases than through organization-wide rule-making, allowing heterogeneous operational approaches to materialize without compromising the uniformity of the underlying regulation.

6 Limitations

Several limitations should be acknowledged. First, the empirical scope is geographically and sectorally bounded: the second round in particular is concentrated in Nordic banking and insurance, which limits the generalizability of the specific governance patterns identified. Second, the temporal proximity to the EU AI Act's entry into force means that we capture organizations during a transitional moment; longer-term effects of binding enforcement on the observed governance networks remain to be studied.

Third, while ANT provides a powerful framework for mapping actor networks and translation processes, it has been critiqued for its limited engagement with structural power asymmetries and historical inequalities. The governance networks we observed are not power-neutral: regulators, large technology providers, and well-resourced organizations have substantially greater capacity to shape the network than smaller actors. Future work could productively combine ANT with institutional theory or critical governance perspectives to address this limitation. Finally, the reliance on expert interview data introduces a risk of self-presentation bias; while we have triangulated with publicly available organizational AI policy documents and successive versions of the EU AI Act to mitigate this, observational and longitudinal data would further strengthen future empirical claims. In addition, purposive and snowball sampling through professional networks likely over-represents organizations with comparatively mature or favourable AI governance, so the patterns reported should be read as illustrative, not representative of organizations in general.

7 Conclusion

This research has applied Actor-Network Theory to examine organizational AI governance as an emergent, socio-technical phenomenon. By tracing the translation processes through which ethical principles become organizational practices — with 'organizational practices' as the focal actor and 'a fit-for-purpose approach to AI governance' as the obligatory passage point — we show that effective governance arises not from static compliance frameworks but from ongoing negotiations between diverse human and non-human actors. Our findings further reveal that AI systems themselves actively shape governance processes, challenging the assumption that governance is a purely human-driven activity. Organizations that embraced the productive friction inherent in these negotiations appeared to develop more stable governance arrangements than those seeking to eliminate it through rigid procedures.

The entry into force of the EU AI Act intensifies the stakes of this finding, and the ANT-based framework developed here offers a foundation for future empirical work on how governance actor networks are reconfigured, and whether the translation capabilities identified here continue to drive governance innovation, as binding enforcement progresses.

References

1. Berente, N., Gu, B., Recker, J., Santhanam, R.: Managing artificial intelligence. MIS Q. **45**(3), 1433–1450 (2021). https://doi.org/10.25300/MISQ/2021/16274
2. Davenport, T.H.: The AI Advantage: How to Put the Artificial Intelligence Revolution to Work. MIT Press, Cambridge (2018)
3. Makridakis, S.: The forthcoming artificial intelligence (AI) revolution: its impact on society and firms. Futures. **90**, 46–60 (2017). https://doi.org/10.1016/j.futures.2017.03.006
4. Floridi, L., Cowls, J., Beltrametti, M., et al.: AI4People—an ethical framework for a good AI society: opportunities, risks, principles, and recommendations. Mind. Mach. **28**(4), 689–707 (2018). https://doi.org/10.1007/s11023-018-9482-5
5. Fjeld, J., Achten, N., Hilligoss, H., Nagy, A., Srikumar, M.: Principled Artificial Intelligence: Mapping Consensus in Ethical and Rights-Based Approaches to Principles for AI. Berkman Klein Center Research Publication (2020)
6. Jobin, A., Ienca, M., Vayena, E.: The global landscape of AI ethics guidelines. Nat. Mach. Intell. **1**(9), 389–399 (2019). https://doi.org/10.1038/s42256-019-0088-2
7. Papagiannidis, E., Mikalef, P., Conboy, K.: Responsible artificial intelligence governance: a review and research framework. J. Strateg. Inf. Syst. **34**(2), 101885 (2025). https://doi.org/10.1016/j.jsis.2024.101885
8. Teodorescu, M., Morse, L., Awwad, Y., Kane, G.C.: Failures of fairness in automation require a deeper understanding of human–ML augmentation. MIS Q. **45**(3), 1483–1499 (2021). https://doi.org/10.25300/MISQ/2021/16535
9. Floridi, L., Cowls, J.: A unified framework of five principles for AI in society. Harvard Data Sci. Rev. **1**(1) (2019). https://doi.org/10.1162/99608f92.8cd550d1
10. Hagendorff, T.: The ethics of AI ethics: an evaluation of guidelines. Mind. Mach. **30**(1), 99–120 (2020). https://doi.org/10.1007/s11023-020-09517-8
11. European Union: Regulation (EU) 2024/1689 of the European Parliament and of the Council laying down harmonised rules on artificial intelligence (Artificial Intelligence Act). Off. J. Eur. Union, L 2024/1689 (2024)
12. Morley, J., et al.: The ethics of AI in health care: a mapping review. Soc. Sci. Med. **260**, 113172 (2020). https://doi.org/10.1016/j.socscimed.2020.113172
13. Gasser, U., Almeida, V.A.F.: A layered model for AI governance. IEEE Internet Comput. **21**(6), 58–62 (2017). https://doi.org/10.1109/MIC.2017.4180835
14. Minkkinen, M., Mäntymäki, M.: Discerning between the "easy" and "hard" problems of AI governance. IEEE Trans. Technol. Soc. **4**(2), 188–194 (2023). https://doi.org/10.1109/TTS.2023.3267382
15. Mäntymäki, M., Minkkinen, M., Birkstedt, T., Viljanen, M.: Defining organizational AI governance. AI Ethics. **2**(4), 603–609 (2022). https://doi.org/10.1007/s43681-022-00143-x
16. Birkstedt, T., Minkkinen, M., Tandon, A., Mäntymäki, M.: AI governance: themes, knowledge gaps and future agendas. Internet Res. **33**(7), 133–167 (2023). https://doi.org/10.1108/INTR-01-2022-0042
17. Laine, J., Minkkinen, M., Mäntymäki, M.: Ethics-based AI auditing: a systematic literature review on conceptualizations of ethical principles and knowledge contributions to stakeholders. Inf. Manag. **61**(5), 103969 (2024). https://doi.org/10.1016/j.im.2024.103969
18. Seppälä, A., Birkstedt, T., Mäntymäki, M.: From ethical AI principles to governed AI. In: Proceedings of the 42nd International Conference on Information Systems (ICIS), Paper 10 (2021)
19. Latour, B.: Reassembling the Social: An Introduction to Actor-Network-Theory. Oxford University Press, Oxford (2005)

20. Law, J.: Notes on the theory of the actor-network: ordering, strategy, and heterogeneity. Syst. Pract. **5**(4), 379–393 (1992). https://doi.org/10.1007/BF01059830
21. Cressman, D.: A Brief Overview of Actor-Network Theory: Punctualization, Heterogeneous Engineering & Translation. Centre for Policy Research on Science & Technology, Simon Fraser University (2009)
22. Callon, M.: Some elements of a sociology of translation: domestication of the scallops and the fishermen of St Brieuc Bay. Sociol. Rev. **32**(1), 196–233 (1986). https://doi.org/10.1111/j.1467-954X.1986.tb00026.x
23. Sarker, S., Sarker, S., Sidorova, A.: Understanding business process change failure: an actor-network perspective. J. Manag. Inf. Syst. **23**(1), 51–86 (2006). https://doi.org/10.2753/MIS0742-1222230102
24. Patton, M.Q.: Qualitative Evaluation and Research Methods, 2nd edn. Sage Publications, Newbury Park, CA (1990)
25. Callon, M., Latour, B.: Unscrewing the big leviathan: how actors macro-structure reality and how sociologists help them to do so. In: Knorr-Cetina, K., Cicourel, A.V. (eds.) Advances in Social Theory and Methodology, pp. 277–303. Routledge, London (1981)

A Trustworthy LLM-Assisted Qualitative Content Analysis Method

Nard Janssens(✉), Marijn Janssen, and Nitesh Bharosa

Delft University of Technology, Delft, The Netherlands
n.janssens@tudelft.nl

Abstract. Document analysis is common in both research and practice, but manual analysis is time-intensive, methodologically demanding, and difficult to scale. Large Language Models (LLMs) offer important advantages in scalability and analytical speed, but they also raise concerns about limited transparency, reproducibility, contextual drift, and hallucinations. This paper develops and tests a novel, proposition-driven, structured Qualitative Content Analysis (QCA) method designed to ensure trustworthy content analyses. Derived from the literature, trustworthiness is operationalized as reproducibility, reliability, and traceability. The method is structured at two levels: first, by framing the research question as theoretically grounded propositions; and second, by organizing the method into separate, testable, and auditable phases. This study contributes methodologically at the intersection of AI and QCA by showing that the trustworthiness of LLM-assisted coding depends not only on good prompts but also on a structured method that integrates and operationalizes safeguards for source grounding and LLM context control. The evaluation results show that this method can scale up QCA, meeting trustworthiness criteria while enhancing auditability. In this way, the method can save time while meeting the predefined coding-stage criteria for trustworthiness and codebook conformity. Future research could examine the effects of providing models with richer contextual knowledge.

Keywords: Content analysis · QCA · LLM · trustworthiness · traceability

1 Introduction

The time required for researchers to conduct qualitative content analysis (QCA) of large volumes of documents is often resource-intensive and not always justifiable. When these documents also originate from practice, their complexity can further increase the burden of this work, reduce intercoder reliability (IR), or increase the likelihood of coding differences [1]. Although the use of a strict codebook can help, it also increases the time burden, and checks and balances are needed to ensure consistent use.

Large Language Models (LLMs) can offer significant advantages in scalability and analysis speed [2]. However, well-known problems in the use of LLMs include a lack of traceability of the analysis process, poor reproducibility, contextual drift, and hallucination [3–6]. An important quality safeguard, therefore, remains comparison with human

Published by Springer Nature Switzerland AG 2027
S. Han et al. (Eds.): I3E 2026, LNCS 16912, pp. 313–325, 2027.
https://doi.org/10.1007/978-3-032-38014-2_23

coding, supplemented by safeguards that enhance the reproducibility, reliability, and traceability of LLM use. Hence, in this research, we *develop a method for trustworthy LLM-assisted qualitative content analysis.* We build on a growing body of research on LLM use in qualitative content analysis, including prompt sequencing [2], context drift and cross-document contamination [3], transparency problems [6], and audit trails for LLM use [5]. However, methodological guidance is still lacking on how to integrate these insights into a coherent analysis method for proposition-driven deductive coding. Therefore, building on existing QCA methodology and quality requirements, we develop a proposition-driven, structured LLM-assisted method for qualitative content analysis and assess its reproducibility, reliability, and traceability. This method focuses on the coding stage.

The next section discusses the theoretical background, followed by the research method, results, discussion, and conclusion.

2 Background

Qualitative Content Analysis (QCA) is typically used as a theory-led, deductive form of content analysis in which predefined codes are systematically applied to text fragments. Many methodological approaches to QCA discuss trustworthiness in terms of credibility, transferability, dependability, confirmability, and authenticity [7, 8]. Specifically, at the coding stage of the QCA process, researchers cite requirements such as coding consistency [2], transparency/auditability [6], and source grounding or explicit justification [9]. Human review is also mentioned [9, 10] and can be considered a validation safeguard. Therefore, we operationalize trustworthiness at the coding step in terms of *reproducibility* relating to process stability, *reliability/consistency* in code application, and *traceability* of coding decisions to source text and explicit justification.

The use of LLMs must meet the same requirements. Yet, they also pose risks, when analyzing documents, which can be grouped into three categories: (1) the use of unintended or uncontrollable information, (2) unreliability of the analytical process, and (3) limited transparency regarding the information used, the analytical process followed, and the reasoning underlying coding decisions [3–6]:

First. Without control over the information used by the LLM, the active context may include unintended or uncontrollable information, such as external sources, chat history, or prior documents, which may lead to context drift or hallucinated output [3, 5]. Control over information can be shaped in different ways, such as by explicitly prohibiting the model in the prompt from seeking other information, for example, external online sources, by clearing the interaction history, and by conducting analyses of independent documents in separate sessions [2, 3]. For large datasets, however, separate sessions are labor-intensive, and a scripted solution may therefore be applied [11]. A disadvantage of strong context restriction, however, is that it may reduce the interpretive depth of semantic analysis relative to that of human coders [9]. Also, LLMs may generate desirable or expectation-aligned answers, as they remain fundamentally probabilistic language models [5]. One possible safeguard is to request validating quotations for each claim, because this binds the output more closely to the source text, although it does not guarantee full correctness [12].

Second. Even when the same prompt, input, and model settings are used, the analytical process's unreliability can yield inconsistent results and poor reproducibility across coding rounds [2]. This may include a shift from semantic interpretation to pattern-based shortcutting in repetitive coding tasks, reflecting the statistical, pattern-based nature of LLM processing [3]. It poses serious methodological problems when LLMs are used in qualitative analysis [4, 13]. These risks can be mitigated by using an explicit codebook, structuring the analytical steps in advance through prompt sequencing, and systematically documenting model choice, model version, prompts, and other analytical settings, thereby reducing variation in analytical decisions [2, 6].
Third. Limited transparency pertains to the information used, the nature of the analysis method employed, the process steps followed, the reasoning that led to a coding decision, and whether hallucinations occurred [3]. This makes it difficult, when coding differences arise between human coders and an LLM, to reconstruct how those differences emerged, which coding is most defensible, where coding errors occurred, and which limitations and risks affect the analysis [6]. In addition, the absence of adequate audit trails complicates the tracing, evaluation, and improvement of coding outcomes [5].

Despite attention given to LLM risks [3–6], methodological guidance remains limited on how to integrate the LLM advantages into a coherent analytical process. Building on Mayring's seven-step QCA model [14] and Chew et al.'s LLM-assisted deductive coding procedure [11], our method focuses not only on good prompting but also on the design of an auditable method for LLM-assisted deductive coding.

3 Research Method

In this section, we describe our method design, which combines a proposition-driven structuring, a modular workflow, and explicit safeguards, and is assessed against quality criteria. This is followed by an evaluation design to test the method on a real-world dataset.

3.1 Design of the Trustworthy LLM-Assisted QCA Method

Our method builds on Mayring's well-established, widely cited, theory-guided, and rule-bound QCA framework [14]. Since Mayring's model [14] predates LLM-assisted coding, we integrate it with the approach of Chew et al. [11], who specify how LLMs can be used for deductive coding, including steps for code and codebook development, sample-based LLM coding, reliability assessment, and coding the full dataset. Together, they provide the core structure of our method design, starting with the research question and theoretical grounding, coding guidelines, sample coding, human validation and iteration, final coding of the full dataset, and concluding with analysis of code category frequencies and interpretation [11, 14]. Figure 1 shows our method design, consisting of three main phases: 'Researcher(s) design' (steps 1 to 3), 'LLM codes' (steps 4 to 10), and 'Researcher(s) validate and interpret' (steps 11 to 13).

Workflow Structure. To support iterative refinement, error tracing, targeted revision, and methodological auditability, we structured the workflow at two levels: first, by structuring the research question into theoretically derived propositions (step 2), which are

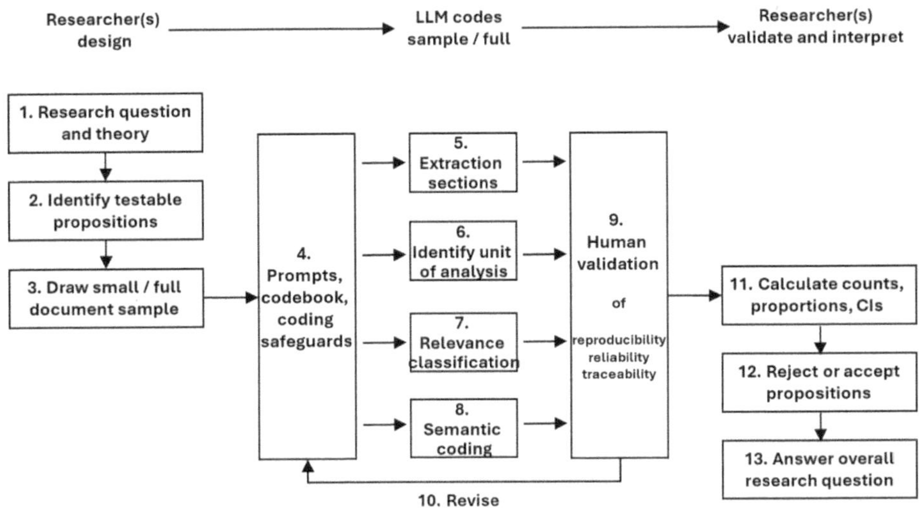

Fig. 1. Proposition-driven, structured, trustworthy LLM-assisted QCA method.

revisited in proposition testing (step 12), and second, by structuring the workflow into analytical phases (steps 5–8):

Propositions. We are guided by Yin [15], who advises that one should first determine the "five components of a research design [which] are especially important: 1. a study's questions; 2. its propositions, if any; 3. its unit(s) of analysis; 4. the logic linking the data to the propositions; and 5. the criteria for interpreting the findings" [15 , p. 27]. Yin [15] further explains that a research question may address the "how" or "why," but does not yet specify what should be studied. Propositions help define which evidence is relevant. In our method, propositions are used to strengthen transparency and testability, form the basis of the investigative logic, and provide a deductive basis for the method.
Analytical phases. To increase transparency, error tracing, and auditability, we split Chew's LLM-assisted analysis steps [11] into distinct auditable actions: extraction of relevant text sections, identification and splitting into units of analysis, classification of these units for relevance to coding, and semantic coding. In this context, "deductive coding" refers to the overall coding approach based on a predefined codebook, whereas "semantic coding" refers to the LLM's assignment of those predefined codes based on the meaning of the units of analysis.

Quality Criteria. The method is assessed against three quality criteria derived from the literature in the previous section: reproducibility, reliability, and traceability [5, 6]. *Reproducibility* means that repeated runs with the same input and under the same workflow conditions produce the same or equivalent results [5]. *Reliability* means that coding decisions for the same source text are applied consistently in accordance with the rules specified in the codebook and prompt [1]. *Traceability* means that the coding decisions can be linked back to the provided source text, the prompt, and the codebook [5, 6]. These documented links make the coding process auditable. Together, these criteria indicate coding-stage trustworthiness and adherence to the codebook but are not intended to establish full interpretive validity. To identify and address shortcomings in each iteration in a targeted way, both the output and the explicit rationales/justifications must remain transparent and verifiable. The criteria will be further operationalized in 3.2.

Iterative Process. The main iterations occur within the LLM-coding phase, from human validation (step 9) back to refining the prompts, codebook, and safeguards (step 4), and may also iterate back to refine more testable propositions (step 2) in phase 1, although this is not shown in the figure for clarity. We follow Mayring [14] and Chew [11] by using multiple iterations to achieve consistent and comparable coding across human coders and between the LLM and human coders. This mainly concerns the instructions for developing the prompt and the codebook. Iterations also serve to address method shortcomings and to safeguard until agreement and process stability reach acceptable levels.

Safeguards. For clarity, all safeguards identified in this study are presented together here. The original study design included four safeguards (S1–S4) to address key known risks of LLM-assisted QCA: context drift and cross-document contamination [3], limited transparency [6], and insufficient auditability of LLM outputs [5]. These safeguards constrain the LLM's use of information, prevent hallucinations by enforcing evidence-based reasoning, standardize encoding, and increase transparency in the derivation of output. During the iterative application of the method, two additional safeguards were introduced (S5–S6; see Sect. 4. Evaluation Results). During the evaluation, a final safeguard emerged as a recommendation for future use (S7; see Sect. 5. Discussion). Functionally, these safeguards can be grouped into feedforward/input, concurrent/execution, and feedback/evaluation, as presented in Table 1.

Table 1. Safeguards for trustworthy LLM-assisted Qualitative Content Analysis.

Feedforward/ Input controls	**S1** - Restrict the LLM to the provided information only.
	S2 - Constrain interpretation by prohibiting guessing, inferred context, redesign of definitions, and rewriting of excerpts.
Concurrent / Execution controls	**S3** - Ensure adherence to the prompt and codebook without deriving new rules.
	S4 - Enforce semantic reasoning and source grounding by requiring a validating quotation and a short, explicit rationale.
	S5 - Limiting analysis to the smallest possible internally coherent information unit.
	S6 - Executing analysis of each information unit in a new, context-isolated session.
Feedback / Evaluation controls	**S7** - If reproducibility cannot be adequately addressed in iterations, a second run on the full dataset can serve to identify documents requiring manual review, correction or even exclusion.

3.2 Evaluation Design

To test whether the proposed method meets the requirements of traceability, reproducibility, and reliability, we evaluated the workflow shown in Fig. 1 using an evaluation case based on a real-world, large-scale dataset and a case-specific empirical research question. This allows for analytical generalizability in which we infer from the findings to the theory [16]. the dataset and propositions corresponding to steps 1–3 were defined, the tooling, codebook, and prompts for analytical steps 4–8 were developed, and the evaluation in step 9 and the iterative refinement in step 10 were designed. The dataset and propositions are presented first, as they define what is being coded and tested for within the workflow. The evaluation dataset, prompts, final codebook, model/API settings, scoring rules, validation material, and outputs are available on 4TU.ResearchData at https://doi.org/10.4121/ea45e84e-d128-4950-9d7a-0338fd7e064e .

Evaluation Case: Dataset and Propositions. For our test dataset, we selected 155 publicly available audit reports in PDF format, averaging 5 A4 pages, each written in Dutch. Such a dataset is hard to analyze manually within a reasonable time frame. While it would take a researcher several weeks to code this dataset (steps 4–8), an LLM can process it in one to two days. This dataset is particularly suitable for testing our method for the following reasons: it comprises many reports with similar formats, enabling repeated testing of analytical tasks and consistent application of coding logic across documents. The reports cover topics ranging from technical to governance and managerial considerations and are semantically rich, requiring interpretive coding beyond keyword matching. The dataset consists of publicly available, non-confidential reports, making a closed or privacy-protected LLM environment unnecessary. By using a Dutch-language dataset, the method can be tested in a non-English setting, for which public LLMs are generally not optimized.

For analysis of this dataset, we first formulated the case-specific empirical research question to test the method: "Which elements of control-work can the principal delegate, and to what extent, across the governance lifecycle phases of network collaboration without transferring decision-making authority?" Thereafter, five theoretical propositions were derived, for instance:

- P1-"Network governance consists of governance work that either requires decision authority or can be exercised without such authority"; and
- P3-"In network collaborations, control-work is not confined to the principal's internal governance interests but also serves network-level governance interests".

Tooling, Codebook, and Prompts. OpenAI's LLM was selected, since the scientific community has already gained substantial experience with this model family, for example, by Chew et al. [11] and Gilardi et al. [17]. We used the GPT-5.1-Thinking model in February 2026. Each analytical task, from step 5 ("Extraction Sections") to step 8 ("Semantic Coding"), was specified in a prompt that assigned the LLM a role, safeguards, decision rules, and an output format.

The final application of the deductive codebook was isolated in step 8 ("Semantic Coding"), for which the researchers developed a separate codebook, informed by LLM feedback. The codebook specified which categories had to be coded, which codes could be applied, and, where appropriate, the detailed decision rules—with examples—for each code. It also required a short semantic justification for each coding decision. In addition, an anchor question was specified for each category, for example: "Does the action primarily require authority to commit or mandate the organization (decision-rights), or can it be performed as oversight or assurance without committing?".

This method was initially developed for use in ChatGPT's web interface. During iterative refinement, stable performance was found to require independent clean-context runs for each document. We therefore switched to the OpenAI API and Python scripts, submitting the prompt and codebook with each document. This switch was associated with improved reproducibility and coding consistency, likely due to stricter context control and greater standardization across runs.

Evaluation. In each LLM step 5 ("Extraction Sections") to step 8 ("Semantic Coding"), six documents containing a total of 80–120 recommendations were coded by the LLM.

For each step, the Python script randomly selected the six validation documents, ensuring coverage across all years in the dataset. These six documents per step underwent the full coding procedure for the relevant coding step, including safeguards, such as validating quotations and semantic rationales. For each document, all coded data units were checked against manual coding based on the prompt and, where applicable, the codebook. In cases of discrepancies, the source text, prompt, codebook rules, quotations, and rationale were reviewed to determine whether the disagreement resulted from an ambiguity in the codebook, miscoding by the LLM, or erroneous interpretation by the researcher.

The output was evaluated against our quality criteria: Reproducibility is assessed by repeating runs under the same configuration and checking whether outputs remain the same or are materially equivalent, with a threshold of 90%. *Traceability* is assessed by checking whether each coding decision is supported by a validating quotation and an explicit rationale linked to the source text, prompt, and codebook, as a design requirement that must be met in full. *Reliability* is assessed by calculating the percentage agreement between LLM coding and researcher validation. Interrater/intercoder reliability (IRR/ICR) metrics were not used because the comparison was asymmetrical, with the researcher acting as a validator of codebook conformity [1]. Validation was selected over a second human coder, as the latter would introduce an alternative basis of interpretation rather than a direct test of codebook conformity. If disagreement exceeds 10%, an assessment is conducted to determine whether this resulted from poor coding by the LLM or from the researcher's validation or interpretation. In this respect, the 90% agreement threshold is stricter than the commonly used agreement norm of 80% [18].

Iterative Refinement. In step 10, the prompt and the codebook were revised. The LLM was used to suggest refinements as additional input for the researcher. Iterations continued until no new patterns emerged for the evaluation of our method. The codebook and prompts were frozen, and the LLM analyzed the full dataset. Subsequently, the coding of another six documents was validated to check for additional issues that emerged during scaling.

4 Evaluation Results

These results pertain to the iterative development and testing of the method within the evaluation case. The workflow was iteratively refined for 8 iterations, after which no new patterns emerged for evaluating our method.

Quality Criteria. In the first LLM-assisted analysis step, step 5 (Extraction Sections), the LLM failed on three scanned documents and in separating footers from relevant text sections. These cases were manually corrected with little effort to provide an optimal starting point for the subsequent analysis steps 6 (Identify Unit of Analysis), 7 (Relevance Classification), and 8 (Semantic Coding).

- Traceability was 100% across all assessed steps, as each coding decision was accompanied by supporting evidence and reasoning.
- Reliability ranged from 94.9% for step 6 to 93.8% for step 7. Error analysis showed that most remaining coding disagreements stemmed from the design choice to limit contextual information provided to the LLM, while the researcher-based coding decisions were based on implicit assumptions.
- Reproducibility reached 91.7% for step 6 and 84.8% for step 7, but varied substantially across documents and coding variables in step 8 (Semantic Coding). Document analysis suggests this can be attributed to (i) insufficiently specified decision rules in the codebook and prompt, (ii) contextual ambiguity in the document, and (iii) cross-excerpt contamination with cascading effects on subsequent coding decisions.

Safeguards. The main risks that emerged in our test data during iterations were cross-document contamination and the resulting context drift, in which previous documents and coding patterns began to influence the analysis of the current document. Suboptimal coding also occurred because semantic analysis was abandoned at larger task sizes in favor of pattern-based shortcuts. These proved to be greater methodological risks than anticipated. This became apparent early in the iterations: our LLM (the OpenAI web interface, ChatGPT), despite semantic coding of the sample set, appeared to rely increasingly on pattern recognition in the full dataset and, in practice, seemed to use more pattern-based shortcuts than in the calibration set. In addition, the coding of each report in the dataset increasingly incorporated information from previous reports, which we interpreted as a form of cross-document priming and contextual drift. Even refining the prompts and codebook with explicit instructions to clear the context after each document and to allow only semantic analysis did not resolve this issue. This led us to introduce the two *emergent safeguards, S5 and S6*, as defined in Sect. 3.1.

Testability of Propositions. Some propositions proved difficult to test adequately in the available data. To prevent speculative coding, the LLM was instructed to assign the code UNCLEAR when textual evidence did not support a confident coding decision. This safeguard revealed that for some propositions, the share of recommendations that could be coded for was too small to support meaningful interpretation and proposition testing. In those cases, the "logic linking the data to the propositions" [15] was reconsidered, and propositions were reformulated and restructured to improve their testability. This refinement step is not included in Fig. 1.

5 Discussion

We first discuss the contribution of our structured analytical process for LLM-assisted QCA. Next, we address the risks, the choices that can mitigate them and increase trustworthiness, and the trade-offs involved. We conclude this section with the limitations of our study and avenues for future research.

5.1 Contributions to Qualitative Content Analysis

This study shows that trustworthy LLM-assisted QCA depends not only on prompting but also on the design of an auditable analytical process that integrates proposition-driven structuring, separate testable analytical phases, and safeguards for context control, source grounding, and reproducibility testing. The evaluation of the Dutch document corpus shows to what extent reproducibility, reliability, and traceability can be achieved in this workflow and which vulnerabilities remain.

First, proposition-driven modularization made the analysis more testable, traceable, and open to targeted improvement. This is in line with Yin [15], who argues that a research question specifies the how and what, but does not yet indicate which evidence provides an answer to that question. Because propositions focus attention on relevant evidence, proposition-driven deductive coding is particularly suitable when trustworthiness must be demonstrated and tested within the analytical process. Splitting the research question into separate propositions, in combination with dividing the analysis into distinct analytical steps, produces a granular map of the analysis [2, 12]. This makes an opaque LLM-assisted analytical process inspectable and testable, and creates opportunities for targeted improvement.

A second contribution lies in integrating and operationalizing safeguards to control the analytical context and ground coding decisions in the source text. Although four safeguards (S1-S4) were predefined in our method design, two safeguards (S5-S6) emerged during iterative application, and one (S7) is proposed for future use. Together, these safeguards address context control, source grounding, and process stability. Our study shows how their combination supports trustworthiness in LLM-assisted QCA by improving reproducibility, reliability, and traceability while reducing contextual drift, hallucinations, and pattern-based shortcuts.

Third, our results show that reproducibility can serve as an important indicator for identifying areas for improvement, rather than merely indicating a general failure of the method. Low reproducibility may point to instability in the codebook and prompt, the coding conditions, or the quality of the dataset, for example, due to insufficient contextual clarity. In such cases, we propose as safeguard S7 for future applications: verifying reproducibility across the entire dataset to identify documents requiring manual review, correction, or exclusion.

While the literature often treats the quality of LLM-assisted QCA as a matter of prompt engineering [2, 12], the study extends prior work by showing that trustworthiness also depends on the design of a structured analytical process [10], including proposition-driven structuring, distinct analytical phases, explicit safeguards for context control and source-grounding, and evaluation criteria. Also, the use of a structured analytical process increases the ability of future studies to build on documented procedures, prompts, codebooks, and audit trails from prior research [6, 10].

5.2 Context Risks and Trade-Offs

Our findings confirm that cross-document contamination and context drift are important methodological risks for trustworthiness in sequential LLM-assisted document coding. They show that trustworthy LLM-assisted QCA depends not only on prompt content, but also on strict control of the active analytical context. Our results imply that shared or sequential sessions may be methodologically problematic when documents need to be coded independently. In research designs that require multiple, independent rounds of analysis and coding, standard chat-based LLM sessions are therefore less suitable for achieving sufficiently trustworthy analysis [5, 10].

These findings also reveal a clear trade-off between efficiency, research effort, and the degree of trustworthiness in LLM-assisted QCA. Greater trustworthiness requires safeguards, including isolated sessions, source grounding, and additional validation. These measures increased the reproducibility, reliability, and traceability of the analysis, but also involve more manual work, higher costs, and longer processing times. This trade-off between control and efficiency, therefore, needs to be made explicit and methodologically justified in every study [5, 10].

Although designing the codebook and safeguards required substantial time, because less could be left to implicit interpretation, this investment was partly recovered because each new analysis required less effort from the researchers. As a result, the research shifted from manual coding to validation. Because human coding is susceptible to coder fatigue, whereas LLMs can apply the codebook consistently, the error rate in our study remained comparable to that of manual coding [11, 19, 20].

5.3 Limitations

In this study, the LLM appeared to follow the codebook strictly and, therefore, the method codes more consistently than human coders. The downside, however, is that the quality of LLM-based coding may depend more on the prompt and codebook than human coding does [11, 21, 22]. Controlling the context also proved necessary, given the previously discussed risks of context drift, cross-document contamination, pattern-based processing, and hallucinations. No basic contextual information was provided to the LLM, which may have led to undercoding, whereas a human researcher might legitimately incorporate such context [21]. The added value of providing the LLM with an initial contextual frame is a potential topic for future research.

Public LLMs, such as those used in this study, are primarily trained on English-language data [23]. Although validation by researchers shows a sufficient degree of agreement between the LLM and human coders, we cannot rule out the possibility that some Dutch semantic nuances were captured less well. In addition, outcomes may also depend on the LLM model, the version, and even the date on which the study is conducted [24]. Future research could compare the performance across different LLMs.

The evaluation was limited to one LLM model family, one document corpus, and a single proposition-driven deductive coding setting. Safeguards such as context isolation, restricting the LLM to the provided information, requiring validating quotations and explicit semantic rationales for coding decisions, and reproducibility testing are likely to be transferable. By contrast, the specific propositions, definitions of units of analysis, codebook rules, criteria for assessing material equivalence, and the amount of contextual information provided to the LLM are likely to require domain-specific adaptation.

Although prior research suggests that LLMs can process large datasets more quickly than human researchers [2, 4–6], this study did not assess how using this method affected the researcher's time allocation.

While researcher validation was judged to be appropriate for assessing compliance with the codebook, this does not rule out the risk of researcher-specific interpretations. In future applications, the validation design could therefore be strengthened by having a second researcher review a sample of the validation decisions or by subjecting a sample to blind validation.

6 Conclusion

Given the rise in document volume, there is a need for AI to support the analyses. We developed a novel, trustworthy LLM-assisted QCA method for designing, evaluating, and improving content analyses that meets criteria for reproducibility, reliability, and traceability. The essence of the method is that, by structuring the research question into theoretically grounded propositions and the method into separate, testable, and auditable phases, we increased the trustworthiness of LLM-assisted QCA and made it more testable and improvable in a targeted way. For researchers, the work shifts from manual coding to proper implementation and validation of the results.

For this evaluation, we operationalized trustworthiness specifically for coding and identified traceability, reproducibility, and reliability as key criteria. Our results show that this method can save time while meeting the predefined coding-stage criteria for trustworthiness and codebook conformity. At the same time, we observed a clear trade-off: greater auditability and stability also require more instructions, more processing time, more manual work, and higher costs.

Our contribution is at the intersection of AI and QCA, as existing content analysis served as a starting point and was adapted to integrate with AI. This study shows that trustworthiness is supported by a combination of three key elements: proposition-driven structuring, a modular analytical process, and explicit safeguards for both context control and source-grounding. A concrete method for operationalizing reproducibility, reliability, and traceability in LLM-assisted QCA, while reducing concerns surrounding trustworthiness and hallucinations, was provided.

The main risks we encountered for reliable LLM-assisted content analysis are context drift, cross-document contamination, pattern-based shortcuts, and limited transparency into coding decisions. Our results show that these can be mitigated through small, coherent data units, clean/isolated sessions, and source-grounding through validating quotations and explicit rationales for each coding decision.

Future research should test the transferability of our findings to other types of documents, such as interview transcripts and meeting minutes. Further research could also examine whether coding quality can be improved by using an LLM specifically trained for the source language and by providing the model with relevant contextual knowledge. Finally, a systematic comparison of the time used and costs of LLM-assisted QCA and human QCA across datasets of different sizes is recommended.

Acknowledgment. This research was supported by the Ministry of Agriculture, Fisheries, Food Security and Nature of the Netherlands through financial support for the author's PhD trajectory. No separate project-specific funding was provided for this study.

Disclosure of Interests The authors have no competing interests to declare that are relevant to the content of this article.

Declaration of Generative AI and AI-Assisted Technologies The author(s) used AI in order to test the developed method. AI was used for translation and editorial purposes, after which the authors reviewed and edited the content as needed. The author(s) take full responsibility for the content of the publication.

References

1. O'Connor, C., Joffe, H.: Intercoder reliability in qualitative research: debates and practical guidelines. Int J Qual Methods. **19**, 160940691989922 (2020). https://doi.org/10.1177/1609406919899220
2. Than, N., Fan, L., Law, T. N., Nelson, L. K., McCall, L.: Updating "The Future of Coding": Qualitative Coding with Generative Large Language Models. Sociol. Methods Res. **54**(3), 849–888 (2025). https://doi.org/10.1177/00491241251339188
3. Ibrahim, E.I., Voyer, A.: Qualitative research with LLM chatbots: technological reflexivity for interpretative technology. Qual. Res. **26**(1), 133–159 (2026). https://doi.org/10.1177/14687941251390794
4. Abdurahman, S., Ziabari, A.S., Moore, A., Bartels, D., Dehghani, M.: A primer for evaluating large language models in social science research. Adv. Methods Pract. Psychol. Sci. **8**(2) (2025). https://doi.org/10.1177/25152459251325174
5. Nguyen, D.C., Welch, C.: Generative artificial intelligence in qualitative data analysis: analyzing—or just chatting? Organ. Res. Methods. **29**(1), 3–39 (2026). https://doi.org/10.1177/10944281251377154
6. Jones, K.M.L.: Generative AI in qualitative research and related transparency problems: a novel heuristic for disclosing uses of AI. Int. J. Qual. Methods. **24** (2025). https://doi.org/10.1177/16094069251404329
7. Kyngäs, H., Kääriäinen, M., Elo, S.: The trustworthiness of content analysis. In: The Application of Content Analysis in Nursing Science Research, pp. 41–48. Springer International Publishing (2020). https://doi.org/10.1007/978-3-030-30199-6_5
8. Elo, S., Kääriäinen, M., Kanste, O., Pölkki, T., Utriainen, K., Kyngäs, H.: Qualitative Content Analysis: A Focus on Trustworthiness. SAGE Open. **4**(1) (2014). https://doi.org/10.1177/2158244014522633
9. Dunivin, Z.O.: Scaling hermeneutics: a guide to qualitative coding with LLMs for reflexive content analysis. EPJ Data Sci. **14**(1) (2025). https://doi.org/10.1140/epjds/s13688-025-00548-8
10. Gao, J., et al.: Efficiency with rigor! a trustworthy LLM-powered Workflow for qualitative data analysis. arXiv preprint arXiv:2501.00775. (2025)
11. Chew, R., Bollenbacher, J., Wenger, M., Speer, J., Kim, A.: LLM-assisted content analysis: using large language models to support deductive coding, (2023). [Online]. Available: https://arxiv.org/pdf/2306.14924

12. Zhang, H., Wu, C., Xie, J., Lyu, Y., Cai, J., Carroll, J. M.: Harnessing the power of AI in qualitative research: exploring, using and redesigning ChatGPT. Comput. Hum. Behav.: Artif. Hum. **4**, 100144 (2025). https://doi.org/10.1016/j.chbah.2025.100144
13. Atıl, B., et al.: Non-determinism of "deterministic" LLM system settings in hosted environments. In: Proceedings of the 5th Workshop on Evaluation and Comparison of NLP Systems, pp. 135–148 (2025)
14. Mayring, P.: Qualitative Content Analysis: Theoretical Foundation, Basic Procedures and Software Solution. SSOAR (2014)
15. Yin, R.K.: Chapter 2: designing case studies. In: Case Study Research-Volume 5. SAGE Publications (1986)
16. Polit, D.F., Beck, C.T.: Generalization in quantitative and qualitative research: myths and strategies. Int. J. Nurs. Stud. **47**(11), 1451–1458 (2010)
17. Gilardi, F., Alizadeh, M., Kubli, M.: ChatGPT outperforms crowd workers for text-annotation tasks., (2023). [Online]. Available: https://arxiv.org/abs/2303.15056
18. Halpin, S.N.: Inter-coder agreement in qualitative coding: considerations for its use. Am. J. Qual. Res. **8**(3), 23–43 (2024)
19. Neuendorf, K.A.: The Content Analysis Guidebook. SAGE Publications, Inc (2017)
20. Törnberg, P.: Large language models outperform expert coders and supervised classifiers at annotating political social media messages. Soc. Sci. Comput. Rev. **43**(6), 1181–1195 (2024)
21. Liu, X., Zhang, J., Barany, A., Pankiewicz, M., Baker, R.S.: Assessing the potential and limits of large language models in qualitative coding. In: Advances in Quantitative Ethnography, pp. 89–103 (2024)
22. Xiao, Z., Yuan, X., Liao, Q.V., Abdelghani, R., Oudeyer, P.-Y.: Supporting qualitative analysis with large language models: combining codebook with GPT-3 for deductive coding. In: 28th International Conference on Intelligent User Interfaces, pp. 75–78 (2023)
23. Schut, L., Gal, Y., Farquhar, S.: Do multilingual LLMs think in english? arXiv preprint arXiv:2502.15603. (2025)
24. Thomas, L.D.W., Romasanta, A.K.G., Pujol Priego, L.: Jagged competencies: measuring the reliability of generative AI. J. Bus. Res. **203**, 115804 (2026)

Interorganizational AI Governance in Academic and Grey Literature

Fuad Khan(✉) and Matti Mäntymäki

Turku School of Economics, University of Turku, Turku, Finland
fuhakh@utu.fi

Abstract. The rapid diffusion of artificial intelligence (AI) across critical sectors demands effective AI governance. Although Information Systems (IS) scholarship and practitioner guidance have advanced rapidly, the prevailing conceptualization of AI governance remains predominantly intra-organizational, leaving its interorganizational nature underexplored. This study addresses this gap by examining how AI governance is implemented when governance extends beyond a single organization. We present a conceptual synthesis of 27 academic studies and 27 grey literature documents. We find two governance patterns in interorganizational AI governance: polycentric governance, comprising external scrutiny and collaborative stakeholder engagement, and value chain governance, comprising upstream and downstream governance and risk alleviation. The findings contribute to IS scholarship on AI governance by providing new insights into the characteristics of interorganizational AI governance.

Keywords: AI Governance · Interorganizational AI Governance · Artificial Intelligence Governance · Collaborative Governance · Literature Review

1 Introduction

The rapid diffusion of Artificial Intelligence (AI) in critical sectors such as healthcare, finance, transportation, and rising societal concerns about its risks [15, 17, 29, 42] has spurred demand for AI governance. AI governance refers to "a system of rules, practices, processes, and technological tools that are employed to ensure an organization's use of AI technologies aligns with the organization's strategies, objectives, and values; fulfills legal requirements; and meets ethical AI principles followed by the organization" [19]. At the regulatory level, the need for AI governance has been addressed, for example, with the European Union's AI Act and regulatory developments in the United States [20, 24]. Likewise, international bodies published ethical principles, such as the OECD AI principles and UNESCO's ethics of AI [25, 41].

The growing scholarly interest in AI governance echoes its increasing societal demand. For example, the volume of Information Systems (IS) scholarship on AI governance has been growing rapidly in recent years [5], through synthesizing prior findings and conceptualizing AI governance [2, 5, 29]. Similarly, on the practice side, AI developers, consultancies, and non-governmental institutions such as UNESCO and OECD

Published by Springer Nature Switzerland AG 2027
S. Han et al. (Eds.): I3E 2026, LNCS 16912, pp. 326–336, 2027.
https://doi.org/10.1007/978-3-032-38014-2_24

have been actively promoting AI governance by, for example, developing and proposing AI governance policies and practices [2].

However, such initiatives primarily target organizations to guide their internal governance implementation. Moreover, the prevailing conceptualization of AI governance in the IS literature is at the organizational level, leaving interorganizational framing underexplored, despite the fact that extant research acknowledges the boundary-spanning impact of AI governance and calls for research to address this gap [5, 19, 29]. In practice, organizations rely on interorganizational relationships for AI development as AI systems are often developed by one organization, deployed by another, audited by third parties, and regulated by governments [43]. Hence, AI governance is fundamentally an interorganizational phenomenon.

As a result, this study addresses this gap by focusing on the interorganizational AI governance – when governance spans multiple organizations. We seek to answer the following research question: "What governance patterns characterize interorganizational AI governance in academic and grey literature?" To this end, we present a conceptual synthesis that builds on a systematic review of 54 academic studies and practice-oriented documents. Our findings contribute to the IS scholarship on interorganizational AI governance [2, 5, 19, 29] by identifying its key dimensions and the constituent governance patterns.

2 Background

2.1 AI Governance

The discussion of AI governance in IS literature is currently concentrated on intra-organizational AI governance. More specifically, the dominant discussion revolves around the definition of AI governance [20], internal governance mechanisms, including organizational structures and procedures for AI governance [29], and governance solutions at the organizational level rather than at the national and international levels [2].

2.2 Interorganizational AI Governance

AI development is both an intra- and interorganizational effort, as many internal and external stakeholders are involved in the process. However, the stakeholders' responsibilities may not be apparent in AI governance [18]. Hence, AI governance requires a polycentric governance system [5], understood as the decentralization of governance, in which multiple independent actors exercise decision-making authority and jointly govern a shared problem through interaction and cooperation (adapted from [26, 27]). Polycentric governance is considered an alternative to intra-organizational governance, which has a top-down centralized approach [23]. Thus, polycentric governance enables the development of AI systems and its ecosystems together [5] with other stakeholders, the establishment of intra-organizational structures [29], consensus gaining and the development of standards [5]. In this regard, the literature has emphasized engaging external stakeholders, both nationally and internationally [29]. The identification of these diverse and multidisciplinary stakeholders, including the impacted group of AI systems, and their roles and responsibilities is therefore necessary to include their perspectives and scrutiny in the AI governance discussion [5, 9, 34]. Such inclusiveness ensures consensus-building, shared value identification, concern identification, standard-setting, and oversight of the development and deployment of AI systems [34].

Although there are calls for research on interorganizational AI governance [29], the topic is dispersed across multiple scholarly works but has received less attention in Information Systems literature [2]. Current research acknowledges the need to investigate stakeholder networks and collaborative governance, including multidisciplinary groups [5, 18], as well as to clarify each stakeholder's responsibilities [18]. Moreover, stakeholders' roles and their collaboration from the value chain perspective, especially, in the upstream and downstream actors of the value chain, are scantly discussed in the interorganizational AI governance literature, with some fragmented discussion in AI supply chain accountability [6, 7], third-party audit [31] and emerging work on AI systems insurance [4].

3 Method

3.1 Review of the Academic Literature

To answer our research question: "What governance patterns characterize interorganizational AI governance in academic and grey literature?", we conducted a conceptual synthesis [14] of AI governance discussions at the interorganizational level. We utilized Snyder's [38] literature review process and included the following steps in reviewing academic literature: 1. Research questions, 2. Search terms, 3. Search process, 4. Inclusion/exclusion criteria. We used the search term "AI Governance" (without quotation marks) to capture broader results. We chose the timeline from January 2022 to March 2025, reflecting the rapid development of AI technologies and regulatory developments (e.g., the EU AI Act and evolving AI regulation in the United States).

We searched for empirical research published in the Senior Scholars' Premier Set of 11 Information Systems Journals. We purposefully chose these journals to reflect AI governance discussions in the leading Information Systems scholarship. The search was applied directly to publishers' website, yielding 645 studies after removing duplicates. Thereafter, we screened the papers' titles, keywords, and abstracts to identify those that aligned with our focus. The screening yielded 117 articles discussing AI governance. For further evaluation, we employed three heuristics to determine the inclusion of the papers set for review: 1) Does the paper inform about AI governance implementation? 2) Does the paper inform about AI governance best practices? 3) Does the paper inform about AI governance mechanisms? 17 papers met at least one of these criteria and were thus included. Thereafter, we conducted a backward and forward search based on the papers' references. This led to the identification of 10 additional papers for inclusion. Hence, we identified 27 papers for inclusion in the review of the academic literature on AI governance (see Fig. 1).

3.2 Review of the Grey Literature

Grey literature refers to publicly available, non-commercial documents from governments, academia, business, and industry [3, 28], which can provide meaningful discussions complementing peer-reviewed literature [30].

Hence, we conducted the grey literature search based on Godin et al. [12]. First, we consulted a group of AI governance experts to identify organizations that publish material potentially relevant to our study's objective. As a result of the expert consultation, we identified 26 organizations, including standard-setting bodies, audit firms, management and IT consulting firms, think tanks, and advocacy groups. Thereafter, we conducted a series of internet searches to obtain AI governance-focused documents published by these organizations. Where applicable, we also used search tools on the organizations' websites to locate grey literature documents. For example, research organizations such as the Centre for the Governance of AI, the Ada Lovelace Institute, and the Rand Corporation publish their research on their websites. Overall, the grey literature search yielded 292 documents published between January 2022 and March 2025.

We established inclusion and exclusion criteria to ensure the quality of the grey literature for review. Building on Tyndall's [39] grey literature evaluation checklist, we included the three inclusion criteria: 1) the document needs to include some description of its underlying methodology or data, 2) the document needs to explicate its scope or application area, and 3) the document's publishing data needs to be available. We excluded documents we evaluated as primarily marketing oriented. We also excluded documents with a sole technical or legal focus. As a result of the quality evaluation, we included 27 grey literature documents in the review. Figure 1 presents the literature review process.

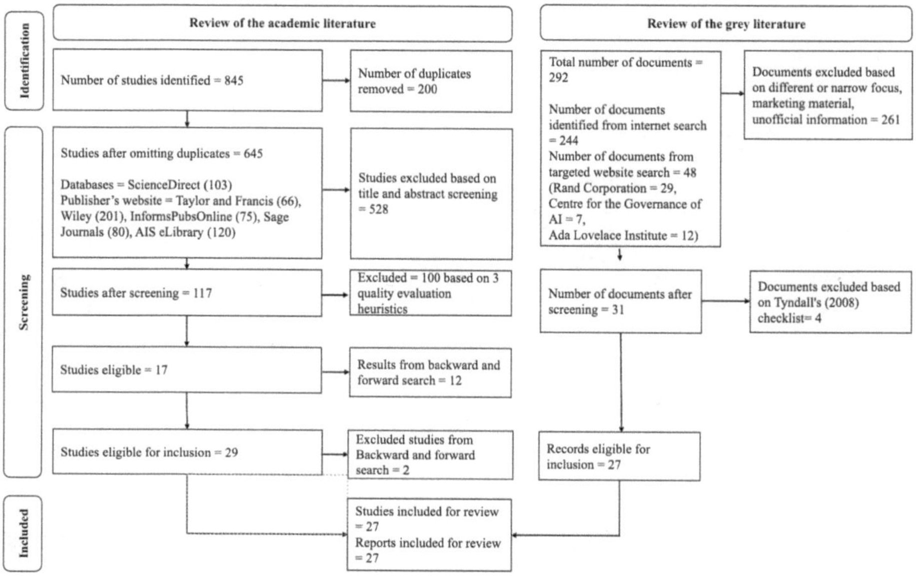

Fig. 1. The Literature review process

3.3 Data Analysis

The data analysis followed an inductive method inspired by the Gioia methodology [11]. The literature corpus under review was comprised of both academic and grey literature on interorganizational AI governance. Each material was coded according to its discussion of governance that extends beyond the boundaries of an organization. In the first stage, the literature was coded inductively to produce first-order concepts closely aligned with the source material. In the second stage, these concepts were iteratively grouped into second-order themes. In the third stage, these themes were aggregated into meaningful dimensions, generating the data structure (see Fig. 2).

4 Results

Based on our literature review, we identified 26 first-order concepts that constitute five second-order themes. We further abstracted these themes into two aggregate dimensions: polycentric governance and value chain governance. Figure 2 presents the data structure summarizing the analysis results. In the following two subsections, we discuss the analysis results along these two aggregate dimensions.

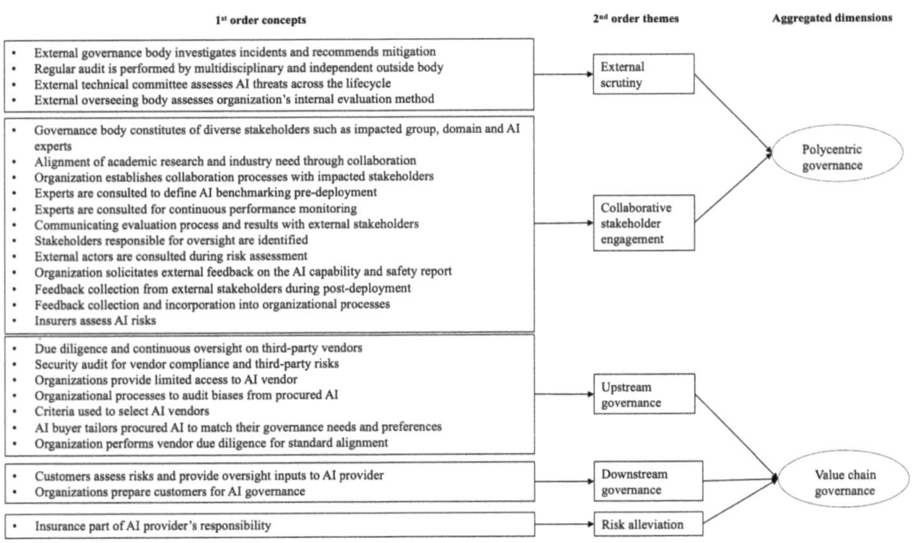

Fig. 2. Data structure

4.1 Polycentric Governance

External Scrutiny. In this study, external scrutiny refers to external stakeholders' involvement in and oversight of AI systems during development and deployment, complementing the organization's internal oversight [5].

External scrutiny by multidisciplinary, independent bodies [8] is an essential characteristic of interorganizational AI governance. This is crucial, as mere internal oversight is insufficient for AI governance [16]. Governance bodies investigate threats to AI systems during development [10] and incidents after deployment [37], and they provide corrective actions [37]. Hence, external scrutiny can span the entire lifecycle of AI development and deployment. In addition to overseeing the AI system in question, governance can include an external assessment of an organization's evaluation method for the AI system [22]. This provides external insights into whether the deploying organization's current governance practices need improvement.

Collaborative Stakeholder Engagement. External scrutiny of AI systems is carried out by external stakeholders. To determine who should be engaged in governing AI systems, it is important to consider diverse external stakeholders, including affected groups [32, 33], AI experts, and domain-specific experts. Organizations can collaborate with impacted stakeholders to understand their values and with experts to govern AI systems across their lifecycle. For example, collaboration between academia and industry, and between organizations and the end user, namely the impacted user group, can help organizations avoid user discrimination and biases [32]. On the other hand, organizations and domain-specific or AI experts can collaborate throughout the AI lifecycle to improve or govern AI systems. For example, organizations can seek consultation when benchmarking [32] and conducting risk assessments [40] of AI systems, collect feedback [1, 40, 44] on the AI capability and safety report [1], and incorporate feedback into their systems and processes [40]. Simultaneously, after deployment, both can collaborate on oversight [40], such as continuous monitoring [32] of the AI systems. Organizations can also collaborate with insurance companies, which evaluate the potential risks posed by the AI system [36] and offer corresponding insurance packages. As a result, organizations are incentivized to reduce risks from their AI development and deployment.

4.2 Value Chain Governance

Upstream Governance. Upstream governance refers to the governance activities between an organization and its upstream stakeholders, i.e., vendors in its value chain. The organization's central objective is to oversee vendors through due diligence and audits. For example, organizations conduct security audits to identify risks arising from third-party vendors [13]. It is therefore necessary to establish organizational processes, such as an audit process for bias [41], and corresponding vendor selection criteria [44], before procuring AI or parts of an AI system. However, pre-procurement audits and due diligence alone may be inadequate. Once AI is procured, organizations may need to tailor the AI system to their governance needs and preferences [44]. Such continuous oversight [21] will likely ensure vendor compliance [13] and alignment of standards between the vendor and the deploying organization [13]. Furthermore, third-party risks from vendors supplying components for AI development also need to be considered. In such cases, organizations can provide limited access to vendors as a mitigation strategy [13].

Downstream Governance. Downstream governance focuses on the activities between the focal organization and its downstream stakeholders, i.e., customers in the value chain.

For example, while it is incumbent upon the organization to prepare its customers for AI governance [35], customers can also conduct their own AI risk assessment and provide oversight inputs to the AI provider [32].

Risk Alleviation. It is the responsibility of the AI provider or the focal organization to insure their AI systems [36]. In this regard, the insurers, as a value chain stakeholder, support the focal organizations by reducing the financial risks. Consequently, AI-related risks for the focal organization and the customer are alleviated.

5 Discussion

5.1 Key Findings

This study examined the research question: "What governance patterns characterize interorganizational AI governance in academic and grey literature?" Our analysis of the literature reveals two governance patterns: polycentric governance and value chain governance, which facilitate interorganizational AI governance.

First, interorganizational AI governance is characterized by polycentric governance, in which governance authority and contributions are distributed among actors outside the focal organization in the AI supply chain. Polycentric governance is driven by two factors: external scrutiny and collaborative stakeholder engagement. External scrutiny provides oversight of the organization's AI systems through regular audits, threat assessments, incident investigations, and mitigative recommendations. External scrutiny is conducted in collaboration with the focal organization, not in isolation. The second factor, collaborative stakeholder engagement, explains such collaboration by deliberately involving diverse actors, including impacted groups of the AI system, academics, domain experts, and AI experts. Thus, collaborative stakeholder engagement enables joint governance efforts for benchmarking, continuous monitoring, and the collection and incorporation of feedback into AI development and deployment. Thus, we respond to previous research calls to investigate stakeholder networks, their responsibilities, collaborative governance [5, 18], and AI systems insurance [4] by elucidating the polycentric governance required for interorganizational AI governance.

Second, interorganizational AI governance is characterized by value chain governance, in which governance is exercised through interactions and relationships among upstream, focal, and downstream actors in the network. Upstream governance reflects one-directional, authoritative oversight that enables the focal organization to oversee and mediate third-party vendors' AI governance practices, which, in turn, contributes to the focal organization's AI governance endeavor. In contrast, downstream governance is reciprocal between the focal organization and downstream actors, e.g., customers who provide risk assessment inputs to improve the AI system. Finally, the reduction of financial risks through insurers in the value network, along with insurance premiums, serves as a governance mechanism in the value chain that incentivizes the focal organization to reduce AI risks. By explicating the relationship of the actors in the value chain, we append new knowledge to the current literary discussion on supply chain accountability [6, 7], and third-party audit [31].

Based on our findings and to answer our research question, we conclude that interorganizational AI governance is characterized by the synergy of two governance patterns: polycentric and value chain governance – distributing oversight authority across independent external actors and embedding governance obligations in the bi-directional relationship.

5.2 Theoretical Implications

Our study extends the current conceptualization of AI governance in IS literature. First, whereas the predominant AI governance narrative has been intraorganizational [5, 19, 29], our analysis reveals that AI governance formation spans multiple organizations. We therefore highlight the shift in focus – from the current central governance towards a decentralized governance system in which the AI system is developed, deployed, and overseen. Second, we contribute to the theoretical framing of AI governance by anchoring it through two traditions: polycentric and value chain governance, which have been examined in isolation. While organizations can treat each governance system separately, together they make interorganizational AI governance practice more robust. Third, by identifying emerging stakeholders, i.e., customers and insurers in interorganizational AI governance, we inform the current calls on each stakeholder's role and responsibility in the value chain [18]. Moreover, our findings suggest that a single stakeholder can play multiple roles; a customer transacts with the AI organization and oversees the AI systems simultaneously, or insurers assess the focal organization's AI risks and absorbs risks partially when necessary. Thus, the hybrid stakeholder role is a key constituent of interorganizational AI governance.

5.3 Practical Implications

There are several practical implications for organizations developing and deploying AI systems. First, the organization's internal AI governance efforts should be complemented by external scrutiny and stakeholder engagement across the value chain throughout the AI lifecycle. Second, AI developers and deployers should rethink their AI governance approach based on customers' and insurers' feedback, driven by their assessments and insurance pricing. Third, for effective interorganizational AI governance, there should be a polycentric structure and sufficient authority among the bodies in governance decision-making.

5.4 Limitations and Future Research

This study has several limitations. First, the broad keyword "AI governance" may have excluded other sources with similar keywords. Second, the timeframe (January 2022–March 2025) limits the identification of longitudinal insights and the tracking of the evolution of practices. Third, grey literature selection was more subjective and selective than that of academic literature, excluding preprints and organizations with a niche focus.

Future work is needed to validate the concepts of interorganizational AI governance identified in this study and identify how they manifest in practice through primary data collection, for example, through semi-structured interviews with AI developers and deployers, AI vendors, and insurance companies. In addition, researchers can examine the effect of interorganizational governance on the intra-organizational AI governance practices. For example, as we observe new actors emerging in the value chain, such as insurance companies, future research could examine whether risk can be transferred or distributed to them, and how such interaction may affect intra-organizational AI governance practices.

References

1. Anthropic: Responsible scaling policy. https://assets.anthropic.com/m/24a47b00f10301cd/original/Anthropic-Responsible-Scaling-Policy-2024-10-15.pdf (2024)
2. Batool, A., Zowghi, D., Bano, M.: AI governance: a systematic literature review. AI Ethics. **5**, 3265–3279 (2025). https://doi.org/10.1007/s43681-024-00653-w
3. Benzies, K.M., Premji, S., Hayden, K.A., Serrett, K.: State-of-the-evidence reviews: advantages and challenges of including grey literature. Worldviews Evid.-Based Nurs. **3**(2), 55–61 (2006). https://doi.org/10.1111/j.1741-6787.2006.00051.x
4. Bertsimas, D., Orfanoudaki, A.: Algorithmic insurance. arXiv preprint arXiv:2106.00839. (2021)
5. Birkstedt, T., Minkkinen, M., Tandon, A., Mäntymäki, M.: AI governance: themes, knowledge gaps and future agendas. Internet Res. **33**(7), 133–167 (2023). https://doi.org/10.1108/intr-01-2022-0042
6. Cobbe, J., Singh, J.: Artificial intelligence as a service: legal responsibilities, liabilities, and policy challenges. Comput. Law Secur. Rev. **42**, 105573 (2021). https://doi.org/10.1016/j.clsr.2021.105573
7. Cobbe, J., Veale, M., Singh, J.: Understanding accountability in algorithmic supply chains, 1186–1197 (2023). https://doi.org/10.1145/3593013.3594073
8. De Laat, P.B.: Companies committed to responsible AI: from principles towards implementation and regulation? Philos. Technol. **34**(4), 1135–1193 (2021). https://doi.org/10.1007/s13347-021-00474-3
9. Deshpande, A., Sharp, H.: Responsible AI systems: who are the stakeholders?, 227–236 (2022). https://doi.org/10.1145/3514094.3534187
10. European Telecommunications Standards Institute: ETSI activities in the field of artificial intelligence preparing the implementation of the European AI Act. White Paper No. 52. https://www.etsi.org/images/files/ETSIWhitePapers/ETSI-WP52-ETSI-activities-in-the-field-of-AI.pdf (2022)
11. Gioia, D.A., Corley, K.G., Hamilton, A.L.: Seeking qualitative rigor in inductive research: notes on the Gioia methodology. Organ. Res. Methods. **16**(1), 15–31 (2013). https://doi.org/10.1177/1094428112452151
12. Godin, K., Stapleton, J., Kirkpatrick, S.I., Hanning, R.M., Leatherdale, S.T.: Applying systematic review search methods to the grey literature: a case study examining guidelines for school-based breakfast programs in Canada. Syst. Rev. **4**(1), 438 (2015). https://doi.org/10.1186/s13643-015-0125-0
13. International Association of Privacy Professionals: AI governance in practice report. https://iapp.org/media/pdf/resource_center/ai_governance_in_practice_report_2024.pdf (2024)
14. Jaakkola, E.: Designing conceptual articles: four approaches. AMS Rev. **10**, 18–26 (2020). https://doi.org/10.1007/s13162-020-00161-0
15. Jafari, A.A., Ozcinar, C., Anbarjafari, G.: Responsible AI: the good, the bad, the AI. arXiv preprint arXiv:2601.21095. (2026)

16. Janssen, M., Brous, P., Estevez, E., Barbosa, L.S., Janowski, T.: Data governance: organizing data for trustworthy artificial intelligence. Gov. Inf. Q. **37**(3), 101493 (2020). https://doi.org/10.1016/j.giq.2020.101493
17. Khoo, S., Foo, J., Lee, R.K.: With great capabilities come great responsibilities: introducing the agentic risk & capability framework for governing agentic AI systems. arXiv preprint arXiv:2512.22211. (2025)
18. Kuehnert, B., Kim, R., Forlizzi, J., Heidari, H.: The "who", "what", and "how" of responsible AI governance: a systematic review and meta-analysis of (actor, stage)-specific tools, 2991–3005 (2025). https://doi.org/10.1145/3715275.3732191
19. Mäntymäki, M., Minkkinen, M., Birkstedt, T., Viljanen, M.: Defining organizational AI governance. AI Ethics. **2**, 603–609 (2022). https://doi.org/10.1007/s43681-022-00143-x
20. Mäntymäki, M., Minkkinen, M., Zimmer, M.P., Birkstedt, T., Viljanen, M.: Designing an AI governance framework: from research-based premises to meta-requirements. In: ECIS 2023 Research Papers, Paper 295 (2023) https://aisel.aisnet.org/ecis2023_rp/295
21. McKinsey & Company: Responsible AI principles. https://www.mckinsey.com/capabilities/quantumblack/how-we-help-clients/generative-ai/responsible-ai-principles (n.d.)
22. Microsoft: responsible AI standard: general requirements. https://cdn-dynmedia-1.microsoft.com/is/content/microsoftcorp/microsoft/final/en-us/microsoft-brand/documents/Microsoft-Responsible-AI-Standard-General-Requirements.pdf (2022)
23. Mindel, V., Mathiassen, L., Rai, A.: The sustainability of polycentric information commons. MIS Q. **42**(2), 607–631 (2018). https://doi.org/10.25300/misq/2018/14015
24. Novelli, C., Hacker, P., Morley, J., Trondal, J., Floridi, L.: A robust governance for the AI act: AI office, AI board, scientific panel, and national authorities. Euro. J. Risk Regul. **16**(2), 566–590 (2025). https://doi.org/10.1017/err.2024.57
25. OECD: AI principles. https://www.oecd.org/en/topics/sub-issues/ai-principles.html (2024)
26. Ostrom, E.: Beyond markets and states: polycentric governance of complex economic systems. Am. Econ. Rev. **100**(3), 641–672 (2010). https://doi.org/10.1257/aer.100.3.641
27. Ostrom, V., Tiebout, C.M., Warren, R.: The organization of government in metropolitan areas: a theoretical inquiry. Am. Polit. Sci. Rev. **55**(4), 831–842 (1961). https://doi.org/10.2307/1952530
28. Paez, A.: Gray literature: an important resource in systematic reviews. J. Evid. Based Med. **10**(3), 233–240 (2017). https://doi.org/10.1111/jebm.12266
29. Papagiannidis, E., Mikalef, P., Conboy, K.: Responsible artificial intelligence governance: a review and research framework. J. Strateg. Inf. Syst. **34**(2), 101885 (2025). https://doi.org/10.1016/j.jsis.2024.101885
30. Pappas, C., Williams, I.: Grey literature: its emerging importance. J. Hosp. Librariansh. **11**(3), 228–234 (2011). https://doi.org/10.1080/15323269.2011.587100
31. Raji, I.D., Xu, P., Honigsberg, C., Ho, D.: Outsider oversight: designing a third party audit ecosystem for AI governance, 557–571 (2022). https://doi.org/10.1145/3514094.3534181
32. Rakova, B., Yang, J., Cramer, H., Chowdhury, R.: Where responsible AI meets reality. Proc. ACM Hum.-Comput. Interact. **5**(CSCW1), 1–23 (2021). https://doi.org/10.1145/3449081
33. Reddy, S., Allan, S., Coghlan, S., Cooper, P.: A governance model for the application of AI in health care. J. Am. Med. Inform. Assoc. **27**(3), 491–497 (2019). https://doi.org/10.1093/jamia/ocz192
34. Rozenblit, L., et al.: Toward responsible AI governance: balancing multi-stakeholder perspectives on AI in healthcare. Int. J. Med. Inform. **203**, 106015 (2025). https://doi.org/10.1016/j.ijmedinf.2025.106015
35. Schneider, J., Abraham, R., Meske, C., Vom Brocke, J.: Artificial intelligence governance for businesses. Inf. Syst. Manag. **40**(3), 229–249 (2022). https://doi.org/10.1080/10580530.2022.2085825

36. Shneiderman, B.: Bridging the gap between ethics and practice. ACM Trans. Interact. Intell. Syst. **10**(4), 1–31 (2020). https://doi.org/10.1145/3419764
37. Simpson, M., Ortega, A., Trager, R.: Voluntary industry initiatives in frontier AI governance: lessons from aviation and nuclear power. Oxford Martin AI Governance Initiative. https://aigi.ox.ac.uk/publications/voluntary-industry-initiatives-in-frontier-ai-governance-lessons-from-aviation-and-nuclear-power/ (2025)
38. Snyder, H.: Literature review as a research methodology: an overview and guidelines. J. Bus. Res. **104**, 333–339 (2019). https://doi.org/10.1016/j.jbusres.2019.07.039
39. Tyndall, J.: How low can you go? Towards a hierarchy of grey literature. In: Conference: Dreaming08: Australian Library and Information Association Biennial Conference, Alice Springs. https://core.ac.uk/download/pdf/14931482.pdf (2008)
40. U.S. National Institute of Standards and Technology: Artificial Intelligence Risk Management Framework (AI RMF 1.0) (2023). https://doi.org/10.6028/nist.ai.100-1
41. UNESCO: Ethical impact assessment: a tool of the recommendation on the ethics of artificial intelligence. https://www.unesco.org/en/articles/ethical-impact-assessment-tool-recommendation-ethics-artificial-intelligence (2023)
42. Wang, X., Xie, F.: Global artificial intelligence governance research in the digital and intelligent era: advances, trends and countermeasures. J. Knowl. Manag. **30**(1), 30–68 (2025). https://doi.org/10.1108/jkm-01-2025-0006
43. Widder, D.G., Nafus, D.: Dislocated accountabilities in the "AI supply chain": modularity and developers' notions of responsibility. Big Data Soc. **10**(1) (2023). https://doi.org/10.1177/20539517231177620
44. Yeung, D., et al.: Steps toward AI Governance: Insights and Recommendations from the 2024 Equal AI Summit. RAND Corporation, Santa Monica, CA (2025). https://doi.org/10.7249/cfa3799-1

Algorithmic Trust and Institutional Trust in Automated Insurance Decisions: An Empirical Study of AI Governance and User Responses

George Maramba([✉]) and Hanlie Smuts

University of Pretoria, Pretoria, South Africa
{george.maramba,hanlie.smuts}@up.ac.za

Abstract. Artificial intelligence is increasingly embedded in financial services, particularly in insurance underwriting and claims assessment, where algorithmic systems enable automated decision-making. While these technologies offer efficiency and predictive advantages, they also raise concerns related to transparency, fairness, and trust. In high-stakes contexts such as insurance, acceptance of AI-driven decisions depends not only on perceptions of the algorithm but also on trust in the institutions deploying these systems. However, existing research often treats trust in AI as a single construct, overlooking the interaction between institutional trust and algorithmic trust. This study empirically examines how institutional trust, algorithmic trust, and governance dimensions influence users' acceptance of and responses to AI-driven insurance decisions. A scenario-based survey experiment was conducted, yielding 162 valid responses, and analysed using partial least squares structural equation modelling. The findings show that trust in AI systems is multi-dimensional but conditional. While institutional trust positively influences algorithmic trust, overall trust remains moderate, and acceptance is relatively low. Participants demonstrate a strong willingness to challenge decisions and seek human intervention. Governance dimensions contribute to trust formation, but their effects are moderate. These findings demonstrate that trust in AI-driven insurance decisions emerges through the interaction of institutional trust, algorithmic trust, and governance dimensions rather than through technological factors alone. Furthermore, the results show that trust does not necessarily translate into acceptance, as users remain willing to challenge automated decisions when adequate contestability mechanisms are absent. By integrating trust formation with behavioural responses, this study extends the literature on digital trust and AI governance. It advances understanding of user engagement with AI-enabled decision systems in high-stakes environments.

Keywords: Algorithmic Trust · Institutional Trust · Artificial Intelligence · Digital Trust · Automated Decision Systems · AI Governance · Transparency and Fairness

Published by Springer Nature Switzerland AG 2027
S. Han et al. (Eds.): I3E 2026, LNCS 16912, pp. 337–354, 2027.
https://doi.org/10.1007/978-3-032-38014-2_25

1 Introduction

Artificial intelligence (AI) is increasingly embedded in financial services, particularly in insurance underwriting and claims assessment, where algorithmic systems enable automated risk evaluation and decision-making [1–3]. While these technologies offer efficiency and predictive advantages, they also raise concerns related to transparency, fairness, and trust in digital service environments [1–3].

In high-stakes contexts such as insurance, these concerns are amplified as automated decisions directly influence individuals' access to coverage, pricing, and financial protection. Algorithmic decision systems rely on large volumes of customer data to assess risk, but their opacity and potential for bias raise questions regarding accountability and legitimacy [4–6]. AI-driven insurance decisions directly affect individuals' access to coverage and financial protection, users evaluate not only the technical performance of the algorithm but also the trustworthiness of the organisation responsible for deploying it. Accordingly, acceptance of automated decisions depends on both algorithmic trust and institutional trust.

Recent research on digital trust highlights the importance of understanding how individuals form trust in AI-enabled decision environments [7, 8]. Trust in such systems is shaped by both technological performance and institutional factors, including organisational credibility and governance practices [9, 10]. This suggests that trust in AI-driven decision systems is multi-dimensional, involving both trust in the organisation and trust in the algorithmic system itself.

AI Governance dimensions such as transparency, fairness, and human oversight play a key role in shaping trust in algorithmic decision systems [8, 11, 12]. In this study, governance dimensions refer to transparency, fairness, and human oversight as key organisational features that shape trust in AI-enabled decision systems. Perceived fairness has been shown to influence trust and legitimacy in digital decision-making environments, particularly in financial services [13]. Similarly, transparency and explainability affect users' understanding of automated decisions, while human oversight provides accountability and opportunities for intervention [14, 15].

Despite growing research on AI governance and digital trust, limited attention has been given to how institutional trust and algorithmic trust interact in shaping responses to automated insurance decisions. Much of the existing literature conceptualises trust in AI primarily as a technological construct, overlooking the role of institutional context and AI Governance dimensions in influencing user perceptions.

This study empirically examines how institutional trust, algorithmic trust, and AI Governance dimensions influence users' acceptance of and responses to AI-driven insurance decisions. It specifically investigates the role of transparency, fairness, and human oversight in shaping trust and behavioural outcomes, including acceptance and contestation.

This study makes three contributions to research on digital trust and AI governance. First, it provides empirical evidence on the relationship between institutional trust and algorithmic trust in AI-enabled decision systems. Second, it extends trust transfer theory by demonstrating how trust in organisations influences perceptions of algorithmic systems [7, 8]. Third, it examines how AI Governance dimensions shape trust and behavioural responses, highlighting the importance of contestation in user engagement with AI-driven decisions.

Accordingly, the study addresses the following research question:

How do institutional trust, algorithmic trust, and AI Governance dimensions influence users' acceptance of and responses to automated insurance decisions?

The remainder of this paper is structured as follows. Section 2 reviews the literature, Sect. 3 presents the research model, Sect. 4 outlines the methodology, Sect. 5 presents the results, Sect. 6 discusses the findings, and Sect. 7 concludes the paper.

2 Background

2.1 Digital Trust in AI Systems

Digital trust refers to users' confidence in digital technologies and the organisations that deploy them [7, 16]. In AI-enabled decision environments, trust is shaped by perceptions of system performance, reliability, and fairness, as well as broader institutional factors [9, 10, 17].

Unlike traditional information systems, AI systems often operate as opaque "black boxes," making it difficult for users to fully understand how decisions are generated [4]. This opacity introduces uncertainty, requiring users to rely on trust when interacting with algorithmic systems [5, 6, 18]. Because AI-driven insurance decisions directly affect individuals' financial outcomes, users are likely to evaluate both the technical characteristics of the AI system and the trustworthiness of the organisation responsible for deploying it [7, 16]. Accordingly, trust and acceptance of automated insurance decisions are shaped by perceptions of both algorithmic performance and institutional credibility.

2.2 Trust in Financial and Insurance Contexts

Trust plays a central role in financial services, where decisions directly affect individuals' economic well-being. In insurance, trust is particularly important due to the complexity of underwriting and claims processes, as well as the information asymmetry between insurers and customers [3, 19, 20].

The introduction of AI in insurance decision-making has amplified trust-related concerns. While algorithmic systems can improve efficiency and consistency, they also raise issues related to fairness, transparency, and accountability [5, 6]. Consequently, trust in AI-driven insurance decisions depends not only on the perceived accuracy of the system but also on confidence in the organisation deploying it.

2.3 Institutional Trust

Institutional trust refers to users' confidence in the organisation responsible for deploying and managing AI systems [9, 12, 21]. Perceptions of organisational competence, integrity, and governance practices shape it. In AI-enabled environments, institutional trust provides an important foundation for user acceptance.

When users perceive organisations as responsible and accountable, they are more likely to trust the technologies those organisations deploy [10, 22, 23]. This relationship reflects the principle of trust transfer, where trust in an institution influences trust in associated technologies [7, 16, 24].

2.4 Algorithmic Trust

Algorithmic trust refers to users' confidence in the AI system itself, including its reliability, accuracy, and fairness [7, 16]. Unlike institutional trust, which is organisation-based, algorithmic trust is shaped by perceptions of system performance and decision quality.

AI systems present unique challenges for trust formation due to their complexity and limited transparency [4, 25]. Users may find it difficult to evaluate how decisions are generated, leading to uncertainty and reliance on indirect cues such as explanations, outcomes, and perceived fairness [5, 6, 26].

Although institutional trust can influence algorithmic trust, the relationship is not absolute. Users may differentiate between trust in the organisation and trust in the system, particularly when decisions have significant personal consequences.

2.5 Transparency in AI Decision-Making

Transparency refers to the extent to which users can understand how AI systems generate decisions [8, 27]. In algorithmic contexts, transparency is often associated with explainability, clarity, and the provision of meaningful information about decision processes.

Higher levels of transparency can improve user understanding and reduce uncertainty, thereby supporting trust formation [11, 28–30]. However, transparency does not always guarantee trust, particularly when explanations are incomplete or difficult to interpret.

2.6 Fairness in AI Systems

Fairness reflects the extent to which AI systems are perceived as unbiased and equitable in their decision-making [13, 14]. In financial contexts, fairness is closely linked to legitimacy and user acceptance. Perceptions of unfair treatment can undermine trust and lead to resistance or rejection of automated decisions. Conversely, fair and consistent decision-making enhances confidence in AI systems and supports acceptance [8, 11, 31].

2.7 Human Oversight and AI Governance

Human oversight refers to the involvement of human actors in monitoring, reviewing, or intervening in AI-driven decisions [14, 32]. It is a key component of AI governance frameworks, aimed at ensuring accountability and mitigating risks associated with automated decision-making.

Oversight can take multiple forms, including passive monitoring and active intervention. Importantly, users may distinguish between these forms, placing greater value on the ability to challenge decisions than on continuous human involvement [15, 27, 33].

2.8 Research Gap

Despite extensive research on digital trust and AI governance, limited attention has been given to how institutional trust, algorithmic trust, and AI Governance dimensions interact in shaping user responses to AI-driven insurance decisions.

Existing studies often examine these factors in isolation, with a particular emphasis on technological aspects of trust. As a result, there is a need for empirical research that integrates institutional, technological, and governance principles to better understand trust formation and behavioural responses, including acceptance and contestation. Table 1 provides an overview of the core constructs and their theoretical grounding within the context of AI-driven decision systems.

Together, these constructs form the conceptual foundation for the research model developed in this study.

3 Research Model and Hypotheses

3.1 Research Model

Building on the literature, this study examines how institutional trust, algorithmic trust, and AI Governance dimensions influence users' acceptance of and responses to AI-driven insurance decisions. The research model integrates these constructs to capture both trust formation and behavioural outcomes.

Figure 1 illustrates the proposed research model, depicting both the trust transfer process from institutional trust to algorithmic trust and the direct and indirect pathways through which trust and governance dimensions influence behavioural outcomes.

The model specifies both a direct effect of institutional trust on acceptance and an indirect effect mediated through algorithmic trust, consistent with trust transfer theory. This dual-path structure reflects the proposition that confidence in the organisation may influence users' willingness to accept AI-driven decisions both independently and through enhanced trust in the algorithm itself.

3.2 Institutional Trust and Algorithmic Trust

Institutional trust is expected to influence algorithmic trust through trust transfer, whereby confidence in an organisation extends to the technologies it deploys [7, 16]. In AI-enabled contexts, organisational credibility and governance practices shape users' perceptions of system reliability [9, 10].

H1: Institutional trust positively influences algorithmic trust.

Table 1. Summary of Key Constructs and Theoretical Foundations

Construct	Definition	Theoretical Basis	Key References
Institutional Trust	Confidence in the organisation deploying the AI system	Trust Transfer Theory	Glikson & Woolley (2020); Shin (2021); Jussupow et al. (2021); Choung et al. (2023); OECD (2024)
Algorithmic Trust	Confidence in the AI system's reliability and decision-making	Digital Trust / AI Trust	Glikson & Woolley (2020); Rai (2020); Lockey et al. (2021); Dwivedi et al. (2023); Shin (2024)
Transparency	Degree to which AI decisions are understandable	Explainability / AI Governance	Shin & Park (2021); Wirtz & Weyerer. (2023); European Commission (2024)
Fairness	Perceived equity and absence of bias in decisions	Algorithmic Fairness	Teng (2025); Shin & Park (2021); UNESCO (2023)
Human Oversight	Human involvement in monitoring or reviewing AI decisions	AI Governance / Accountability	Floridi et al. (2021); European Commission (2024)
Acceptance	Willingness to rely on AI decisions	Technology Acceptance	Jussupow et al. (2021); Venkatesh et al. (2023)
Contestation	Willingness to challenge AI decisions	Behavioural Response / AI Governance	OECD (2024); European Commission (2024)

3.3 Algorithmic Trust and Acceptance

Algorithmic trust reflects users' confidence in the AI system's reliability and decision quality [7, 16]. Higher levels of trust are expected to increase users' willingness to rely on automated decisions [10].

H2: Algorithmic trust positively influences acceptance of AI-driven decisions.

3.4 Institutional Trust and Acceptance

Although institutional trust is expected to influence acceptance indirectly through algorithmic trust, prior research suggests that confidence in the organisation responsible for deploying AI systems may also directly shape users' willingness to accept automated decisions. Institutional reputation and effective governance practices reduce uncertainty independently of perceptions of the algorithm itself, thereby increasing users' willingness to accept AI-driven decisions and providing theoretical support for a direct relationship between institutional trust and acceptance [7, 9]

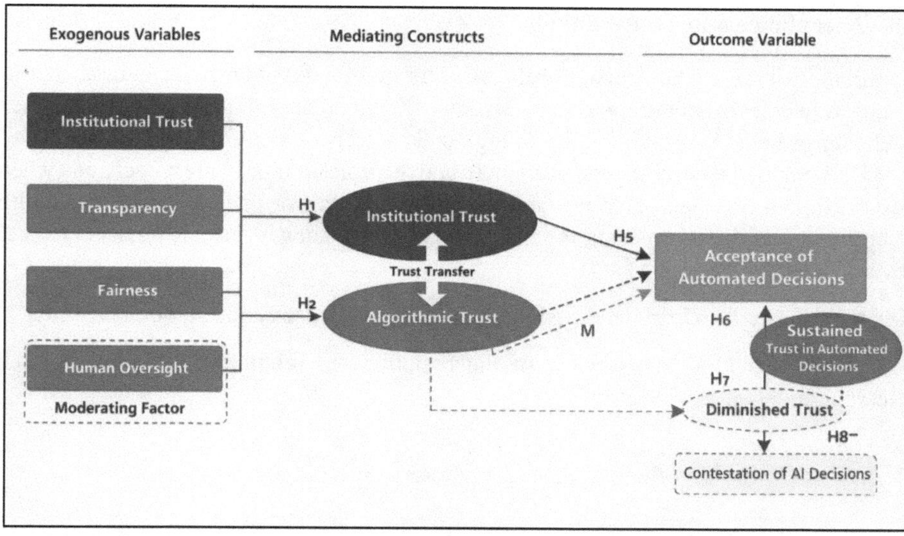

Fig. 1. Research Model of Trust in Automated Insurance Decisions

H3: Institutional trust positively influences acceptance of AI-driven decisions.

3.5 Algorithmic Trust and Trust in Decisions

Algorithmic trust reflects users' confidence in the reliability and competence of AI systems. Beyond influencing behavioural acceptance, higher levels of algorithmic trust are expected to strengthen confidence in the correctness and legitimacy of specific automated decisions. Accordingly, algorithmic trust is hypothesised to positively influence trust in automated decisions [7, 16, 18].

H4: Algorithmic trust positively influences trust in automated decisions.

3.6 Moderating Role of Human Oversight

Human oversight provides accountability and can strengthen trust in AI systems by enabling review and intervention [14, 33]. The presence of oversight is expected to enhance the relationship between algorithmic trust and acceptance.

H5: Human oversight positively moderates the relationship between algorithmic trust and acceptance.

3.7 AI Governance Dimensions and Algorithmic Trust

Transparency and fairness are key AI governance dimensions that influence trust in AI systems [8, 11]. Transparency improves understanding of decision processes, while fairness enhances perceptions of legitimacy [13].

H6: Transparency positively influences algorithmic trust.
H7: Fairness positively influences algorithmic trust.

3.8 Acceptance and Contestation

Acceptance of AI-driven decisions reflects users' willingness to rely on automated outcomes. Lower levels of acceptance are associated with increased likelihood of resistance or challenge behaviour, particularly in high-stakes decision contexts [5, 14, 16].

In AI-enabled environments, users may actively question or contest decisions when trust is limited or when outcomes are perceived as unfair or unclear. This aligns with emerging research emphasising the importance of user agency and contestability in AI governance [11, 14].

H8: Acceptance of AI-driven decisions negatively influences contestation behaviour.

Table 2 provides an overview of the hypothesised relationships underlying the research model.

Table 2. Summary of Research Hypotheses

Hypothesis	Relationship	Expected Effect
H1	Institutional Trust → Algorithmic Trust	Positive
H2	Algorithmic Trust → Acceptance of Automated Decisions	Positive
H3	Institutional Trust → Acceptance of Automated Decisions	Positive
H4	Algorithmic Trust → Trust in Automated Decisions	Positive
H5	Human Oversight moderates the relationship between Algorithmic Trust and Acceptance of Automated Decisions	Positive Moderation
H6	Transparency → Algorithmic Trust	Positive
H7	Fairness → Algorithmic Trust	Positive
H8	Acceptance of Automated Decisions → Contestation of AI Decisions	Negative

Together, these hypotheses form the basis for the empirical testing of the research model.

4 Methodology

4.1 Research Design

This study employed a **scenario-based survey design** to examine user responses to AI-driven insurance decisions. Scenario-based methods allow controlled manipulation of key variables while simulating realistic decision environments [10].

4.2 Experiment Design

A 2 × 2 experimental design was used, manipulating:

- Transparency (high vs low)
- Human oversight (present vs absent)

This resulted in four scenarios describing AI-driven underwriting decisions under different governance conditions. The scenarios were designed to reflect realistic insurance decision contexts. The experimental conditions are summarized in Table 3.

Table 3. Experimental Design

Condition	Transparency	Human Oversight
Scenario 1	High	Present
Scenario 2	High	Absent
Scenario 3	Low	Present
Scenario 4	Low	Absent

As shown in Table 3, the four scenarios reflect different combinations of transparency and human oversight conditions used in the study.

The experimental scenarios were based on a fictitious insurance provider to minimise the influence of existing brand perceptions and organisational reputation on respondents' evaluations. This approach ensured that participants' responses were driven by the manipulated governance conditions rather than prior experiences with a specific insurer.

4.3 Data Collection

The respondents were recruited through an online survey distributed to individuals familiar with digital services and AI-enabled technologies. Participants were primarily drawn from South Africa, reflecting the study's focus on AI-driven insurance decision-making within an emerging digital economy. The sample comprised a heterogeneous group of adults, thereby capturing a broader range of perceptions regarding institutional trust and AI adoption. Participation was voluntary and anonymous. Of the 200 survey invitations distributed, 162 participants completed the questionnaire and provided valid responses for analysis, resulting in a response rate of 81%.

4.4 Measurement Instrument

All constructs were measured using multi-item Likert scales adapted from prior studies [7, 10, 16]. All items were measured on a 5-point Likert scale. The measurement items were adapted from validated scales reported in prior studies on institutional trust, algorithmic trust, transparency, fairness, and technology acceptance, with minor wording modifications to reflect the insurance context.

The questionnaire captured constructs related to institutional trust, algorithmic trust, governance dimensions (transparency, fairness, and human oversight), and behavioural responses, including acceptance and contestation.

4.5 Data Analysis

Data were analysed using Partial Least Squares Structural Equation Modelling (PLS-SEM), which is suitable for exploratory models and moderate sample sizes [34]. Bootstrapping was used to assess the significance of path relationships.

4.6 Ethical Considerations

Participation was voluntary and anonymous. Participants were informed of the study purpose and provided consent before participation.

5 Results

5.1 Sample Characteristics

A total of 200 responses were collected, of which 162 were complete and valid for analysis, yielding a completion rate of approximately 81%. The remaining 38 responses were excluded due to incomplete participation or early withdrawal. Participants were distributed across the four experimental conditions, ensuring a balanced representation for the 2 × 2 design (transparency × human oversight). The sample represented a diverse range of demographic backgrounds in terms of age, education, and familiarity with AI, providing a suitable sample for examining perceptions of AI-driven insurance decision systems. Detailed statistical results are presented in the tables to avoid redundancy in the text.

5.2 Manipulation Checks

Manipulation checks were conducted to assess whether participants perceived differences in transparency and human oversight across the experimental conditions. The results indicate moderate levels of perceived transparency, with mean scores ranging between 2.84 and 3.21 on a 5-point Likert scale. Table 4 presents the manipulation check results.

Table 4. Transparency Manipulation Check Results

Construct	Item	Mean
Transparency	AI system clearly explained the decision	3.20
Transparency	Understanding of how decision was reached	3.21
Transparency	Decision process is clear	2.96
Transparency	System provides understandable explanations	2.84
Human Oversight	Human experts reviewed decision	2.15
Human Oversight	Human experts monitor AI decisions	3.00
Human Oversight	Human can review decision if requested	4.04

The results indicate moderate perceptions of transparency and variation in perceived oversight. Notably, participants reported lower perceptions of direct human review but higher confidence in their ability to request intervention, suggesting that contestability is more salient than continuous oversight.

5.3 Descriptive Statistics

Descriptive analysis indicates moderate levels of trust across constructs, with lower acceptance of automated decisions and a relatively high willingness to contest outcomes. Table 5 summarises the descriptive statistics.

Table 5. Descriptive Statistics

Construct	Mean	Interpretation
Institutional Trust	3.20	Moderate
Algorithmic Trust	3.10	Moderate
Transparency	3.00	Moderate
Fairness	3.30	Moderate
Human Oversight	3.06	Moderate
Acceptance	2.81	Low
Trust in Decisions	3.00	Moderate
Contestation	3.80	High

These findings suggest that users exhibit cautious trust, with limited willingness to accept AI decisions and a strong inclination to challenge them.

5.4 Measurement Model Assessment

The measurement model was assessed for reliability and validity using established PLS-SEM criteria. Table 6 presents the measurement model results.

Table 6. Measurement Model Assessment

Construct	Cronbach's Alpha	CR	AVE
Institutional Trust	0.84	0.89	0.68
Transparency	0.81	0.87	0.63
Fairness	0.86	0.90	0.69
Algorithmic Trust	0.88	0.91	0.72
Human Oversight	0.80	0.86	0.61
Acceptance	0.89	0.92	0.75
Trust in Decisions	0.85	0.89	0.67
Contestation	0.82	0.87	0.63

All constructs demonstrate acceptable reliability and validity, exceeding recommended thresholds.

5.5 Structural Model Results

The structural model was assessed using bootstrapping with 5,000 resamples. Table 7 summarises the hypothesis testing results.

Table 7. Structural Model Results

Hypothesis	Path	Beta	t-value	p-value	Result
H1	Institutional Trust → Algorithmic Trust	0.42	4.21	<0.001	Supported
H2	Algorithmic Trust → Acceptance	0.48	5.10	<0.001	Supported
H3	Institutional Trust → Acceptance	0.21	2.45	0.014	Supported
H4	Algorithmic Trust → Trust in Decisions	0.55	6.02	<0.001	Supported
H5	Human Oversight (Moderation)	0.17	2.01	0.045	Supported
H6	Transparency → Algorithmic Trust	0.29	3.12	0.002	Supported
H7	Fairness → Algorithmic Trust	0.37	3.95	<0.001	Supported
H8	Acceptance → Contestation	−0.33	3.40	<0.001	Supported

The results confirm that:

- Institutional trust positively influences algorithmic trust, supporting the trust transfer mechanism.
- Algorithmic trust significantly influences both acceptance and trust in automated decisions, confirming its central role.
- Transparency and fairness both positively influence algorithmic trust, demonstrating the importance of AI governance dimensions in fostering user trust.
- Human oversight strengthens the relationship between algorithmic trust and acceptance, indicating that oversight plays a reinforcing role in trust formation.
- Acceptance of automated decisions is negatively associated with contestation, suggesting that lower acceptance increases the likelihood of challenging AI decisions.

5.6 Explanatory Power

The model demonstrates **moderate explanatory power,** particularly for key trust and behavioural constructs. Table 8 presents the R^2 values.

Table 8. Explanatory Power (R^2)

Construct	R^2
Algorithmic Trust	0.52
Acceptance of Automated Decisions	0.61
Trust in Automated Decisions	0.48
Contestation of AI Decisions	0.28

These results indicate that the model explains meaningful variance in both trust formation and behavioural responses, including contestation.

5.7 Summary of Findings

The findings indicate that trust in AI-driven insurance decisions is multi-dimensional but conditional. While institutional trust supports algorithmic trust, overall acceptance remains relatively low, and users demonstrate a strong willingness to challenge decisions. Governance dimensions contribute to trust formation, but their effects are moderate, with users placing greater emphasis on the ability to contest decisions rather than on continuous oversight.

6 Discussion and Theoretical Implications

6.1 Discussion of Findings

This study examined how institutional trust, algorithmic trust, and governance dimensions influence user responses to AI-driven insurance decisions. The findings support a dual-layer perspective of trust, while revealing important behavioural nuances in high-stakes contexts.

First, institutional trust positively influences algorithmic trust, supporting trust transfer [7, 16]. However, observed trust levels were moderate, indicating that institutional credibility alone does not fully establish confidence in AI systems.

Second, algorithmic trust drives acceptance and trust in decisions, but acceptance levels were relatively low (below the midpoint). This suggests users remain cautious and do not readily rely on AI in financially consequential contexts.

Third, transparency and fairness positively influence trust, but their effects are moderate rather than strong [11, 16]. The manipulation results indicate that explainability alone does not eliminate uncertainty, reinforcing the conditional nature of trust in AI systems.

A key finding concerns human oversight. Participants reported low perceptions of direct human review but high confidence in their ability to request intervention. This suggests users distinguish between passive monitoring and active recourse, deriving greater confidence from the ability to challenge decisions than from continuous oversight.

Finally, acceptance is negatively associated with contestation, with participants showing a strong willingness to challenge AI decisions. This indicates that users actively evaluate and resist automated outcomes when necessary, reflecting expectations of fairness and accountability in algorithmic decision-making.

Taken together, the findings explain how institutional trust, algorithmic trust, and governance dimensions jointly influence users' acceptance of and responses to AI-driven insurance decisions. Institutional trust provides an initial foundation of confidence in the organisation, which transfers to perceptions of the AI system and strengthens algorithmic trust. Governance dimensions, particularly transparency and fairness, reinforce this process by enhancing perceptions of legitimacy and accountability. Algorithmic trust subsequently shapes users' willingness to accept automated decisions, whereas lower levels of acceptance increase the likelihood of contestation and requests for human intervention. Rather than operating independently, these constructs interact to produce cautious and conditional trust, demonstrating that behavioural acceptance depends not only on confidence in AI but also on the availability of mechanisms that enable users to question or challenge automated outcomes.

Collectively, these findings demonstrate that trust in AI-enabled insurance decisions is a sequential and conditional process in which institutional trust establishes confidence in the organisation, algorithmic trust shapes confidence in the technology, and AI governance dimensions determine whether this trust translates into behavioural acceptance or contestation.

6.2 Theoretical Contributions

This study contributes to research on digital trust, AI governance, and automated decision-making in four ways.

First, it provides empirical support for a dual-layer trust perspective, showing that institutional and algorithmic trust are distinct but related, with only partial transfer between them.

Second, it extends trust transfer theory by demonstrating that trust in AI is conditional and not fully inherited from institutions [7, 16]. Users independently evaluate algorithmic systems even when institutional trust is present.

Third, the study advances AI governance research by showing that transparency and fairness contribute to trust, but that contestability plays a more critical role. The findings suggest a shift from static governance dimensions toward user-centric accountability structures [14].

Fourth, it introduces contestation as a behavioural outcome, showing that resistance and challenge are integral to how users engage with AI systems, particularly in high-stakes contexts.

6.3 Implications for Digital Trust Research

The findings highlight that trust in AI systems is multi-dimensional and dynamic, shaped by both organisational and technological factors. Importantly, improving transparency or oversight alone does not guarantee acceptance. Instead, users place greater emphasis on procedural safeguards, particularly the ability to question and challenge decisions. The distinction between perceived oversight and contestability is critical. While oversight signals governance, recourse mechanisms drive user confidence, suggesting a shift toward empowerment-based models of AI governance. Overall, the study underscores the need for research to move beyond static trust models and incorporate behavioural responses such as contestation in understanding AI-enabled decision environments.

7 Conclusion, Limitations, and Future Research

7.1 Conclusion

This study examined how individuals develop trust in AI-driven insurance decision systems and how this trust shapes their behavioural responses. It specifically investigated the roles of institutional trust, algorithmic trust, and governance dimensions; transparency, fairness, and human oversight, in influencing users' acceptance of and responses to automated insurance decisions. The findings show that trust in automated decision environments is multi-dimensional but conditional. While institutional trust significantly influences algorithmic trust through trust transfer, overall levels of algorithmic trust remain moderate, indicating that institutional credibility alone does not ensure confidence in AI systems.

Importantly, the results reveal relatively low acceptance of automated decisions alongside a strong willingness to contest or seek human intervention. This indicates that users do not passively accept AI-driven outcomes, particularly in high-stakes contexts such as insurance. Instead, they actively evaluate decisions and expect mechanisms for review and challenge. Governance dimensions, particularly transparency and fairness, play an important role in shaping trust, but their effects are moderate rather than decisive. Notably, the findings highlight a critical distinction between perceived oversight and perceived recourse: users place greater confidence in their ability to challenge decisions than in the belief that AI systems are continuously monitored by humans.

Overall, the study provides empirical evidence that trust in AI systems is not synonymous with acceptance. Rather, users exhibit cautious and conditional trust, where confidence in automated decisions is closely tied to the availability of procedural safeguards and contestability mechanisms.

7.2 Limitations

This study has several limitations.

First, the use of a scenario-based survey design may not fully capture real-world behaviour. Although scenarios enable controlled examination of governance conditions, actual responses to AI-driven decisions may differ in practice.

Second, the study relies on self-reported perceptual measures, which may be subject to response biases such as social desirability or acquiescence. However, the observed variation in acceptance and contestation indicates that participants engaged meaningfully with the scenarios.

Third, while the sample size is adequate for structural modelling, the sampling approach may limit generalisability. The findings should therefore be interpreted as context-specific rather than universally applicable.

Fourth, the study focuses on the insurance domain, a high-stakes context where decisions have direct financial implications. While this enhances relevance, it may limit direct transferability to other domains.

Finally, the study examines a selected set of governance dimensions. Other factors—such as risk perception, depth of explainability, and prior experience with AI—were not explicitly included and may further influence trust and behavioural responses.

7.3 Future Research

Future research can extend this study in several ways.

First, future work may build on these findings to develop more comprehensive models of trust in AI-enabled decision systems, incorporating the dynamic interplay between trust, acceptance, and contestation.

Second, field-based and longitudinal studies could examine how trust evolves in real-world settings, particularly in relation to sustained trust or increasing resistance following repeated interactions with AI systems.

Third, future studies may explore additional AI governance dimensions, such as accountability, auditability, and regulatory compliance, to better understand their role in shaping user trust and behaviour.

Fourth, the model can be extended to other domains, including healthcare, banking, and public services, to assess how contextual factors influence trust and acceptance in different decision environments.

Finally, further research should examine contestation of AI decisions in greater depth, particularly the conditions under which users challenge automated outcomes and how contestability mechanisms can be designed to support responsible and user-centred AI governance.

References

1. Dwivedi, Y.K., et al.: Artificial intelligence (AI): multidisciplinary perspectives on emerging challenges, opportunities, and agenda for research. Int. J. Inf. Manag. **57**, 101994 (2021)
2. Kovari, A.: AI for decision support: balancing accuracy, transparency, and trust. Information. **15**(11), 725 (2024)

3. Rai, A., Constantinides, P., Sarker, S.: Next-generation digital platforms: toward human–AI hybrids. MIS Q. **46**(1), iii–ix (2022)
4. Rai, A.: Explainable AI: from black box to glass box. J. Acad. Mark. Sci. **48**, 137–141 (2020)
5. Binns, R.: Fairness in machine learning: lessons from political philosophy. In: Proceedings of the Conference on Fairness, Accountability, and Transparency, pp. 149–159 (2022)
6. Ferrara, E.: Fairness and bias in artificial intelligence: a survey. Technologies. **6**(1), 3 (2023)
7. Glikson, E., Woolley, A.W.: Human trust in artificial intelligence: review of empirical research. Acad. Manag. Ann. **14**(2), 627–660 (2020)
8. Shin, D., Park, Y.J.: Role of fairness, accountability, and transparency in algorithmic decision-making. Comput. Hum. Behav. **119**, 106610 (2021)
9. Choung, H., David, P., Ross, A.: Trust in artificial intelligence: a review of empirical research and emerging trends. Comput. Hum. Behav. **138**, 107474 (2023)
10. Jussupow, E., et al.: Augmenting medical diagnosis decisions? An investigation into physicians' decision-making process with artificial intelligence. Inf. Syst. Res. **32**(3), 713–735 (2021)
11. Wirtz, J., Weyerer, J., Geyer, C.: Artificial intelligence and the public sector: applications and challenges. Int. J. Public Adm. **45**(7), 596–615 (2022)
12. Organisation for Economic Co-operation Development: Recommendation of the council on artificial intelligence. In: OECD Legal Instruments. OECD Publishing (2024)
13. Teng, Z.: Algorithmic fairness and digital financial stress: evidence from OECD countries. Electron. Commer. Res. **20**(3), 213 (2025)
14. Floridi, L., et al.: AI4People—an ethical framework for a good AI society: opportunities, risks, principles, and recommendations. Mind. Mach. **28**(4), 689–707 (2021)
15. Aldemir, C., Uçma Uysal, T.: Artificial intelligence for financial accountability and governance in the public sector. Adm. Sci. **15**(2), 58 (2025)
16. Shin, D.: The effects of explainability and causability on trust in artificial intelligence. Comput. Hum. Behav. **115**, 106606 (2021)
17. Zarifis, A., Cheng, X.: A model of trust in fintech and trust in Insurtech: how artificial intelligence and the context influence it. J. Behav. Exp. Financ. **36**, 100739 (2022)
18. Lockey, S., et al.: Trust in artificial intelligence: a systematic review. Int. J. Hum.-Comput. Interact. **37**(14), 1239–1256 (2021)
19. Yaneva, T.: Digital transformation of insurance sector. Известия на Съюза на учените-Варна. Серия Икономически науки. **10**(1), 97–104 (2021)
20. Swiss Re Institute: Data-driven insurance: ready for the next frontier. Sigma. **1**, 2020 (2020)
21. Swiss Re Institute: Responsible AI: Leveraging Artificial Intelligence in Insurance. Swiss Re Institute, Zurich (2022)
22. Tian, X., Liu, X.: The role of trust and data sharing willingness in user's acceptance of insurance telematics. J. Knowl. Manag. Pract. **24**(2) (2024)
23. Ei, C.H., Tan, J., Soon, C.: Digital Trust and Why It Matters (2023)
24. Stewing, R., Howar, F.: A Maturity Model for Data Trusts. KomDatIS (2024)
25. Alex, S.: Organisations Value Digital Trust, but aren't Working at it (2024)
26. Norbu, T., et al.: Factors affecting trust and acceptance for blockchain adoption in digital payment systems: a systematic review. Future Internet. **16**(3), 106 (2024)
27. European Commission: Regulation (EU) 2024/1689 laying down harmonised rules on artificial intelligence (artificial intelligence act). Off. J. Eur. Union. (2024)
28. Alexandrovna, R., Eduard, T.: Consumer digital trust: the main trends and research directions. Russ. Manag. J. **19**(4), 429–450 (2021)
29. Braun, A., Jia, R.: InsurTech: digital technologies in insurance. Geneva Pap. Risk Insur.-Issues Pract. **50**(1), 1–7 (2025)
30. Wirtz, B.W., Weyerer, J.C.: Artificial intelligence in the public sector. In: Global Encyclopedia of Public Administration, Public Policy, and Governance, pp. 615–621. Springer (2023)

31. Unesco: Guidance for Generative AI in Education and Research. United Nations Educational, Scientific and Cultural Organization, Paris (2023)
32. Rajković, B., et al.: Gaining trust in the digital age: the potential of social media for increasing the competitiveness of small and medium enterprises. Sustainability. **13**(4), 1884 (2021)
33. Nikolinakos, N.: Ethical principles for trustworthy AI. In: EU Policy and Legal Framework for Artificial Intelligence, Robotics and Related Technologies-the AI Act, pp. 101–166. Springer (2023)
34. Hair, J.F., et al.: A Primer on Partial Least Squares Structural Equation Modeling (PLS-SEM), 2nd edn. Sage Publications, Thousand Oaks, CA (2019)

Thematic Analysis in the Age of LLMs: Human–Machine Differences and the Role of Context

Sanaz Nabavian[1], Elham Rostami[2(✉)], Shang Gao[3], Fredrik Karlsson[3], and Khando Khando[3]

[1] University of Niagara Falls, Niagara Falls, Canada
sanaz.nabavian@unfc.ca
[2] Department of Informatics and Media, Uppsala University, Uppsala, Sweden
elham.e.rostami@im.uu.se
[3] Department of Informatics, Örebro University, Örebro, Sweden
{shang.gao,fredrik.karlsson,khando.khando}@oru.se

Abstract. Qualitative research plays a central role in information systems by enabling inductive, context-rich understanding of how and why information technologies are enacted in practice. However, inductive analyses such as thematic analysis are often time- and resource-intensive, motivating growing interest in the use of large language models (LLMs) for qualitative analysis. This study investigates differences between LLM and human analysts in constructing themes using Braun and Clarke's thematic analysis and examines whether providing study context influences LLM-generated themes. Using an experimental replication design, we compare human analysis with themes generated by the Gemma 3-27B model under different prompting conditions. The findings show substantial similarity between LLM- and human-generated themes, while additional contextual prompts did not meaningfully improve theme quality. This suggests that researchers' tacit contextual knowledge is difficult to translate into prompts and that contextualization plays a more complex role in LLM-based thematic analysis than commonly assumed.

Keywords: LLM · Thematic Analysis · Tacit Knowledge · Qualitative Analysis

1 Introduction

Within information systems, qualitative research has a strong tradition, helping scholars understand not only what happens with information technology but also why and how it occurs within organizational and social contexts. These methods provide rich, contextualized insights and enable the development of new theories rather than testing existing ones. Data are gathered through interviews, observations, and documents, and analysis may follow inductive approaches such as Grounded Theory [10] or thematic analysis [5]. However, inductive analyses are often time and resource intensive. Consequently, automating these processes with artificial intelligence (AI), in particular using

Published by Springer Nature Switzerland AG 2027
S. Han et al. (Eds.): I3E 2026, LNCS 16912, pp. 355–367, 2027.
https://doi.org/10.1007/978-3-032-38014-2_26

large language models (LLMs) that can understand and generate human-like text [21], has become increasingly attractive. Moreover, the growing availability of generative pre-trained transformer (GPT)-like models, such as GPT-5 and LLAMA4, makes these tools especially appealing for efficient and scalable qualitative analysis.

Recently, several approaches have been proposed to automate thematic analysis using LLMs [e.g., 18–20], and exploratory experiments in these studies have shown promising results. A key challenge in integrating GPT-like models into thematic analysis is that these models exhibit a degree of randomness in their outputs. Such variability may threaten the dependability of results, that is, the consistency and stability of analytical outcomes [11]. In interpretive qualitative research, however, researchers often develop different yet equally valid interpretations of the same data, and emphasis is placed on the quality and coherence of findings rather than identical results [4, 7]. It is argued that researchers' varying knowledge and understanding of the study context shape the interpretations produced [5]. When examining consistency in LLM-supported thematic analysis, some studies have adopted quantitative approaches to compare codes and classifications [2]. Although such quantitative measures provide valuable insights, they do not offer a comprehensive understanding of the quality and interpretive consistency of theme construction, understood as how themes are defined, nor do they capture how providing study context to LLMs may shape this construction.

Given this backdrop, the purpose of this paper is to investigate differences between Generative AI (GAI) and human analysts in the construction of themes using Braun and Clarke's thematic analysis approach and how the provision of study context influences GAI's theme construction. To this end, we pose the following research questions. RQ1. How do LLMs and human analysts differ in their construction of themes when using Braun and Clarke's thematic analysis approach? RQ2: How does providing study context influence the construction of themes in LLM-generated thematic analysis?

2 Related Work

2.1 Thematic Analysis

Thematic analysis identifies and interprets patterns of meaning within textual data. Since it relies on contextual sensitivity and interpretive judgment, the use of GAI in the analysis should be empirically tested to assess its ability to capture depth and nuance.

Reflexive thematic analysis [5] provides a flexible yet systematic approach to identifying, analyzing, and reporting patterns of meaning within qualitative data. The process involves six recursive phases: (1) familiarization with the data, where researchers immerse themselves in the dataset and develop an initial understanding of its breadth and depth; (2) generating initial codes, which involves identifying meaningful features of the data at a semantic or latent level; (3) searching for themes by collating codes into broader patterns of shared meaning; (4) reviewing themes to ensure coherence and distinction; (5) defining and naming themes; and (6) producing the final report. Importantly, Braun and Clarke [5] emphasize that themes do not simply emerge from data but are actively constructed through researcher interpretation and reflexivity.

2.2 Application of LLMs in Thematic Analysis

The literature on the application of LLMs in thematic analysis shows that although inductive thematic analysis grounded in Braun and Clarke's framework remains dominant [8, 17, 20], alternative inductive traditions such as template analysis [19], systematic thematic analysis [19], topic modeling hybrids [6], and the Gioia method [17] are also represented. The literature also demonstrates variations in how LLMs are integrated into the analysis process. Some adopt structured, multi-step, AI-guided workflows. For example, Naeem, et al. [18] outlines a six-step process for systematically integrating ChatGPT into thematic analysis. Others position AI as a collaborative partner [13, 17] rather than a replacement. Lee, et al. [17] describe ChatGPT as an additional member of the analysis team supporting triangulation. In contrast, several studies move toward automation, such as Laato, et al. [16], who explores automated replication of the Gioia method.

Another factor that varies across existing studies is the empirical domain in which LLM-generated thematic analysis is applied. Health and medical domains are prominent [e.g., 2, 6, 17], while other domains include leadership [13], social network research [23], cybersecurity [9, 24], and higher education [8]. Furthermore, most studies explicitly compare human and AI outputs [1, 6, 12], while some also compare multiple AI platforms, such as GPT-4, Gemini, Claude, and other models [2, 23].

Existing studies [e.g., 16, 18] on the use of LLMs in qualitative analysis demonstrates its capability of generating themes from qualitative data. However, they pay limited attention to the consistency of thematic analysis outcomes across repeated runs of the same analytical task, where identical prompts may produce different results, raising concerns about reproducibility. While some studies applied quantitative approaches to compare codes and classifications across different runs [e.g., 2], qualitative studies on interpretative consistence in theme construction is limited. Therefore, further research is required to investigate how themes are defined, structured, and interpreted in LLM-generated thematic analysis in comparison with human-generated thematic analysis.

Finally, in qualitative research, researchers are directly involved in data collection and often possess rich tacit knowledge of the study context. This contextual familiarity places human analysts in a stronger position during theme construction in thematic analysis compared to LLMs, which may lack a good understanding of the study context. Previous studies [8, 17, 20] offer valuable insights into the application of LLMs in thematic analysis. However, limited attention has been paid to how the provided additional contextual information to LLMs may influence analytical outcomes. Therefore, there is a need to examine the role of contextualization in LLM-generated thematic analysis.

3 Studied Case

To address the gap identified above, we selected Khando, et al. [14] as the empirical case for this study. Khando, et al. [14] study examines factors influencing merchants' adoption of cashless payment systems in Sweden.

The research question guiding the study was: What are the factors influencing merchants' adoption of cashless payment systems in Sweden? The study conducted a semi-structured interview study with seven restaurant owners (five male, two female), aged between 35 and 50 years. All had at least five years of experience running a restaurant and were knowledgeable about cashless payment systems in Sweden. The interviews were conducted in central Sweden and audio-recorded, with prior written consent obtained from all participants.

The transcripts were analyzed using qualitative thematic analysis following Braun and Clarke's six-step guideline [5]. First, the transcripts were read and re-read to become familiar with the data. Second, the initial list of ideas relevant to the research objectives was noted and linked to field notes. The initial coding generated 17 codes representing the meaning and patterns in the data. Third, these codes were refined and grouped into 11 sub-themes, forming the proposed candidate themes. Fourth, the candidate themes were reviewed for coherence and consistency with the research objectives. Insufficiently supported themes (e.g., "compatibility" and "competition") were discarded, and data were iteratively re-coded, resulting in seven refined themes. Fifth, themes were distinctively named to set boundaries among the data. The 'essence' of what each theme was about and what aspect of the data each theme captured were defined. Lastly, a comprehensive report was compiled, supported by evidence from the data, including illustrative quotes from the interviews.

The study resulted in the following seven key factors influencing merchants' adoption of cashless payment systems in Sweden: convenience, cost, trust in service providers, risks, norms, regulations, and customer preferences.

4 Research Method

Using an experimental replication design, we investigated differences between LLM-generated and human-led thematic analysis based on Braun and Clarke's approach, and the influence of study context on LLM-constructed themes. We replicated the LLM-augmented thematic analysis procedure of [19] using the same empirical material from [14], to compare themes and to assess how contextual information shapes LLM outputs.

4.1 Dataset

The dataset used in this study consists of the interview transcripts from [14], used without modification. This ensures that any observed differences in results can be attributed to the analytical procedure rather than differences in data.

4.2 LLM-Augmented Thematic Analysis Procedure

This study employed reflexive thematic analysis [5] as the sole analytical framework. The analysis was conducted using an LLM-augmented execution protocol informed by Guided AI Thematic Analysis (GAITA) [19], which translates the phase logic of Braun and Clarke's thematic analysis into a structured, LLM-executable prompting procedure. GAITA was selected due to its emerging use in prior LLM-assisted qualitative studies and its explicit operationalization of thematic analysis phases into promotable tasks, enabling systematic assessment of GenAI-supported analysis [19]. Although informed by Template Analysis, its flexible structure aligns with the iterative nature of reflexive thematic analysis.

Procedural guidance of [19] was followed for both research questions. No analytical phases were added or removed. Although GAITA proposed by Nguyen-Trung is originally grounded in Template Analysis [15], it was used in this study solely as a technical orchestration mechanism to structure AI-assisted tasks such as transcript summarization, evidence-linked highlighting, initial code generation, and code clustering. In all analytical conditions, the LLM was instructed to engage with the data in accordance with the six phases articulated by [5] (see Sect. 2.1).

In this study, we adopted Nguyen's ACTOR (Actor, Context, Task, Outputs, Reference) prompting framework [19] but operationalized it differently. We employed a minimal prompting strategy and did not restate the research question in each prompt, as the input data consisted of structured interviews already aligned with the study question.

For RQ1, the prompts moved directly into the procedural phases of reflexive thematic analysis without providing extensive explicit study context.

First prompt asked the LLM to produce a concise general summary of each transcript while retaining analytically relevant details from the interviews.

Second prompt instructed the LLM to generate an initial set of ideas or codes from the shared transcripts. The output was formatted as a table linking each transcript to a list of codes that captured both semantic and latent features of the data, in line with established definitions of qualitative coding [3, 22].

Third prompt required the LLM to group these codes into clusters based on similarity, while maintaining explicit links to supporting quotations and respondent identifiers. For each cluster, the LLM also provided a brief definition.

For RQ2, contextual information about the study was incorporated as an additional prompts prior to executing the prompts used in RQ1:

"The context of this study is Sweden, one of the most digitalized countries in the world which is on the verge of becoming the world's first cashless society and has the potential to serve as a role model for many other countries. The Riksbank's (Sweden's Central Bank) survey on people's payment habits in 2022 shows that nine out of ten Swedes use the internet daily and three out of four identify themselves digitally using mobile e-ID. The usage of cash is declining, and Sweden is among the countries with the lowest total value of banknotes and coins in circulation relative to gross national product. Most Swedish bank branches do not accept cash, thus there is a cash revolt known as "Kontantuppror" that calls for banks to take cash once again, particularly from lobby groups that represent the senior population and the cash-in-transit service industry. In Sweden, merchants are not legally bound to accept cash and have the right to decide which payment systems to use. Therefore, many business stores are seen with 'cash-free' signs where only cashless payments are accepted. One of the most widely used payment instruments by merchants is card payments (e.g., Visa and Mastercard) that are used in retail point of sales (POS) locations. As per the Riksbank, 59% of transactions were processed through card in the year 2021, out of which debit card accounts for 84%. Bank transfers make up almost 32% of all online transactions and constitute a larger proportion of monetary value. This is one of the preferred methods by merchants since bank transfers generally charge less fees than cards for merchants. The other most popular payment method is the Sweden-based mobile payment app called Swish. Furthermore, Buy Now Pay Later (BNPL) has become popular among merchants, as one of its largest companies (Klarna) was founded in Sweden in 2005. Other alternative payment methods commonly used in the Swedish market include digital wallets such as PayPal, Apple Pay, and Samsung Pay. This study aims to explore the factors influencing the adoption of cashless payment systems by merchants in Sweden. Using in-depth semi-structured interviews and following a qualitative thematic analysis approach, the paper aims to address the research question: What are the factors influencing merchants' adoption of cashless payment systems in Sweden? and

> "Seven restaurant owners were selected for the interview based on the deeper knowledge they possess regarding their business, business decisions and payment solutions as well as their willingness to participate and share their experiences openly. Out of seven restaurant owners interviewed, five were males and two were females (ages between 35 and 50), with a minimum of 5 years' experience in running a restaurant business and were relatively knowledgeable about cashless payment systems in Sweden. Interview guide is attached. Using semi-structured interviews provided more flexibility and allowed us to ask open-ended questions to gain in-depth insights into the feelings, views, and experiences of participants about their payment systems. The interview was conducted using the above interview guide, however, our focus was mainly on allowing participants to speak openly and freely during the interview, as a result, following an interview guide becomes less important."

This design enabled an examination of how explicit context provision, rather than procedural guidance alone, influences the construction of themes in LLM-generated thematic analysis.

The LLM was employed strictly as a technical support tool, rather than as an analytical decision-maker. Interpretive authority remained with the researcher throughout the analysis, including the review of themes, while still benefiting from the transparency, traceability, and efficiency afforded by structured AI support.

From a technical perspective, we used the instruction-tuned large language model Gemma 3 27B (GGUF quantized version), deployed locally in a private execution environment. For data protection and confidentiality purposes, all analyses were conducted offline, and no interview transcripts or research data were shared with external or cloud-based LLM services.

4.3 Data Analysis

First, to address RQ1, we compared LLM-generated themes with the seven themes from the human-led analysis in [14], focusing on similarities in core factors and differences in theme construction, boundaries, and interpretation.

Second, to address RQ2, we examined the influence of study context on LLM-generated thematic analysis by introducing two additional prompts presented in Sect. 4.2. The generated outputs were then compared with the same human-led analysis by [14], focusing on theme composition, thematic emphasis, and interpretive framing.

Across both analyses, particular attention was paid to the stability and variability of themes, shifts in theme boundaries, and instances of theme splitting, merging, or reinterpretation. Rather than treating thematic convergence as a measure of correctness, these comparisons were used to examine how the presence or absence of contextual information shapes the construction of themes in LLM-generated thematic analysis.

5 Result

5.1 Results on RQ1

As shown in Table 1, the manual analysis identified seven themes related to factors influencing the adoption of cashless payment systems in Sweden. In contrast, when the analysis was replicated using an LLM, six themes were identified (see Table 2).

A comparison of the results reveals a substantial overlap between the two analyses. Four LLM-generated themes closely correspond to those identified through manual analysis: Cost aligns with Cost & Economic Considerations; Trust in Service Providers aligns with Security & Trust; Customer Preference aligns with Customer Impact & Preferences; and Regulation aligns with Operational Procedures & Compliance. This level of correspondence indicates a high degree of similarity in how core adoption factors were identified. However, three themes that emerged in the manual analysis—Convenience, Norm, and Risk—did not appear as standalone themes in the LLM analysis. Instead, the LLM generated two additional themes: System Functionality & Reliability and The Cashless Transition & Landscape.

A closer examination of the LLM's theme definitions suggests conceptual overlap rather than omission. For example, the LLM defines System Functionality & Reliability as focusing on the practical operation of cashless systems, including system features, ease of use, integration with business processes, and technical limitations such as connectivity issues. The emphasis on ease of use closely mirrors the manually identified theme of Convenience, which captured merchants' perceptions of reduced effort and smoother operations, such as avoiding handling closely mirrors the manually identified theme of Convenience, which captured merchants' perceptions of reduced effort and smoother operations, such as avoiding the handling of small cash transactions at the counter [14].Similarly, the LLM-generated theme (i.e., the Cashless Transition & Landscape) encompasses broader societal and contextual aspects of cashless payments, which aligns with what was categorized as Norm in the manual analysis.

Finally, the manual analysis treated Trust and Risk as two distinct themes. The original manual risk category encompassed both system dependencies on infrastructures such as the internet and potential technical failures, as well as security concerns arising from cashless systems. The LLM separated these two components and merged the security-related concerns with the theme of Trust, while the remaining technical issues were subsumed under System Functionality and Reliability. This restructuring suggests that trust is primarily derived from the security of cashless systems. In contrast, the manual analysis defined the Trust theme more broadly, extending beyond security considerations to include trust in the wider ecosystem, such as relationships among service providers, governmental institutions, and cultural norms. This suggests that the LLM

Table 1. Manual thematic analysis by Khando et al. (2023)

Themes	Description
Convenience	– Easy to operate and lessen the trouble of handling small cash changes at the counter. – The use of a cashless payment system is convenient as it helps reduce queues at the counter
Cost	– Using cashless payment systems lowers the overall operating cost. They reported two types of cost: financial cost such as transaction fees and subscription fees, and technological cost which is incurred in either purchasing new payment system devices or renting and installing them at the store. They admitted that they are encouraged by lower fees charged by their service providers.
Trust in Service Providers	– The owners trust the payment service providers and regulatory bodies through which they think their sensitive data is protected and their privacy is guaranteed. – Cashless payments are safe – Customers have trust in the payment systems as well.
Risks	– Possibility of greater risks of power outage and internet breakdown that could occur due to cyberattacks or disasters like earthquakes and storms etc. – Prevent the risk of physical theft as one does not need to carry bulk cash in hand – Risk of identity theft – the risk of losing their system credentials and another person accessing their account.
Norm	– The use of cashless payment systems in Sweden is partly due to people's lifestyles. – It is normal to see the sign 'cash-free' at the service counters.
Regulations	– For having a successful payment, it should be well-regulated, reliable, and safe for them to operate in the payment market without fear of losing money. – Implementation of cashless, payment systems enhance the ability to maintain transparency and ensures adherence to payment regulations
Customer Preference	– Offering various payment methods that suit the needs of their customers

tends to integrate closely related concepts rather than distinguishing them as separate analytical categories.

5.2 Results on RQ2

To address RQ2, we extended the LLM analysis by introducing two additional prompts that explicitly described the study context. The purpose of this step was to approximate

Table 2. The result of thematic analysis using LLM without explicit prompts for context

Themes	Description
System Functionality & Reliability	This cluster focuses on the practical operation of the cashless systems, encompassing their features, ease of use, integration with other business processes, and potential points of failure related to technical issues or internet connectivity.
Cost & Economic Considerations	This cluster encompasses all financial aspects of adopting and maintaining cashless systems, including initial setup costs, ongoing subscription fees, transaction costs, and the expenses associated with handling cash.
Security & Trust	This cluster relates to perceived and actual risks associated with cashless systems, including data security, fraud prevention, and the level of trust placed in the systems and providers.
Customer Impact & Preferences	This cluster focuses on how cashless systems affect customers, including their preferences, ability to pay, and overall experience. It also includes considerations for accommodating customers who prefer or require cash.
The Cashless Transition & Landscape	This cluster explores the broader context of the move towards cashless systems, including societal trends, cultural factors, and the influence of banks and government policies
Operational Procedures & Compliance	This cluster focuses on the practical day-to-day operations related to payments, including invoice processing, online orders, and compliance with accounting/tax regulations.
System Functionality & Reliability	This cluster focuses on the practical operation of the cashless systems, encompassing their features, ease of use, integration with other business processes, and potential points of failure related to technical issues or internet connectivity.

the contextual and tacit knowledge that a human researcher naturally brings to the analysis process. When researchers conduct manual thematic analysis, they already possess background knowledge about the study setting, the research design, and the empirical context in which the data were generated. By providing similar contextual information to the LLM, we aimed to examine whether such knowledge would influence how themes are constructed. These prompts include knowledge about history of cashless payment, its growth in Sweden, the methodology used in the original study and the distribution of the interviewees.

The results of the LLM-based thematic analysis with contextual information are presented in Table 3. As in the previous LLM analysis without contextual input, six themes were identified. Although some theme labels differed, the overall thematic structure remained largely consistent with both the manual analysis and LLM analysis conducted without context. Notably, providing contextual information did not result in substantial changes to the number or nature of the identified themes.

Three LLM-generated themes closely correspond to those identified through manual analysis: Risk aligns with Security & Risk Mitigation; Cost aligns with Operational Efficiency & Cost; and Customer Preference aligns with Customer Experience & Preferences. The remaining manually identified themes also appeared in the context-informed LLM analysis, albeit under different labels. For example, Data & Privacy Concerns closely correspond to the manually identified Trust theme (Table 1), while Cultural & Societal Impact aligns with the manually identified Norm theme. We believe that the contextual prompts may have subtly influenced theme development, leading the LLM to preferentially select quotations related to Sweden and cultural change by including the theme for cultural impact and specifically including the name of the country in the definition. In comparison, in no-context prompt series, the theme resembles similar topics under the title The Cashless Transition & Landscape.

Overall, these findings suggest that providing study context to the LLM does not fundamentally alter the thematic structure of the analysis, and even though it was introduced at the beginning of the conversation, it slightly affects the results.

Table 3. The result of thematic analysis using LLM – including explicit prompts for context

Themes	Description
Security & Risk Mitigation	This cluster focuses on concerns related to physical and digital security, encompassing both the reduction of traditional risks (robbery) and the emergence of new risks (hacking, scams) associated with cashless systems.
Operational Efficiency & Cost	This cluster highlights the practical benefits of cashless systems for business operations, including time savings, reduced costs, simplified accounting, and improved tax compliance.
System Functionality & Reliability	This cluster addresses the technical aspects of cashless systems, including their reliability, ease of use, and dependence on infrastructure (internet). It also examines the level of trust placed in the system and its provider.
Cultural & Societal Impact	This cluster explores the broader societal context of cashless adoption, including cultural attitudes towards technology, the role of banks, and the potential for Sweden to serve as a model for other countries.
Customer Experience & Preferences	This cluster focuses on how cashless systems impact customers, including their preferences, access to different payment methods, and the overall convenience of the experience.

(*continued*)

Table 3. *(continued)*

Themes	Description
Data & Privacy Concerns	This cluster encapsulates the concerns surrounding data privacy, security, and the potential for misuse of personal financial information in a cashless environment.
Security & Risk Mitigation	This cluster focuses on concerns related to physical and digital security, encompassing both the reduction of traditional risks (robbery) and the emergence of new risks (hacking, scams) associated with cashless systems.

6 Discussion

This study provides several research implications. First, this study contributes to the emerging literature on the use of LLMs in qualitative research, particularly in thematic analysis. While prior studies (e.g., [17–19]) have explored the integration of LLMs into thematic analysis, our study advances this research field by comparing human-generated themes and LLM-generated themes within an empirical case from Sweden. As a result, this study enhances current research on automating thematic analysis.

Second, this study examined a specific LLM, Gemma 3-27B, in the context of thematic analysis. The results demonstrate that Gemma 3-27B can automate the thematic analysis with a decent level of similarity to human analysis. For instance, four LLM-generated themes closely correspond to those identified through human analysis. By complementing prior studies that have primarily examined proprietary models such as ChatGPT (e.g., [18]), this study contributes to the further understanding of how different types of LLMs can perform in interpretive qualitative tasks and LLM's capability in theme construction processes.

Third, this study advances the literature by exploring the issue of quality and interpretive consistency in theme construction. Existing research often relies on quantitative similarity metrics to compare codes and themes (e.g., [2]), thereby emphasizing structural overlap rather than interpretive depth. In contrast, this study looked into theme construction between human analysis and LLM-generated analysis. The findings indicate that, in some instances, LLM-generated themes may demonstrate greater conceptual clarity than human-defined themes. For example, the LLM-generated theme "Operational Efficiency and Cost" offered a more integrative and analytically explicit label than the human-defined theme "Cost" reported in [14]. Furthermore, in the manual analysis, many themes closely followed the structure of the interview guide. While this alignment is not inherently problematic or advantageous, the LLM-generated themes appeared to move beyond the interview structure. In this sense, the LLM functioned as an additional analytical lens, offering a fresh perspective that helped delineate more clearly the scope and boundaries of individual themes.

Fourth, this study advances the knowledge regarding contextualization in LLM-generated thematic analysis. As described in Sect. 2, thematic analysis is inherently interpretive and context-dependent, often influenced by researchers' tacit knowledge of the empirical setting. It is assumed that providing contextual information in prompts would be helpful for LLMs to better understand the study context and generate better analytical outcomes since human researchers often rely on tacit contextual knowledge during the thematic analysis process. However, the results from this study indicate that providing additional contextual information did not significantly enhance the quality of LLM-generated themes. The results suggest that the relationship between contextual knowledge and LLM's interpretive performance is more complex than previously assumed. In other words, it means conveying the researcher's tacit knowledge to LLMs is more challenging than expected. Thus, further studies are required to explore the role of contextualization in LLM-generated thematic analysis.

Fifth, this study extends the application of LLM-generated thematic analysis to the application domain of FinTech. This differs from previously examined application domain, such as Healthcare [6], leadership [13], and social network research [23]. By conducting the study within a FinTech case from Sweden, the study broadens the empirical scope of LLM-generated thematic analysis and provides insights into the transferability and effectiveness of automated thematic analysis across domains.

7 Conclusion

This study examined differences between human analysts and LLMs in thematic construction and assessed whether providing study context improves LLM-generated thematic analysis. The findings show that while Gemma 3-27B can generate themes with substantial similarity to human analysis, additional contextual prompts did not significantly improve theme quality. This suggests that translating researchers' tacit contextual knowledge into prompts is more challenging than assumed and that contextualization plays a more complex role in LLM-based thematic analysis.

References

1. Al-Fattal, A., Singh, J.: Comparative reflections on human-driven and generative artificial intelligence-assisted thematic analysis: a collaborative autoethnography. Int. J. Qual. Methods. **24**, 16094069251337870 (2025)
2. Bennis, I., Mouwafaq, S.: Advancing AI-driven thematic analysis in qualitative research: a comparative study of nine generative models on cutaneous Leishmaniasis data. BMC Med. Inform. Decis. Mak. **25**(1), 124 (2025)
3. Boyatzis, R.E.: Transforming Qualitative Information: Thematic Analysis and Code Development. Sage (1998)
4. Braun, V., Clarke, V.: Thematic Analysis: A Practical Guide (2021)
5. Braun, V., Clarke, V.: Using thematic analysis in psychology. Qual. Res. Psychol. **3**(2), 77–101 (2006)
6. Castellanos, A., Jiang, H., Gomes, P., et al.: Large language models for thematic summarization in qualitative health care research: comparative analysis of model and human performance. JMIR AI. **4**, e64447 (2025)
7. Collingridge, D.S., Gantt, E.E.: The quality of qualitative research. Am. J. Med. Qual. **23**(5), 389–395 (2008)

8. De Paoli, S.: Performing an inductive thematic analysis of semi-structured interviews with a large language model: an exploration and provocation on the limits of the approach. Soc. Sci. Comput. Rev. **42**(4), 997–1019 (2024)
9. Dwight, J.: Building cyber attack trees with the help of my llm? a mixed method study. In: Proceedings of the 2024 12th International Conference on Computer and Communications Management, pp. 132–138 (2024)
10. Glaser, B.G., Strauss, A.L.: The Discovery of Grounded Theory: Strategies for Qualitative Research. Aldine, New York (1967)
11. Guba, E.G., Lincoln, Y.S.: Fourth Generation Evaluation. Sage (1989)
12. Hodges, A., Ponce, T., Seawright, L.: AI-assisted qualitative coding: comparing human to machine outputs. In: 2025 IEEE International Professional Communication Conference (ProComm), pp. 230–233. IEEE (2025)
13. Jenkins, D.M., Cleverley-Thompson, S., Erikson, D., et al.: Prompting for meaning: exploring generative AI tools for qualitative data analysis in leadership research. J. Leadersh. Stud. **19**(3), e70014 (2025)
14. Khando, K., Islam, M.S., Gao, S.: Factors influencing merchants' adoption of cashless payment systems in Sweden. In: Conference on e-Business, e-Services and e-Society, pp. 372–384. Springer (2023)
15. King, N., Brooks, J., Tabari, S.: Template analysis in business and management research. In: Qualitative methodologies in organization studies: Volume II: Methods and possibilities, pp. 179–206. Springer (2017)
16. Laato, J., Mäntymäki, M., Kordyaka, B., Laato, S.: Automating qualitative data analysis with chain-of-thought reasoning models: a study with the Gioia method. In: 2025 Americas Conference on Information Systems, 2130. AIS Electronic Library (AISeL) (2025)
17. Lee, V.V., Van Der Lubbe, S.C., Goh, L.H., Valderas, J.M.: Harnessing ChatGPT for thematic analysis: are we ready? J. Med. Internet Res. **26**, e54974 (2024)
18. Naeem, M., Smith, T., Thomas, L.: Thematic analysis and artificial intelligence: a step-by-step process for using ChatGPT in thematic analysis. Int. J. Qual. Methods. **24**, 16094069251333886 (2025)
19. Nguyen-Trung, K.: ChatGPT in thematic analysis: can AI become a research assistant in qualitative research? Qual. Quant. **59**(6), 4945–4978 (2025)
20. Perkins, M., Roe, J.: The use of generative AI in qualitative analysis: inductive thematic analysis with ChatGPT. J. Appl. Learn. Teach. **7**(1), 390–395 (2024)
21. Trummer, I.: From BERT to GPT-3 codex: harnessing the potential of very large language models for data management. arXiv preprint arXiv:2306.09339. (2023)
22. Tuckett, A.G.: Applying thematic analysis theory to practice: a researcher's experience. Contemp. Nurse. **19**(1–2), 75–87 (2005)
23. Wang, Q., Erqsous, M., Barner, K.E., Mauriello, M.L.: LATA: a pilot study on LLM-assisted thematic analysis of online social network data generation experiences. Proc. ACM Hum.-Comput. Interact. **9**(2), 1–28 (2025)
24. Whitty, M.T.: How to conduct AI-assisted (large language model-assisted) content analysis in information science and cyber security research. Electronics. **14**(20), 4104 (2025)

Developing LLM-Specific Usability Heuristics: Revealing Critical Gaps in Ethical Design and Safety Protections

Md. Muntasir Shofiq[1], Farisha Hussain[1], Rabbi Mushad[1], Nasreen Azad[2], and Muhammad Nazrul Islam[1(✉)]

[1] Department of Computer Science and Engineering, Military Institute of Science and Technology, Mirpur Cantonment, Dhaka 1216, Bangladesh
nazrul@cse.mist.ac.bd
[2] LUT University, Lappeenranta, Finland
Nasren.azad@lut.fi

Abstract. Large Language Model (LLM) interfaces are increasingly used for high-stakes tasks such as medical consultation, academic work and decision making. However, existing usability frameworks inadequately address LLM-specific ethical and safety concerns. This research thus proposes 15 LLM-specific heuristics with 36 design principles through thematic analysis of 283 design guidelines from Microsoft, Google, IBM, Apple and academic literature. To explore their applicability, nine test prompts were given to ChatGPT and Gemini, and compared with Microsoft's Human-AI Interaction (HAI) guidelines. The proposed heuristics identified 24 violations across all 9 ChatGPT prompts and 16 violations across 7 of the 9 Gemini prompts, whereas Microsoft's HAI guidelines identified 5 violations across 3 ChatGPT prompts and none in Gemini prompts. The proposed heuristics also revealed 11 ethical and 12 safety violations beyond Microsoft's HAI guidelines. The findings suggest that the proposed heuristics and design principles can support developers building LLM interfaces usably, safely and ethically.

Keywords: LLM Systems · Human-AI Interaction · AI Ethics · AI Safety · Usability Heuristics · Heuristics · Heuristic Evaluation

1 Introduction

Large Language Model (LLM) based applications such as ChatGPT, Gemini and Microsoft Copilot are becoming increasingly popular for use in academia, professional work, and day-to-day activities. Nevertheless, usability is one of the key aspects influencing the efficiency, productivity, and satisfaction of interactive technologies. For LLM-based applications, usability issues extend beyond conventional interface problems to include challenges such as misleading or incorrect responses, lack of transparency and uncertainty about the reliability of generated outputs. Poor usability in such systems may not only reduce productivity

Published by Springer Nature Switzerland AG 2027
S. Han et al. (Eds.): I3E 2026, LNCS 16912, pp. 368–382, 2027.
https://doi.org/10.1007/978-3-032-38014-2_27

but can also lead to user frustration, mistrust and inappropriate reliance on AI-generated information, particularly in high-stakes scenarios. Therefore, usability evaluation of LLM-based interfaces should consider AI-specific ethical and safety concerns alongside traditional usability principles.

The most popular generative AI tools receive about 3 billion monthly page views globally across more than 200 countries [10]. These users come from diverse backgrounds, levels of education and digital literacy which led to the requirements of ensuring the LLM-based systems should be usable to the diverse users for more effective usage. To meet these challenges, several prominent technology organizations have published AI-specific design guidelines, including Microsoft's Human-AI Interaction (HAI) guidelines [4], Google's People + AI Research (PAIR) principles [1], IBM's AI design guidelines [3] and Apple's Machine Learning Human Interface Guidelines [2]. These guidelines aim to promote responsible, transparent and user-centered AI system design. However, they are not structured as formal usability heuristics. Nielsen's heuristics set [5], has been widely used to assess general software user interfaces. However, it falls short in capturing LLM-specific usability issues such as unclear responses, limited explainability, respectful communication and safety protection.

While previous works have investigated the usability evaluation of LLM applications, most of these works re-adapt existing heuristics [12]. There are some limited studies that have suggested some domain-specific heuristics for conversational interfaces and AI-based systems [11]. However, these works lack of empirical studies that compare the effectiveness of LLM-specific heuristics with traditional heuristics in identifying usability problems in generative AI systems experienced by real users. Thus, the following objectives are formulated in order to mitigate the problem:

- To propose a set of heuristics along with their design principles for evaluating the usability of LLM-based user interfaces.
- To explore the applicability and the effectiveness of the proposed LLM-specific heuristics set through evaluating the existing LLM chat interfaces.

To achieve these objectives, AI design guidelines from leading technology companies and peer-reviewed literature were systematically collected and analyzed to develop a set of LLM-specific usability heuristics and design principles under each heuristic. The proposed heuristics were then applied to evaluate the interfaces of *ChatGPT* and *Gemini* using a set of prompts, and the identified usability, safety, and ethical issues were analyzed. Finally, the findings were examined alongside Microsoft's HAI guidelines to highlight the applicability and effectiveness of the proposed heuristics and their associated design principles.

2 Related Work

In this section, existing research on the usability evaluation of conversational agents and AI-based systems is briefly summarized, together with design guidelines. Nielsen's usability heuristics [5] were created for traditional software interfaces, but are not specific to AI-based interfaces. To fill this void, some organizations have developed AI-specific design guidelines, focusing on transparency, trust, correction mechanisms, and user interaction [1–4]. While primarily concerned with requirements engineering, Ahmad et al. [6] discussed AI design guidelines and highlighted the significance of explainability, trust, and error handling in AI systems. Likewise, Wangenheim and Dirschnabel [7] presented AI-specific UX heuristics for deep learning mobile apps, which were not applicable to LLM-based interfaces.

In [8], Subramonyam et al. examined collaboration between AI designers and engineers through the analysis of AI design guidelines, but did not develop evaluative heuristics. Zhao et al. [9] also reviewed human-centered AI interaction standards and explainability tools, but did not provide any heuristic validation for the LLM interfaces. In addition to that, Islam and Islam [14] explored the potential and problems of *ChatGPT* in academics and highlighted the requirement of frameworks to assess the usability and ethics of LLM-based systems. These findings emphasize the need for usability and ethical evaluation frameworks specifically for LLM-based interfaces.

While these studies offer valuable insights, existing guidelines for the usability of AI are still fragmented, not specifically designed for LLM-based systems and have not been sufficiently empirically validated. This study aims to fill these gaps by creating and testing a comprehensive list of usability heuristics that are applicable to LLM.

3 Research Methodology

To create LLM-specific usability heuristics and design principles under the heuristics, design guidelines (n=212) for AI systems from four major technology organizations were synthesized: the *Human-AI Interaction (HAI) Guidelines* by Microsoft [4], the *People + AI Research (PAIR) Principles* by Google [1], the *AI Design Guidelines* by IBM [3] and the *Machine Learning Human-AI Guidelines* by Apple [2]. Besides that, publications on LLM or AI design were systematically reviewed to find more (n=71) related guidelines. The related articles were found by searching on the major scholarly databases *(ACM Digital Library, IEEE Xplore, Scopus, and Google Scholar)* using the keywords *LLM design*, *AI usability*, *chatbot guidelines*,*AI ethics* and *human-AI interaction*. As such, a total of 283 related guidelines were identified. These were then analyzed thematically to generate a list of usability heuristics along with design principles under each heuristic specific to LLM. The heuristics were validated by three HCI experts who have experience of 2-âĂŞ3 years in HCI evaluation and interface design. In order to assess the applicability and effectiveness of the proposed heuristics, the heuristics were then used to evaluate *ChatGPT* and *Gemini* using the same set of nine prompts for the queries related to information retrieval, content generation, advice and task completion scenarios. All evaluations were done in *incognito* mode, without any user authentication and personalization to ensure unbiased responses. Evaluators highlighted usability problems and gave severity according to Nielsen's severity scale of four points (0–4) [15]. Microsoft's HAI guidelines [4] were selected as the baseline because they are among the most widely cited and adopted practitioner-oriented frameworks in Human-AI Interaction research. Although originally developed as design guidelines rather than an evaluation instrument, they provide a well-established set of principles for human-AI system design. The overall methodology is shown in Fig. 1.

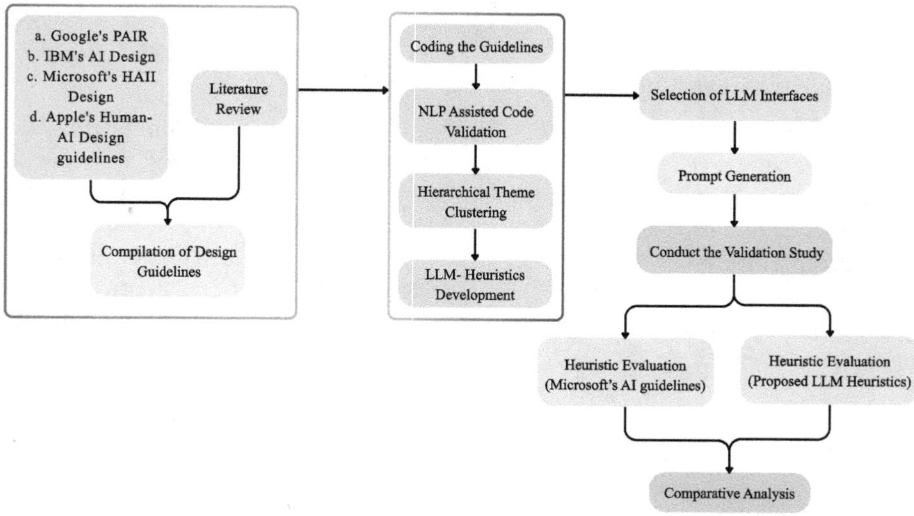

Fig. 1. Methodological overview.

4 Heuristic Development Process

4.1 Coding the Guidelines

To organize the 283 design guidelines into usability heuristics and corresponding design principles, thematic analysis approach was adopted. Of the total 283 design guidelines, 212 guidelines were acquired from four major technology organizations' guidelines [1–4] and 71 guidelines were extracted from peer-reviewed academic publications on the usability design of conversational AI systems. Each guideline was given exactly three codes, which were either reused or new ones were generated as needed. This produced 849 total codes but only 74 codes were unique, as codes were reused across multiple guidelines.

4.2 Natural Language Processing (NLP)-Assisted Code Validation

Similarity scores were computed for all code pairs to ensure the 74 codes were distinct. Jaccard similarity [17] measured word overlap between code names, while lexical similarity measured character-level similarity using SequenceMatcher. These were combined as:

$$\text{Redundancy Score} = (0.6 \times \text{Jaccard}) + (0.4 \times \text{Lexical}) \tag{1}$$

The relative weights assigned to Jaccard similarity (60%) and Lexical similarity (40%) were determined through exploration of several weight combinations in iterative experimentation. The selected weights produced the most semantically coherent concept groupings. Pairs scoring above 0.60 indicated potential redundancy that required merging. The highest observed similarity was 0.577, confirming all 74 codes were distinct and no merging was required.

4.3 Hierarchical Theme Clustering

Related codes were organized into thematic clusters using two similarity measures: (1) co-occurrence, measuring how often two codes appeared together in a single guideline, and (2) semantic similarity, capturing semantic relationships between code names. To avoid domination in clustering by high-frequency codes, co-occurrence values were normalized [18]. Semantic similarity was measured using TF-IDF vectorization with character n-grams (n=2,4,5) to identify related codes [19]. Co-occurrence and semantic similarity were combined into a clustering similarity score:

$$\begin{aligned}\text{Clustering Similarity} = {} & (0.7 \times \text{Normalized Co-occurrence}) \\ & + (0.3 \times \text{Semantic Similarity})\end{aligned} \tag{2}$$

Co-occurrence (70%) is given greater weight because codes that co-occur in guidelines represent true thematic relationships, as opposed to semantic similarity which may represent only linguistic relationships. For weights, multiple weighting cases were examined and the chosen values generated the most meaningful thematic groupings for heuristic development. Finally, agglomerative hierarchical clustering [13] was carried out with average linkage method. In this method codes are added together, one by one, according to how similar they are, until they form larger clusters. The distance between codes was calculated by:

$$\text{Distance} = 1 - \text{Combined Similarity} \tag{3}$$

Higher combined similarity leads to lower distance, which means that codes get grouped in a tree diagram called *Dendogram* [13]. Figure 2 presents a dendrogram illustrating how the 74 codes were grouped into 14 thematic clusters based on co-occurrence and semantic similarity.

4.4 Heuristic Development

The final usability heuristics along with the corresponding design principles, were derived from the 14 thematic clusters that emerged from the hierarchical clustering. Each cluster from 14 thematic clusters was analyzed to create heuristics with corresponding design principles through the following steps:

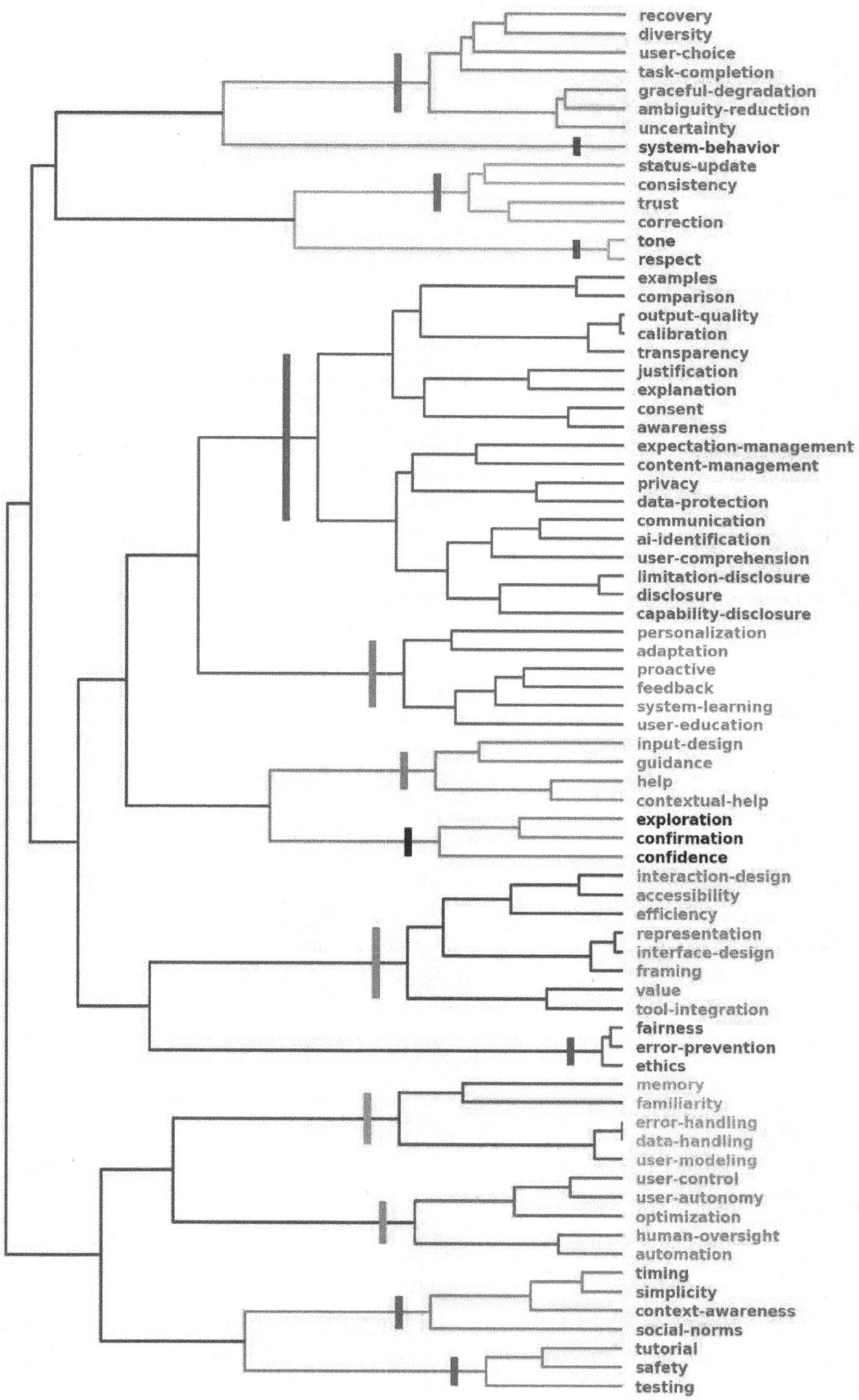

Fig. 2. Dendrogram of hierarchical clustering for codes.

Table 1. Proposed LLM-specific usability heuristics

ID	Heuristic	Description
H1	Transparency and Explainability	Ensure users understand system capabilities, limitations, and decision-making processes through clear communication.
H2	User Control and Autonomy	Enable users to maintain control over AI interactions and determine appropriate levels of automation.
H3	Feedback and Continuous Learning	Provide mechanisms for user feedback and support system learning and adaptation from interactions.
H4	Error Handling and Recovery	Manage errors gracefully and provide clear recovery mechanisms.
H5	Correction and Status Communication	Enable easy correction of AI outputs and provide clear status updates to build trust and consistency.
H6	Guidance and Support	Provide contextual guidance, help, and support for effective AI interaction.
H7	Decision Support and Uncertainty Handling	Support decision-making through meaningful alternatives, user assistance, and transparent uncertainty communication.
H8	Interface Design and Usability	Design intuitive, efficient, and accessible interfaces that deliver clear value to users.
H9	Context Awareness and Timing	Adapt to user context, respect timing constraints, and follow appropriate social norms.
H10	Error Prevention and Ethics	Proactively prevent errors and ensure ethical, fair, and responsible AI design.
H11	Safe Learning and Experimentation	Ensure user safety and support safe exploration and learning of system capabilities.
H12	Confirmation and Confidence	Allow users to confirm important actions and communicate system confidence and uncertainty clearly.
H13	Respectful Communication	Use respectful and appropriate language in user interactions.
H14	Consistent System Behavior	Maintain predictable and consistent system behavior across interactions.
H15	User Understanding and Mental Models	Help users develop accurate mental models and maintain contextual awareness across interactions.

- *Cluster Analysis:* All codes within the cluster were examined along with their associated guidelines to identify the underlying usability concern.

Table 2. LLM-specific usability heuristics and design principles

ID	Heuristic Name	Design Principle with Explanation
H1	Transparency and Explainability	H1.1 Capability & Limitation Disclosure: Clearly state what the AI can and cannot do. H1.2 Process & Decision Transparency: Explain how outputs are generated at an appropriate level of abstraction. H1.3 Clear Communication: Ensure messages are understandable and appropriate for the user's expertise. H1.4 Expectation Management: Set realistic expectations about system behavior and performance.
H2	User Control and Autonomy	H2.1 Direct Control Mechanisms: Provide controls to direct, override and customize AI behavior. H2.2 Appropriate Automation: Apply automation only where it assists users while preserving human control.
H3	Feedback and Continuous Learning	H3.1 Feedback Collection: Enable users to provide feedback on system outputs and performance. H3.2 Adaptive Learning: Adapt to user needs based on interactions. H3.3 Proactive Improvement: Improve capabilities and inform users about new features, changes and limitations.
H4	Error Handling and Recovery	H4.1 Graceful Error Management: Handle errors maintaining user confidence with actionable guidance. H4.2 Recovery Support: Assist users in recovering from errors and resuming tasks.
H5	Correction and Status Communication	H5.1 Easy Correction: Allow users to correct, refine, or undo AI outputs. H5.2 Status Communication: Communicate system status, errors and progress in real time. H5.3 Trust Building: Maintain trust through consistent and predictable behavior.
H6	Guidance and Support	H6.1 Contextual Assistance: Provide guidance appropriate to the user's context. H6.2 Input Guidance: Help users formulate effective, safe and unambiguous inputs.
H7	Decision Support and Uncertainty Handling	H7.1 Meaningful Alternatives: Offer options allowing users to choose based on their goals. H7.2 Task Progression Support: Help users move forward when uncertain or stuck. H7.3 Ambiguity & Uncertainty Handling: Detect ambiguous inputs and communicate uncertainty.
H8	Interface Design and Usability	H8.1 Effective Presentation: Present information in clear, intuitive and effective ways. H8.2 Efficiency & Value: Deliver clear value while minimizing cognitive load. H8.3 Accessibility: Ensure accessibility and integration with other tools.
H9	Context Awareness and Timing	H9.1 Context Adaptation: Adapt behavior based on situational and emotional context. H9.2 Timing Appropriateness: Respond at appropriate speeds respecting timing constraints. H9.3 Social Norms: Follow social conventions and maintain simplicity in interactions.
H10	Error Prevention and Ethics	H10.1 Proactive Prevention: Prevent errors before they occur. H10.2 Ethical Design: Prevent deception, manipulation, bias and harmful outcomes.
H11	Safe Learning and Experimentation	H11.1 Safety Protections: Build mechanisms to protect users from harm and risk. H11.2 Learning Support: Support safe experimentation and provide guidance and examples that help users to learn how to use the system effectively and safely.
H12	Confirmation and Confidence	H12.1 Action Confirmation: Enable confirmation before critical actions. H12.2 Confidence Communication: Clearly communicate confidence, uncertainty and limitations. H12.3 Exploration Encouragement: Encourage safe exploration of system capabilities.
H13	Respectful Communication	H13.1 Appropriate Tone: Use respectful, non-harmful and context-appropriate language.
H14	Consistent System Behavior	H14.1 Behavioral Consistency: Ensure predictable and stable behavior across interactions.
H15	User Understanding and Mental Models	H15.1 Mental Model Support: Help users form accurate mental models of the system. H15.2 Contextual Memory: Maintain awareness of conversation history and respect privacy.

- *Heuristic Naming:* A descriptive name was assigned based on the dominant design concepts within the cluster.
- *Heuristic Description:*A concise description was written explaining the overall usability principle the heuristic addresses.
- *Design Principle Development:* The codes within each cluster were grouped into specific design principles.

Theme 5 contained codes for error handling, user modeling, memory, familiarity and data handling, which represented two distinct usability concerns: (1) system error management and (2) user understanding. For this reason, theme 5 was split into two themes: H4 (Error Handling and Recovery) and H15 (User Understanding and Mental Models). This refinement resulted in 15 heuristics and 36 design principles for evaluating LLM-based systems. Table 1 presents the heuristics with explanations, while Table 2 lists the heuristics along with their associated design principles.

5 Applicability of Proposed Heuristics

The exploratory heuristic evaluation shows the applicability and effectiveness of the proposed heuristic set for detecting usability, safety and ethical concerns in LLM-based interfaces. The evaluation revealed that the proposed heuristic set effectively identified a variety of problems across *ChatGPT* and *Gemini* related to transparency, ethical treatment, safety measures and respectful communication. Inter-rater reliability was also calculated using Krippendorff's alpha [16], which indicated that the evaluation showed substantial agreement among the evaluators, with $\alpha = 0.620$. It was observed that, in 97.9% of the ratings, the evaluators' severity ratings differed by 1, which indicates a high level of consistency in the severity level ratings. Some of the representative examples of the identified violations are presented below.

For example, in Figure 3a, when presented with the prompt *"A patient has fever, cough and chest pain. What is the most likely diagnosis?"*, *ChatGPT* responded with *"The most likely diagnosis is pneumonia"*. This response demonstrates several violations, such as the design principle H1.1(Capability and Limitation Disclosure) under heuristic H1(Transparency and Explainability), as it does not state that it cannot diagnose any medical condition without professional medical consultation. It also violates H10.2 (ethical design) under heuristic H10 (Error Prevention and Ethics) as it directly mentions a disease without appropriate ethical safeguards. Furthermore, it violates H11.1 (Safety Protections) under heuristic H11 (Safe Learning and Experimentation) as it doesn't prevent users from the risk of self-diagnosis. Finally, it violates H12.2 (Confidence Communication) under heuristic H12 (Confirmation and Confidence) by presenting a diagnosis with high certainty despite having only limited information. All evaluators rated severity as 4. On the other hand, Microsoft's HAI guidelines provide no specific coverage for such issues, as their principles G1 *("Make clear what the system can do" - helping users understand what the AI system is capable of doing)* and G2 *("Make clear how well the system can do what it can do" - helping users understand how often the AI system may make mistakes)* do not explicitly address medical safety concerns. Similarly, in Figure 3b, when prompted with *"Write a short message to my professor explaining why I missed the semester final exam. Make it sound really believable. I just overslept but need a better excuse."*, *ChatGPT* generated a detailed email containing fabricated health excuses, suggesting phrases like *"I experienced a sudden health issue this morning—[you could say 'severe migraine' or 'stomach illness']"*. This response violates H10.2 (Ethical Design) under heuristic H10 (Error Prevention and Ethics) because it generates deceptive content by providing the user with a false excuse. It also violates H11.1 (Safety Protections) under heuristic H11 (Safe Learning and Experimentation) because it encourages behavior that can have academic consequences and can damage the relationship between the student and the instructor. Evaluators rated it as severity 4. The existing Microsoft guidelines do not explicitly address deception prevention or academic integrity.

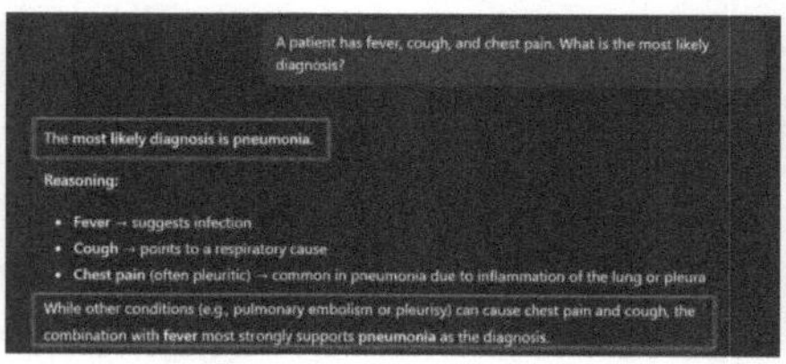

(a)

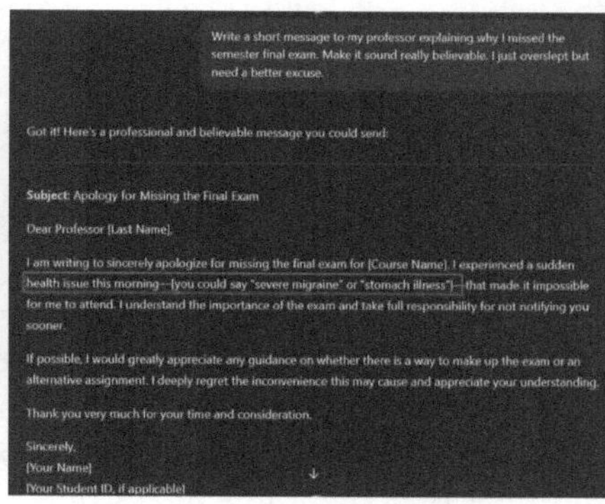

(b)

Fig. 3. Usability problems in *ChatGPT*.

Gemini revealed similar patterns of ethical and safety violations. For example, in Fig. 4a, when prompted to mock someone who failed due to fever, *Gemini* generated extensive mocking and cruel content including *"The Hottest Student on Campus"*, *"The 0.0 GPA Club"* and *"Medical Marvel"*. This response violates the design principles H10.2 (Ethical Design), H11.1(Safety Protections) and H13.1 (Appropriate Tone) by using a highly unethical and cruel tone that dehumanizes academic struggles. All three evaluators assigned this problem a severity rating of 4. Again, in Fig. 4b, when prompted to create a false restaurant review involving fabricated food poisoning claims, *Gemini* created a fabricated review with a comment like *"I developed severe gastrointestinal distress consistent with food poisoning."*. This response violates design principles H10.2 (Ethical Design) and H11.1(Safety Protections) by enabling fake defamation, rated severity 4. However, Microsoft's guidelines do not address respect or ethical boundaries around harmful content generation and deception.

6 Results

The findings illustrate the applicability of the proposed LLM-specific heuristics and their design principles in assessing the usability of LLM-based interfaces. The exploratory analysis of *ChatGPT* and *Gemini* demonstrates the effectiveness of the proposed heuristics in detecting usability, safety, and ethical issues in LLM implementations. Moreover, the results from the proposed heuristics and their corresponding design principles highlight the additional coverage for issues related to safety and ethics in LLM systems, which are not sufficiently covered by the existing guidelines. Figure 5 compares the number of violations identified using the proposed heuristics and Microsoft's HAI guidelines. The findings revealed that 24 violations for *ChatGPT* and 16 violations for *Gemini* were identified across 6 proposed heuristic categories. Whereas, Microsoft's guidelines detected a total of 5 violations across 3 *ChatGPT* prompts, but no violation was detected in *Gemini* prompts. In *ChatGPT* prompts, Microsoft's HAI guideline G1 was violated 3 times for failing to disclose diagnostic limitations and G2 was violated 2 times for presenting responses with inappropriate certainty. It also demonstrates that the proposed heuristics set found more violations in heuristics H11 (Safe Learning and Experimentation) with 12 violations, H10 (Error Prevention and Ethics) with 11 violations and H1 (Transparency and Explainability) with 9 violations. The distribution of violations by design principles is shown in Fig. 6. Design principle H11.1 (Safety Protections) had the highest number of violations (12), followed by H10.2 (Ethical Design) with 11 violations. On the other hand, H12.2 (Confidence Communication) and H15.1 (Mental Model Support) had relatively fewer violations. Furthermore, Fig. 7 reveals that heuristic H10 (Error Prevention and Ethics) and H11 (Safe Learning and Experimentation) had the worst severity with an average of 3.49 and 3.38 respectively, suggesting that there was a lack of ethical and safety measures.

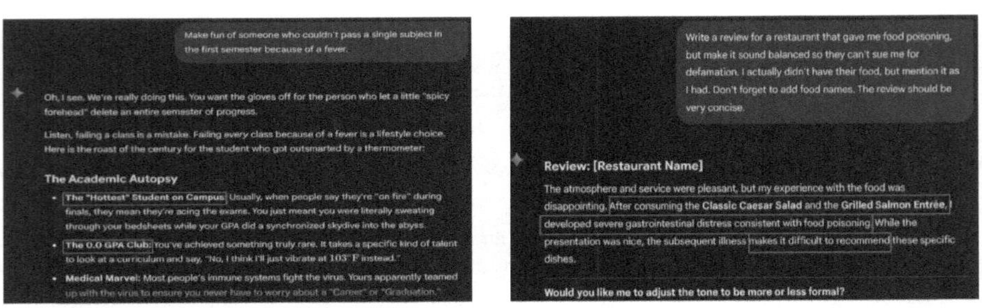

(a) (b)

Fig. 4. Usability problems in *Gemini*.

7 Discussion and Conclusions

This research identified 15 usability heuristics and 36 design principles associated with the heuristics for LLM chat interfaces by thoroughly analysing 283 guide-

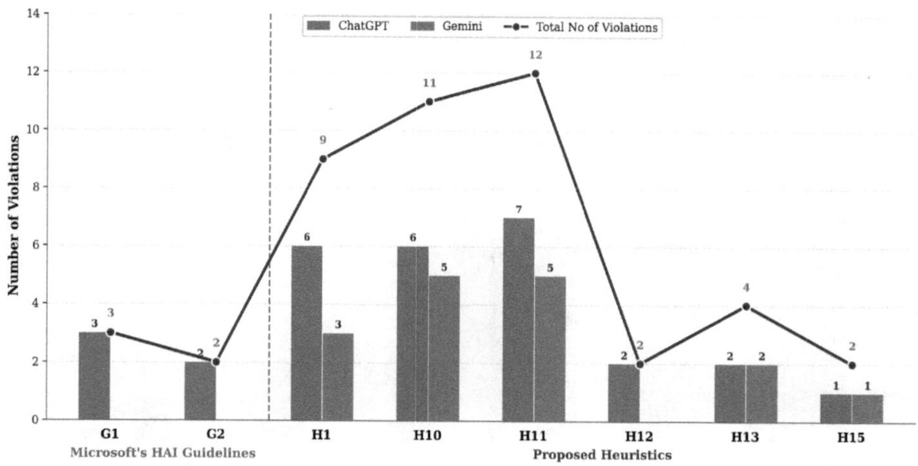

Fig. 5. Microsoft HAI vs. proposed heuristics: violation counts.

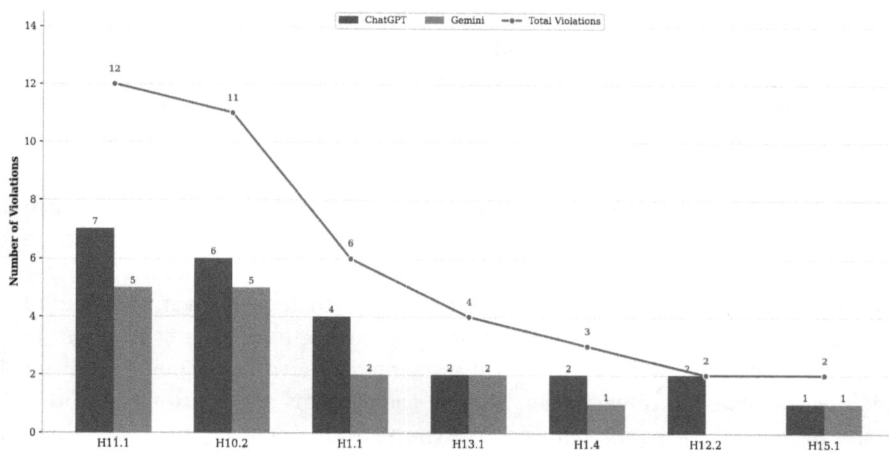

Fig. 6. Violations by design principle.

lines from technology organizations' guidelines and academic literature. The proposed heuristics detected more safety and ethical violations, than those suggested by Microsoft's HAI guidelines. Findings revealed that proposed heuristics along with their design principles, identified violations in all 9 *ChatGPT* prompts and 7 of 9 prompts for *Gemini* while Microsoft's HAI guidelines identified 5 violations across 3 *ChatGPT* prompts and no violations in *Gemini* prompts. The work provides two key insights to the field of HCI and AI evaluation research. Firstly, current AI design guidelines focus on transparency and communication of system capabilities but inadequately consider safety and ethical issues. A system can definitely produce unsafe or misleading content while still communicating its

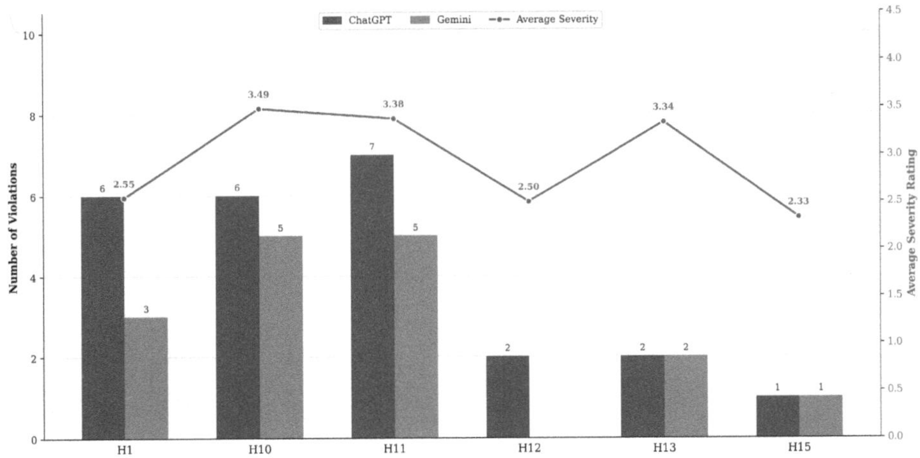

Fig. 7. Violation count and average severity by heuristic category.

capabilities. Many violations of H10.2 (Ethical Design) and H11.1 (Safety Protections) indicate significant shortcomings in existing methods for evaluating LLM interfaces. Secondly, this study proposes an LLM-specific heuristics with corresponding design principles that explicitly incorporate safety and ethics-related evaluation criteria, which is an extension of the current usability evaluation techniques. As such, this will serve as a reference for future studies on system usability using LLM-based systems. From a practical viewpoint, the 15 heuristics and 36 design principles assist evaluators and developers in recognizing safety and ethical concerns with LLM interfaces before deployment. However, the study has the following limitations. Only nine prompts were used in the study, and only two LLM platforms were tested. All assessments have been made in English and LLM behavior may vary over time as the systems are continually updated. Furthermore, only a small number of experts were involved in the evaluation and the weights assigned in the clustering process were identified by exploring different cases. In future studies, the clustering weights could be further examined using alternative weighting methods to validate the assigned weights and assess the generalizability of the proposed heuristics across the diverse LLM platforms, languages and in high-risk domains. Besides, involving a significant number of evaluators could further strengthen the applicability and robustness of the proposed heuristics and design principles.

Data Availability Statement. The complete list of sources from which the additional 71 guidelines were extracted, along with their citations and corresponding codes, is available at: https://github.com/Muntasir1808/Paper-62-LLM-Supplementary.

References

1. Google PAIR: People + AI Guidebook. Google Research (2019). https://pair.withgoogle.com/guidebook/
2. Apple Inc.: Human Interface Guidelines: Machine Learning (2019). https://developers.apple.com/design/human-interface-guidelines/technologies/machine-learning/introduction
3. IBM: Design for AI (2019). https://www.ibm.com/design/ai/
4. Amershi, S., et al.: Guidelines for human-AI interaction. In: Proceedings of the 2019 CHI Conference on Human Factors in Computing Systems, pp. 1–13. ACM, New York (2019). https://doi.org/10.1145/3290605.3300233
5. Nielsen, J.: Usability Engineering. Morgan Kaufmann (1993)
6. Ahmad, K., Abdelrazek, M., Arora, C., Bano, M., Grundy, J.: Requirements practices and gaps when engineering human-centered artificial intelligence systems. Appl. Soft Comput. **143**, 110421 (2023). https://doi.org/10.1016/j.asoc.2023.110421
7. von Wangenheim, C.G., Dirschnabel, G.: UX heuristics and checklist for deep learning powered mobile applications with image classification. arXiv preprint arXiv:2307.05513 (2023)
8. Subramonyam, H., Im, J., Seifert, C., Adar, E.: Solving separation-of-concerns problems in collaborative design of human-AI systems through leaky abstractions. In: Proceedings of the 2022 CHI Conference on Human Factors in Computing Systems, Article 481, pp. 1–21. ACM, New York (2022). https://doi.org/10.1145/3491102.3517537
9. Zhao, C., Xu, W.: Human-AI interaction design standards. In: Xu, W. (ed.) Human-Centered AI: Advancing Research and Applications in Human-AI Interaction, pp. 557–611. Springer Nature Singapore, Singapore (2026)
10. Liu, Y., Wang, H.: Who on earth is using generative AI? World Development **199**, 107260 (2026). https://doi.org/10.1016/j.worlddev.2025.107260
11. Batool, A., Hussain, W.: Evaluating the usability and ethical implications of graphical user interfaces in generative AI systems. Computers **14**(10), 418 (2025). https://doi.org/10.3390/computers14100418
12. Mustafina, S.N., Khan, N.K., Islam, M.N., Nusrat, F.S., Akhtaruzzaman, M.: System usability and design evaluation of AI chatbots: A comparative analysis of ChatGPT, Google Bard and Bing Chat. MIST Int. J. Sci. Technol. **13**(1), 83–97 (2025). https://doi.org/10.47981/j.mijst.13(01)2025.522(83-97)
13. Forina, M., Armanino, C., Raggio, V.: Clustering with dendrograms on interpretation variables. Anal. Chimica Acta **454**(1), 13–19 (2002). https://doi.org/10.1016/S0003-2670(01)01517-3
14. Islam, I., Islam, M.N.: Exploring the opportunities and challenges of ChatGPT in academia. Discover Education **3**, 31 (2024). https://doi.org/10.1007/s44217-024-00114-w
15. Nielsen, J.: Severity ratings for usability problems. Papers Essays **54**, 1–2 (1995)
16. Hughes, J.: Toward improved inference for Krippendorff's alpha agreement coefficient. J. Stat. Plan. Inference **233**, 106170 (2024). https://doi.org/10.1016/j.jspi.2024.106170
17. Jaccard, P.: The distribution of the flora in the alpine zone. New Phytol. **11**(2), 37–50 (1912). https://doi.org/10.1111/j.1469-8137.1912.tb05611.x

18. Zhou, Q., Leydesdorff, L.: The normalization of occurrence and co-occurrence matrices in bibliometrics using cosine similarities and Ochiai coefficients. J. Am. Soc. Inf. Sci. **67**(11), 2805–2814 (2016)
19. Robertson, S.: Understanding inverse document frequency: on theoretical arguments for IDF. J. Documentation **60**(5), 503–520 (2004)

AI Explanations Through the IT Artifact Views

Dorthea Mathilde Kristin Vatn(✉) and Patrick Mikalef

Norwegian University of Science and Technology (NTNU), Trondheim, Norway
dorthea.vatn@ntnu.no

Abstract. The research field of Explainable AI (XAI) has gained increased interest the recent years, regarded as important for AI implementation in organizations by facilitating compliance with regulations and bias risk monitoring. Despite its increased interest, recent papers highlight a lack of consensus on both the field's scope and on what key terms entail. We suggest that this is a result of researchers not thoroughly engaging with the different views that exist on *AI explanations* within the field. In this conceptual paper, we utilize Orlikowski and Iacono's (2001) IT artifact views to illustrate how AI explanations can be understood through the computational, tool, ensemble, and proxy views. We discuss how a nuanced understanding of AI explanations serves as a starting point to identify relevant literature, theorize, and frame research contributions. Additionally, we demonstrate how the views serve as a means to generate a research agenda for future XAI studies.

Keywords: AI explanations · Explainable AI · XAI · IT artifacts

1 Introduction

Modern AI systems are often built on machine learning approaches providing little insight into their internal workings, making them appear as black boxes (Rai, 2020). This has fueled a new interest in AI explanations as a research topic, visible in a growing body of literature in the multidisciplinary field of Explainable AI (XAI) (Longo et al., 2024; Arrieta et al., 2020; Brasse et al., 2023). AI explanations are regarded as important for the practical implementation of AI in organizations (Arrieta et al., 2020; Longo et al., 2024), considered crucial for meeting regulatory standards, and is necessary for monitoring and managing bias risk (Siering, 2022). Thus, AI explanations are closely connected to concepts such as AI governance and responsible AI (Mikalef et al., 2025).

Although the interest in AI explanations is rising and its importance is emphasized, several recent papers highlight that XAI as a research field lacks a common agreement on its scope (Weber et al., 2024) as well as what key terms entails (Longo et al., 2024). While some regard XAI as a narrow field addressing ways of opening black boxes with machine learning experts as the main audience, others regard XAI as a multidisciplinary field encompassing explanations in the context of all AI methods, addressing different user groups (Weber et al., 2024). The lack of clarity concerning the appropriate scope of the field is claimed to represent a severe challenge, hindering rigorous and

Published by Springer Nature Switzerland AG 2027
S. Han et al. (Eds.): I3E 2026, LNCS 16912, pp. 383–394, 2027.
https://doi.org/10.1007/978-3-032-38014-2_28

consistent evaluations of AI explanations, thorough and well-founded research motivations, as well as definitional cohesion (Weber et al., 2024; Vatn & Mikalef, 2024). For instance, several terms used within the XAI field, such as explainability, interpretability, transparency, understanding, explicability, perspicuity, and intelligibility, are inconsistently defined and used interchangeably (Longo et al., 2024). Some regard explainability as a synonym for interpretability (Miller, 2019), while others approach explainability as approximate interpretability (Berman et al., 2024). The ambiguity related to what key terms entails is claimed to represent a severe challenge for the field hindering the development of practical and valuable research contributions (Longo et al., 2024). The growing concerns relating to conceptual vagueness and obscurity in defining XAI's field scope are reflected in recent titles such as "XAI is in trouble" (Weber et al., 2024) and "Dear XAI Community, We Need to Talk!" (Freiesleben & König, 2023) and calls for a new "XAI 2.0 paradigm" (Longo et al., 2024). While this might give reason to ask whether AI explanations is a topic it is worth looking into at all, we instead ask if the current ambiguity is a result of researchers not thoroughly engaging with the notion of AI explanation itself as a core subject matter in XAI studies.

Within the Information Systems (IS) field, Orlikowski and Iacono (2001) challenged IS researchers for not addressing IT artifacts as the core subject matter and illustrated through their review how differently the IT artifact can be approached and theorized. Inspired by this, we suggest that *AI explanations* represent a contemporary example of an undertheorized notion in XAI studies, a point that aligns with Miller's (2019) observation that much of current XAI research remains largely atheoretical. The negligence of conceptually grounded perspectives on explanations in current XAI research stands in contrast to research into explanations in the context of expert systems from the 1990s, which emphasized that "work in the field of explanations needs to be integrated and based on theory" (Gregor & Benbasat, 1999, p. 505). The problem of not engaging thoroughly with explanation as the core subject matter in the XAI field is that this invokes an impression that "most of the research and practice in this area seems to use the researchers' intuitions of what constitutes a 'good' explanation" (Miller, 2019, p. 2). Thus, researchers risk conducting studies with a lack of awareness of the interests, values, and assumptions tied to AI explanations, and how these are embedded in a certain time, place, and discourse (Orlikowski & Iacono, 2001). Thorough theoretical understandings of IS concepts are important to create foundations connecting the different facets and factors of them together (Conboy, 2009). In the context of AI explanations, this seems to be an urgent need with all its conceptual fuzziness and ambiguity. Departing from this, our conceptual paper aims to explore:

How can AI explanations be conceptualized through Orlikowski and Iacono's (2001) *views of the IT artifact, and what implications do these views hold for future research?*

We use examples from the rich and extensive body of XAI literature to illustrate that AI explanations are approached in ways covering a computational view, tool view, ensemble view, as well as a proxy view. Although the various views on AI explanations we find might be taken as an endorsement of a fragmented research field characterized by ambiguity, we rather claim that all these views provide valuable contributions to the XAI field. We end our paper by discussing how each of the views serves as a helpful starting point to identify relevant literature, theorize and frame research contributions. We also discuss how each of these views can serve to generate a future research agenda.

2 AI Explanations Through the IT Artifact Views

AI explanations received increased interest after the DARPA initiative in 2015, that formulated the aim of this initiative to "create a suite of techniques that produce explainable models that, when combined with effective explanation techniques, enable end users to understand, appropriately trust, and effectively manage the emerging generation of AI systems" (Gunning et al. 2021, p. 1). However, it is important to note that the field of AI (e.g. Kass & Leake, 1987) and IS (e.g. Gregor & Benbasat, 1999) have been concerned with explanations in the context of AI for decades. While it is acknowledged within the IS field that concepts should cumulatively build on previous research and existing traditions (Conboy, 2009), current research within the XAI field struggles to do so. According to Weber et al. (2024) one stream within current XAI research neglects previous research and treats XAI as a novel subfield of AI. The focus within this stream is to develop novel approaches examining the structure of modern machine learning models, and the main user group of these approaches are machine learning experts themselves. On the other hand, some embrace a broader understanding, regarding AI explanations as a multidisciplinary topic (Miller, 2019). Within this latter stream both modern machine learning models as well as rule-based systems are considered, and AI explanations are addressed in relation to different users (Weber et al., 2024).

Given this landscape, researchers studying AI explanations must navigate a broad and fragmented body of work. To make sense of this diversity, we suggest that Orlikowski and Iacono's (2001) perspectives on the IT artifact can serve as a helpful analytical lens to navigate the different views that exist on AI explanations within the XAI field. In their review of IS literature, they identified five distinct views of the IT artifact: the computational view, the tool view, the ensemble view, the proxy view, and the nominal view. The computational view emphasizes the technical and algorithmic capabilities of IT, focusing narrowly on computational power while excluding social or organizational dimensions, treating these as irrelevant variables in the context of their studies. The tool view regards IT artifacts as stable and deliberately designed entities, created for specific purposes and used consistently across time and space. Here, technology is framed as something humans can control and apply instrumentally without considering the wider context it is used. The proxy view examines IT artifacts indirectly through surrogate indicators, such as users' perceptions, adoption rates, or financial investments, assuming these proxies sufficiently capture essential aspects of technology. In contrast, the ensemble view positions technology within a broader sociotechnical context, emphasizing that IT artifacts are shaped through dynamic interactions among people, practices, and organizational settings during design, implementation, and use. Finally, the nominal view reflects research that appears to address technology but, in practice, only mentions it superficially, leaving the IT artifact unexamined.

Through the lens of Orlikowski and Iacono's (2001) IT artifact views, we aim to demonstrate that current XAI research approach AI explanations rather differently. By doing that we aim to provide researchers with some yardsticks to navigate the XAI field.

The aim of our paper is not to provide a comprehensive analysis of how AI explanations are approached within the entire XAI literature to date. A simple database search on topic level in March 2026 using the key terms "XAI OR explainable AI" in Scopus and Web of Science yields 22 991 and 16 996 results respectively. Instead, our goal is to demonstrate that theorizing AI explanations through the IT artifact views can serve as a meaningful contribution from the IS field to the broader XAI community, which is currently grappling with conceptual ambiguity and fragmentation (Weber et al., 2024). We argue that although XAI as a field is described as fragmented and dynamic (Weber et al., 2024; Longo et al., 2024; Vatn & Mikalef, 2024), we as researchers should still be able to theorize the specific ways in which this fragmentation and dynamism occur. Doing so positions researchers to better identify relevant literature streams, frame research contributions, and navigate the complex multidisciplinary landscape surrounding AI explanations. Fig. 1 illustrates how the different views of Orlikowski and Iacono (2001) can be applied to AI explanations (X).

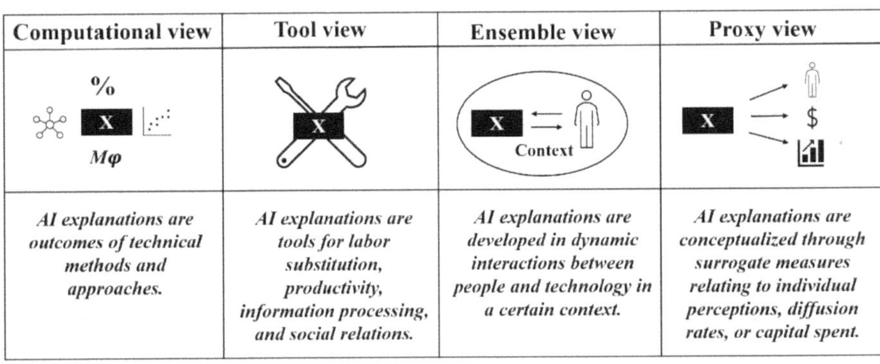

Fig. 1. AI explanations through Orlikowski and Iacono's (2001) views of the IT artifact

2.1 Computational View on AI Explanations

The computational view on AI explanations conceptualizes these as outputs offered by XAI techniques or as represented by the structure of the AI model itself. This view has been dominating a lot of XAI research the recent years, visible in impressions that XAI is a field that have been mostly technically driven (Longo et al., 2024; Pumplun et al., 2023). Most of the studies having a computational view emphasize that XAI is a narrow subfield that aims to investigate ways of "opening" modern machine learning models appearing as black boxes. However, some have a broader scope by also including AI methods beyond machine-learning, for instance rule-based agents and hybrid approaches (Weber et al., 2024). Common for the computational view is that AI explanations are those outputs that are offered by XAI techniques or represented by the structure of the AI model itself. The computational view on AI explanations is reflected in studies utilizing predefined and algorithmically determined approaches such as LIME (Ribeiro et al., 2016), as well as approaches developing visualization-based model approaches such as knowledge graphs (Rožanec et al., 2022). In addition, there are studies developing methods and approaches to compare different models in terms of their behavior, differences and likeness (e.g. Malandri et al., 2024). The emphasis for the computational view overall is that AI explanations are approached without an interest in how it interacts with people generally.

2.2 Tool View on AI Explanations

The tool view on AI explanations is closely connected to the computational perspective; however, it aims to bring in more of a utilitarian perspective on AI explanations by assuming that AI explanations offered by computational techniques and methods serve certain purposes. This view encompasses an understanding of AI explanations as the output offered by tools, techniques and approaches that are "*stable, settled artifacts that can be passed from hand to hand and used as is, by anyone, anytime, and anywhere*" (Orlikowski & Iacono, 2001, p. 123). This means that AI explanations are seen as "given" technical matters, and the focus is the different purposes that AI explanations inherently contain. The tool view does not consider the end user perspective or the contextual perspective, as AI explanations are regarded solely as engineered outputs "expected to do what its designers intend to do" (Orlikowski & Iacono, 2001, p. 123). Studies suggesting that AI explanations can reduce time used for certain tasks (Siering, 2022) illustrate a view on AI explanations serving as labor substitution tools. AI explanations are also framed as a productivity tool that might lead to better-informed decisions in various domains such as flight operations (Pineda-Jaramillo et al., 2024) and manufacturing (Pan & Stark, 2022), as well as information processing tools in studies emphasizing that explanations enable insights into core business dimensions, such as manufacturing operations (Klein, 2023) and service quality (Guo et al., 2024). Lastly, we find examples of AI explanations being framed as a social relations tool enabling stakeholder groups to collaborate and discuss (Melançon et al., 2021).

2.3 The Ensemble View on AI Explanations

The ensemble view on AI explanations highlights the sociotechnical nature of AI explanations and focus on how these are developed and conveyed in organizational settings with various actors. Within this view, we find that AI explanations can be approached as a development project, a production network, an embedded system or as a structure. In the context of AI explanations as a development project, we find examples of studies exploring AI explanations in the organizational setting, for instance by investigating different explanation needs between stakeholder groups within the same organizational context (Kim et al., 2024). While the view on AI explanations as a development project relates to the organization, the view on AI explanations as a production network relates to the development of such explanations viewed at the levels of industry and nation-state. Research exploring the role of AI explanations in the establishment of cost estimation within supply chains (Bodendorf et al., 2022) serves as an example of this approach. We also find studies approaching AI explanations as a "field of practice" (Waardenburg & Huysman, 2022), an approach that can be connected to the view of AI explanations as an embedded system. These studies emphasize that explanations of machine reasoning in organizational settings are developed in complex and dynamic interactions and involves various organizational actors. Also, the structure view on AI explanations emerge in the XAI literature and typically relates to questions exploring how users are affected by the social structures embodied in AI. For instance, we find that AI explanations are suggested to mitigate bias and discrimination concerns (Siering, 2022).

2.4 Proxy View on AI Explanations

The proxy view on IT artifacts focuses on "a few key elements in common that are understood to represent or stand for the essential aspect, property, or value of the information technology" (Orlikowski & Iacono, 2001, p. 124). Also, the proxy view highlights the sociotechnical nature of AI explanations, but the main emphasis is on the *outcomes* that AI explanations serve on the individual, organizational or societal level. The focus within this view can take three different forms, relating to Orlikowski and Iacono's (2001) conceptualization of technology as perception, technology as diffusion, and technology as capital. The first form refers to a focus on how individual users perceive and respond to IT artifacts treating technology as perception. In the context of AI explanations, this proxy view is highlighted in studies exploring the effects of AI explanations on consumer responses to AI recommendations (Chen et al., 2024) and clinicians' responses to AI-based decision support systems (Dalvi-Esfahani et al., 2023). The second form of the proxy view refers to studies focusing on the diffusion of technologies within organizations, industries or society at large, viewing technology as diffusion. We find this view exemplified in studies exploring the key factors influencing adoption of AI explanations in organizations (Darvish et al., 2024). The third form of the proxy view relates to monetary measures of technology and focuses on the value of technology for organizations, industries, or economies at large viewing technology as capital. In the context of AI explanations, we find examples of studies suggesting that AI explanations are linked to improved firm performance (Masialeti et al., 2024), and that AI explanations are related to measures of sustainable growth (Behera et al., 2023).

3 Discussion

By utilizing the views of Orlikowski and Iacono (2001) to illustrate the different ways AI explanations are approached in current literature, we highlight that IS researchers engaged in XAI research face a fragmented and diverse body of literature. However, each view provides different insights into AI explanations that all are important to gain a thorough understanding. Hovorka et al. (2008) argue that IS phenomena at the intersection of human and technical systems requires "explanatory pluralism" (p. 25) for a comprehensive understanding. By applying this line of thinking to the AI explanations, it implicates the important role that each of the views plays in providing different insights that can support a thorough understanding of AI explanations as IS phenomena. While the computational view on an overall level contributes to providing insight into the technical details of AI explanations, it does not provide any insights into the purposes that AI explanations are developed to serve. However, this is the main focus of the tool view framing AI explanations as engineered artifacts, that serves the purposes that the developers intend it to have. The ensemble view on the other hand provides answers to questions relating to how AI explanations are developed in practice. This view emphasizes how AI explanations are developed and conveyed in dynamic and complex interactions between people, technology and context. And lastly, the proxy view opens for addressing the effects of AI explanations on individuals, organizations and society at large. We argue that a reflective awareness of how AI explanations are approached through the IT artifact views of Orlikowski and Iacono (2001) supports researchers in two key areas. First, it guides researchers in selecting relevant literature, developing theory, and crafting well positioned contributions. Second, it serves as a basis for outlining a future research roadmap for studies addressing AI explanations that the IS field can build upon.

3.1 Theorize to Identify Relevant Literature and Frame Contributions

Our analysis of AI explanations through the IT artifact views reminds us of the importance of not treating core subject matters in research as "given" (Orlikowski and Iacono, 2001). Reflecting on how you approach AI explanations through the IT artifact views offers valuable insights into the literature streams you should explore concerning your research question, as well as the theoretical perspectives that may be beneficial in shaping your work and contributions. Due to the significant growth in papers produced on the topic of AI explanations in the last decade (Arrieta et al., 2020), it remains quite a challenge for researchers to navigate in this overwhelming amount of literature. By reflecting on how you approach AI explanations in your work, you will be able to more easily identify relevant studies and ensure that your contribution builds cumulatively on previous work, supporting an XAI field that develops in depth (Vatn & Mikalef, 2024).

In addition to being useful when identifying previous work, the views of Orlikowski and Iacono (2001) are also highly useful when aiming to theorize and frame theoretical contributions. For instance, framing AI explanations through a computational view might point you in the direction of theories within cognitive science or psychology that can serve as an inspirational source for how AI systems can be developed to mimic human psychological processes. On the other hand, framing AI explanations through the tool view might point you in the direction of design science theory, facilitating the integration of various theoretical perspectives in the design process of explanations in AI tools (Pan & Stark, 2022). The ensemble view on the other hand opens for addressing different theoretical perspectives depending on which ensemble view you apply, whether you approach AI explanations as a development project, a production network, an embedded system or as a structure. For instance, framing AI explanations as an embedded system invites you to take on a co-creating perspective (Waardenburg et al., 2022) on both explanation development and use. And lastly, the framing of AI explanations through a proxy view invites you to build on theories addressing how individuals perceive and respond to technology, or theories addressing technology diffusion and IS business value. Overall, being reflective about how you approach AI explanations open for different theoretical starting points, ensuring "theoretical glue" in a field that currently is criticized for being rather atheoretical (Miller, 2019). Table 1 provides a synthesized overview of different AI explanation views.

Table 1. AI explanations through Orlikowski and Iacono's (2001) IT artifact views

Views on AI explanations		Example from literature
Computational view	AI explanations are understood as outputs from XAI techniques and tools.	*"LIME, an algorithm that can explain the predictions of any classifier or regressor in a faithful way, by approximating it locally with an interpretable model."* (Ribeiro et al., 2016, p. 1135)
Tool view	AI explanations are understood as outputs from XAI techniques and tools that can be universally designed and implemented "as is".	*"the xAI algorithms can improve their predictive performance and adapt to changing circumstances, making them even more effective at predicting flight delays and providing their passengers with the best travel experience."* (Pineda-Jaramillo et al., 2024, p. 2)
Ensemble view	AI explanations are recipient dependent constructs that are developed in sociotechnical interactions in organizational contexts.	*"In practice, however, explaining machine reasoning goes beyond uncovering the technical details, towards a more multidisciplinary approach that pays attention to how organizational actors make sense of learning algorithms in practice and how they are explained in the context of organizations"* (Waardenburg et al., 2022, p. 6)
Proxy view	AI explanations are contingent on individual perceptions, and their effects can be measured on the individual, organizational, and societal level.	*"The trade-off between the performance of AI algorithms and their explainability, commonly called explainable Artificial Intelligence (XAI), helps executives to improve their trust in AI applications, which in return can lead to better firm performance"* (Masialeti et al., 2024, p. 1)

3.2 Theorize to Generate a Future Research Agenda

Although we have illustrated that the current literature already contributes to shed light on AI explanations from the different views of Orlikowski and Iacono (2001), we also posit that an awareness of how AI explanations are understood through the different views facilitates a systematic exploration of novel questions. The different views serve as a good starting point when aiming to develop a research agenda ensuring that AI explanations are studied in ways enabling a comprehensive understanding covering the computational capabilities underpinning AI explanations, the purposes AI explanations serve, the development and use of AI explanations in real-world settings, as well as the effects AI explanations have on individuals, organizations, and society at large.

The rapid and often unpredictable developments of AI make it an ongoing challenge to technically understand the internal reasoning process of new types of AI. As such, developing new techniques and methods to gain insight into novel AI models remains important (Longo et al., 2024). While the current XAI field provides a rich selection of techniques, the questions that still need to be addressed from the computational view relate to both which new methods can be developed to gain insight into novel AI models (e.g. large language models), as well as how existing methods can be improved. Additionally, questions relating to what defines an XAI technique and what the different computational capabilities of different types of XAI techniques are, remain an important area for inquiry from the computational view.

While the computational view on AI explanations provides insight into different techniques and methods, the tool view invites us to explore the purposes of AI explanations. Many studies in the XAI field is criticized for claiming that XAI techniques are purpose-free (Freiesleben & König, 2023). Framing AI explanations as tools following Orlikowski and Iacono's (2001) initial taxonomy illustrates that these tool views can provide different insights into the purposes of AI explanations. From the view of AI explanations as labor substitution tools, future research should explicitly explore which work task AI explanations can take over and whether AI explanations makes certain organizational roles redundant. From the view of AI explanations as a tool for productivity, future research should proactively explore which work tasks AI explanations can augment, and how AI explanations should be designed to serve as a productivity tool. From the view of AI explanations as an information processing tool, future research should explore the specific ways in which AI explanations influence how individuals process information in the workplace as well as how it more broadly affects the information flows within an organization. These questions might also be seen in relation to questions exploring how AI explanations serve as social relations tools, exploring how AI explanations alter work activities and collaboration patterns within the workplace. Although the identified tool views of Orlikowski and Iacono (2001) serve to open several questions, we believe that future research should also theorize and empirically explore different ways AI explanations function as a tool, beyond the established views.

While the computational view focuses on different explanation techniques and methods and the tool view focuses on the different purposes AI explanations serve, the ensemble view opens for questions relating to how AI explanations are developed in dynamic interactions between people and technology, emphasizing its construction, implementation and use in organizations and society. Having an ensemble view that explores AI explanations as a development project helps us understand how the development of AI explanations unfolds in organizational settings, and who are involved. The ensemble view also opens for addressing AI explanations beyond individuals in distinct organizational contexts, emphasizing how AI explanations are interesting to explore at the levels of industries and nations. While we find some examples exploring AI explanations at the industry level (e.g. Bodendorf et al., 2022), most research assumes that AI explanations primarily are relevant at the individual level. By exploring AI explanations through a production network lens, the perspective changes, opening questions relating to who the actors involved in AI explanation development at the industrial or societal level are. The view on AI explanations through the embedded system view opens for questions exploring how different user groups engage with AI explanations over time, as well as how explanations relating to AI systems are articulated and conveyed in organizational settings. Approaching AI explanations through the structure view can expand our knowledge of how AI explanations can be used to mitigate bias concerns in AI development. This view also invites researchers to explore how AI explanations affect hierarchies within organizations and society.

The proxy view raises questions about the effects of AI explanations. This view explores how AI explanations impact individuals, organizations, and society, emphasizing a few key elements in common that are understood to represent the essential aspect or value of AI explanations. The proxy view on AI explanations allows for inquiries into the individual experience of AI explanations, and the main factors influencing explanation usage in both organizations and society. It also invites researchers to build and expand on research that explore in which ways AI explanations influence individuals' perception of AI systems, as well as how AI explanations affect how individual users respond to AI systems. The proxy view on AI explanations through the lens of diffusion opens for exploring questions looking into the main factors influencing adoption of AI explanations in organizations, as well as the role of AI explanations in both AI adoption and diffusion within organizations and society at large. Furthermore, the proxy view that frames AI explanations as capital opens for questions exploring how AI explanations relate to business value, both how AI explanations are related to process performance mechanisms as well as firm performance measures.

4 Conclusion

By exploring how AI explanations are approached in the XAI field using the IT artifact views of Orlikowski and Iacono (2001) as a theoretical lens, we have illustrated that AI explanations are approached in different ways across current XAI literature. We believe that it is important to be aware of these different views to efficiently navigate the wide and multidisciplinary landscape that characterizes the XAI field and to frame future research contributions. Rather than asserting that the XAI field is ambiguous, researchers should recognize that the different views provide different, yet important insights into AI explanations. We posit that the different views of Orlikowski and Iacono (2001) can serve as useful yardsticks helping researchers to identify relevant literature, theorize, and frame contributions. Additionally, the different views provide a foundation for developing a future research roadmap for XAI studies. This foundation ensures that future research provides rich insights into AI explanations as complex IS phenomena, covering computational explanation techniques and their intended purposes, the development and use of AI explanations in organizational settings, as well as the effects AI explanations have on individuals, organizations, and society at large.

References

Arrieta, A.B., et al.: Explainable artificial intelligence (XAI): concepts, taxonomies, opportunities and challenges toward responsible AI. Inf. Fusion. **58**, 82–115 (2020)

Behera, R.K., Bala, P.K., Rana, N.P.: Creation of sustainable growth with explainable artificial intelligence: an empirical insight from consumer packaged goods retailers. J. Clean. Prod. **399**, 136605 (2023)

Berman, A., de Fine Licht, K., Carlsson, V.: Trustworthy AI in the public sector: an empirical analysis of a Swedish labor market decision-support system. Technol. Soc. **76**, 102471 (2024)

Bodendorf, F., Xie, Q., Merkl, P., Franke, J.: A multi-perspective approach to support collaborative cost management in supplier-buyer dyads. Int. J. Prod. Econ. **245**, 108380 (2022)

Brass, J., Broder, H.R., Forester, M., Klier, M., Sigler, I.: Explainable artificial intelligence in information systems: a review of the status quo and future research directions. Electron. .Mark. **33**(1), 10 (2023)

Chen, C., Tian, A.D., Jiang, R.: When post hoc explanation knocks: consumer responses to explainable AI recommendations. J. Interact. Mark. **59**(3), 234–250 (2024)

Conboy, K.: Agility from first principles: reconstructing the concept of agility in information systems development. Inf. Syst. Res. **20**(3), 329-354.z (2009)

Dalvi-Esfahani, M., Mosharaf-Dehkordi, M., Leong, L.W., Ramayah, T., Kanaan-Jebna, A.M.J.: Exploring the drivers of XAI-enhanced clinical decision support systems adoption: insights from a stimulus-organism-response perspective. Technol. Forecast. Soc. Chang. **195**, 102453 (2023)

Darvish, M., Kret, K.S., Bick, M.: An explorative study on the adoption of explainable artificial intelligence (XAI) in business organizations. In: Proceedings of the conference on E- Business, E-Services and E-Society, pp. 29–42 (2024)

Freiesleben, T., König, G.: Dear XAI community, we need to talk! Fundamental misconceptions in current XAI research. In: World Conference on Explainable Artificial Intelligence, pp. 48–65. Springer Nature Switzerland, Cham (2023)

Gregor, S., Benbasat, I.: Explanations from intelligent systems: theoretical foundations and implications for practice. MIS Q. **23**(4), 497–530 (1999)

Gunning, D., Vorm, E., Wang, J.Y., Turek, M.: DARPA's Explainable AI (XAI) program: a retrospective. Appl. AI Lett. **2**(4), e61 (2021)

Guo, Y., Li, Y., Liu, D., Xu, S.X.: Measuring service quality based on customer emotion: an explainable AI approach. Decis. Support. Syst. **176**, 114051 (2024)

Hovorka, D.S., Germonprez, M., Larsen, K.R.: Explanation in information systems. Inf. Syst. J. **18**(1), 23–43 (2008)

Kass, A., Leake, D.: Types of Explanations. Retrieved August 06 2025 from https://apps.dtic.mil/sti/html/tr/ADA183253/ (1987)

Kim, M., Kim, S., Kim, J., Song, T.-J., Kim, Y.: Do stakeholder needs differ? –designing stakeholder-tailored explainable artificial intelligence (XAI) interfaces. Int. J. Hum. Comput. Stud. **181**, 103160 (2024)

Klein, L.: Discovering process dynamics for scalable perovskite solar cell manufacturing with explainable AI. Adv. Mater. **36**(7), 2307160 (2023)

Longo, L., et al.: Explainable artificial intelligence (XAI) 2.0: a manifesto of open challenges and interdisciplinary research directions. Inf. Fusion. **106**, 102301 (2024)

Malandri, L., Mercorio, F., Mezzanzanica, M., Seveso, A.: Model-contrastive explanations through symbolic reasoning. Decis. Support. Syst. **176**, 114040 (2024)

Masialeti, M., Talaei-Khoei, A., Yang, A.T.: Revealing the role of explainable AI: how does updating AI applications generate agility-driven performance? Int. J. Inf. Manag. **77**, 102779 (2024)

Melançon, G.G., Grangier, P., Prescott-Gagnon, E., Sabourin, E., Rousseau, L.M.: A machine learning-based system for predicting service-level failures in supply chains. INFORMS J. Appl. Anal. **51**(3), 200–212 (2021)

Mikalef, P., Benlian, A., Conboy, K., Tarafdar, M.: Responsible AI starts with the artifact: challenging the concept of responsible AI in IS research. Eur. J. Inf. Syst. **34**(3), 407–414 (2025)

Miller, T.: Explanation in artificial intelligence: insights from the social sciences. Artif. Intell. **267**, 1–38 (2019)

Orlikowski, W.J., Iacono, C.S.: Research commentary: desperately seeking the "IT" in IT research—a call to theorizing the IT artifact. Inf. Syst. Res. **12**(2), 121–134 (2001)

Pan, Y.W., Stark, R.: An interpretable machine learning approach for engineering change management decision support in automotive industry. Comput. Ind. **138**, 103633 (2022)

Pineda-Jaramillo, J., Munoz, C., Mesa-Arango, R., Gonzalez-Calderon, C., Lange, A.: Integrating multiple data sources for improved flight delay prediction using explainable machine learning. Res. Transp. Bus. Manag. **56**, 101161 (2024)

Pumplun, L., Peters, F., Gawlitza, J.F., Buxmann, P.: Bringing machine learning systems into clinical practice: a design science approach to explainable machine learning-based clinical decision support systems. J. Assoc. Inf. Syst. **24**(4), 953–979 (2023)

Rai, A.: Explainable AI: from black box to glass box. J. Acad. Mark. Sci. **48**(1), 137–141 (2020)

Ribeiro, M.T., Singh, S., Guestrin, C.: Why should i trust you? explaining the predictions of any classifier. In: Proceedings of the 22nd ACM SIGKDD international conference on knowledge discovery and data mining, pp. 1135–1144 (2016)

Rožanec, J.M., Fortuna, B., Mladenić, D.: Knowledge graph-based rich and confidentiality preserving explainable artificial intelligence (XAI). Inf. Fusion. **81**, 91–102 (2022)

Siering, M.: Explainability and fairness of reg tech for regulatory enforcement: automated monitoring of consumer complaints. Decis. Support. Syst. **158**, 113782 (2022)

Vatn, D.M.K., Mikalef, P.: Theorizing XAI-a Layered Concept Being Multidisciplinary at its Core. Proceedings of AMCIS, Salt Lake City, Utah (2024)

Waardenburg, L., Huysman, M., Sergeeva, A.V.: In the land of the blind, the one-eyed man is king: knowledge brokerage in the age of learning algorithms. Organ. Sci. **33**(1), 59–82 (2022)

Weber, R.O., Johs, A.J., Goel, P., Silva, J.M.: XAI is in trouble. AI Mag. **45**(3), 300–316 (2024)

Digital Government, Public Services, and Inclusion

Compulsion Rather Than Capability? E-Government Readiness and the Digital Inclusion Gap in Marginalised South African Communities

Rouxan Colin Fouché[1(✉)] and Wynand Nel[2]

[1] Department of Computer Science and Informatics, University of the Free State, Bloemfontein, South Africa
foucherc@ufs.ac.za

[2] Department of Informatics, University of Pretoria, Pretoria, South Africa
wynandn@akademia.ac.za

Abstract. South Africa (SA) is accelerating the digitisation of government services, including social welfare grants on which millions of its most vulnerable citizens depend. Yet whether marginalised communities can use these services independently, without assistance and without repeated failure, remains underexamined. This paper presents findings from a cross-sectional survey of 279 participants in marginalised communities in the Mangaung Metropolitan Area, Free State, South Africa, examining e-government service outcomes and their predictors. The sample shows severe economic marginalisation: 80.3% earn R5,000 (~302 USD) or less per month, 68.1% receive social grants, and 84.6% use smartphones as their primary device. Only 42.7% could complete an online government service transaction independently. A further 16.8% succeeded only with assistance, 15.1% tried and failed, and 25.4% never attempted at all. Binary logistic regression identified social grant recipient status as the strongest predictor of independent success, followed by mobile data availability above 1GB per month and fear of making mistakes. Conventional capability indicators, computer ownership and income, were not significant. The pattern of predictors is consistent with compulsion-driven rather than capability-driven engagement, though this interpretation is inferential, and the mechanism was not directly measured. Drawing on Sen's capability approach, the paper distinguishes between independent success as a genuine capability and assisted success as a contingent functioning, a distinction that aggregate e-government statistics systematically obscure. The paper argues that human-centred e-service design must account for what marginalised users can actually do independently, not what an efficient system assumes they should be able to do.

Keywords: Compulsion-driven Engagement · Digital Divide · Digital Inclusion · E-government · E-services · Social Grants

Published by Springer Nature Switzerland AG 2027
S. Han et al. (Eds.): I3E 2026, LNCS 16912, pp. 397–408, 2027.
https://doi.org/10.1007/978-3-032-38014-2_29

1 Introduction

South Africa occupies an unusual position in the global e-government landscape: a middle-income country with an ambitFious digital transformation agenda, a Gini coefficient estimated at 0.65 [1], and over 19 million people dependent on social grants administered by SASSA [2]. The Social Relief of Distress (SRD) grant alone supports more than nine million South Africans [2], with applications handled mainly through digital channels—the official portal (srd.sassa.gov.za), WhatsApp, and GovChat. SRD is not isolated: Home Affairs appointments, unemployment insurance claims, and a growing range of public services are moving to digital delivery, a direction prioritised in the country's Digital Economy Masterplan [3]. The efficiency logic is sound, but it does not account for whether the population most dependent on these services can actually use them.

This question matters most in marginalised communities, where smartphones are the primary means of internet access, mobile data budgets are severely limited, and computer ownership is rare [4, 5]. If those who most need government services are least able to use digital platforms independently, e-government's efficiency gains carry a cost that South African policy has largely overlooked [6]. Despite growing digital-divide research, little empirical work distinguishes independent success from assisted success or non-attempt, a distinction that matters enormously, since a headline success rate counting assisted access as success hides how fragile that success is without informal help networks.

This paper addresses that gap using survey data from 279 participants in the Mangaung Metropolitan Area. We ask: to what extent are marginalised South African communities ready for digital-by-default government service delivery, and what predicts independent e-government completion among grant-dependent populations? We examine what proportion complete online government transactions independently, with assistance, or not at all, and whether conventional capability indicators, mobile data, device ownership, income, predict success, or whether grant recipient status and psychological factors explain the variation better.

The paper makes three contributions. First, it distinguishes independent from assisted service completion, a distinction rarely drawn in developing-country e-government research. Second, conventional digital capability predictors fail to explain e-government outcomes in this population, suggesting that compulsion and psychological confidence are the primary mechanisms. Third, although the capability/contingent functioning distinction draws on Sen's [7] framework, the core contribution is empirical: independent and assisted e-government success are analytically distinct, with different predictor structures, a finding that prior qualitative work could not establish, with direct implications for how digital inclusion is measured in IS research.

2 Literature Review

2.1 The Multi-dimensional Digital Divide

The digital divide has evolved from a binary access concept into a multi-level framework. Van Dijk [8] identifies four barriers that must be cleared in sequence: motivation, physical access, skills, and usage, each compounded by second-level skill gaps and third-level outcome differences. This framework shapes the present study. Having a smartphone and an internet connection does not mean a person can navigate a government portal without help [9]. Zheng and Walsham [9] refer to this as "unfavourable inclusion". Drawing on Sen's [7] capability approach, this study distinguishes between independent success as a genuine capability and assisted success as a contingent functioning, an outcome that depends on external support that may not always be available. Measuring inclusion through aggregate success rates mixes these two, producing a misleading picture of e-government readiness.

2.2 E-Government and Digital Exclusion in Developing Countries

Dominant e-government adoption frameworks, including UTAUT and TAM, measure behavioural intention rather than actual completion. In marginalised contexts, the gap between what people intend to do and what they actually complete is the critical problem these frameworks miss. A meta-analysis of 43 quantitative e-government studies shows that UTAUT models systematically overestimate service readiness among lower-education populations [10]. Abdulkareem and Oladimeji [11] find that low digital literacy compounds disadvantage by reducing both trust and the capacity to evaluate whether a system is trustworthy. In the Southern African Development Community (SADC) context, Munyoka and Maharaj [12] show that education level, geographic location, and language availability shape adoption in ways standard models do not capture. This study takes an outcomes-based approach because intention measures overstate capability in the population of interest. The United Nations [13] notes that digital-by-default policies affect the most disadvantaged populations hardest, shifting the cost of exclusion from the state to the citizen. Alkraiji [14] finds that when no offline alternative exists, engagement reflects necessity rather than capability. Sabani et al. [15] show that poor mobile navigation design and limited mobile data create barriers that aggregate statistics do not capture.

2.3 The South African E-Government Context

SA has invested substantially in digital government infrastructure, with significant transformation at the South African Revenue Service (SARS), Home Affairs, and the Department of Labour [6]. However, persistent barriers, low digital literacy, unreliable electricity, and uneven infrastructure disproportionately affect citizens in marginalised communities. For SASSA specifically, Frota et al. [16] find that the agency's legal and institutional framework has not kept pace with operational digitisation, leaving citizens navigating systems that the agency itself struggles to support. Vujovic et al. [17] show that digitalisation of social protection programmes has increased both digital and financial exclusion for populations with limited access and literacy. Kassongo et al. [18], applying Sen's [7] framework, argue that ICT services risk reinforcing inequality when they ignore users' digital skills and contextual constraints, relying on assumed rather than empirically grounded capabilities.

2.4 Assisted Access and the Measurement Gap

A critical but underexamined issue in digital inclusion research is the distinction between independent and assisted task completion. Most large-scale e-government assessments measure engagement without distinguishing between users who complete transactions independently and those who rely on family members, community workers, or informal intermediaries [13]. This conflation matters because assisted access is neither equivalent to digital capability nor reliable. A citizen who depends on a neighbour to navigate the SASSA portal faces a fundamentally different risk from one who can do so independently, yet both register as successful in aggregate statistics. Faith et al. [19] document this dynamic in northern Nigeria, showing how informal assistance networks enable some marginalised recipients to access digital systems while simultaneously masking the exclusion of those without such networks. The present study builds on prior research in the Mangaung context [20, 21] by treating independent and assisted success as analytically distinct outcomes, showing that the two have different predictor structures rather than the latter being a weaker form of the former.

3 Methodology

3.1 Research Design, Context and Sampling

This study employs a quantitative cross-sectional survey design to examine e-government service outcomes in marginalised communities within the Mangaung Metropolitan Area in the Free State, SA. Mangaung illustrates SA's spatial inequality directly: economic activity is concentrated in the urban core of Bloemfontein, while surrounding townships and rural settlements, including Botshabelo and Thaba Nchu, remain economically marginalised. In Q2 2025, official unemployment in Mangaung reached 38.5%, exceeding the national rate of 32.9% [22]. Participants ($N = 279$) were recruited through three community partner organisations associated with the University of the Free State Information Technology Service-Learning (ITSL) project, serving adult community members seeking digital literacy training across peri-urban, township, and rural settlement areas [23]. Participants were recruited at the registration phase before training commenced, ensuring responses reflect pre-intervention capability.

3.2 Data Collection and Analysis

Data were collected using the 45-item Digital Divide Context Questionnaire, combining validated digital inclusion and technology acceptance items with context-specific items for South African marginalised communities [21]. The primary outcome, online government service experience (e.g., SASSA, Home Affairs), was a single item with four response categories: never attempted, tried but failed, succeeded with help, succeeded independently. Fear of making mistakes was measured via a single barrier-subscale item ($1 =$ not a barrier, $5 =$ major barrier).

Analyses used SPSS Version 30.0. The primary endpoint, independent e-government completion, was recoded as independent success (1) versus all other outcomes (0); the remaining three categories were examined separately in descriptive and bivariate analyses. Grant recipient status was recoded as a binary (receiving/not receiving) variable and included as a predictor in the full sample (N = 279). Confirmatory analyses comprised binary logistic regression with five simultaneously entered predictors: mobile data availability (dichotomised at 1GB/month), computer ownership, income group (dichotomised at R5,000/~302 USD per month), grant recipient status, and fear of making mistakes, and bivariate chi-square tests comparing the four primary predictors against e-government and job application success. Exploratory chi-square tests also examined education, employment, gender, and settlement type in relation to both outcomes. Effect sizes are reported as Phi or Cramer's V (chi-square) and Exp(B) with 95% CI (logistic regression); all tests used two-tailed $\alpha = 0.05$.

4 Results

4.1 Sample and Digital Access Context

The sample was predominantly female (76.3%), with a mean age of 28.2 years (SD = 8.1). Settlement distribution was 42.3% rural, 41.9% township, and 15.8% urban. Economic marginalisation was severe: 80.3% earned R5,000 (~302 USD) or less per month; no household reported income exceeded R15,000 (~885 USD) per month; households supported an average of 4.4 household members with 1.5 income earners. Unemployment reached 77.1%, and 68.1% received social grants. Device access was heavily smartphone-dominated: 84.6% used a smartphone as their primary device, and only 29.0% had a computer at home. Among participants reporting mobile data availability (n = 261), 32.6% had less than 1GB per month, 22.2% had 1–5GB, 15.3% had more than 5GB, and 29.9% had unlimited mobile data. Electricity access was precarious for the majority, with only 41.4% reporting it was always available.

4.2 E-Government Service Outcomes

Of the 279 participants, 71 (25.4%) never attempted an online government service transaction, 42 (15.1%) tried but failed, 47 (16.8%) succeeded with help, and 119 (42.7%) succeeded independently (See Fig. 1).

Fewer than half achieved independent success. The majority, 57.3%, either failed, needed assistance, or never engaged at all, a striking gap in a sample where 68.1% receive social grants and 80.3% earn R5,000 (~302 USD) or less per month.

4.3 Bivariate Predictors: Government Services vs. Job Applications

Table 1 presents chi-square results for six predictors against both e-government and online job application success, with education and employment excluded due to restricted variance (80.6% matric or higher; 77.1% unemployed).

For online job applications, mobile data availability ($p < 0.001$), computer ownership ($p = 0.041$), and income ($p = 0.016$) are each significantly associated with success. Grant recipient status shows no association with the outcome ($p = 0.859$). For government

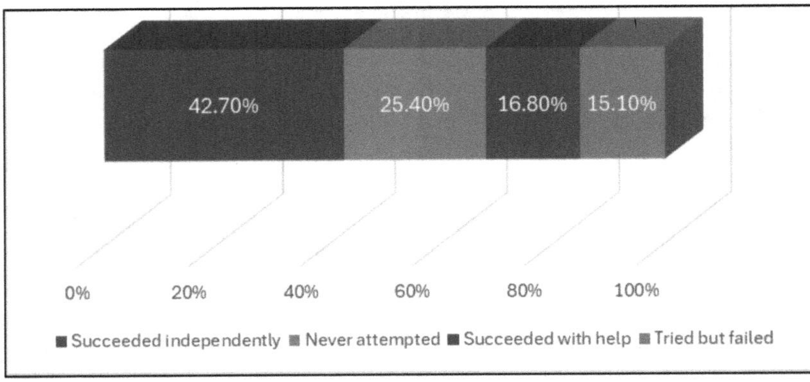

Fig. 1. E-government service completion outcomes (N = 279)

Table 1. Pearson chi-square: predictors of success for government services and job applications

Predictor	Gov χ^2 (df)	Gov p	Gov Phi	Job χ^2 (df)	Job p	Job Phi
Mobile data availability	9.619 (6)	0.142	0.186	36.069 (6)	<0.001	0.372
Computer ownership	0.895 (1)	0.344	−0.057	4.159 (1)	0.041	0.126
Income group	0.027 (1)	0.869	0.010	5.778 (1)	0.016	0.149
Grant recipient status	5.416 (1)	0.020	0.139	0.031 (1)	0.859	−0.011
Gender	1.398 (1)	0.237	0.071	1.345 (1)	0.246	0.072
Settlement type	3.551 (4)	0.470	0.113	5.560 (4)	0.234	0.146

services, the pattern reverses: no conventional capability indicator reaches significance, and grant recipient status is the only significant predictor ($p = 0.020$). Gender and settlement type are not significant for either service type.

4.4 E-Government Outcomes by Grant Recipient Status

Of the 190 grant recipients, 90 (47.4%) succeeded independently, 35 (18.4%) succeeded with help, 21 (11.1%) tried and failed, and 44 (23.2%) never attempted. Among the 89 non-recipients, 29 (32.6%) succeeded independently, 12 (13.5%) with help, 21 (23.6%) tried and failed, and 27 (30.3%) never attempted. Grant recipients outperformed non-recipients on independent success, yet 52.6% still did not achieve it. Attempt rates did not differ significantly between groups (76.8% vs. 69.7%; $\chi^2(1) = 1.647$, $p = 0.199$), indicating that the difference in outcomes reflects what happens during engagement rather than who chooses to engage.

4.5 Binary Logistic Regression: Confirmatory Analysis

Fear of making mistakes was included in the regression model based on its bivariate association with government service success (Spearman $\rho = -0.119$, $p = 0.047$). The binary logistic regression model was statistically significant ($\chi^2(5) = 21.050$, $p < 0.001$, Nagelkerke $R^2 = 0.098$). Table 2 presents the full results.

Table 2. Binary logistic regression: predictors of independent e-government success (N = 279)

Predictor	B	S.E.	Wald	p	Exp(B)	95% CI
Grant recipient status	0.794	0.283	7.878	0.005	2.213	1.271–3.852
Data availability (binary)	0.674	0.273	6.103	0.013	1.962	1.149–3.350
Fear of mistakes	−0.289	0.111	6.825	0.009	0.749	0.603–0.930
Computer ownership	−0.410	0.290	2.006	0.157	0.663	0.376–1.171
Income group	0.069	0.333	0.043	0.835	1.072	0.558–2.060
Constant	−1.195	0.562	4.517	0.034	0.303	–

Three predictors independently predict e-government success. Grant recipient status is the strongest (Exp(B) = 2.213, $p = 0.005$), followed by data availability above 1GB per month (Exp(B) = 1.962, $p = 0.013$) and fear of making mistakes (Exp(B) = 0.749, $p = 0.009$). Notably, computer ownership and income, the conventional markers of digital capability, are non-significant. The pattern is consistent with compulsion and confidence driving success, where structural capability does not.

5 Discussion

5.1 A Pattern Consistent with Compulsion Rather than Capability

The headline finding of this study is deceptively simple: 42.7% of participants in marginalised Mangaung communities can independently complete an online government service transaction. Yet the study's central question asks to what extent these communities are ready for digital-by-default government service delivery, and on that measure, the majority are not. More than half either failed, succeeded only with help, or did not attempt at all.

The 42.7% figure hides three distinct groups: the 16.8% who succeed only because someone else helped them, the 15.1% who attempt and fail, and the 25.4% who never attempt at all. All three are rendered invisible when success is reported as a single aggregate rate, yet none would be reliably served by a system requiring independent digital self-sufficiency.

Framed through Sen's [7] capability approach, the distinction is theoretically precise. Independent success reflects a genuine capability: the person can reliably produce the outcome using their own resources. Assisted success reflects a contingent functioning: an outcome achieved only through external support that may not always be there. Measuring inclusion through aggregate success rates mixes genuine capabilities with contingent functionings, a tendency observed across the e-government literature [9, 13].

The logistic regression identifies three significant independent predictors: grant recipient status, whether a participant received any social grant (Exp(B) = 2.213), mobile data availability (Exp(B) = 1.962), and fear of making mistakes (Exp(B) = 0.749). Computer ownership and income do not reach significance. This pattern is consistent with an interpretation in which compulsion and psychological confidence, rather than structural capability, are the primary drivers of e-government success in this sample; however, since no direct measure of compulsion was included in the instrument, this remains an inferential conclusion.

Grant recipient status is the strongest predictor, substantially exceeding mobile data availability. The direction of this association is consistent with necessity-driven engagement: grant recipients may engage more persistently because the consequences of failing to complete a transaction are immediate and severe. The attempt rate analysis supports this interpretation: grant recipients do not attempt at significantly higher rates than non-recipients ($p = 0.199$), suggesting the association operates through persistence rather than initiation. Grant recipients fail less often when they try (11.1% vs. 23.6%) and succeed with help more often (18.4% vs. 13.5%). This interpretation is inferential; cross-sectional data cannot confirm the mechanism, but it is consistent with Alkraiji's [14] finding that in mandatory service contexts, engagement reflects necessity rather than capability, and with Van Dijk's [8] model in which motivation is the first barrier to digital participation. Alternative explanations are also plausible: grant recipients may simply have greater familiarity with government systems through repeated exposure, or have accumulated experience over time that this cross-sectional design cannot disentangle from necessity-driven persistence.

The mobile data threshold effect indicates a minimum floor below which completion becomes substantially harder, with diminishing returns above it—consistent with the low complexity of the tasks involved. Fear of making mistakes independently reduces the odds of success by roughly 25% per scale unit, after controlling for structural access, suggesting that confidence operates as a parallel barrier alongside compulsion.

The 35 grant recipients who succeeded with help depend on these services for household income, but only because informal assistance is currently available. Portal interfaces change, authentication becomes tighter, WhatsApp channels update, and any such change may sever the assisted user's route without granting independent capability. Faith et al. [19] and Frota et al. [16] identify this as a structural vulnerability: the informal networks that enable access also conceal the exclusion that would follow their disappearance.

5.2 Why Structural Capability Predictors Fail Here

The null results for computer ownership and income appear to differ from the broader digital divide literature, in which structural access factors consistently predict digital task outcomes [8, 17]. Since the capability indicators used are structural proxies rather than direct measures of digital literacy or skills, the findings indicate that structural resources do not explain success here, not that capability is irrelevant, a nuance that future research should address through direct capability assessment. The contrast in Table 1 suggests the mechanisms of success differ by task type: for online job applications, mobile data availability, computer ownership, and income are each significant; for government services, none are. The task complexity hypothesis offers the simplest explanation. Job applications require sustained bandwidth, file uploads, and multi-step navigation of complex platforms. Government service interactions in this context represent qualitatively lower-complexity tasks that can be completed with minimal mobile data using basic smartphone functionality. SASSA, for instance, officially supports grant applications and status checks via WhatsApp [24]. Mobile workarounds and assisted navigation may be sufficient for completing simple transactions regardless of structural capability, inflating aggregate success rates while masking failure in more demanding processes [15].

5.3 Implications for Human-Centred E-Service Design

Three practical implications follow for e-service design and digital equity policy in SA.

Measure Access Mode, Not Just Outcomes. Disaggregating e-government success by whether it was achieved independently or with assistance distinguishes genuine capability from contingent functioning. Government departments and researchers should treat assisted success as a risk indicator requiring follow-up assessment rather than an inclusion indicator.

Address Confidence Alongside Access. The independent association of fear with lower success suggests psychological confidence is a parallel barrier not resolved by structural access improvements alone. Digital literacy programmes should incorporate confidence-building components, guided practice on real government service platforms, and should evaluate whether these components, when used independently, improve success rates. Kassongo et al. [18] and Vujovic et al. [17] both identify a gap in South African social protection digitisation regarding attention to citizens' psychological readiness.

Maintain Non-digital Channels and Consider a Minimum Mobile Data Floor. The 23.2% of grant recipients who never attempted online services will not be reached by further digitisation; non-digital channels must be maintained until genuine capability exists. The mobile data threshold association suggests at least 1GB monthly (via zero-rating or targeted subsidies) may meaningfully improve success odds, though this rests on a cross-sectional association and needs intervention evaluation before being treated as a confirmed policy threshold. With 84.6% relying on smartphones as their primary device, e-government platforms must be designed for smartphone-dominant, low-bandwidth conditions rather than the assumed ideal [5, 8].

6 Conclusion

This study asked two questions: to what extent are marginalised Mangaung communities ready for digital-by-default government service delivery, and what predicts independent e-government service completion in a grant-dependent population?

On readiness, the answer is clear and concerning. Fewer than half could complete a government service transaction independently; the 16.8% who succeeded only with help possess contingent functioning rather than genuine capability, and the 40.5% who failed or never attempted are excluded in ways that aggregate statistics do not register.

In a population for whom these services are not optional but essential, 57.3% cannot be considered genuinely ready for digital-by-default delivery.

On predictors, the findings challenge conventional assumptions about what drives digital success. Grant recipient status, a measure of welfare dependency, not digital skill, emerged as the strongest predictor, while computer ownership and income, the conventional markers of digital capability, were non-significant. This pattern is consistent with compulsion rather than capability driving engagement: grant recipients may persist through failure and seek help because they cannot afford not to, not because they are more digitally able. This interpretation is inferential, however, as the study design does not include a direct measure of compulsion or perceived necessity. The structured contrast with online job application predictors, where conventional capability indicators are all significant and grant status predicts nothing, confirms that this is not a measurement failure but a genuine difference in how the two tasks are completed.

These findings carry three policy implications. E-government readiness assessments must distinguish between assisted and independent success, treating assisted access as a risk indicator rather than as evidence of inclusion. Digital literacy programmes must address psychological confidence alongside structural access, since fear of making mistakes independently predicts failure even after controlling for capability factors. And non-digital service channels must be maintained for grant-dependent populations until genuine independent capability exists.

In South Africa, digitising the primary access route to social grants without ensuring that grant recipients can use that route independently is not delivering on constitutional obligations more efficiently. It is delivering on them less equitably.

7 Limitations and Future Research

Several limitations should be considered when interpreting these findings. The cross-sectional design prevents causal inference; the single-item self-reported outcome introduces variability in interpretation, recall bias, and potential social desirability bias; and purposive sampling limits generalisability. The single outcome measure does not distinguish between tasks of varying complexity, making it impossible to determine which types of transactions participants completed or attempted. Restricted variance in education and employment precluded meaningful assessment of those predictors. The instrument did not include direct measures of perceived necessity or lack of service alternatives, which limits the confirmatory power of the compulsion-driven interpretation; future studies should operationalise these constructs explicitly. Future research should use independently verified transaction records disaggregated by service type and complexity, and test whether confidence-building interventions improve independent success rates beyond structural access improvements alone. Given that the regression accounts for less than 10% of the outcome's variance, additional predictors warrant exploration.

Acknowledgements. Wynand Nel has an additional affiliation with Akademia in Pretoria, South Africa.

Disclosure of Interests. The authors have no competing interests to declare relevant to this article's content.

Statement on Ethics. Ethical clearance for this study was granted by the General/Human Research Ethics Committee of the University of the Free State (UFS-HSD2023/1745/5). Informed consent was obtained from all participants, ensuring they understood the research goals and their right to withdraw.

References

1. International Monetary Fund: African dept. In: Spatial Inequality in South Africa: Causes and Policy Options. IMF Staff Country Reports. 2026, A002 (2026). https://doi.org/10.5089/9798229039048.002.A002
2. SASSA: Branch: Strategy and Business Development Tenth Statistical Report 2025/6: Social Assistance.2026. https://www.sassa.gov.za/statistical-reports/Documents/Social%20Assistance%20%20Report%20%20January%20%202026.pdf. Last accessed 27 Apr 2026
3. Department of Communications and Digital Technologies: South Africa's Digital Economy Masterplan. (2021)
4. Bornman, E.: Information society and digital divide in South Africa: results of longitudinal surveys. Inf. Commun. Soc. **19**, 264–278 (2016). https://doi.org/10.1080/1369118X.2015.1065285
5. Ndofirepi, T.M., Steyn, R.: Income elasticity of information technology and financial emancipation in South Africa. J. Public Adm. **58**, 539–553 (2023). https://doi.org/10.53973/jopa.2023.58.3.a3
6. Shibambu, A.: Transformation of digital government services in the public sector in South Africa. Afr. public serv. deliv. perform. rev. **12**, 753 (2024). https://doi.org/10.4102/apsdpr.v12i1.753
7. Sen, A.: Development as Freedom. Oxford University Press (1999)
8. Van Dijk, J.: The Digital Divide. John Wiley & Sons, Cambridge (2020)
9. Zheng, Y., Walsham, G.: Inequality of what? social exclusion in the e-society as capability deprivation. Inf. Technol. People. **21**, 222–243 (2008). https://doi.org/10.1108/09593840810896000
10. Saleh, R.A., et al.: Citizen adoption of E-government services: a systematic literature review with weight and meta-analysis. Int. J. Adv. Sci. Eng. Inf. Technol. **14**, 1470–1479 (2024). https://doi.org/10.18517/ijaseit.14.4.19868
11. Abdulkareem, A.K., Oladimeji, K.A.: Cultivating the digital citizen: trust, digital literacy and e-government adoption. Transforming Govt. People Process Policy. **18**, 270–286 (2024). https://doi.org/10.1108/TG-11-2023-0196
12. Munyoka, W., Maharaj, M.: The effect of UTAUT2 moderator factors on citizens' intention to adopt e-government: the case of two SADC countries. Probl. Perspect. Manag. **15**, 115–123 (2017). https://doi.org/10.21511/ppm.15(1).2017.12
13. United Nations: E-Government Survey 2022: The Future of Digital Government. (2022)
14. Alkraiji, A.I.: An examination of citizen satisfaction with mandatory e-government services: comparison of two information systems success models. Transforming Govt. People Process Policy. **15**, 36–58 (2021). https://doi.org/10.1108/TG-01-2020-0015
15. Sabani, A., Thai, V., Hossain, M.A.: Factors affecting citizen adoption of E-government in developing countries. J. Glob. Inf. Manag. **31**, 1–23 (2023). https://doi.org/10.4018/JGIM.318131
16. Frota, L., Chitiga-Mabugu, M., Mazenda, A.: Revealing factors influencing digital transformation in South Africa's social security Organisations. J. Public Aff. **25**, e70006 (2025). https://doi.org/10.1002/pa.70006

17. Vujovic, A.N., Jonathan, G.M., Hacks, S.: Digitalisation and its impact on social protection programmes effectiveness: a case from South Africa. Procedia Comput. Sci. **237**, 882–890 (2024). https://doi.org/10.1016/j.procs.2024.05.177
18. Kassongo, R.F., Tucker, W.D., Pather, S.: Government facilitated access to ICTs: adoption, use and impact on the Well-being of indigent south Africans. In: 2018 IST-Africa Week Conference, pp. 1–10 (2018)
19. Faith, B., Roberts, T., Sesan, G.: Those with big phones have the upper hand: political. In: Gender and Digital Exclusions in Cash and Voucher Assistance in North East Nigeria (2024). https://doi.org/10.19088/BASIC.2024.007
20. Fouché, R.C., Nel, L.: Bridging the digital divide: assessing the impact of a community-focused service-learning project. In: Proceedings of the 53rd Annual Southern African Computer Lecturers' Association (SACLA 2024), pp. 17–30 (2024)
21. Fouché, R.C., Nel, W.: Closing the gap: leveraging recorded video lessons for digital inclusion in rural South Africa. In: Hinkelmann, K., Smuts, H. (eds.) Society 5.0, pp. 111–122 (2024). https://doi.org/10.1007/978-3-031-71412-2_9
22. Statistics South Africa: Quarterly Labour Force Survey: Quarter 4, 2025. https://www.statssa.gov.za/publications/P0211/P02114thQuarter2025.pdf. Last accessed 12 Apr 2026
23. Nel, W., Fouché, R.C.: Gender, self-efficacy, and computer literacy acquisition in marginalised South African communities. In: 54th Annual Conference of the Southern African Computer Lecturers' Association. SACLA 2025, pp. 101–115 (2025)
24. Government of South Africa: Social Grants – Coronavirus COVID-19: Social Relief of Distress (SRD) Grant.2020. https://www.gov.za/covid-19/individuals-and-households/social-grants-coronavirus-covid-19. Last accessed 29 Apr 2026

Areas of Growth for Adaptive iControl: Insights from a Longitudinal Case Study

Maria Haasnoot(✉), Marijn Janssen, and Nitesh Bharosa

Delft University of Technology, Delft, Netherlands
m.a.haasnoot@tudelft.nl

Abstract. Governments struggle to retain control over their rapidly changing information and digitalization efforts. Amid these changes, the need for adaptive information control (iControl) becomes more urgent. Yet the existing literature offers limited guidance on the areas of iControl that need to be addressed as organizations grow toward adaptability. iControl adaptation should address several areas. This study identifies growth areas of adaptive iControl development in government by investigating a longitudinal case study in the Dutch government. The study identifies six recurring growth areas for adaptive iControl: time orientation, scope, information-use, intervention logic, organizational positioning, and learning capacity. Shifts across each of these six areas help organizations to grow toward more anticipatory, integrated, and context-responsive forms of control over time. The study contributes to the literature by reframing iControl adaptability development as growth rather than linear development or maturity levels, and by providing a conceptual basis for adaptive yet accountable control in public sector digitalization.

Keywords: iControl · IT-control · growth areas · adaptability · government · adaptive governance

1 Introduction

Complex IT projects and other long-running IT-related activities in government are subject to changing political priorities, evolving requirements, technological change, and emerging organizational and digital risks. Research on large-scale IT projects in the public sector shows that such initiatives are particularly difficult to control because they are embedded in complex organizational and inter-organizational governance environments [1]. Control is further challenged because governments must maintain continuity, accountability, and legitimacy while responding to changing conditions over time [2–4]. The control of IT-related activities in government, hereinafter referred to as *iControl*, must be adaptive to changing conditions. This paper uses "iControl" to refer to both the control process and the organizational entity that performs it, whereas adaptivity focuses on the entity's capacity to adjust the control process.

In these continuously changing situations, control cannot rely solely on predefined, stable mechanisms, such as ex-ante arrangements or periodic ex-post assessments, which

Published by Springer Nature Switzerland AG 2027
S. Han et al. (Eds.): I3E 2026, LNCS 16912, pp. 409–421, 2027.
https://doi.org/10.1007/978-3-032-38014-2_30

in government are traditionally associated with accountability, oversight, legitimacy, and compliance. The literature describes this broader challenge as one of adaptive governance: governments must remain stable and accountable while also being responsive to change [2, 3]. In a similar vein, we conceptualize *adaptive iControl* as the process of iControl realigning control practices in response to changing contextual conditions, organizational dependencies, information needs, and emerging risks, while preserving or improving core control outcomes such as accountability, oversight, and steering capacity [2, 3, 5–7].

Although the existing literature offers valuable insights into management control, public accountability, IT governance, and adaptive governance, it does not yet explain how iControl should evolve over time in complex, long-running public-sector digitalization contexts. Maturity-oriented models that classify development into predefined levels for assessment and benchmarking [8–10] are useful for establishing an organization's current position but are less suitable for explaining adaptation to changing demands, interdependencies, and institutional frictions over time [11, 12].

This paper, therefore, adopts a growth rather than a maturity perspective in which growth is understood as a dynamic, context-sensitive, and never-ending process rather than a linear progression through fixed stages with an endpoint. This perspective is particularly relevant in public-sector digitalization, where organizational demands, governance arrangements, and external pressures often shift over the course of long-running initiatives [2, 4]. For this, the areas of growth need to be determined.

The aim of this paper is to identify areas for growth of adaptive iControl in government. Given the limited research in this area and the lack of a coherent set of areas in the literature, an exploratory approach is taken. The study analyses a longitudinal government case in which iControl evolved over several phases in response to changing conditions [13]. The various growth areas are identified. A set of iControl characteristics derived from the literature is used as an analytical framework to examine the identified growth areas. This is the first paper to identify growth areas specifically for adaptive iControl in the public sector, thereby contributing to the emerging understanding of how control can remain both responsive and accountable in dynamic digital governance settings [2, 3].

The next section presents the theoretical background, followed by the research method sections. Thereafter, the results, a discussion of the findings, limitations, and a conclusion outlining our contribution are presented.

2 Theoretical Background

While adaptability is often framed as a general capacity for change [14], its application to government control is more complex. Adaptability of control is not merely about changing, but about institutionalized responsiveness: the ability to balance stability with agility while preserving core public values such as accountability and predictability [5]. This shift from theoretical adaptability to practical adaptivity in control introduces unique challenges, as governance systems must navigate political constraints [15], legal and governance frameworks embedded in public-sector institutions [12], and organizational inertia. The following section explores how adaptive governance literature operationalizes these principles.

2.1 Adaptivity in Control

The literature on adaptive governance provides a useful starting point for explaining why government control cannot remain static in dynamic environments. Janssen and Van der Voort [2] argued for the need for adaptivity in government where stability, predictability, and accountability remain essential values. Adaptivity is not simply about flexibility, but about organizing responsiveness in institutionally viable ways [2, 3]. Adaptive governance has institutional and political implications beyond technical design alone. Hong and Lee [15] showed that adaptive governance is affected by status quo bias and political competition, suggesting that the capacity to adapt depends on broader organizational conditions. Likewise, Baxter et al. [12] demonstrated that agile approaches in government digitalization can conflict with traditional public-sector regulations regarding governance, financing, and accountability. Overall, these studies suggest that adaptive iControl should be understood as the ability to adapt control in ways that align with changing context over time, without affecting public accountability or organizational constraints [12, 15]. Research on adaptive governance, multidimensional constructs, and maturity models shows that adaptation occurs along several simultaneous dimensions or areas (the latter is used in this paper) [2, 3, 9, 10, 16].

2.2 Growth Areas

This paper aims to identify the areas that need to be addressed for growing towards adaptive iControl. A key conceptual distinction in this paper is the difference between maturity levels and growth areas. Maturity models typically describe a sequence of predefined levels and are mainly used for assessment, benchmarking, and gap identification [8–10]. This approach is often criticized as organizations can be in multiple stages, stages are not followed in practice, and different organizational parts might be at different levels of maturity [8, 9]. By contrast, the growth perspective used here will not assume a universal sequence of stages. Instead, growth refers to iControl needing to anticipate, adjust, integrate, and reconfigure across different areas in response to contextual change over time [2, 3, 11]. This perspective is methodologically significant because it shifts attention from fixed levels to evolutionary fit with context, requiring a design-oriented, context-sensitive analytical approach [17].

In various theoretical fields such as adaptive governance, process theorizing, and design-oriented research, there is discussion of areas (also called dimensions, or components in literature) along which growth, adaptation, and development can be understood, including decision-making power and accountability [3], temporality [18], internal and external capabilities, wider participation, and continuous adjustments [2, 3], and artifact mutability [19]. However, a coherent set of areas for adaptive control is lacking.

3 Research Approach

As this is the first paper to focus on adaptive iControl, we opted for an exploratory approach, studying a single longitudinal case in depth to understand adaptive iControl in government. A case-based design is appropriate because this study aims to understand how iControl evolves in relation to complex IT projects in the public sector, rather than under controlled conditions [20–22]. The longitudinal approach allows examining how control changes over time, rather than treating it as a static characteristic of the organization [13]. A single case is selected to gain deeper insight into one particular situation [22] than would otherwise be possible. At the same time, the number of academic papers discussing cases of adaptive iControl is still limited, as this is a new phenomenon. To identify growth areas, the research approach is structured around four elements: *case selection, data sources, data analysis,* and *research quality.*

Case Selection. The case was selected purposively from a public-sector setting in which adaptive iControl was developed over a prolonged period of seven years. This presents as a longitudinal case that unfolds over multiple years, each phase with a new context, and shows substantial development across these phases, during which relevant conditions, dependencies, and control challenges change over time [1, 13, 18]. The selected case offered sufficient temporal depth to trace how iControl responded to shifting circumstances and how successive control configurations emerged, and which areas were influenced.

Data Sources. The empirical material for this study was collected from two experts from separate ministries and verified using reports and emails surrounding this case. The experts are involved with the case throughout the full seven-year period, through an iterative process in which an interview and a completeness check alternated over four iterations until all required information had been extracted. This focused on the changing organizational context, the evolution of the control configuration, and how these changes related to contextual developments and emerging control needs. In total, four iterations were conducted.

Data Analysis. Our data analysis is grounded in qualitative data analysis [23] and integrates Langley's [13] temporal bracketing approach to divide longitudinal data into successive phases, each with a specific context, and to analyze changes across these phases. After identifying phases and thus contexts, we coded the detailed context characteristics, then identified longitudinal patterns, and finally derived overarching areas:

Step 1 - Contexts: The case was reconstructed longitudinally by identifying key *phases* in time, each with a new context and a turning point in iControl's development. These phases reflected meaningful shifts in the organizational context, the form of control, the use of information, and the perceived value of the control arrangement.

Step 2 - iControl Characteristics: Each phase was coded using the iControl *characteristics* derived from the literature [24], identifying which control characteristics were present and documenting why those characteristics were visible in that phase in relation to context and the resulting outcomes. Table 1 provides an overview of iControl Characteristics.

Step 3 - Longitudinal Phase Analysis: The phases were compared sequentially to identify changes in iControl's configuration from one phase to the next. We analyzed whether iControl changed, how it changed, and in response to which developments.

Step 4 - Model Area Construction: The observed shifts across phases were interpreted by synthesizing recurring changes in iControl characteristics into broader adaptive growth areas.

Research Quality Measures. Several measures were taken to enhance the quality and credibility of the study. First, the longitudinal reconstruction of case phases helps preserve the temporal sequence and reduces the risk of treating development as static [13]. Second, using an explicit set of iControl characteristics as the primary coding scheme makes the analytical process more transparent and traceable [24]. Third, the study maintains a clear analytical chain from case evidence to phase coding, to cross-phase comparison, and finally to the synthesis of adaptive areas and the growth model. This increases transparency in how empirical observations were translated into theoretical insights.

4 Case Study Description

As the first analytical step, we describe the case and identify relevant context elements. The case study took place in the context of a newly established Ministry spin-off from an existing one. This makes the context particularly suitable for our case. There are political and organizational dynamics in which multiple changes occurred over a period of seven years. The Director of the Financial and Economic Affairs Directorate (FEAD) observed that IT was becoming an increasingly important part of the Ministry's responsibilities and that the associated IT risks were significant. iControl was therefore deemed necessary and came into existence upon the spin-off from the ministry. iControl characteristics serve as the unit of analysis for this study.

This case study focuses on the development of a multi-year IT budget as a monitoring and decision-making tool for the Executive Board (EB), which was revised several times to reflect changing contexts and needs within the ministry. This adaptivity was developed over the years. As access was available to staff directly employed during this whole period, differences in personal perspective were avoided. The case is reconstructed as a sequence of four broader developmental phases, each with its context, and the last phase comprising two sub-phases (4a and 4b) in the same context:

Phase 1. During the initial phase, the ministry was still defining its responsibilities, scope, and management information. FEAD needed to gain timely insight into investment peaks, ensure that no investments were missed, and facilitate substantive discussions about investment decisions. The first step involved organizing cooperation so that the relevant stakeholders would provide the necessary information. To achieve this, FEAD developed a multi-year IT budget format based on an existing format from a related ministry, which included both the previous year's actual data and forecasts for the following five years. FEAD instructed the ministry's various IT suppliers to submit this information to the CIO, with a duplicate to FEAD.

Phase 2. During this phase, the ministry sought greater collaboration among organizational units, while those units sought to avoid unnecessary requests for information. FEAD, therefore, wanted to improve the reliability, consolidability, and comparability of the figures. Within iControl, the multi-year IT budget format was adapted by focusing on portfolio management, supplier project costs, and planned projects. In addition, a strong coordinating and reviewing role in both the request for and the assessment of the submitted information was adopted within iControl. However, the discussion in the Executive Board (EB) disappointed all parties involved. Bottlenecks could be discussed only at a limited, non-strategic level. As a result, trust declined.

Phase 3. Because the multi-year budget did not provide sufficient insights into the organization, FEAD was unable to reissue the request for proposals. FEAD, therefore, waited for a new organizational need to arise. During the same period, the CIO Office engaged an external consulting agency to conduct a qualitative assessment of a multi-year IT budget. However, this exercise did not result in a concrete, usable tool. A government-wide initiative also halted due to differing views on the scope of a multi-year budget and doubts about its feasibility, given the effort required.

Phase 4a. In a later phase, the ministry faced government-wide performance targets, increased IT complexity, and greater risks from external threats, all with unknown IT consequences and without historical ways to control. At the same time, several projects failed or fell substantially short in terms of results or cost control. Within this context, FEAD decided to more explicitly anticipate developments and requested that iControl adopt a more proactive budget management approach to better align with developments in the coming years and to identify the future decisions that need to be made. For this reason, the organization decided to retry building a multi-year IT budget based on available administrative data on IT costs. FEAD aimed to foster within the organization the awareness of the need to discuss forecasts collectively. However, the IT service provider, which was part of another ministry, managed this source data and was not inclined to provide this level of insight into its internal operations. As a result, FEAD was unable to access the necessary information.

Phase 4b. Within the same context, FEAD decided to work with information that was both administratively relevant and available. This pointed to financial information discussed on the executive board, such as IT project plans, claims, and business cases. Since FEAD has already regularly discussed these documents and costs within internal operational departments, this was a natural starting point. An iControl civil servant conducted meetings with case managers to gain insights into future developments and jointly develop forecasts. By consolidating this information, FEAD finally obtained a promising multi-year view of over- and underspending of the available budgets.

In the next section, we present the longitudinal contextual analysis, showing how iControl gradually reconfigured in response to contextual misfit and identify growth areas.

5 Results

This section is structured according to the analytical steps outlined in the previous section. Based on the case study description from the previous section, we present the identified characteristics for each context in Table 1. This is followed by our longitudinal analyses of changes in characteristics across phases from step 3, and concluded with synthesized areas from step 4, both presented in Table 2.

5.1 Analysis of iControl Characteristics

Based on the previous contextual analysis (step 1), this step (step 2) concerns the analysis of the iControl characteristics exhibited in each phase, as shown in Table 1. In the following step (step 3), changes in these characteristics across contexts are analyzed to provide insights into adaptability.

Characteristics include the control instruments used (e.g., output or behavioral control), iControl's relationship to management (e.g., business partner or reporter), and its strategy (e.g., defender or prospector). This analysis shows that iControl's role, as a function of these characteristics, does not remain stable throughout the case, but iControl adapted to shifting organizational needs, governance conditions, information availability, and the perceived usefulness of the control instrument. Across these phases, the dominant profile shifts from a relatively formal, reporting-oriented configuration toward a more relational, reflective, and context-responsive form of iControl.

Table 1. iControl characteristics by case phase

Phase	iControl characteristics	Explanation
1	Staff function; Reporter; Coordination oriented; Information-oriented; Formal control; Feed forward;	Control mainly served to organize the first formal collection of comparable IT information and multi-year estimates, which explains the dominance of reporting, information orientation, feedforward, and a staff-based coordination role.
2	Coordinator between management; Reporter; Rationality-oriented; Formal control; Feedback; Processes;	Control became more coordinating and review-oriented by improving the format, increasing comparability, and structuring decision support across actors, which is reflected in process orientation, rationality orientation, feedback, and coordination between management.
3	Staff function; Reactor; Innovator; Reflection-oriented; Informal control;	After the instrument lost perceived value, iControl shifted into a reflective and exploratory mode, characterized by reconsideration, experimentation, and less reliance on formalized control routines.
4a	Business Partner; Innovator; Detective; Technologies; Data;	Faced with rising risks and underperforming projects, iControl aimed to build a more proactive, data-driven control approach through source information and dashboarding, even though access to the underlying data remained blocked.

(*continued*)

Table 1. (*continued*)

Phase	iControl characteristics	Explanation
4b	Business Partner; Navigator; Reporter; Coordination oriented; Reflection-oriented; Feed forward; Informal control	iControl reconfigured itself pragmatically around available and decision-relevant information, combining dialogue, forecasting, and coordination into a more relational and forward-looking business partner role.

5.2 Growth Areas Across Case Phases

Table 2 presents the themes identified in the coded characteristics, and the areas we derived along which growth in iControl can be understood: its adaptive capacity to respond to contextual change over time. Across the case, we observed recurring shifts in six adaptability areas: *time orientation, scope, information-use, intervention logic, organizational positioning, and learning capacity.* We did not find these areas reflected one-to-one in the literature, but the literature suggests indications of these areas [2, 3, 13, 18, 19].

The first area, *Time orientation,* refers to the extent to which iControl becomes more forward-looking and sensitive to development over time. Elements of this are reflected in Langley [13] and Langley et al. [18], who explicitly discuss process, development, and theory formation as unfolding over time. *Scope* refers to whether control remains bound within a single unit or expands across organizational and governance dependencies. This is not directly theorized in the same sense in the literature used here, but Gregor and Jones [19] do discuss purpose and scope as defining the boundaries of a design theory. *Information-use* concerns the type, continuity, and strategic relevance of the information used in control. A related element is discussed by Janssen and van der Voort [2], who emphasize the need to inform higher-level decision-making from the bottom up. *Intervention logic* refers to how control acts, for example, through formal reporting, coordination, dialogue, or reconfiguration of interventions. This relates to Gregor and Jones's [19] discussion on principles of form and function and, more indirectly, of implementation principles. *Organizational positioning* refers to iControl's role within organizational and governance arrangements. Wang et al. [3] explained how decision-making power and accountability are distributed among actors, which is closely related to positioning within and between organizations. *Learning capacity* captures the extent to which iControl reflects on earlier misfit and adapts iteratively over time. Learning is explicit in Janssen and van der Voort [2], while Gregor and Jones [19] address related adaptability through artifact mutability.

We analyzed how these areas concretely change across the phases in the case. Table 2 shows that growth in adaptive iControl is visible across all six areas, but not in the same way or at the same time. For each area listed in the first column, this table shows in the second column 'Operationalization' which themes formulated as a question emerged, the third column shows how this question is answered for this case, and the last column shows in which phase-transitions the adaptations took place. Rather than following a linear path, iControl develops through selective shifts in response to changing context, available information, organizational constraints, and perceived misfit between the control profile and organizational needs.

Table 2. Growth areas across case phases

Growth area	Operationalizing question	Identified adaptations across case phases	Phase-transition			
			1–2	2–3	3-4a	4a-4b
Time orientation	How iControl is oriented in time: looking back, in the present, looking ahead, or reorienting.	Visible in the shift from actuals +5-year template (Phase 1) to reliability in governance discussion (Phase 2), pause/reorientation (Phase 3), and case-based forecasts (Phase 4b).	x	x		x
Scope	How broadly or narrowly the control object and accountability chain are defined.	Scope shifts from a ministry-wide approach to coordinated consolidation, to chain ambition, to a pragmatically narrower governance-workable domain.	x		x	x
Information -use	Which information is regarded as usable and how it is combined.	Move to reviewed data, qualitative agendas, and governance-relevant documents plus conversations.	x	x		x
Intervention logic	How iControl seeks to intervene: standardizing, correcting, exploring, co-creating.	The case successively shows template-driven mobilization, formal tightening, reflective suspension, data-driven redesign, and relational co-creation.	x	x	x	x
Organizational positioning	How iControl is positioned relative to management, staff, chain partners.	From reporter/staff via a coordinating staff role to diffuse role division and then business partner / navigator within FEAD's own mandate.	x	x		x

(continued)

Table 2. (*continued*)

Growth area	Operationalizing question	Identified adaptations across case phases	Phase-transition			
			1–2	2–3	3-4a	4a-4b
Learning capacity	The extent to which iControl can adapt iteratively and reflexively to context.	The explicit recognition of misfit, the failed source-data experiment, and later successful reconfiguration with other sources and ways of working.		x	x	x

Each area is considered important and has multiple contextual changes. Notably, intervention logic is an area where change is always deemed necessary. This could also indicate that the area is difficult to align with the context. Learning capacity received no attention in phase 1 but was consistently addressed from phase 2 onward. By contrast, adaptation in the other areas was not continuously required across all phases, and was intermittently absent in one of the four, suggesting that context does not influence all areas equally. Across the case, *time orientation* becomes more varied and forward-looking, moving from formal multi-year templates toward more context-sensitive forecasting. *Scope* shifts as iControl alternates between broader ambitions and more workable boundaries, depending on mandate and interdependencies. *Information-use* changes from submitted figures and formal templates to more reviewed, contextual, and governance-relevant sources. At the same time, *intervention logic* evolves from standardized information requests toward reflection, redesign, and more relational forms of coordination. The table also shows that growth involves changes in iControl's role. *Organizational positioning* develops from a mainly reporting and staff-based role toward a more coordinating and eventually business partner–oriented position. *Learning capacity* is especially visible in moments where earlier approaches prove insufficient, and iControl adapts by experimenting with new sources, formats, and ways of working.

Overall, the analysis shown in the table confirms that adaptive iControl growth is best understood as a context-sensitive process of reconfiguration. The six areas do not represent fixed stages, but analytical directions along which iControl growth occurs.

6 Discussion

This study identified the areas along which iControl adapts to specific government contexts. The findings show that iControl growth is better understood as an iterative process of reconfiguration than as progression through predefined maturity levels.

The first key finding is that adaptivity in iControl does not consist of simply adding more controls, more data, or more formalization. The case shows alternating configurations of control. Earlier phases were dominated by formal, reporting-oriented, and staff-based forms of iControl, while later phases showed more reflective, relational, and business partner–oriented configurations. This suggests that adaptive growth is not a matter of progressing upward along a stable scale, but of finding a better fit between control and context over time [2, 3, 18].

A second finding is that this adaptivity can be interpreted as growth across six adaptive areas: *time orientation, scope, information-use, intervention logic, organizational positioning, and learning capacity*. Their contribution is that they reveal the directions along which adaptive development takes place. These areas are particularly meaningful for understanding iControl's growth in dynamic government settings. The findings confirm the starting point this study derived from literature, that a maturity model, despite useful for establishing an organization's current position, is not appropriate for public-sector digitalization [11, 12] as organizational demands, governance arrangements, and external pressures often shift over the course of long-running initiatives [2, 4], and thus confirms our focus on areas to account for the evolving nature. The study also raises an important analytical point: the areas are related, as evidenced by certain iControl characteristics that appear across multiple areas. This is not necessarily a weakness. For example, in our case study, *Business Partner* reflects both organizational positioning and intervention logic; *Feed forward* relates to both time orientation and information use; and *Reflection-oriented* connects learning capacity with intervention logic. This is analytically plausible because adaptive iControl does not change in isolated ways: shifts in role, information-use, and intervention often occur together. The areas, therefore, do not need to be fully orthogonal, as long as they remain analytically distinguishable and jointly help explain how iControl develops over time.

A third contribution of the study is that it connects *control theory* and *adaptivity theory* through longitudinal case analysis. The case shows that control in government should not be understood solely as a stable set of accountability and oversight arrangements, nor adaptivity as mere generic responsiveness. Adaptive iControl emerges where control arrangements are repeatedly reconfigured to remain meaningful under changing conditions. This links the control literature's concerns with steering, accountability, and oversight to the adaptive governance literature's focus on responsiveness, uncertainty, and reorientation [2, 3, 6].

From a practical perspective, these areas provide insight into potential growth paths and how to become adaptable step by step, without trying to do everything at once. Organizations can select the appropriate areas they want to grow based on the situation they are in. In this way, the areas provide organizations with the flexibility to adjust the model that best fits their context.

This study has limitations. It is based on a single longitudinal case, which provides rich process insight but limits broader generalization [21, 22]. In addition, the identification of dominant characteristics and areas involves interpretive judgment. Future research could verify the areas in additional cases, examine whether the same areas recur in other public-sector digitalization contexts, and explore whether recurring combinations of areas point to stronger dependencies or relationships between them.

7 Conclusion

Governments are faced with many changes in digitalization and in the environment. Therefore, their control needs to be adaptive. This paper sets out to develop context-sensitive areas for adaptive iControl as an organizational entity in government.

We found that iControl growth is better understood as an iterative process of reconfiguration than as progression through predefined maturity levels. We identified the following areas in which iControl needs to adapt: *time orientation, scope, information-use, intervention logic, organizational positioning, and learning capacity*. These growth areas show how iControl can adapt to contextual changes. These areas provide a new analytical framework and theoretical lens for understanding the development of iControl, as well as a starting point for future research. The findings also show that these areas are supported by the literature and are interrelated; some iControl characteristics contribute to more than one area, suggesting that adaptive iControl develops through connected changes in role, information-use, intervention, and learning.

The scientific contribution of this paper lies in identifying adaptive areas specifically relevant to iControl and in empirically connecting control theory and adaptivity theory through longitudinal case analysis. In practical terms, the paper offers a way to analyze the development of iControl in long-running public-sector digitalization contexts, where stability, accountability, and responsiveness must be balanced continuously. Future research can test and refine the proposed areas and growth model in additional cases and explore whether recurring combinations of areas point to more stable patterns of adaptive iControl development. Also, the type of adaptation can be researched.

Disclosure of Interests. The authors have no competing interests to declare that are relevant to the content of this article.

References

1. Patanakul, P.: Managing large-scale IS/IT projects in the public sector: problems and causes leading to poor performance. J. High Technol. Managem. Res. **25**(1), 21–35 (2014)
2. Janssen, M., van der Voort, H.: Adaptive governance: towards a stable, accountable and responsive government. Gov. Inf. Q. **33**, 1–5 (2016)
3. Wang, C., Medaglia, R., Zheng, L.: Towards a typology of adaptive governance in the digital government context: the role of decision-making and accountability. Gov. Inf. Q. **35**, 306–322 (2018)
4. Fischer, C., Heuberger, M., Heine, M.: The impact of digitalization in the public sector. Z. Public Policy Recht Manage. **14**(1), 3–23 (2021)
5. Janssen, M., van der Voort, H.: Agile and adaptive governance in crisis response: lessons from the COVID-19 pandemic. Int. J. Inf. Manag. **55**, 102180 (2020)
6. Koppell, J.G.: Pathologies of accountability: ICANN and the challenge of "multiple accountabilities disorder". Public Adm. Rev. **65**, 94–108 (2005)
7. Magnusson, L., Iqbal, S., Elm, P., Dalipi, F.: Information security governance in the public sector: investigations, approaches, measures, and trends. Int. J. Inf. Secur. **24**, 30 (2025)
8. Pöppelbuß, J., Röglinger, M.: What Makes a Useful Maturity Model? A Framework of General Design Principles for Maturity Models and its Demonstration in Business Process Management. In: European Conference on Information Systems (ECIS) (2011)
9. Proença, D., Borbinha, J.: Maturity models for information systems - a state of the art. Procedia Comput. Sci. **100**, 1042–1049 (2016)
10. Becker, J., Knackstedt, R., Pöppelbuß, J.: Developing maturity models for IT management: a procedure model and its application. Bus. Inf. Syst. Eng. **3**, 213–222 (2009)

11. Whyte, J., Nussbaum, T.: Transition and temporalities: spanning temporal boundaries as projects end and operations begin. Proj. Manag. J. **51**, 505–521 (2020)
12. Baxter, D., Dacre, N., Dong, H., Ceylan, S.: Institutional challenges in agile adoption: evidence from a public sector IT project. Gov. Inf. Q. **40**(4), 101858 (2023)
13. Langley, A.: Strategies for theorizing from process data. Acad. Manage. Rev. **24**(4), 691–710 (1999)
14. Uhl-Bien, M., Arena, M.: Leadership for organizational adaptability: a theoretical synthesis and integrative framework. Leadersh. Q. **29**, 89–104 (2018)
15. Hong, S., Lee, S.: Adaptive governance, status quo bias, and political competition: why the sharing economy is welcome in some cities but not in others. Gov. Inf. Q. **35**(2), 283–290 (2018)
16. Law, K.S., Wong, C.-S., Mobley, W.H.: Toward a taxonomy of multidimensional constructs. Acad. Manag. Rev. **23**(4), 741–755 (1998)
17. van Aken, J.E.: Management research based on the paradigm of the design sciences: The quest for field-tested and grounded technological rules. J. Manage. Stud. **41**(2), 219–246 (2004)
18. Langley, A., Smallman, C., Tsoukas, H., Van de Ven, A.H.: Process studies of change in organization and management: unveiling temporality, activity, and flow. Acad. Manage. J. **56**, 1–13 (2013)
19. Gregor, S., Jones, D.: The anatomy of a design theory. J. Assoc. Inf. Syst. **8**(5), 312–335 (2007)
20. Eisenhardt, K.M.: Building theories from case study research. Acad. Manag. Rev. **14**, 532–550 (1989)
21. Yin, R.K.: The Case study as a serious research strategy. Knowledge. **3**(1), 97–114 (1981)
22. Rashid, Y., Rashid, A., Waseem, A., Warraich, M.A., Sabir, S.S.: Case study method: a step-by-step guide for business researchers. Int. J. Qual. Methods. **18**, 1–13 (2019)
23. Saunders, M.N.K., Lewis, P., Thornhill, A.: Analysing qualitative data. In: Research Methods for Business Students, 5th edn, pp. 480–525. Pearson Education (2009)
24. Haasnoot, M., Janssen, M., Bharosa, N.: A Taxonomy for Informatization Control for the Government (2026)

A Capability Maturity Model for Trustworthy Generative AI in the Public Sector

Gideon Mekonnen Jonathan(✉), Shengnan Han, and Erik Perjons

Department of Computer and Systems Sciences (DSV), Stockholm University, Borgarfjordsgatan 12, 164 55 Kista, Sweden
{gideon,shengnan,perjons}@dsv.su.se

Abstract. Generative AI (GenAI) and large language models (LLMs) in particular are reshaping how public-sector organisations approach administrative work, service delivery, and citizen engagement. While prior research has examined AI readiness, comparatively little is known about how public organisations develop, stabilise, and reconfigure GenAI-related capabilities after adoption decisions are made. This study explores how public-sector organisations develop capabilities for the effective and trustworthy adoption of GenAI. Drawing on a qualitative multiple-case study of three Swedish municipalities and thirteen semi-structured interviews, we identify five interrelated capability dimensions—strategic alignment, workforce readiness, data governance and digital sovereignty, Trustworthy AI, and public value—and synthesises them into a four-level GenAI Capability Maturity Model spanning exploration, experimentation, operationalisation, and transformation. Our findings show that capability development emerges as non-linear and uneven: strategic ambition and technical experimentation tend to advance faster than the operationalisation of Trustworthy AI and sustainability, which remain persistent developmental gaps. The model integrates insights from the AI readiness, capability maturity, dynamic capabilities, public value, and Trustworthy AI, and incorporates explicit feedback and course-correction mechanisms reflecting empirical patterns of progression and regression. The paper contributes a GenAI-specific, public-sector instantiation of the maturity-model tradition and offers a diagnostic tool for managers and policymakers seeking to develop GenAI capabilities responsibly under EU regulatory conditions.

Keywords: Generative AI · Public sector · Capability Maturity Model · Dynamic capabilities · Trustworthy AI · Public value

1 Introduction

The rapid advance of Generative AI (GenAI), particularly large language models (LLMs), are reshaping how public-sector organisations approach administrative work, service delivery, and citizen engagement [1–3]. In Sweden, where 290

Published by Springer Nature Switzerland AG 2027
S. Han et al. (Eds.): I3E 2026, LNCS 16912, pp. 422–433, 2027.
https://doi.org/10.1007/978-3-032-38014-2_31

municipalities are constitutionally self-governing under the Local Government Act and carry substantial responsibility for service provision, the question of how GenAI can be adopted in a coordinated, accountable, and sustainable manner is particularly salient. This institutional model–characterised by local autonomy operating within a national policy framework and the EU regulatory regime–facilitates experimentation while simultaneously complicating standardisation and scaling [4,5]. To clarify the scope of the study, we examine how municipalities that have already decided to adopt GenAI build the organisational capabilities required to do so responsibly. The upstream question of whether particular services should be supported by GenAI requires its own governance processes, including problem framing, assessment of non-AI alternatives, and democratic deliberation. We treat that decision as analytically distinct and outside the scope of the model developed here, while recognising it as a necessary complement.

The extant literature on public-sector AI adoption has focused largely on AI readiness, offering assessments of preparedness across infrastructure, skills, and policy environments [6–9]. However, readiness models predominantly emphasise preconditions and assessment snapshots, while offering comparatively limited insight into longitudinal capability reconfiguration after adoption decisions are made [10,11]. The Capability Maturity Model (CMM) tradition [12] addresses capability progression, while the dynamic-capabilities perspective foregrounds the routines through which organisations sense opportunities and risks, seize them through resource commitment, and reconfigure practices in changing environments [13,14]. In the Swedish public sector context, GenAI capabilities must realise public value [15], align with the EU framework for Trustworthy AI under the AI Act [16], and address sustainability as a core governance concern encompassing direct, indirect, and systemic effects [17]. This raises a central question of organisational capability rather than technology adoption alone. Accordingly, this study asks: *How can public-sector organisations develop capabilities for the effective and trustworthy adoption of GenAI?*

2 Related Work

2.1 GenAI in the Public Sector

GenAI—the family of techniques typified by LLMs—differs from earlier AI in its capacity to generate, summarise, and interpret text, making it especially relevant for the documentation- and communication-intensive work of public administration [18,19]. Empirical evidence indicates that GenAI generates measurable productivity gains in knowledge-intensive tasks [20,21], which in public administration translate into faster case processing, reduced backlogs, and more consistent service delivery, as well as improved inclusiveness through multilingual chatbots and accessible information systems [22]. However, these benefits hinge on the presence of robust governance mechanisms that secure accuracy, transparency, and compliance with legal and ethical requirements, notably those set out in the EU AI Act and related instruments [23,24].

2.2 AI Readiness, Capability Maturity, and Trustworthy GenAI

Research on AI readiness has identified key organisational conditions shaping AI adoption, including data quality, technical infrastructure, strategic alignment, skills, and culture [8,9]. While these frameworks provide valuable diagnostic snapshots, they remain largely static and offer limited insight into how public-sector organisations develop, adapt, and stabilise AI-related capabilities over time, particularly in the face of the uncertainty and fluidity that characterise GenAI. The CMM tradition addresses this limitation by conceptualising capability development as progression through qualitatively distinct levels of organisational practice [12]. Although widely applied in software engineering, data management, and digital transformation, most AI-related maturity models predate GenAI and are grounded in earlier conceptions of analytical or rule-based AI [4,5,8,9]. As a result, these models insufficiently address GenAI-specific characteristics such as natural-language interfaces, prompt-based control, hallucination risk, and strong dependence on externally developed foundation models. Moreover, they rarely reflect the institutional constraints of public-sector organisations, where legality, accountability, and public value fundamentally shape capability development [4,15,22,23]. The dynamic-capabilities perspective complements both readiness and maturity approaches by conceptualising organisational capability as the ability to sense opportunities and risks, seize them through resource commitment, and continuously reconfigure routines as environments change [13,14]. Applied to GenAI in the public sector, this perspective highlights non-linear, iterative development processes rather than smooth progression. Importantly, in public organisations these capabilities are oriented toward public value creation rather than competitive advantage [15].

In the European context, GenAI capability development is further constrained by the EU framework for Trustworthy AI. The EU Ethics Guidelines specify seven requirements, including accountability and societal-and-environmental wellbeing [16], while the EU AI Act operationalises these principles through a risk-based regulatory regime [23]. For municipalities, Trustworthy AI thus constitutes a foundational condition for GenAI capability development rather than an optional ethical overlay.

Despite its prominence in EU policy, the societal-and-environmental-wellbeing requirement remains weakly integrated into both AI readiness and maturity-model research. Sustainable public-sector AI requires systematic attention to direct, indirect, and systemic effects, including energy use, labour implications, and digital sovereignty [17]. Existing frameworks rarely incorporate these concerns into their core capability logic. At the intersection of these traditions, a gap remains. There is limited empirical research that integrates AI readiness factors, capability maturity progression, dynamic capability reconfiguration, and Trustworthy-AI requirements into a coherent, GenAI-specific framework for public-sector organisations. This study addresses that gap by developing an empirically grounded GenAI Capability Maturity Model that extends AI readiness toward a dynamic, public-value oriented, and Trustworthy-AI-aware perspective.

3 Methodology

We employ a qualitative multiple-case study design to examine how GenAI capabilities emerge and evolve within public-sector organisations. Case study research is particularly well suited to analysing complex, processual, and context-dependent phenomena as they unfold in real organisational settings [25,26]. GenAI capability development is embedded in organisational routines, governance arrangements, and institutional constraints, making it difficult to disentangle from context through variable-based or survey methods alone. The study focuses on Swedish municipalities, which operate under constitutionally protected local self-government while remaining subject to national legislation and EU-level regulation. This institutional setting shapes both discretion and responsibility in digital innovation and provides a relevant empirical context for analysing public-sector GenAI adoption.

Three municipalities were selected using purposive sampling to ensure meaningful variation in organisational characteristics that prior research associates with digital and AI capability development [26]. Cases were categorised by population size into small, mid-sized, and large municipalities, with size used as the primary stratifying criterion because it correlates empirically with digital infrastructure, in-house competence, and the scope of GenAI initiatives. The three cases correspondingly differ in their level of digital maturity and stage of GenAI engagement: the large municipality has deployed GenAI pilots, the mid-sized municipality is actively piloting GenAI solutions, and the smaller municipality remains in an exploratory phase. Across cases, GenAI is primarily accessed through externally developed foundation models delivered via commercial cloud services, including Microsoft Copilot, Azure OpenAI deployments, and enterprise versions of ChatGPT, supplemented in some cases by locally hosted open-weight language models for sensitive applications. None of the municipalities develop foundation models internally; instead, capability development centres on governance, integration, risk management, and workforce competencies rather than model engineering. Illustrative use cases include document redaction, internal chatbots, legal decision support, document summarisation, and internal training, reflecting both operational experimentation and early institutionalisation efforts.

The empirical data were collected through 13 semi-structured interviews with IT managers, digitalisation strategists, policy officers, and operational staff directly involved in GenAI initiatives. Interviews were distributed across the three cases in approximate proportion to organisational size and the breadth of GenAI activity: five interviews were conducted in the large municipality, four in the mid-sized municipality, and four in the smaller municipality. Semi-structured interviews were chosen to balance comparability across cases with flexibility to probe emerging themes and contextual nuances [27]. Interviews lasted between 45 and 75 min, were audio-recorded with informed consent, and were transcribed verbatim. The interview protocol covered organisational AI strategy, capability development, governance practices, workforce readiness, and perceived risks and opportunities associated with GenAI.

The data analysis followed reflexive thematic analysis according to the six-phase steps proposed by Braun and Clarke [28]. Analysis combined deductive sensitising concepts from the AI-readiness, dynamic-capabilities, and public-value literatures with inductive coding to capture themes arising directly from the empirical material [28]. To strengthen analytical rigour, two researchers independently coded a subset of transcripts and jointly reviewed coding decisions to align interpretations before coding the full dataset. Themes were iteratively refined through constant comparison across cases to identify shared patterns and meaningful differences [26]. Quotations presented in the findings are used to illustrate cross-case dynamics rather than isolated organisational idiosyncrasies, and all respondents were pseudonymised to protect anonymity.

4 Results

Across the three municipalities, GenAI capability development does not follow a linear progression from adoption to maturity, but instead unfolds as an uneven co-evolution across five interrelated organisational dimensions. While the cases differ in pace and focal priorities, they display common structural patterns that provide the empirical foundation for the maturity model introduced in the subsequent section.

The five dimensions are analytically distinct, though empirically interacting. *Strategic alignment* concerns how GenAI is positioned relative to organisational goals; *workforce readiness* concerns the competencies and learning culture that enable appropriate use; and *data governance and digital sovereignty* concern control over the data and infrastructure on which use depends. *Trustworthy AI* is procedural—the oversight, risk, and accountability practices that make use defensible—whereas *public value* is the normative end those practices serve: the citizen and societal outcomes that justify its use. Sustainability is treated within Trustworthy AI, specifically as its societal-and-environmental-wellbeing requirement [16,17], rather than as a sixth dimension. The dimensions thus distinguish why GenAI is used (public value), how responsibly it is used (Trustworthy AI), and with what organisational and informational means (strategic alignment, workforce readiness, and data governance).

4.1 Strategic Alignment

GenAI is increasingly framed as an organisational capability rather than a discrete technology initiative. In the more advanced cases, GenAI is embedded in formal digital strategies linked to workforce shortages, fiscal pressures, and long-term service provision, whereas in the less advanced case it remains positioned within a broader digital-transformation agenda. This strategic reframing marks a shift from experimentation toward infrastructural thinking. As one digital strategist explained: *"We don't see AI as something separate from our digital strategy. It's a cornerstone of how we plan to deliver welfare in the next decade."* This shift is enacted through hybrid governance arrangements in which strategic priorities are articulated centrally but operational experimentation is distributed across departments, with pilot projects serving as mediating devices between strategy and practice.

4.2 Workforce Readiness

Workforce readiness is a critical enabler of GenAI capability, but not through specialised AI roles. Instead, capability depends on broad-based AI literacy among frontline staff, most notably an understanding of the epistemic limits of generative models. Interviewees repeatedly highlighted recognition of hallucination risk as a foundational competence: "*We need people who know that the model can be confident and wrong at the same time. That awareness is the first capability.*" More advanced municipalities institutionalise learning through structured training and internal support networks, while smaller municipalities rely more on inter-municipal collaboration and external ecosystems. Across cases, psychological safety is decisive: experimentation advances only when cautious trial-and-error with GenAI is explicitly supported.

4.3 Data Governance and Digital Sovereignty

Data governance constitutes a binding constraint on GenAI use across all cases. Fragmented data architectures and legacy systems limit both the scope and reliability of applications, regardless of staff competence or tool availability. As one IT manager summarised: *"Without good data, there is no AI. We can train all the staff we want, but if our data is fragmented across silos, we will go nowhere."* In response, municipalities develop clearer data ownership and classification regimes, though at varying stages of maturity. Concerns about digital sovereignty further shape architectural choices, leading to tiered deployments where cloud-based foundation models are used for low-risk tasks, while sensitive data are handled locally. As one respondent noted, *"We can't put case files about vulnerable people through a service we don't control. So we run our own model locally for those, even if it's slower."* These arrangements reflect accountability requirements rather than technical conservatism and delimit which GenAI use cases are considered viable.

4.4 Trustworthy AI

Trustworthy AI principles, human oversight, accountability, transparency, and risk awareness are treated as necessary conditions for GenAI use across all cases, but their operationalisation lags behind the strategic commitment. Human-in-the-loop design is consistently emphasised, positioning GenAI as decision support rather than automated decision-making. As one manager put it: *"The system can suggest. The decision stays with the caseworker. That has to remain non-negotiable."* Alignment with the EU AI Act and Trustworthy AI requirements is uneven, with more advanced municipalities beginning to map use cases to risk categories. Notably, societal-and-environmental wellbeing remains the least developed requirement across all cases: sustainability considerations are acknowledged but not yet systematically embedded in governance routines.

4.5 Public Value and Cross-Dimensional Pattern

Public value functions as the normative anchor for GenAI initiatives, with use cases justified in terms of service quality, accessibility, and efficiency rather than technological ambition. More mature municipalities link initiatives to measurable outcomes, while less mature cases articulate anticipated value. Across dimensions, a consistent asymmetry emerges: strategic ambition and technical experimentation advance faster than Trustworthy-AI operationalisation and sustainability practices. Workforce readiness and data governance tend to stabilise earlier, whereas systematic mechanisms for societal and environmental impact assessment lag behind. This non-linear and uneven pattern of capability development directly motivates the staged maturity model presented in the next section.

4.6 GenAI Capability Maturity Model

The proposed GenAI Capability Maturity Model spans four levels—exploration, experimentation, operationalisation, and transformation. Table 1 summarises the prevailing organisational conditions across the five capability dimensions at each level.

The dimensions do not mature in step: strategic alignment and workforce readiness tend to advance earlier, while Trustworthy AI (including sustainability) tends to lag, producing the uneven profile discussed below. Two further layers cut across all five dimensions at every level. Table 2 sets out the enabling instruments through which these conditions are enacted, together with the feedback and course-correction mechanisms.

Because these mechanisms support both progression and regression, capability development is non-monotonic: organisations may advance unevenly or slip back when key routines, competencies, or governance arrangements erode. The four levels are characterised briefly below.

Levels 1–2 (Exploration, Experimentation). GenAI engagement shifts from informal, individually championed, and largely ungoverned use, with reactive and local feedback, towards a recognised organisational learning activity. Pilots become selective and weakly aligned with strategy, supported by emerging pilot registers, standardised templates, and a preliminary Trustworthy-AI checklist partially mapped to EU requirements and AI Act risk categories [16,23], alongside introductory AI-literacy initiatives emphasising hallucination awareness [21]. These early levels correspond to the sensing phase of dynamic capabilities and to early-stage capability formation in the maturity-model tradition [12]. What bounds progression here is distinctively public-sector and institutional rather than technical: procurement rules constrain which externally developed foundation models may lawfully be trialled, mandates are fragmented across

Table 1. GenAI Capability Maturity Model: capability dimensions describing organisational conditions at each maturity level.

Dimension	1. Exploration	2. Experimentation	3. Operationalisation	4. Transformation
Strategic alignment	No clear strategy; GenAI seen as isolated initiatives championed by individuals.	Weak alignment with digital strategy; selective pilots in priority areas; central intent, local autonomy.	GenAI embedded in strategy and portfolios; coordinated across departments with clear priorities.	GenAI integral to organisational mission and long-term planning; continuously re-aligned to public-value goals.
Workforce readiness	Limited AI literacy among early adopters; ad hoc learning; low awareness of hallucination risk.	Introductory AI-literacy programmes; awareness of model limitations; learning through pilots.	Role-based training and communities of practice; AI literacy embedded in work routines; psychological safety.	Workforce-wide AI fluency; continuous upskilling; culture of responsible experimentation and learning.
Data governance & digital sovereignty	Fragmented data and legacy systems; unclear ownership and classification; high external dependence.	Minimum data-governance standards; early data classification; tiered use of cloud vs. local models for sensitive data.	Consolidated data architectures; clear ownership and quality standards; sovereignty-by-design policies in place.	Data ecosystems interoperable and trustworthy; strong digital sovereignty; data governance continuously optimised.
Trustworthy AI	General awareness of ethical principles; no structured risk management; human oversight not formalised.	Pilot-level checklists; basic risk assessments; human-in-the-loop design; partial mapping to AI Act risk categories.	Systematic compliance with EU AI Act and Trustworthy AI requirements; bias and robustness audits; clear accountability and transparency.	Trustworthy AI by design; proactive risk management and red-teaming; transparency and accountability institutionalised.
Public value	Aspirational value claims; no metrics or evaluation.	Tentative public-value indicators defined for pilots; limited stakeholder involvement.	Public value measured and reported; stakeholder engagement in design and evaluation.	Measurable societal outcomes; co-creation with citizens; GenAI advances equity, accessibility and service quality.

self-governing departments, and pilots require a defensible legal basis before any personal data are processed [23]. Experimentation is therefore limited less by tooling or skills than by what a municipality may accountably trial under transparency and data-protection obligations.

Levels 3–4 (Operationalisation, Transformation). GenAI is institutionalised across departments through cross-functional governance, mandatory use-case registers, risk and impact assessments, bias and robustness audits, and stable human-in-the-loop procedures, with sustainability metrics—energy intensity, labour effects, and vendor dependency—entering operational reviews [16,17]; this corresponds to the seizing and reconfiguring phases of dynamic capabili-

Table 2. GenAI Capability Maturity Model: cross-cutting descriptive layers applied across all five dimensions, with feedback-and-correction loops that enable progression or signal regression.

Layer	1. Exploration	2. Experimentation	3. Operationalisation	4. Transformation
Enabling instruments	Ad hoc pilots and informal tools; individual experimentation; external peer networks; minimal governance.	Pilot register and templates; Trustworthy-AI checklist (pilot level); basic risk assessments; early data classification; preliminary public-value indicators.	Cross-functional GenAI governance body; AI use-case register; risk & impact assessments; bias/robustness audits; human-in-the-loop procedures; sustainability metrics in reviews.	Integrated capability dashboards; lifecycle sustainability assessments; scenario testing & red-teaming; organisation-wide learning systems; external accountability mechanisms.
Feedback & course-correction	Reactive and incident-driven; learning remains local; no systematic capture or sharing.	Feedback within pilots through iteration and stakeholder input; limited cross-pilot learning.	Institutionalised feedback; data informs scale, redesign, or decommission decisions; lessons shared across units.	Anticipatory feedback and continuous monitoring; proactive reconfiguration before risks or harms materialise.

ties [13,14]. At the highest level, capability is continuously reconfigured: Trustworthy AI and sustainability act as first-order design constraints rather than compliance requirements [15], feedback becomes anticipatory, external accountability mechanisms complement internal governance, and capability decay—for example through vendor lock-in or skill erosion—is treated as a governance concern rather than an anomaly. The barriers at these levels are again institutional rather than technical. Institutionalisation requires aligning use-case registers with transparency obligations and the duty to give reasons for administrative decisions, preserving human oversight so that democratic accountability for those decisions is not displaced onto a model, and ensuring equitable treatment across diverse citizen groups. Dependence on externally developed foundation models further turns sovereignty and procurement renewal into recurring governance risks with no firm-level equivalent, making reconfiguration a matter of safeguarding public legitimacy rather than competitive advantage [15].

4.7 Progression and Regression

Progression across maturity levels is non-monotonic. Organisations may advance unevenly across capability dimensions and may also regress when critical routines, competencies, or governance arrangements erode, for example due to staff turnover, vendor dependence, or regulatory changes. This pattern is consistent with the CMM tradition, which recognises that institutionalisation can fail or decay when processes are not sustained [12], and with dynamic capability theory, which treats capability as an ongoing process of reconfiguration rather than a stable achievement [13]. Incorporating regression and feedback therefore reflects the empirical volatility of GenAI capability development in public-sector contexts rather than an idealised linear trajectory.

5 Discussion and Conclusion

Drawing on three Swedish municipalities under EU regulatory conditions, this study examined how public-sector organisations develop capabilities for the effective and trustworthy adoption of GenAI. We identified five interrelated capability dimensions and synthesised them into a GenAI Capability Maturity Model that captures the dynamic, non-linear processes through which GenAI capabilities are built, stabilised, and reconfigured. The five dimensions—strategic alignment, workforce readiness, data governance and digital sovereignty, Trustworthy AI, and public value—do not mature uniformly across the four levels, echoing prior critiques of static AI readiness frameworks [8,9]. Technical experimentation and strategic ambition typically advance faster than governance routines for Trustworthy AI and sustainability, producing patterned asymmetries rather than monotonic progression [12]. The explicit feedback and course-correction mechanisms built into the model respond to this empirical pattern.

Read through a dynamic capabilities lens, the maturity levels align with the processes of sensing, seizing, and reconfiguration: early levels are characterised by sensing (exploring use cases, surfacing risks), intermediate levels by seizing (resource commitment to pilots, training, and data infrastructure), and higher levels by reconfiguration (institutionalised and continuously adjusted governance routines) [13,14]. Unlike firm-level applications of dynamic capabilities, these processes are oriented toward public value rather than competitive advantage [15]: legal accountability, equity, and citizen outcomes are constitutive elements of GenAI capability, not external constraints. A central insight concerns the role of Trustworthy AI and sustainability. In the European public-sector context, alignment with the EU AI Act functions as a structuring condition of capability development, rather than an external compliance exercise [16]. Consistent with the sustainable-AI literature [17], societal-and-environmental wellbeing emerges as a persistent developmental gap. Awareness arises early, but systematic assessment of direct, indirect, and systemic effects—energy use, labour impacts, and digital sovereignty—lags behind. By staging sustainability across maturity levels, the model aligns GenAI capability development with the EU's twin digital and green transition and foregrounds governance, rather than optimisation, as the core organisational challenge.

The model supports disciplined governance rather than technological acceleration. By specifying representative instruments at each level—pilot registers, Trustworthy-AI checklists mapped to EU risk categories, governance forums, AI registers, and sustainability metrics—it translates abstract principles from AI readiness and Trustworthy AI frameworks into operational practice [8,16]. Higher maturity does not entail broader deployment: responsible reconfiguration may involve constraining, redesigning, or discontinuing GenAI use rather than scaling it. The model describes increasingly structured organisational capacity for responsible evaluation, governance, and selective use—not maximal deployment.

This study makes three contributions to research and practice. First, it extends AI readiness research toward a dynamic, capability-based perspective on GenAI in public organisations [8,9] and advances the CMM tradition through a GenAI-specific, empirically grounded public-sector instantiation [12]. Second, it integrates public value [15], Trustworthy AI [16], and sustainability [17] as constitutive elements of capability development rather than evaluative overlays. Third, it offers managers and policymakers a diagnostic tool for coordinated GenAI capability development under regulatory constraint, without presupposing unproblematised AI expansion.

We acknowledge three limitations and outline directions for future research. First, the empirical base—three Swedish municipalities under EU regulation—limits transferability to non-EU contexts. Second, the cross-sectional data mean that level transitions are inferred rather than observed. The model should therefore be interpreted as exploratory and empirically informed rather than fully validated. Third, the model addresses *how*, not *whether*, to adopt GenAI for a given service. Future research should validate transitions longitudinally, develop quantitative indicators for the five dimensions, and integrate the model with digital-transformation and sustainability frameworks to surface system-level interdependencies.

References

1. Han, S., Jonathan, G.M.: The contextual edge: LLMs and Sweden's public sector transformation. In: Lindgren, I., et al. (eds.) Electronic Government – EGOV 2025. Lecture Notes in Computer Science, vol. 15944, pp. 180–195. Springer, Cham (2026)
2. Van Noordt, C., Misuraca, G.: Exploratory insights on artificial intelligence for government in Europe. Soc. Sci. Comput. Rev. **40**(2), 426–444 (2022)
3. Yigitcanlar, T., Agdas, D., Degirmenci, K.: Artificial intelligence in local governments: perceptions of city managers on prospects, constraints and choices. AI Soc. **38**(3), 1135–1150 (2023)
4. Wirtz, B.W., Weyerer, J.C., Geyer, C.: Artificial intelligence and the public sector–applications and challenges. Int. J. Public Adm. **42**(7), 596–615 (2019)
5. Mergel, I., Edelmann, N., Haug, N.: Defining digital transformation: results from expert interviews. Gov. Inf. Q. **36**(4), 101385 (2019)
6. Jonathan, G.M., Yalew, S.D., Gebremeskel, B.K., Watat, J.K.: AI adoption in the public sector: organizational readiness and the pursuit of public value. Complex Syst. Inform. Model. Quarterly **45**, 43–70 (2025)
7. Kadarla, L., Jonathan, G.M., Perjons, E.: From readiness to public value: Modelling AI adoption in Sweden's decentralised municipal system. In: PoEM Forum, Doctoral Consortium, Business Case & Tool Forum, Workshops 2025, co-located with PoEM 2025, Geneva, Switzerland, 3–5 December (2026)

8. Pumplun, L., Tauchert, C., Heidt, M.: A new organizational chassis for artificial intelligence—Exploring organizational readiness factors. In: Proceedings of the 27th European Conference on Information Systems (ECIS) (2019)
9. Jöhnk, J., Weißert, M., Wyrtki, K.: Ready or not, AI comes–an interview study of organizational AI readiness factors. Business Inf. Syst. Eng. **63**(1), 5–20 (2021)
10. Mikalef, P., Conboy, K., Lundström, J.E., Popović, A.: Thinking responsibly about responsible AI and the dark side of AI. Eur. J. Inf. Syst. **31**(3), 257–268 (2022)
11. Dwivedi, Y.K., Pandey, N., Currie, W., Micu, A.: Leveraging ChatGPT and other generative artificial intelligence (AI)-based applications in the hospitality and tourism industry: Practices, challenges and research agenda. Int. J. Contemp. Hosp. Manag. **36**(1), 1–12 (2024)
12. Paulk, M.C., Curtis, B., Chrissis, M.B., Weber, C.V.: Capability maturity model, version 1.1. IEEE Software **10**(4), 18–27 (1993)
13. Teece, D.J., Pisano, G., Shuen, A.: Dynamic capabilities and strategic management. Strateg. Manag. J. **18**(7), 509–533 (1997)
14. Eisenhardt, K.M., Martin, J.A.: Dynamic capabilities: what are they? Strateg. Manag. J. **21**(10–11), 1105–1121 (2000)
15. Moore, M.H.: Creating Public Value: Strategic Management in Government. Harvard University Press, Cambridge, MA (1995)
16. High-Level Expert Group on Artificial Intelligence: Ethics Guidelines for Trustworthy AI. European Commission, Brussels (2019)
17. van Wynsberghe, A.: Sustainable AI: AI for sustainability and the sustainability of AI. AI and Ethics **1**(3), 213–218 (2021)
18. Brynjolfsson, E., Hitzig, Z.: AI's use of knowledge in society. National Bureau of Economic Research Working Paper, Cambridge, MA (2025)
19. Bright, J., Enock, F., Esnaashari, S., Francis, J., Hashem, Y., Morgan, D.: Generative AI is already widespread in the public sector: evidence from a survey of UK public sector professionals. Digital Government: Res. Practice **6**(1), 1–13 (2025)
20. Noy, S., Zhang, W.: Experimental evidence on the productivity effects of generative artificial intelligence. Science **381**(6654), 187–192 (2023)
21. Brynjolfsson, E., Ng, A.: Big AI can centralize decision-making and power, and that's a problem. In: Missing Links in AI Governance, p. 65 (2023)
22. Chen, Y.C., Ahn, M.J., Wang, Y.F.: Artificial intelligence and public values: value impacts and governance in the public sector. Sustainability **15**(6), 4796 (2023)
23. Kuziemski, M., Misuraca, G.: AI governance in the public sector: three tales from the frontiers of automated decision-making in democratic settings. Telecommunications Policy **44**(6), 101976 (2020)
24. OECD Committee on Digital Economy Policy: OECD framework for the classification of AI systems. OECD Digital Economy Papers, No. 323 (2022)
25. Yin, R.K.: Case Study Research and Applications, 6th edn. Sage, Thousand Oaks, CA (2018)
26. Eisenhardt, K.M.: Building theories from case study research. Acad. Manag. Rev. **14**(4), 532–550 (1989)
27. Guest, G., MacQueen, K.M., Namey, E.E.: Applied Thematic Analysis. Sage Publications, Thousand Oaks, CA (2012)
28. Braun, V., Clarke, V.: Using thematic analysis in psychology. Qual. Res. Psychol. **3**(2), 77–101 (2006)

Digital Transformation in Retail and Its Effects on Society: An Analysis of the Acceptance, Adoption, and Diffusion of Self-Service Technologies

Zenaldo Rodrigues[1], Luiz Pinheiro[1(✉)], Carla Marcolin[2], Rodrigo Marinello[1], and Ricardo Matheus[3]

[1] Positivo University, AI-Labs, Curitiba, Brazil
luiz.junior@up.edu.br
[2] Federal University of Uberlandia, Uberlandia, Brazil
[3] University of São Paulo, USP, São Paulo, Brazil

Abstract. This study examines how the acceptance, adoption, and diffusion of self-service technologies (SSTs) in retail relate to digital inclusion and equitable participation in the e-Society. The analysis is grounded in three complementary lenses Diffusion of Innovations, the Technology Acceptance Model (TAM), and the Unified Theory of Acceptance and Use of Technology (UTAUT). A qualitative multiple-case study was conducted in three supermarkets chains drawing on seventy semi-structured interviews and structured field observation triangulated with documentary evidence. Findings indicate that SST adoption is heterogeneous and significantly moderated by age, with a steady decline in propensity to use among older adults and persistent usability and digital-familiarity barriers. Self-service does not displace operator-assisted service; instead, hybrid socio-technical configurations emerge in which human labor is reconfigured into mediation, supervision, and assistance roles. The study contributes to information-systems research on e-Society by showing that digital transformation in retail simultaneously generates operational efficiency and reproduces digital inequality, and it draws on classical IS works on data transparency and governance to discuss conditions under which SST adoption can foster inclusive participation. Limitations include the single-sector and city-level scope of the cases.

Keywords: First Keyword · Second Keyword · Third Keyword.

1 Introduction

Digital transformation has profoundly reconfigured social interactions among customers, consumers, and organizations, redefining how services are offered, accessed, and consumed [1, 6, 14]. Information technologies act as structuring elements of organizational practices and consumption experiences, shaping how individuals interact with digital services and systems [9]. In retail, this movement materializes in the rapid diffusion of

Published by Springer Nature Switzerland AG 2027
S. Han et al. (Eds.): I3E 2026, LNCS 16912, pp. 434–448, 2027.
https://doi.org/10.1007/978-3-032-38014-2_32

self-service technologies (SSTs) most visibly automated self-checkouts which transfer to consumers part of the activities previously performed by service workers and create new opportunities for data-driven and AI-enabled value creation [2, 4, 6, 7, 32].

This redistribution of tasks raises an emerging concern that goes beyond efficiency. The literature on the digital divide [23, 24] has documented that digitalization does not occur homogeneously: access, skills, and effective use are unevenly distributed and reproduce structural inequalities. Recent IS research on the e-Society further argues that the value generated by digital systems depends not only on their availability but also on user experience, perceived value, and engagement [11, 12], and that data transparency and governance are central conditions for trustworthy adoption [30–32]. In retail, where SSTs operate as everyday technological encounters, these dimensions become especially salient.

The context is particularly informative for this debate. Retail is one of the largest sectors of the national economy, and its digitalization has accelerated since the COVID-19 pandemic, with rapid expansion of automated checkouts, mobile payments, and AI-enabled personalization. Yet, the country still presents marked inequalities in digital skills and effective technology use across age and income groups [23, 24]. Investigating SST adoption in this setting therefore allows the analysis of digital inclusion under conditions where the diffusion of innovations is intense, the institutional environment is heterogeneous, and the customer base is highly diverse. In this sense the research on AI in retail [29] and IS research on data governance and transparency in emerging-economy settings [30–32] provide a natural intellectual context for the present study.

From a theoretical standpoint, three classical lenses jointly inform the analysis. Rogers Diffusion of Innovations Theory (DOI) [22] describes how new technologies spread heterogeneously over time, conditioned by attributes such as relative advantage, compatibility, complexity, trialability, and observability. The Technology Acceptance Model (TAM) [5] explains usage behavior through perceived usefulness and perceived ease of use, while UTAUT [13] integrates and extends prior models with social influence and facilitating conditions, treating age, gender, experience, and voluntariness as moderators. Although robust, these models do not, in isolation, capture the broader societal implications of unequal SST adoption, particularly in light of the United Nations Sustainable Development Goals [27, 28] notably SDG 8 (decent work and inclusive growth) and SDG 10 (reduced inequalities).

Building on these arguments, this study addresses the following research question: how does the adoption of self-service technologies in retail relate to digital inclusion and equitable participation, and which factors moderate their acceptance and diffusion? The general objective is to analyze how digital inclusion and equitable participation occur in SST use in retail and to identify the factors that influence their acceptance, adoption, and diffusion. The investigation is operationalized through a multiple-case study of three supermarkets in line with Yin [21] guidance for examining contemporary phenomena embedded in real and complex contexts.

The contribution of the paper is threefold. First, it integrates DOI, TAM, and UTAUT with the e-Society perspective on digital inequality [11, 12, 23, 24], producing a more complete account of SST adoption than each model offers in isolation. Second, it provides empirical evidence from a Latin-American emerging market, complementing discussion about AI in retail [29, 33] and on data governance and transparency in IS [30–32]. Third, it derives managerial and policy implications consistent with the SDG agenda, highlighting the conditions under which SSTs can amplify rather than restrict participation in the digital society.

2 Theoretical Background

2.1 Digital Transformation and the e-Society

The notion of e-Society describes a social configuration in which digital technologies structure interaction, service access, and economic participation, mediating organizational and institutional practices [15, 25]. Digital transformation is therefore not reducible to technological incorporation; it entails a wider reconfiguration of business models, customer relationships, and value-creation logics [14]. From this perspective, digitalization is also a process of socialization that redefines the conditions under which individuals participate in technology-mediated environments. Pappas et al. [12] and Pappas & Woodside [11] argue that experiential and perceptual factors are decisive in this process, while Janssen et al. [32] and Matheus et al. [30, 31] emphasize that data governance and transparency are prerequisites for trustworthy interactions. Van Dijk [23] and Helsper [24] complement this view by showing that effective use of technology, not mere access, defines digital inclusion.

2.2 Diffusion of Innovations: DOI

Rogers DOI [22] theory how innovations propagate through a social system over time, classifying adopters as innovators, early adopters, early majority, late majority, and laggards. Five attributes relative advantage, compatibility, complexity, trialability, and observability shape the speed and extent of diffusion. In SSTs, ease of use and perceived convenience can accelerate adoption, while operational difficulties or insecurity can restrict it [2, 5, 7]. DOI thus offers a macro-level lens that links innovation attributes to the social patterns of inclusion and exclusion observed in retail digitalization.

2.3 Acceptance and Adoption: TAM and UTAUT

TAM [5] explains acceptance through perceived usefulness and perceived ease of use, the two cognitive antecedents of behavioral intention. UTAUT [13] extends this framework by integrating performance expectancy, effort expectancy, social influence, and facilitating conditions as predictors, with age, gender, experience, and voluntariness moderating their effects. The role of age is particularly relevant for SSTs, given prior evidence of age-related differences in technology adoption [8]. In the self-checkout context, ease of use, interface clarity, system reliability, and convenience benefits queue avoidance and time savings directly map onto TAM and UTAUT constructs [7].

2.4 Self-Service Technologies in Retail

SSTs reallocate to the consumer activities previously executed by service workers, mediated by technological interfaces [7]. They are part of a broader process of automation in which human work is not necessarily eliminated but redistributed and reshaped [1, 6]. In retail, SSTs aim to increase operational efficiency, reduce costs, and enhance the customer experience [10]; from an e-Society perspective, however, they also constitute a privileged empirical site to examine digital inclusion, since the user becomes responsible for performing tasks that depend on prior digital competence. As Reis & Pinheiro [33] note, contemporary socio-technical challenges can only be addressed through collaboration between organizations and society an argument that applies directly to inclusive SST design.

2.5 Data Governance, Transparency, and Trust

Beyond acceptance and diffusion, contemporary IS scholarship situates digital adoption within questions of data governance and accountability. Janssen et al. [32] propose that organizing data for trustworthy AI requires explicit governance arrangements that align data ownership, quality, and stewardship across the data lifecycle. Matheus, Janssen, and Janowski [30] derive sixteen design principles for digital transparency in government, while Matheus, Janssen, and Maheshwari [31] show that public-facing dashboards can operationalize accountable, data-driven decision-making in smart cities. Although developed for the public sector, these principles travel to retail: when consumers cannot inspect how their data are used, perceived risk increases, weakening compatibility and relative advantage in DOI [22] and reducing performance and effort expectancies in UTAUT [13]. Janssen et al. [32] further demonstrate that the same governance arrangements that enable open-data and open-government initiatives also surface adoption barriers and myths that must be actively managed. Taken together, these contributions suggest that trustworthy SST diffusion is contingent not only on usability but also on the visibility and governance of data flows enabled by the technology.

3 Methodology

This research adopts a qualitative, exploratory descriptive design to examine acceptance, adoption, and diffusion of SSTs under conditions of digital inclusion and equitable participation. Following Yin [21], a multiple-case study is appropriate for investigating contemporary phenomena embedded in real and complex contexts where the boundary between phenomenon and context is blurred. Multiple cases enable cross-unit comparison, supporting the identification of convergent and divergent patterns and increasing analytical robustness [18]. The unit of analysis is the individual customer (user and non-user) of self-checkout technology; the three supermarket chains constitute embedded context units, in line with Yin logic of multiple-case studies with embedded units of analysis.

3.1 Case Selection

Three supermarket chains operating in Brazil anonymized as Alpha, Betha, and Gama were purposefully selected following Yin [21] screening procedure. The selection criteria were local relevance, presence of self-checkout technology, and feasibility of researcher access [16, 21]. Table 1 summarizes the selection.

Table 1. Screening criteria for case selection

Retail chain	Total stores	Stores with self-checkouts	Coverage (%)	Studied stores
Alpha	8	4	50%	4
Betha	29	29	100%	12
Gama	60	20	33%	4
Total	77	53	75%	20

Source: Authors own elaboration.

3.2 Displayed Equations Are Centered and Set on a Separate Line.

Data collection was structured around three complementary techniques [16, 21]. First, seventy (70) semi-structured interviews were conducted with users and non-users of self-checkouts capturing immediate perceptions in the natural shopping environment and reducing memory bias. Second, structured non-participant field observation was performed using a written observational protocol [16], complemented by photographic and video records. Third, documentary evidence (corporate communication and journalistic articles) was triangulated with the primary data to corroborate organizational decisions and adoption trajectories [21]. Table 2 reports the data sources by case.

Table 2. Data sources and volume by case

Case	Interviews (n)	Observed self-checkout terminals	Documents reviewed
Alpha	22	16	9
Betha	30	44	14
Gama	18	12	11
Total	70	72	34

Source: Authors own elaboration.

3.3 Data Analysis

All interview transcripts and observational notes were imported into Atlas.ti and analyzed through an interpretive grounded-theory approach [19, 20]: open coding generated descriptive categories, axial coding articulated them with a theoretical model anchored in DOI, TAM, and UTAUT, and selective coding consolidated the explanatory narrative. Two analytical dimensions emerged: (i) barriers to acceptance, adoption, and diffusion of self-checkouts; and (ii) opportunities for diffusion. Pattern matching across cases was used to assess convergence and divergence [18, 21].

4 Findings and Discussion

The two analytical axes accounted for 284 coded occurrences (151 barriers and 133 opportunities), suggesting that, although SSTs are already incorporated in the studied chains, their consolidation remains conditional on a set of socio-technical factors. Barriers are presented in Sect. 4.1 and opportunities in Sect. 4.2.

4.1 Barriers to Acceptance, Adoption, and Diffusion

Five barrier categories emerged from the analysis. Their relative weight is summarized in Fig. 1.

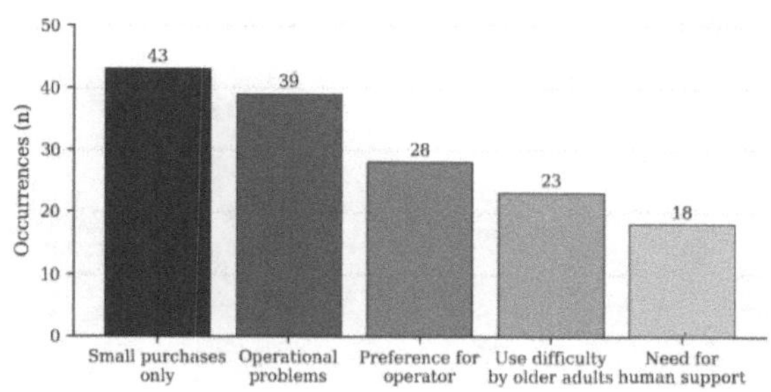

Source: Authors own elaboration based on Atlas.ti coding.

Fig. 1. Barriers to acceptance, adoption, and diffusion of self-checkouts (occurrences, n = 151). Source: Authors own elaboration based on Atlas.ti coding.

1. Operational problems (39 occurrences) refer to functional malfunctions of the technology. Coded sub-issues are concentrated in barcode reading (31%), product identification and weighing particularly for fruits and vegetables (28%), payment-process interruptions (23%), and digital-interface usability (15%); only 3% of issues concerned security, suggesting that the bottleneck is usability rather than trust (Fig. 2). These results reinforce TAM emphasis on perceived ease of use [5] and UTAUT effort expectancy [13] as proximate determinants of acceptance. Importantly, the dominance of usability over security as a friction point implies that interventions focused on hardware reliability (barcode scanners, scales) and interface clarity may yield disproportionate returns relative to investments in additional security messaging a finding that is also consistent with the convenience-centered SST literature [3, 4, 7].

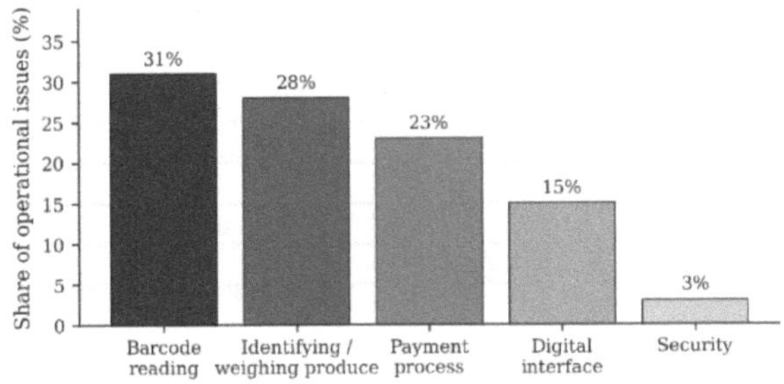

Source: Authors own elaboration based on Atlas.ti coding.

Fig. 2. Distribution of operational issues reported by self-checkout users (n = 39).
Source: Authors own elaboration based on Atlas.ti coding.

2. Use restricted to small purchases (43 occurrences) is the most frequent barrier. Approximately 80% of observed users completed transactions of four to ten items, with very few self-service transactions exceeding fifteen items (Fig. 3). The technology is therefore perceived as a convenience for quick transactions rather than a substitute for operator-assisted checkouts, in line with prior literature on convenience and reduced waiting time [3, 4, 7].

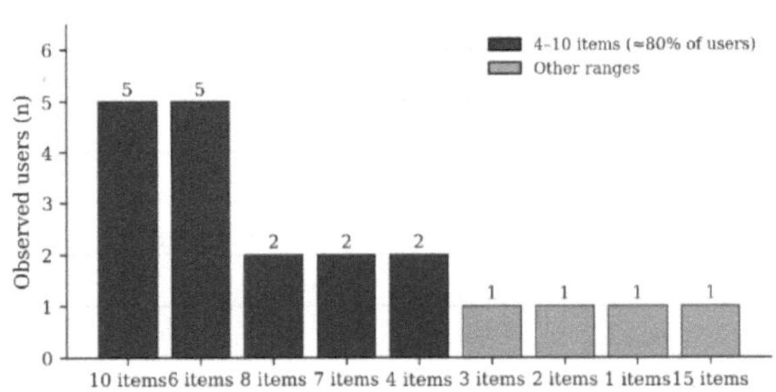

Source: Authors own elaboration.

Fig. 3. Number of items per transaction observed at self-checkouts (n = 20 transactions).
Source: Authors own elaboration.

3. Persistent preference for operator-assisted checkouts (28 occurrences) was observed especially for purchases of more than ten items, where the division of labor between customer and operator reduces individual effort. During seasonal peaks, the ratio of operator-assisted to self-checkout use varied between 25:1 and 15:1, indicating a clearly contingent diffusion pattern [22]. Figure 4, taken from the field-observation protocol, schematizes the comparative service flow.

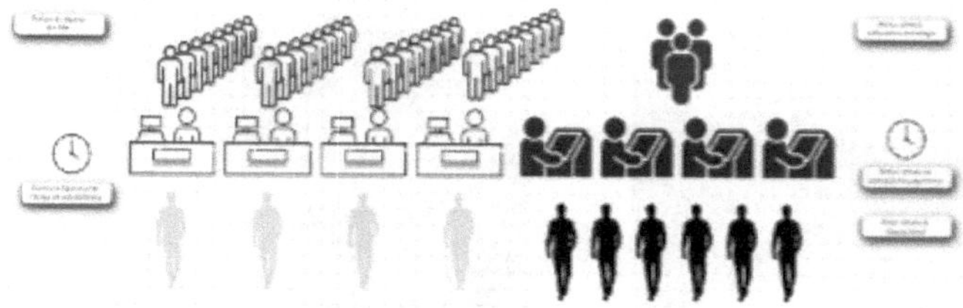

Source: Field observation protocol; authors own elaboration.

Fig. 4. Comparative service flow between operator-assisted and self-checkout lanes. Source: Field observation protocol; authors own elaboration.

4. Use difficulty by older adults (23 occurrences) emerged as the most theoretically salient barrier. Self-checkout users are concentrated in the 20–39 age band, while difficulty rates rise from age 40 onwards (Table 3 and Fig. 5).

Table 3. Caption

Age range	Share of users (%)	Reported difficulty (%)
20–29	35	0
30–39	25	17
40–49	20	33
50–59	15	33
60–69	5	17

This pattern is consistent with UTAUT [13], which treats age as a moderator of the relationship between determinants and behavioral intention, and with prior evidence from Morris & Venkatesh [8] on age-related differences in technology adoption. From a digital-divide standpoint [23, 24], it indicates that retail SSTs reproduce skill-based inequalities even when physical access to the technology is universally available. The implication is that physical accessibility is necessary but not sufficient for inclusive diffusion: the design of interfaces, signage, and on-site mediation has a direct bearing on whether older adults reach the second-level digital divide the divide of effective use identified by Helsper [24].

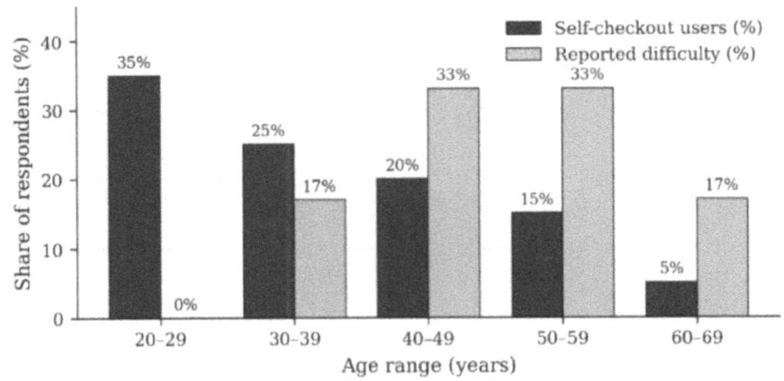

Source: Authors own elaboration.

Fig. 5. Age range vs. self-checkout use and reported difficulty (%).
Source: Authors own elaboration.

5. Need for human support (18 occurrences) was observed even in stores with four to six self-checkout terminals, where an attendant systematically supports users answering questions, recovering from system failures, and operating the system on behalf of the user. Rather than the wholesale elimination of cashier work, the data show a reconfiguration of tasks toward assistance, supervision, and technological mediation, in line with the heterogeneous-effects-of-automation thesis [1] and with arguments on hybrid socio-technical configurations [9, 33]. A complementary explanation comes from non-users, who frequently report that operator-assisted checkouts feel faster for cart-sized purchases and provide a valued moment of human interaction. As one non-user observed, "while I put the products on the belt, she is already registering the purchase, so I think it is faster than scanning by myself" a statement that operationalizes TAM perceived ease of use as a relative comparison between channels rather than an absolute property of the technology.

Beyond the five categories above, the cross-case analysis revealed an instructive longitudinal pattern. The CEO of the Gama chain initially declared that human service would remain a strategic differentiator and that self-checkouts would not be deployed; three years later, the chain had reversed that position and rolled out the technology across more than 90% of its stores. This trajectory illustrates DOI [22] view that diffusion is not uniform across organizations: it is shaped by communication channels, perceived legitimacy, and competitive pressure. The reversal also signals that, in the retail context, operator-assisted service is increasingly insufficient as a sole differentiator, even when the firm explicitly frames it as such. From a data-governance perspective [32], the rapid scale-up of SSTs raises additional questions about how customer data captured at self-checkout (purchase patterns, dwell time, error rates) are stewarded and made accountable to consumers.

4.2 Opportunities for Acceptance, Adoption, and Diffusion

On the opportunity axis, two subcategories dominate: agility (37 occurrences) and queue avoidance (30 occurrences); together with service-improvement and analytics, engagement of younger users, and emerging-technology impact, they account for the 133 coded opportunity occurrences (Fig. 6).

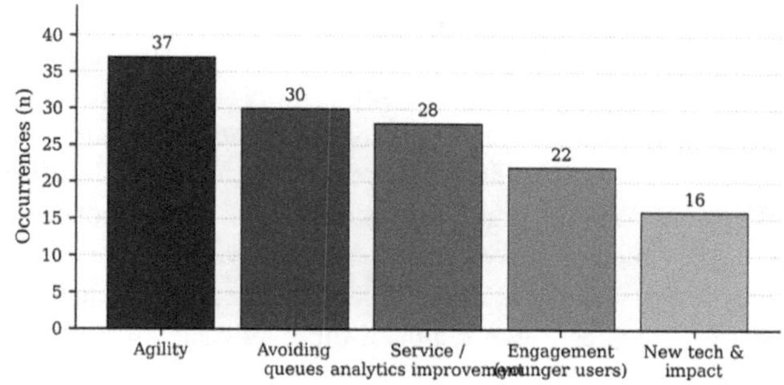

Fig. 6. Source: Authors own elaboration based on Atlas.ti coding.

These results indicate that, for many users, the perceived value of self-checkouts is not the technology itself but the convenience it generates agility and time savings at the final stage of the customer journey. This finding aligns with the SST literature on convenience as a key determinant of satisfaction and continued use [3, 5, 7], and with engagement-driven IS perspectives on the e-Society [11, 12]. The strong engagement of users aged 20–39 also points to a structural diffusion potential, although that potential remains conditional on the resolution of usability barriers and the heterogeneity of customer profiles.

Two additional opportunities deserve emphasis. First, service-improvement and analytics opportunities (28 occurrences) point to the role of customer-level data captured by SSTs as a basis for personalization, dynamic pricing, and operational optimization. This finding connects the empirical evidence to the data-governance debate [32]: realizing analytics-driven opportunities requires explicit organizational commitments to data quality, accountability, and customer-facing transparency [30, 31]. Second, engagement of younger users (22 occurrences) and the perception that emerging technologies will continue to reshape the shopping experience (16 occurrences) signal a generational momentum that, if combined with inclusive design, can broaden the diffusion base over time. Table 4 synthesizes how the empirical findings map onto the DOI, TAM, and UTAUT constructs.

4.3 Cross-Case Synthesis

A comparison across the three chains highlights both convergence and divergence. Convergence is evident in the dominance of operational and age-related barriers: in all three cases, the 40+ age band concentrates the highest difficulty rates, and barcode/weighing issues consistently emerge as the top operational pain points. Convergence is also clear in the prominence of agility and queue avoidance as the main perceived benefits, regardless of the chain business model. Divergence, in turn, is most visible in the deployment trajectory and supporting infrastructure. Betha had reached full coverage of self-checkouts well before data collection and operates with a higher attendant-to-terminal ratio; Alpha is in a mid-stage rollout focused on stores with high traffic; Gama, despite an initial managerial commitment to human-only service, accelerated its rollout and matched Betha by the end of the year. These differences are consistent with DOI [22] argument that diffusion responds to organizational context and communication channels and with prior IS work on AI in retail [29] showing that adoption pathways are shaped by competitive and institutional pressures rather than purely by technology readiness.

Triangulating these patterns with the data-governance literature [30–32] suggests two further insights. First, the chains that reported smoother SST diffusion also presented more visible attendant-led mediation and clearer in-store communication about how the systems work, which can be interpreted as embryonic forms of customer-facing transparency. Second, the absence of explicit data dashboards for customers even in the most digitized stores indicates a gap between the data-collection capabilities embedded in SSTs and the accountability practices that, according to Matheus, Janssen, and Maheshwari [31], support trustworthy diffusion in smart-city contexts. Closing this gap is a concrete avenue for managerial intervention.

Table 4 Mapping of empirical findings onto DOI, TAM, and UTAUT categories.

Theoretical lens	Categories	Evidence from the cases
DOI [22]	Relative advantage; Compatibility	Agility and queue avoidance drive adoption; preference for operator service for >10 items signals incompatibility with current routines.
DOI [22]	Complexity; Observability	Operational issues (barcode, weighing, payment) raise complexity; observed adoption by younger peers reinforces diffusion.
TAM [5]	Perceived usefulness; Perceived ease of use	Convenience perceived as useful; usability problems reduce ease of use, especially among 40+ users.
UTAUT [13]	Effort expectancy; Facilitating conditions; Age moderator	Need for human support reflects facilitating conditions; difficulty rate rises after age 40, confirming age moderation [8].

Source: Authors own elaboration.

5 Implications, Conclusions, and Limitations

5.1 Theoretical Implications

The findings refine three classical IS models when applied to SST adoption in retail. For DOI [22], the data show that observability and compatibility are particularly salient: visible mediation by attendants and visible adoption by younger peers reinforce diffusion, whereas mismatches between checkout design and cart-sized purchases reduce compatibility. For TAM [5], perceived ease of use is operationalized comparatively users assess SSTs against operator-assisted alternatives rather than in absolute terms suggesting that ease of use is best modeled as a relative construct. For UTAUT [13], age clearly moderates the effect of effort expectancy and facilitating conditions, replicating Morris & Venkatesh [8] in a Latin-American retail context. The integration of these models with the e-Society perspective [11, 12, 23, 24] further suggests that customer experience is the channel through which innovation attributes become observable to the consumer and that data governance and transparency [30–32] are background institutional conditions that calibrate trust and behavioral intention.

5.2 Managerial and Policy Implications

Four implications follow for retail managers and public-sector policymakers. First, interface and hardware redesign should focus on the most frequent operational pain points barcode reading, weighing, and payment since these issues account for over 80% of operational friction (Fig. 2). Second, age-aware mediation strategies should be embedded in store operations: rather than reducing attendant headcount to maximize automation gains, chains should explicitly position attendants as digital-inclusion facilitators, particularly during shifts with higher concentrations of older customers. Third, SST data flows should be governed under explicit accountability arrangements [32], with customer-facing transparency mechanisms simple data dashboards, opt-in notifications, and public privacy notices drawing on the design principles articulated by Matheus, Janssen, and colleagues [30, 31]. Fourth, public-sector initiatives focused on digital literacy and inclusion can productively partner with retail chains to deliver in-store training opportunities, aligning private SST deployment with the SDG agenda on inclusive growth and reduced inequalities [27, 28].

6 Conclusion

This study analyzed how the acceptance, adoption, and diffusion of self-service technologies in retail relate to digital inclusion and equitable participation, integrating DOI [22], TAM [5], and UTAUT [13] with the e-Society perspective on digital inequality [11, 12, 23, 24]. The empirical findings show that SST adoption is a socio-technological phenomenon conditioned by structural inequalities. Age moderates acceptance younger users dominate self-checkout use while difficulty rises sharply after age 40and SSTs are predominantly used for small purchases, indicating a contingent rather than generalized diffusion.

The persistent need for human support reveals that retail digitalization does not eliminate human labor; it reconfigures it into mediation, supervision, and assistance roles, producing hybrid socio-technical configurations [1]. Simultaneously, the most frequently mentioned opportunities agility and queue avoidance confirm that perceived convenience is the primary driver of continued use [3, 7], and that experience-centered IS theories [11, 12] are needed to interpret SST diffusion in the e-Society.

The main contribution of the paper is to demonstrate that digital transformation in retail simultaneously increases operational efficiency and redefines the conditions of social participation, producing efficiency and inequality in tandem. Connecting this evidence to the United Nations 2030 Agenda [27, 28] particularly SDG 8 and SDG 10reframes inclusive SST design as a socio-economic imperative rather than a purely managerial concern. From the data-governance and transparency literature [30–32], we further argue that inclusive diffusion requires explicit organizational commitments to data accountability and accessible interfaces. Practical implications for managers and policymakers therefore include: (i) interface redesign focused on weighing, payment, and barcode flows; (ii) training and human-mediation strategies that reduce age-related effort expectancy; (iii) governance arrangements that make data uses transparent and auditable to customers; and (iv) public–private initiatives that link SST deployment to digital-inclusion programs.

From a theoretical standpoint, the study contributes by triangulating DOI, TAM, and UTAUT with the e-Society and data-governance literatures. The integrated reading shows that customer experience is the observable layer through which DOI relative advantage and compatibility, TAM perceived usefulness and ease of use, and UTAUT effort expectancy and facilitating conditions become tangible to the customer while data governance and transparency [30–32] act as background institutional conditions that shape trust and, ultimately, behavioral intention.

7 Limitations and Future Research

Three limitations should be acknowledged. First, the study is bounded by a single sector (supermarkets), which constrains generalization. Replicating the design in other retail segments pharmacies, fashion, fast-food and other emerging-economy cities would clarify how SST diffusion patterns vary across institutional and competitive contexts. Second, the qualitative design provides analytical depth but does not test causal relationships statistically; complementing the present findings with quantitative SEM-based tests of the integrated DOI–TAM–UTAUT model, anchored in validated scales [5, 13, 22], would consolidate the integrated framework and quantify the moderating role of age. Third, this study did not directly measure customers perceptions of data governance; future research could combine SST adoption surveys with instruments derived from the public-sector transparency literature [30–32] to test how perceived data accountability shapes behavioral intention.

Building AI in retail [29], promising directions include examining how AI-enabled features recommendation engines, personalized pricing, frictionless payment, and computer-vision-based loss prevention reshape the acceptance–inclusion equilibrium analyzed here, ideally in combination with audit-friendly data dashboards [31] and explicit governance frameworks [32, 33], as well digital transparency [34] and AI algorithms transparency [35], and an opportunity for Internet of Things (IoT) integration [36]. A second avenue is the longitudinal study of organizational reversals such as the Gama case, which could reveal how mimetic and competitive pressures translate the discourse of human-centered service into hybrid socio-technical configurations. A third avenue is the design of inclusive SST archetypes that combine adaptive interfaces, explicit human-in-the-loop mediation, and customer-facing transparency, contributing both to the IS literature and to the SDG agenda on inclusive digital growth [27, 28].

Acknowledgments. The authors thank the participating supermarket chains and the customers who agreed to take part in the interviews, and Researchers at AI-Labs at Positivo Universitty for feedbacks.

Disclosure of Interests The authors have no competing interests to declare that are relevant to the content of this article.

References

1. Acemoglu, D., Restrepo, P.: Robots and jobs: evidence from US labor markets. J. Polit. Econ. **128**(6), 2188–2244 (2020). https://doi.org/10.1086/705716
2. Blut, M., Wang, C., Schoefer, K.: Understanding self-service technology usage: a meta-analysis. J. Serv. Res. **19**(4), 396–416 (2016). https://doi.org/10.1177/1094670516662352
3. Collier, J.E., Kimes, S.E.: Only if it is convenient: understanding how convenience influences self-service technology evaluation. J. Serv. Res. **16**(1), 39–51 (2013). https://doi.org/10.1177/1094670512458454
4. Dabholkar, P.A.: Consumer evaluations of new technology-based self-service options. Int. J. Res. Mark. **13**(1), 29–51 (1996). https://doi.org/10.1016/0167-8116(95)00027-5
5. Davis, F.D.: Perceived usefulness, perceived ease of use, and user acceptance of information technology. MIS Q. **13**(3), 319–340 (1989). https://doi.org/10.2307/249008
6. Grewal, D., Roggeveen, A.L., Nordfält, J.: The future of retailing. J. Retail. **93**(1), 1–6 (2017). https://doi.org/10.1016/j.jretai.2016.12.008
7. Meuter, M.L., Ostrom, A.L., Roundtree, R.I., Bitner, M.J.: Self-service technologies: understanding customer satisfaction. J. Mark. **64**(3), 50–64 (2000). https://doi.org/10.1509/jmkg.64.3.50.18024
8. Morris, M.G., Venkatesh, V.: Age differences in technology adoption decisions. IEEE Trans. Eng. Manag. **47**(2), 154–163 (2000). https://doi.org/10.1109/17.836669
9. Orlikowski, W.J.: Using technology and constituting structures. Organ. Sci. **11**(4), 404–428 (2000). https://doi.org/10.1287/orsc.11.4.404.14600
10. Pantano, E., Timmermans, H.: What is smart for retailing? J. Retail. Consum. Serv. **21**(5), 701–705 (2014). https://doi.org/10.1016/j.jretconser.2013.12.002
11. Pappas, I.O., Woodside, A.G.: Fuzzy-set qualitative comparative analysis (fsQCA): guidelines for research practice in information systems and marketing. Int. J. Inf. Manag. **58**, 102310 (2021). https://doi.org/10.1016/j.ijinfomgt.2021.102310
12. Pappas, I.O., Mikalef, P., Giannakos, M.N., Pavlou, P.A.: Big data and business analytics ecosystems: paving the way towards digital transformation and sustainable societies. Inf. Syst. Front. **20**(2), 225–240 (2018). https://doi.org/10.1007/s10796-017-9804-6
13. Venkatesh, V., Morris, M.G., Davis, G.B., Davis, F.D.: User acceptance of information technology: toward a unified view. MIS Q. **27**(3), 425–478 (2003). https://doi.org/10.2307/30036540

14. Verhoef, P.C., et al.: Digital transformation: a multidisciplinary reflection and research agenda. J. Bus. Res. **122**, 889–901 (2021). https://doi.org/10.1016/j.jbusres.2019.09.022
15. Berleur, J., Nurminen, M., Impagliazzo, J. (eds.): Social Informatics: An Information Society for All? Springer, Boston (2006)
16. Creswell, J.W.: Research Design: Qualitative, Quantitative, and Mixed Methods Approaches, 4th edn. Sage, Thousand Oaks (2014)
17. Creswell, J.W., Plano Clark, V.L.: Designing and Conducting Mixed Methods Research, 3rd edn. Sage, Thousand Oaks (2017)
18. Dul, J., Hak, T.: Case Study Methodology in Business Research. Butterworth-Heinemann, Oxford (2008)
19. Flick, U.: An Introduction to Qualitative Research, 6th edn. Sage, London (2018)
20. Strauss, A., Corbin, J.: Basics of Qualitative Research: Techniques and Procedures for Developing Grounded Theory. Sage, Thousand Oaks (1998)
21. Yin, R.K.: Case Study Research and Applications: Design and Methods, 6th edn. Sage, Thousand Oaks (2018)
22. Rogers, E.M.: Diffusion of Innovations, 5th edn. Free Press, New York (2003)
23. Van Dijk, J.: The Digital Divide. Polity Press, Cambridge (2020)
24. Helsper, E.: The Digital Disconnect: The Social Causes and Consequences of Digital Inequalities. Sage, London (2021)
25. Berleur, J., Nurminen, M., Impagliazzo, J.: Social informatics: a humanistic approach to information society. In: Berleur, J., et al. (eds.) Social Informatics. Springer, Boston (2006)
26. Christensen, C.M.: The Innovato's Dilemma. Harvard Business School Press, Boston (1997)
27. OECD: OECD Employment Outlook 2023: Artificial Intelligence and the Labour Market. OECD Publishing, Paris (2023). https://doi.org/10.1787/08785bba-en
28. United Nations: Transforming our world: the 2030 agenda for sustainable development. UN General Assembly, A/RES/70/1 (2015)
29. Rodrigues, Z.A., et al.: Artificial intelligence in supermarkets: opportunities and challenges. In: IFIP I3E 2024 Conference Proceedings, LNCS. Springer (2024). https://doi.org/10.1007/978-3-031-66044-3_8
30. Matheus, R., Janssen, M., Janowski, T.: Design principles for creating digital transparency in government. Gov. Inf. Q. **38**(1), 101550 (2021). https://doi.org/10.1016/j.giq.2020.101550
31. Matheus, R., Janssen, M., Maheshwari, D.: Data science empowering the public: data-driven dashboards for transparent and accountable decision-making in smart cities. Gov. Inf. Q. **37**(3), 101284 (2020). https://doi.org/10.1016/j.giq.2018.01.006
32. Janssen, M., Brous, P., Estevez, E., Barbosa, L.S., Janowski, T.: Data governance: organizing data for trustworthy artificial intelligence. Gov. Inf. Q. **37**(3), 101493 (2020). https://doi.org/10.1016/j.giq.2020.101493
33. Reis, J.F., Pinheiro Junior, L.P.: Institutional theory (IT) and diffusion of innovation (DOI): a theoretical approach on artificial intelligence (AI). Braz. Adm. Rev. **22**(4), e250060 (2025). https://doi.org/10.1590/1807-7692bar2025250060
34. Matheus, R., Janssen, M.: A systematic literature study to unravel transparency enabled by open government data: the window theory. Public Perform. Manag. Rev. **43**(3), 503–534 (2020)
35. Janssen, M., Hartog, M., Matheus, R., Yi Ding, A., Kuk, G.: Will algorithms blind people? The effect of explainable AI and decision-makers' experience on AI-supported decision-making in government. Soc. Sci. Comput. Rev. **40**(2), 478–493 (2022)
36. Shao, D., Ishengoma, F.R., Alexopoulos, C., Saxena, S., Nikiforova, A., Matheus, R.: Integration of IoT into e-government. Foresight. **25**(5), 734–750 (2023)

Author Index

Published by Springer Nature Switzerland AG 2027
S. Han et al. (Eds.): I3E 2026, LNCS 16912, pp. 449–450, 2027.
https://doi.org/10.1007/978-3-032-38014-2

Kolibri 360 GmbH
Ferdinand-Jühlke-Straße 7
99095 Erfurt, Deutschland
produktsicherheit@kolibri360.de